SURREY RECORD SOCIETY

Volume XXXIX

SURREY PROBATE INVENTORIES

1558–1603

Transcribed by D. M. Herridge

SURREY RECORD SOCIETY

2005

Surrey Record Society, 130 Goldsworth Road, Woking GU21 6ND

ISBN 0 902978 14 4

Produced by Arrowsmith, Bristol
Printed in Great Britain

CONTENTS

FOREWORD

DOROTHY MARION HERRIDGE 1924-2004

Impetus for the preparation and publication of this volume came from members of the Domestic Buildings Research Group (Surrey). In the course of recording and studying the older buildings in the county they had found inventories of great value. In 1986 the Group published an **Index of Surrey Probate Inventories 16th to 19th Centuries,** compiled by two members, Joan Holman and Marion Herridge. The work of transcribing for publication the inventories of the reign of Elizabeth I was then undertaken by Marion Herridge. Realising the importance of relating the inventories to the wills with which they belong, Marion also undertook this additional task. It brought her, as it will the reader, closer to the testators whom she came to regard as friends. The comprehensive indexes and glossary were compiled with the assistance of Pat Heather who also created the layout of the text.

Although the final stages of seeing the volume through the press have been undertaken by other members of the Record Society, in conception and through many years of work this is Marion Herridge's book, and the Society dedicates it, with gratitude, to her.

To mark the special circumstances of this volume, the Society has decided to use the Gollancz Bequest to fund its publication. The Fund was left by Marguerite Gollancz, former Editor of the Society, to further the Society's work. Miss Gollancz, who was County Archivist of Surrey for many years, always encouraged researchers to publish; Marion's sterling efforts on these 445 inventories and wills in a variety of 16th century hands, undertaken in her later retirement years for no other purpose than to make the information available to others, meet that vision perfectly.

Shirley Corke
Vice-President, Surrey Record Society

ACKNOWLEDGEMENTS

The editorial team would like to thank all who helped in bringing Marion's work to publication. Special thanks are due to Pat Heather for the original creation of the word-processed text and indexes. Nothing has been omitted or altered in Marion's text and we hope Marion would have approved of the final result.

Our thanks to the British Library for their permission to use part of Christopher Saxton's 1575 map of Surrey on the dustjacket. Thanks also to Hampshire Record Office for their kind permission to use photographs of three original inventories which Marion had asked for specifically in order to exemplify certain elements in the taking of inventories.

We gratefully acknowledge Lt Colonel Godwin Austen of Shalford for his kind permission to include the delightful early 17th century elevations of Shalford church and houses.

Our thanks too to David Hooper from Arrowsmiths for his continued help and advice in preparing the volume for the press.

Maggie Vaughan-Lewis
Shirley Corke
David Robinson

ILLUSTRATIONS

(Illustrations appear following page 264)

EDITORIAL NOTE

THE ARRANGEMENT OF THE INVENTORIES IN THIS VOLUME

Unless otherwise stated the references at the end of each entry for the inventory and (where given) the will are for documents among the probate records of the bishopric of Winchester held at Hampshire Record Office (eg *1558 B 62 Will, 1558 B 63 Inventory* identify the year and the series). Some re-organisation has occurred at Hampshire (HRO) since the original references were noted and it is advisable to check if wishing to quote in future work. Other changes include:

GLRO = Greater London Record Office *now* London Metropolitan Archives

PRO = Public Record Office *now* The National Archives

GMR = Guildford Muniment Room *now* Surrey History Centre (including LM Loseley Mss and G references)

SRO = Surrey Record Office *now* Surrey History Centre (including K references)

The inventories are arranged and numbered in chronological order of the date of the exhibition of the inventory in the ecclesiastical court. If there is no evidence of this having occurred, the date of the probate or of the witnessing of the will or inventory is used.

A summary of the clauses of the will (where it survives) follows the transcript of the inventory. In many cases this provides evidence of ownership of property, and of disposals of goods made before death or before the making of the inventory, and places the inventory of household goods and farming or trade equipment in a wider context. The family circumstances and relationships of the testator are also often made clear.

Where the deceased's occupation is only given in the will, it has been incorporated in the heading of the inventory.

In the numeration sequence two numbers were not used: [15] and [224]

Original spelling has been retained except for parish names which are modernised.

Sums of money have been rationalised using the form £0 0s 0d without punctuation.

BIBLIOGRAPHY

Inventories

Holman, Joan and Herridge, Marion, *Index of Surrey Probate Inventories, 16th –19th centuries* (Domestic Buildings Research Group (Surrey), 1986)

Carlin, Martha, *London and Southwark Inventories 1316-1650* (IHR, 1997)
(This volume contains an excellent select bibliography on mediaeval and modern personal inventories pp. xxi-xxiii)

Abdy, Barbara, *Probate inventories for Epsom and Ewell from 1561 to 1834*, (Nonsuch Antiquarian Society, 2001)

Harries, Joan, *Crondall In The Time Of Elizabeth I, A Study Based On The Probate Inventories* (Farnham Museum, 1987)

Heselton, Kenneth Y., *Sunbury household effects 1673-1724 (probate inventories)* (Sunbury & Shepperton Local History Society, occasional publications, 2, 1976)

Havinden, Michael Ashley, *Household and farming inventories in Oxfordshire 1550-1590* (HMC Joint Publication no 10 / Oxfordshire Record Series Vol 44, 1965)

Wills

Webb, Cliff, *Union index of Surrey probate records which survive from before the year 1650.* (British Record Society, 1990)

See also The National Archives online index to wills proved in the PCC. (www.documentsonline.nationalarchives.gov.uk)

Gibson, J., *Probate Jurisdictions: Wills and Where to Find Them* (Federation of Family History Societies, 4th edition 1994)

Camp, A. J., *Wills and their Whereabouts*, (private publication, 1974)

Cox, Jane, *Affection Defying the Power of Death: wills, probate and death duty records,* (Federation of Family History Societies, 1993)

Scott, Miriam, *Prerogative Court of Canterbury Wills and other Probate Records* PRO Guide 15, (Public Record Office 1997)

Riden, Philip, *Probate records and the local community* (Alan Sutton, 1985)
Arkell, T, Evans, N and Goose, N., *When death do us part, understanding and interpreting the probate records of early modern England* (Leopard's Head, 2000)

Probate Accounts

Spufford, Peter, *Probate accounts of England and Wales K-Z,* (British Record Society Index Library 113, 1999)

Bower, Jacqueline, *Probate accounts*, Short guides to records, No. 34 (Historical Association, 1994)

Diocesan material

Willis, Arthur, *Winchester Consistory Court Depositions 1561-1602,* (Willis, 1960)

Willis, Arthur, *Wills, administrations and inventories with the Winchester Diocesan Records,* (Willis 1968)

INTRODUCTION

THE NATURE AND VALUE OF PROBATE INVENTORIES

'Tis opportune to look back upon old times, and contemplate our forefathers' wrote Sir Thomas Browne in 1658.[1] In an article in *The Historian* in summer 2002, defending the study of her subject, the distinguished historian Dr Marjorie Reeves told fellow practitioners *'The first use of history today therefore begins with a search for roots'*. This volume is for those who (as she put it) *'find their real reward comes in bringing back to memory ordinary people who have no place in national history and therefore would otherwise be lost'... 'It is only as writers of history set out to get as close as possible to the reality of past lives that there is any nourishing truth to be found for the present'.*[2]

Lists of the household goods and paraphernalia of those recently dead, particularly of the humbler sort, can bring the reader very close to the daily lives of those who used them.

These probate inventories tell us virtually nothing of relevance to the old style dynastic, administrative and nationalistic history, (though 'a Musket with all his furnyture, a bowe with a shef of Arrowes', in an upper room in the house of a noted Guildford vintner in April 1588 (**263**) conjures up a Dad's Army ready to face invaders brought by the Armada). Insofar as they take us into the workshops and storerooms of craftsmen and tradesman they are evidence for economic history, if at a local level. Active women, many of them widows, have a place in women's studies. But these lists are essentially domestic. They take us through the rooms in cottages and farmhouses, and the occasional mansion. We learn what items of furniture they contained, and what equipment was used in the storage and preparation of food in kitchen, stillroom and dairy. In barns and outhouses lie the tools and implements used in farming and cognate activities, as well as animals. Brief summaries of the wills to which the inventories were an adjunct are provided to set testator, house and contents in a family and wider financial and social frame.

Dr Reeves has accurately identified where the interests of many of the non-professionals who undertake their own searches in historical sources now lie. As more and more of the records of routine administrative processes are made available fewer of our former citizen ancestors are lost to memory. The direct and lateral descendants of four hundred and forty four men and women who lived in Surrey during the reign of the first Elizabeth will now be able to find out about the furniture and other belongings of an ancestor, possibly even identify the house or cottage where that person lived. Village histories will acquire depth, whether in areas still rural or eaten up by suburbia. The settlements along the Thames which are now wholly urban will reveal early stages in their change of nature.

The testamentary process

By this time the distinction between a will, devising land, and a testament, moveable goods, was blurred, and it was usual to combine the two in a single Will and

[1] Sir Thomas Browne, The Epistle Dedicatory to *Hydriotaphia,* 1658
[2] Marjorie Reeves, 'The Uses of History in 21stc.', *The Historian,* No 74 Summer 2002

Testament. Although the royal courts retained jurisdiction over heritable land (though not leases), all other procedures concerned with a testator's disposition of his possessions were the responsibility of the ecclesiastical courts. This was because the 'last will' was inseparably associated with the final, deathbed confession, whereby the testator prepared himself or herself to meet God. The future of a soul was at risk. So important was this confession considered that anyone who died without making a will, intestate, could not be buried in consecrated ground, and his property could be forfeit. Because of the stigma attached to dying without a will a note of intended bequests given by word of mouth before two witnesses would be accepted and treated as a 'nuncupative' or 'nuncupatory' will. The church was also concerned to see that the wishes of the deceased should not be set aside by possibly aggrieved or disappointed relations, and treated the executor (required by a testament) as its agent in ensuring that the testator's wishes, as expressed in the will, were correctly carried out.

The 'will and testament' was written out, sometimes by a professional scribe, or a notary, and often at the dictation of the testator. He or she signed it in the presence of witnesses, whose signatures then authenticated both will and the testator's signature. It would name one or more executors, and also frequently an overseer or overseers, whose authority outlasted that of the executor, which terminated with the probate of the will. After the testator's death the will would be taken to the ecclesiastical court by the executors. The official of the court would issue a bond requiring the executors to produce an inventory and valuation of the deceased's moveable possessions and to keep an account of all their transactions. The inventory would then be prepared by two appraisers, usually two neighbours, or two men working in the same trade. There would be two copies.

Once the inventory with valuation, and the executors' accounts had been approved by the court official, probate would be granted, and the will entered in the register of the court. The probate act, (a note of proof) would be entered in the Probate Act Book, while the bond, the inventory and accounts were filed with the records of the court. The executor could then proceed to the payment of expenses incurred since the death, and start distribution of legacies and payments of any outstanding debts. Until the estate was wound up the executor was responsible for the deceased's dependents, and must again keep full accounts. In the case of intestacy Letters of Administration were issued at the stage when probate was granted. The final stage usually lasted between nine months and two years. If not completed within two years an official called the Apparitor was sent out to see what was happening. A fee was due to the court, nothing if value of goods was under £20, thereafter graduated.

Church courts in Surrey

The structural system of courts was the same throughout England, and in all dioceses the archdeacon's courts were the lowest level. In the diocese of Winchester there were two of these, the archdeaconry of Surrey and the archdeaconry of Winchester. The next level up in the hierarchy of the bishop's courts was his consistory court at Winchester. Wills could be proved by either the bishop or his commissaries when the archdeacons' courts were inhibited, normally during the months March to May. Neither officials nor courts were necessarily resident in one place, and might sit in parish churches in Surrey towns to conduct business, including proving wills.
The wills of those who owned no property outside the diocese in which they lived could be proved in any court of their bishop. Wills of those who owned property in more than one diocese would use the archbishop's court in the province concerned, in the case of Surrey the Prerogative Court of Canterbury. Those who lived in a

Peculiar of the Archbishop of Canterbury had in any case to use his court. The archdeaconry courts had no jurisdiction over Administrations of the goods of those who died intestate, though they could validate an Administration with will annexed. There are glimpses of the system at work in the pages of text that follow. What looks like a complex system seems to have caused few delays, and the inventory was usually prepared within a few days of the death. Rather longer could elapse before the will was proved. That there were inherent difficulties is shown by a note written on one copy of the will of William Luffe, probably of Frensham, proved on 30 May 1582: "this will was soe defaced by reason of rayne being carried from Guildford to Winchester from the visitation the xxxith of May 1582 in a Cloke bagge". Another copy had to be made. (**182**).

Probate records for Surrey: their survival and present whereabouts

The probate records of the Archdeaconry of Hampshire and of the Consistory Court of the Bishop of Winchester are now held in Hampshire Record Office in Winchester. The survival of both wills and inventories in these series is good for this period, and the majority of the inventories in this book are from these sources.

The records of the Archdeaconry of Surrey and of the Bishop of Winchester's Commissary Court are held in the London Metropolitan Archives, London EC1. The survival rate is not good. Only a few early inventories here will be found to have come from these series.

No probate accounts of any Surrey court have survived.

Records of the court of the Peculiar Deanery of Croydon are in Lambeth Palace Archives.

Records of the Prerogative Court of Canterbury are in The National Archives (Public Record Office) at Kew. Images of the registered wills in series PROB 11 (1381-1858) are now available online on the TNA website www. nationalarchives.gov.uk.

A few inventories in private collections including the Loseley manuscripts (LM) are to be found in Surrey History Centre, Woking.

Surrey People as revealed in their inventories during the reign of Elizabeth I

Because the survival of inventories in Surrey at this period is desultory and the methods of taking them not uniform they cannot profitable be used for any sort of systematic or statistical study. There are other uncertainties. The reasoning in the minds of appraisers when setting valuations is of course incalculable, and some may have been influenced by the pitiable circumstances of a deceased neighbour's heir. The valuation put on crops would have depended to some extent on the nature of the soil, as well as the standard of husbandry, and where beasts were concerned must have been affected by their age and condition as well as the time of year when the inventory was taken. A flock of sheep that must be fed through the ensuing winter would be worth less in October than the same flock in May. Nonetheless a few tentative conclusions suggest themselves, backing up generally accepted developments in the country as a whole.

Going on the comparative values assigned to animals and crops, as well as the quantity and quality of household utensils, it looks as though the standard of living in Surrey, including in areas of not notably fertile land, is rising during the period.

Taking the cost of beasts as a rough example, in 1561 four oxen were valued at £4, four horsebeasts at £1 10s, and sixty wethers and tegs with twenty ewes and lambs at 10s [**22**], while in 1603 six oxen are entered at £14 10s, two mares and three colts at £8.13s 4d [**426**], and thirteen ewes and lambs at £8 18s (**421**). The first valuation is undated but was probably taken during the winter, the second was made on 7 May and the third on the 4 May. Oxen were still the normal draught animals throughout the period, and the most valuable of the beasts in a small farmer's inventory. Steers were coming in at the end of the century. Horses were comparatively rare, being expensive to feed. Other indications of greater affluence must be the appearance of books and silver spoons, still exceptional, in unexpected places. Certainly the inventories become longer, and the descriptions in them more detailed, though this could be due to tighter regulation by officials. Many of the earliest inventories here list objects without naming the rooms in which they were found; this is unusual by 1603.

The temptation to draw conclusions from the occupations attributed to the deceased in wills or inventories has to be resisted, particularly since no occupation at all is entered for one hundred and thirty people. It is perhaps surprising to find that during these forty five years the deaths occurred of only one clothier, collier, dyer, fuller, mason, miller, shepherd (with no sheep) and victualler, though unquestionably many households carried out some of these activities at home. The frequently listed domestic "querns" must have been used for grinding their own grain into flour, for example. Two glovers and two coopers seem possible, as do three shoemakers, two tilemakers, two tanners, three saddlers, four carpenters and eleven weavers. There were a number of looms in farmsteads, greatly outnumbered by the wheels for spinning wool or linen. If, as is likely, most farmers were also craftsmen, many others may be concealed, voluntarily or involuntarily under the catch-all description of husbandman (eighty six names), yeoman (seventy eight names) or even labourer (eleven names). There are five instances of people with two occupations [**46, 60, 131, 206, 429**].

This preponderance of tillers of the soil illustrates the extent to which Surrey was still overwhelming a rural county, albeit including part of London, a flourishing county town and several market towns. It is not easy to determine what differentiated a yeoman from a husbandman. It did not depend on what you were worth: William Dynes of Godalming who described himself as a husbandman died with goods worth £272. He was evidently a farmer on an unusually large scale, and he named among the overseers of his will his loving friend the gentleman Valentine Costillion, a leading local landowner. In the long list of his goods is a bottle of Aquavita, one of the rare instances of liquor mentioned outside a public house (**401**). Conversely, William Collen of Thursley, with goods valued at £7.15s 4d is a yeoman (**23**). It looks as though one could tentatively conclude that while the labourer owned no land, and the yeoman did (sometimes a copyhold), the husbandman was often leasing his farm, but there are so many exceptions it is probably a mistake to try to discern a rule of thumb covering the whole county.

The moment when the yeoman of one generation has children who choose to call themselves gentlemen has not yet arrived. There are very few gentlemen in this volume, though some who were surely gentry prefer to call themselves yeoman. The inventory of John Steven of Cannon Court in Fetcham was taken by Robert Sandes of Fetcham, gentleman and two others who are called yeoman: Thomas Roger of Bookham Court and Richard Blundell. The long inventory demonstrates that Steven had a large estate, with six horses to pull his carts, as well as six bullocks. Among the products of this estate was home-made cloth (**359**). An odd yeoman is

Bartholomew Williamson of East Clandon who had no farming equipment but owned books, silver spoons and pins, and three gold rings, and looks like a professional money lender (**420**). The inventory of Sir Edward Bray of Cranleigh, unquestionably a gentleman, is unfortunately very damaged (**8**). The most sumptuous household equipment is that of John Hull, gentleman, of Hambledon, whose long inventory is also damaged, though a second list of silver only, which includes elaborately decorated vessels, is complete (**47**). It is difficult to resist the conclusion that something odd was going on after Hull's death, when William More of Loseley, not named in the will as executor of overseer, became involved. A letter from Richard Bydon, Hull's cousin, to More describes Mrs Hull as a 'stout wench' who will not go out of the house unless she is carried out by force. (LM Cor 3/31 & 45).

Most widows have few goods, and are among the poorest people whose inventories are here. There are exceptions. A few widows of gentlemen are at the other end of the scale. Katherine Vine, of Shackleford in Godalming, had a large and well-equipped mansion. Her goods, valued at £120 8s 8d, included a map and a side saddle (**379**). Alice Mychel of Frensham also had a side saddle with two girths as well as a 'Rodesadell' (road saddle for long journeys) with stirrups and girths. Her other goods, all valued at £20 10s 1d, included a 'cote of mail with six earthen cruches' (**415**). This perhaps looks more like a cherished bygone than a useable piece of military equipment. Joan Kidwelle of Rotherhithe, the widow of Richard, had a well-equipped house with the 'painted cloths', which are found in some rooms in very many other dwellings, in all her six rooms (**261**). One of witnesses to the will of Jone Beste of Gatton was Mistress Cicely Arundell 'one of the Quene's Highnes Maides' (**70**).

Weapons kept in the house are surprisingly common. Evidently those men whose names were on a muster list and who might be summoned to turn out kept their pikes and halberds to hand. Gentlemen had swords and daggers. Slightly surprisingly parsons' cupboards held the arms of gentlemen: Hambledon a sword and dagger (**270**) and St Nicholas Guildford a Scottish dagger, a sword and another dagger and a soldier's coat (**369**). The presence of bows and arrows explains the existence of the fletcher Henry Copsell of Lingfield (**4**), who died before Elizabeth came to the throne and lived in the remoter eastern part of the County. The light armour called Almain Rivets appears in several houses.

The assumed large size of William Dynes' and John Steven's farms is exceptional. Most of those whose living came from cultivating the ground appear to have had a small acreage; this is an unavoidable deduction from the number of acres under the plough and the number of beasts. Occasionally a will provides hard information about landholdings. Henry Sponner [or Spooner] a yeoman of Abinger, who lived in the wooded southern part of that parish, 'below the hill', evidently owned or leased a number of pieces of woodland, and timber must have provided part of his income (**438**). There are traces of evidence to suggest that the same pattern applied to people living in other heavily wooded areas of the county, usually in the Weald. Examples are Richard Davye the sawyer of Shere (**350**) and Richard Ticknor, yeoman, of Wonersh (**361**). The existence of woodworking tools including axe, wedges, beetle, chisel, wimball [?] and chains in many barns indicate an involvement with wood, if only to provide for the domestic hearth. Thomas Hart of Windlesham described himself as 'yeoman and carpenter' (**429**).

There is evidence of the production of charcoal, the essential fuel for the towns along the Thames. The collier Roger Mathew of Chadsworth, Thames Ditton (**322**) may have been making, or possibly simply collecting, charcoal from the southern parts of the county where William Elwyn of Horne had two olde coleweynes (**59**) and William Todham, also of Horne, one colle weayne (**149**). There were forty colesacks in the Stonehowse of Jefferie Smith, yeoman, farming in Sutton, whose goods totalled £204 4s 6d (**375**).

Where they are itemised the lists of household and farming equipment, 'implements of huswivery and implements of husbandry'(**416**) show everything needful for the activities that would make a family self-supporting to a remarkable degree. They could feed and clothe themselves on perhaps not more than a hundred and twenty acres. A number of cereal crops were grown (of which wheat was the most valuable), all usually in comparatively small quantities on from two to nine acres each: rye, oats, barley, wheat, and also in some cases peas, and tares. In a rare geographical reference we find Thomas Lawson, husbandman, of Walton-on-Thames growing 'two acres of payse and tayres next to the wharffe' (**412**). Unusually Richard Styllwell of Eashing near Godalming was reported to be growing beans and roots - 'Serten benys and Rotys in the garden' (**377**).

The almost ubiquitous querns or grinding stones prepared flour from home-grown grain, the mixed heap of wheat and rye – often grown together - in one barn perhaps indicating the nature of that particular family's bread. The 'one grindstone with the winche' (**422) was** probably for sharpening axes and other tools, and Nicholas Walker of Kingston, yeoman and smith, had a malt quern (**60**). Outside were oxen, steers, cows and calves, sheep, pigs, poultry, and often several 'stalls' of bees. William Phillip of Windlesham had ten and a half hives in his garden (**343**), and there were 14 stalls in another garden, in Puttenham (**193**). In a larger establishment the bakehouse and brewhouse would be a separate building close to the main house, while indoors (or sometimes in the yard) a cheese press, and churn, buckets, kneading trough for bread-making and the salting and powdering troughs required to prepare joints of meat for preservation. Flitches of bacon, joints of meat, cheeses and other stores were usually kept in lofts. A wide variety of cooking equipment and dishes, plates, bowls, and cutlery was always to hand, the vessels for the table being of wood, pewter or brass. Approaching the top of the prosperity scale a few silver spoons sometimes appear (**57, 60, 433**). Slightly further up come silver bowls, and further still salt cellars and standing cups (**92, 263, 434**).

In addition, for the already hard-worked female members of the household there was almost always at least one spinning wheel, often with cards and unspun wool, and frequently also a linen wheel, sometimes with flax to hand. John Marner snr of Thursley should probably be added to the twelve people who were weavers (or had been so in their working lives} had 'two loomes with the appertunances' in his house (**354**). John Barnard of Dorking is another (**231**). The weaver Peter Mannte of Runfold in Farnham had three looms, seven gears and a pair of warping bars (**49**).

The inventories of tradesmen, usually in towns along the Thames or in the market towns elsewhere in the county include some of the richest and most prosperous people in Surrey at the time. It is clear that Guildford, on the Portsmouth Road, county town, the usual seat of the Assizes and where parliamentary elections took place, was the most important place outside Southwark. It was home to rich businessmen, mostly of families long established in the governing oligarchy of the town. Nicholas Smalpeece, sometime mayor, was a member of a family that had been providing mayors since 1502. He was a haberdasher, and the long list of the contents of his shop indicates that he specialised in hats: many different elegant and expensive varieties, including for children as well as adults, are described. His household establishment was very large and exceptionally well equipped, and he had a farm, as well as a dyehouse, presumably using the water of the river Wey. The total value of the items in his inventory, which included a silver gilt salt and five silver goblets and twenty five silver spoons was £522 8s 10d (**405**).

Simon Tally of Guildford is described as a vintner, and he seems to have been also associated with an inn. He, like Nicholas Smalpeece, lived in style, and owned even more silver items, including three salts. His inventory totalled £291 15s 2d (**263**). The large and rather grand house (with hall, great chamber, three other chambers and a gallery as well as working rooms and a cellar) of George Glover, clothier, was well furnished. In 1561 we are still just in the great days of the Surrey cloth industry. As well as equipment in the shop there were thirty Kerseys valued at £57, and wool and yarn in the house valued at £94 0s 8d. Glover was owed £18 for kerseys by Fransis Barnard of London. He was evidently selling cloth which had been made by local weavers working at home whom he supplied with yarn. Total value £233 7s $8\frac{1}{2}$ d (**27**). The Guildford saddler Thomas Northall had a son Thomas who was vicar of Kirdford (**145**). Rather less prosperous was the shoemaker Richard Forde, whose goods were valued at £60 4s 8d (**26**). In connection with the cloth industry we should notice that a little further down the river Wey, at Ripley, was the fuller John Stanton, who also farmed at Ryde Farm and leased the George Inn in Ripley. His inventory value was £195 17s 3d (**397**).

Among notable tradesmen in other towns should be mentioned George Whittingham of Farnham, innkeeper of the Antelope and also of a larger, unnamed inn. The equipment and fittings of both are described in detail. The larger had much wainscot, and many named chambers, including the great, the broad stairs, the chapel, and the red, yellow and green. Among the many other rooms were a brewhouse, a taphouse containing four hogsheads and eight kilderkins of beer, and a cellar with two hogsheads of 'wine white', claret, and five gallons of sack. The total value here was £194 17s 8d (**443).** The silver items among the goods of the Farnham yeoman George Osborne (valued at £37 6s) cease to be surprising when his will reveals that he owned land in three counties (**434**). Of two glovers in Farnham, Henry Martin (**370**) and John Kent alias Newbury (**394**), only the latter's inventory provides evidence of what was to be found in a successful glover's shop, as well as covering his household and farm. Total value £103 18s 10d.

Books appear infrequently, and with one exception, only the Bible is named. The exception is, however, interesting. It occurs in a Farnham inventory, that of Thomas Warner, who was involved in the cloth industry and had a dyehouse. He was well off, owning a silver salt, a silver goblet and six silver spoons. In his parlour was 'one bibell of the largest volume, one booke called Calven's Instuticiones with two other books', valued together at £1. The total value of his belongings was £204 11s. He died in 1571 (**92**). It may be of relevance that two other tradesmen in Farnham had bibles: Richard Francklyn, a shoemaker (**427**), and James Raunger a weaver, who also owned 'six other books' (**435**).

The clergy, curates as well as incumbents, appear frequently in the inventories, writing wills as well as witnessing them all over the county, sometimes for each other. The vicar of Carshalton, for example, wrote the nuncupative will of the dying Robert Frayn in 1584 (**194**).

In 1589 the parson of Albury was witness to the will of the labourer William Mathewe, whom he buried two days later, recording the fact that his parishioner had been the victim of manslaughter by Henry Chesman (**269**).

Almost all the clerics whose inventories are in this volume have books, with bibles among them. Thomas Key, parson of St Nicolas Guildford, had books in his study valued at £6, and also three old maps (**369**). John Brownewend parson of Long Ditton, who evidently wanted to be able to read and write in bed, had a 'desk of burd made to go into the bedd'. His 'Lyberarie of bokes' was valued at £5 (**388**). No book is mentioned in the rather skimpy inventory of Richard Lucas the parson of Horley in 1561, but part of the document may be missing (**31**). In 1589 the parson of Hambledon, whose library was worth 10s, left five shillings to buy a bible for the parish (**270**). In the inventory of John Maudesley, curate of Bramley, the bakehouse is immediately followed by the bookehouse, containing books valued at £1. The books were bequeathed to his son Samuel (**414**).

In the earlier part of Elizabeth's reign very few laymen have books. In 1550 the books of John Clemente of Nutfield are valued at 3s 4d, in a total valuation of £80 0s 4d (**17**). In his will of 1565 John Bonyon of Chobham left all his books to a son (**52**). No value was allotted to the three books of William Beston of Southwark, gentleman, though 'an old Bible' was valued at 4s (**166**). The book, pen and inkhorn which belonged to John Browne of Cranleigh and Alfold in 1574 may be a book to write in rather than to read (**129**). After this date 'books' become increasingly common in the inventories of better-off laymen, though in what quantity is doubtful, as appraisers seem puzzled by books. All Simon Tally's books were valued at 5s 4d in 1588. In 1591 Margarett Brigman, widow and Dutchwoman living in Southwark, had 'certain bookes' valued at 10s (**292**). By the end of the century bibles are more frequently to be found among the possessions of humbler people.

A tradesman who owned two bibles and 'other small books' in 1603 was Arthur Talbot, bricklayer, of Kingston-upon-Thames. Unusually there were curtains with rods in most of his windows. He had evidently made a career out of the 'Great Rebuilding' taking place during increased prosperity at the end of the sixteenth century. He is called a bricklayer, but he owned several houses and the material in his backside builder's yard suggests that he was at least on the way to being a developer, the equivalent of a speculative builder today. Total value £124 5s 2d (**441**). Other Kingston men used the river Thames: Peter Buckland of Kingston, waterman, had a row barge and two wherries (**175**); Geffrey Warde of Southwark, also a waterman, had a wherry and a 'cocke and a rode' (a row boat? He had oars and sculls) (**219**), and Richard Jennings of Kingston was a fisherman who leased an eyot in the parish (**267**). A Byfleet yeoman left sixpence to Combes the ferryman at Shepperton (**436**). The shipwright John Waters of Rotherhithe lived in lodgings (**122**).

Trades whose practitioners have left inventories include a tilemaker of Frensham (**25**), a shepherd in Carshalton (**266**), a weaver in Send (**24**), a dyer in Ash (**437**), a tailor in Puttenham (**413**) and another in Witley who had a 'presin iron' (**141**), a matchmaker of Long Ditton (**382**), a fuller of Ripley (**397**), a tanner in Reigate (**223**), a clothier in Godalming (**237**), a carpenter of Richmond, who made himself a four-poster bed (**396**), and a Lambeth blacksmith using sea coal (**346**). It is worth noticing the amount of glass in the inventory of John Hoke of Chiddingfold (79). Only one musician has an inventory: John Mors of Guildford, who lived in two rooms with his wife Jowse and whose bass viol was valued at 10s (all his goods £5 14s 6d). His appraisers were prominent Guildford men, John Derrick snr and John Derrick jnr, Thomas Derrick and John Abbott (**432**). The only other instance of a musical instrument is the virginals in John Hull's house in Hambledon (**47**). Unusual occupations were the loriner, making metal parts for harness (**241**), and the wareburner, who appears also to be engaged in some craft connected with metal (**331**).

As usual Southwark housed some of London's half-hidden secrets, and was home to foreigners including a cooper, Cornelius Eggen, born in Falkenberg (**258**). We also find a gentleman, Tristram Blabye, owning £2 6s 8d worth of books, and running a school (**332**) and a well-set up widow who left everything to her faithful servant, including the shop, which from its listed contents could only have been a hairdresser's or a barber's. As there were no razors listed the former seems, improbably, more likely (**411**). There was a Southwark barber, Robert Woodward, who had as appraisers a citizen and vintner of London and a gentleman (**124**). Distinguished residents were John Mounger, citizen and mercer (**159**), and William Beston, citizen and girdler (**166**).

There is evidence for the movement of London money into rural Surrey. Before 1588 copyhold land in or near Kingston had been sold – and was not yet paid for – to Thomas Fletcher, citizen and merchant taylor (**253**), and a farm, perhaps in Woking, had been leased before 1572 to John Mounger, citizen and mercer (**159**). There are scraps of useful incidental information: when Peter Mantte made his will on 19 October 1563 he named his wife his executrix and residuary legatee unless 'it so happen that my wyffe doth fayll in thys plage that now is wyth us' (**49**). Could this plague, overloading the officials, explain the absence of any inventories in 1564? That diet was not as monotonous as one might expect is demonstrated by a spice mortar and pestle (**60**), and the 'table that hath a hole in it with chopping herbs' (**57**). Unexpected objects appear: a 'klocke' in 1569 (**76**), and a 'whelde' chair in 1572 (**159**).

Touching and familiar details are to be found. Family disagreements were not unusual, in days when young wives often died young and second families were normal. Thomas Harding made provision for the possibility that his wife and son might not be able to live in the same house (**368**). A concerned and careful widow hoped that she had made the arrangements in her will such that there would be a state of 'quietnesse' after her decease (**195**). Devoted fathers urged their widows to keep their sons at school till they had mastered reading and writing, and accounts, and could be apprenticed (**73** and **223**).

INVENTORIES

1558

Christian Botley 1

of Lingfield, widow of Roger; taken by John Gaynsford, gentleman, Thomas Kedor, Nycholas Saspe and Robert Dane, 17th April 1558.

	£	s	d
8 kene	9	6	8
2 bullockes of 2 yeres age	1	6	8
3 bullockes of one yeres age	1	0	0
A mare and a Colte	1	0	0
12 sheppe and 3 Lambes	1	10	0
Hodges, 2 shotes and a sow hodge		6	8
Wheat in the barne 2 quarters		13	4
2 acres of wheat on the grounde		13	4
Otes and malte in the howse		8	0
A ffether bed and the apparentes ther to bellongynge	1	0	0
4 payer of shetes		13	4
A great Cawdern, A brase pann, 4 ketlles, one brasse potte and one skellett, A chaffynge dysche and a latten bason	1	0	0
The pewter and the salt sellar and Candellstickes		6	8
Tubbes, trestles, Chestes, a ffat and other Woden vesselles, tables and all maner of other implementes of Houshold as pott hooke, fire jack, grydirne		13	4
Hir apparell		16	0
In Redy money	1	0	0
	21	14	0

Note: The Will was written on 24th November 1556 and proved on 27th April 1558. The executor was her son-in-law Richard Underhill and the overseers appointed were John Gaynsford and Robert Dane. Specific bequests of cattle and chattels were made to Annys, John, Johane and Margaret Wood, to John and Robert Standford and to the wife and daughter of Richard Underhill, both named Johane. Katherine, a daughter of the testatrix was also a beneficiary and it was made plain that all bequests of her late husband were to be fulfilled. Special arrangements for the future of John and Annys Wood were left to the executor to carry out, he to be residuary legatee. The three named witnesses were John Gaynsford, gent., Robert Dane and Harry Jamys. Probate was granted at Kingston, the executor having been duly sworn to the truth of the documents.

Ref: 1558 B 62 Will 1558 B 63 Inventory

Jone Burgies 2

of Kingston-upon-Thames, widow; taken by Andrewe Langdon, John Robynson and William Wood of the said town, yeomen, 26th April 1558.

	£	s	d
A fether bedd, a bolster, a Coverlett and a pillowe		13	4
A kowberd		10	0
A tornyd cheyre and a stone morter			8
3 pewter platteres		2	0
3 pewter disshes and 3 sawseres		2	3
A pewter quart pott and a pewter pynt pott		1	4
A pewter bason and a pottill pott		3	4
3 olde candellstickes and a pewter salte celler		1	4
2 kettiles, a Skymmer and a spitt		1	0

2 olde brasse pottes		5	0
On gown furrid with blacke shankes		6	8
A gowne lynyd with seint thomas wusted		13	4
A gowne lynyd with blacke cotton		3	0
An olde wusted kyrtell and an olde reade kyrtill		6	8
2 olde petycottes		4	0
Too syngle railes and too kercheres		2	0
2 sillver spoonys and a maser	1	6	8
A payre of silverhookes, a litle silver pynne and a silver Ryng		1	10
A payre of Jeatebeades gawdid with silver		1	0
A payre of Shietes		5	0
[*£5.10.5*]	5	11	1

Note: The Will was written on 7th April 1558 and Probate was granted to the executor named in the Will three weeks later on 27th April. Bequests of particular items of clothing were made to Jone Emes, her son's wife and to John Byggnell's daughter Anne, who was also given three items of pewter and a brass pot. Anne's two brothers and two sisters, John, Joan, Matthew and Elizabeth, were each given a pewter platter. Jone Burgies' son, John Emes, was given a short-legged brass pot, a pair of towen sheets and the gown lined with black cotton. The residue was to go to the executor, her son-in-law, John Byggnell. The witnesses were William Mateson, William Russell and John Bayse.

Ref: 1558 B 89 Will 1558 B 90 Inventory

John Cole, Cooll **3**

of Limpsfield, husbandman; taken by Robert Chapman, Wylliam Cooll, Robert Hards and John Chapman, 25th April 1558.

	£	s	d
In the hall			
A tabell, a furme and A Cheyre		1	4
A byll, A naxe		1	0
To brasse poots		4	0
To kettells, fower Chaeffars		6	8
Thre platters, fouer pewtter desshes, to saltts		6	0
To Candellsteyks, one Chaeffynge deashe of latten		1	8
In the parller			
One fether bede wethe a bowlster, to pyellous, a blayngket, A kyuffaryng and a payr of shetes		16	0
In the upere Chamber			
One tone, to keyllers, to standynge barells, to ferkence, fowr Chests, thre pyer of shettes		7	0
In the Key Chen			
To tabele clothes		15	0
One featte, to towbs, A greddean, A fyrrack, A brandIarn, A speet, A knead trouf, muildyng bourd, Cheyse lath		7	0
10 bowndells of floks, one bottell of lether		2	4
the Cattells			
5 Keyne, 2 healffers of to years owld, one boull, to wenyears, thre shepe, 7 hooghs, one mare	9	0	0
	12	8	0

Note: The Will dated 26th January was proved on 27th April 1558 at Kingston. The testator named his wife, Thomasine, as executrix, residuary legatee of all moveable goods and temporary tenant of his house and land called Riddone. The overseers, John Lambe and Robert Chapman, were given 6s 8d for their pains. The testator asked to be buried in Limpsfield churchyard. He gave 6d to the high altar there, 13s 4d to the church and 20d to the poor. His son Richard and his daughters Christian and Jone, were each to receive a 2-year-old heifer within 18 months after his decease. His sister's son, Mores Metherste, was to have a similar bequest at the age of 16. Richard in addition was given a ewe and a lamb. The testator's round table was given to John Cole's mother, but the great table was to be considered a stander in the house, together with the board bed in the parlour and the settle in the upper loft. These last three items do not feature in the Inventory. A bequest of £3 at the age of 16 was to be paid to Christian by her mother, but a like bequest at the age of 18 to Jone was to be paid by Richard, who by then would presumably have inherited Riddone at the age of 22. If Richard were to die or to produce no lawful issue, his two sisters were to inherit the property. In case the upkeep of Riddone was unsatisfactory or the legacies were unfulfilled, the overseers or the children were to take appropriate action as allowed by local custom. The witnesses were Robert Sole, William Coole, Henry Walles, John Winge, Robert and John Chapman. John Cole was buried at Limpsfield on 1st February 1557/8.

Ref:1558 B 140 Will 1558 B 141 Inventory

Henry Copsell **4**

of Lingfield, fletcher; taken by John Holmden and Raynold, Robt[-]d and Harry James, with others. [*undated*]

	£	s	d
6 kenne	8	0	0
3 bullockes of one yer and vanntage	1	10	0
Haye and Corne on the grounde	1	0	0
A mar and a Colt	1	0	0
5 hodges	1	2	0
2 matresselles and Coverletes to the same belongyne		6	8
2 Cawdernes		10	0
3 kettelles		3	4
A chaffer and an Irne pot		4	0
2 chaffyng dyshes		3	4
5 plateres, 2 pewter dyshes, 4 sawseres, 2 tyn saltes and an aquavite bottell		8	0
3 Candellstyckes		1	8
2 spytes, a grydirne, pothayngyes		2	4
9 payer shetes, 3 table Clotes	1	10	0
A Cobbard		10	0
All maner of howeshold, all maner of tolles of howshold and armowr, all maner calbers, stoles, tables, ffates, chestes and other wodden vessel		10	0
Henes, gesse and pultrey		3	4
Hys apparell		5	0
In redy money		2	0
	17	11	8

Note: The Will was written on 1st June 1558 and proved on 9th November the same year. The testator was a widower and he left instructions that his two daughters, Joan and Margaret, should stay in the house for a whole year. Then Joan was to be tenant for four years, followed by his son John for the remainder of the lease of the farm, if the overseers John and Raynold Holmden should consider him fit to take charge. The son was to have the profit from the farm in any case. The remaining goods and chattells were to be divided equally between the three children after Joan had taken two of the three bullocks, a bay mare, a cupboard and a chest. Witnesses to the Will were two women, Annys Borkett and Jane Wudenell of Docketes. His daughter Joan was to be executrix.

G.L.R.O. Ref: DW/PA/5/1558/70 Will & Inventory

John Lewer 5

of Newdigate, husbandman; taken by Thomas Nudegate, gent. and John Chandeler, 3rd October 1557.

	£	s	d
8 Kyen	8	0	0
2 bullockes	1	0	0
2 calves		10	0
A sow and 2 hogges		10	0
6 pigges		4	0
5 lambes		8	4
Corne, otes and haye	1	0	0
A cote, a dublet, a paire of hoss		3	4
A trifte and a broche			8
A flockebede, 2 blanckettes, a coverlet, 3 paire of shetes and a bolster		10	0
[*£12.6.4*]	12	6	8

Note: The Will written on 30th August 1557 was proved at Guildford on 28th April 1558. The testator's wife Mary was named as residuary legatee and executrix. He asked to be buried in the churchyard of Newdigate and, that the poor people might better pray for his soul and those of others, he ordered his wife to provide bread, drink and cheese. A cow was left to each of his 5 children, Thomas, John, Nicolas, Jone and Agnes. The witnesses were John Harris, the curate; Thomas Nudigate, gent.; and John Chanler, yeoman.

Ref: 1558 B 386 Will 1558 B 387 Inventory

---

[*] **Tolley** 6

of Charlwood; taken by John [*]burge [*] and Christofer Kempsall, 7th A[*pril*] 1558.

Two fetherbeddes, 2 bolsters, 2 [*], [*] Clothes, 2 testers, the one of greene and the other white.
4 pillowes and 4 pilloweberes
2 old mattresses and 2 corse bolsters
3 paire of flaxen shetes and 2 paire of Hempen
A dosen of Napkins, a diaper table cloth, a plaine table Cloth, and 2 towelles
4 gownes, one of worsted and 2 of [*]
2 old clokes, one of fryse? [*a dowe*] and the [*other*] of cloth, a g[*]ycote and a fryse cote, 2 pa[*ire*] of hose and 2 dublettes of fustian
2 shertes of Lynnen, a taffete Hat and a cap
A sword and a buckler, an arr[*] sworde and a dagger
Old hanginges
A ioyned bedstede and one plaine bedstede
3 chestes
2 turned chestes and 4 ioyned st[*ooles*]
A round table, a long table
2 pottes, one bigger then the other, a posnett
A frienge panne
A drypinge panne
A great old caldron, a hanginge [*] and a litle kettle
2 paire of pothangers, a paire of pothookes, a spitt, a trevet, a paire of s[*mall*] cobirons, a grydiron
6 platters, 6 dyshes, 6 saw[*cers a*] bason and a salt celler of pewter

4 kandelstikes, one chafinge dish and a skomer
A dosen of pewter spoones
2 dosen of trenchers and a dosen wooden dyshes
3 erthen Jugges and a pewter pott
4 ale barrelles
6 mylke pannes, 2 mylking [*]
6 tobes
An axe and a bill
3 Seves and a shawle
2 sowes and 4 shotes
6 hennes and a cocke
2 sakkes
A geldinge, a brydle and a sadle
On Nagge
54 shepe, old and yonge
4 Kyne and 2 hefers
5 two yereling bullokes
5 wenyers
Summe total
Whereof laid owt for the buriall
At the monethes day
For rent
To Anne Guylingner
To Thomas Guylingner
To Gibbes of Nutfeld
To James Edward
For skoolinge of his children
For a lettere of administracion
For expences in London in fetching of the said lettere
Summe
So remaineth
Exhibited by Margerie Tolley [*]st of [*] 1558

No trace of a Will has yet been found. P.R.O. Ref: PROB 2/340 Inventory

---

1559

Sir John Bekeham□ 7□

of Farnham, vicar; taken by John Rawnse, George Osborne, Wyllyam Byknell and Rychard Ubley, with others, 16th January 1558/9.

	£	s	d
A fether bede, a bolster, a Koverlit, 2 blankettes, 3 pyllos and 5 payr of shettes	2	10	0
A worsted gowne	1	10	0
A clothe gowne	1	6	8
A cloke	1	0	0
A cotte		10	0
A dobelet and a payr of howsse		4	0
2 olde frysse gownes		4	0
A hatt, a cappe and a typat		13	4
2 coffers		5	0
3 shyrttes		4	0
A dager and a Rappeyer		2	0
A mare, sadell and brydell	1	0	0
A payre of buttes		1	0

Bokes		2	0	0
	[*£11.10.0*]	11	15	8

Note: The Will dated 3rd November 1558 was proved on 18th January 1558/9. Shortly before dying in office the testator had written: "By me Syr John Beckham Vicar of ffarnham". He gave 13s 4d to the new founding of the fourth bell at Farnham and half as much to be doled to the poor of the parish at his burial. Margaret Estis was given 10s, a pair of his best sheets and another gift, unfortunately illegible as it had been written of the outer edge of the mutilated document. A cousin John Forby was to deal with a quantity of malt and £3 in money besides. After the corn and malt had been sold and the expenses paid, the residue of the sale was left to his widowed sister Margaret and after her to his 2 nieces. Gifts of money and books were bequeathed to other clerics, William Lyon and his son Hillary Lyon and Sir Robert Newman, vicar of Chobham. Sir Mathew Bromeley, curate of Elstead, was left the best cloak and Harry Battell was given a shirt. Edward Brewar was given money and the residue of the estate, he being appointed executor. Witnesses were Richard Ubley, Harry Battell and Thomas Haryson. Part of the Parish Register is missing, but as a new vicar was invested on 20th December 1558, John Bekeham's burial must have preceded this date.

Ref: 1558 B 32 Will 1558 B 33 Inventory

Sir Edwarde Braye **8**

of Cranleigh, Knight; taken by Simon Braye, [*] S[*], Thomas Kynner and M[*], [*] 1558.

[**document in very poor condition, stained and mutilated*]

	£	s	d
[*] and shews	2	0	0
A cheste		3	0
1 bla[*]		3	0
[*]		6	8
[*] Brasse potte		6	8
A Carte		7	0
[*] Hempe		8	0
[*] aufe	1	0	0
34 [*]en	5	13	4
	10	7	8
Debtes owynge to the sayde Edwarde Braye			
In the handes of Master Thatcher	20	0	0
In the handes of Master Braye	13	13	4
In the handes of Master Selwyn	15	0	0
In the same Selwyns handes	6	0	0
In the handes of Wyllyam Segar, Clerke in Sussex	6	0	0
	60	13	4
Summ total	71	1	0

[*Signed by*] Francis Harwarde 14th April 1559

Note: The Will, written on 16th August with a codicil added on 10th September 1558, was proved on 3rd March the following spring. The joint executors were Lady Jane Bray, his third wife, who was the residuary legatee and George Browne who was given the best of the two-year-old geldings. The overseer was Mr Caryll, who was given the testator's own gelding used for riding. Jane Bray, his wife's goddaughter, was left £100 and Reynold Bray £20 for a chain. The poor folk of Cranleigh, who were to carry the coffin to the funeral service thought fitting for the patron of the living, were each to have 12d. Lady Jane was to have the life tenancy of all the property in Cranleigh, which would then pass to his son, Edward Bray. The manor of Coneyhurst in Ewhurst was left to the son provided that the remaining debt of £60 was paid over to Thomas Bishop of Henfield, gent. and that John Caryll and George Browne, the other two signatories to the bond, were not troubled. Also the testator's son Edward was in no wise allowed to interfere with the management and sale of the wood and underwood on any part of the land, which was left entirely to the discretion of the executors to provide the money for the legacies and for the needs of Lady Jane. Edward would forfeit his inheritance if the will or codicil were disobeyed in any particular.

At the time of Sir Edward's burial in Cranleigh on 1st December 1558, Edward, the son of his father's second marriage, was already 40. He and his stepmother, Lady Jane, had recourse to law and much of the very large land holding was subsequently sold by both parties.

P.R.O. Ref: PROB 11/42A Will PROB 2/739 Inventory

Thomas Chesman **9**

of Wotton. *[no appraisers given and undated]*

	£	s	d
20 wethers	3	0	0
12 eowes	1	4	0
All his Apparrell		10	0
In his pursse			8
	4	14	8

Note: Two copies of the Will, written on 10th April 1559, differ slightly in the wording and spelling. The wethers, at that time "in the keeping of John Gadd of Puttenham", were to be equally divided among his immediate family: his brothers Percival and John and his sisters Joan and Alice. The residue of the estate was left to the executor, Robert Henryson, who was granted Probate on 20th April 1559. Witnesses to the will were John Germayne and the rector of Wotton, Romayne Agnet.

G.L.R.O Ref: DW/PA/5/1559/13/1 Will and Inventory

William Chittey **10**

of Godalming, Eashing, husbandman; taken by John Inwoode of Godalming, Stephen Stoner of Eashing and Henry Edwardes, 13th June 1559.

	£	s	d
3 small kettels		5	0
A skilliet, a posnet and a girdiron		1	8
Pewter vessell 6 peces		5	0
Spones of pewter half a dozen		1	0
Certayne tryne vessell with a pecke		2	4
A letherne bottell			6
3 Stappins		2	0
An axe and a bill, 2 augers, 2 wimbles and a Iron wage with a trivett		3	4
In the chamber			
A flock bed and althinges therunto belonging	1	6	8
3 shites		2	8
His wearing gere		5	0
2 shetes		2	0
A kerchewe, a rayle and a worsted aporne		2	0
A cople of oxen	3	6	8
3 steres	3	13	4
2 bollakes	1	13	4
2 kyne	2	0	0
A mare, a colte and a geldinge	3	0	0
43 shepe	4	6	0
The corne in the barne		14	0
2 acres and a halfe of Wheate and two acres and a half of Rye in the fyld	1	13	4
An acre and a halfe of peson and as much of feches	1	0	0
5 acres of barly	1	5	0
7 acres of otes	1	0	0

2 tode of woole	1	12	0
3 hogges and a halfe		17	0
4 pygges		8	0
A weane with weales and a dounge potte		8	0
A plowe and a harowe		5	0
7 boshels of malte		9	4
5 boshels of barly		5	0
An hoste heare, 2 sackes and a bagge with a spyning whele		7	0
A barrell and a pannell		1	0
In monye	15	0	0
[*Another sum of money written in another hand*] £46.3.2	31	2	2

Note: The Will dated 21st May was proved on 16th June 1559. Robert Crofter stood proxy for his kinsmen John and William Chittey, executors, in their minority. The overseers of the will were Robert Chittey of Hurtmore and John Hammond, a neighbour, of Eashing.

G.L.R.O Ref: DW/PA/5/1559/62/1 Will DW/PA/5/1559/62/2 Inventory

---

Sir Myles Codde **11**

of Weybridge, Parson, but died in Southwark; taken by Willyam Kenningeham and Thomas Everidge, 22nd November 1558.

In the Chambre of his kinsmans Howse, Robert Norton	£	s	d
A ffetherbed and a bolster and a pillowe	1	0	0
A coverlett and 2 blanckettes		10	0
2 payre of shetes		5	0
7 yardes of white course brode clothe		15	0
13 yardes of broade clothe blewe	4	5	0
One prestes Goune of blacke, faced with Tawney saye and lyned with ould clothe	1	0	0
A nother Goune of puke, faced with Russeles woursted		10	0
A nother Goune, faced with Russells woursted and lyned with Buckeram		8	0
A verye owlde Goune		5	0
A dublett of woursted		2	6
A nother dublett of mockeadoo		2	0
A Canvas Trusse		1	0
2 payre of blacke hose		7	0
2 owlde Jackettes of clothe and an owlde clocke		12	0
2 preste cappes and one owlde hatte		1	4
His bookes greate and smale	1	0	0
A Cubbarde of Waynskote		5	0
A latten basonne and two Candellstickes		5	0
A basone of pewter and a pewter dyshe, one porringer of pewter and 2 Sawecers and 3 Tynnen bottelles		5	0
A brasse potte and a chaffer of brasse and a kettell		5	0
A ffryinge panne and a Gryderon, 2 payre of pottehockes, a Spytte and a payre of Rackes		2	4
In Reddy monney	16	0	0
A sylver sponne		5	0
3 Coultes and a Mayre	4	0	0
A saddell, a brydell and 2 payre of stirroppes		1	0
	32	12	2
In debtes			
John Cooke of Okinge	2	6	8

Thomas Lawerence of Stanes	2	0	0
John Machim of Walton	1	6	8
Nycholas Sponde	1	0	0
	6	13	4
	39	5	6
Debtes due to the testator			
Richard Cooke of Okynge	2	6	8
Nicolas Sponge	1	6	8
Thomas Obye of Warlton	1	6	8
[*blank*] Smythe of London	6	13	7
	50	18	7

Note: The Will was written on 31st October 1558 and proved on 2nd April 1559. As priest and parson of St. Nicholas, Weybridge he carried the courtesy title of Sir Myles and asked that he should be buried in the chancel before the high altar, to which he bequeathed 6s 8d. Robert Norton was left £40 and all his cattle and horses. Thomas and Robert Norton, sons of his cousin, were to have £2 apiece out of their father's gift. Norton's servant, Nycolas Weston, was left 5s and Jayne, the maid, 20s. Kinsmen living in Harpswell, Lincolnshire were to have gifts of money at the discretion of the executor, the first named Robert Norton, who was to inherit the residue of the estate. William Nott of Dytton was to have £2 for his duties as supervisor. Witnesses to the will were Andrew Smyth, Thomas Grayson, clerk, John Barton and Richard Tompson.

Ref: 1559 U 036 Will 1559 U 037 Inventory

John Frysbee **12**

of Morden, husbandman; taken by Nycholas Smythe, Thomas Heryngman and John Mantle, 23rd December 1558.

	£	s	d
4 kyne	4	0	0
A horse	1	0	0
A mare		13	4
5 wether tegges		6	8
2 Hogges		6	8
5 acres of wheate	2	0	0
Brasse and puter	1	6	8
Spyttes and cobyrons		3	4
Sheetes and table clothes	1	6	8
One fetherbed and 2 mattresses	1	0	0
Coverlettes and blankettes to them belongyng		13	4
One table, one cubborde, a fourme and chestes	1	0	0
In money	2	0	0
Debtes owyng	1	10	4
[*£17.7.0*]	17	10	0

Note: The Will was written and the Inventory taken on the day of the testator's death, 23rd December and Probate was granted to Joan Frysbee, the widow, six months later on 30th June 1559. It seems possible that his executrix, his wife Joan, had been widowed once before, leaving her with 3 children, John Goryng, Joane Goryng and Alis Goryng, who were each given 20s in the Will. The testator left bequests to his sister Ellen and to the son and daughter of another sister, Anne Palmer. George Myller was to take care of the livestock, both for them and for his own two sons Lennard and John Myller. The clothes were bequeathed to the testator's brother Thomas Frysbee and to a certain Henry Cotes. The lease of 2 acres of land in Mitcham was given to the aforesaid brother, Thomas. Nycholas Smythe, his landlord and George Myller, his brother-in-law were appointed overseers. Richard Myles and John Mantyll witnessed the writing of the Will.

GLRO Ref: DW/PA/5/1559/117 Will and Inventory on same document.

Nycholas Goryng **13**

of Morden, labourer; taken by Nicholas Smythe, Thomas Heryngman and John Mantyll, 2nd February 1558/9.

	£	s	d
10 kyne	6	13	4
A horse		13	4
10 sheepe	1	0	0
Brasse and puter	1	0	0
Spyttes and cobyrens		2	0
Lynnen and beddyng	2	0	0
Two acres of wheate		13	4
One hogge		3	4
	[*12*	*5*	*4*]

Note: The Will, dated 2nd February 1558/9, is interesting because the bequests include 6 kine, two each to the testator's 3 children Alice, Jone and John, who were to receive the profits from Nicholas Rolande of Merton, [-] Goldsmith of Merton, Rychard Randolfe and John Tyler, all of whom "hyred" cattle and sheep from him. Monetary bequests were added to the livestock and the residue was bequeathed to his wife, Jone, who was to be executrix. The first two appraisers of the goods were appointed overseers. Richard Myles and William Mathew were witnesses. No date of Probate was recorded on this copy of the Will.

G.L.R.O. Ref: DW/PA/5/1558/118 Will and Inventory

Richard Peerson **14**

of Pitfold in Frensham; taken by Nycholas Baulden, Rychard Payce and Rychard Boxoll, 26th May 1559.

	£	s	d
3 kyne	3	0	0
2 bolokes		13	4
10 schepe	1	0	0
4 smale hogges		8	0
A Cauderyn		4	0
3 ketelles, a pote		3	0
7 peces of pewter		7	0
2 Canstykes, a frying pan		1	4
2 floke beddes		7	0
2 bolsters, 2 koverlettes		6	0
2 pere of scheattes		4	0
2 Cofers		2	0
2 pere of blaynkettes		4	0
Hys werying gere		13	4
4 hennys, a Coke		1	8
2 duckes, a malard		1	0
A broache, a Anndyryn		1	4
2 Vates, a kever and other Vessylles		3	4
	8	0	4

Note: The Will and Inventory were written on the same day and Probate was granted to the executrix, his widow Julyan, on 12th October of the same year. The church at Haslemere was given 20d and the management of the residue was left to Julyan to do what was convenient. John and Richard Peerson, Jone Betisworth and Jane Payne, their 4 children, were all married with children, each family being left 2 sheep. Jane Payne was left a flock bed and John Peerson's daughter, Jone was left a year-old bullock. The witnesses were Richard Boxoll and John Gase.

Ref: 1559 U 239 Will 1559 U 240 Inventory

Johan Tornor **16**

of Ham, widow; taken by Martyn Chapman and Thomas Ball, 29th January 1558/9.

	£	s	d
A kowe	1	6	8
10 shiepe		18	0
A fetherbedd		13	4
2 brasse pottes		5	0
3 pewter disshes, a platter and a pewter pott		4	0
2 payre of Shietes and foure kercheres		2	4
A flocke bedd		2	0
2 chestes		1	8
2 petycotes and an olde gowne		6	0
An olde helyng			4
	3	19	4

Note: This is a single document with no indication of a will or administration.

G.L.R.O. Ref: DW/PA/5/1558/276

1560

John Clemente **17**

of Nutfield; taken by Andrewe Ledger, Robert Kellycke and Willyam Kellycke, 1st October 1560.

	£	s	d
5 Oxen	9	0	0
6 Kyne and a heffor	6	16	0
4 steres	4	0	0
4 beasse	2	13	4
Two bullockes		16	0
2 horses	2	0	0
15 sheape	1	10	0
7 hogges and 6 pigges	1	0	0
Poltrey		5	0
Hay praysed at	3	0	0
Barley praised at	2	0	0
Pees valued	1	0	0
Oates valued	1	6	0
Wheate and rye	2	0	0
Weyne, wheales, yokes, ropes, plowe and Harrowes	1	13	4
Newe Wheles and Whele tymber	6	0	0
Toles	1	0	0
Newe tymber	1	6	8
A fether bedd in the greate lofte wyth a payre of blankettes, a coveringe, a boulster and 2 pillowes	1	0	0
The fether bedd in the litle lofte with a payre of blankettes, a coveringe, a boulstoor and a payre of pillowes	1	6	8
4 mattresses, 5 blankettes, three coveringes, three boulsters and 2 pillowes	1	13	4
18 payre of sheates	2	0	0
2 christeninge sheates, 2 celers, 2 payre of pillowbers, 6 table clothes, 12 table napkyns and three towells	1	0	0
6 chests		6	8
A cubbarde		6	8
For Wooll		5	4

For all the brasse		1	13	4
All the latten			6	8
All the pewter			8	0
All the wodden vessell			5	0
For the cheses		2	0	0
For all the yron implementes in the kytchyn			5	0
For tables, formes, chayres and stoles			2	8
For a stayned clothe and 4 cusshens			1	8
For bookes			3	4
For a woollen wheale and for hempe, flaxe and yarne			2	0
For the wood in southe parke		13	1	4
For wood at Horne beinge in the Lawe		[*no value given*]		
For a payre of scales and waightes and old yron and all other implementes of the house			6	8
For saddells and brydells			5	0
For newe yron		1	0	0
For all his weringe raymente		2	0	0
In redye money		1	12	0
A silver spone			4	0
Bakon			4	0
	[*£79.5.8*]	80	0	4
Debtes owinge to the testator				
Nicholas Beste of Nutfelde oweth		1	13	4
	[*£80.19.0*]	81	13	8

Note: The Will, written on 16th April 1559, was proved on 5th October 1560 and the Inventory was exhibited on 31st December by Robert Clemente, son of the testator. Robert and his mother Agnes were appointed joint executors and residuary legatees. John asked to be buried in Nutfield churchyard and he gave to the aforesaid Robert his lease in Hatchers and Wilkins Field. Richard, another son, was to have 5s for his trouble to be taken as overseer of the Will. He was given his grandfather's great brass pot, a feather bed, useful bedding and cooking utensils. The other children had bequests of money. William, Katherine and Ann, were to have £3, £6 and 4 marks, respectively. Katherine was to have an additional 40s, previously bequeathed to her by her uncle Richard. Every godchild was to have a shilling. A grandson, John Buchin, was given a 2-year-old bullock. The burial was recorded on 1st October 1560.

G.L.R.O. Ref: DW/PA/1560/7/6 f 246 Will. S.R.O.(K) Ref: 3089/10 Inventory

---

Robert Lylley **18**

of Wotton, yeoman; taken by William Byrchett, Thomas A Stone, Robert Wursfold and John Robenson, 8th December 1560.

	£	s	d
In the Chamber			
A ffetherbed with the ffurnyture		10	0
2 fflockebeddes with the ffurnyture		10	0
8 pare of shettes		10	0
5 Chestes		3	4
A carpett		2	0
The Chesse in the howsse		5	0
Hys apparrell		10	0
2 Tabell Clothes and 2 Towelles		1	8
	2	12	0
In the Kechen			
A lyttell Cawdron		4	0
3 old pannes		3	0

4 old kettelles		4	0
A Chafingdyshe, a bason and 4 Candelstyckes		3	4
5 pewter platters		3	4
9 pewter dysches		3	0
4 sawcers and 2 Salt Sellers		1	4
A nold Cobberd		1	0
2 lyttell brasse pottes and a Chafer		4	0
2 potthanggers, a Trevett, a Cobiron and a spitte		2	0
A Gyrdiron			6
All the Wodden Vessell		6	8
2 dryncking Cuppes			4
A Malt querne and Muster querne		4	0
A Chyp Axe, a Ryp Axe, a Cart Axe, a hatchett, a byll, 2 pronges and 3 Awgers		4	0
2 lyttell old bottelles			6
A Showell, a spytter and a mathowke		1	0
3 old Sakes		1	4
7 baken flyches		7	0
A Tabell, 2 Tresselles and a forme		1	4
A Cherne			6
	2	16	2
In the Barne and yerde			
Of Wheat and otes in the sheff	1	13	4
of Hay	2	0	0
7 kene	8	0	0
2 Steres	2	10	0
2 hackfordes	1	0	0
2 Twelmonthinge bullockes		12	0
2 lyttell mares and a Colt	1	0	0
8 hogges		10	0
3 Gesse and a Gander		1	8
1 shepe		1	4
The pultrey		2	6
2 harrowes		3	0
A lyttell Cart		1	8
	17	15	6
	23	3	8

Note: Witnesses to the Will, written on 4th October 1560, were Wylliam Byrchett, Robert Worsfold and Thomas Marten, with others unnamed. Probate was granted to the only executrix, Joan the widow, in the same year though no date is visible, the document having been repaired. The lease of their home was left to the said Joan for life or until she remarried, in which case it was to go to Robert, son of the testator. William and the previously mentioned Robert and two daughters Elynor and Margaret, had bequests of livestock. A third daughter Agnes was given a small hog and 2 cheeses; a fourth daughter Joan was to be given 6s 8d if she asked for it, otherwise the money was to go to the son, William. Rychard Marter, son of the testator's wife by a previous marriage, was to have 4 sheep and Margaret Leghar the maid was given a young calf. Wylliam Byrchett and Robert Worsfold were appointed overseers.

Ref:1560 U 182 Will 1560 U 183 Inventory

1561

John Banester **19**

of Chertsey; taken by Richard Warner, Rychard Whetleye and John Warner. [*undated*]

	£	s	d
In the chamber	£	s	d
A flocke bedde, a bolster, a pelowe, a peyre of blankettes and a coverlett		16	0
A selynge of the bedde and two hedde clothes		2	0
Thre peyre of canvas shettes, owld		9	6
Two owlde table clothes, the one dyaper		2	4
Two owld Cercheirs		1	0
6 sherttes, 4 of Canvas and two of Holonde		6	0
A Rayle, a pelowbere and an aperne		2	0
Redye moneye		16	0
Two owlde cotes and a gyrkyne		8	6
Two Dublettes and two peyre of hosynne		6	0
A pece of clothe of 7 yerdes coler puke		13	4
Two yerdes of wyght Kerseye		3	4
One hatte and a cappe		2	0
Two stone and a halfe of fryse wolle and 6 pownde of lambes wole and lockys		11	6
24 lytelle cheses		5	2
Two chestes		1	8
Fower platteres, one dyshe, a sawser, two candelstekes, 5 spones and a salte seler		5	0
Thre kettelles of brasse and a skelett		3	2
Two brasse pottes, a trevett and a drypping panne		9	0
Thre bowles, a kever, 6 dyshes and halfe a bushell		2	0
A cobberd, two axies and a spade		2	4
A lytell stande for ale, a sterer and a fowrme			8
A spynnynge whele, very owlde			4
Two kyene, two stere bolockes and a mare cowlte	3	3	4
Wetheres and yeowse - 43 and 6 lambes	3	10	0
Thre hogges and 2 pyggee shottes		9	4
Malte a quarter		10	0
A cockee, 4 hennes, a capon and a gosse		2	6
One acre of mede called the Broke		6	0
Two acres of very smale rye		10	0
Two acres of smale ottes		5	0
[*£15.5.0*]	16	5	0

Note: The Will was dated 3rd July 1561 and Probate was granted on 25th August to the executrix, Agnes Harme, represented by the rector of Weybridge. An uncle John Melleste and a brother William Banester were appointed overseers. Two other brothers Richard and Robert had bequests of money and goods, as did William. Twelve unnamed children of close relatives were given a shilling apiece. This gift involved 5 belonging to "Uncle Warner", 4 belonging to "Uncle Melleste" and 3 to "Cousin William Banester". The most personal bequest was that of the testator's best coat and doublet and a chest with all the contents that had been his before his mother's death. This gift went to his brother Robert. The brothers William and Richard were to receive their 20s legacy from Fynche of Chertsey. Several other small legacies were made to "Aunt Melleste", to "Cousin Alice Banester", to Thomas Peter and to Izabel Roke. He asked to be buried in the churchyard of Chertsey, leaving 6s 8d to the poor men's box there. Agnes Harme was appointed residuary legatee and the 2 overseers were to have 5s each for their trouble. The witnesses were Roger Notyngham, parson of Weybridge; John Meleste, William Hudnett, William Banester and others unnamed.

Ref: 1561 B 14 Will 1561 B15 Inventory

John Byckenall **20**

of Puttenham; taken by George Merlyn, Thomas Withall, William Ludger and John Clyfton, 5th May 1561.

	£	s	d
On kow	1	0	0
On stere	1	0	0
On hecfur		10	0
3 twelmonthynges bollockes		15	0
On mare		6	8
3 coltes		15	0
30 shepe	3	0	0
On sowe and 5 shottes		12	0
In brasse	1	0	0
In pewter		13	4
3 candylstyckes		1	0
In the barne			
Corne	1	0	0
3 akers of Whete	1	0	0
On aker of barle		3	0
On helve of otes		1	4
On aker of fatches		1	8
On floke bedd with on coverlett and on bolster		10	0
3 pare of shettes		6	0
His apparell in wollyns and lynnins		13	8
On youke and on cheyne and a solter and culter and strappes		2	0
On byll and on shovell and axe		1	0
Two colfers		1	8
On table and a forme and two tresteles and on table cloth		3	0
On pothanger and on pothoke and on broche and a gredyron		1	4
Item on keve and on faett with all other Lomber		5	0
[£14.12.8]	15	4	0

Note: The Will was written on 31st March and Probate was granted to the executrix, his widow Kateren, on 21st May 1561. His son Richard, still a minor, was left the iron gear, some livestock and the land, which was to be managed for him by the overseers if the said Kateren should die before Richard came of age. Two other sons, John and Nicolas and two daughters, Kateren and Agnes, had smaller bequests. The executrix was to enjoy the land and the residue of the testator's goods for life. He appointed his brothers Edward and John Byllynghurst to be overseers. The witnesses were Mathew Bronnely, clerk; John Clyfton, William Ludger and others unnamed.

Ref: 1561 B 24 Will 1561 B 25 Inventory

John Cacot **21**

of Bletchingley. *[no appraisers given and undated]*

	£	s	d
In the Hall			
A table, 2 tressells and a forme		2	0
A chayre and tooe 3 foted stoles			8
A Cobberd in the halle		5	0
An olde paynted clothes		2	0
Brasse in the howse	1	0	0
The latten in the howse		5	0
The pewter in the howse		10	0

Spytts, pothowks, anderns, gridern	1	0	0
In the Kytchene			
Bruing vessell and a trowff to knead in		6	0
In the Chamber			
One fether bed, 4 pillowes, 2 bowlsters	1	0	0
Thre matterysys, 4 Coverletts, 6 blanketts	1	6	8
In sheets 15 payre	2	0	0
4 tabelclothes, 6 napkyns, 2 pillowbers		13	4
A stayned clothe over the bedd		1	8
4 cheasts		10	0
3 Cotes, a chamlet Jerkyin, a freas gowne, a lether doblet, 2 payre of hose	2	0	0
Bred corn and malt corn in the howse	1	0	0
6 oxen	12	0	0
4 horses, one mare and 2 Colts	6	13	4
A long Cart, a dong Cart and a payre of weales	2	0	0
5 kyne and 3 heyfords	6	13	4
9 hoggs	1	10	0
9 score ewes and wethers	24	0	0
Wheat standing of the grownd to the valew of	8	13	4
Barley standing of the ground to the valewe of	1	0	0
Otes standing of the grownd to the valewe of	1	10	0
In money	1	0	0
A plow and plowyerns and 2 harrows to the valewe of		10	0
[*N.B. Three totals written and a fourth deleted*]	77	12	4

Note: The Will was written on 10th May 1559. Probate was granted on 17th July 1561. Marryan, wife of the testator, was given £10 to be paid in four equal instalments at Michaelmas. Wheat and malt were to be handed over by one son, Thomas and the household goods were to be divided equally between Marryan, Thomas and the other son Richard. The aforesaid sons were appointed executors and residuary legatees, but the testator had certain anxieties about the future. A cow was bequeathed to Marryan and the lease of the Parsonage to Thomas. However, the overseers Thomas Cacot and Nicholas Syllyard were ordered to divide the goods fairly, if the two sons failed to agree on their shares. Richard and Marryan had been warned against meddling with the parsonage lease and the corn. A grandson Richard Nellyngham, son of a daughter Margery, was to be paid £2 10s at the age of 21 and an equal amount the following year. Jone Whyser, the daughter of Richard Whyser, was to receive £1 under similar conditions, the total of £7 to be paid by the executors. William Burges and George Nele were witnesses.

Ref: 1561 B 27 Will 1561 B 28 Inventory

William Chanell 22

of Wonersh; taken by Hary Chawner, John Gosden, Thomas Strete and Henrye Baker, [*no month or day given*] 1561.

	£	s	d
A table, a paire of trestelles, a forme, a Coborde, a painted clothe with stoles and quisshans		10	0
His apparell		5	0
In his purse		5	0
2 beddes, a bedstede with thappurtenances	1	3	4
A cawdron, 4 olde Kettelles and 3 pottes	1	5	0
24 peces of pewter, 2 salte sellers and a pewter potte		18	0
4 canstickes, a scommer		3	0
A spitt, a cobyron, a grydiron		2	0
2 vates with other woden vessell		6	8

A bill, an ax with other olde iron		2	6
In the Rofe			
Bacon and beafe		13	0
2 spinnyng tornes and a skynner		1	2
In the barne			
Rie		15	0
Wote malte		2	6
4 hors bestes	1	10	0
4 oxen	4	0	0
A wene, a plough and thappurtenances	1	0	0
4 Kien, 2 bullockes	4	0	0
6 swine		10	0
5 acres Rie	1	13	4
60 wethers and tegges, 20 yewes and lambes		10	0
7 acres otes	1	1	0
[*£30.6.6*]	30	16	6

Note: The Will, dated 15th July 1560, was proved on 21st May 1561 by his wife Felys, the executrix, who was to have an interest in the house and lands called Lee and Heylands, maintaining them in good order for 14 years. At that time their son Thomas was to inherit the property, being allowed meanwhile to keep his bequest of 5 wethers and 5 ewes on the copyhold land. Another son John was left £10 at the age of 25 and their 4 daughters Felys, Agnes, Johanna and Margaret, were left £4, £2 13s 4d, £2 and £2, respectively. The overseers were Thomas Chawner of Barnet and Henry Baker of Albury. There were some minor bequests of money and instructions that the surviving children should share the property if their mother should die. The witnesses were the two overseers, together with Henry Chawner, Edward West, Walter Punter and others.

Ref: 1561 B 33 Will 1561 B 34 Inventory

Willyam Collen **23**

of Thursley, yeoman; taken by George Byrche. [*undated*]

	£	s	d
A Cow		18	0
An other Cow		16	0
A twelmontinge bullocke		8	0
A wayninge calfe		4	0
A mare		16	0
20 shepe	2	13	4
6 lambes		8	8
A sow, 5 shutes		10	0
A flocke bed, a coverlet with thappertenances		6	8
A bras pot		3	4
A cawdron, 2 kettelles		5	0
4 platters, 2 pewter dishes		3	0
A salte and canstickes			9
2 tubbes			8
A table and a forme			8
Dishes and a ladell			7
[*£7.14.8*]	7	15	4
Dettes that he did ow	1	15	1

Note: The Will written on 16th April was proved on 21st May 1561. The residuary legatee and executrix was the testator's wife Joan. No overseers were named. He asked to be buried in the churchyard of Thursley. Of the 3 sons, John the elder was given a teg; Harry had a teg and a pewter dish; and John the younger had a ewe, a lamb and a brass pot. Daughter Elizabeth had a ewe, a lamb and a cauldron; her sister Joan had a ewe, a lamb and a kettle. His wife was to dispose of anything else as should "seme good in her eyes". The Witnesses were Richard Collanes and Johan Deyner.

Ref: 1561 B 36 Will 1561 B 37 Inventory

Petter Davy **24**

of Send, weaver; taken by Thomas Frauncis, Robert Smale and Robert Boughton, 14th April 1561.

	£	s	d
In the Halle			
A table, a furme and a cuborte		3	4
2 flock beddes and all that belonge to them	1	6	0
4 payre of sheittes		10	0
In brasse and pewter	1	6	8
Old twbbes and vessels		6	0
In wolle 10 pounds		5	0
4 peces of watchett kerseye	6	0	0
His Lombes and all that long to it	1	10	0
In baken		10	0
12 hogges	1	4	0
His pultrey		3	0
6 acres of Reye sowen	1	0	0
4 acres of ottes sowen	1	0	0
7 kyne	10	0	0
2 yong styre	3	0	0
5 yong bwlockes	2	0	0
2 mares and a colte	2	0	0
4 calfes		13	4
20 shepe	2	13	4
His apparrell	1	0	0
[*£36.10.8*]	36	10	10

Note: The Will, written on 3rd April, was proved on 21st May 1561. The residuary legatee and executrix was the testator's wife, Joan. The overseers Thomas Davy and Robert Smale were given 20d apiece. He asked to be buried in the churchyard of Send and he gave 8d to the poor men's box there. Two cows, 3 sheep and 20s in money at the age of 14, were given to each of his 3 daughters, Marie, Joan and Alice. Witnesses were Richard Davy, John Evans, Robert Boughton and the 2 overseers.

Ref: 1561 B 43 Will 1561 B 44 Inventory

Oliver Fanner **25**

of Frensham, tilemaker; taken by Thomas Tryge, John Hardyng and William Eyd, 8th March 1561.

	£	s	d
In his chamber			
A flocke bed, a boulster, a coverlet, a payer of shetis, a shred helyng and all his aparyll	1	16	0
Too tableclothys, thre coffers, a Cobard, a tabell, a forme		7	4
In bras, a pot, 3 kettyllis, too olde pannys, a letyll skelet	1	0	0
3 platers, 3 pothangers and too candylstykes		4	0
In the barne			
Of rey, otys and haye		13	4
A cowe, 4 hecfers	4	0	0
2 maris		13	4

fyftye shepe	5	0	0
10 hogges	1	0	0
22 pound of yerne		14	0
A poudryng trowe, a knedyng trowe, 3 tobis, a boule		4	0
A naxe, a byll, a tryfte, a gyrdyerne, a payer of pothangers and a payer of pothokes		3	4
[*£15.15.4*]	15	14	4

Note: The Will, dated 14th Feb 1561, left twopence to the mother church (Winchester) and fourpence to Frensham church. The testator's wife Jone, three sons and two daughters, were beneficiaries in the way of livestock. The wife and a son Oliver were to share the residue and to be executors. Another son Harry was to inherit a house and land called Byrchyn Reyd. Names of the other children were John, Jone and Annys. The overseers were Thomas Tryge and John Hardyng, both of Sprakely. The aforesaid overseers, together with Wylliam Eyd, Christopher Byne and others unnamed, acted as witnesses. Probate was granted on 21st May 1561 at Guildford.

Ref: 1561 B 211 Will 1561 B 212 Inventory

Richard Forde **26**

of Guildford, shoemaker; taken by William Marter, Anthony Lewesdale and Nicholas Parkhurst, 24th February 1560/61.

	£	s	d
The Hall			
One cupbord, 2 tables with a forme		5	0
The stoles with the Cushins, a steyned cloth, a carpet with the cupbord Cloth and a chare		6	8
The yron stuff in the chympney		2	0
The chamber over the hall			
2 flockbedes with a matteres, 3 bedstedes with all that belongeth thereunto	1	6	8
4 coffers with a table		5	0
12 payre of shettes, 2 of locrum and tenn of Canvas	1	10	0
The table clothes, a towell and napkins		6	8
2 payre of pillowbers		2	0
The chamber over the parlor			
A fether bed with a matteres and all that belongeth thereunto		12	0
A counterpoynte with 2 pillowes and the steyned clothes		15	0
The chamber over the entrye			
One bed with all that belongeth to it		5	0
The chamber over the shope			
A coffer		1	4
A Dycker and a half of lether	4	10	0
A quarter of barley		10	0
2 busshell of tares		2	8
2 howberdes		1	0
In the parlor			
A fether bed, a matteres and all that belongeth thereunto	1	6	8
2 coffers with the steyned clothes		3	0
The buttery			
12 latten candlestickes and 2 chafing dishes		12	0
6 pewter pottes and 4 saltes		8	0
The pewter vessell	1	10	0
The kitchin			
7 brasse pottes, a chafer and a posnet	1	10	0
3 brasse pannes		5	0

6 kettles and a skymer		13	4
A gerdiron, a payre of tonges and a kettle		2	6
3 spittes and a Cobbiron		1	6
A Cawdron		10	0
2 payre of pothokes with a tryvet and tonges		2	0
2 vates, the keves and other bruyinge vessell		15	0
In the shopp			
The shoes in the shope with the leases and other stuff	1	6	8
A grinstone		1	4
4 horsbeastes	4	0	0
2 oxen and 2 steares	6	0	0
Wheat and Rye sowen in the ground	8	0	0
Wheat and barley in the barne	8	0	0
A Carte, a plowe, a harrowe and all thinges thereunto belonginge	1	10	0
One cowe	1	6	8
The hogges, 3 sowes and 3 pigges		15	0
Other Lumbre		5	0
In Redye money	6	0	0
For leases	4	0	0
	60	4	8

Note: The Will was written on 28th January and proved on 21st May 1561. The testator asked to be buried in St. Mary's churchyard, Guildford, at the discretion of his wife Thomasyn, his executrix, to whom he gave the residue of his goods and 2 acres of land, bought of Mr. Combes, next to the Dean acre. His 4 children, or the survivors of John, Walter, Richard and Joan, were given £10 apiece at the age of 21. His wife's son, daughter-in-law and granddaughter, Henry, Joan and Agnes Berye, were given 6s 8d apiece. The Forde children were to have equal shares in half the brass, pewter and bedding. The overseers Mr William Snellyng and John Frye were charged with the investment and care of the £40 bequeathed to the children. The witnesses were John Bagfett, Nycholas Parkhurst, Edward Sackfeld and Peter Wye. The burial was recorded on 5th February 1560/61.

Ref: 1561 B 64 Will 1561 B 65 Inventory

George Glover **27**

of St Mary's, Guildford, clothier; taken by James Hill, William Cranle, John Astreat and Robert Dawborne, 15th July 1561.

	£	s	d
In the halle			
One foldynge tabell with a frame, one forme, one Cobbard, one Rounde tabell, one Chayre and to yonyd stolles	1	0	0
One Carpit of Dornyx, one grene banker and 11 Coschens		10	0
The hanggyns in the halle contayning 30 yardes		10	0
The halle	2	0	0
In the greate chambar			
The hanggyns in the cha[*m*]bar contayninge 36 yardes		12	0
A tabell with 2 trestelles, 2 forms		5	0
A Carpit lynid with solewych		10	0
A grene wendow cloth and 2 coschens		1	0
A litell Counterbord and one standynge trestell		1	4
2 Cofers		4	0
2 Joyned bedstedes	2	6	8
A brysell tyke fetherbed with a bolster	1	10	0
One arres coverlett	1	13	4
One payre of blankettes		6	0
5 Cortayns of grene sey and Rede	1	0	0

One fetherbed with a bolster	1	0	0
A payre of blankettes		3	0
One coverlett of Red lyste and blew		6	8
in the chambar	9	19	0
In the second chambar			
The hanggyns in the chamber contayninge 20 yardes		6	8
One teyster of Rede and yelow lokeram and 2 litell Coschens		3	0
A playne bedstede with standynge pellars		2	0
One floke bed with a bolster, one coverlett of Red lyst and blue and one blankett		12	0
5 fustian pyllowes with fethers		5	0
One litell floke bed, 2 pillowes with flokes, one old coverlett		8	0
3 cofers		3	0
One litell bedstede, one Jonyd chayre and a boyette		3	4
in the second chamber	2	3	0
In the thyrd chambar			
A bow with arrowes		3	0
One Jacke, one gorcete and one stole		3	0
2 swordes, one dagger and one bucler		4	0
2 pykes and one yavelen		2	0
One cheserake with a borde			8
2 old Cofers and one blake bill		1	4
in the thyrd chambar		14	0
In the gallere			
One bedstede			8
One flokbed with a bolster, one coverlet of lyste yarne and one paynted tester		7	0
in the gallere		7	8
Lynen and napere			
14 payre of Canvas shettes	1	15	0
One payre of holand shettes		13	4
One payre of lokram shettes		6	0
6 holand pellowbers		12	0
6 tabell Clothis of canvas		6	0
One tabell clothe of lokram		3	0
One tabell clothe of Diaper and one tuell of diaper and one dosen of diaper napkyns	1	6	8
One playne tuell and 6 napkyns		3	0
2 Cobbard Clothis of holand and one Cobbard clothe of lokram		8	0
of linen and nappre	5	13	0
In the buttre and seller			
17 plattars, 13 potengers, 12 sausers, 4 disshis, 2 basons, one pote, 2 saltselers, 4 cuppes and one flat pece, all pewter weynge all the some one hunderde fore poundes at 6 pence the pounde	2	18	0
One bason with one eure, 2 floure pottes and one chamber pote, all pewter		6	8
7 Canstykes		5	4
13 tobbes, vattes and barrelles and 3 dosen trenchers		5	0
the buttre and seller	3	15	0

In the kechen

4 pottes of bras, 2 chafers, 2 chaphindiches, one boll and one brasen morter, all weynge 94 pounds at 3 pence the pounde	1	3	6
One bras pane, one greate caudren, 4 smale caudrens, 2 skymers and 2 ladelles, weynge all the som of 49 pounds at 4 pence the ponde		16	0
2 broches, 2 pothangers, one longe Iron bare, one fyre scholfe, one fryinge pane, one payre of tonges, 3 payre of pothokes, one drypynge pane, one fryynge pane, one grydier, one payre of anndirons and one tryvet weynge all 154 pounds at 1 penny the ponde		12	10
In other olde Iron aboute the house 505 pounds at ½ penny the pounde[*1.1.0½*]		4	10½
2 tabelles, 3 trestelles, one forme and one litell standynge borde		4	0
One trow with a cover, 3 stolles, one Cope, one axe, one hachet and 2 drypynge pans of whyt plate		2	2
in the kechen [*3.19.6½*]	3	3	4½

In the mens chambar

One bedsted, one flokebed, one bolster, one blanket and a sprede		5	0
2 old Cofers, one basket with teaselles, one byll, one stilitory of lede and one old bedstede		8	0
2 todes of flokes		4	0
the mens chambar		17	0

In the bakhouses

One longe trow, one boltyngwych, one old Cofer and a ches prece		3	0
2 fyre rakes of tymber	1	14	0
In old tymber and bordes	1	0	0
5 lodes of fagottes		12	0
in the bake housis	3	9	0

In the yarde and baksyd

8 lodes of wod there and in the wode by extimacion		16	0
1 thousand of tyle		10	0
in the yard and baksid	1	6	0

In the shope

7 payre of fullar shers	3	0	0
One payre of small shers and 8 burlynge Irons		1	8
2 sherbordes		2	0
A prese with 5 followars and 8 dosen of prese bordes	1	3	4
10 corse of handelles		5	0
2 straves, one Rake hede with a rope and the yre gere to the same		1	4
2 hogeshedes, 2 plankes, one olde forme and a lytell standyng borde		1	8
in the shope	4	15	0

Thynges forgotton

In smalle nessesary thynges in dyvers placis of the house as shellvis, tobes, barrelles and many other smale thynges by extimacion to the valew of		5	0

Grayne and hey in the feld

3 akers of barle and 3 akers of tarris	2	0	0
3 lodes of hey	2	5	0
	4	5	0

In cattalles

2 geldynges	2	0	0

2 kyne		2	10	0
One sowe			5	0
	in cattalles	4	15	0
Money and plate				
In money in the house		20	0	0
6 silver sponis		2	0	0
In money lyinge in the handes of Fransis Barnard of London for kersis		18	0	0
In money owynge to George Glover		2	0	0
In money before hande payd upon bargyns of wolle		50	0	0
	fourescore and twelfe poundes	92	0	0
Kersis in clothe in the house				
30 kersis		57	0	0
Wole and yarne in the house				
4 todes of Russet yarne		6	0	0
One tode of White yarne		1	10	0
45 pounds of Corse Russet yarne		1	0	0
20 pounds of White yarne		1	0	0
9 pounds of White lyste yarne			4	0
5 todes of weget yarne		8	0	0
4 todes of Cullerd woll		5	6	8
14 todes of whyt woll		14	0	0
		94	0	8
	[£234.2.10½]	233	7	8½

Note: The Will was written on 22nd April and proved by his widow Jane on 4th June 1561. She was to manage all the property in Guildford, Godalming and other parts of Surrey for 6 years following his death, when it was to be given to a male child if such should be born. If a daughter were born she was to be given £50. This money was to be handed over to his daughter Agnes if no younger sister had been born or reached marriageable age. Agnes was to inherit property in St. Mary's parish, Guildford, then occupied by Agnes Mychell and £50. The testator's brother Henry was given his best gown, coat and doublet. The overseers were to be the Mayor of Guildford at that time and John Austen. A sum of 13s 4d was bequeathed towards the building of the Free School. John Austen wrote the will, witnessed also by John Tomson, Nycholas Parkhurst, John Bagfett and Edward Sakfelde. The burial of George Glover, clothier, was recorded on 25th April 1561.

Ref: 1561 B 72 and 73 Will 1561 B 74 Inventory

Thomas Haywarde **28**

of Runfold in Farnham, weaver; taken by John Joure, Richard Hitchecocke, Wylliam Stoner and Richard Butcher, 25th January 1560/61.

	£	s	d
The Halle			
A Table, a paire of Tresselles, a forme		1	4
The chamber			
One flocke bedde, a bolster, the stedle		6	8
A coverlet, a paire of blanketes and 3 paire of Sheates		13	4
2 coattes, 2 paire of hose, a doblet, a petycote, 2 canvas shirtes and a hatte		16	0
2 letle coofers		2	0
The buttery			
3 platers, 5 potengers, a basen, a sauser, a salte, 3 candlestickes and halfe a dosen spones		10	0

A caudron, 2 brasse pannes, a potte and 2 kettelles, 2 letell possenettes and a friinge panne, 2 broches, a pothangers	1	6	8
3 barrelles and a tubbe with other lumbery ther		3	4
The shoppe			
A lume and 4 geres, a paire of warping bares		13	4
3 carsye yerons of vellstuffe	3	10	0
A toode of flyeswooll		13	4
3 kyne and syxe other smale bestes	6	13	4
2 mares	1	6	8
10 ewes	1	0	0
A dosen smale swyne		13	4
At the roufe a hooge and a halfe of baken		5	0
Corne upon the gronde 2 Acres		6	8
The corne in the barne and a loade of heye		13	4
Halfe a score of poltery		2	0
Halfe a carte and halfe a plowghe and all that therto pertennethe	1	0	0
	[*20*	*16*	*4*]

Note: The Will was written on 1st December 1560, but was not proved until 2nd July 1561 by the executrix, his wife Agnes. The eldest son William was given a cauldron and a broach. Nicholas, the second son, was to inherit £2 13s 4d at the age of 21; Joan, Katherine, Margaret and Alice, were to inherit the same amount on their wedding days. The residue of the goods and chattels was left to his wife, but the business of finding money for the legacies was left to the discretion of the overseers, Rycharde Hitchecocke and William Stonner. George Osborn, Rychard Butler and others unnamed, witnessed the Will.

Ref: 1561 B90 Will1561 B 91 Inventory

Harry Hedger **29**

of Thursley; taken by Rychard Boxolde and John Styllwell, 10th February 1560/1.

	£	s	d
One Cowe	1	0	0
One bolocke of 2 yeres olde		10	0
Debtes owynge to hym	7	18	0
Hys aparrell		13	4
	10	1	4

Note: The Will was written on 14th January and proved on 2nd July 1561. The cow and £1 were given to Thomas Talmion and the bullock was given to Richard Talmion, his son. Peter Hedger was given £1 and William Hedger was to keep the £1 he already had. Three men were each given a shilling: John Collyns of Crogeat, Father Mower and John Collyns of Wilkes. Elizabeth Padwyke was to have 5s and 1s was given to Elizabeth Greves and to Florence Boxolde. The residue was to go to Susan Hedger, his mother and John Hedger, his brother, the two executors. The witnesses were the appraisers of the goods and chattels, Richard Boxolde and John Styllwell.

Ref: 1561 B 92 Will 1561 B 93 Inventory

Crystofer Lamboll **30**

of Ockham, yeoman; taken by Thomas Adowne, gentylman, John Freland of Brownes and John Sayer, 8th April 1561.

	£	s	d
Twoo flokbeddes and All thynges therto belongyng		10	0
In pewter vessell		6	0
6 payer of Shetes		10	0
In Apparell		6	8
4 Chestes		3	0

An olde Cubbord		2	0
Twoo Cawdorns and three pannes	1	0	0
A pott and A posnett		2	0
2 Spyttes, A payer of Cobberdes, A payer of potthangers, A gredyorn, A Trevet, 5 Iron wedges and An olde Sythe		3	0
Certyn Tubbes and bruyng vesselles		1	6
In Cattell, Fyve kyen and three Bullokkes	5	0	0
4 horses	1	0	0
7 hogges		10	0
In Corne Apon the grounde, fower Acres		7	0
	10	1	2

Note: The Will dated 8th March was proved on 21st August 1561. The testator asked to be buried in the churchyard of Ockham. His joint executors and equal residuary legatees were his two sons, Robert and John. No overseers were appointed. Robert Gregory, clerk and John Busshe were the only named witnesses.

Ref: 1561 B 111 Will 1561 B 112 Inventory.

Sir Richard Lucas **31**

of Horley, vicar; taken by Richard Bristow and John Goodman, 13th April 1561.

	£	s	d
One bed with all that belongethe there unto	2	6	8
One other bed with all that belongeth there unto	1	13	4
7 payre of shettes	2	6	8
3 gowndes, 2 coppes, 3 payre of hose, one dublet, 1 hatte, 4 shyrttes, 2 typpettes, 3 payre of shooes, the purse and hys gyrdell and the mony in his purse	10	13	4
2 chestes, one cheyre, one Rounde tabell		6	8
Thre pewter dyshes, 3 platteres of pewter and 6 pewter dyshes, 2 porryngers [*illeg.*] and one panne of brasse, one presse one tabell and one forme	2	0	0
[*illeg.*]	1	6	8
	20	13	4

Note: The Inventory was written with the customary title "Sir" for a vicar, but this was omitted in the Will, dated 21st March 1560/61. The testator asked to be buried in the chancel of Horley church. Five shillings was given towards repairs both there and at Burton. The largest bequest of £6 13s 4d was made to his brother Rennell Lucas and no other obvious relatives were mentioned. Richard Coply's wife and children were to have 1s apiece and Elisabeth Selden was given 5s, as were the three overseers, Richard Hewes, Harry Shawe and Edmund Hewett. Two of these men witnessed the Will, John Shawe replacing Harry Shawe; they were joined that day by others unnamed. The executrix and residuary legatee was Agnes Dawes, widow, to whom Probate was granted on 28th April 1561.

Ref: 1561 B 122 Will 1561 B 123 Inventory

Water Mabanke **32**

of Hambledon, mason; taken by John Hull, John Cheswyke, John Denyer and Henry Ropply, on Ascension Eve 1561. [*14th May 1561*]

yn the hall	£	s	d
A table and a forme		1	8
A Cobborde		3	0
5 platters and 2 dysshis and 3 saucers		3	4
3 saltseles		3	0
2 canstykes and a chafyngdyshe		1	6

A olde tynn botell			2
12 olde sponnys			2
2 bras pootes		4	0
3 kettelles and a lyttyll pap pan		2	0
Wooden platteres dysshis and ladeelles			2
3 boolles		1	0
A broche			4
A peyre of pothokes			2
A lyttell trevet			2
yn the kechyn			
A Cheyer			4
A Knedyng troo, 2 tubbes and a butter cherne		1	8
2 hamers and 2 trowelles		1	0
A shovell			3
A torne and a skaner			4
yn the chamber			
2 flokbedes, 2 sleese helynges and 2 peyre of sheettes		13	4
2 coottes and other his waryng gere		10	0
3 cofers		3	0
A byll and a dager		1	4
2 Tabell cloothes		2	0
Catell			
3 kyne	3	0	0
dettes that he dyd owe			
Paid to Master Hull		13	4
To Rycharde Chety		10	0
To John Elyot of Godalmyng		5	0
To Edwarde Byrlle		4	0
To Rycharde Flutter		3	4
To John Marcaunte			5
dettes dewe to Water Mabanke			
Master Scarlet owith	2	0	8
Raffe Mabank owith		13	4
	[6	*4*	*10]*

Note: The Will dated 4th February was proved on 21st May 1561 at Guildford. The testator asked to be buried in the churchyard of Hambledon. To the relief of the poor he gave 12d and to the mother church of Winchester 4d. Five gifts of 10s in money were given to John and Water Edwards, his present servants; to Richard Cheti, a former servant; to Johane Colen, his daughter; and to Elizabeth Colen, his goddaughter. The residuary legatee and executor was John Colen. A sum of 3s 4d apiece was left to the supervisors Master John Hull, gentleman and John Cheswyke. Three named witnesses were John Twersly, Thomas Handfelde and George Smyther.

Ref:1561 B 124 Will 1561 B 125 Inventory

Robert Mowse **33**

of Tandridge; taken by John Humffrey, Roger Heath, John Mentell and Thomas Isted, 27th March 1561.

	£	s	d
Cattell			
3 kyne	3	0	0
3 heffer bullockes	1	10	0
2 mares		8	0
One black balde horsse		6	8
4 hogges		13	4
12 Goattes	2	2	4

Tenne poultrey	4	2
All the Brasse	7	0
On Irone ketell and one frypane	2	0
All the pewter	5	0
2 brandIrons and a spytt	3	4
A Couberd	2	8
An old fetherbed, a blankett, a bolster and a Coverlett	10	0
All the lynnen	8	0
His apparell	10	0
All the chestes	3	0
All old woden tubbes	1	4
Old Iron	1	0
All the fodder for cattell	4	8
The monye in his pursse	2	0
[*£11.4.6*] 11	0	4

Note: The Will dated 15th March was proved on 16th April 1561. The testator asked to be buried in the churchyard of East Grinstead or wherever he should happen to die. The residuary legatees and executors were his 2 sons, Thomas and George. The elder was to have the property called Boxsures and the younger to have Blykes, both in Tandridge. He left small sums of money to his brother Anthony and nephew John; to Margery Person, a granddaughter; and to Edward Lege, a godson. Sums of 6s 8d were left to the overseers Thomas Isted and Nycholas Swane. His married daughter, Joan Person, was to have a third part of the household stuff and some livestock. His younger daughter Elizabeth was given livestock and Thomas's son Mathew was left a table and a cauldron. Probate was granted to Thomas Mowse and to Anthony Mowse, the guardian of George Mowse the other executor. The end of the Will is mutilated and part is missing. Two named witnesses were John Humfrye and Edward Stanford.

Ref: 1561 B 135 Will 1561 B 136 Inventory

Thomas Moyr **34**

of Alfold; taken by James Hurste of Alfold and Robertte Moyr of Cranleigh, 13th June 1561.

	£	s	d
6 oxyne, on with a nother	10	0	0
3 kyne, on with an other	3	0	0
On kowe and calfe	1	6	8
3 Bullokys, on with another	2	0	0
3 horss Bestys	1	16	8
6 yeus and a Rame		14	0
4 lambys		5	4
17 swyne	2	6	8
On weyne, a plough, yokys and cheyns and harousse	1	0	0
6 Acars whette	1	10	0
8 Acars ottys	1	6	8
In the barne			
On lode off hey		5	0
2 whyp says		4	0
In the halle			
Bras, 7 ketylls and brass pott and posnett	1	0	0
12 pecys off puter, a latyne Basyn and 2 salt sellers		8	8
3 candylstykys		1	0
2 potthangers, a broche and trevette and a payr o potehokys,			
2 fryinge panys, on Ax and a byll and a beke, 3 Awgers,			

2 wymbylls, on drawynge knyf, a hand sawe, a pronge	7	0
2 olde cobordys, a joynyd tabyll and a sete	13	4
On war byll		6
One flokbed, 4 payre off shettys, on pylowe	13	4
One olde helyng		6
All wodene vessyll	6	8
5 pound of wolle	2	6
2 lether Botylls	1	0
6 henys and a coke	1	6
On drypynge pane		2
On tabyll clothe		6
2 spynynge whylls and a payr off cards		8
[*£29.12.4*] 30	2	6

Note: The Will dated 2nd June was proved on 2nd July 1561. The testator left half his goods and cattle to his wife Anne. He asked to be buried in Alfold churchyard and left 4d to the poor men's box there. Sums of 3s 4d were given to the executors Robert Jakmane and John Browne. His daughter Joan was to have a bullock and a ewe and a lamb, as well as 6s 8d. The same amount of money was to go to his son Robert and to his daughter Gillian. His godchildren were left 4d apiece. The residue was to be shared equally between his other 3 sons and 2 daughters, John, Edward, Harry, Alys and Elizabeth. Witnesses to the will and the inventory included John Westbroke, Robert Jakmane, John Browne, John Moyr, Tomas Constabyll, Enyry Gonshote and John Fuller.

Ref: 1561 B 137 Will 1561 B 138 Inventory

Jhone Mychell **35**

of Chertsey, widow; taken by John Warner and John Evyenes and witnessed by John Myllyst, John Beryman, Thomas Chapman and others, 25th February 1560/61.

	£	s	d
6 kyne	4	0	0
48 sheppe one with a nother	4	0	0
16 Lambes		13	4
Thre Bolloxkes of to yeres old	1	1	0
To bolloxkes of 3 yeres old		16	4
A Colte of a yere		2	1
In the Chamber			
And old fether bead, A bolster and that dothe pertayne therunto		10	0
In hyre Pursse 10 shillings and a old flocke beade and that dothe pertayne ther to		16	8
In the lofte			
2 old matterys, Fouer olde bead steaddes		14	0
To olde Payntyd Clothes, to testers		5	0
A great chest, old, to Smallechestes		5	6
A olde Coubbarde, a old cheyer		1	8
Foure olde Brasse Pottes		9	0
And olde cawderyn, to old kyttylles, A lyttyll chaffer, 5 Smale Round Pannes, to old Lyttyll Kyttelles		6	2
5 Smale Bolles and boldyshes, 5 olde Toubbes, 2 Fryinge panes, To spyttes, 2 old Cobbe Ieryns, 5 uppe staves, a Trevytt		7	4
A Salte Troffe, the cover, a chese presse with the chesse mottes, old Loumber in the kyttchyen and a olde Whelle		3	1
In the halle			
A coubehard, a long Table, to Payer of tresselles, a forme,			

	£	s	d
A chayer, to Joynt Stollys		8	4
A lattyne Bassyen, a chaffynge Dyshe, 5 old Canddyll Styx, old payntyd clothes		4	8
12 olde pewter platters, dyshes and Sawsers, 12 trene dyshes with trenchers and spones		4	6
4 Payer of shettes, to old pyllowbers, A coursse Table clothe		4	6
to Frockes, 2 pettye cottes, old, with a Rounde Goune lyned with bockerome	1	0	0
A Kercher and Raylles, to neckyngers, 16 lockeryme Smockes		6	8
A newe flocke beade		6	8
The plowe with the yockes and harrowe		6	0
	[17	*12*	*6]*

Note: The Will was dated 26th February 1559/60 and probate was finally granted on 24th April 1561 to Richard Whettlye, the executor. Although he bore a different surname, he was to receive the residue of his mother's estate, being deliberately named as her son. Richard's two daughters, Ann and Joan, were each to have a cow, a sheep, a brass pot, a platter and 2 pairs of sheets. Alice Whettlye, John Whettlye's daughter, was given a lamb and Thomas Douglas a small cow bullock. Her servant Joyce Sewer was given 16d. The godchildren, a manservant Nycolas Whettlye and the house boy Raynold Key, were each given 12d. John Beryman and John Myllyst were appointed overseers. The vicar of Chertsey, the poor men's box there and the mother church of Winchester, were left 12d, 3d and 2d in that order. Named witnesses were John Whettlye, Wylliam Crockford and Thomas Chapman.

Ref: 1561 B 139 Will 1561 B 140 Inventory

William Roger **36**

of Fetcham; taken by John Hudson, John Blundell and John Griffyn. *[undated]*

	£	s	d
One fether bed		13	4
One flockebed, one matres		9	4
One mattres		2	0
5 bolsters		6	8
4 coverletes		10	0
3 paire of blancketes		8	0
12 paire of shetes	2	13	4
5 bedstedes		5	0
One bedhangar		2	0
3 payntede clothes		10	0
2 cotes		10	0
One worstede dublet		5	0
2 paire of hoss		5	0
One paire of shues			8
3 shirtes		4	0
One capp		1	8
One cheste		2	0
One coborde		4	0
2 tables, 2 formes		5	0
2 chayres		2	0
3 ioyned stoles		2	0
Pewter	1	6	8
2 bras pottes		10	0
2 cawdrons	1	0	0
6 pannes		12	0
2 kettelles		5	0

2 spittes		4	0
2 tryvetes		3	0
2 drypinge panes		2	0
one fryinge pan		1	0
7 canstickes, 1 chafingdishe		5	0
4 paire of shetes		2	0
5 awgers, one handsay		3	0
2 Jakes		4	0
Tubbes		6	0
2 yolfates		2	0
One kened trow, a charne		1	4
Dishes and trenchers		1	0
Dosen tynnen spones		1	0
One ax, one byll		1	0
Pothangars, pothokes		1	2
7 horss	10	0	0
One mare		6	8
3 coltes	2	0	0
4 oxen	6	0	0
2 steres	2	0	0
One stere		13	4
6 kyen, one bull	7	0	0
6 bullockes	3	0	0
2 wayninge calfes		6	8
3 hogges		10	0
7 shotes		14	0
4 pigges		2	8
Gees and galles		3	6
5 henes, one cocke		2	0
10 duckes, 2 mallardes		2	0
3 score wethers	9	0	0
40 yews	4	0	0
20 lambes	1	0	0
20 quarters barley	9	0	0
8 quarters whete	6	0	0
8 quarters otes	2	0	0
2 quarters peasen and tares	1	0	0
1/2 quarter beanes		5	0
20 acres whete and Rie	6	13	4
Plowes and cartes and all thinges belonging thereunto	2	13	4
[*£84. 4. 8*]	60	0	0

Note: The Will, dated 1st January, was proved on 21st May 1561 at Guildford by the executors, his wife Agnes and his son Thomas, who were to be residuary legatees. The considerable store of grain was carefully apportioned, by the quarter and the bushell, together with livestock, to his son Walter, to his daughter Mary, to Elynor Stephan, to Alis Carter, to Edward Bray and to Elizabeth Shore. The executors were to occupy the farm together, but if his wife remarried Thomas was to take sole charge and she was to move out. The overseers were his brother Robert Roger and John Hudson, who witnessed the Will, together with Thomas Francis.

Ref: 1561 B 166 Will 1561 B 167 Inventory

John Saker **37**

of East Betchworth, husbandman; taken by Christopher Whyte, Henry Harman, Thomas Wood and Christopher Tailor, 26th April 1561.

	£	s	d
The whole brasse	1	0	0
7 platters of pewter		4	0
One hetchell		1	4
One spyte with a pothanger with a trevet and a gridyron and 2 paire of sheares		1	8
Ould Iron with bills, hammers and other such trasshe		3	4
Ould towles of ould yron		5	0
A fether bed with a boulster and a coveringe, 2 blankettes		13	4
A paire of shetes		2	0
A chist		2	0
3 oxen	6	0	0
2 kyne	2	0	0
5 ewes with 3 lambes		13	4
5 hogges		13	4
4 pigges		4	4
A wayne		2	4
A yoke with the rope		1	0
In barelye unthresshed by estimacion 10 busshels		13	4
In wheate unthresshed by estimacion		1	0
Layed out in chardges		2	8
[*£13.4.0*]	13	5	8

Note: The Will dated 12th April was proved on 8th May 1561. His three daughters Alice, Gillian and Annys, were to benefit from his estate after his immediate debts had been paid and the house had been repaired sufficiently. Nicholas Parker, the executor, was to have the management of the land and control over the rents obtained. The custody of the three girls and payment of money to each of them on reaching the age of 17, was also under Nicholas Parker's control for 10 years. Christopher White was named as overseer; he witnessed the writing of the Will, together with Christopher Taylor, William Westbroke, John Browne and Francis Beckytt.

Ref: 1561 B 176 Will 1561 B 177 Inventory

Henry Selwode **38**

of Holy Trinity, Guildford, painter; taken by Symon Lyne and Arnolde Champion, 22nd May 1561.

In the hall	£	s	d
One Cupborde		6	8
The h[*a*]nginges in the hall		1	0
One table, 3 stoles and A cheyre		1	8
Onc carpett, olde and 6 Cusshins		1	4
8 pewter platters		6	8
12 pewter Dyshes		6	0
6 Sawcers		1	6
6 Porryngers		2	0
4 pewter Saltes		1	0
4 pewter pottes		2	0
5 pewter cuppes		1	0
8 latten candlestykes		2	8
A latten bason and Ewer		1	0
All the brasse		5	0

	£	s	d
One broche and A drippinge pann			6
2 payre of pothangers, one paire of pothokes, one Andiorn and A fier sholve		1	8
In the chamber over the entrye			
3 flockbeddes and all that belongeth therto		15	0
10 payre of canvas shetes		10	0
4 Chestes		2	0
An olde furnes		2	0
For thre tubbes and other lumbrye		1	0
One lease of a house beinge in St. Marye parishe	8	0	0
A bucken tubbe, 3 kevers and 2 bruynge vesselles		1	0
A testor of A bedd, 3 curteynes and the steyned clothes in the chamber over the entry		2	0
	11	14	8

Note: The Will was written on 7th November 1560 and proved by the executrix and residuary legatee, his wife Amy, on 6th December 1561. He gave 4d to the poor men's box of his parish. Out of the annual rent of 25s paid by the tenant Thomas Palmer of a tenement in South Street, Guildford, he asked his wife to pay Margaret and John Warner, his daughter and son-in-law, 1 shilling annually, his wife enjoying the remaining proceeds of the lease. William Mownger was given the great kettle and Richard Laxstyn his best working stone. The 2 appraisers were witnesses to the will, together with William Farlay, Richard Laxtyne and George Sherard, the curate.

Ref: 1561 B 180 Will 1561 B 181 Inventory

John Shudde **39**

of Shere; taken by George Redford, Edmond Kyryell, Nicholas Seman, Thomas Mongar, with others, 3rd January 1560/61.

	£	s	d
One steer	1	0	0
Two kyene	1	10	0
2 hayford bullockes	1	4	0
2 Waynyar Calves		16	0
One Maere	1	0	0
10 Hogges	1	3	4
64 Sheep	7	9	4
2 bosshelles Wheat		6	0
6 bosshelles Rye		12	0
2 quarters barley	1	1	4
3 quarters ottes		12	0
4 Akers Rye	1	0	0
2 loddes of haye		12	0
One brasse pott		4	0
3 lyttell kettylles		5	0
One possnet and one skellet pan			10
3 candelstyckes		2	0

	£	s	d
2 pewter platters, 4 pewter dysshes, 2 Sawcers, 2 porryngers, 2 saltt sellers, one pewter coope and one goblet of pewter		4	8
One olde fether bed, 3 flockbeddes, 2 bolsters of canvas and 2 pyllowes	1	0	0
3 olde keverlydes, 2 peyer of blankettes		15	0
3 peyre of Canvas Shettes, 2 tabelclothes of canvas		6	8
2 Joyned bedsteddylles		13	4
One Coobborde and one lyttell Rounde tabell		10	0
One Tabell, 5 Joyned stoolles and 2 chayers		5	0
3 chestes		3	0
One lyttell buckyngtub, 2 kyvers, one olde stobbyn, one steane, one dossen trenchers and one dossen sponnes		2	6
3 lyttell broches, 2 Andyerons, one lyttell Tryvett, one fryengpan, one cobyeron, one peyre of tonges, one fyer pan, one gyrdyeron		6	0
All Hys workynge toolles	1	0	0
One swearde, one woodknyffe, one bowe and syx Arrowes		3	4
2 pronges, 3 Sythes, 4 syckelles, one olde Harrowe		2	0
3 newe plowes with other ploughe tymber		6	8
7 hondred of hoopes		18	0
All Hys wearynge Rayment		13	4
In Redye money in Hys pursse		5	0
	26	12	4

Note: The Will was written on 15th December 1560 and proved by the executors, Harry Appesley and Thomas Frances, on 21st May 1561. George Redforde was appointed overseer. Among the bequests was a complete named set of new clothes for his servant Jone Shudde, comprising: "one frocke of my gray russet clothe redie made to her backe one peticote of the same clothe if there be so much or elles to have her peticote of my white clothe"; 2 canvas smocks, 2 canvas aprons, 2 lockram kerchiefs, a pair of hose and a pair of shoes. She was also given a ewe sheep. The testator gave instructions for the fair division of his working tools between Thomas Frances and Richard Dendy. His wife Anne was to have his goods and a life interest in the rents of his lands. The upbringing of his daughter was to be in the hands of the executors, who were to take charge of the rest of the goods. Eventually the lands in Shere were to go to a godson John Shudde and the lands called Parkhatch in Hascombe and Shalford to Thomas Shudde. Upon their inheritance they were to pay £4 to John and Joan, the children of the testator's brother Thomas. On the day of his burial in Shere churchyard, the poor were to be refreshed by a kilderkin of beer and bread baked from a bushel of wheat. Witnesses to the Will were George Redforde, Olyver Redforde, Nicolas Seymour and Thomas Monger.

Ref: 1561 B 189 Will 1561 B 190 Inventory

Bartyllmew Steyll 40

of Frensham, husbandman; taken by Bartyllmew Hardyng, Wyllyam Eyd and Simon Hardyng, 6th January 1561.

	£	s	d
In his chamber			
A bed, one shete and his aparell		6	8
A cautherne, 3 kettylis, a pot	1	6	8
9 pecys of pewter		6	8
3 coffers, a chayer, two tryftes, a gerdyerne, 4 wedgis, one sythe, 2 axes, 2 byllis		13	4
Too tabyllis, one forme, 2 kevys, 2 fatys, 2 kevers one boule, 2 bocatis with other lombry	1	0	0
In bacon at the Rofe			
Thre flyches		6	8
Corne and haye		13	4

A letyll carte		2	0
Too maris		13	4
Too bolokes	1	0	0
6 shepe		12	0
7 hogges		10	0
5 staule of beis		9	0
9 hennis and a coke		3	4
	8	3	0

Note: The Will dated 22nd December 1560 was proved on 21st May 1561 at Guildford. The testator's son Richard was named as executor and residuary legatee, he to have the land after one year and before which time Joan, wife of the testator, was to have the benefit. Subsequently she was to be paid 6s 8d annually for life and she was given valuable bequests, including his own old mare, good young livestock, the bacon in the roof and corn in the barn. Her son William was to share a hive of bees with his mother. His sons William and John and his daughters Jone, Anys, Alis and Cataryne, were beneficiaries of goods and livestock not all mentioned in the Inventory. The 4 other hives of bees were given to the 3 youngest daughters and to his son John. He and William were given a wether teg and the youngest girls a ewe. Household goods divided between the girls included a pot and pan of brass, frying pan, pappe pan, platter, posnet and a bed hanging. His brother Robert was given 2 bushels of oats, tools, clothes, a bullock and 5s. John Hardyng of Sprakly and Harry Huntingford were to have 3s 4d for their pains taken as overseers. The 3 appraisers of the Inventory acted as witnesses to the Will. After the burial in Frensham churchyard, 4d was to be paid into the church and 2d to the mother church at Winchester.

Ref: 1561 B 199 Will 1561 B 200 Inventory

Christopher Thorne **41**

of Ewell, husbandman; taken by James Codyngton, Thomas Alderton, Bonaventure Tayler and William Pecock, 22nd April 1561.

	£	s	d
One Cote		4	0
One dublett and one paire of hosen		2	8
2 Shertes		3	4
3 ffether bedes with 3 bolsters	2	0	0
2 Coverlettes with one blankett		6	8
3 testers paynted		3	0
Tenn payre of Sheetes	1	13	4
2 pilloberes		1	8
One old dyaper table Clothe and one other table Clothe		5	0
3 brasse pottes		10	0
2 brasse pannes		3	4
2 brasen Chafers		1	8
3 brasen Kettelles		3	4
A Chafing dysshe of Latten			8
2 Latten basons		1	0
7 Latten Candelstickes		2	4
14 pewter platters		14	0
4 pewter disshes		2	0
2 pewter pottingers with 2 Sawcers			8
2 quarte pottes of pewter			8
2 Iern Spittes		1	0
2 Cobbierns		1	0
One drippyng pann of Iern			4
One pothanger of Iern			6
4 paynted hangynges		4	0

3 bedstedes		2	0
One Coberd		5	0
3 Chestes		6	0
2 tables with 2 tressalles and one forme		3	4
Certen old tubbes		1	0
2 horses	1	0	0
2 Oxen	3	6	8
4 Steares	3	6	8
2 heyfers and one Cowe	3	0	0
27 wether Sheepe	5	6	0
17 Ewes and 2 Tegges	1	18	0
Tenn Lambes		16	8
8 hogges		15	8
A Carte		10	0
A plowe with the reppes and 2 harrowes		5	0
A Culter and a Share		1	8
4 akers of Wheatt	2	0	0
4 akers of Rye	1	0	0
8 akers of Barley	2	0	0
One aker and a halfe of Otes		5	0
One aker of Tares		3	4
Halfe an aker of pease		1	8
	33	19	10
Dettes whiche the said Christopher Thorne dyd owe att the tyme of his deathe			
To the Churche of Ewell	1	15	0
To Nicholas Waterer	1	3	8
To William Tyrrell, Gent.		18	10
To Edmond Hyde, Gent.		4	0
To John Kyngston		5	0
To Bonaventure Taylor		5	0
	4	11	6

Note: The Will was written on 23rd February and probate was granted two months later on 23rd April 1561. No rooms were noted in the inventory, but his wife Joan was left all the stuff in the parlour and his son-in-law Robert Thomson was left 2 oxen and also the feather bed in the parlour loft. These two people were left the residue of the goods and chattels and were made executrix and executor. Bequests of ewes and lambs were to go to Sebyne Baker; Elyzabeth More; Dorothy, Elyzabeth and William Smith; Catherine, Ellen and Luke Burges; and Annys Mathew. Thomas and Elyzabeth Alderton were to have a gift of barley and the aforesaid Sebyne Baker also was given a calf. None of the goods were to be shifted before Michaelmas next. The named witnesses were Thomas Basmor, Nycolas Waterer, Thomas Alderton, Robert Thomson and William Agland.

Ref: 1561 B 206 Will 1561 B 207 Inventory

William Whyte **42**

of Dorking; 24th February 1559/60. [*no appraisers given*]

	£	s	d
8 Ewes	1	6	8
8 Rames, tegges and wethers	1	1	4
A Cowe	1	6	8
A steare	1	0	0
A twelmonthynge bollocke		8	0

8 hyll of wheat	1	0	0
12 busshelles of barllye		18	0
On Coatte		6	8
Another Coatte		3	4
2 old Coattes		3	0
4 shyrttes		4	0
2 kettelles		5	0
A sake		1	0
On stone of wolle		4	8
12 pond of yarne		9	0
A gyrddell and a dagger		1	4
and a purse			1
[*£8.18.9*]	9	9	9

Note: The Will was dated 23rd February 1559/60, giving all the wheat and wool to the testator's mother, half the barley lying at William Holland's to his brother Clement and the rest of the barley to his master William Nettelfold, who was asked to be overseer. Small bequests were made to his sister Margaret, to his goddaughter, to John and Joan Maydman and to Anne Shoe. To the poor he left 5s. Marjary White was to be executrix and residuary legatee and was commended to the good offices of his master. William Whyte, a young man, was buried at St. Martin's, Dorking, on 24th February 1559/60. William Nettelfould, Raffe and Joane Mose and Annet Umfrye, were witnesses to the Will, which was proved on 20th May 1561.

Ref: 1561 B 225 Will 1561 B 226 Inventory

Thomas Wyght **43**

of Shere; taken by John Parkhurste, John Risbriger, Larannce, with others. [*undated*]

	£	s	d
28 Sheep	4	4	0
Onne horse		10	0
Syxe hogges	1	0	0
6 hennes and a cocke, 2 gese		3	4
One fether bedde with the fornature		16	8
One flockbedd with the furnature		6	8
3 pare of shetes		10	0
One cotte, a pare of hose and a doblet and a Sherte and a cappe		15	0
In Redye money		6	8
3 brase potes, 2 posnetes		16	8
4 panes, 3 kettells, 2 chek panes	1	0	0
Achafindys, a basen, a scimer, 2 candelstikes		3	4
7 platers, 3 pewter dyses, 2 sauseres, 2 saltseer, a dosen of spones		7	0
A tabell, a forme, a pare of trestells, a cheyer, 3 coferes		6	0
3 fattes, a cyfor		5	0
2 bules, a busell, halfe a dosen dyses		2	0
Halfe a dozen of sieves		1	0
2 sythes, a ayxe, a byll, a broche, one cobbyrone		5	0
Halfe a naker of Wheat, 2 akeres of Rye		13	4
	[*12*	*11*	*8*]

Note: The Will was dated the last day of March 1560, but probate was not granted at Guildford until 21st May 1561 when Alis, the widow, sole executrix and residuary legatee, presented the inventory. He requested that he should be buried in Shere churchyard. His copyhold lands in the parish of Lee passed to his son William and from the profits of the same lands 20s was to be given at the age of 21 to John, Harry and Edward, his 3 other sons. His daughters Joan and

Margery were each to have 2 sheep and specific pots and pans. John Parkhurst was appointed overseer. Sir Raphe Bunteley, clerk; Thomas Munger, clothworker; together with John Risbridger, Richard Maybancke, Robert Cranley, Lawrence White (here given his surname) and others, were witnesses. Ref: 1561 B 223 Will 1561 B 224 Inventory

---

1562

John Peter□ **44**

of Capel; taken by John a Stone and Thomas Stapylhurst, 31st March 1562.

	£	s	d
Eyght kene and heyfers	8	0	0
Two bolockys	1	6	8
Two yeris bolockes	1	0	0
Thre bolockes of one yere old	1	1	0
One stere		18	0
A mare and two cooltys	2	0	0
Hoogys and pyggys	1	0	0
Whete growynge on the ground		15	0
Wotes growynge on the ground		10	0
Bakon In the Rouffe	1	10	0
Brasse		13	4
Pewter		6	8
The cobourde		3	4
Woddyn vessyll		5	0
Beddyng		13	4
Hys waryng geare	1	0	0
A bylle and axsys and other ege toolys and all other trumpere		5	0
	21	7	4

Note: The Will dated 27th January was proved on 4th May 1562. The testator's wife Jone was appointed executrix and residuary legatee. A shilling each was left to the overseers, Wylliam Young and Wylliam Stere. Careful and specific gifts of livestock were made to his 3 sons John, Edman and Robard and to his 4 unmarried daughters, Alys, Joan, Elysabeth and Annys Peter. If any of his children were to die before the age of 21, the survivors were to be heirs to that share. John Stere and John Peter were the only named witnesses.

Ref: 1562 B 102 Will 1562 B 103 Inventory

Thomas Stere **45**

of Capel; taken by Edward Netylfold, Robard Swan and Wylliam Stere, 19th February 1562.

	£	s	d
Foure oxen and thre steres	8	0	0
One cowe	1	0	0
Two heyfers	1	6	8
Foure bolockes of one yere old and the vantage	1	6	8
Two maers and a coolt	2	0	0
The wene, the ploughe, the harro and yokes with all thyngkes perteynyng to it	1	6	8
A sowe and her pyges suckyng		8	0
The hey	1	6	8
The corne grouyng uppon the ground	1	13	8
Two bosheles of whete		4	0
4 bosheles of Rye		6	8
Wotys		15	0

Bakon		2	0	0
A floke bed with all thynges perteynyng to it			6	8
Two other beddys			10	0
A cobourd			3	0
Foure ketyles			10	0
The pewter			4	0
Tubbys wyth other wodden vessel			2	0
The pot hangers			1	0
A byll and an ax with other hedge tolys			2	0
A table and a fourme with all other trompere			2	0
Hys aparell			13	8
Two chestys			1	0
	[*£24.9.4*]	24	10	4
[W*ritten on the Will*:] My dettes				
and I do owe my brother Wylliam			19	0
I do owe John Hether		1	0	0
I owe my brother John		1	14	0
I have owing of Hew Mullford		1	6	8
and the seid Hew Mullford hath Contracted with the seid Thomas Stere to discharge the seid Thomas and his Executors of a bond for 4 lode of borde				
I do owe to John Pallmer			16	0
		[*£5*	*15*	*8*]

Note: The Will dated 22nd January was proved on 4th May 1562. The testator's wife Agnes was appointed executrix and residuary legatee. William Stere, his brother, was named as overseer. A sum of £2 each was given to Margaret and John and £1 each to his other daughter Agnys and to his other sons Thomas and Ellys. His godchildren were left 4d apiece. The three witnesses were his brother Wylliam Stere the elder, Robert Sheffield and John Cooke.

Ref: 1562 B 126 Will 1562 B 127 Inventory

1563

Jone Hawle **46**

of Farnham, widow and Innholder; taken by John Over, Thomas Wellche and Thomas Wallker, 2nd November 1563.

In the halle	£	s	d
A tabell and a forme wythe a chayar		5	0
A lettell syd tabell and a fforme, a pare of trestelles, 2 stolles, 2 mattes ffor benchys and a pare of playenge tabelles		4	0
2 angerys, 2 pares of potte hangerys and 2 perys of pottehokes, and a pare of bellowyes, 2 ffyar shovys, a pare of tonges		3	0
6 cossynes		2	0
3 paynttyd clottherys and a Jenyd bord ffor the bake		5	0

19 0

In the parlar			
A tabell, a pare of trestelles, a fforme, 4 gynyd stolles and a cheyar wythe a matte for the benche		4	0
Coberde		5	0
2 standynge bedys wythe 2 testarys, 2 conter paynes, 2 quyllettes wythe 2 blankettes, 2 ffetther beddes wythe a matterys and 2 staynd Clotherys wythe 2 bollsterys	2	0	0
2 Carpyttes		8	0

	£2	17	0			
In the Chambar over the parlar						
A tabell, a pare of trestelles, 3 fformes and a settelle, 2 gynyd stolles, a gyned bedestedyle and a trokell bede, a ffether bede 2 ffloke bedes wythe 2 bollstarys, 2 covelyghtes, a blancatte 2 mattes ffor bedes and 3 stayned Clotherys				1	13	4
the Chamber over the gatte howse						
2 bedestedylles wythe 2 floke bedes, 3 bollsterys, 2 Coverlyghtes wythe a presse, 2 stayned testerys and a staynd Clothe					13	0
the C[*h*]amber over the buterye						
A bede stedylle wythe a ffloke bede, a coverlyght, a fforeme					3	0
In the Chambar over the kechne						
2 bede stedylles and 2 s[*p*]enynge torryne[*s*]					2	0
In her parlar						
2 bedestedylles, 2 fforemys, a chayar, 2 fflokebedes, 2 bollstarys, 2 coverlyghtes wythe a blankatte, 2 staynd Clotherys, 2 testerys ffor bedes				1	0	0
3 Cofferys and 2 Chestes, 2 belles, 4 ollde sordes, a whyte bascatte					5	0
6 cosshenys					3	0
7 pellowyes					7	0
4 paryrys of lockerem sheetys and a hollon shette				1	0	0
2 Cobard Clothers, 2 touewelles of lockerem					3	0
10 parys of Canvas shettes				1	0	0
5 pelloberys					5	0
6 napekynes					2	0
6 tabelle Clotherys of Canvas					7	0
A tabelle Clothe of lockereme					2	0
6 touewelles of Canvas					2	0
A tynnen bottell						8
				£7	8	0
In the butterye						
2 Cobardes, a pare of trestelles wythe a lettell tabell, a settell wythe the shellvys					4	0
10 platterys, 7 pottyngerys, 16 ssesserys wythe 2 Chamber pottes and 6 sallttes, 3 C[*h*]ayferdes of putter				1	6	8
4 wyne quarttes, 4 bere quarttes and 8 bere pytt pottes, 2 wyne pyntes and a hallfe pynte					12	0
8 Canttykes and 2 Chaffendyshes of brasse, a braysyn mortter wythe a pestelle					10	0
	£2	2	8			
In the kechen						
A Callderyne					10	0
A panne					5	0
A kettell at gayge					2	4
11 kettelles					13	4
5 brasse pottes and a belle, 2 skememerys and a strayner				1	0	0
A pare of Koberttes, 3 bochys, 4 drepynge pannes and 2 ffryenge pannes, a gerdyreyne, a pare of andyerynes					13	4
5 bolles, a kever and a trowe wythe other kynd of lomber					6	0
	£3	10	0			
In the osterye						

A bedstedylle wyth a matterys, a wight testar, a coverlyght, 4 boshelles and a halfe boshelle and a peke wythe other kynd of lomber		8	0
In the baryne			
For haye	3	10	0
For 25 boshelles of ottys	1	0	0
For woode and fagattes		13	4
A hoge		3	4
A cowe at gayge		10	0
All her Aparrell	1	12	0
£7 16 8			
	25	3	4

Note: The Will written on 9th October 1563 was proved on 23rd November. Her only son Richard was appointed executor. Harry Stocker and William Bycknell, as overseers, were to have authority to divide the unbequeathed residue of the estate equally among the five children. Richard, Gillian and Jone, were given beds and Annys More's children were given kettles. Elizabeth was just to have her fifth share, but if any of the five proved discontented with his or her lot, it was to be taken away and divided amongst the amenable. Four named witnesses were George Osborne, Robert More, Harry Stocker and William Bycknell. Jone Hawle's burial was recorded on 17th October 1563.

Ref: 1563 B 80 Will 1563 B 81 Inventory

John Hull 47

of Hambeldon, gentleman; taken by John Twyforde, John Cheswicke senior and others, 20th January 1563. [* *Very large ragged holes eaten through the rolled document.*]

	£	s	d
In the hall			
Two standinge Tables with twoo fformes		5	0
An olde Cupborde		2	0
An olde Redd hanginge		1	8
Two warrbylles of one makinge		1	0
A fforest byll			10
Two javelens		1	4
A moule staff			6
A pronge for himself			4
A Sworde		1	8
A Skeyne for himself		3	4
A Cloth with Adam and Eve			6
An old benche Cloth			4
3 bowes of Ewe		1	8
3 of Wytche hasyll		1	0
A Quyver of lether with 6 beringe Arrowes		1	8
A Wyck [* *] Arrowes		1	0
3 sh[* *]			4
A th[* *]			2
A [* *]			2
[* *]		6	8
[*.*]		1	0
[*.*]			[*illeg*]
In the old parlor			
[* *]		6	8
[* *]		6	8
[* *]		3	0

[* *]			8
An old [* *]			4
An olde grene hang[*]		1	0
Two tables of pyctures one of [*] [*the oth*]er of the Regyment of France		1	4
A payer of grete Iron Anndirons		3	4
A payer of playinge Tables		1	0
Shaftes and Arrowes 28 payre		1	8
A long Settell			6
A grete olde Chest with a locke		1	4
A payer of Iron Tonges and an Iron forke		2	0
A lytle Cloth paynted with two pyctures			6
A payer of Vyrginalls		10	0
6 Cussyons of pound garnetts	1	0	0
A stand [* *] Counters			8
An olde [* *]			4
In the newe Parlor			
Fyrst A [* *] bedstedd, a Close st[*oole*] [* *]ed, a ffether [* *] Co[* *]	1	6	8
[* *]		13	4
[* *]		1	8
In the Chamber over the newe parlor			
One ff[* *] ffether B[*ed*] [* *] a pyllowe	1	0	0
2 olde ffether bedds W[* *]rydds and a blankett		16	0
A lytle ffoldinge table to wry[* *]		1	0
A Close Stole			8
A Settell		1	0
An olde Chest			3
A batell axe			8
A cote of fente covered with worsted and a hatt to the same		6	8
A lytle Crosbowe with a bender		3	4
In the grete kychyn			
11 broches		11	0
2 Potthangers		1	0
2 other potthangers to move of and on		1	0
3 paye[*r*]			8
A sly[*ce*]			8
Two [* *]			6
A [* *]		1	0
[* *]			8
[* *]			8
[* *]		1	8
[* *]			8
11 br[* *] and the worst viz 6 of the best [* *] A pece	1	10	0
2 Chaffers in the house and one at Mr Stubses		10	0
7 kittells lytle and grete, that is to saye 3 of the byggar sorte 10s and the other four at 4s		14	0
4 Latten basons, 2 grete and two small		11	4
2 brasse pannes		6	8

A lytle brasse pan with a sockett		1	4
2 brasen Ladells		1	0
2 Pappe pannes		1	8
A Posenett that lacketh a fote			8
A Cullend[*er*]			6
A Po[*]			2
A [* *] tte brasen morter [*]		5	0
[* *]		2	0
[* *]		6	8
In the butterye			
[* *]		2	6
3 g[*]		2	0
3 grea[*te*] [*Candestyckes*]		3	0
7 other Candesty[*ckes*]		3	4
A Stonen Morter with a Pestel			8
A Shoynge Horne with a Cheyne			6
An old Cawdron of brasse		1	8
29 platters of all Sortes	1	13	8
20 Dyshes of all sortes		16	8
16 Sawsers		8	0
3 chargers		6	0
Two basons, 2 Ewers		6	8
5 plate trenchers		2	0
10 Pottengers [* *] broken		6	8
4 W[* *]		5	0
2 [* *]		1	8
5 [* *]		1	0
[* *]			10
[* *]		2	6
[* *]		1	8
In the grete Chamber			
[* *]ed, 3 Iron Rod [* *] [B]lankett and a Counterpoynt q[* *]	3	6	8
A grete Sypres Chest	1	0	0
A Chest of ffyrr		2	0
A Chest of Wenscott		2	0
An olde Courte Table			6
A pycture of the Savyor		2	6
A grete glasse to loke in, garnysshed with Pomander		3	4
An old Redd hanginge of small valewe		1	4
There is in the saide Chest of ffyrr 2 table clothes of Damaske worke and a Towell of the same	1	3	4
A ffyne C[* *] of Dyaper otherwyse called Dyaper Na[*]		6	8
10 ot[* *] be answered the Rest [*]		1	0
[* *]		1	0
[* *]] and the thy[* *]		6	8
A T[* *]		5	0
A ffayr Chrystny[*nge*][*]	1	0	0
A payer of ffyne Hollon [*]		6	8
An other payer of fynes Shete[*s*]		5	0
An other paire not fellowes		3	4
A payer of shetes		3	4
A bearinge Shete		1	0
A Damaske Coverpane			[*no price*]

A payer of Shetes that goeth abrode	[*no price*]	
In the Closett		
Two basons of Glasse	[*no price*]	
A glass bowle paynted	[*no price*]	
2 Wodden [*]	[*no price*]	
In the lytle Chamber where a presse standeth		
In the [*] vellett and yelowe imbrothery [*] Damaske	3	0
2 [*]	5	0
[*]	2	0
[*]	6	8
2 q[* *]	6	0
One w[* *]	3	0
A grete Redd Cush[*ion*]	2	6
6 olde [*] of Tapstery in	1	0
6 other of the harte in the y[*]	2	0
A Wyndowe Clothe for the grete Chamber Wyndowe	2	6
In the Chamber over the butterye		
A Standinge bedstedd with a Tester of Wenscott	10	0
A grete Chest	2	6
An Iron Rodd for the Wyndowe Curten	[*no price*]	
In the Chamber over the Larder		
A standinge bedstedd with a Tester of Wenscott	10	0
An Iron Rodd for the Wyndowe Curten	[*no price*]	
In the Larder		
A powdry[*nge*] T[*rough*]	2	0
4 S[* *]		8
A benc[*h*]		2
2 P[*]	1	8
[*]		6
[*]	1	0
A hi[*]		6
An olde [*]		10
In the newe kychyn		
Kyvers and [*]	5	0
A grete Vate		8
A Chese presse		8
An olde heare cloth	1	0
An olde furnes	3	4
In the boultinge house		
A boultinge hutche		6
A knedinge trough	1	0
A mouldinge table		8
A Shelf		2
3 old tr[* *]		6
A Range		6
2 br[* *]	1	0
A [* *]		10
[* *]		6
A [* *]	3	4
In the olde mylke house		
Two [* *]	1	0
In the garden		
T[* *]	6	8

In the newe lodginge: In the Chamber			
A standing [*] [*fe*]ther bedd, a bolster, 2 blanketts, a coverlett of Tapstery [*wor*]ke, a pillowe and a truckell bedsted	1	10	0
In the lytle chamber			
A Standinge bedstedd with a ffether bedd, a bolster, 2 blanketts, a coverlytt of Shrydds		13	4
In the Chamber over the grete Chamber			
A playne bedsted			8
An olde Chest			8
An olde harnes for a Horseman	[*no price*]		
An old kerf Sawe		2	0
In the lytle Chamber called Gyles Chamber			
A playn[*e bedste*]d, a bolster and a Coverynge		3	4
Cattell			
5 [* *]	15	0	0
6 [* *]	7	0	0
A [* *] calfinge tyme in [* *]	8	0	0
One [* *]ynne		10	0
5 Twelvemonthing [*] 4 cowe bullocks	1	13	4
One Redd Heyfer bullock q[* *]		6	0
Horses, mares, geldings			
Two Geldings used to drawe before oxen	2	0	0
An amblynge Mare Culler baye	1	13	4
A lytle bay Curtall		13	4
Two Geldings Culler baye	4	0	0
A Done Mare	1	13	4
Shepe that dydd remayne in Mr. Hulls owne Hands			
Shepe of all sortes	8	3	4
12 Hoggets	1	15	0
16 [*] whereof remayninge at Cost	2	10	0
Necessary Toles for Husbandrye			
[* *] 3 Cheynes and [*]		18	0
2 [* *] bylls, two Sythes with w[*] 3 beckes, a crosse becke, Augers of all sortes [*] wymble, a pub sawe, an ades, two Drawinge L[* *]uts, 4 Wedges of Iron, a paire of Pyncers [* *]yun of Iron, a Clevinge Axe for pale, a byl[*l*] [* *] Iron beame with Scales		6	8
4 Ledden Weyghts		5	0
A lytle Dong [*]		2	0
Plate of sylver and gylte			
A Syl[* *]	[*not valued*]		
13 [* *]	[*not valued*]		
a [* *]	[*not valued*]		
a [* *]	[*not valued*]		
a [* *]reyinge	[*not valued*]		
a S[* *]ynge	[*not valued*]		
a lytle goblet of Syl[*]	[*not valued*]		
All which plate last above wrytten Do Remayne in the hands of the above named Richard Bydon [* *]ers or where [**]e			
A whyll [* *] sylver-cheyne			
A R[* *] deceased			

Corne in the ffelde

C[* *]ylleds

sowen[* *]kent and

conteyned in [*]

Corne in the barn

Rye 22 bushells

Ottes grete and small 7 qua[*rters*] grete at 8d the bushell	2	18	0
and small 4 quarters at 5 [* *] come	1	9	4

[*no total on Inventory*]

John Hull INVENTORY 2:

of Hambledon, gentleman; taken by Symon Talley, Nicholas Slade and John Austen, 30th June 1564.

In the custody of Richard Bydon

Six sylver spones with knopps gylte, six square like pendens, one with a Mayden hedd and ffyve with Round gylte knopps wreathed weinge 13oz. and 3qr.

One lytle Mazer banded with sylver and gylt and a knobbe of Sylver and gylte with a face in blewe, ye knobbe sett over with lede, which with the wode and lede therof doth way 7½ oz. good weight

A lytle salte seller of silver parcell Gylte syxe square weinge 11oz.

Summa 32 ounces and a quarter

In the Custody of William Morgayne

One standinge Cupp of Sylver and Dubble gylte with a Cover, with a Tygers hedd and the lettres I. H. in Romayne lettres in bosse and Graved weinge 25 oz. quarter and half quarter

A Newe salte of Sylver, Duble Gylte Rounde with a peper boxe in the topp, foted with mermaydes weinge 16 oz. good weight

Somma 41½ ounces a quarter and a half quarter

In the Custody of the saide William Morgayne

One playne Goblett parcell gylte weinge 13½ oz and a quarter

Somma patet 55½ ounces a quarter and a half quarter [***no values given***]

Note: The Will dated 1st October 1562 was proved on 15th April 1563. The testator appointed his son Gyles to be executor and residuary legatee and he gave £3 apiece to his overseers Mr Richard Bedon and Mr William Morgaine. They were to levy a charge on the estate to see him decently buried in Hambledon Church and to bestow a suitable amount on the poor. He gave 12d to the church at Winchester and 5s for repairs to St Peter's, Hambledon, with 6s 8d to the church box for poor relief. Gyles was to have his gold signet ring and most of the plate listed in the 2nd Inventory except the mazer, which was to go to Richard, the other son. Gyles was to have the dun ambling mare. Richard was to have lands in Hascombe and Dunsfold called Gylls, Corechambers and Borstookes, at the age of 21, the rents from which were to be used meantime by the overseers to pay for the schooling of the two boys. The heir Gyles would inherit lands in Hambledon, Chiddingfold, Dunsfold and Godalming under the same condition. Wool money was to be used and invested to provide for the 3 daughters. For Constance £20 was to be levied at once on the sheep cared for by John Cheswicke. Jane and Mary would inherit £20 at the age of 19. Jane and a certain Alens Love were to use the profit from the land to the south of the house to maintain and keep the home and its contents until Gyles came of age. A servant Gyles Cooke was given 6 sheep and a life interest in the rent of a house called Estberthing-land, occupied by Edward Denyer. The testator's sister was given a cow. His brother Thomas inherited a black gown and coat. Alens Love was given 8 ewes and all his godchildren 4d. Giles was to inherit all the sheep at John Cheswicke's when he had paid the £60 to his sisters and discharged any debts. The witnesses were John Cheswicke senior, Henry Cheswick, Henry Ropplye and Henrie Eliot.

G.M.R. Ref: LM 2011/42 Will LM 1095/1 and LM 1095/2 Inventories

Harry and Alice Juer **48**

of Runfold in Farnham; taken by Robartt Whytte, John Mabanke and Thomas Champion, with others, 2nd November 1563.

	£	s	d
in the Hawle			
A borde, a forme, a payntyd Klothe		1	8
in the Chamber			
A olde flocke bede, a bedstedle, 3 olde Cofferes		5	0
2 shetes, a tableclothe, a towell, 2 kerchers and a Rayle, a Woman's Cape, a gowne, a olde frocke, a doblett, a olde cotte and a pettycotte	1	6	8
in the Kyttchen			
A potte hangeres, a fryenge pan, a gerierne, 3 olde pewter plateres, 3 pewter dyshes, 3 sauseres, a sawlte, 3 olde canstyckes, halfe a dosen of sponys		10	0
A lyttell olde Cawderne, 3 olde Lyttell Kettelles and a skymer		6	8
Hys workynge towlys		1	8
7 shepe		17	6
A cowe and a younge bolock and a yonge Cowlte	2	0	0
Sawlte and hunye and a bottell		1	8
Peasun and Rye		5	0
A naker of barlye and haye		10	0
2 Akeres of whette in the grownde and the th[*i*]rde of a nother aker		13	4
[*£6.19.2*]	6	19	10

Note: A Will was written by Alice, already a widow, on 18th October 1563. Her main concern was for the christian upbringing of her children. This charge she entrusted to her friends Thomas and Annys Champion, whom she appointed joint executor and executrix. The Will was proved on 13th November 1563, when the administration of the estate was passed on to Annys Champion. The witnesses were John Chesse, Robartt Lawde, Peter Mawnte, Annys Hambleden and Margarett Bell. Harry Juer's burial was recorded on 19th October and that of Alice on 21st October in Farnham.

Ref: 1563 B 102 Will 1563 B 103 Inventory

Peter Mantte **49**

of Runfold in Farnham, weaver. [*no appraisers given and undated*]

3 looms, 7 gears, 2 flockbedes with the apparell, fyve brase pottes, 4 kettelles, 12 peces pewter, fyve Chestes, 2 broches, 2 kneding kevars, syxe tobbes, a koubarde, an old kuledern, a posnet and a pan, 32 quyllyng whelles, a payr of warping barse, there (sic) payre of sheates, a frok, a gowne, 3 yardes of new Cloth and 2 kowes. [*no values given*]

Note: The Inventory was written below the Will, dated 19th October 1563. On the back of the Will was written "Henry Capp of Farnham, joyner and Mychall Wright of Farnham, lynnen draper". On 13th November 1563 Henry Cappe was sworn to the truth of the Inventory and was granted letters of administration. Allys, wife of the testator, was appointed executrix and residuary legatee, unless "it so happen that my wyffe doth fayll in thys plage that now is wyth us". Allys had had a son Richard and an unnamed daughter by a previous marriage to one Franklen. The aforesaid Richard was left the best brass pot by his stepfather. The testator named only one of his three children. Alice was given the trestles, a board, a form, the best cupboard and 2 platters. If her mother died, the unnamed stepdaughter would only inherit if Peter's three children died too. The testator asked to be buried in Farnham churchyard. When he appointed the 2 overseers he gave an old cauldron to Thomas Coytt with 6 of the best boards in the house and Henry Capp was rewarded with 2s. John Chesse wrote the Will, which was witnessed by Thomas Webb and

Rychard Denocke. Peter Mawnte's burial was recorded on 25th October. Ref: 1563 B 125 Will and Inventory

---

1564

[*no inventories*]

1565

Nicholas Alyngham **50**

of Horley, husbandman; taken by Richard [*only name remaining of the appraisers, as parts of the document are missing.*] 19th January 1564/5.

	£	s	d
4 keen	[*4*	*0*	*0*]
3 small Bullockes	1	6	8
One mare	1	0	0
11 Shepe	1	2	0
3 small hogges		5	0
Hennes, Duckes and geese		3	4
Otes and Hey in the Barnes	1	0	0
Wheat on the ground		10	0
Pewter Vessell		3	4
Brasse		10	0
In Beddynge		16	0
Lenen		15	0
His Reymente		6	8
In money		1	0
Bylles, Axes and other Romblement		5	0
	12	4	0

Note: The top of the Will is also badly mutilated, but 17th January 1564/5 is a possible date and probate was granted on 1st June. Apart from 12d each to the overseers, Ralph Laker and Edmund Huat, the bequests were solely to members of the immediate family. A sum of £4 was to go to his son Ralph at the age of 16, or failing him to his son John, or failing him to his daughter Margery at 14 years. She was to have 40s, 2 sheep and 2 lambs, at the age of 14. The executrix was to be Johane, his wife, who was also to inherit the residue. The Will was witnessed by the two overseers and Rychard Alyngham.

Ref: 1565 B 1 Will 1565 B 2 Inventory

Margaret Amy **51**

of Cranleigh, widow; taken by John Mercer, Peter Amy, Henry Gretes, Robert Lloyd, with others, 2nd May 1565.

	£	s	d
7 kyne	4	13	4
7 heycfers	2	6	8
3 yerlynges		10	0
A mare	1	0	0
A olde horse		5	0
18 yewes with theyr lambs	3	0	0
4 tegges		8	0
6 swyne		12	0
9 peces off brasse		13	4
8 peces off pewter		6	8
One Candelsticke			8

One old cobborde	2	0
One old fether bed and flocbed with theyr apportenances	13	4
3 olde cofers	3	0
Trene vessels and lumbre	3	0
The corne in the grounde	6	8
One broche, a trevet and pot hangynges	1	4
In ploughe stoff	2	0
Her apparell	10	0
[*£15.17.0*] 15	18	0

Note: The Will of the late Richard Amy's widow was written on 10th April and proved by Elizabeth Amy on 2nd June 1565. Richard Amy, brother of Elizabeth, was the other executor named by their mother, the testatrix. William, another son, was left £1. All the goods and chattels were to be divided among the other children: Richard, Cicely, Elizabeth, Mawdlen, Ellen and Katheryne. Those who survived to lawful or marriageable age were to share what there was. John Mercer, Peter Amy and Harry Greteste, were the named witnesses.

[*Minor differences in spelling in the two copies of each document.*]

Ref: 1565 B 3 and 4 Wills 1565 B 5 and 6 Inventories

John Bonyon **52**

of Chobham, yeoman; taken by Wyllyam Chennell, Rycharde Hyller, Robert Norwode and Thomas Hudnet, 28th May 1565.

	£	s	d
2 brasse pottes		5	0
Certen olde bras pannes		8	0
4 candellstyckes		1	8
Pewter		13	4
6 olde pewter pottes		2	8
3 olde broches and a payre of Andyarns		2	4
On olde trift, a grydyarne, a fyer shovell, pott hanggeres and potthockes		1	8
One meshingefatte, 4 kewlers, 2 boles, on boltinge hutche, on knedyng trowe, 4 barrelles		13	4
2 tables and 3 formes with treseles		5	0
3 cheares, 1 stoole		2	8
5 chestes		4	6
One musted querne, one candell molde, one trowghe and 2 tallow pannes, on Iarne morter, on payre of skales with weghts and 2 tallowe Knyves		16	0
3 saltes, 2 dosen of spones, dysshes and trenchers		1	6
2 bylles and 2 shovelles			10
One hogges heade of vargis		6	8
4 standinge beddestedes		3	4
3 flocke bedes, one fether bede and one mattrys with bolsters and pyllowes	1	10	0
3 coverletes and 3 blanckets		10	0
6 payre of shetes and 3 table clothes	1	0	0
One olde geldinge		10	0
2 sowes and 6 Lyttell pygges		10	0
2 flytches of bacon		4	0
2 hennes			8
Hys weringe rayment		6	8
In his purse		1	8
	9	1	6

Note: The Will was dated 15th May 1565 and probate was granted to the executrix, Agnes, his wife on 2nd June. Although he is quoted as a yeoman at the beginning of the Will, his son Davye was given "all my workyng toles that Apertayneth or belongeth to a Chandler". Another son Robert was given all his books. An unmarried daughter Alys was to receive a platter. The two married daughters, Agnes Stott and Elizabeth Sturte, were each to have a pewter dish. The residue was left to his wife. The vicar of Chobham, Thomas Brodehurst, was the only named overseer. The two witnesses were Robert Norwood and Rychard Sheperd of Woking.

Ref: 1565 B 21 Will 1565 B 22 Inventory

Rycharde Marlyn 53

of Chobham; taken by Walter Atfelde, John Atfelde, John Rempnant and Thomas Butt, 30th April 1565.

	£	s	d
Money in his purse		1	0
Theapparell of hys bodye		13	8
Brasse and pewter		10	0
Two bedes		13	4
Two Chestes		2	0
A trevet, A gredyarne, A broche and A potthangger		2	6
The trene vesselles		1	0
4 Kyne	2	13	4
Two bullockes of A yeare oulde		10	0
3 shepe		5	0
3 shootes		5	0
Two Akeres of Corne		13	4
	6	10	2
Margret Marlyn			
The apparell of the sayde Margret deceasyd Aprysed at one cassocke and 2 pettycotes	1	0	0
More 4 payre of shetes		13	4
Her lynnyne geare		10	0
	[2	*3*	*4]*
	8	13	6

Note: A will of Margret Marlyn, late wife of Rycharde Marlyn deceased, was dated 27th May 1565 and probate was granted on 2nd June. The witnesses were Thomas Brodehurst, vicar of Chobham and John Atfelde, with others. Presumably her inventory was added to that of her late husband without a later date being noted. All three deeds were written in the same hand. The clothing of the couple, their household. and animal stock, were bequeathed to close relatives of two generations. Her brothers Richard and Thomas Wood were beneficiaries, as were her brother Nicolas and her sister Jone Byrchet. The Atfelde family: Nicolas and Walter, brothers-in-law and their children Elizabeth, Owyn, Nicolas and Allyne, were also beneficiaries. The elder Nicolas was named as executor and Walter was to fulfil the duty of overseer.

Ref: 1565 B 58 Will 1565 B 59 Inventory

Thomas Morrell 54

of Merton, tailor; taken by Richard Woodnet and Nicholas Clarke, 30th January 1564/5.

	£	s	d
Two bullockes	1	8	0
One old mare		10	0
in the hall			
Two old cupbordes		6	8
One chayre		1	4

	£	s	d
4 stooles		1	4
Payntted clothes		2	0
in the parler			
Two chestes		4	0
Paynted clothes		2	0
in the fyrst chamber			
Two fetherbeddes and bolsters	1	0	0
Two bed stedles		4	0
One presse		3	0
4 chestes		4	0
Paynted clothes		4	0
Two shred coverles		5	0
in the second chamber			
Two olde mattresses		2	0
Two bedstedles		2	0
Two old coverynges		2	8
Paynted clothes		2	0
8 payre of shees of hempe	1	0	0
in the keychyn			
3 brasse pottes		10	0
4 olde kettles		8	0
5 candlestickes		4	0
4 puter platters and dishes and sawcers		5	0
5 puter pottes		3	0
One spyt, a payre of cobyrons and a gyrdyron		2	0
	7	16	0
Debtes			
I owe unto my brother in law Rafe Chylmyd		4	0
I owe unto Goodman Clarke for 2 bushells of wheate		[*blank*]	
I owe unto the bruer for olde debte	1	0	0
I owe unto Mr. Steeven of Kyngstone		7	0
I owe in new debte unto the bruer		10	4
I owe for my halfe yeares rent		8	0
	2	9	4

Note: The Will, the list of debts and the Inventory, were written on one document on the same day. The will was proved on 1st June 1565, leaving the residue of the estate to the executrix, his wife Jone. The overseers appraised the goods and chattels listed in the inventory. The unnamed children of the testator were left 20s apiece, to be paid to them before any subsequent marriage of his wife. Were the widow to remarry, her future husband was ordered to secure money for the children's legacies beforehand. Rafe Chylmyd, brother-in-law of Thomas Morrell, was left a white fustian doublet. He and John Mantyll had witnessed the signing of the will and two days later, on 2nd February, Thomas's burial was recorded.

Ref: 1565 B 67 Will and Inventory

Richard Oliver **55**

of Godalming, innholder; taken by Henri Chitty, William Hooke and Arnolde Champion the elder, 29th May 1565.

	£	s	d
In the Hall			
A table, one ffourem, one Chayer, 2 ioyned Stoles		5	0
One Cubberd		5	0
Paynted Clothes		2	0
In the parlowr			
One Table, 2 formes, one Chayre, one Rowne table	1	0	0

One dosen of Smale Cushens		4	0
One Joyned Bedsted with a truckell bedsted	1	0	0
2 ffether bedes and a fflocke bed and 2 fether bolsters	2	0	0
2 payer of blankettes, 2 Coverlettes, one of tapestri and the other of Dornyckes and a Carpett	1	10	0
Paynted Clothes		3	4
In the Chamber over Hall			
2 Joyned Bedstedes with the hanginges		13	4
2 ffether bedes and 2 fether bolsters	1	13	4
2 blanketes with 2 Coveringes		13	4
2 quyltes		8	0
A Round table, 2 Joyned stoles		3	4
The paynted Clothes		6	8
In the Chamber over the parlowr			
Two Joyned bedesstedes wherof one standinge bed and the other a truckell bedsted	1	13	4
2 fether bedes with 2 fether bolsters	1	13	4
3 blanketes, 2 Coverlettes, one Quylte	1	10	0
3 Curtens to one bed of Seye		10	0
2 Litell tables, one Carpett, one Litell fourme, one Chayer, 4 Joyned Stoles		13	4
Paynted Clothes		6	8
[£16.14.0]	16	19	0

Note: Unusually, only the year 1565 appeared by way of date at the beginning of the Will. Three children were still young and provision was made for legacies to be paid in case the wife Annis, the executrix, should marry again. The son John was to have £10 at the age of 18 or 19, his lawful age and years of discretion and the two daughters Jane and Alice were to be given £5 on reaching the age of 16. All these bequests were to be advanced to the day of their mother's marriage, if this were to happen. Witnesses were Goodman John Smythe senior, Richard Bridger, Nicholas Wyllson; and Henry Hooke, the landlord, who was also named as one of the two overseers. The other was Goodman John Perior. The date of Probate was missing.

Ref: 1565 B 76 Will 1565 B 77 Inventory

Robart Taylor **56**

of Horsell, husbandman; taken by John Wodrof and Robart Symond. [*undated*]

	£	s	d
His aparell		13	4
Money remayning in his purse		5	0
2 tabuls with formes and stooles		3	4
2 beddes with shetes, Coverlettes and other thynges therunto belongyng	1	0	0
6 chestes		6	8
Tabull Clothes and towels		2	0
All the brasse and pewter	1	10	0
Bruyng vessels with bolles		6	8
2 spyttes with Cobberdes and potthangers		6	8
5 kyen and 4 bullockes of too yere olde	4	6	0
Too laboryng nagges	1	6	8
19 Shepe	1	6	0
7 acres of Rye	1	6	8
4 acres of otes		13	4
8 hogges		16	0

	£	s	d
All his workyng toolles		2	0
6 hens		2	0
Dethes	1	1	0
	14	12	4

Note: The Will was dated 21st May 1565 and Probate was granted a week later on 2nd June. Alice, wife of the testator, was appointed executrix and her son Thomas Strudwick was given a cow and 21s. The money featured in the Inventory and was to be recovered from Water Cotter of Thames Ditton, in payment for a white faced red cow as agreed, on All Saints Day next following. Robert's sister Joan was left 6s 8d and his godson George Pycsam 6d. To the poor men's box and to the repair of Horsell church, was bequeathed 2s apiece. All other bequests went to 4 members of the Hyllar family: to Wyllyam went his best coat and a bullock; to John, his best shirt and a bullock; to Rychard, a shilling; and to John, son of Harry, 6d. Alice Taylor, his wife, was residuary legatee. The overseers were Master Reden and Bartholomew Taylor, the testator's brother. John Wodrofe, Robart Symon and John Hone, acted as witnesses.

Ref: 1565 B 105 Will 1565 B 106 Inventory

Anthony Worthyngton **57**

of Horsell, husbandman; taken by Henry Myddelborow, John Wapshott, Rychard Edmed and John Payne, 13th April 1565.

	£	s	d
In Redie monne		10	0
The apparell of his bodie		13	4
Halfe a dossen sylver spones		10	0
Tables, trestelles and formes		3	0
A kobborde In the haull and two cheyars		5	0
In brasse		13	4
In peuter		6	8
Broaches, Andyarnes, pothangers, fryenge panns and dryppenge panns		2	0
Thre fether bedes with all that belongeth unto theym	3	0	0
One owld flocke bed lyeng under a fether bed		1	4
In lynnen clotthes		6	8
6 koffers		6	0
The hangynges In the hall and chambers		3	4
In tubbes, boulles, payles and other lumber In the house		3	4
5 acrs Rye upon the grounde	1	5	0
8 kene and one heffer	6	0	0
Thre wannynge calves		10	0
One mare and two other toudes	1	6	8
14 ews and tegges		18	8
Thre hogges and threy shootes		10	0
A goose and a gander		1	0
Thre henns and a cocke		1	4
	17	16	8

Note: The Will dated 26th February was proved on 2nd June 1565. The residuary legatee and executrix was the testator's wife Margaret, but it was the job of the overseers, John Theyar of Horsell and John Atwood of Woking, to take charge of the elder son John and his inheritance. They were to manage the affairs and give account when John reached the age of 21. Most of the household goods were given directly to John, together with the remaining term of years of the lease of the house and land. The younger son Henry was to be his brother's heir if John should die and if Henry died the next heir was to be Richard, son of Uryan. The testator's brother Uryan was to take charge of a mare colt and an acre of rye on behalf of his nephew and to return the animal and produce the crop in good time. John was to have "A table that hath a hole in hyt wyth choppynge yerbes". The overseers were to redeem the silver spoons from Richard Edmed for £1

6s 8d and small debts were to be repaid to Mr Savege and John Stansted. His wife's son Henry Newbery was given a ewe and a lamb. The parish church of Horsell and the common box there were each given 4d. Three named witnesses were Nycolas Savege, clerk; John Spong and Uryan Worthyngton.

Ref: 1565 B 125 Will 1565 B 126 & 127 Inventories

1566

William Amias **58**

of Reigate, husbandman; taken by Richard Amias, Robertt Gattes, Nycholas Braye, John Grene, John Polyn, Thomas Gattes and Wyllyam Lymden, 22nd May 1566.

		£	s	d
The Cattayell				
4 Oxen		7	0	0
4 kene		4	0	0
4 tooyerelyng bollokes		2	0	0
3 bollokes of 4 yere olde		1	4	0
7 hogges			14	0
2 meres and a stonid Coltte		2	0	0
All the powltrye a bought the howsse			10	0
2 Wenes, one plowe with yeokes, Reppes, chaynes with shucheleke		1	0	0
The corne on the grounde				
8 Akeres of Whette		4	0	0
9 akeres of ottes		2	5	0
	[*£24.13.0*]	24	19	8
The stuffe in the halle, as bras and pewter				
2 Caudrens, 3 kettelles, a posnett and a braspott		1	0	0
6 platters, 7 dysshes, 5 sawsers, 3 sallt seleres, 2 candellstikes and one quart pott			16	0
A frieng pan, a skomer, a trefte with potthokes and pott hangeres			1	8
The chambber				
A cobberde and 4 olde chestes			13	4
In the [*che*]stes 10 payer of shettes		1	13	4
In the saied chestes 4 tabell clothes with all other lenin			6	8
One ffether bedd with all thinges theruntoo belonginge		1	6	8
2 other beddes more for howsholde with all thinges ther un too belonginge			10	0
His rayment		1	0	0
In other trene vessell with tubbes, barelles, whelles and shuch rombellmente			10	0
In axis, bylles, sythes, shovelles, spittes with all shuche leke			1	8
	[*£7.19.4*]	7	11	11
	[*£32.12.4*]	32	18	7
Dettes that he dyd owe				
too Glover of Waddon			10	0
too Jhon Cruse and Rychard Charlwood		1	10	0
too Jhon Amias ffor a Kowe		1	6	8
too Mr Dalender of Bokland		1	10	0
too Harye Henn of Nodgatte		1	0	8
too Thomas Gattes		5	0	0
too George Astrette of Reygate			10	0
		[*11*	*7*	*4*]

Note: The 2 overseers, his brother Richard Amias and his brother-in-law Robert Gattes, were witnesses to the Will written on 11th May 1566 and appraisers of the Inventory on 22nd May. His wife Margaret was appointed sole executrix and residuary legatee. There were bequests of 10s apiece to his 5 children, divided into 2 groups. The survivor or survivors were to be heirs. William and Elizabeth were in the first group and Robert, Elizabeth and Joan, were in the second . Probate was granted to the executrix on 24th May. The burial of William Amias had been recorded a week earlier on 17th May.

Ref: 1566 B 3 Will and Inventory

William Elvyn 59

of Horne; taken by Richard Smythe, William Roughie, Richard Stimford and John Lambe, 15th April 1566.

	£	s	d
In the House			
One table, a forme, trestols and stooles		3	0
A Cubbord		10	0
2 Chestes		3	4
		16	4
In Bedding			
One fetherbed and all therunto belonging	1	13	0
3 Mattresses with thappurtenances	1	10	0
7 pair sheetes	2	6	8
15 yerdes of wollen cloth	1	10	0
Lynnen yerne		6	8
	7	6	4
Corne in the house and grounde			
7 quarters of otes and malte	1	15	0
One acre of whete	1	0	0
	2	15	0
Brasse, pewter and latin			
In Brasse all together	2	0	0
In Pewter plates, dishes, Salltes and spoones		13	4
One Chafingdishe and 5 Candlestickes		4	0
	2	17	4
Cattall			
6 oxen	12	0	0
6 Steers of 4 yere old	8	0	0
6 kene and Calves	8	0	0
2 harfers of 4 yeres	2	0	0
5 bullockes of 3 yere old	3	6	6
One haffer of 2 yeres		12	0
One twelve monthing		8	0
21 shepe	2	10	0
2 Mares	1	6	0
8 Hogges	1	0	0
	39	2	6
In the Barne			
In Wheat and otes	2	0	0
bourdes and plankes		6	8
	2	6	8
2 olde Coleweynes with wheles, yokes and tightes and other furniture therto	2	0	0
2 spittes, 2 trefotes, one cobiorne, one grydiorne,			

	£	s	d
pothokes and hangers, a fier Rake		6	0
Woodden vessell	1	0	0
A Querne		6	8
Axes and billes		2	0
Apparell to his bodie	1	6	0
	5	0	8
	60	4	10

Note: The Will was dated 10th March and proved 23rd May 1566. A sum of £14 was bequeathed to his son William and £12 each to his daughters Grace and Alice. The poor of the parish were left 5s between them and his godchildren were to have 8d each. His kinsman John Chawcroft was left a two-year-old bullock, not the best nor the worst and his servant Edward Tye was to have one of the best sheep. Alice Jelly was given a sheep, not one of the worst. The executrix, Joan his wife, was to have the residue. Witnesses to the Will were William Rohye [Roffey] of Burstow, John Lame of Horne, John Lane and the widow Joan Mantell. The overseers were Thomas Chart of Horne and John Chawcroft.

Ref: 1566 B 68 Will 1566 B 69 Inventory

Nicholas Walker **60**

of Kingston-upon-Thames, yeoman and smith; taken by John Hale alias Andrewes, Richard Bowyer and Roger Wright, weaver, of Kingston, 10th May 1566.

	£	s	d
In the Hall			
A table, a carpet, the trestelles and a forme		5	0
A benche with a ioyned backe		1	0
4 chaires		2	0
A cubberd		8	0
8 Cusshens		8	0
A bason, an ewer, 2 cups and twoo Saltcellers of pewter		5	0
The old paynted clothes about the hall		2	6
A payre of Andyrons		2	6
A fyer shovell, a paire of tonges and A paire of Crepers		1	4
In the Butterie			
11 pewter platters		7	4
A bason with 11 pewter disshes		5	0
11 sawcers and 4 pewter porringers		4	0
4 quart pottes, 2 pinte pottes and A pottle pott		4	0
A wine quart pott, a wine pinte pott And 8 Candelstickes		5	0
A laten bason, a chafinge disshe, A spice morter and A pestell		5	0
A Chambre pott of pewter			4
In the kytchin			
4 brasse pottes, grett and small		10	0
A brasse panne		1	4
5 small kettelles		2	6
A paire of small rackes of yron		1	4
A fryinge pann and 2 grydirons		1	4
2 posnettes, one old chafinge disshe and a foote for the same		1	8
4 spittes, 2 pott hangers, A paire of pott hookes and a drippinge pann		2	6
An old Styll		1	0
An yron peele			4
A chafer and a brasen ladle		2	0
An old cubberd, a bowltinge hutche, twoo tubbes and A busshell		2	0
A Stone morter, A woodden pestle, twoo shredinge knyves and A paire of bellowes		1	0
In the chambre over the kitchin			

A malt querne and old bourdes endes		6	8
In the utter chambre			
A ioyned bedsted and 4 bolsters		8	0
2 old coveringes, 2 old paynted clothes and one old blankett		4	0
A chaire, a fourme and 2 old chestes		1	4
In the chambre over the Hall			
A ioyned bedsted		13	4
2 fetherbeddes, 2 coveringes and a bolster	1	6	8
A truckle bedd and a fetherbed with a coveringe And a bolster	1	6	8
6 pyllowes		6	0
A ioyned presse		5	0
5 chestes		13	4
A rounde table		2	0
A paire of Alman Revettes		5	0
In the backesyde			
All the wood and old tymbre there		10	0
In lynnen and naperie stuff			
12 paire of sheetes	1	10	0
5 table clothes		5	0
2 dossen of table napkins		8	0
2 towelles		1	4
For dettes due and payable with other implementes of the Shoppe	15	0	0
A silver goblet, a maser and half a dossen of silver spones	2	0	0
[*£30.5.4*]	29	14	4

[*Written in a different hand was the widow's name and next to it an unusual personal mark*]:

Allis Walker of Kyngston uppon temys

Note: The Will written on 26th September 1565 was proved on 26th June 1566. Alice, wife of the testator, was named as executrix and residuary legatee. No mention was made of surviving children. The overseers, John Jenyns and George Snellynge the elder, had a number of bequests to carry out, for which they were to have 10s apiece. A sum of £1 was bequeathed to the churchwardens of Kingston for the maintenance of the church and as payment for digging his grave and putting the ground to rights again. The Free Grammar School, poor relief, the great bridge of the town and the stone wall at the west end, were to have the benefit of his Kingston properties and their rents or money from their sale, either immediately after his decease or after that of his wife. One house was occupied by James Frese. His own house was subject to a life tenancy by Alice and a plot of ground in Gygehill, purchased from Owen Bray Esq., was to be sold immediately. The testator's more personal bequests were suited to the needs or pleasure of his servants and friends. Annys Tomell was to have £1 in addition to her wages and a feather bed and bolster. Thomas Grace, another servant, was given a little anvil, a pair of bellows behind the door and a hand hammer. Thomas Warthowe was the better for a hundredweight of iron, a doublet of doe's leather and to be forgiven his debts. George Frank was given an iron bar. One pound went to Thomas Taylor of Bookham and 6s 8d to Nicholas Carpenter. John Wynter was forgiven his debts and given the best cloak and jacket. Another jacket went to Umfry Okar and the fox-furred gown was given to Austen Bursey. John Wynter, Humfrey Okar and Elizabeth Wallen, were inscribed as witnesses to the signing of the Will, under which were the signatures of Thomas Atterbury, George Snellyng, John Jenyns and John Wynter. There was also the mark of a cross over the words "by me Nycolas Walour". His burial was recorded at Kingston on 13th February 1565/6. Ref: 1565 B 112 Will 1565 B 113 Inventory

1567

John Bet **61**

of Fetcham; taken by John Blundel, Thomas Blundell, John Marter and Jorge Gryffen, 13th April 1567.

	£	s	d
6 kynne	4	10	0
4 boollokes of two yere old	1	6	8
One boollooke of 3 yeare old		8	0
3 boollookes of one yere old		12	0
8 yousse and 8 lambes	1	1	0
11 drye shepe	1	0	0
A steare		14	0
8 swyne		13	4
6 shutlynges		4	0
A 11 akers of Wynter Corne in the felde	3	0	0
12 ackers of peasse and tares	1	16	0
3 akeres of otes		6	0
3 quarters of whet within the howsse	1	16	0
3 quartteres of malte	1	6	0
5 quarteres of barllee	2	0	0
Haulffe a quarter of otes		2	0
2 lode of horsse mete		12	0
A ffether bed		13	4
18 peyer of Shetes	2	8	0
3 blanckess		8	0
A bed heller		4	0
5 tabell Clotes		8	0
2 brasse potes		10	0
A brasse pan and 2 ketteles		10	0
5 peuter platters		5	0
3 peuter dysshes		1	6
2 saussares			8
2 salte selleres			6
A Chaffyng dysse			10
2 Canstyckes		1	0
A spyt and the Cob Iron		1	0
A fryeng pan and a gredyan			8
A pothook and a pot hangar			8
An ax			8
A War byll			8
Hys Rayment		5	0
In hys porsse at the oure of hys deth		3	4
A Cooberd and a Cheste		4	0
A table and a forme		1	8
A Cheyer			4
All old toobs and lumbber		10	0
A Carte with the weles	1	0	0
A dunng pot with the weles		5	0
Two plowes		3	4
Two harrowes		2	8
Two yokes and two Chaynes		2	6
Two flyches of Backon		4	0

A sythe			1	0
Two sakes			1	0
Three attempts at the total	[*£30.5.4*]	*32*	*6*	*2*

Note: The Will was dated 10th December 1562. No date of Probate has been traced in 1567. He gave 3s 4d to the repair of the church. Henry Bet was given a two-year-old bullock and 2 ewes. Elizabeth Gooddear was to have 2 ewes. His sons, John Bet the elder and John Bet the younger, as executors, were to share the residue in brotherly love. Witnesses were John and Thomas Blundyll, Arnold Merches, John Adenne and Rayffe Peter.

Ref: 1567 B 15 Will 1567 B 16 Inventory

William Birle **62**

of Hascombe; 4th May 1567. [*no appraisers given*]

		£	s	d
The table and the fourme standing in the hall			1	4
2 painted clothes hanging in the halle			1	4
The Cobberd and the chaier standing in the hall			5	0
2 andiarns a spit and a trevet			1	8
2 pewter pottes, 2 saltes and certaine pewter vessells			6	8
Certaine latten basons, canstickes			1	8
A fetherbed with that belonge unto yt			10	0
A flockbed with that belonge to het			5	0
A borded bed, a mattresse, a Chest			3	4
His wering gere		1	0	0
8 paier of shetes			16	0
Brasse and other lumber		1	0	0
A furnes with certain tubes			10	0
2 quarters malt		1	13	4
Certaine Rye unthresshed			13	4
Horse Coltes and Arnes		3	6	8
Certaine cartes and a ploughe			13	4
3 Kyne and 2 Calves		2	0	0
Feftye and 16 Lambes		5	0	0
9 akers Wheate and Rye		3	0	0
9 akers Wheate and Ry		2	5	0
6 akers barly		1	6	0
12 akers, pese otes and ters		2	0	0
4 hogges and 5 pigges			6	8
4 duckes, 6 hends			2	0
A bote and a chaine			5	0
A bill, an axe, a Wanne, a busshell			2	0
	[*£27.15.4*]	30	3	4

Note: The Will, dated 20th April 1567, provided money at specified stages to 3 daughters, Alice, Catherine and Thomasine and to 2 sons, John and William. The care of the youngest daughter, Thomasine, was committed to her brother, Thomas, the executor and residuary legatee. The overseers appointed were John Mower and Walter Sherlock. The named witnesses were Henry Pulter, William Russell and William Flowers. No date of Probate was written on either document.

Ref: 1567 B 19 Will 1567 B 20 Inventory

Bartholemew Hardynge **63**

of Westend in Frensham, husbandman; taken by Thomas Trygge and Symone Hardynge, 28th April 1567.

In the chamber	£	s	d

Hys aparyll, one bede and that belongythe to hym, two olde bedis 3 coverletis, 6 payer of shetis	4	6	8
One grete cheste, 3 coffers, 8 pound of wooll		10	0
In the hall			
One table, one forme, one chayer, one cobard with stolis, one olde payntyd clothe		6	0
In the kechyne			
Of bras one cawtherne, thre potis, 3 kettylles, one pane, one broche, one gyrdyrne, one posnet, one frynge pane, one pothokes, one pothangers	1	6	8
Of pewter thre platers, foure potyngers, one saucer, one dyshe, too saultis, 12 sponys, too candylstykes, one floure pot		8	0
2 fatis, one keve, one kever, one trowe, too boulys with tobys and other lombry	1	0	0
Too sythys, too axes, one byll, one shovyll, too weggis, one becke, too augers, too payer of shepesherys		6	8
Too spynynge whelys, one payer of wolen cardys		2	0
4 stall of beys		8	0
Too kyne with there cavys	2	0	0
3 baryne kyne, one heffer, one bulche	3	6	8
2 yerlynge bullockes		10	0
2 marys, one coullte	2	0	0
7 hogges		13	4
15 yoes with there lamys	3	0	0
8 wethers	1	9	4
12 tegges		18	0
In the barne			
3 busshelles of Rey		3	4
In the fylde grouynge			
3 acars of whete and Rey	1	0	0
8 acars of otys	1	6	9
A letyll carte and Ropys with harnys and too harows		5	0
12 felde wattylles		2	0
6 henys and a coke		2	0
	25	9	8

Note: The Will was written on 8th April 1567 and the testator's wife Anys was appointed executrix. The overseers were John Hardynge of Sprakely and William Eyd of Westend. The mother church of Winchester was given 2d and the local poor men's box of Frensham 4d. One son Richard was given £6 13s 4d and he and 3 brothers, Bartyllmew, Thomas and John, were given livestock, as were his 2 sisters Chrystane and Joan. Anys, the widow, was residuary legatee. No date of probate was written on either document, but on the back of the Will were debts owing to the testator: 3s 4d from Rychard Brodbryge and the 40s from Master Beydone which a certain Mr Vync had agreed to pay before witnesses. Named witnesses to the Will were John and Wyllyam Hardynge, Wyllyam Eyde and Chrystofer Beane.

Ref: 1567 U 167a Will 1567 U 167b Inventory

John Harper alias Harfell **64**

of Blundelles in Wonersh, yeoman; taken by Henry Chalner, John Byknolde, Richard Hamonde and William Astrete, 2nd May 1567.

In the Hall	£	s	d
One table, one forme, one paire of trestilles, one olde cupborde and one olde chaire		5	0

in the Chamber				
2 olde bedstedes, one verey olde flokbed with a bad coverlett one blankett and one shete, one olde cofer wyth out lok and his apparell		1	5	0
in an other Chamber				
Certen Tubbes to brewe in and other woodden vessell			13	4
in the Kychen				
Brasse, pewter and latten		1	0	0
One broche, one byll, one axe and certen other tooles			4	0
Corne and malte				
Of Rye by estymacion	14 busshelles		15	0
Small otes	5 busshelles		1	8
Of oten malte 16 busshelles, of barlye malte 4 busshelles			11	0
Bakon in the Ruoff			1	8
Money in his purse			3	4
8 hennes and one cok			1	8
Cattell and corne in the ffields				
6 oxen and steares, 6 kyne and 2 yerlyng bullokes		12	0	0
Six olde shepe and 16 lambes		10	0	0
2 horse beastes		1	0	0
One wayne, one plowe, sithes and other necessaryes of husbandry			13	4
Fyve hogges			13	4
5 acres of wheat and Rie 9 acres of otes and one acre of peasen		4	0	0
		33	8	4
Debtes oweng to the said John Harper for the most parte Desperate				
Fyrst Robert Marche oweth for certen plowe Iorneis		1	2	0
John Mower 3 plowe Iorneis			5	0
John Shyrlok				[*blank*]
Nicholas Mawborne for the caringe of 3 lodes of stuff				[*blank*]
Thomas Tanworth for the caryeng of 3 lodes of Ryndes				[*blank*]
John Whitmore for the earing of 6 acres of Lande				[*blank*]

Note: Both documents gave Blundells as the property, but the Will written on 7th April 1567 gave the name of John Harfell and the Inventory dated 2nd May 1567 gave the surname Harper. In the Will, John Harfer, Richard Harper and Harry Harfell, are all plainly written, this last named as "my sonne". Later "Henry and William my sonnes" were named as executors. Any doubts or variances between them were to be settled by the overseers, John Gosden and Thomas Astrete. Henry had a small share compared with his brother, the residuary legatee, but they were to use equally the store of corne and malt and to see a number of small bequests honoured. The testator asked to be buried in the churchyard of Wonersh and he gave 12d to the poor men's box there. Henry Whetmore was given 12d also. The best cauldron went to the testator's daughter Alice Marche. Ralph Marche was given a ewe lamb, as were three godchildren, John and Alice Astret and John Harfer. Richard Harper was given a ewe lamb too. The bequest to Harry Harfell was a cow, a table, a form and a kneading trough. Thomas Bycnolde, Richarde Hamonde, Harry Chalner and Joseph Kichen, acted as witnesses. No date of Probate was recorded. The burial of John Harfell of Blundells was recorded on 28th April 1567.

Ref: 1567 B 64 Will 1567 B 65 Inventory

Nycholas Hyll **65**

of Ewhurst, husbandman; taken by Thomas at Ryde, yeoman and Henry Naldred, yeoman, 25th April 1567.

	£	s	d
The goodes in the halle			
One table and tresselles and fforme, one owld cheyr with other owld trashe		1	0
One lytell owld Cawtherne with other worne brasse		6	8
One Flyche of baken and martelmas byffe		2	6
One Chaffyng Dyshe, 3 pewter platters and 2 sawcers with 2 salte cellers and 5 other pyces of pewter		4	0
One potte hangger with sirtyn tryen dishes and other tryen vessell		1	0
The goodes in the Chamber			
3 owld trashe beddes wyth the poor and simple furneter to the said beades and 3 owld Coffers	1	0	0
the goodes In the mylk howse			
Sirteyne owld Tubbes and one owld Fryng pane, one lynnen whyelle and owld [-]		3	0
A Cock with 6 henes		2	4
Hogges and pygges	1	0	0
The goodes in the yerd			
One weyne with 2 owlde peyr of whgyelles, 2 harrows and one Cheyne, 2 yerne wedges, byll and axe, on plow wythe other owlde yerne		15	0
6 kene and Callves	6	0	0
4 helffkers	2	13	4
6 yerlynges	2	0	0
4 oxen	6	0	0
In the Fyld			
3 akers and better of wheatt at 18 shillings the aker	2	18	0
6 akers of ottes at 8 shillings the aker	2	8	0
In redye money in his purse		4	0
His apparrell		10	0
2 horse beastes	1	0	0
	27	8	10

Note: The Will was written on 15th April 1567 in favour of his 3 children, Johane, Elyoner and his son Rychard, the executor. Wyllyam Perkine of Ockley was appointed overseer. The daughters were each left a cow, a year-old bullock, a third of the household stuff, the corn and grain and the hogs. His son was left the residue of the estate, which comprised a similar third share of the goods and all the farming gear and remaining stock. The witnesses were Henri Naldred, Robarte Stent and Ralph Dalton. No date of Probate was given.

Ref: 1567 B 81 Will 1567 B 82 Inventory

John Rawstricke **66**

of Kingston-upon-Thames, saddler; taken by Rafe Godfrey and Robert Chelsham, 16th April 1567.

	£	s	d
In the hall			
Thre chayres		1	8
A table with the trestelles and a fourme		1	0
A litle round oysterbourd and two litle stooles			8
4 platters of pewter		3	4
2 pewter disshes, 3 sawcers, 2 salte sellers, one porringer and a cupp of pewter		1	8

	£	s	d
2 pewter quarte pottes		1	8
2 laten candelstickes		1	0
2 kettelles and a litle posnet of old brasse		1	6
A fryinge pan, a spit, a gridiern and A drippinge pan of white plate		1	4
A Pronge			6
A bill			6
Certeyn bowlles, woodden platters and treen disshes		1	8
		16	6
In the bedd chamber			
A black cloke stitched rounde abowt wyth sylke		10	0
An old cote of violet colour		2	0
An old dublet of chamlet		2	4
2 Jerkins, the one of white fryse, the other of lether		2	8
4 rounde clothe capps		3	4
A payre of white hose		4	0
An old cloke of blew colour		1	0
2 shirtes of canvas		2	0
10 paire of sheetes	1	6	8
2 mattresses, A bolster, 3 pilloes and a coverlett		10	0
A bedsted and 3 chestes		3	4
A calves skin, a peece of white lether and certeyne peeces of white and red lether		3	4
The paynted clothes abowt the chamber		1	0
Old lumber in the hall and the chamber		2	0
Certeyne skaynes of lynnen yarne and two wheeles		4	0
	3	17	8
In the Shoppe			
A cubberd		2	8
A new hedstall and all the other Wares in the shoppe	1	6	8
All the tooles, a cutting bourde and a stoole		2	0
Certeyn brydell bittes, snaffells and stirops		8	0
5 payre of spurres		1	8
A grey litle nagge	1	0	0
	3	1	0
	7	15	2

Note: The Will was written on 24th March 1566/7 and named his wife Katherine as his executrix. The overseers, Henry Bowrer and James Dodson, were given 3s 4d apiece. No surviving children were mentioned. A number of small monetary bequests were given and careful provision was made for a life interest in rent and property for the aforesaid Katherine, who was to inherit the residue of the estate. Robert Norton was left a parcel of ground at the Chappell and an interest in an acre of meadow at Bonnar Hill and a close of another acre of meadow at Chappel Mill, while his wife Elizabeth Norton lived. Arrangements were made for Thomas Benson's son Mathew to inherit the land later. If all failed then it was to go to John Starr of Kingston, one of the Queen's Yeomen-in-Ordinary of the Household and to George Snelling the elder of Kingston, mercer. Seven named witnesses were Thomas Benson, George Snelling the elder, Henry Bowrer, James Dodson, William and Henry Stoughton and Edward Butler. No date of Probate was given.

Ref: 1567 B 129 Will 1567 B 130 Inventory

Steven Sherube **67**

of Wrecclesham in Farnham; taken by Nycholas Ede, Thomas Serell, Rychard Brodbrige and Hary Battell, with others, 28th June 1567.

	£	s	d
The halle			

	£	s	d
An old volding table, a fforme, 2 Joyned stolles and a chayre and a paynted clothe with a backe of Joyners work		10	0
4 olde kosshens		1	0
The chambre			
A ffether bede with a bolster and a tester and all other thinges therunto belonging	1	0	0
A nold cobard		5	0
4 Coffers		6	8
His aparell	1	0	0
4 payre of shettes and a lone shete		4	6
A payre of lokram pelowbers		1	0
In a nother chambre			
2 bedstedes, 2 old fflokebedes with 2 bolsters with all thinges petayninge ther unto		15	0
2 payre of tresselles			8
In the Buttrie			
7 platters, 4 potingers, 3 sawsers and 3 pewter disshis		6	8
4 Kandilstikes of bras, on salt seller and a dossen of pewter spones		1	10
In Woden Vessell as barelles and tobbes		5	0
In the Kychin			
2 andirens, a trivett, a payre of potthangers, a potehoke, a girdiren and a broche, a skymmer and a drippynge pan and a fryynge pan		6	8
3 bras pottes		10	0
A nold cadorne and 3 pannes and a pappe pan		10	0
In the elinge howse			
2 olde trowes, one coverid, a kneding kyver and a bolting wyche, a vatte, 2 brewynge tubbes and 2 old tubbes		6	8
3 old bockettes, 2 bolles, 2 chese fattes and a buttercherne		1	0
In a nother old chambre			
An old bedstedle and olde hanginge		1	8
A beame of Irene, a payre of skales, 3 smalle weyghtes of ledde		3	4
In the shoppe			
A lome with all thinges belonging to a lome		12	0
2 spynynge whelles and a relle and a payr of olde cardes		2	0
3 olde bylles and an axe		2	0
3 Iron wegges		1	0
A Iron bownd cart	1	3	4
2 yokes and 2 chaynes and other thinges belonginge to a plought and a payr of stroppes		6	8
Harnis and Roppes		1	0
Corne in the fylde			
Whette and Rye 5 acres	1	13	4
An aker and a hilve of barley and 3 acres of ottes and 2 acres of pesse		16	4
Shepe			
14 wether sheppe	1	12	8
7 tegges and 5 yowse	1	0	0
12 lambes		16	0
Cattell			
A noxe and a stere	2	0	0
2 kyne	1	6	8
2 letyll bolockes, a yerlynge and a waynyere		10	0
A colte		5	0

A kock and 7 henes		1	8
5 hogges		10	0
	19	16	4

Note: At the end of the Will, written on 14th April 1567 and proved three months later on 14th July, there appeared a list of debts owed by the testator: to Nycholas Edde £1, to Robert Sherubbe £1 13s 4d and to Richard Hichkoxe 10s. He asked to be buried in Farnham churchyard and gave 6d to the poor men's box there. His wife Annys, 3 sons and 5 daughters, were beneficiaries. Most of the items noted in the inventory were bequeathed; for instance, the "backe of Joyners work" from the hall was left to John, the eldest son. John, the younger son, was to have the loom and all connected with it. Annys, the two Johns and a third son Thomas, were appointed executors and residuary legatees. Of that generation only Thomas and his sister Sybil had no children. Each of the 13 grandchildren was given a sheep. John the eldest was father to Elizabeth, Margery and Steven Sherube. John the younger was father to Richard and Annis. Joan Coteral was mother to Elizabeth and Hugh. Elinor was the mother of Annis Chestelyn. Annis Barkeshier was the mother of Joan Barkeshier. Alice Brodbridge nee Sherubbe had been married 3 times and had produced Joan and John Hethe, Richard Bagin and James Brodebridge. The testator's wife was given leave to spend the legacies left to her children should she fall upon hard times. Nycolas Ede of Froyle was appointed overseer and the named witnesses were Thomas Serill, Richard Brodbridge, Harry Battell, John Holoway and John Fesseley. The burial was recorded on 6th May 1567.

Ref: 1567 B 148 Will 1567 B 149 Inventory

Thomas Webb **68**

of Farnham; taken by Thomas Walker, Robert Whyte and Thomas Parker, 20th May 1567.

	£	s	d
A table, a formme and 2 stooles, a payer of trestles and a painted cloth		2	0
2 platters, 2 pottengers, a quartpot, a pynt pot, a water pott, a salt and a bottell		3	4
One yerne pot, 3 kettelles, 3 skelletes, 3 candlestyckes, a chafyng dyshe, a skymmer, a ladell and a mortar		7	0
A payere of tonnges, one andyrone, a cobyerone, a brotche, a payere of pothowkes and pot hanngers, a gerdyerone, a fryenge panne, a dryppinge pann and a tostinge pronnge, a showinge horne		3	0
2 ale barrelles, 2 old towbbes, 2 lytle kyvers, a pecke, 2 tryene platters, a gayene bole, 2 lytle baskettes, a breade graete and a letherne bottell		2	0
A bedstedle, a bed hannginge, a flocke bed, one bostere, 4 pyllowes, 3 blanketes, one old coveringe and a bed matt		5	0
2 paere of sheetes, 3 walletes, 3 cappe kercheifes, 2 shertes, one rayle, 2 halfe kercheifes		6	0
A paere of smale skaeles, 30 pound of led, 3 1/2 pound of brasene wayghtes, 3 payere of sheape sheares, a mattocke, an axe, 3 yerone wedges, 2 shovelles, an auger, a skyppet and a skoope, a hammer, a wymble with other lumber		7	0
4 hyves and a halfe and 12 empty hyves		8	0
A grynestone, halfe a loade of woode, 2 ladders and a lytle forme, a whyele barowe, a payere of knyves, a waste gerdell, a hatt and a cappe		5	0
A Cote and a Jerkyne, a paere of hose, anold cloke, an old smocke, anold kertle, a nold petycote and anold save garde		6	8
	2	15	0

Money layd oute by me William Webb in the tyme of the

sycknes of the said Thomas Webb and his wyffe and at there buryalle		17	0
Theise ar the dettes knowen that the said Thomas Webe dyd owe			
To William Alley of London grocer	3	18	0½
To John Thomas of London grocer	9	12	0
To Robard Baedgene of Bentlye	3	5	0
To George Wattes of ffarnham		2	0
To John Rogers of ffarnham		4	4
To John Lanawaye of ffarnham as he saythe	2	0	0
To John Huat of ffarnham		1	2
To John Wylde of ffarnham		1	0
To Thomas Parker of ffarnham		1	0
To Thomas Reade of ffarnham			7
	[20	*2*	*1½]*

Administration on 16th July 1567 granted to William Webb of Farnham.

Ref: 2567 D 3/127

1568

Robert Andrew 69

of Kingston-upon-Thames. [*no appraisers given and undated*]

	£	s	d
2 aceres and 3 yardes of barly	1	6	8
2 aceres of tarsse		13	4
Haffe a hacer of pesse		4	0
A rede bollock of to yere ollde		12	0
A bollcke of a yere ollde		8	0
2 oll kene	1	2	0
A colltt of 2 yere olld		8	0
A sowe		3	4
6 hensse and a coke		2	6
2 gesse and a gandere		2	0
15 colles		1	0
Hysse on werynge gere		10	0
In hys chamber			
2 matterysse		5	0
4 pare of shettes		8	0
and a tabwll clothe		1	0
2 chesse and a choffer		3	4
2 bollsteres and 2 chwferynge		6	8
2 bedstedylles		1	4
A tabwll and a forme and a pare of stretylles		2	0
[*£7.0.2*]	7	5	10

Note: The Will was dated 1568 and proved on 11th May in that year. The executrix and residuary legatee was his wife Joan. Thomas Hunt was named as overseer. His son Harry and his daughter Rose were treated equally. Each was given £3 3s 8d, an acre of barley and a bullock. They were to share the 2-year-old colt and if one child died the other was to inherit that share too. The witnesses were Thomas Benett, John Gelys, Robert Brade and Thomas Tummell.

Ref: 1568 B 3 Will 1568 B 4 Inventory

Jone Beste **70**

of Gatton, widow. [*no appraisers given and undated*]

[N.B. "The notte of ale the goods" is a long list of 53 items with no values given, followed by the names of 5 men and property held by them for her. To save space the items have been written here across the page instead of one per line.]

2 tabelles, 1 chear, 1 brasse potte, 1 potte hangger, 1 cobbyar, 1 trevat, 1 spete, 1 letel cadderne, 4 cettels, 1 panne, 3 bolles, 1 bottel, 2 chafeng deshes, 3 cansteke, 1 salte seler, 2 porengers, 1 saser, 4 platters, 1 basone, 1 tonelle, 1 ovenne pelle, 1 barelle, 1 wollon whelle, 1 lennan whelle, 1 cherne, 2 woddon deshes, 1 tangcord, 1 chopeng knyfe, 1 grate, 1 cobarde, 2 chestes, 1 matres, 1 keveryng, 1 blancatte, 1 bollester, 1 kertel, 3 petycotes, 4 shetes, 1 yarde of new cloth, 2 neckerchers, 1 tabell cloth, 2 smokes, 3 apernes, 5 kerchars, 2 cappes, 1 hatte, 1 payar of sleves, 1 coshene, 1 bedde stedelle, 2 paynted cloth, 1 folde pecher, 2 payar of bedes, 5 payar gloves, 1 sow hoge, 1 hene

In the hands of Hary Beste 1 oxse, 1 cowe
in the handes of Thomas Beste 4 shepe and 1 lame
in the handes of Recharde Beste 4 sheppe and 1 lame
in the handes of Nekeles Wodde 1 oxse, 1 cow, 2 bolocse, 1 horse
in the handes of Roberde Beste 4 shepe, 16 boshelles whett,
1 letor gake

Note: The nuncupative Will was dated 27th June 1558 and probate was granted after almost 10 years on 11th May 1568. Two copies of the Will have survived with variation of the spelling of names and articles. The grain, stock and a few articles of clothing, were left to 9 family beneficiaries and to the maid of the testatrix. The executor and residuary legatee was Richard Best, one of 3 men of that surname deliberately specified as her sons. The other 2 were Henry and Thomas. Henry Best, his unnamed wife and their daughter Joan, were named first in the list of bequests. Nicholas Wode of Chipstead was to hand over an ox to the aforesaid Henry, but the cow, also in his keeping, was given to his own daughter Agnes Wode. Isode and Cicely, daughters of the testatrix and two of her sisters, unnamed but living in Carshalton and Croydon, were given a bushel of wheat apiece. Robert Best was given a russett petticoat and Julian Best, her maid, was given the best kirtle. Four sheep were to go to Thomas the third son. The named Witnesses were Dame Elizabeth Coply, widow; Mistress Cicely Arundell "one of Quene's Highnes Maides"; also John Wintersall, gent.; John Long, yeoman; and Richard Beste.

Ref: 1568 B 18 and 19 Will n. c. 1568 B 20 Inventory

Thomas Meede **71**

of Worplesdon, tilemaker. [*no appraisers given and undated*]

	£	s	d
A coote		12	0
A Jerkine		1	8
A payre of hoose		1	8
A cappe		1	4
A lokaram shirt		2	0
A trowell			2
An old coote			8
		19	6

Note: The Will was dated 11th April 1568. Three dozen of bread were to be distributed at the funeral. The gift of a toft or parcel of land called Parkhurst and the newly built house, was made for life to John Russell the elder, as a mark of friendship. This property had come to Thomas's father Henry Meede and his wife Johanna, in the gift of William Russell, gent. and Isabel, his wife, on the 5th November 1544. The rents and profits for 10 years were to go to Jane Russell, the daughter of the said John Russell, yeoman and the house was to be occupied by Robert Clifton for life. Eventually on the death of his father, the property was to go to John Russell the youngest son and his heirs for ever. Robert Porter and William Underwood were to be overseers and the aforesaid John Russell the elder was to be executor and residuary legatee. Myles Ayrey, curate to the rector of Worplesdon, wrote the document. The other three witnesses were Robert Clifton, William Crichlowe and Thomas Boylet.

Ref: 1568 B 149 Will 1568 B 150 Inventory

Thomas Otwey **72**

of Ashtead; taken by Rychard Blondell, James Otwey, John Hammont, and Edward Otwey, 9th May 1568.

	£	s	d
2 kowes	2	0	0
2 calves		8	0
Oen bullocke		8	0
2 smale brasse pottes		5	0
3 olde kettles		5	0
2 pewter dishes		1	8
4 wod platters and a dosyn trenchers			3
3 olde chestes		2	0
A flocke bedde with thappertenances		10	0
2 olde cootes and a payre of hoosyn		3	0
4 bushelles of wheate		6	8
2 bushelles of malte		3	4
Oen acre of grene maslyn		10	0
A Acre of barlye		6	8
Half acre of peyse and tayres		2	6
A table and a furme			8
A tubbe		1	4
Oen henne			6
2 olde axes, 2 billes, 2 bill-huckes		2	6
A laten candlesticke			8
A yearthen cruse			2
In money		6	8
	6	4	7

Note: The Will was written on 27th April and proved on 11th May 1568 by the executors, his son John Otway and a certain Raufe Kirkham, who were residuary legatees. His son Christopher was given the cow and £3 6s 8d and his son Henry was given the bullock and the same amount of money. The fourth son James was given £5. The poor men's box of Ashtead was to have 3s 4d and Edward Mathewe and Raufe Goofe were each to have 6d. Two of the witnesses were Thomas Francke and James Otwey.

Ref: 1568 B 161 Will 1568 B 162 Inventory

1569

Richard Basyngton **73**

of Camberwell, yeoman; taken by Thomas Babes and Christofer Stockye, 16th May 1569.

	£	s	d
One table bourde and one fourme		2	0
On cubbourde		5	0
16 peces of peortter, one chafyngdeshe 4 candelstyckes, one morter		15	8
Two cheares			6
3 brasse pottes, two possenettes, 5 kettles, two frying pannes	1	0	0

In coperye ware as tubbes, payles, bolles, dyshes, tancardes and one chrene		5	0
3 spyttes, one gredeiron, one payre of pottehokes, one payre of coberdes, one payre Anndelrons		4	4
One fetherbed wythe the coveryng and bolster	1	0	0
One cubbourde		6	8
Two bedsteddes, one mattras and one coveryng		5	0
5 chestes, 3 stoles and one fourme		11	0
6 payre of shetes and 4 table clouthes and 12 napkens	1	6	8
Two coates, two payre of hosen, one dublett, one hatt, 4 shurtes	1	5	0
8 paynted clouthes		14	0
4 kyne, one bolloke and one calfe	5	11	0
One horse		13	8
One sowe wythe 3 pygges		5	0
One cocke wythe two hennes		1	0
	14	11	6

Note: The Will dated 16th April was proved on 23rd May 1569. The executrix and residuary legatee was Agnes, wife of the testator. She was to keep his son Richard at school until he was old enough to write and read and then bind him apprentice in agreement with the 2 overseers, Master Richard Gesse and Evans Crokes. A sum of £5 was left to Richard at the age of 16. The testator's brother John was left 6s 8d and the overseers were left 3s 4d apiece. A shilling each was left to Agnes and Ales Crosse, to Richard and Margaret Brytayne, to both of Evans Crokes' children, to Richard Stockye and to Isabel Fyeld. A similar sum was left to Randulphe Bekett, curate, one of the 4 named witnesses; the others were Thomas Babes, Thomas Crofte and Rychard Symons. An entry of the burial of Richard Basyngton was made on 3rd May 1569 in the Parish Register of St. Giles, Camberwell.

Ref: 1569 B 14 Will 1569 B 15 Inventory

George Byrche 74

of Witley, clerk and vicar; taken by Henry Adam, clerk, parson of Hambledon, Thomas Stent and Stephen Peytoo, 23rd May 1569.

	£	s	d
in the chamber			
A Joyned bedsted		6	8
An olde fether bed, a bolster, an olde coverlett, a payre of blankettes and a payre of sheetes		13	4
8 payre of olde sheetes, one dosen of course napkyns and 2 table clothes	1	0	0
4 coffers and chestes		10	0
His Apparell: one olde gown and one other gown, a cote, a dublet, a payer of hose and a hatt	1	10	0
In his purse in mony		3	4
An olde ffether bed and that belongeth		10	0
in the hall			
An olde table, a form and 4 stooles		4	0
A cobborde and 2 olde cheyres		5	0
in the kytchyn			
6 pewter platters, a bason, 5 pewter dyshes, 3 potengers, 2 sawcers and a salt		12	0
A dripping panne, 4 broches, 4 litle anndirons, a fyre panne and a tryfte		5	8
3 candlestickes		2	0
2 oldebrasse pottes and a litle posnet		4	0

3 Litle Kyttelles		6	0
3 old Tubbes and a Keler		1	4
A latten basen		1	4
A broken Ladle of brasse and Iron			2
2 olde carpettes		2	8
A mare		6	8
An acre and a halfe of grene otes		5	0
Grene barly		3	4
All his bookes		5	0
A colt	*[no price given]*		
[£7.17.6]	7	16	8
Dettes which he owed at the houre of his deathe			
To Mr. Keyes citezen of London	2	0	0
To a poticar in Bucklersbury		5	4
To John Byloroughe of London		15	0
To Agnes Pointell widow of Stretford Bowe	2	3	4
For a close of grounde and one orcharde for the rent thereof for halfe a yere		10	0
To Richard Westbroke, bocher, of Godallmyng			8
To William Chitty, mercer, of the same town			4
To Thomas Poyntell of the same towne for wheat and pease		3	6
To the sayde Thomas more for money lent hym to pay the queenes monye for the Tenthe		4	10
[£6.3.0]	6	2	8
To William Poyntell of Lymhouse in the parishe of Stepnye besyde London	*[no amount]*		
Ther was owing unto hym at the houre of his deathe for tything Lambes and other reckoninges to the uttermost that we can Learn the value of	1	5	0

Note: The Will written on 12th October 1568 was not proved until 24th May 1569. His wife Alice, the executrix, inherited the whole estate except his books which were given to the overseer, his son-in-law Thomas Pointell. Henry Adam, parson of Hambledon, witnessed the testator's signature. Ref: 1569 B 31 Will 1569 B 32 Inventory

1570

Robert Altham **75**

of Tooting Bec, yeoman; taken by Robert Lyvesey, gent., Willyam Morraunt, Edward Seer and John Buttes, yeomen, 24th April 1570.

In the hall	£	s	d
A table with a frame		2	0
An olde Cownter table			8
A Cubborde		3	4
A forme to the table			6
3 olde chayres			8
4 quishens and an olde Benker of tapistrie		1	8
A pare of tables			4
A basyn and an ewer		1	4
A laver			8
A cubbord cloth and a towell		1	0
The paynted clothes and 3 Stooles		1	4
A maser edged with silver		3	4

In the parlor			
A ioyned bedsteade, a fetherbed and bolster, a Coverlett, 1 pare of blankettes, one pare of Shetes and curtens for the bedd		13	4
One Cubbord, one olde greate chest, one olde Settle, a wicker chayre		4	0
2 Candlestyckes, one pewter pott, a drynkyng cupp of stone, an old chayre, the paynted clothes, 2 bowe pottes of pewter		3	4
A bowe, a sheafe of arowes, a scottish capp and a scull, an olde Sworde		3	0
1 gowne, 1 lyvery coate, 2 dublettes, theone fustyan and the other worsted, 2 pare of hose, 3 shertes and a hatt	1	0	0
In the Chamb[*er*] over the parlor			
A ioyned bedsteade with a testor of olde bare velvett, a fetherbed, a bolster, 2 pillowes, 1 pare of blankettes with lowe Settles aboute the bed		10	0
2 broken chestes, 3 pilowberes, 18 napkyns, 2 pare of shetes, 2 towelles, 3 table clothes, the paynted clothes		13	4
in the Buttrye			
19 pewter platters		6	8
6 pewter dishes		1	6
15 porrangers		2	6
8 saucers		1	0
4 brasse pottes, 3 litle		4	0
5 brasse pannes		6	8
1 Cawdron, old		1	4
2 kettles		1	4
1 chafer, 1 chafyng dish, 1 Collander and 1 latten for a custard		1	8
4 quart pottes, 1 pottell pott, 2 pynte pottes and a litle drynkyng pott all of pewter, 1 latten basyn, one chamber pott, 1 warmyng panne, 2 latyn basyns and 5 Candlestickes		6	0
In the kitchen			
2 brasse pottes, 1 caldron, 2 kettles, 2 skillettes and a Skymmer		4	0
3 dripping pannes, 1 gyrdyron, 6 spyttes, 1 spyce morter and 2 latten candlestickes		6	0
1 grene sauce morter			2
1 pare of rackes, two pare of pott hangers, 1 pare of Andyrons and a chese presse		5	4
1 Trivett, 1 pale, 1 chirme and other Lumber		1	0
In the boltyng house			
A boltyng tubbe, 1 kneading tubbe, 1 buckyng tubb, 3 washing tubbes, 1 litle stand and other Lumber theare		1	0
In the servanntes chamber			
1 bedsteade, 1 olde fetherbed, 1 olde Settle, 2 bolsters, 2 blankettes and a coverlett and a towne quilt		3	4
1 Almayne rivett, 1 pyke, 2 back pieces of an alman rivett, 1 pare of Splyntes and 1 pare of gauntletes and 2 old swordes		3	4
1 playn bedsteade, olde, 1 old mattresse, 1 old bolster, 1 old shete, 1 old coverlett and 1 old quilt and 1 old forme		2	0
In the yarde			
One olde Carte, 1 plough with share and culter and 2 harrowes		10	0
In the Stable			
6 lame horses and olde harnys for them	2	3	4
Other Cattall			
5 mylch kyne	4	0	0
2 shootes and 1 sowe		8	0

	£	s	d
4 hennes		1	4
In corne			
4 acres of grownde sowen with rye	2	0	0
4 acres sowen with otes	1	0	0
	17	5	4

Administration was granted to Margaret, relict, on 11th May 1570. Ref: 1570 Ad 2

William Baker **76**

of Dunsfold; taken by Nicholas Mawborn, Henry Baker, William Jackman and William Legcher, 15th June 1569.

	£	s	d
A table and a forme		2	0
An ould paynted cloth		1	0
2 Cottes, a girkyn, a doblet, a payr of hosen and a klocke		13	4
12 peces of ould peuter vessels		6	8
A ghafynge dys, 3 candelstikes and 2 oulde salte sellers		2	0
One potte, 3 oulde kettels with other ould brasse		6	8
2 toubes, 2 firkins, with other woden vessels		1	6
A spitte			6
2 flocke beddes		11	8
2 ackres of ottes		5	4
one ould ghest			6
fyve payr of ould shettes		10	0
A tabel cloth and a towel		1	0
An ould Cartte		2	0
A weniard Calf and 2 pigges		6	8
	3	10	10

Administration was granted to Pernelle, relict, on 12th June 1570. Ref: 1570 Ad 6

Thomas Chittey **77**

of Ockley; taken by Thomas Eversed, Richard Tydy and Henry Ame, 11th May 1570.

	£	s	d
Two quarters of otes		8	0
One saw with that therunto belongeth		6	8
Two sythes		3	4
Five ells of canvas for a bed		3	4
Two payre of shetes		8	0
One axe and one byll with other Implements		1	4
His waring gere		10	0
Of Readye money in his purse		1	0
	2	1	8

Note: The Will dated 20th March was proved on 12th May 1570. No overseers were named. The residuary legatee and executrix was Agnes Butler. The testator asked for 5s to be bestowed at his christian burial and he gave his old wearing gear to the poor folk who had helped him. His best clothes went to his brother and a 10s debt owed by his father was forgiven. His master Mr Tidy was given his best scythe and a quarter of oats. Another quarter was left to his master's household. Small sums of money were left to Alice Jutton, Edmund Lipscomb and William Nightingale. The witnesses were Richard Weller and Richard Tidy. The Will was proved at Guildford. No christian names had been given to his father or brother.

Ref: 1570 B 66 Will 1570 B 67 Inventory

John Constable **78**

of Ockley; taken by John Wyllet, Richard Tydy, Richard Amias and John Pullen, 25th April 1570.

	£	s	d
Three kine	3	0	0
Three two yerelinge heckfers, 15 shillings apece	2	5	0
Two twelfmonthings, 8 shillings apece		16	0
One mare	1	0	0
Syx twelfmonthinge tedgs		16	0
Two hodgs and foure pidgs		10	0
One acre of wheate and one acre of rye		13	4
One acre and a halfe of otes		13	4
One flocke bed with all that therunto belongeth	1	0	0
One matteris with all that therunto belongeth		10	0
Eyght payre of shetes	1	0	0
All the brasse and peuter	1	10	0
Foure Chestes		4	0
Two table Clothes and two table napkins		3	4
Syx busshels of oten malt		4	0
Tubs, barrills, bylls, axes with all other Implementes		13	4
His waringe gere		13	4
Of Readye money in his purse		3	4
[*£15.15.0*]	13	17	0

Note: The Will dated 6th April was proved on 12th May 1570. The residuary legatee and executrix was the testator's wife, Agnes. A sum of 3s 4d apiece was given to the overseers Richard Tydye and John Chisman. Twopence was bequeathed to the Mother Church of Winchester and 12d to his goddaughter Alice Byxlye. Careful provision was made for the payment of £4 to his son John at the age of 21, at which time the young man would take over, either from his mother, or from his uncle Nicholas Constable, the eight acres of land called Palmers field and Ferris Grove. Meantime the testator's father was to receive 8s a year from the said parcel of land. The overseers witnessed the Will, as did Richard Constable, William Worsfould and the writer John Eversed.

Ref: 1570 B 82 Will 1570 B 83 Inventory

John Hoke **79**

of Chiddingfold; taken by John Osbarne, Wylliam Strowdwyke, Henry Strowdwyke and John Rapley. [*undated*]

	£	s	d
His apparryll		6	8
In the parler			
A flokebed with althynges belongyng		13	4
The stayned clothes, a cobbord, 2 chestes		10	0
In the lowfftes			
The beddyng and stayned clothes	2	0	0
The tabyll, the cubbord, a stayned clothe, 4 pewter dysshes 3 eryd dysshes		13	4
In the kechyn			
Brasse	1	0	0
2 spytes, 2 awndyrons and a pothanger		5	0
5 pewter plateres		4	0
Tubbes and trowes and boles and dysshes and bordes		10	0

2 spynyng wheles		1	0
Barrylles and tubbes and a chese presse		10	0
In the buttere			
Stobbynes and 3 glasse potes and other thynges		6	0
Owld saddyles		1	1
Glassys	1	0	0
Fortye quarternes of glase	2	0	0
5 akeres off rye	2	0	0
10 akeres off ottes	2	0	0
Shettes and 2 tabyll clothes and other lynyn	1	0	0
A owld carte and a yoke and a chayne		4	0
Woll		6	8
5 shottes		10	0
Gese and pultre		3	4
2 oxen, 5 kene, 3 bullukes	10	0	0
2 horse bestes	2	0	0
A lease being 14 yeres to cum	14	0	0
	42	4	4

Administration was granted to Margarete, relict, on 9th October 1570. Ref: 1570 Ad 28

Robert Marshar **80**

of Wrecclesham in Farnham; taken by Thomas Serell, Nycolas Shambell, William Ede and Symon Marner, 28th March 1570.

	£	s	d
The Chamber			
A ffether bed, a bolster, 4 pare of sheytes and a Coverlyte, 2 fflocke beddes, 2 bolsters, 2 Coverleytes and a blanket, 3 Chestes	1	9	8
A testor of a bed		1	0
his apparell			
2 pare of hose, 2 Jerkyns, one Cote, A hatt, 2 sheyrtes with the reste of his wearynge Geare	1	0	0
the haule with suche things as ar therin			
2 Saltes, 4 platters, 5 pottingars, 3 sausars And a pewtar potte, 18 Spoones		6	8
One tabell in the haule Joyned with a cupbord in the same tabell, a fforme, a cupborde		13	4
Another tabell in the haule		1	0
The kychen with suche thinges as ar therin			
5 ketelles, 2 Cawdrons, 2 Brasse pottes, A skillot, a pappe panne, 4 Candelstyckes, a Skymmer, a ffryenge panne, A Tryfte, 2 Andyrons, a pare of Tonges, a Spytte, 2 pare of pothanngers, 2 pare of potte howkes	1	3	4
6 Tubbes, 2 ffates, a Bultyng hutche, a powderynge Troghc, a Busshell, a Sede Codde, A Chese presse with other necessaryes		12	0
2 Dowsen trenchers, one dowsen dyshes, 2 Boles, 2 Bole dyshes, 2 Buckettes, 3 Bottelles		2	0
2 Chayers and a Cradell		1	8
Cattaile in the ffelde			
18 shepe, A Colte	2	0	0
2 workynge Steres	2	0	0
4 Kyne	2	13	4
A blacke heckefowrd Bullocke of 3 yeres olde		10	0
A Brended Bullocke of one yere olde		6	0
2 bullockes		10	0

2 Mares		13	4
A Sowe and 2 pygges		5	0
An yron Bownde Carte and 2 woode ropes, a Court rope, 3 Chaynes and a pare of yron Stroppes, 2 plowghes, 2 harowes with all other necessaryes belonngynge to the same plowghe and carte and a lytell watar Carte	2	0	0
A Grynestone, 2 Sythes and a Cradell, 6 yron wedges, 2 billes, 2 Axes, A hatchat, A ffolde pytchar, 12 wattelles		10	0
10 Acres of wheate and Rye Sowen in the ffealdes, 14 busshelles of Otes and 2 busshelles of ffetches	2	10	0
[*£19.8.4*]	19	11	10

Note: The Will was written on 30th January and proved at Guildford on 12th May 1570. Thomas Serell and William Ede had been made overseers with a reward of 12d each. His wife Alyce and John, one of his 4 sons, had been made executors and they "to go haulfe in my lanndes, tylladge and corne and haye and they to occupy together as long as my said wyfe liveth". This son John also had a half share with his mother of the principal farming gear and on his own account, furniture and stock. His brothers Henry and Allen were given specific stock and so were the two sisters Katheryne and Joan, but whereas John inherited the full share at his mother's death, brother Nycholas was given £5 at the age of 22. The overseers and Henry Battell were 3 named witnesses. On 14th February 1569/70 the burial of Robert Marsher was recorded.

Ref: 1570 B 280 Will 1570 B 281 Inventory

John Northall **81**

of Guildford, saddler; taken by Herry Parkhurst, Robert Tredcroft and Thomas Seman, 20th March 1569/70.

	£	s	d
In the hall			
A table, a forme and a payr of tressells		2	4
A Cubberd		3	0
A payr of Andyrons, a payr of tonges and a payr of pothokes		2	6
A brusshe			3
In the Chamber			
A Joynbedstedle		5	0
A truckell bed		1	0
A chest			8
The paynted clothes		5	0
A flock bed		5	0
An other flock bed		2	0
A bolsters and 3 pyllowes		4	0
A Coverlet and a payr of blankettes		3	4
2 payr of shetes		4	0
In An other chamber			
A bedsted, A matrys, a shete, a Coverlet		6	8
2 table clothes		1	0
In the buttry			
Pewter vessell		4	0
A quart pott and A pynt pot of pewter		1	8
2 Candle styckes			8
Half a dossen of spones			3
In the kychen			
A brasse pott		3	8
A skellett of brasse			8
A frying panne			4
A kyttle		1	0

Dysshes, trenchers and a Ladle of wod			2
A dofh Tubbe, a vyrkyn and a booll		1	8
A byll			8
His Aparell		3	4
In Redy mony in his pursse			6

12th May 1570 Administration granted at Guildford to Anne, relict [*the word executrix scored through*].

In the shoppe			
2 new sadles		12	0
The making of A sadle		1	0
A packsadle tree and a syd sadle tre		3	0
4 byttes and a payr of styrropes		2	0
A male pyllen			5
2 payr of gyrtes			10
11 hedstales		7	4
7 payr of Raynes		2	4
Senewes and heare			8
A hyd of Lether coryed		11	0
A coler of Lether			6
Bokells and Curbes			2
Ules in the shoppe		1	0
Wod in the gate		2	6
	5	9	1
Owynge unto Christopher Mellershe	6	0	0
George Austen	1	0	0
Rychard Cox	1	0	0
Henry Parkhust	1	0	0
George Myles		5	0
James Shawe	1	0	0
Thomas Seman		16	0
John Schotchar		5	0
Henry Myhell	3	0	0
Anthony Barns		10	0
Braborn the tanner		10	0
Baldynge the tanner		4	0
Robert Mason	1	5	0
Olyver Chert		10	0
Myles Poole		5	0
John Hole	2	0	0
	19	10	0

Beside the Queen's Majesty's dewe which is unknowne

The grant of Administration had been written by George Acworth at Guildford at the bottom of the front of the document. Ref: 1570 Ad 42

Note: John Northall's burial had been recorded 2 months previously on 10th March 1569/70 in Holy Trinity parish register.

James Westbroke **82**

of Compton next Guildford; taken by William Children, gent., Thomas Turnere, George Merline, John Turnere and Thomas Brodbridge, 25th April 1570.

In the haall	£	s	d
A table, 2 benches and a forme		2	6
2 coopbordes and 2 shelfes		12	0

In the chambers			
3 flockebeddes, 3 Coverletes, 2 blanketes, 4 bedsteedles, 2 fethere bolsteres, 1 flocke bolstere and 2 pillowes	1	0	0
2 caldrens, 3 kettels and a pane		16	0
2 brase pootes and a chaffere		10	0
1 latten basane, 2 lattan candlstickes and a brasane laddle		3	0
5 pewtere platters, 3 pewter dishes, 2 sawsers, 4 saltseellers and 4 dosen of tynnen spones		16	4
A payere of poothangers, a payere of potehookes, a broche, an andirone, a drippinge panne, a chaffingdishe, 2 triftes, a friing pane and a girdirone		5	0
3 table clothes, 2 payere of locorame sheetes, 2 payere of canvas sheetes and 2 table napkins		10	0
4 chestes		4	0
A quartere of wheat	1	0	0
2 quarters of barley		18	8
3 quarters malt	1	11	0
5 bacone hooges in the Roofe	1	5	0
In the barne			
By estimatione 4 quarters Rye	2	16	8
4 quarters barley in the barne by estimation	1	17	4
A wagane with irone bound wheels, a plowe with yokes, cheynes and all thinges therto pertayninge and one payer of wheeles bandes, tow old dungpootes without wheeles and 2 harrowes	3	14	0
3 axes, 2 billes, 2 showels with Certayne othere Implementes and tryffels belonginge to husbandrye		6	0
All his apparell and his wife's	3	0	0
His dager and his girdle		1	0
Money in his purse		10	0
Certayne tubbes, stobins and standes with certayne othere tr[*u*]mpery and lumber in the kychine		10	0
4 stones potes and 4 dosen of trenchers			10
4 oxene	6	13	4
5 Kyne	5	0	0
4 heckfers, one yonge bulle and a steare	4	0	0
Towe geldinges and 2 mauers	4	0	0
17 ewes and 14 lambes	3	0	0
53 wethers	7	10	0
32 teeges	3	0	0
All the swine	2	0	0
10 acars of wheat upone the grounde	6	13	4
5 acars of Rye	2	10	0
10 acars of barley	3	0	0
8 acars of small ootes	1	12	0
6 acars of pease		16	0
3 acars of taers		8	0
A lesse for terme of yeres of Westberrie Lordshippe 15 yeres to come		[*blank*]	
	72	12	0

Note: The Will was written on 22nd April and exhibited two months later, on 22nd June 1570, his son William having been made executor and residuary legatee. William More Esquire, the lord of the manor of Westbury in Compton, was given 6 wethers, desiring him to be good to the Westbroke children: William, John, George, Thomas and Agnes. Names of cows, colours and ages of other beasts and horses and details of fields, crops, articles of household and farming goods and of clothing, were all set down in the bequests to family, servants and neighbours. Thomas, the testator's brother and Richard Inwarde were named as the 2 overseers. Field names of arable land bequeathed to the children were in total: 5 acres of barley above Marlpits; 5 acres of wheat in Crab Tree Croft beneath the old hedges, one of them above the old ditch; 1 acre of peas in Downside; 3 lands of vetches in Fowler's Croft; and 3 acres of oats in Sheeplands. The testator's brother Thomas was to have the care and keeping of his nephew Thomas and his inheritance till the age of 21. If the boy were to die, then half the goods were left to his uncle and the other half equally to his 3 brothers and his sister. Thomas Westbroke, William Wheler and Florence Punter, three servants of the testator, had various bequests of livestock, money, grain and clothing. Joan Wodier, Richard Inwood's wife, Henry Cawrties, Edward Punter and two brothers-in-law Peter and Edmund Smith, were all given articles of clothing suited to their needs. A widow Ellen West and Thomas Turner's wife, each inherited 3s 4d. Thomas Turner and Thomas Brodbridge witnessed the Will. The overseers obtained letters of administration in 1570 and the copies of the Will and Inventory were exhibited again on 23rd October 1574 when the executor came of age.

Ref: 1570 B 473 Will 1570 B 474 Inventory

John Winne **83**

of Wrecclesham in Farnham, labourer; taken by Nicholas Shambles, RobertTrigge, John Holoway, Rychard Brodebridge and Symond Marner, 28th March 1570.

	£	s	d
The hall			
2 platters 3 pottingers, 3 sawcers, 1 saltseller, 4 spoones, 6 trenchers a table, a pepercorne, a paire of sheyres		5	6
A pottehanger			4
The kitchen			
A Cawdron, 1 panne, 2 kittles, a frying panne		5	0
A broche, 1 trifte, 3 tubbes, 1 kyver, 1 ould trowe		2	0
The chamber			
A flocke bedd, 1 boulster, 2 coverletts, 2 bed bedstedds		8	4
The linnen			
2 paire of shetes,1 table cloth		5	4
The bacon			
3 small hogges of Bacon		7	8
Barely and peason			
4 bushels of bareleye and 3 bushels of peason		6	4
The corne in the fielde			
3 hilves of wheat, 3 hilves of rye and half an acre of fetches		5	4
Shepe and neate			
26 shepe	2	13	4
Hoggelings			
6 hoggelings		9	0
A byll, 1 axe, 1 hatchet, 3 sithes, 1 spinninge tourne and 1 pair of cards		3	0
A lease of a howse and halfe yardelande therto apperteyninge lyinge in Wreclesshame		8	0
			0
	[*13*	*11*	*2*]

Note: The Will was written on 8th February and proved about 3 months later, on 12th May 1570. Joan, his wife, was made executrix and residuary legatee. His sons John and Symond were left sheep and cattle. If the children were to die, then his wife and his mother were to share the bequests equally. One third of the current season's corn was bequeathed to his mother. The 2 overseers appointed were his brother Robert Winne and Richard Brodebridge. 3 appraisers, John Holoway, Simond Marner and Nicholas Shambles, were named as witnesses, as were William Cheynell, William Gunter and John Shrubb. The Will was proved in Guildford. The burial in

Farnham on 28th March 1570 coincided with the date of the making of the Inventory.Ref: 1570 B 485 Will 1570 B 486 Inventory

1571

Robert Bundell **84**

of Thames Ditton; taken by John Freland, John Tayler, John Roger and George Byrde, 12th May 1571.

	£	s	d
3 Feyther Beddes, 5 bolsters, 5 pyllowes	2	0	0
1 Mattres		3	4
2 Coverlettes, 2 Blankettes		6	8
7 payre of Shettes	1	0	0
2 Tabylclothes, 3 Napkyns, 2 pyllowebeares, 2 toweles		6	8
2 Crisnyng shettes		6	8
2 Carcheves, 3 Rayles		4	0
3 Bedstedes, 5 Chestes		12	0
2 Cotes, 3 Gyrkyns, 1 Canves Dowbelett, 1 payre of hose		12	0
9 platters, 6 dysshes, 5 sawsers, 4 podengers, 2 Saltsellers, 2 quart pottes, 1 pynt pott, 2 Basons, 1 Ewer		16	0
1 Sword 1 Woodknyfe		3	4
1 Banker		1	0
5 kettylles, 3 pannes, 4 Brassepottes, 1 Cawdron	2	0	0
8 Candylsteckes, 1 Bason, 1 Chafyngdysshe, 1 morter, 2 pottes of laten		10	0
3 Spyttes, 2 Gyrdeyens, 2 payre of Tonges, 1 fyer panne 2 pott hangers, 2 payre of pott hokes, 1 Trevett, 1 payre of Cobyens, 1 dryping panne, 2 frying pannes		6	8
2 Axes, 3 bylhokes, 2 hedgeing bylles, 1 hammer, 1 payre of pyncers, 5 Augurs, 1 addes, 1 oxcheane, 1 payre of Strapps		3	0
3 Cubbordes, 2 Joyned Stoles, 1 Chare		10	0
Old hangenges		2	0
3 leyther Bottelles		1	0
8 pounds of Towe		1	4
2 Sackes		2	0
1 mattehock, 1 Spade, 1 Busshell		2	0
Tubbes and Bowles, Dysshes, Trenchers and Spones		3	4
2 payre of Fetters, 2 lockes		1	0
1 Cart, 1 Harrowe, Harnes and Ladder	1	1	0
1 Horse, 1 Mare	2	0	0
2 kene, 1 bullock	2	6	8
2 pegges and pultre		3	0
1 acr of wheat, 1 acr of Rye, 1 acr peyse, 1 acr of hottes	1	0	0
Money in hys purse		4	0
[*£17.8.8*]	17	13	8

Note: The Will was written on 1st May 1571 and proved 3 weeks later. His daughter Margaret was given some livestock and she and Elizabeth Whyttyngton were each given a comprehensive share of household goods and half of his late wife's linen. Thomas Okley's wife and Edward Bundell had small bequests. The residuary legatees and appointed executors were his 2 sons, George and Roger, but as they were minors at his death, the overseers Thomas Okely of Esher, husbandman and Thomas Twyne of Thames Ditton, carpenter, bound themselves well and truly to administer the estate. The witnesses to the Will were George Byrd and Thomas Frannces.

Ref: 1571 B 30/1 Will 1571 B 30/2 Inventory

Julyan Elyot **85**

of Catteshall in Godalming, widow; taken by Wyllyam Atred, Henrry Whelar of Catsyll, Wyllyam Chyttye of Godalmynge and Thomas Wellar of Catsyll, 19th May 1571.

	£	s	d
In the hall			
A foldynge table, a forme, 2 chayres, a old carpat, 4 koshyns, a cobarde and coubard cloth and a paynted cloth	1	3	4
In the parler			
A fether bed with a playne bedstedell with a coverlet the best, a blanket, 6 pyllows, 2 bolsters, a bed hangyn with the paynted clothes, 2 chestes and 3 playne kofers	4	0	0
A holyn shet, a lokoren payre of shetes and 7 payre of canvas shetes, 2 canvas table clothys and a lokorome table clothe, a payre of holyne pillobers, 4 table napkyns	1	16	8
all her aparrell			
A gowne, a kertell and round kertell and 3 cassokes, 2 petycotes, a hat and a cap, 3 neckerchers, 3 hedkerchers and 3 rayles, 2 cap napkyns wythe all the rest of her aparell	3	17	0
In the parler at the end of the house			
A table, a forme, a cobarde, a playne Join bedstedell, a fether bed, a coverlett, a payre of blanketes, a boster with the pay[*nted*] clothes in the parler	2	13	[ ]
In the lofte over the parler			
A olde fether bed and a old coverlet, a payre blanketes and a bolster and a bedhanger	1	5	0
In the chamber			
A flocke bed, a old coverlet and a bolster, a bedstedell and the paynted clothes for the chamber		18	[ ]
In a nother lofte			
A old table and tressels, half a tod of whyt wooll, 20 pound of dyed lyste, 3 olde cofers	1	1	4
In the servantes chamber			
A old bedstedell, a flocke bed, a payer of blanketes and a coverlet and a bolster		10	0
all the brasse			
2 cawdrons, 3 brase potes, 3 prase panes, 5 kytels, a posnet, a fryeng pane	2	15	0
all the pewter In the pantry			
14 platers, 6 pewter dysshes, 7 sacers, 3 saltes, 6 canstykes, 2 chafyndysshes of latyn and a latyn basyn and a morter, a quart potte of pewter and pynt pot of pewter, 2 stonynge potes a dosyn spones	2	4	0
In the kychyne			
A pothokes, a pothangers, one angeryn, 2 strevetes, 3 broches, a fyre showell and a dryppynge pan, one small furnys	1	3	4
The bacon In the roufe	2	0	0
In the kychyn chamber			
A knedtrow, a boultyn huche, 2 bruinge fates, one kew, 4 barrelles, 3 stabyns, a bokyn tob, one kyver, 2 bolles, one ches prese, 2 chesmotes		16	6
In the kychyn lofte			
2 quarters of malt, one barely and one of otes and 3 busshels of rye in the hous shressed		19	0
The Rye In the barne	3	0	0

A busshell and a peck, a sedlyp, a wylle, a byll and axe, 2 showelles, 4 agors, a draenge knyf, a hachat and a becke		6	8
2 gaynes of grecc		2	0
4 oxen, a horse, a mayr, a colt	10	0	0
4 kyne, 2 stears	8	0	0
8 bullockes	5	6	8
2 vens, 2 payres of whels, a dong ven, 3 yockes and 3 chaynes, 2 harrowes and a plowe and that belongethe to it	2	6	0
3 score wethers and 30 tegges and 20 ewes and 20 lames	16	13	4
10 hoges, 6 veynyars and 9 suckynge pyges	2	9	0
A coke and capon, 6 hens, 6 duckes and a malard		5	0
For certen lease lande	10	0	0
In redye mony In the howse	3	0	0
Thomas Weste do owe the some	17	0	0
Wyllyam Gylforde do owe	2	0	0
Harry Tannar of Lydlynge		5	0
Harry Woodes	1	0	0
Wyllyam Nell		5	0
[*£109.0.10*]	109	0	6

Note: The Will dated 18th April was proved on 21st May 1571. The residuary legatee and executor was William, the son of the testatrix. A sum of 3s 4d was left to each of the overseers, William Atred, Harry Tanner of Hurtmore and William Chyttye of Godalming, clothier. Of her plenty the widow gave generously to her children, to servants, to neighbours and to the poor: money, clothing, household goods, livestock, timber, rye and malt. Joan and Margaret, the 2 married daughters, were left £5 each. Alice, the youngest, was left £20 and instructions for the clothes suitable for her wedding day and amongst other things, the gift of the coverlet still on the loom. Thomas West, her son by a former marriage, was a beneficiary. Her third son Robert was left £20, as well as goods and chattels and the £4 due to him in his father's day. Her godchildren and those of her late husband were also remembered with the gift of 6d each. Her unnamed grandchildren were each given a ewe and a lamb. Robert Beldome and John Chytty, servants, were each left 6d above their wages. Ann Hamonde and Rychard Atred were left 20d. A variety of gifts went to Alice Grover and Harry Tanner, sister and brother of the testatrix, who asked to be buried in Godalming churchyard and gave clothing and 20s to the poor. No witnesses were recorded.

Ref: 1571 B 59/1 Will 1571 B 59/2 Inventory

Richard Gylman **86**

of Bletchingley, gentleman; taken by John Chamley, gent., John Chyldmell and Henrye Marten, 17th May 1571.

	£	s	d
In the chamber			
A Joyned bedsted with a fetherbedde, a bolster, 2 pyllous, a payer of blancketes, a coverlet and curtens of buckeram, redde and yellowe	5	6	8
A trundell bedde with a wooll bedde, a bolster with fethers, a blancket and a coverlet	1	6	8
A Joyned presse	2	0	0
3 carpetes, a coverlet and a blancked and 2 cusshens	1	10	0
A square Joyned table		5	0
A Joyned chest		8	0
The backe chamber			
A fether bed, 2 blanckettes and 2 pyllows	2	0	0
A square Joyned borde with a carpet		2	6
A chest		2	0

	£	s	d
Paynted clothes		13	4
The parlor			
A longe table with a fframe		16	8
A courte cupborde Joyned		5	0
The wenscot	5	10	0
2 Joyned formes		5	0
5 turned chayers		3	4
A curten of grene and redde saye		3	4
A payer of Andyernes, a fyre rake and a potthanger		5	0
The hall			
A table		2	6
The kychyn			
A Cawderne	1	3	4
A brasse panne		8	0
3 ketelles, 2 posnetes, a chafyngdyshe, a skymmer, a fryenge panne and a Drypynge panne		12	0
8 porrengers		4	0
6 plate dysshes and 6 sawcers		5	0
6 pewter platters		10	0
More 8 pewter platters and dysshes		10	0
3 pewter candelstyckes and one of latten		5	0
2 basons and one ewer of pewter		6	0
2 pewter saltes and 2 spyttes		2	0
A tryvet and 2 chamber pottes		5	0
A Joyned cupborde		5	0
A raper, a sworde and a dagger		5	0
Halfe a dossen of small cusshyns		2	0
Naprye			
10 payer of shetes and 2 payer of pyllowebers	4	0	0
4 playne table clothes		16	0
20 table napkyns		12	0
One towell		3	0
A cupborde clothe frengyd		3	0
All other lumber in other oute chambers	2	0	0
Cattell and corne			
3 kyne	5	0	0
A geldynge	2	14	4
A mare and a colte	2	0	0
A nagge		10	0
An other colte	1	13	4
A sowe with 3 pygges		10	0
Haye		5	0
Rye 3 acres	2	0	0
Barlye 2 acres	1	6	8
20 lode of tymber	5	10	0
In faggot, barcke and wood	5	0	0
A lease of certen grounde	2	0	0
[£62.10.8]	62	10	4

Note: The Will was written on 10th April 1571 and proved on 22nd May of that year. George Snelling of Kingston, linen draper and John Chilmede of Bletchingley, clerk, bound themselves well and truly to administer the estate. Alys, the wife, was appointed executrix. A sum of 10s was left to the poor of the parish and the other bequests concerned the inheritance of 3 separate properties amongst his wife and children. The son Thomas was to have most of Mychenell in

Bletchingley and Venters in Burstow, but if part of Mychenell was not handed over, then the son Nicholas was to have Venters and Bakars in Bletchingley. A sum of £20 was to be set aside for the unborn child his wife was carrying and she was to enjoy all the property until the children reached 21 years. The overseers were his brother Thomas, his cousin Anthony Gylman, his 2 brothers-in-law George Snelling and Davye Yevans and an uncle Henrye Marten. The sixth man was John Turner the younger. Witnesses were Antonye Gylman, gent., George Snellynge and Thomas Gylman, with others unnamed.

Ref: 1571 B 80/1 Will 1571 B 80/2 Inventory

Richard Hedger **87**

of Thursley, husbandman; taken by John Boxsolld the elder of Heyfeylld, John Boxsolld of Hedge and Wylliam Greevett, 16th May 1571.

	£	s	d
All His Aparell		10	0
On olld flock bed with that belongeth therto		10	0
3 oulld coffers		6	0
On littell caudron		3	4
3 littell kettelles		2	0
2 panes		2	0
On pott and 2 posnettes		4	0
6 platteres, 2 pewter dyshes		7	0
On dosen of spowens, on candellstycke, on sallt		1	0
On keve, on fatte, on tubbe		4	4
3 alle tubes and 4 other tubees		3	0
On littell kever, 3 littell boulles		1	0
2 speinnyg whelles, on belle		1	0
On pott Hageres, on spitt, on Axe, on byll and all other yron gere		2	4
On table, on forme, 2 trestelles		1	0
On oulld sythes		1	2
On oulld Harowe			8
On Kowe, on callff	1	2	0
2 Hecferes	1	6	8
On sowe, 4 littell showetes		6	4
On Acre and Hallf of corn Ry in the fyelld		10	0
5 Acres of ottes in the feyelld		16	8
On littell Hors		4	4
3 Hennes and on kcock		1	4
2 littell bowell dyshees, on ladell and the Rest of the thynges			6
	7	7	8

Note: The Will written on 28th April was proved on 21st May 1571. The executrix and residuary legatee was his wife Maud. William Greevett and John Boxsolld the elder of Heyfield, were named as overseers and given 12d apiece for their pains. The testator asked to be buried in Thursley churchyard and then divided most of his moveable household goods amongst his 6 children: Harry, Thomas, John, George, Agnes and Joan. The cauldrons, bowls and tubs were given according to their capacity to avoid any possible mistake. The "shoutt lying with farrow" given to Joan was listed 3 weeks later in the Inventory as a sow "with 4 littell showetes". The testator made clear his wish that the children's mother Maud was to have the use of all their bequests as long as she should live. A loft was mentioned in the Will only, when a coffer was given to the eldest son Harry. No witnesses were recorded.

Ref: 1571 B 90/1 Will 1571 B 90/2 Inventory

John Monnyarde **88**

of Horne; taken by Walter Tyckner, William Leaggar and Thomas Chart, with others, 16th April 1571.

	£	s	d
In the Halle			
A Cowbord	1	0	0
4 Cettelles, 2 pannes, one brass pott and one yearne pote, 2 possenetes, one skellet, one Chaffyng dyssh		10	0
8 pewtar platars and dyshes, 5 sasars		9	0
One gyryarne, one treavet, on fyoure Rake, one pott Hanggar, one payere of pot Hokes, one plate of yearne		2	6
One grate, one speate, one fleashe hocke, 2 axes and on byll		2	4
2 saltes			8
On payere of belowes			8
Paylles, dyshes, treanchers and Wooden plattars		2	0
In the Lofte			
One floke bede, one Coverlet, on blancket, on bolstar, one bed stedell and the selynge		16	0
On Mattrys, one Coverlat, on blancat, 2 pelowes		10	0
12 payere of shetes	1	8	8
One fryce Cote, one payere of Hose, 2 shertes		5	0
Rofe Hempe		2	0
Lynnyn Yearne		5	0
3 Chesstes		6	8
A pyce of Wolen clothe	1	0	0
Corse lynyne yearne		3	4
In the ground Chambar			
On Cawthorn		5	0
2 Kyldarkyns with other owld tobbes		10	0
On fatt		1	8
2 Hodges of baken		13	0
3 Whilles		3	0
8 gallynnes of greace		8	0
On Cheslathe, 3 Hoppes and Veselles to put mylke in		1	8
The Cattel			
5 Kenne and one steare	6	13	0
One Horse		13	0
30 shepe, great and small	4	10	0
A sowe, 3 pygges and one shote		10	0
A talbele and form, one Cheyar and 2 stolles		2	6
Halfe an A Care of Rye		6	8
[£22.1.4]	22	1	5

Note: The Will was written on 11th September 1570 and his wife Betteriss, the residuary legatee, was appointed executrix. The overseers were Walter Tycknor and John Chapman. The testator's 7 children, John, Peter, Wyllyam, Robert, Thomas, Emmye and Kattren, were each left £1 6s 8d to be paid on their twentieth birthdays. A brass kettle and a cupboard were bequeathed to the two girls, in that order, upon the decease of their mother. Probate was granted on 22nd May 1571. The widow and Walter Tyckner bound themselves well and truly to administer the estate. The 4 witnesses were Walter Tycknor, Wyllyam Leager, John Chapman and John Alffrye.

Ref: 1571 B 124/1 Will 1571 B 124/2 Inventory

Richard Osborne **89**

of Haslemere; taken by Rycharde Boxsolde, John Brygar, Henry Stede and Walter Gase, 19th May 1571.

In the Hale	£	s	d
A table, two tressule, a forme, a coberde, a chear and other stolfe		5	0
A bedstedule, a bolstere, two coverletes and a blankete		4	0
A flokebede, a bolstere, a coverlete, a bedstedule and a tesstar		10	0
4 chaste		5	0
All the Wodun fessele		7	4
5 platers, 3 pottengears, two sasers, 2 salte and a pote		7	0
3 kettuls, a braspute, posnete and two kandelstyke		9	0
3 spenyge whele and a Rele		2	6
A spete wythe a fote, a pote hangare and a paire of potehouches		2	0
A nax, two bylle, a shufule and a hammar			
A payar of shears, a pressyngiar, a sorde, a dageare		3	4
A fleche of bakun		3	0
4 shetes, two table clothes		10	0
Hes Aparrele		16	0
Two kyene	2	6	8
A horsbeste	1	0	0
Two soue hoges		10	0
The leas of the howse	1	0	0
	9	0	10

Administration was granted to Agnes Osborne, the widow and John Grove, husbandman, also of Haslemere, on 21st May 1571. Ref: 1571 Ad 30

Nicholas Parker **90**

of East Betchworth, Brockham, husbandman; taken by Edmonde Munter, John Elsey and Robert Saker, 11th May 1571.

	£	s	d
In hys purse		5	0
One Cote, one payre of hose with other weryng gere		10	0
In the chamber			
4 bedstedes with bedynge there	3	0	0
In the Hal			
2 olde tables		13	4
In the Kychene			
In peuder And brasse with other lummerment	1	0	0
In Cattell			
10 oxen	10	0	0
10 kyne	5	0	0
7 twoyerlynges	2	6	8
3 threyerlynges	1	4	0
In twelmonthlynges 8	2	0	0
In horsses			
1 Geldyng and 2 Mares	2	0	0
2 Coltes		10	0
In Shepe			

One hundred shepe	10	0	0
In Sowes and Pyges			
In hoglynges, sowes with yonge pyges	1	0	0
In Corne			
20 Acres of weat and Rye	6	13	4
12 acres of barlye and 10 of Otes	3	13	4
10 Acres of peace And teares	1	0	0
1 Corne wayne and one wayne with the necessaries	1	0	0
[*£51.15.8*]	51	5	8

Note: At the end of the Will, written on 12th April and proved on 22nd May 1571, appeared the following:-

Detes

Jelian Sakeres and An Saker the dowghter must have out of thys my goodes for there fatheres bequest the some off £10 apece for there porcion that was out of there fatheres goodes that was committed to me they beyng yonge.

Deue to the smyth		8	0
Due to Henry Kempe		6	8

Detes owyng to me
due to Reayve

Mr Dorrell dothe ow me	1	12	0
Allyngam of Horley doth ow me for hay		6	0
Wylyam Taylor doth owe me for hay		4	0

The testator asked to be buried in Betchworth churchyard. Annes, his wife, was to be residuary legatee and she was required to see the fulfilment of his will in right and conscience. John Bell and Christopher Taylor were appointed overseers; John Bell and Robert Saker, husbandmen of Betchworth bound themselves to administer the estate. Nicholas Scorier, his servant for 19 years, was rewarded with £10 and 20 sheep, in return for those he had brought when he entered Parker's service. Roger Stuarde, whom he called his brother, was given £1. The 3 children of the late William Saker were mentioned: John was to have the £3 still due to him by his father's bequest; a ewe sheep was given to the said John and to his two sisters Gelian and Ann Saker and also to John West, Mary Snelling and Thomas Bell. The only witnesses named were Robert Saker and John Cowdrie. The burial of Nicholas Parker was recorded on 19th April 1571.

Ref: 1571 B 137/1 Will 1571 B 137/2 Inventory

Hugh Tew **91**

of Farnham, shoemaker; taken by Thomas Welshe, Thomas Gates, John Tyrry, John Browne, Thomas Rosier and others, 28th January 1570/71.

	£	s	d
The hawle			
A Framed table and one other table, 2 formes, 1 chaire, 3 Joined stooles, a payre of trestells and a payre of playinge tables		18	0
6 cusshines, 3 paynted clothes with 3 inche bourdes	1	3	0
A payre of Andirons, 2 paire of potthangers		5	0
The Shoppe			
Mony for the ware of the shoppe sould	13	13	0
The seller			
A beame with a paire of scales and weightes		6	8
A coriinge panne		6	8
A pytche barrell with other lumbery			8
A lynnen whele and a paire of hanpers		2	0
The Kytchen			
A cawdron		18	0

A little brasse panne		3	4
4 kittles		10	0
2 brasse pottes		9	0
A chafinge dishe			5
4 pewter water pottes		5	0
A morter of brasse with a Iron pestle		5	0
2 broches		3	4
A drypinge panne, a gyrdiron, a brason ladell, a skymmer, 2 payre of potthookes, a fleshe hooke and a slyce, a fryinge panne		3	0
A cowpe for hennes			6
A fyre panne, an oven pele of Iron and a tallowe knyfe		2	0
12 pewter platters	1	0	0
One bason		1	6
7 pottingers and a platter		4	0
6 poridge pewter Dishes		2	6
9 sawsers		1	6
A frute dishe, a pewter cuppe to drinke with		1	0
3 saltes		2	6
8 spones			4
A boultynge hutche and a kever		1	0
A table, a stand, a forme with other lumberye		2	0
A parelor			
2 framed tables and a forme		12	0
A standing bedstedle and a truccle Bedstedle		13	4
2 fether beddes, 2 bowlsters, 2 coverlettes, 2 bed mattes with one paynted clothe	2	0	0
The chamber over the parlor			
A standynge bedstedle, a truccle bedstedle with a tester for the bedstedle		10	0
A fether bed, 2 fether boulsters, a flocke bed, a Quilt, to owld coverlittes, a flocke boulster with 2 bed mattes	1	5	8
An Andiron			8
3 Joyned stooles and a Fourme		2	6
2 painted clothes		2	0
Another chamber			
A bedstedle with a tester over hym		5	0
A fether bed, a boulster, a flocke bed, a Quilt an a coverlett	1	6	8
Another chamber			
A bedstedle, a flocke bed for servantes		2	6
Another parlor			
A standinge bedstedle		3	0
One oulde bedstedle			6
A flocke bed, a fether bowlster, 2 Quiltes, 3 pyllowes and a coverlett		16	0
A cubberd		10	0
5 candlestickes		2	0
A chayre			10
a Joyned chest		6	0
4 other chestes		5	0
The napery			
One owld locrome shete		2	0
5 payre of other oulde shetes		12	0
2 owlde pillowe beares			8

	£	s	d
The Butterye			
5 pewter quarte pottes, 1 pewter pint pot		7	0
3 pewter Drinkinge cuppes		2	0
A stand, 4 bordes, 2 dozen trenchers with other lumbry		1	1
3 tubbes withe the other lumber		2	0
The ostrye			
10 busshels of wheate		17	6
Bushell and a pecke		2	6
3 tubbes, a payre of tressells, 3 bowrdes, a kyver with other lumber		3	4
A welbuckkett, a rope, a cheyne and a Iron handle for the well winche		3	4
A fate, 2 tubbes, a paire of ould tressells, a hatchett, a ould axe, an owld bill, a table withe other lumber		8	0
The Barne			
4 lodes of hey	2	0	0
Cattaille and other thinges without the howse			
A sow and 3 shuttes		12	0
A whele barrowe			6
A grindstone		2	6
[*£36.1.0*]	36	3	0

On 6th October 1571 John Pore exhibited the inventory for obtaining Letters of Administration. Ref: 1571 Ad 45

Note: The document had been used for some writing practice. Inside we read the name Hugh Tue and on the cover Hugo Tew. Almost a year previously the parish register record for 25th October 1570 shows that Hugh Too was buried on that day. Constance, his wife, followed him the next days.

Thomas Warner **92**

of Farnham, [*clothier*]; taken by George Osborne, Nicholas Burlace, Thomas Mabancke and Thomas Tredcrofte of Farnham, 20th May 1571.

	£	s	d
In the hall			
2 tables standinge uppon fframes, 1 other tabell standinge uppon tressells with 2 formes, 3 stoles and 2 turned chayres	1	0	0
1 cupberde with the stained clothes in the halle		6	8
1 paire of Andyerns of Iron, 1 backe of Iron, 1 fyer shovell, 1 fyer forke, 2 pothangers and 1 paire of tongs		10	0
In the parlor			
1 tabell uppon a frame, 2 formes, 1 other square tabell, 3 stoles	1	0	0
A Settell of waynscot		10	0
A standinge cupberde with a presse	1	0	0
The stained clothes aboughte the parlor	1	3	4
5 lyttell carpettes		16	8
6 turky quissions and 6 other quissions		13	4
1 plate candelsticke		1	0
1 bibell of the largest volume, 1 booke called Calvens instuticions with 2 other bookes	1	0	0
In the Chamber over the parlor			
2 standinge bedstedes, 1 with a tester of waynescot, the other without, 1 truckell bedstede, 1 lyttell tabell and a presse with bordes	1	1	8
3 chestes and 1 lyttell cofer		10	0
1 fether, 4 flock bedds with theire bowlsters and 6 fether pillowes	2	3	4
4 coverlettes of liste and 4 blanckettes		16	4

Stained clothes in the same chamber with a holberde, bill and a brushe		13	4
2 gownes and his other apparrell	2	13	4
In the Inner chamber			
2 Bedstedes, 1 cheste, 1 flockbed with 2 listen coverlettes, 1 cradell		6	8
In the chamber over the entrye			
2 standing beddes, 1 with a testor of waynescot, the other with dorneckes with theire testors	2	0	0
2 tables uppon frames with 3 stoles and 1 cofer		13	4
The stained clothes there	1	6	8
1 fetherbedde with his bowlster, 2 flockbeddes with 1 bowlster and 1 blancket	1	18	0
1 counterpointe of Arys	2	0	0
1 coverlet of Dornex		6	8
In the menns chamber			
2 materisses, 2 listen coverletes with 2 olde bedstedes		6	8
Lynnen napry			
1 paire of hollonde shetes, 1 paire of lockerom shetes, 5 paire of canvas shetes and 6 paire of olde canvas shetes	1	16	8
2 Dyaper tabell clothes and 4 canvas tableclothes	1	0	0
6 Dyaper napkyns, 1 towell of Dyaper and 6 canvas napkyns		6	8
4 paire of pillobers		5	0
Plate of Silver			
1 silver salte parcell gilte	2	6	8
1 silver goblet	2	0	0
6 silver spones	1	6	8
In the kytchen			
1 lyttle furnes		16	0
4 brass pottes, 3 skylletes of Brasse	1	2	0
4 brasse pannes and 4 brasse kettels	1	6	8
1 brasen morter, 1 chafinge dishe and 1 skymmer		6	8
1 paire of greate cobIrons, 1 greate trivet, 1 grydyern, fyve broches, 5 spittes, 1 drippinge panne, 1 oven pele of Iron, 1 colerake and 2 paire of pothookes	1	3	4
A tabell with bordes and shelfes		2	6
In the buttrye			
6 lattyn candelstickes		5	6
1 bason and ure, silver fashion and 2 other basons		6	8
2 greate chargers of pewter		5	4
24 platters, 8 pewter dishes, 8 Sawsers, 6 frute Sawsers, a standinge pece for frute and 2 peces of pewter for wyne	2	5	0
6 eared pewter dishes, 4 quarte pottes, 2 pinte pottes, 6 flouer pottes and 2 copps of pewter		11	0
3 tynn bottels, 3 stone Jugges covered with pewter, chestes, shelves and other lomber in the buttrye		5	0
In the brue housse			
Vates, kyvers, tobbes, barrells, buckets, vyrkyns, baskettes and other lomber	2	0	0
In the wolle lofte			
30 todde of Wageot woolle	37	0	0
Kearsies ordynarymad alreddy in clothe	26	13	4
20 browne blewes made in clothe	50	0	0
4 white kearsy yarnes	4	10	0

Remnanntes of clothe in housse	1	10	0
In the woodehousse			
Wodde ware and oylle	7	10	0
In the shoppe			
2 shere bordes with the handells, sheres and shoppe geare, viz. 8 paire of greate sheres, 6 paire of clipping sheres with other lomber in the shop	3	0	0
Teasells and flockes belonging to the shoppe	2	3	4
A presse with bordes and tabell belonging to the same	1	0	0
In the Dye housse			
One furnesse, 2 woodefates, planckes, bordes and other thinges theire	13	6	8
2 paire of rackes in the backeside	1	13	4
Corne in the barne	1	6	8
Corne in the garner	2	0	0
Corne in the fieldes	1	10	0
A baye geldinge	2	6	8
2 kyne	2	0	0
1 Sowe hogge		6	8
Woode in the wodyarde			
Wood and cole	2	0	0
	204	11	0

Note: The lengthy Will written on 4th April was proved on 22nd May 1571, his wife Agnes having been made executrix and Thomas Chaper, clothier and John Kent, glover, both of Farnham, appointed overseers. Provided that Agnes remained a widow, she was to inherit the house and range of buildings, including the dye house, fire house, furnaces and vats, connected with his work. His son Robert was to inherit all from his mother at her death or marriage. In case of default by death or lack of a male heir, the other sons Nicholas, Thomas and Phillip and their male heirs, in that order, were to inherit; and as a last resort the 2 daughters Elizabeth and Rebecca and their heirs would inherit. A house bought from Robert Terry and other property formerly called Michinalls in Farnham, bought from Thomas Tredcroft, were left first to Phillip and subsequently to Nicholas, Thomas, Robert, Elizabeth and Rebecca under the same conditions of inheritance. Household goods and money were left to his wife and children, to Farnham church and to the poor of the parish. John Burlacy wrote the Will, also witnessed by Nicholas Burlacy, Thomas Chaper, John Kent, Thomas Tredcrofte and Robert Warner. In the parish register on 13th April 1571 the burial of Thomas Warner, the eldest, was recorded.

Ref: 1571 B 196/1 Will 1571 B 196/2 Inventory

Francis West **93**

of Haslemere; taken by Rycharde Boxsolde, John Brodfold and Walter Gase, 7th May 1571.

	£	s	d
In the halle			
A forme, two chears, a pothangar, two Anirunes a fyarrake and a fyar toungs		3	4
All the brase fessele	1	0	0
A iurune pote, a trevete, a gerdirune, a potehangar and a paire of potehoke		6	8
7 stofe of tessuls		14	0
All the peuter fessele	1	10	0
5 lattene candelstyke, two paire of skales		4	8
A Irune beame and 40 lb. of ledon weyts		5	0
All the wodune fessele		3	0
A spenyge whell and a rele		1	4
A floke bede, a bolstar, two covarlets, two			

	£	s	d
blankats, a tesstar, a hedclothe and a bedstedule	1	0	0
6 fether pellos		10	0
A floke bede, a bolster, 3 coverlets, two blankets, a tesstar, a hedclothe	1	10	0
5 stayne clothes		6	8
3 cheste		5	0
17 shets, 3 table clothes, 3 pellobears, 5 table napkens	2	13	4
All hes aparrele	1	10	0
All hes workyng toules		13	4
Dettes due to be payed	5	9	0
	18	5	4

Administration was granted to Elizabeth West, widow, on 21st May 1571. Bound: John Farendon, husbandman and John Bradfold of Haslemere, weaver. Ref: 1571 Ad 47

Robert Wysdome **94**

of Capel, bachelor; taken by Robert Wyllet and John Stere, 5th May 1571.

	£	s	d
He had in his pourse the daye of his Deathe		1	1
Wylliam Byxley his executor had of his goodes Remayninge in his handes	5	5	8
All his Raymet	1	0	0
	6	6	9

Note: The Will dated 5th May was proved on 21st May 1571. The residuary legatee and executor was William Byxley. The 2 overseers John Vaughan, curate of Capel and Thomas Staplers were each given 4s. The executor and Thomas Staplers bound themselves to see the testator's estate well and truly administered. He gave 8d to Capel church and 12d to the poor of the parish. The executor was to bestow 6s 8d at the burial in the churchyard. Jane Wysdome, his sister, of Broadwater in Sussex was left 20s. His bequests to Thomas Staplers and to three widows, Stere, Hether and Pace, were given in groats, the old silver coins worth 4d each at the time. The 2s payment for making 24 rods of dyke was to be recovered from Robert Maydman and paid to William Deane. Other small monetary gifts were made to Annes Eliot, William Deane's servant, to Annes Staplers and to John Dirket. A sum of 4d was to be recovered from both John and Thomas Staplers. The 2 overseers were the only witnesses named.

Ref: 1571 B 212/1 Will 1571 B 212/2 Inventory

1572

William Channell **95**

of Wrecclesham in Farnham, husbandman; taken by Thomas Serle, Richard Brodebridge, John Holoway and Simon Marner, 5th December 1571.

In the hall	£	s	d
A form and an old paynted cloth, an old chayr and 2 old stolles		1	4
2 shelffes			6
The chambre			
All his apparell		13	4
2 simple fflocke beddes		8	0
3 old bolsters and 2 letell pillos		2	8
3 payr of shettes		9	0
2 old keverletes		5	0
A bede testur		2	0
3 bedstedes		3	0
2 old chestes and 3 coffers		6	0
A brusshe			4

2 old table clothes		1	0
A bras potte		6	0
A nother bras potte		2	8
A possnete		1	0
A bras pan		4	0
A grete Kytle		6	0
A littele Kytele		1	8
2 littele Kyttelles and a pappe pane		1	4
2 old candelstikes			8
A salt seller, a dosson of spones			8
4 platters and 1 potinger and 2 sawsers and a pewter potte		4	8
2 payr of pothokes and a broche		1	6
A nolde gyrdeyren and a trivet			6
A frying pan and 2 payr of shers		1	1
2 Kevers and a trow and 2 olde tubbes and a chesse presse		3	0
A Ware byll and a bottell		1	0
A bosshell and a Butter cherne		1	0
4 barelles		1	4
Trene disshes and trene plattes and irenne pottes with other old lumbre		1	8
2 spinyng wheles and a payr of cardes		1	8
A sithe,a naxe and a byll and a showffull and other towles		6	0
Corne in the barne	1	15	0
Corne in the ffyld sowed 4 acres	1	10	0
Cattel			
2 Kyne	2	0	0
2 steres	2	0	0
A hecfford and a weneinge caffe		13	4
A horse beste		6	8
30 smalle shepe	3	0	0
5 swyne	1	5	0
A yoke and a chayne		2	4
Koxe, hennes and gesse		3	4
8 olde watteles		3	4
[*£17.18.3*]	16	7	6

Note: The Will was written on 6th November 1571 and proved on 7th May 1572. Joan, his wife, was named as executrix and given the tenancy of his property until their son Robert should reach the age of 21. The overseers, John Holoway and Simon Marner, were given power to administer the 2 freehold tenements for the benefit of the next heirs, if there were any deaths in the family. Household goods and animals were bequeathed to the aforesaid Robert and his brother John and to their three sisters Joan, Alice and Mabel. The testator's wife Joan was to inherit the residue. One of the witnesses was Mr Daniel Croft, vicar of Farnham. Others were Richard Brodebridge, Harry Battell and the overseers. The widow and John Shrubb of Wrecclesham bound themselves well and truly to administer the estate. The burial of William Channell of Wrecclesham was recorded on 9th November 1571.

Ref: 1572 B 18/1 Will 1572 B 18/2 Inventory

John Holt **96**

of Alfold; 7th April 1572. [*no appraisers given*]

	£	s	d
7 Ken and 5 caves	10	0	0
2 twoeering hecfors	1	10	0
One threeryng hecfore	1	0	0
Tew earelynges	1	0	0

One mar and a sokyng colt	1	0	0
8 ewes and ther lames	1	2	0
4 teges		10	0
One sowe and 9 shutes	1	0	0
Two Akers of Rye	1	6	8
A kerte for one horse		2	0
3 hens and one koce		1	4
One hors harowe		3	0
In the hawll			
One taball and one forme, one cheare, one gynestole		5	0
One cobberde		1	8
In the kechen			
4 kettells and 2 skelletes and a posnet and one letell braspot and a shafare	1	0	0
Of petter fessell 2 plates, 6 peter Desshes and 3 sacers, 1 sallt, 2 kanstikes		10	0
One troe, a bultynghuche with other wuden fessell		12	0
2 pothokes, one gerdy[earn] and Andyearn		1	8
8 hogges and 1 fleche of baken, one pes of martellmas beffe	1	6	8
One malt qworn and 2 harrowe tres		4	0
Two axes, 2 billes, one hachete, 4 agars, on drayng nyf, 4 plans, 2 arren wegges, 2 shovels		4	4
In the Lowght			
The fyrst Lowght, 2 floke bedes, 2 bolsters, 2 pelowes, 2 hellynges, 3 blanketes, 2 bedstedels	1	6	8
1 cover		1	0
3 paynted clothes		1	0
2 payr of shettes, one tabel cloth		5	0
in the chambar			
3 bad bedes, 2 bedstedeles, 2 blanketes, 1 bolster, one pelowe, one Helyng, on qeullt		15	0
hes Rayment			
One cott, one Doblat and a payre of hose and a cape and a shert		10	0
In hes pors		3	0
Off Otes 6 boshels		2	0
2 sythes and one sned		4	0
4 sekeles			8
3 botelles		1	4
one broshe			3
one sake and a bage		1	0
	[27	*1*	*3]*

Administration on 7th May 1572 of the goods of the deceased was granted to Thomas Puttock and Elizabeth, his wife, the daughter of the said deceased. Obligation: bound the said Puttock and Oliver More of Alfold, husbandman, to pay to Jane, Margaret, Catheryn and Thomas, the children of the deceased, their equal portions when they came of age.

Ref: 1572 Ad 13

John Lypscombe, senior **97**

of Abinger; taken by John Chaunler, Antonye Tydie, John Longhurst, Raffe Sponer and Rychard Lyllie, 25th February 1572.

	£	s	d
His Apparrell		16	0
7 Kynne	7	0	0
4 smalle bollockes	2	0	0
26 shepe	2	12	0
2 hogges		8	0
Ann old Horse		5	0
Haye		12	0
Two quarters of wotes		8	0
5 old flockbedes		16	8
5 old Coverlietes		16	8
8 paire of shettes		8	0
6 Hogges of Baconn	1	10	0
6 peces of pewter, 2 sacers and two Candlestyckes		6	8
A Chaffyng dyshe		1	0
All maner of brasse	1	13	4
A Cobord and A table		6	8
4 Chestes		5	0
3 dosen of treene vessels with such Lyke ymplementes		13	4
2 harrowes		2	0
A spitte		1	0
A trefvett		1	2
2 axes and 2 bills		2	0
2 old sythes		1	0
A shovell and A spitter		1	0
2 hennes and A Cocke		1	4
[*£21.7.10*]	21	7	9

Note: The Will dated 16th May 1567 was proved 5 years later on 7th May 1572. The executor and residuary legatee was his son Thomas. The overseers Robert Worsfolde and Richarde Lylye were left 2s for their pains. The testator's eldest son John was given 4 marks (£2 13s 4d), the cupboard and table in the hall and a cow. Another son William was given £5 and a 3 year old heifer. A sum of 6s 8d was given to the testator's brother Edmund. Both daughters were married; Margaret, the elder, married to John Evershed, was left 20 florins (£6 13s 4d) and the greatest cauldron. Her son John was left a brass pot and 9 florins (£3) at the age of 20. Katherin the younger daughter was left 20 florins and was given the lesser cauldron. The biggest pot and the pothooks went to her son Thomas. Felip (Philippa?) the servant was given £2 besides her wages and Henry Raven was given a 3-year-old heifer. Every godchild was to have a shilling. After his burial in the church or churchyard at Abinger, the sum of 20 florins was to be distributed among the poor at 2d each, as far as it would stretch. The witnesses were Antonye Tydie and Edward Sone.

Ref: 1572 B 61/1 Will 1572 B 61/2 Inventory

Robert Machyke **98**

of Thursley, yeoman; 21st April 1572. [*no appraisers given*]

	£	s	d
In the Hall			
One tabull, 2 tressyls, a furne and 2 stoles		1	8
One owlde cobberd		2	0
A paier of pote hanggers, a spite, a trevet, a gredyern,			

a payer of potehokes		3	4
2 brase potes, 2 panes and 2 kettels		13	8
4 platters,sallsellers, a saser, 5 spones		4	0
His aparell		13	4
2 bedstedels, 2 paier of blankets, a coverlet and 2 bolsters		9	0
2 shetes and a bed hangger		8	6
7 yardes of cloth		9	4
3 owlde chiste		2	6
2 axssis, 2 byles, 2 shuvels, chysyll and a nagar		1	8
Carte, a plowe and all that therto belonggeth		10	0
2 tobes, 2 paiels, 6 dyshis and 6 trenchers		2	8
9 stalles of bees	1	0	0
3 steres, 4 kyne and 3 bollokes	6	13	4
One geldyng, 2 mares and one colte	2	0	0
19 shype, 5 lambes	2	3	0
One showe, 5 shotes and 6 pyges		13	0
3 akers of rye and 5 akers of otes	1	8	4
6 hoges of bacon	1	3	4
[*£19.2.8*]	17	19	4

Note: The Will was written on 7th June 1566. The testator asked to be buried in Thursley churchyard and gave 4d to the poor men's box. His son Richard was given the best ox, the best cow, his bed and bedding, a brass pot, a pewter platter, a scythe and a kneading trough. His house and the ground around it were bequeathed to Anys, his daughter-in-law, towards the upbringing of her children until the heir came of age, keeping all in good order meanwhile. She was to have an equal share when his goods were divided amongst his children living at the hour of his death. However, John Dendy and Elizabeth, his wife, were to have nothing to do with any part or share of the goods or cattle, unless he changed his mind on his deathbed. Small bequests of money, utensils, stock and implements, were bestowed upon Harry, a son, Beatrice, a daughter and Richard, his son's son. The tables, trestles, forms and shelves, were to remain in the house by his specific order. The executors were named as Richard and Harry, the sons. The overseers Richard Collins and Nicholas Woodyer were given 2s 6d apiece. The witnesses were Richard Machyke, William Boxall of Highfield, William Grevet and the vicar of Witley, George Byrche. Probate was granted to the executors on 7th May 1572.

Ref: 1572 B 66/1 Will 1572 B 66/2 Inventory

Sence Starr **99**

of Tolworth in Long Ditton, widow; 1572. [*no appraisers given*]

	£	s	d
5 Keene	6	0	0
One bullocke		6	8
One sowe		3	4
7 shepe	1	0	0
2 acres of whete	1	0	0
poultrie		1	8
The Linnen clothes		6	8
The wollen clothes	1	0	0
The beddinge		10	0
Brasse and pewter and other suche stuffe	1	0	0
12 bushels of wotes		6	0
	[*11*	*14*	*4*]

Note: The Will was written on 4th February and probate was granted to the executors on 8th May 1572. No mention was made of the sow or the poultry, but all the other stock and crops were specifically bequeathed to members of the Starr family and four other people: Joan Dytton, Elisabeth Mylles and Margaret and Elisabeth Fulkes. The oats were shared equally between her eldest son John and Margaret Fulkes, who were given the major part of the estate. Thomas and Margery Starr, the executors, were given the 2 acres of wheat and 2 kyne. William, the youngest son of the testatrix, was given one cow. Daniel Ware wrote the Will which was witnessed by Thomas Rogers and Hew Mylles. No overseers were named. The burial was recorded on 17th March 1571/2 at Long Ditton.

Ref: 1572 B 96/1 Will 1572 B 96/2 Inventory

Alice White **100**

of Brockham in East Betchworth, widow; taken by John Woodman, John Elsay, Robert Sakeres, John Kemp and others, 26th March 1572.

	£	s	d
In hyr purse		1	11
In Apperrell		6	8
In shetes and linnin	1	0	0
Two fetherbedes	1	0	0
Thre Chistes		3	4
In the hall and the kycheing	2	13	4
In kyne 4	4	0	0
4 Oxen	6	0	0
4 two yere olde bullokes	2	13	4
2 twelmonthinges		13	4
One geldyng or olde horse with one lyttyll mayre	1	6	8
In Eues and other shepe	2	0	0
Yownge hogges		13	4
4 Acres of Corne	2	0	0
1 Acre of pease and tares		2	0
One Corne wayne with a plow		10	0
In otes in the chamber in the house with the Rest that is in the house	1	6	8
For one lease In value besyde the Rent as we Judge		2	0
	26	12	7

Note: The Will was written on 14th August 1571 and proved on 8th May 1572. Specific goods named and bequeathed in the will were not listed in the inventory, but her son William and daughter Margaret were given greater shares that the other three children, John, Ellyn and Katryn, who were to have only their fifth share of the brass, pewter and iron. The clerk's wife and son were given small bequests, as were John, the son of William Westbroke, Nicholas Saker, Ann Heathfield and Thomas Munke. The overseers were to be John Woodman and John Westbroke. The son William was to enjoy the remaining years of the lease of Woolstons and to be the sole executor. The Will was written by George Brokewell, the vicar and was witnessed by John Kempe, Henry Charlwood, Wyllyam Bachelor, John Wytt and others unnamed. Alice White was buried on 25th March 1572 at Betchworth.

Ref: 1572 B 113/1 Will 1572 B 113/2 Inventory

1573

Peter Bonwick **101**

of Horley; taken by Necolas Bray and Henry Braye. [*undated*]

	£	s	d
In lether	30	0	0
In tane	5	0	0
10 fates	4	0	0
In shafes and knyves and other thynges	1	0	0

[*40* *0* *0*]

Note: The nuncupative Will was dated 22nd June 1572 and proved 27th April 1573. His father, Richard Bonwick of Horley, yeoman, was the only beneficiary and he it was who entered into the Administration Bond. From the inventory it would appear that Peter was a tanner. The list of goods was written on an inner fold of the Will. Ref: 1573 B 14

Henry Boxsold **102**

of Elstead, husbandman; taken by Thomas Boxsold, John Bedell and Steven Penycod, 2nd December 1572.

	£	s	d
His a parell	1	0	0
One flocbead and all thynges there to belongynge		13	4
2 coffarse		2	0
Mor the brase and one gyrdyren		12	0
All the coper stofe		2	8
2 troese		2	8
2 bokets, one bole, trenchers and dysses		1	0
Ieren wegges, axese and 1 treft		4	0
One sake, one bage and one chese prese		1	6
One olde cobard		2	0
2 tabells, one forme, 2 stoles		2	0
The pewter and 1 canstek		2	4
Pothangars			6
2 sythes		2	0
The Rye in the baren		13	4
The wotes in the baren	1	0	0
The Rye in the fylde		8	0
12 wattellse		3	4
1 pannell, one Pronge, 2 harose		3	2
5 kyne	5	0	0
One lyttell coue		13	4
4 bollocs	1	0	0
2 horse bease	1	1	0
6 hyfes		12	0
4 skore and 10 shepe at foure mark the skore	12	0	0
8 hogs		6	0
The hense and koce		1	2
	26	9	4

Note: The Will was dated 1571 with no month or day and probate was granted to John Boxsold, the youngest son, on 29th April 1573. Both he and Richard Bradbridge of Wrecclesham, husbandman, bound themselves well and truly to administer the estate. The poor men's box of Elstead was given 12d and the church there 4d. The testator's servant Joan Brown was given the choice of a cow and 6 sheep, or 40s. The eldest son John and his 5 children, Harry, Thomas and three unnamed daughters, had bequests of livestock, as did his daughter Joan Upfold and her 4 children, Harry, Thomas, John and Joan and also the 3 children of John the youngest son, Agnes, Margaret and Harry. Gifts of sheep were made to Harry and Agnes Eede; of 12d to his goddaughter Juliane Gosden; and of a bushel of rye apiece to his godson John Patfold and to John Hichburne. William Luffe and Martin Mannt were appointed overseers. The residuary legatee and executor was to be John Boxsold, the youngest son. The 5 witnesses to the Will were the two overseers, both the sons named John Boxsold and a certain John Wylkynson.

Ref: 1573 B 15/1 Will 1573 B 15/2 Inventory

Robert Clebroke **103**

of Ockham, parson; taken by John Sayer, Thomas Ham, Thomas Lee, Mathew Fayerchild, with others of the neybors, 1573.

	£	s	d
A table and 2 formes		2	6
One Joyned bedstedell and 3 other bedstedelles		13	4
5 chestes		3	4
2 cubbardes		10	0
2 chayers and 3 stoles			8
2 fetherbedes and 2 flockbedes and 5 boulsters	2	6	8
2 coverlyhtes and 3 blankettes		13	4
4 payer of shetes		6	8
His werynge Rayment	2	0	0
His bokes		6	8
20 pound of Woll		10	0
3 oulde brasse pottes, a cadron and 3 kettelles, 2 skellettes, one skymer, a chafynge dishe and 2 candellstikes	1	1	8
5 pewter platters, 7 pewter dishes, 3 sacers, 2 saltes and 8 spones		8	0
2 payer of coblrons, 2 spittes, a tryvett, a frying pan, a pott hanger and potthokes, a grydlron and tongues		5	0
A bultynge hutche and knede troughe		2	0
A fate, 3 kylderkyns, 2 stobyns and fyve ould tubbes		6	8
A chorne and booles and chese motes and a chese presse		4	0
A bill, one axe, 2 shovells, one pronge, a bottell, sakes and seves, a busshell, a peck, one clense seve, one hoste hare, a wimble, a hamer		8	8
Woden platters and trenchers			6
4 kyne	5	6	8
5 bullockes of one yere ould	3	0	0
3 mears and a colte	4	13	4
3 wenynge calves		18	0
24 yewes and lames	2	8	0
3 acres of Rye	1	10	0
Whete and malt in the howse	2	6	0
Hodges and pidges	1	0	0
Pultry and duckes		3	4
A saddell and brydell		4	0
One stale of bees		2	0
One ould carte with wheles, traces and colers		3	4
Monye in his purse		2	8
[£32.7.0]	30	7	0

Administration: On 27th June 1573 the Inventory was exhibited by Thomas Steven of West Clandon, representing Margery Clebroke, relict of the deceased. Ref: 1573 Ad 8

Note: The burial was recorded on 11th June 1573.

William Ede **104**

of Wrecclesham in Farnham, husbandman; taken by Symon Marnar, John Newlynne and Rychard Brodbrydge, 29th April 1573.

	£	s	d
In the haule			
A table, a fforme, 2 Stooles		1	0
One Cupbowrd and a olde Chayer		1	8

His apparell		6	8
In the Chamber			
A fflocke bedde, 2 olde worne coverleytes and 2 bolsters		13	4
3 pare of sheytes and a table clothe		6	0
3 olde Coffers		2	0
3 painted Clothes		2	0
2 bedstedelles		2	0
For olde tubbes, one trowe and old boles		2	0
A Spytte, a ffryenge panne and a drippinge panne		2	0
For brasse and pewter		10	0
An Andyron and a lytle tryffett with a pare of pothanngers		1	4
An axe, a bill and other smale towles		2	4
A Sawe		10	0
2 Canvas Sheyrtes		2	0
[*£3.4.4*]	3	12	8

Note: The Will, written on 4th April, was proved on 29th April 1573 in favour of the executrix and residuary legatee, his wife Margery. He asked to be buried decently in the churchyard and left his freehold house and lands in Wrecclesham for life to Margery and then to his son Roger. The overseers Rychard Brodebridge and John Shrubbe were left 6d each. They witnessed the Will with others, including Hary Battell, John Newlyn and Simond Marner. The burial was recorded at Farnham on 10th April 1573.

Ref: 1573 B 42/1 Will 1573 B 42/2 Inventory

Richard Fagatere **105**

of Pirbright; taken by Edwarde Burle, John Remnant, Richard Collowey, Nicholas Gadd and others, 18th May 1573.

In the Hall	£	s	d
A table, a forme and a cubbord		10	0
A litle table and a forme		4	0
6 stooles		2	0
A fetherbedd and a bolster		10	0
2 coverletes and a paier of blanketes		8	0
4 paynted clothes		6	0
2 flocke beddes, 4 pillowes and 2 bolsteres		16	0
3 coverletes and 2 blankettes		5	0
2 paynted clothes		2	6
His apparell	2	3	4
The money in his purse	1	14	0
His wives apparell	1	6	8
9 sheetes	1	0	0
3 table clothes and a wallet		6	0
10 chestes		10	0
12 platteres, 2 peowter dishes and a bason		15	0
4 sawseres, a pottinger, 2 peowter pottes and 2 saltes		2	4
3 brasse pottes		16	0
3 brasse pannes		8	0
3 candlestickes		1	0
A chafinge dishe, a morter and a skymmer		5	0
A cawtherne and 6 kettels		16	0
2 fryenge pannes, a grideyron and a spitt		2	0
A cubbord		3	4
2 Cobbyrons, 2 pott hookes and 2 potthangeres		5	0
A shewinge horne			4

4 bottels and a cappe case		4	0
A paynted cloth		1	8
A Knedinge trowghe		2	0
4 tubbes		3	0
A chesse presse			8
A Keyve and a butter cherne		1	8
A paier of bootes and 2 paier of shewes		2	0
3 bowles		2	0
10 dishes and 2 trenne platteres			4
2 dossen of spones		1	0
2 stone pottes 3 [*blank*] and a lanterne		1	2
A spynninge whele and 3 paier of cardes		4	0
A paier of sheres, a pecke and a busshell		1	0
4 Axes and 2 bills		2	0
A pronge			6
2 Augers, a drawinge knyfe, a handesawe and a wymble		1	6
A hammer, 2 chestes and a paier of pynsers			8
Olde yron		2	0
For shovels		1	0
2 gryndinge stones		2	8
3 sythes and a donge racke		5	0
A Heare clothe		1	4
Boordes and planckes		8	0
2 harrowes		8	0
A cart with yron bownde wheles	1	0	0
A donge pott and a paier of wheles		3	4
The plowghe, the chaynes, the yokes, the stropes and the ploughe yrons		6	8
The corne in the barne	1	0	0
4 acres of wheat and rye	2	0	0
Otes upon the grounde		6	8
3 Mares	3	0	0
A paier of roopes		1	0
2 stales of Bees		6	8
4 Kyne	5	6	8
2 steers	2	6	8
One heyfor bullocke		6	8
Sheepe	1	0	0
5 hogges		6	8
A cocke and 6 hennes		2	4
A wood knife and a dagger		1	0
2 Geese and 1 gander		1	0
Bakon and beefe in ye roofe		2	4
4 sackes		2	0
A bowe and arrowes		1	8
3 Seves			6
A sadle, a bridle, a pannell, a cart sadle and a whele barrowe		4	0
4 bedd steades		3	0
A ladder and a sead codd		1	0
In wooll		3	4
4 syckles			8
Harnys, collers and halteres		3	4
	35	12	10

Note: The Will written on 7th May was proved on 30th May 1573, the administration being granted to the overseers, Robert Russell and John Baker of Pirbright, during the minority of the 3 executrixes, Amye, Jane and Anne, daughters of the testator. His son Thomas was to have a very generous share of the goods, chattels and farm implements; he was also to have the freehold land if he was prepared to give his 3 sisters the profit of his own copyhold land for 5 years, in exchange for their 22-year interest in the said freehold land. A servant Elizabeth was given the best wether sheep. The poor of Pirbright had 3s and the overseers 3s 4d apiece. George Hawford, clerk, was one of the witnesses with Thomas Martyn, the overseers and others unnamed.

Ref: 1573 B 43/1 Will 1573 B 43/2 Inventory

Thomas Foxe **106**

of Surbiton in Kingston-upon-Thames, yeoman; taken by John Gold, John Duck and Gregory Bell, 12th May 1573.

	£	s	d
An acre of wheat in the grounde		10	0
An acre of Rye		10	0
An acre of barley and a half		10	0
Two acres and 3 quarters of peazes and tares		18	4
Two Mayres	2	0	0
One stere		13	4
A Litle chest		1	8
In mony	3	0	0
	8	3	4

Note: The nuncupative Will was written on 10th May and probate was granted on 20th May 1573. Mary Steward, the daughter of William Steward of Kingston, was left £3, a mare, a steer and half the crops on 6 acres of land in Surbiton. The residuary legatees and executors were his brothers Robert and James Foxe. The 2 witnesses were William Steward and Gregory Bell. The executors and William Steward, all husbandmen of Kingston, bound themselves faithfully to administer the estate of the deceased, whose burial had been recorded on 10th May 1573.

Ref: 1573 B 48/1 Will 1573 B 48/2 Inventory

Thomas Fulston **107**

of Frensham; taken by William Valler, William Eade, Richard Boxsall, William Summer and others, 22nd March 1573.

	£	s	d
His apparrell	2	0	0
Foure beddes with ther appurtenances	3	6	8
Five chestes, on coffer and five bedstides		12	0
2 Tables, on litell cobberd, 2 forms, on cheier		5	0
2 Trowes, 2 Vates, a boltinge which, a chese presse with all other lice ware	1	0	0
A brasse pott, on cawdren with all other brasse vessell	2	0	0
A Dosen platters and potte chargers, 6 sawsers, Dosen spones, 4 candelstickes, 2 saltes, 4 cupps		13	4
Shovells, axses, billes, broches, andiers, pothokes, pot hangers with other Iron geare		10	0
Thre hoges of Bacon with some hanged bief	1	0	0
2 Table clothes		2	0
Cheses		6	8
A cart, a plowe, harrowes with all thinges therto belonging		16	0
A Saddell, a bridell, a pannell		5	0
Sithes and Riphokes		4	0

20 busshelles of harde corne	1	16	8
Threscore busshelles of Otes	1	10	0
Hey		16	0
A Dosen ofwattels		3	0
30 cowples	4	0	0
Forty Drie Shepe	4	13	4
2 Ladders		1	0
8 acres of corne	2	0	0
4 oxsen	6	0	0
2 steres	2	6	8
5 kynne and bulle	8	0	0
6 bullockes	4	0	0
6 calves	2	0	0
2 Mares	3	0	0
A old mare and a geldinge		13	4
Hogges	2	0	0
Geese and powtry		5	0
A tode of woolle		13	4
A Torune and the cardes and a realle		1	8
[£57.0.8]			
Dettes owinge the testator			
Thomas Elmes of Farnneham Bowcher oweth him	3	6	8
Richarde Wooddich oweth		12	0
Dettes that the testator oweth: To John Hardinge of Sprakley	9	0	0
[£51.19.4]			

Note: The Will dated 12th February was proved on 29th April 1573. The residuary legatee and executrix was the testator's wife Johane. A sum of 2s 8d each was given to Richard Harding and Richard Boxall, the overseers. The testator's brother William had a bequest of £6 13s 4d, while his sister Johane and his brothers Robert and Nicholas were each given a ewe. His brother-in-law John Harding had a heifer and his godson Abraham Harding had a ewe. The testator's 2 daughters Johane and Constance were each left £3 6s 8d. The cathedral church of Winchester was given 4d and the poor of his own parish where he asked to be buried were left 12d. No witnesses were recorded.

Ref: 1573 B 52/1 Will 1573 B 52/2 Inventory

Robart Fylden **108**

of Southwark, St. Saviour; taken by John Mors and Thomas Morwell, 18th April 1573.

	£	s	d
4 peayr of sheets, 3 shurtes, 8 table nappkeines, 2 table clothes, ffyve pellowbeeres, 2 tabel touwells		10	0
Thre ffether beades with ther ffournnetour	2	0	0
One Couborde, 2 tabeles, 4 Joyned stoules		10	0
7 chistes		6	0
2 cheyers and one coubourd		2	0
ffyftene pewter pootes		10	0
52 peces of peweter, platters and dishes, saccers and pootingers	1	0	0
Sixe lattine Canlstykes, 2 brasse poots, tenn cettlls and skelltes		10	0
One waringe panne, one lattin chaffynge dishe		2	0
All the payntted clothes ffore the house		5	0
Twoo quysheins			8
	5	15	8

All here dettes Commethe to the somme of ffyve pound

Note: The Will dated 6th April was proved on 27th April 1573. The residuary legatee and executrix was his wife, Annis. She was to decide where he was to be buried and the testator desired and trusted her to be good to his daughter, Joan Yvans. The three Witnesses were Richard Harman, the curate; John Ameres, a grocer dwelling in Fenchurch Street; and John Realfe, a hat maker. The burial was recorded on 14th April 1573.

Ref: 1573 B 45/1 Will   1573 B 45/2 Inventory

Gyles Fynnes **109**

of Tandridge, carpenter; taken by George Coper and Wylliam Taner, 16th April 1573.

	£	s	d
5 kene withoute calves	6	6	8
In the garet loft			
All the bourdes and quartes with other thynges		3	4
In the inward loft			
All the ioyned workes, boardes and quarters		16	8
An yron wynche for a grenstone		1	8
A trefett, a payer of feters, a horse locke and a yron chane		4	0
All hys carpenters toles		12	8
Old yron		1	8
And thre of old yron			6
Foure old pewters platters		2	4
2 chestes		4	0
Hys apparell		10	0
	[*9*	*3*	*6*]

Note:The Will dated 14th April was proved on 22nd May 1573. The residuary legatees in equal shares were his children, the executor Thomas being the only one named. John Hethe and John Hunt, the overseers, were given absolute authority to divide the goods, chattels and money, as they thought fit. The testator asked to be buried in the churchyard of Tandridge. Witnesses to the Will were Oliver Bagthwayte, curate; Nicolas Whyte and his wife; and Anne Andrew. The executor and the curate bound themselves well and truly to administer the estate.

Ref: 1573 B 47/1 Will   1573 47/2 Inventory

Robert Hardewyn **110**

of Byfleet, yeoman; taken by Richarde Harme, Roberte Cheinell, John Harme and Walter Rodgers, parishioners of Byfleet, 4th April 1573.

	£	s	d
In Ready money in his purse		1	0
6 Tegges and 25 wethers	2	0	0
17 Ewes and 17 Lambes at 3s 4d the Cowple	2	16	8
4 Tegges		1	4
2 kyene	2	0	0
One Stere	1	6	8
4 oxen	6	13	4
A Cowe and a calfe	1	6	8
In the barne			
In Rie 16 bushells	1	12	0
In Otes 8 bushells		4	0
In haie		10	0
A Carte and wheles		6	8
A dounge potte and ffrethinges		1	4
2 yokes			6
3 Reapes		2	6
A pare of stroppes			10

A Ladder			2
2 harnesses and Collers			6
A plowe, A Coppes and A Locke, Culter and Share		3	0
A Shovell, A spade, A bill, A hatchette and an Axe		2	0
8 plaines with Ireons and 4 without Ireons, 20 Cheselles, A Tennant Sawe, 2 hand sawes, 3 awgers, etc.		8	0
12 acres Rie upon the grownd	6	0	0
4 acres Otes	1	0	0
A mare of 2 other Jades	2	3	0
A Sowe and 8 pigges		4	0
7 Shutes		14	0
3 biggar hogges		7	0
8 hennes and A Cocke		3	0
3 brasse pottes, one bigger then the other		7	0
4 kettles, one panne, A ketche pan and a friengpan		8	0
6 dishes of pewter, 6 platters, one sawcer and 1 salt seller		9	0
6 pewter spones			6
5 Candlestickes of latten		2	4
A Joined Cupborde	2	0	0
A Joined Table with A Cupborde underneathe		5	0
6 Joined stooles		4	0
A longe Table and twoe Joined Tresselles		3	0
A longe ffowrme			2
Painted Clothes in the Hall and 2 Cushions		2	0
A Table and A Cheste under the same		3	4
2 Chestes with 2 lockes		3	0
A Joined bedstead carved		5	0
A Tester of painted cloth with a ffringe		1	0
A fflocke bedde of Canves, A Tike bolster with ffethers and 2 pillowes of ffethers		6	8
A Coverlette woven		5	0
A blankette		2	0
A Truckle bedstead		1	8
A helien and A bolster		1	4
The painted Clothes in the Chamber		3	4
6 pare canves shetes		14	0
A Diaper Towell		3	0
2 Canves Table clothes		3	0
2 Table napkins of Diaper		2	0
A Joined bedstead	1	0	0
A fflockbedd, A Tike bolster of ffethers and 1 pillowe of ffethers		5	0
A Coverlette of Dornix		6	8
A fflockbedde, a bolster and A Coverlette		3	0
A wodden beame and Skailes to the same		2	0
31 pounds weighte in leaden weightes		2	6
In Tubbes, stobbins, kivers, booles, buckettes, erthen pottes and suche other lumber and wodden dishes and Trenchers and Chesemotes		16	0
12 stalles of Bees	1	0	0
7 Emptie Hives		1	9
2 bedd postes and A dowble quarter			8
13 bordes		4	0
A Dragge			4
An oxe harroe and a horse harroe		16	0

	£	s	d
A Carte ladder and 2 Ropes		1	4
2 pare of potthangers and A pare of pottehokes		2	0
A farne sithe and 3 Sickles		1	0
A Broche			8
A Girde Ireon			6
A blacke coate, A Cloke, A Jerkin, a sackclothe Dublette, a pare of hosen and 2 shirtes of Canves	1	0	0
The Dounge in the gate		3	4
A Colte	1	0	0
A Seade Codde			3
	44	10	6

Note: The Will dated 18th March was proved on 29th April 1573. The residuary legatee and executrix was his wife Johan. John Slifelde of Byfleet, husbandman and William Waterer, the parson, were each given 2 bushels of rye as overseers. The testator gave 12d to the poor of Byfleet, in which churchyard he asked to be buried. His married son James was to have the plough, both the horse harrow and the ox harrow with their gear and a seedcod, after the said Johan's decease. At that time Robert and Mary, James's 2 children, would each inherit 10s. The testator's married daughter Johan, the wife of Edward Chyttie, would inherit £5 in 2 years' time. At the age of 24 or when they married, the other 4 children, Robert, Thomas, Anne and William, were to inherit sums of £5, £6, £5 and £6 13s 4d, respectively. Property consisting of the house, garden, orchard and land in Walton-on-Thames, was left to his wife Johan for life. It was to pass to son Robert and his heirs and failing issue from him, to Thomas, William, or the testator's legal heirs, in that order. The widow, John Slivyn and Richard Harme, husbandmen, bound themselves to see the administration carried out and the deed was taken to Guildford on 20th May with the bond. Witnesses to the Will were the overseers, of Byfleet and William Porter, the younger, of Weybridge.

Ref: 1573 B 63/1 Will 1573 B 63/2 Inventory

John Isam **111**

of Horsell, yeoman; taken by Robert Russell, Harre Melest and Richard Edmedd, 28th May 1573.

	£	s	d
2 flockbeedes, 2 bolsters and a blankate		5	0
4 paynted clothes		1	4
2 pewtere platters and 5 pewtere dishes		2	4
All the treenne vessells		1	0
A payer of strappes and capsses, 2 Round pynnes of Irone and 2 Augers, 4 cart clowtes, an owld byll, 2 howkes, a hand sawe, a wimbell and a spook shawe		2	4
3 bedstedels		2	0
One great cheste		2	6
1 littell chest			6
2 formes, 7 bordes, 1 planke, 2 tressels, one hutche, one littell tabell and 2 baskets		2	0
One maare		10	0
One blacke bullocke of thaige of one year		12	0
2 Kine	3	0	0
One cowe	1	12	4
A saddell and a hanger		6	8
11 sheepe	1	0	0
1 horse and a breddell		16	0
[£8.16.0]	8	6	0

Exhibited by Henry Robynson 16th October 1574.

Note: The Will dated 30th October 1572 was proved on 20th May 1573. The residuary legatee and executrix was the testator's wife Agnes. A sum of 3s 4d was given to his brother Thomas Clifton the elder of Worplesdon and the same to William Russell of New Windsor, the 2 overseers. These trusted yeomen were to take charge of the rents and profits from his property in Old Windsor for the ensuing 4 years to pay the legacies in orderly fashion. One pound each was left to the poor men's boxes of Old and New Windsor, with an extra 6s 8d for repairs of Old Windsor church and 10s for highway repairs between Russell's Lodge and Windsor Town. A sum of £6 13s 4d was left to his godson William Russell, a son of the overseer. One pound each was left to John Russell, Gabriell Russell and their eldest sister and also to George and Eleanor Clifton, children of the other overseer. Thomas, the son of Thomas Clifton the younger of Worplesdon, was left a like sum. Francis Clifton, another son of the overseer, was singled out to inherit the lands in Old Windsor. The witnesses were Joseph Kichin, Robert Purse and Thomas Purse.

Ref: 1573 B 77/1 Will 1573 B 77/2 Inventory

Christopher Lyllye **112**

of Abinger, husbandman; taken by Richard Lyllye, John a Stone, Christopher Aylerd and John Nye, 19th May 1573.

	£	s	d
The best cote		5	0
An other cote		2	0
A dublet		1	0
A payer of hosen		3	0
1 shert		1	0
1 bed, 2 bolsters, 1 blanket and 1 keverlet		10	0
An other bed with that belongethe therto		5	0
6 payer of sheetes		10	0
3 old chestes		3	0
An other bed with that belongethe therto		4	0
An other bed with that belongethe therto		3	8
1 cubberd		3	0
The baken left in the roofe		5	0
3 peuter dishes and 1 salt		2	4
5 ketteles and a brase pote		18	0
3 new cheeses		1	0
1 latin candelsticke			4
Woden boules, blatters with all other woden vessell		5	4
1 axe, 1 hatchet and a bill		2	6
1 table and a forme		1	0
Potehookes and pote hangers			8
1 iron spite			8
2 sakkes		1	4
Half a quarter of wheet		10	0
1 old fryinge pane with 1 drippinge pane			8
1 girdiron			6
4 tubbes		6	0
2 litell closes of wheet	1	0	0
1 crofte of otes		13	4
6 milche kene without calves - 4 nobles apeece	8	0	0
A bull 2 yeares of age		13	4
2 twelvemonthinges		13	4

1 weninge calffe			4	0
A mare and a colt		1	10	0
3 hogges			13	4
10 sheepe and 4 lambes - 18 pence a peece		1	1	0
Timber that was to workinge			16	0
A grindstone				4
A spiter and a shovell				8
A horse harrow			1	8
A payer of sheeres				4
	[*£20.13.4*]	19	5	8
Dettes owinge by the seid Christofer the sume of		3	0	0

Note: The Will was written on 24th April and proved on 20th May 1573. A cow was given to each of three sons, Richard, Robert and William and to his daughter Margaret. His landlord's son Richard Hill was given a cow, a sheep and a lamb. The residuary legatees and executors were Annys, his wife and John, another son. His overseer was his brother Richard Lyllye who was one of 2 named witnesses, the other being Robert Worsfold. The burial was recorded on 12th April 1573.

Ref: 1573 B 85/1 Will 1573 B 85/2 Inventory

George Marlyn **113**

of Puttenham, husbandman; taken by John Byllynghurste, Bartylmewe Hardyng, Rychard Wooddes and Robert Warner, 6th January 1573.

In the halle	£	s	d
One Table, a forme, a chayre and a stole		3	4
An olde Cubberd		3	4
4 Pewter platters, 2 Pottengers, 2 sawsers and one salte seller		8	0
One Chaffyng dyshe and 2 candylstyckes		1	0
in the chamber next the halle			
One Bedstedell, one fetherbedd, on flock bedd and other thynges belongyng to them	1	10	0
2 Coffers		3	4
2 Cottes, two dublettes, 3 shertes, two payre of showes, a hatte, a Cappe, two payre of hose and a cloke	2	0	0
in the backe chamber			
2 Beddsteddes and two olde beddes		10	0
Three payre of shetes, two table clothes		11	0
In the kytchen			
Two olde brasse pottes and a posnett		6	8
A brasse panne, a lytle cawdern and two olde kyttylles		13	4
One broche, two lytle Andyrons, a payre of pott hangers and a frying panne and Gyrdyron and a payre of potte hookes		3	4
One maltyng ffate and a yell ffate, a knede trowe, a salte trowe, two ale stabbyns, a Barrell, a worthe boule with other tubbes		6	8
A busshell, a sacke, a gryndstone, a buckett		1	8
In the Barne			
6 hyle of Wheate		12	0
10 hyle of Rye		13	4
A lode of Smale Otes		9	0
A lode of haye		9	0
A lode of tares		5	0
A lode of pease		7	0

	£	s	d
4 quarters of Barley	1	12	0
In the ffyldes			
15 acres of Wheate	6	0	0
8 acres of Rye	2	13	4
In the gates			
4 Oxen	5	6	8
4 keyne	4	13	4
3 Bullockes and 3 calves	2	0	0
4 olde horse and a Colte	3	0	0
10 smale hoogges	1	0	0
20 wether shepe, 20 Ewes shepe and fourtye tegges	9	6	8
A Carte and wheles and a donge potte		13	4
A plowe, two harrowes, 2 yokes, 2 chaynes, two horse harnes and 12 watles		10	0
One sythe, one byll, one Axe, two shovels, a pycke axe and pronge and a donge spytt		4	0
5 hennes and a Cooke		1	6
in the olde house			
Two awgers and a handsawe, a chyssell, a lantorne and a payre of sheres		1	0
Halfe a dosen of dysshes, a ladle, a dosen of trenchers, a dosen of spones and a pepper querne			10
A spynyng whele and a bottell		1	0
A wache Byll and a hanger		1	8
[*£47.2.4*]	47	3	4

Letters of Administration were granted to Alice Marlyn, relict of the deceased, on 29th April 1573. The widow herself and Richard Woode of Puttenham, husbandman, bound themselves well and truly to administer the estate. Ref: 1573 Ad 20

Note: The burial of George Marlin had been recorded in Puttenham on 29th October 1572.

Thomas Martyn **114**

of Compton; taken by Edwarde Smyth, Gylbert Massante, Richarde Bull, Richarde Prinishe, Richard Overton and Symon Poole, 24th March 1573.

	£	s	d
In the haule			
An olde folding table, 2 formes, thre chaiers, a backestole and stained clothe		10	0
Thre Cubberdes		13	4
In the bedd Chamber			
Fower flocke beddes, 4 bolsters of flockes, 1 pillowe of fethers, 4 white yarne coverlettes, 2 white lynen testers, one chequer Coverlett and three bedsteddes	2	13	4
In the lofte			
A greate cheste and 10 cofers	1	6	8
Napery and lynen			
Fyve payer of canvas shetes, 4 pillowes, 4 table clothes and other lynen	2	6	8
Apparell			
Hys apparell and 1 pece of wollen cloth		18	0
brasse and pewter			
Pewter vessell		13	4
5 pannes and 4 kettells	1	10	0
Brasse pottes	1	16	8
4 candelstickes		1	0

wodden vessells			
A granarde and all other treen vessells	2	6	8
Old Iren and leden weightes		10	0
Corne in the felde			
Wheate 13 acres, fetches 1 acre 1 half and 1 yarde meale	8	10	0
Corne in the baron			
2 quarters of barley		13	4
Cattall and corne			
2 Kyne and a bullocke	2	13	4
3 horses, a sowe and 6 yonge hogges	3	8	0
Shepe 53	6	0	0
Plowes, harrowes, welbucket, welrope, cartes, sackes and winoing shete	1	13	8
3 flyches bacon and 2 paier of shetes	1	4	8
10 acres barley in the felde	4	0	0
Pesen 1 acre ½, otes 2 acres ½	1	4	0
Fier wood in the barton and in the wodd		16	8
Hennes and cockes		2	6
Duckes and mallardes 4		1	0
A bedstede, a rounde table, 2 trowes and a broche and a roler	1	6	8
[*£46.19.6*]	40	8	2
Dettes hereof to be taken out	6	13	4
Dettes of To. Martin	6	13	4

Memorandum

£34 to be devided into partes by discretion of the L[*ord*] Bisshopp of Winchester, his chancellor and neigbors of Compton.

[There must have been some discussion before finalising the deliberations of the officials. A short dated paragraph was scored across by 10 diagonal lines. More detailed instructions appeared below.]

18 July 1573. Administration of the goods of the deceased is granted to Thomas Marten and Richard Marten sons of the same Thomas etc. sworn.

Bound the said 2 of Compton for the administration.

Surety for Thomas: Oliver Lynny of Netherington in the parish of Micheldever, yeoman
and John Complyn of Old Stoke alias Stoke Charity, husbandman,
for Richard Marten: William Williams
Peter Prior of Compton, husbandman.

18th July 1573 Administration of the goods of the deceased was granted with the exception of £21 belonging to George, Thomas and Johane Marten, children of the said deceased, sworn by Christiane, widow of the said deceased.

Bound: the widow and Richard Bull of Northstoneham, husbandman. The same day aforesaid £21 was distributed thus: George Marten £8; Thomas Marten the younger £6 10s; Jone Marten £6 10s; and the administration of the remaining estate was granted to Thomas Marten the elder and Richard Marten, sons of the deceased. Ref: 21M 65/D3/141

Edward Matthewe **115**

of Woking; taken by John Wattes, John Childe, Edmond Bonce and Richard Russell, 28th April 1573.

	£	s	d
The Redy mone in his poursse		5	0
All his Aparell		6	8
To lyttell fflocke bedes with that belonges to them		13	4
To olde bedstedes		1	0
To pare of olde Canvas shettes		2	0

To olde Canvas tabelclothes		1	4
Olde paytted Clothes		2	6
4 olde Chestes		3	4
One Tabell and A fourme		1	0
Tyn sponnes trenchers and dysshes			6
To Lether bottelles		1	0
A nolde Cupbourd		3	4
All other Woodden vesselles		2	6
A kned Troughe		1	0
A hand baskett			2
A Chese presse			6
A Spinnyng whele and Cardes			8
A nolde Axe and A nolde bile and A hammer			8
There Stoules			4
The brasse		5	0
The peuter		4	0
4 Candylstickes and A nolde Chaffyng dyshe		1	4
One Lyttell spitt and to lyttell Cobyornes		2	0
One Gryddyorne and A ffrying pane			8
A Drinckyng Cruse			1
4 Skrubde oxen	6	13	4
3 Toudded mares	1	10	0
A Longe Cart and A Donnge Cart	1	0	0
One plow, one Harro, yokes and Chenes		5	0
3 kyne, one bulloke and A wenyng Calfe	3	3	4
A bowe and 6 Arrowes		2	0
One Smalle hogge		1	4
One Gousse and A Gander		1	0
5 Henes and A Coke		2	0
The Corne and Wootes on the ground	1	0	0
	16	17	11

Note: The Will dated 22nd April was proved on 20th May 1573. The residuary legatee and executrix was the testator's wife Jone. A sum of 2s was left to Thomas Davy the overseer; 5d was left to the poor men's box of Woking and 8s was to be bestowed at his burial in the churchyard. John, Thomas and Richard Matthew, the 3 sons of his brother Nicholas, were major beneficiaries, the first two each being ordered to pay £1 to Richard. John had to pay a like sum to the testator's sister Margaret and to his maid Annys Bedell. His shooting bow and most of the farming gear were left to the said John, though Thomas had the second pair of oxen and a mare. Rose Skett, another maid, was left a weaning calf. His clothing was carefully apportioned to 4 people; the best went to Richard, the son of his kinsman John Matthew. The clothing made of russett went to John Daborne, his servant; to Wylles, the poor man; and to Thomas Bedford. A groat (4d) each was left to Annes Waters, his goddaughter and to John Gryffeth. Named witnesses were Thomas Davy, John Gryffythe and Rychard Bedford.

Ref: 1573 B 87/1 Will 1573 B 87/2 Inventory

George Payne **116**

of Horley; taken by Henrye Shooe, Rycharde Bonnycke and Thomas Roffye, 18th April 1573.

	£	s	d
8 Oxen	17	0	0
6 steeres	12	0	0
4 kyen and 3 heaffers	9	6	8
3 heaffers of 3 yeare olde	3	0	0

7 twelve monthinges	3	0	0
2 geldinge and one mare	4	0	0
sheepe and 6 lambes	1	0	0
8 hogges	2	0	0
6 Acres of wheate and Rye	3	0	0
12 Acres and A half of Oates	3	0	0
Wheate and barlye in the barne	3	0	0
Weanes with wheeles, plowes and harrowes, yokes, tyghtes and dungcortes	5	0	0
One gryndinge stone		1	0
15 loades of Tymber	2	10	0
In woode, felled, Cutt and standinge	2	0	0
Malte, Oates and barlye	1	6	8
Bacon and Beefe	1	10	0
Brasse and pewter	2	0	0
Yron pottes, spittes, drepinge pannes, brandyrons, one Fyerplate, A hempe yron, A gredyron, A fyerrake, A paire of belloes	1	0	0
One ffate with tubbes and woodden vessell	1	0	0
A Querne and A knedinge troffe		4	0
One Cheese slade, mylke vessell and A fewe sawen boardes		10	0
Axes, bylles with other tooles of husbandrye		10	0
One Cobarde		10	0
16 paire of sheetes and other lynnen	4	0	0
2 featherbeddes, one Chaffebed and A mattres	2	0	0
Bolstars, Pillowes, Coverlettes and blanckettes	2	10	0
Bedstedels, one tabell with foormes, stooles and Chayres		10	0
Hennes, geese and Duckes		6	0
A wollen wheele, A lynnen wheele with Cardes and a hetchell		3	0
His Apparell	1	10	0
His purse and gyrdell and money in his purse	1	0	0
[*£90.7.4*]	91	17	4

Note: The Will written on 25th October 1568 was proved on 27th April 1573. His wife Joane was made residuary legatee and sole executrix. The testator left 5s to be divided between the poor of the parishes of Horley and Charlwood, where he had land. Small amounts of money were left to his godchildren and to 5 named servants, Julyan Webb, John Burstowe, Mabell, Nicolas Mylles and Alice Tullye. Livestock was left to the servants William Sanndes and James Burstowe. The profits from his land in Charlwood called Weasers were to go to his wife for a term of 7 years and then to his son Richard, who was also left £20. Provision of £10 was made for any child of his who might be borne by his wife. Three nephews, George, Richard and Thomas, the sons of Thomas Payne, were mentioned to ensure that the land was inherited by members of the family. The overseers were Thomas and Edward, brothers of the testator and Richard and Robert Mylles, the brothers of the executrix. Three named witnesses were Willyam Browne, vicar of Horley; John Kerrell and John Shooe.

Ref: 1573 B 104/1 Will 1573 B 104/2 Inventory

Henry Punter **117**

of Send; taken by Robert Small and Robart Howghton, 1st April 1573.

	£	s	d
Mony in his purse		3	4
His apperell		13	4
2 fether bedes	1	6	8
2 flokbedes		13	4
4 Coveringes, one pare of blankes	1	4	0

A pare of locroome Shettes and 5 pare of Canvas	1	0	0
One table clothe		1	0
3 Small Cawderns and 3 Small pottes of bras,			
3 kettelles, 2 lyttell pans	1	13	4
All of pewter		10	0
3 Candelstikes		2	0
fryne panes			6
2 gyrdyarnes			6
2 spyttes		1	8
4 olde tubbes		1	0
4 bolles		1	0
5 chestes		5	0
One Cowbard		5	0
One table with a Forme			6
Paynted clothes in all the howsse		2	0
One knedinge trowgh		1	0
In Corne in the barn - 12 bushells		18	0
In the Felde growinge 7 acres of Rye	1	15	0
Ottes in the Felde 2 acres		6	8
6 kyne	7	0	0
One bulloke of 2 yees of age		10	0
2 bullokes of one yer of age		12	0
4 weyners calves		13	4
2 mares, one Colte of 2 yere olde, one colt of 1 yer of age	1	10	0
10 ewes and lames	1	5	0
7 hogges	1	3	4
4 pigges		2	0
6 hennes and a Coke		1	8
4 gesse		1	0
	[24	*3*	*2]*
Received of the executors - 4s 10d	*[24*	*8*	*0]*

Note: The Will written on 31st March was proved on 20th May 1573. The residuary legatee and sole executrix was the testator's wife Mary, who received a life interest in a close of freehold land called Hoke in Send. On her decease the land was willed to a son John and his heirs for ever. The other 4 children, Henry, Thomas, Joan and Johan, were each left a cow and a sheep with lamb, to be given to them as soon as the first child should reach the age of 15. The overseer was Thomas Chenell of Albury and the witnesses were Richard Smith, John Shurlock and the vicar of Send, Richard Harwood, who wrote the will.

Ref: 1573 B 116/1 Will 1573 B 116/2 Inventory

Agnes Reves **118**

of Frensham, widow; taken by William Ede, Thomas Heathe, Olyver Inwoode and Thomas Ede, 25th February 1572/3.

	£	s	d
Here apparell, lynen and wollen	1	0	0
A ffethar bedde and a fflocke bedde		13	4
3 pare of sheytes and 4 blanketes, 2 olde Coverleytes			
and 3 fflocke bolsters	1	0	0
3 Coffers		3	4
One old Cupbowrde with olde Tubbes, bowles and Barrelles		5	0
For pewtar, Brasse, 2 Spyttes, one Andyron, a ffryenge panne,			
a pare of potthowkes and pothanngers, an olde prownge,			
a warre bill, one olde hedgynge bill and an axe	1	2	0

Cattaile			
A Geldinge and a Colte	1	4	0
Fyve Kene and a heckefowrde	6	6	4
3 bullockes	1	3	4
20 wethars and wethar shepe	3	0	0
13 Ewe shepe	1	14	8
7 Tegges at 18 pence a tegge		10	0
28 Ewes and lambes that were John Lygears	3	6	8
2 pygges		1	0
In the barne			
6 bushells of Rye		10	0
8 bushells of smale Otes		3	0
6 hennes and a cocke		2	0
In haye		3	0
Corne in the ffelde		10	0
2 hyves of Bees		4	0
A pare of olde wheles, an olde Carte, a harrowe and a harnesse		5	0
2 olde bedstedelles			8
A lease ffor certaine lanndes in Frensham aforesaid of certaine yeres yete to come and not determyned	4	0	0
[*£27.7.4*]	27	12	4
Oute of which Inventory ys to be alowed for the Charges of the ffuneral	1	0	0
Also that ys geven to the poore by the testamente of the said Agnes		6	8
For the probate of the testamente			[*blank*]
For a mortuarye			[*blank*]

Note: The Will written on 29th December 1572 was proved on 29th April 1573. The residuary legatee and executor was Richard Broadbridge, son of the testatrix. Two other Broadbridge sons were William and James. Another son was William Ledger. Two daughters were Johane Vanner and Johane Knight. Grandchildren named were Richard Broadbridge, Benet Broadbridge, Annis Knight and Richard Knight. Margery Burden and a former servant Johane Brown were also beneficiaries. The testatrix was explicit in her numerous bequests and instructions: she asked to be buried in Farnham churchyard and bequeathed an immediate gift of 20d to the most needy of the parish, to be repeated on Good Friday of 3 subsequent years. Five named witnesses were Richard Knyght, Oliver and Hary Vanner, Hary Battell and Edward Gregory. No overseers were appointed. There is an entry in Farnham parish register of the burial on 24th February 1573 of Annis Reaves, so her wishes were honoured.

Ref: 1573 B 120/1 Will   1573 B 120/2 Inventory

Thomas Reynolde, the elder **119**

of Strowde in Egham, husbandman; taken by Wyllyam Bolton, Thomas Stere and John Felde, 10th March 1572/3.

	£	s	d
14 yewes at 3s 4d a pece	2	6	8
15 teges at 2s 4d the pece	1	15	0
One lytle tege		1	0
A mare and a Colte	1	6	8
A Cowe	1	2	0
A blacke bulloke		10	0
The Crope of corne on the grounde		12	0
In the barne			
Thre bushells of Rye		5	0
Thre bushelse of barlye		3	6

In the hall			
A Cobbard		1	0
Tow brase potes		3	4
A kytle		2	6
5 pewtter platters		2	6
A saltsellar and a candlestyke			8
A matris and tow bolsters and thre pyllowes and tow olde hellynges		5	0
Thre payre of shetes and a pyllow bere		6	0
A bedsted and a pecke			8
Thre chestes		3	0
Tow lynnan hangynges over the bedes		1	4
One cheste and tow toobes		1	0
Olde Ireone		1	4
A fanne		1	0
	[*9*	*11*	*2*]
The detes that Thomas Reynold dothe owe mounteth to	4	18	11

Note: The Will written on 23rd February was proved on 29th April 1573. Administration of the goods and chattells was granted to Robert Skyte and William Rowell, who had been appointed guardians of the two executors and residuary legatees, the testator's daughters Annys and Mabell, during their minority. The testator's wife Alse was left a cow, a bullock, a hog, some rye and barley and enough household goods for her to be independent. The freehold house and land and also the indenture holding, were left to Mabell and her heirs for ever; were she to have no heirs, the property was to be inherited by Annys. The overseers were Rychard Tayllar and Rychard Skydmore. John Heywode, clerk and William Colton, husbandman, both of Egham, bound themselves to see the estate properly administered. The 5 witnesses to the Will were Robarte Skyte, William Rowell, Thomas Haryson, Adame Tutchate and John Mabonke.

Ref: 1573 B 121/1 Will 1573 B 121/2 Inventory

Dorothy Snellinge **120**

of St. Mary's, Guildford, widow; taken by Robart Jepsonne, George Myles and Rychard Smalpece, 12th May 1572.

	£	s	d
in the bede chamber			
1 Joyned bedsted, one flocke bed with a bolster and a fustyan pyllo with fethers	1	9	7
A mat of sedge, a coverlyte of lyst, 1 payre of blanktes		5	6
in the corne loft			
8 busshels of wheat, 4 busshels of barley and one off ottes	1	0	4
in the buttry			
One brasse pot, 1 kettell of brasse, 2 platteres, two pewter dysshes, 2 sacesers		8	6
A brasen morter with a yron pystell, 2 candellstickes and a dryppinge pan of plat with a broche		3	11
2 andirons, 1 pothangers, 1 payre of pothokes, one gyrdiron and a peele of yron		3	0
A bruinge tub, 3 kevers, 2 stenes, a vyrken, one pypken, 1 lyttell tub, 2 lyttell boules, a chamber pot		4	0
A fryinge pan, 1 peck, 1 halfe peck, 2 bucketes, 6 dysshes of wood, 1 dosson of trenchars and foure stonne crusses		1	11
One chest, 1 cassocke, 1 gowne, 1 peticote, two kertels and one sylke hat	2	14	8
A chest, 3 payre of sheetes and a payre of pyllobers		12	4
A dossen peces of lynnen for her Atyar		10	0

	£	s	d
In her pursse in redie money		6	8
In debtes that William Cranly, her brother doth owe her	20	0	0
In debtes that Robard Cranly her brother dothe owe her	25	0	0
	53	0	5

Note: The Will written on 5th May 1572 was not proved until 29th April 1573. The residuary legatee and executrix was her niece Jonne Cranley, daughter of the testatrix's brother William. She was also to inherit two sums of £20 owed by the testatrix's two brothers William and Robard. The remaining debt of £5 owed by Robard was to be paid equally to William's 3 sons, Thomas, John and William. A sum of 10s was left to the poor men's box and 3s 4d to the repair and maintenance of the church. Specific articles of clothing were left to the testatrix's sister Alyce Dunns, her two nieces Alyce and Idden Dunns, her brother Harry Cranley and her sister-in-law Jane Cranley. The overseers were her brother William Cranley and Harry Parkhurst. Of the 3 witnesses, Rychard Smallpece and Tomas Snellynge signed and William Cranley made his mark. The burial was recorded on 9th May 1572.

Ref: 1573 B 131/1 Will 1573 B 131/2 Inventory

Thomas Warner **121**

of Wonersh, yeoman; taken by John Gosden, Richard Babbe, Richard Fakener and Thomas Jowre, 21st April 1573.

	£	s	d
In the hall			
One table, one forme, 2 old chaires and one painted cloth		3	0
One spynnyng whele and one paire of olde wollen cardes			8
In the kichen loftes			
One bedsted, one olde flock bed and one painted cloth		3	10
One table, one forme and certen boordes		1	6
Certen other lumber			4
In the yelding house			
13 barrelles and other Tubbes, 2 bolles and one olde wheele		6	8
In the botrie			
One cupboorde and certen stobbins		8	6
In the kichen			
One troughe, one bolting hutche, one kever, one busshell, one moulding boord, other woodden vessell and certen sheeffes		7	0
In an other botrie			
One side saddle and other lumber		6	8
In the newe lofte			
2 cuisshins, one cofer and a chaire		2	6
In the bed chamber			
2 bedstedes, one fetherbed, one bad flokbed, one mattris, 2 coverlettes and 3 blankettes	2	0	0
2 cofers and certen painted clothes		5	0
Brasse, lattyn, pewter, etc.			
One brasse pott, an yron pott and a posnet of brasse		8	0
3 kettles, one Skellett and a Skymmer		3	4
3 candlestickes, one chafing disshe and a morter		3	8
18 peces of pewter		13	4
2 paire of pothangers, one paire of pothooks, one paire of cobirons, one Anndyron, one fier prong, one paire of tonges, one toasting yron, 2 broches, one trivet, and a gridyron		5	4
2 dripping pannes and a frieng panne			8
Napery			
6 paire of shetes, 5 table clothes, 4 table napkins and			

4 towelles				13	4
His apparell, etc.					
His apparell			1	6	8
Money in his purse				1	0
Cattell, etc.					
Two horse beastes and a cowe			3	0	0
4 hogges				8	0
Hey in the barne				10	0
Woode in the gate				6	8
Summe	£12 5 8				
	whereof				
oweng by the said Thomas Warner to divers persons as appereth by a bill of parcelles by his owne confession				10	10
To Mr Carrill for rent			1	0	0
To Mr Stoughton for rent				1	8
Summe of the debtes	£1 12 6				
And so remayneth clere			10	13	2

Note: The Will written on 6th April was proved on 20th May 1573. The residuary legatee and executrix was the testator's wife Johane. Robert Wakeforde, a friend and neighbour, was appointed overseer. He was a witness together with Thomas Crosse and Joseph Kichen, vicar of Wonersh. A certain James Sharpe of Guildford, draper and the widow, bound themselves well and truly to administer the estate. A sum of 4d was left to the poor men's box of Wonersh. The widow was to have the use of the household goods brought to Wonersh. Robert, Elizabeth and Mary Warner, his 3 children, were to have equal shares of the goods in the keeping of Robert Doddesworth of Worplesdon. The burial was recorded on 18th April 1573.

Ref: 1573 B 139/1 Will 1573 139/2 Inventory

John Waters **122**

of Rotherhithe, shipwright; taken by George Stagg, Evan Pryce and John Hall, 2nd May 1573.

	£	s	d
In Reddye monye	11	15	0
His Apparrell and 2 peces of pewtar with other odde thinges	2	0	0
	13	15	0
Debptes owinge by the sayde Waters			
To Rother Willyams his host for his borde and lodginge	5	4	0
[*Therefore remains*	*8*	*11*	*0*]

Note: The Will was written on 20th July 1570 and administration of the goods and chattels was granted to Roger Williams of Rotherhithe, waterman, on 6th May 1573. The testator left 40s to his "wyfe if she be alyve, if dead the same 40s to William Stampe, her sonne". His best cloak was bequeathed to Roger Williams. A table cloth, linen in the chest, all the pewter and a skillet were bequeathed to his host's wife Elynn. The minister Thomas Addy was given 13s 4d and one of the best shirts. John Stevynson was to have all the working tools. Sums of 13s 4d were bequeathed to Anthony Lawrence and to John Childe, carpenter. The sum of 3s each was left to Wydow Harding, Goodwyfe Stodare and Goodwyfe Blande. Two shillings apiece was left to Goodwives Whitehed, Coole and Chapman and to "Old Browe". The preacher at the burial was left 3s 4d. These bequests totalled £5. There is no mention of any overseer or witness.

Ref: 1573 140/1 Will 1573 B 140/2 Inventory

Edward West **123**

of Godalming, dyer; taken by Wyllyam Chyttye, John Woodes and Nycholas Bylynghurste, 16th [*no month given*] 1573.

	£	s	d
In the hall			
A table, 2 Joyned formes, a Round table, 4 Joyned stoules and a chayre, a coubard and a paynted clothe	1	19	0
In hys chamber			
A stannynge bedstedell, 2 floke bedes, a coverlet, a payre of blanketes, 2 playne cofers and the paynted clothes	1	13	4
Mony in hys purse		5	0
All hys aparell		16	0
In the lofte over the hall			
A playn bedstedell, a flocke bed, a coverlet and a payre of blanketes, a trokyll bedstedell and a flocke bed, a payre of blanketes and a shryden coverlet	1	4	0
In a nother lofte			
A planke, a payre of tressells, a presse and a cofer		6	8
In the buttreye			
A dosyn of pewter platers, old and new, 6 pewter dyshes, 4 potyngers, 2 sasers, 3 pewter potes, 3 candilstyckes, 2 barels, a kefer, a tob, a dosyn of spones and a dosyn and a halfe of trenchers	1	5	0
all his Lynen			
A Hollen sheet, a locormne table clothe, 2 canvas table clothes, 2 payre of towells, one of them hollen and the other locorom, 3 payre of canvas shetes, a locorom sherte and 2 canvas shertes and a payre of pyllowbers	1	3	4
In the kechyne			
4 brase potes, one brase skyllet, 3 kytels, on pan, a cawdrow, a fryinge pane, 2 brochys, 2 angerons, a dryppynge pane, 2 pot hangers, 2 pothokes, 2 tryftes and a gyrderne	2	19	8
In the kechyn chamber			
A bultynge huche, 2 bockyng toobes, a bruinge fate and a kev, 4 boles, a powdryng tob, cumsynge tub, a kned trow, 3 old baryls, 6 bourdes, 6 quarters		15	2
In the Dyhowse			
Gryninge weed		5	4
A pare of beame and scales		2	8
8 lodes of tald wood and 3 lodes of fagates	1	4	0
[*£13.19.2*]	13	19	6

Note: The Will dated 4th February was proved on 20th May 1573. The residuary legatees and joint executors were Harry Chowter and his wife Jonne. A sum of 13s 4d was bequeathed to the overseer Wyllyam Chytty of Godalming, clothier. Richard Hamonde, John Woodes and others unnamed, witnessed the will. The testator's sister Katheryne was given a plain bedstead, a flock bed and the bedding. All his unnamed godchildren were left either a pewter platter or a dish. The sum of 6s 8d was left to the poor.

Ref: 1573 B 141/1 Will 1573 B 141/2 Inventory

Robert Woodward **124**

of Southwark, barber; taken by Bryan Pattensone, citizen and vintner of London and Robert Draper of the Borough of Southwark, gentleman. [*undated*]

	£	s	d
In the parcke Chamber			

One bedsted with a testerne, a materes, a blanket with a olde cheste and fform and a coverlet and the glase wendowe there	1	0	0
In the Chamber underneathe the same			
2 chestes with other lomber and a glase wendowe		5	0
In the bedd Chamber			
One bedstede of waynskote Selled with a trunelbed, the hangins and glase windowe, 2 chares and a chest	3	6	8
One ffether bedd, a mattres, one blancket, 2 pillowes withe 2 dornex Coverletes	1	10	0
In the Kechen			
2 iron potes, 2 copper potes, 2 Brase kettelles, one brase morter, 2 chafing deshes, 4 candellstickes, 3 Spittes, a payr of small Rackes, A grediron, one payre of pote houckes with the puther and glase windowe there with other lomber	3	6	8
In the hall			
The cubbarde, the hanggyns, table, setelles, forme, 4 charres, the glas, the curtaynes and houckes, a chaffer of brase, fyer shovell and tonges with 6 kussynes	4	10	0
In the shoppe			
11 baysenes, 4 barberes pottes, a wessynge ketell, a greate glase, the warmynge pane, the hangeynes, the glas windowe there with Lumber	5	0	0
In Aparrell			
A gowne of newe russet lyned with Cotten ffaced with budge, hes lyvery Cote, dublet, hose and a cloke	3	0	0
In Lynnen			
4 payre of shetes, 3 table clothes, 2 towelles, one dussen napkens, barbere clothes and 2 dussen of holland clothes	3	6	8
The lesse of the house ffor 10 yeres yet to cume that he dwelles in	10	0	0
In monye nechell		[*blank*]	
	35	5	0

The Inventory was exhibited by Ann Woodward, the Administratrix, on 28th May 1573.

Note: The signatures of both appraisers were written in good style. The burial was recorded in the Parish Register of St. Saviour, Southwark on 27th April 1573.

Ref: 1573 Ad 36

1574

Thomas Dakin **125**

of Seale, Clerk and Curate; taken by Edward Craneley, Wylliam Brombye, Wylliam Herryson and Peter Whealer, 8th July 1574.

	£	s	d
Bedyng and all that belongethe therto	2	0	0
Brase and puter withe a speyt and one cobeyron and 2 candystykes	1	3	4
One table and one forme with 3 chayres and cushyns with other lumberment		10	0
3 Kyne	4	0	0
60 sheype	8	10	0
1 sowe and 2 pyges		4	4
His purse and gyrdyll with his Rayment 30 shillings, monye in his purse 10 shillings	2	0	0
	18	7	8

Note: The Will was written on 28th June and proved on 20th July 1574. The residuary legatees and executors were Harry and Thomas Hall, who had separate bequests of £2 apiece. Gifts of money also went to the poor men's box of Seale, to the mother church of Winchester, to Peter Whealer and his daughter Ayles and to the testator's 3 servants Margaret and William Mychenor and Margaret Dollye. Gifts of livestock went to the children of Rychard Mychenor, Peter Whealer, Harry Hall, Thomas Hall and Hew Cooke and to Joane Hampton and Ayles Hall. The overseers were Hew Cooke and William Brombye. The will was written by Antonye Pourythe, curate of Ash. Two other named witnesses were Hugh Cooke and Edward Cranley. The same Hugh Cooke of Lassam, gentleman and Henry Hall of Seale, husbandman, bound themselves well and truly to administer the estate. The burial was recorded thus: "Thomas Dakyn, clearke, curate of Seale and fermore of the parsonage there, was buried ye first of July 1574".

Ref: 1574 B 62/1 Will 1574 B 62/2 Inventory

Thomas Hayward **126**

of Wrecclesham in Farnham, weaver; taken by Rainolde Baldinge, John Grover, John Hollaway and Barthelmew Mathew, 26th April 1574.

	£	s	d
In the Haule			
A Table, A painted cloath, 2 bordes and one plancke		3	6
2 plauters, 2 potengers, a sawser, 2 Spones, a candlesticke, a litle brasse panne, 2 litle kettles, 2 frienge pannes, 2 Trene Disshes, a broche and A paireof pottehookes		7	10
In the Chamber			
A coat, a paire of hose, a flocke bedde, a bolster, a coverlet, a blanket and three Sheetes		13	4
2 old Bedstedes and 2 old coofers		3	4
In the bultinge house			
A kyver with other olde lumbrie Stufe, as bordes and suche like		3	4
2 Busshelles of coorse vetches		2	7
In the Barne			
A litle stacke of Otes and a litle heie	1	1	0
4 Kyne, two bulloxe, 2 wenyers and two coltes	8	0	0
22 shepe	2	6	8
Two hogges		8	0
Fyve hennes and A cocke		2	4
On the ground 2 acre rie	1	3	4
An olde table cloth			7
A spininge whele and cardes			10
	14	16	8

Note: The Will was written on 28th May 1570 but was not proved until 2nd October 1574. His wife Johan was to be the executrix and residuary legatee for life. At her death the 3 Hayward daughters Agnes, Johan and Clare, were to share the inheritance equally. The overseers were to be John Pofelie and Richard Buecher. Under the Will of a certain John Buckeham proved 8 years before 1570, Thomas Hayward had been made guardian and keeper of the 3 Buckeham daughters, Margaret, Agnes and Johan. The terms of that settlement were not attached to the Will or Inventory. Three named witnesses were Rainolde Baldinge, Symon Roger and Robert Tridge. The Parish Register records the burial on 23rd January 1573/4 of Thomas Heward.

Ref: 1574 B 94/1 Will 1574 B 94/2 Inventory

Thomas Penvey **127**

of Chiddingfold, miller; taken by Richard Brodfold, Thomas Shorter, John Hole and William Eve, 21st June 1574.

£ s d

In all kynd of corne and graynes		16	0
A mare and a collte	1	13	4
A Colt of a yeare old	1	10	0
A Sowe and 3 pygges		7	0
11 gease		3	0
A geldynge	1	13	4
The grasse		3	0
Hennes and Dwckes		2	0
All the beaddes and beadstedles and all that there unto belongeth	4	0	0
4 old cheastes		5	0
2 old Cwbbordes		10	0
3 tables and 3 foarmes		7	0
3 old cheyres and a stoole		3	0
All the paynted clothes		2	0
All the woodden vessels		15	0
3 broches		2	6
All the brasse and pewtter	3	15	0
The andyrnes and potthwckes		10	0
2 old frey pannes		2	0
Cwppes, transors and sponnes		1	0
All his edge tooles		1	4
A grynestone		1	0
All his apparell		10	0
An old sadle, brydle and bootes		3	4
An old Carte and a donge potte		2	0
Hoockes and Sykles		2	0
[*£17.19.10*]	18	0	2

Note: The Will was dated 26th May 1564 and proved on 2nd October 1574. The residuary legatee and executrix was the testator's wife Eme. A shilling was given to the overseers William Eve, tanner and Thomas Shorter of Chiddingfold. Christopher Cobbe who wrote the will was left 1s and 3 other witnesses, William Rudges, Thomas Taplin and Thomas Grene, were left 6d each. The testator gave 2d to the mother church of Winchester, but asked that the ringers at his burial in Yateley should each have 4d and that 4 poor men should have a similar sum. The poor of the parish were left 3s 4d. On the day of his burial 2 bushels of wheat and a barrel of beer were to be bestowed in Chiddingfold. He left a yearly charity, to commence after his wife's decease, of 6s 8d to be divided evenly between the poor and the mending of the highways of Chiddingfold. The executrix and Thomas Toplys of Yateley, husbandman, bound themselves well and truly to administer the will.

Ref: 1574 B 127/1 Will 1574 B 127/2 Inventory

1575

Thomas Allen **128**

of Pitfold in Frensham; taken by John Cover, Richard Boxould, Robert Wheler, John Bridger and Barthelemew Harding, 5th May 1575.

	£	s	d
All his apparrell		10	0
One flockbed, a boulster, a paire of blankettes, a Payre of Shetes and a Coveringe, etc.		10	0
An other Paire Shetes, a paire of blanketes, a boulster and a Shred Coveringe, etc.		5	0
3 Table Clothes		2	0
One Cheste		2	0

	£	s	d
8 Peces of Pewter		5	0
One ould Caldren, 3 ould kettles, a latten bason, a brasse pott, a Candlesticke, a little brasse panne	1	0	0
One broche, a friingpane and potthangers		2	0
3 ould axes and a Byll, an ould syethe, 3 Iron Wedgies and a gryndlestone		3	4
4 ould paynted Clothes		2	6
A table and forme with all other lumbery ware		6	8
A horse harrow		1	0
A paire of Shepe sheres			2
2 ackars of Rye, 4 ackers of otes	1	13	4
58 Sheepe	7	6	8
5 Lambes		6	0
2 Kyne, the one hath a Calf	3	0	0
2 heyfers and 2 bullockes	3	0	0
A little Nagge		13	4
3 hogges and 9 pigges		10	6
A goosse and a gander with 7 yonge		2	0
4 hennes and a Cocke		1	8
	20	3	2

On 22nd June 1575 Alice the widow was sworn to the truth of the above inventory. She bound herself, together with Robert Wheler of Haslemere, husbandman, to declare any further goods or chattels which might in future come to her hands, possession, or knowledge. An instruction at the bottom of the document requests that it should be sent to Robert Cover, a mercer in Farnham, for Alice Allen. Another note gives a list of legal fees. The administration cost 3s 6d, the seal 4d, the obligation 12d, the carrier 4d and another charge 1s 7d; total 6s 9d.

Ref: 1575 Ad1

John Browne **129**

of Cranleigh "and Late Inhabityng in the parishe of Alfold", May 1574.[*no appraisers given*]

	£	s	d
2 brasse pottes wyth 4 Kittells		13	0
One plater, 2 pewter dysshes, 2 sacers, one salter with 15 spones		4	6
2 Candlestickes		1	0
One spitte, 1 brand Iron		3	4
A friyng pann and A grydeiron		1	4
An axe, a byll and a spitter		1	8
1 Handsawe, 1 Chesell and 1 auger			8
One scummer, a grate, one paire of sherres and 2 paire of Cisers		1	6
One Hooke, 4 kyttells, 1 olde axe, an olde fyer pan, 1 yron peele, trewell, a wimblestocke, a staffe with a litle shovell one the ende with A boke, pen and ynke Horne		2	0
15 earthen potes		1	0
One Tubbe, 1 stobyn, one pipken, 1 bokett, 6 bolls, 2 trene platers, 13 trene dyshes, 18 trenchers, 1 Ladle, 1 pot Lyd and 1 mustard pot		1	8
One glas bottle and 2 other glasses			3
2 bascates 1 browshe and one shoying horne with 2 Cusshens		1	1
2 flock bedes, 3 flocke bolsters with one fether bolster and one flock pillow	1	0	0
2 Coverlytes and 3 blanketes		10	0
2 bedd testars		2	0
7 kercheifes, 5 neckearcheifes, 2 pillowbeares, 2 Canvas Aprens, one knyt purse, 2 table clothes, one Canvas Wallet, 1 worsted apron,			

one lynsay woolsay Apron, 1 paire of worsted sleves, A payre of fustian sleves and a pece of new Cloth		15	0
One sacke, 1 sworde, 1 dager, 2 Chestes, 1 foscer, 1 sworde girdle		4	0
One almery, one litle forme, one Chayre and one litle Chayre		1	0
One sythe with that therto belongethe		2	4
One trevete with other olde yron		1	8
3 Basketes, a fewe fethers, 1 syve		1	0
2 Lomes, 2 quilling tornes, 11 paire of geres, 2 spyndles withe 6 paire of shaftes	1	6	8
One sadle, A sowe and a troughe		4	0
2 paire of Canvas shetes		8	0
	[*6*	*8*	*8*]

Administrators of the estate were Thomas Tydye and John Hurst for the benefit of Alice Browne, daughter of the old man deceased. They were bound by the deed dated 28th April 1575.

Note: John Browne's death is recorded as having taken place in May 1574.

Ref: 1575 Ad 10

Agnes Chaundler **130**

of Haslemere; taken by Rychard Boxould, Walter Gasse and John Warner, 30th May 1575.

	£	s	d
One flockbed and all thinges belonginge to hit		10	0
2 short plankes, A chaire and a forme			8
One brasse pott		3	4
3 kettles		9	0
2 Coffers		1	4
A platter, a candlestike, 2 pottengers and 2 sacers		2	10
2 tubbes with other Lumberye stuffe		5	0
A fringepane, a broche with other ould Iron		2	0
One axe, a byll, a hachett and a hammer		1	4
A spynnynge whele and the rele			4
Hir apparell		13	4
2 Ladders with certayne Cleftes		1	8
7 boordes		3	4
	2	14	2

Note: The Will was written on 13th May and was proved by the executor John Warner, brother-in-law of the testatrix, on 22nd June 1575. She asked to be buried in Haslemere churchyard and gave 20d to the poor men's box there. A sum of 12d was given to Walter Gasse, the overseer. The best kettle was bequeathed to a goddaughter Agnes Martin and the other two kettles to Joan Lanaway. The residue was to be inherited by the executor. An instruction ordered the Will to be sent to the parson at "Hedley in Hamshier for John Warner there". The bond was taken in the name of the executor, a husbandman. There followed a list of charges totalling 3s 10d: probate 6d, the seal 4d, the obligation 12d, the exemplification of the Will 2s. Walter Gasse and Agnes Lanaway had witnessed the Will.

Ref: 1575 B 10/1 Will 1575 B 10/2 Inventory

Robert Geale **131**

of Byfleet, bachelor and day labourer; taken by Roberte Cheniell, Richarde Harme, John Harme, Thomas Peter, Edwarde Colier and Walter Rodgers, parishioners and householders of Byfleet, 24th April 1575.

	£	s	d
In Ready moneye in his purse		15	6
Twoe canves shirtes		2	0

A Sacke clothe Dublette		5	0
One newe pare of showes and 2 olde pare		2	0
An olde canves Trusse, an olde ffrisse Jerken, an olde pare of Russette hosen, A pare of Russette stockinges and twoe ffelte hattes		5	4
An olde Russette coate without Sleves and an olde canves trusse		1	0
An Ashen staffe with a pike			6
	1	11	4

On 18th May 1575 the goods and chattels of the deceased as appeared in the Inventory were handed over to the two "Guardians" Robert Chanell and George Harme, for the benefit of the poor of the parish.

Ref: 1575 Ad 26

John Gosden **132**

of Wonersh, yeoman; taken by Thomas Astrete of Farnehill, John Bicknolde, John Chalner and Henry Harper, 25th April 1575.

in the Hall	£	s	d
One folding table, one forme, one turnd chaire, 2 bad stooles, and one painted cloth		6	0
One small cupborde		3	4
in the parlor			
One table, 2 ioyned formes, one turned chaire, one ioyned stoole and 6 old cuisshins		5	0
One cupboorde in the same parlor		13	4
The chamber over the parlor			
2 playne bedsteddes, 2 flockbeddes, 2 blankettes and 2 olde coverlettes	1	0	0
4 cofers and 2 bad presses		6	8
5 paire of course sheetes, 6 table clothes, 3 table napkins, 4 towelles and 3 pilloberes	1	0	0
His apparell	2	10	0
Money in his purse	1	10	0
One paire of Almayne Rivettes, one paire of splintes, one Scull, one Jacke, one bowe and sheaf of arrowes, one swoorde and one dagger	1	3	4
4 shelves			6
Two Remnants of wollen cloth conteyneng 2 yardes and a half		4	0
in the servantes chamber			
2 bad bedstedes, one old flockbed, 2 payre of olde blankettes, 2 bolsters and 2 old cuverlettes		10	0
One bridle and saddle		4	0
in the Ale chamber or botrye			
One powdring trowghe one powdring tubbe, one kever, 5 ale stubbins, one litle caige and one boorde to cover a troughe		10	0
the larder howse			
2 litle barrelles, one old tubbe, 4 woodden bottelles, 2 tankerdes, 3 stone cuppes, whereof 2 with kovers		5	0
the boulting howse			
One knead troughe, one boulting hutche, an old trowghe, 6 old tubbes, 2 old chirnes, one old busshell, one barrell and 5 boordes		13	4
the milke howse			
One chese presse, one old kever, 9 erthen pottes and 2 erthen milke pannes		8	0

	£	s	d
in the kichen			
One bad furnace, one litle cawdron, 2 brasse pannes, 6 kettles of all sortes and 2 skellittes	1	10	0
2 brasse pottes and one posnett		10	0
2 broches, 2 cobyrons, 2 chopping knives, 3 pott hangers, one paire of potthooks, one trivet, one gridiron and one paire of tonges		6	8
One malt vate, 2 kevers, one bolle, one chirne, one fourme, 2 standes and one oven piele		4	0
Pewter, etc.			
8 pewter platters, 3 disshes, 3 sawcers, one bason and one salt seller and 12 spoones	1	0	0
3 latten candlestickes, one latten bason and one chafingdishe		5	0
5 fliches of bakon and 2 of beefe	1	0	0
in the shoppe			
All the tooles there	1	0	0
in the barne			
By estimacon 30 hiles of Rye there	2	0	0
Hey and Otes there		13	4
Barlie by estimacon 3 busshelles		4	0
Cattell, etc.			
7 Kyene and 5 calves	10	0	0
4 oxen and 2 steares	10	0	0
One heckfare and A bulle	1	13	4
4 yerling bullockes	2	0	0
6 horsebeastes	5	0	0
One sowe and 8 sucking pigges and 6 other hogges	1	0	0
All the pultrie about the house, tenne in number		2	0
35 wether shepe	6	0	0
24 ewes and tegges and 20 lambes	4	10	0
Tymber lieng in Long deane		6	8
Tymber and shengle lieng in litle hilles and Gaston	6	0	0
On olde cart, one olde weyne, 2 old dong pottes and 2 paire old wheles		5	0
One other cart and shod wheles, one old donng pott, one olde paire of shod wheles and one litle drag	2	6	8
Plowghes, yokes, cheynes, harrowes, sithes, billes, beckes, mattockes, axes, shovilles, Ropes, etc.	1	0	0
By estimacion 12 acres of Rie and wheat in the fieldes	6	0	0
By estimacon 8 acres of otes and 1 acre and half of peason	3	0	0
	79	4	2

Note: The burial was recorded the day after the Will was written on 16th April and probate was granted on 18th May 1575 to the executors, his wife Johan and his eldest son Henry, who together were to inherit half of the residue of the estate. A promise of half the goods and chattels to his son Philip, made at his betrothal, was to be honoured. Minor bequests of 5s were made to the poor men's box, to his servants Johan Gosden the elder and John West. John and Walter Strete, his sons-in-law, were made overseers, the former being given £5. All his grandchildren were given a lamb and his godchildren 4d. One granddaughter Johan, the child of Henry Gosden, was singled out to receive the annual rent of 20s from a newly acquired property in Ewhurst bought from Mathew Acolles. Three of the witnesses were Joseph Kichen, vicar of Wonersh, William Tickner of Woodhill and William Astrete, Tailor.

Ref: 1575 B 28/1 Will 1575 B 28/2 Inventory

Robert Lake **133**

of West Molesey, husbandman. *[no appraisers given and undated]*

	£	s	d
Wheate and rye fortenne akers	12	0	0
Seaven akers off Barleye	4	13	4
Syxe akers off pesone and teares	2	0	0
Fowere horse	5	6	8
Fowere oxen	10	0	0
1 steare beinge 2 yeares oulde	1	0	0
4 kynne	5	6	8
30 sheppes	3	0	0
Eyght swyne	1	4	0
Thre geese		3	0
Pultrie		5	0
Fower fether bedes with all therto belonginge	7	0	0
A dussone payre of shetes	1	16	0
4 brase potes		13	4
4 pannes		12	0
Thre dussone of pewder	1	4	0
4 pewder potes		2	0
2 salt sellers		1	0
Ten candylstyckes		13	4
Two payre of pot houkes		1	4
Syxe chystes		12	0
A dusone of tre dyshes and two tre platters			8
Two dusonne of Tynne sponnes		1	0
2 cupbordes		6	0
3 kettels and one caldrone		13	4
Fyve speites		5	0
A payre of tonges and two gardyeadens		3	0
Thre table clothes and thre towells		10	0
A dussone table napkyns		8	0
Two chayres and halfe a dussone off Joynte stoolles		8	0
An hackney sadell and a brydle		3	4
A shode carte	1	6	8
A dunge carte		5	0
Fower horse harnes		4	0
Two yokes and their cheynes		8	0
A ploughe, culter and shares		6	8
A ten pounde of wull and a payr off wullen cardes	1	0	0
Two payre of yrone cobberns		5	0
	64	7	4

Note: The Will was dated 15th May 1563 and probate was granted twelve years later, on 22nd June 1575, to the executrix the widow Isabell, in the person of James Cornford, yeoman. Two bushels of rye were to be delivered to Richard Best after the next harvest. The testator had three sons, but only land enough for bequests to two of them. Charles was to have Baldens Hawe and Arthur a close beside Heversam Lane, but their mother was to occupy the ground until they came of age. Francis was to have a steer, the best cupboard and table from the hall. The residue was to go to Isabel. Witnesses were Richard Allcocke, clerk, Thomas ffysher, Thomas Woods and others. Instructions were written on the outer fold "To be sent to the Griffyn to Mr. Love at Kingston for James Cornford of West Molesey". No overseers had been mentioned in the Will.

Ref: 1575 B 41/1 Will 1575 B 41/2 Inventory

John Mantill **134**

of St George the martyr, Southwark, joyner; taken by Robert Peacock, fletcher, Thomas Coxe, victualler and John Pym, fletcher, all of the same parish, 6th April 1575.

				£	s	d
In the Halle						
One old tabell, 2 olde strestelles and 1 old forme					2	0
1 olde cubbord with one olde carpet					3	4
4 pewter dyshes					2	1
2 olde pewter saltes						3
3 pynte potes of pewter					1	0
1 olde cheste						6
1 olde chayre and 1 old watch bill						5
The old staynd clothes about the halle					1	8
	£0	11	3			
In the chamber						
2 olde bedsteddes					2	6
2 old featherbeddes, 2 old bolsters, 3 old matryses and 2 olde coverynges					13	4
1 old spyngyng whele with other olde lumbermente					2	2
	£0	18	0			
In the workynge chamber						
4 olde sawes					2	6
1 olde hatchet, 2 olde hammers and 4 olde Awgers					1	2
4 planes, 2 genytes, 4 old cheselles					3	2
2 old persers wyth other old working tooles and other old lumbermente					3	4
An Iron holdfaste						6
An old bedsted						6
A working borde						8
A lytell gryndstone						6
	£0	12	4			
In the kytchin						
1 olde bedsted wyth an old featherbed, a bolster, 2 olde pillowes, 2 old blanketes and one olde coverynge					13	4
A lytell foldyng tabell					1	10
2 old chare and 2 olde chestes					4	0
10 olde pewter platters					6	8
2 old pewter basyns					1	4
5 pewter dyshes					2	1
9 olde pewter sawcers					2	3
5 old pewter quarte potes and one olde pynt pott					4	2
2 potengers and 6 pewter spones						7
4 olde Kettelles					3	0
1 olde brasse pott					1	4
2 olde skylletes						7
1 laten chafyngdyshe						9
6 olde laten candelstickes					2	0
3 olde drypingpannes of Iron					1	2
4 lytell spyttes					1	4
2 pothangers, 1 olde gredyron and one olde breadgrate						6
1 olde fryeng panne, 1 pare of tonges and one pare of olde andyrons					1	2
12 trenchers, 1 old brushe and one old peperquearne						4
A lytell spyse morter with a pestell						5
1 olde chopinge knyfe and a choping bord						4

2 olde tubbes and one olde pale						4
	£2	9	6			
Lynnen						
4 pare of olde shetes					4	8
3 olde tableclothes					1	6
6 olde napkyns					1	0
	£0	7	2			
Apparrell						
1 olde gowne, one olde frysecoate, one old dowblet, one olde pare of hose, one old capp and 2 olde shyrtes					5	2
	£0	5	2			
				5	3	5
Detes which I John Mantill do owe						
to Mr. Beestone for 7 barrelles of beare				2	12	8
to John Ede for 12 barrelles of ale and one kylderkyn				4	8	0
to Water Willyames					3	0
to Hew Drew					1	6
for rente of my howse for a hole yeare				1	6	8
				[*8*	*11*	*10*]

On 26th April 1575 the Administration of the goods and chattels was granted to Jane, widow and relict of the deceased. She herself and Robert Peacock of St. George's, Southwark, fletcher, were bound well and truly so to administer, having been sworn to the truth of the above Inventory. Ref: 1575 Ad 34

Steven Petoe **135**

of Bramley in Shalford, yeoman; taken by John Smyther, brewer, Richard Caringham and John Steedman, 17th May 1575.

	£	s	d
In the Hale			
One table, one foram, two stooles, one chayer, one paynted clothe		4	0
In the Parlor			
Two fetherbedes, two bolsters with all thinges pertayning unto them	2	13	4
In the Parlor Chamber or Butterye			
8 peuter platters, 8 pewter disshes, 5 sausers, one salte seller and tw[*o*] candlestickes		15	0
In the baking chamber or boulting house			
Two caldrons, two panns, two brasse pottes and one cettle	2	6	8
In the Kytchin			
Two hogges of bacon		14	8
Twelve busshels of oaten malte		8	0
Three broaches and a payer of pothangers		5	0
His apparrell			
His wearing clothes	1	0	0
Abrode in the gate, fieldes or barne			
A plowe, harrowes, yokes and chaynes, a seade codde, bills, axes, shovels, augars and sives		19	0
Two yeltes		6	8
7 shootes		14	0
One yoke of oxen	4	0	0
8 bullockes	9	0	0
Two mare and three coultes	4	0	0
5 Kyne and calves	7	10	0
20 weathers	4	0	0

	£	s	d
18 tegges	2	14	0
Fower ewes and lambs		13	4
7 lambs		11	8
In Corne			
5 acres of Rye	3	0	0
8 acres of oates	2	13	4
Three stales of bees		5	0
In the barne			
Three hiles of Rye		10	0
6 busshells of oates		3	0
	49	6	8

Note: The Will was dated 24th April and proved on 18th May 1575. The joint executors were his wife Joane and his daughter Joane. Sums of 5s each were left to the overseers John Braborne and John Palmer. The testator left his property in Hambledon, that in Chiddingfold and the implements of husbandry stored in the barn there, together with the household stuff he had brought to Bramley, to his daughter Joane. The 2 ladies were each left a half share in the livestock. He asked to be buried in Shalford and gave 3s 4d to the poor of both Shalford and Bramley. Gifts of livestock went to John Tickner, his son-in-law and to each of the Tickner children, to William Bridger, to the goodwife Gastone, to Isabell Burghe and to his servant Joane Newes. Small gifts of money went to Steven Taylor and Thomas Mellershe. Clothing was left to Thomas Newes, the clerk of Bramley and to Nicholas Huatt. The witnesses were John Sweeting, vicar of Shalford, John Smither the younger, Thomas Newes and Richard Brumbeye.

Ref: 1575 B 66/1 Will 1575 B 66/2 Inventory

Thomas Turner **136**

of Compton beside Guildford; taken by Thomas Washingtone, Herre Verey, Herre Robynsone, Walter Turner and Edmund Smith, 27th April 1575.

	£	s	d
In the haall			
One table and one forme		2	0
1 trifte and 1 pothangers			6
7 pewtere platters		8	0
5 pewtere dishes, 6 sawcers and 4 saltsellers		8	6
5 latten candellstickes and 2 latten chaffingedishes		6	0
2 Caldrones and 2 brase pannes	1	6	8
10 littell kettels	1	2	0
3 brasse potes and a posnet	1	6	8
2 olde friinge pannes, a dripingpane and a broche		2	0
In the Kitchine			
2 trowghes with Certayne tubbes and other lumbrye		10	0
A broche, a trifte, a bill, ane axe with other workinge tooels		2	8
In the Chambere			
One fether beede, 1 Coverlet, 1 bedhanger and 1 olde bedstedl	1	0	0
3 olde flockebeedes, 3 old coverlets and 2 old beedstedells	1	6	8
11 payere of olde sheetes	1	2	0
3 Coffers		3	0
All hys apparell		6	8
Money in his purse		1	0
1 Cowe	1	6	8
2 olde mares	1	6	8
2 acars of Rye one the grondd	1	6	8
24 sheepe and 4 lambes	3	0	0
1 quarter of barley in the howse		8	0
5 littell swinne		12	6

	17	14	10

Note: The Will was written on 8th January and proved on 19th September 1575. A residuary legatee and the named executor was Walter Turner, son of the testator. The overseers were Herre Robinsone, John Turner, son of the testator and Edmund Smith. The only monetary bequests were 4d to the poor men's box at Compton and 20s each to two of his five daughters Milisante and Ezabell. His married daughter Katherine was given a pair of canvas sheets and a bushell of barley; her sister Johane had the same. Margaret was given one loceram sheet. Thomas and Juliane Turner of Dunsfold, children of John Turner, were to share a ewe. His godchildren, Edward, son of Edmund Smith; Elizabeth, daughter of John Innes of Pirbright; and Johane Innes, were each given a ewe. The 4 unmarried daughters, Eline, Margrete, Milisant and Ezabell, were to have an equal share with their unmarried brother Walter of the unbequeathed moveable goods in the house and kitchen and in addition these girls were left 4 ewes apiece. Witnesses to the signing of the Will were Thomas Brodbridge, Walter Turner junior and Myels Veyrey.

Ref: 1575 B 88/1 Will 1575 B 88/2 Inventory

John Waterer **137**

of Shalford, tailor; taken by John Stidman, John Smether, Richarde Chalingiame and John Paulmer, 17th May 1575.

	£	s	d
In the Haule			
A table, a forme, a paynted clothe, 2 cubbordes		19	0
A chambre			
A Joyned bedstede with a ffether bed, 2 bolsters, 2 pelowes, 2 blankettes, a healinge, a joyned cubburd, 2 Cooffers, a testerne paynted	3	0	0
A letle chambre			
A bedstede, 2 flock bedes, a bolster, 2 pelowes, a Cushune, a payre of blanketes, a healinge, a shoppe borde		16	0
An other chambre			
2 bedstedes and a cheste		2	0
A mylke house			
A payre of trestelles, a borde, a shelfe, 4 bolles with other trumprye		3	4
In the butterye			
A brasse potte, a kettle, 4 stabbins Pewter. 6 platters, 6 sawcers, a bacene, a peweter dishe with other trumprie	1	6	8
the Kyttchene			
2 kettelles, a shpitte, a frying panne, a chese presse, a wollen wheele, a payre of potte hangers		5	0
A bultinge hutche		3	4
Bakone in the rooffe		10	0
Naperie			
A table cloth, 3 payre of sheetes		8	0
Wearinge geare	1	0	0
The money in his purse		2	0
Cattell			
A mare and a colte	1	5	0
6 yerelinge bullockes and a Cowe	5	0	0
also 3 Ewe tegges		9	0
and 4 Calves weaniers	1	6	8
Corne			
5 akers of Rye	3	6	8
Otes, 7 akers	2	0	0

Hogges			
Showtes, yonge 8		10	0
A Carte and a payre of wheeles		6	0
A Cocke and 3 henns		1	4
[£23.0.0]	23	1	0

Note: The Will was dated 19th April and proved on 18th May 1575. The testator appointed his mother-in-law Johan Elyotte residuary legatee and executrix. She was to have the profits from his properties and to bring up his children John, Johan, Agnes and Jane, until they reached the age of 20. The overseers, Stephen Peato and John Tickner, were each left 3s 4d and were instructed to sell enough of the moveable goods and chattels to defray the expense of his funeral and payment of his debts. The freehold house and land called Water House in Shalford and Dunsfold, which he had inherited from his father Robert, was left to his son John. His daughter Johan was to inherit Bonners, Pollershawe and Blackbrook, in Shalford, lawfully purchased, but if she died without issue the 3 parcels of land were to go to John. Agnes and Jane were to inherit jointly land called Norland in Shalford, lying below the way leading from Bramley to Cranleigh. If neither they nor their heirs survived, the land was left to the testator's own right heirs. The witnesses were Henry Adam, curate, William Chalner, Harry Parvis, tailor and Edward Elyotte.Ref: 1575 B 91/1 Will 1575 B 91/2 Inventory

---

1576

John Astlett **138**

of Runfold in Farnham, husbandman; taken by Rychard Hycheckoke, John Astreate, Wyllyam Stonner and Robartt Fylder, 21st May 1576.

	£	s	d
in the hawle			
2 tables, 2 formes, 2 payer of tresteles		3	4
2 payer of Cotterells, on awndeirne		1	8
On Chayer, 2 stoulys			8
in the parler			
On flockebed, on bolster, on coverlett, on blankett, on olde bedstedle		13	4
On Cubarde		5	0
2 Chestes		3	4
in the lofte over the parler			
On olde fether bede, on Coverlett, on blancate, on bolster, on olde bedstedle		8	0
On Cheste		1	0
Hys apparrell	1	0	0
in the buttrie			
2 keveres, on fatte, on bushell, 4 alle barrelles		6	8
3 sackes, on bage		1	8
7 plateres, 8 pottengeres, 3 sawseres, on earedyshe, on sawlte, 12 sponys of pewter		18	0
2 lattyn basuns, on Chaffynge dyshe, 2 Candellstyckes		2	0
The naprie			
5 payer of shetes, 2 whytte bedselynges, 2 table Clothys, 2 tuelles	1	5	0
in the kyttchyn			
2 Cawthernes, 3 pannys, 2 brasse pottes, on skellett, 3 kettelles, on brassine morter	3	0	0
2 brochys, 2 triftes		3	0
Olde dripynge pann, on frienge pann		1	0
2 olde axis, 2 hedgynge byllys, on wedge		1	4
Trein dyshys, trencheres and ladell			6
5 hennys, on kokrl		2	0
7 duckes, on mallarde		1	4

8 hogges of all sortes	1	0	0
60 sheppe and lambes	8	0	0
3 kyne	4	0	0
4 stearys	6	0	0
2 yearelynge bullockes	1	0	0
3 wanyre bullockes		15	0
2 flettchys of baken		2	0
6 bushelles of Rye		10	0
4 Akeres of Rye on the grounde	1	0	0
4 Akeres of wheatte on the grounde	1	0	0
5 akeres of barreleye	1	5	0
4 akeres of peace		13	4
4 akeres of smoalle ottes		13	4
On ierbonnde cart, on ploughe with yokes, Chaynys, harnys, Collores, harrows and all thynges thatt belonges theare to	2	0	0
	36	17	6

Note: The Will was written on 28th May 1574 but was not proved until 5th June 1576. The residuary legatees and executrixes were the testator's wife Idythe and his daughter Annys. The overseers were Wyllyam Stonner the elder and Robert Fylder. After making a gift of 12d to the poor men's box at Farnham church, the next bequest of all the gear for cultivation of the ground went to Thomas Astlett, the eldest son. Thomas Astlett, the younger son, was given a cow, some grain and household articles. Wyllyam Astlett, another son, had a cow and 20 sheep. The daughter Annys had a heifer and 2 ewes. Apart from the farming gear, the bequests were to be held over until the widow's death and if the elder Thomas gave any trouble, his share was to go to William and Annys instead. The 2 overseers witnessed the will, as did John Stynte and John Robynsone. The widow and Robert Fylder of Runfold, yeoman, bound themselves well and truly to administer the Will. The burial at Farnham was recorded on 6th May 1576.

Ref: 1576 B 2/1 Will 1576 B 2/2 Inventory

William Brodebridge **139**

of Tilford in Farnham; taken by Rychard Hardynge, James Marten, Olever Hardynge and Rychard Novell; 4th May 1575.

	£	s	d
in the halle			
2 tables and a forme		1	8
A nold Cobard		6	8
A pote hangers and a payr of pothokes			6
4 old stooles			2
A gyrd Iron and a chaffyng disshe			4
in the Buttry			
3 pecis of old pewter and a salte seller			8
A candelstike			6
A Cadorne, 2 olde pannes, a nolde kettile, a bras possnet and 2 skyllettes		15	0
3 alle tubbes, a nold powdringe tubbe, 3 trene bolles, disshes and spones and a fryinge pane		2	6
A broche			6
His apparell		13	4
in the Chambre			
A fflockebede, a bolster and that belonginge ther unto		16	0
3 Olde Coffers		3	0
A bowe and arrowes			6
A nolde fflockbed		1	8
A table Clothe			4

2 spynning whelles and cardes		1	0
2 olde Coffers		1	0
A Knedynge kever		1	4
A byll, a naxe, a showffull and 2 olde sithes and a hachett and a nawger		5	0
A koke and hennes and chikynes		1	4
Corne and Cattell			
2 acres and a halffe of Rye sowen apon the grownd		16	8
2 kyne and 2 hecffores	4	0	0
29 sheppe and 6 lambes	4	10	0
A leasse in Tylfford	6	0	0
[*£18.19.8*]	18	18	8
Item there moste be deducted of thys Invitory for dettes owynge	2	0	0

Note: The Will was written on 26th April 1575, a week before his burial and was proved on 10th May 1576. The testator's only monetary bequest was 6d to the poor men's box of Farnham, in which churchyard he asked to be buried. His brother Richard Brodebridge and James Martyn were to be overseers. His wife Joyce and 2 sons, William and Benet, were to be executors and legatees of the whole estate, with the exception of a term of years of a lease in Tilford, which was to go directly to the 2 sons and their assignees for ever. William was to have the first choice of his third part of all the goods and chattels, the other two parts going to Benet and Joyce. The 2 overseers witnessed the Will, as did Rychard Novell, Oliver Hardynge, Edward Camplen and Henry Battell.

Ref: 1576 B 14/1 Will 1576 B 14/2 Inventory

Eden Feld **140**

of Frensham, late the wyffe of Olyver Fyld; taken by John Hardinge, Henry Huntyngford, John Smyth, Thomas Bockrom and John Denynge, 11th April 1576.

	£	s	d
His apparrell		13	4
The beddynge		6	8
2 sylver Rynges and 2 Carcheffes		2	4
A Coubbord and a Coffer		3	0
In the backe Chamber			
Old Tubbes, vates and a trowe		10	0
In the haule			
A Catheron, 5 kettelles, 5 skyllettes, a Chafynge Dyshe, a Candellstycke		13	4
In a backe Lofte			
2 Covers and a bedsted		2	4
7 pewter Dyshes, a sausser		4	0
A broche, an Andeyron, 2 Trevettes and a sythe		4	0
A nawger, a drawinge knyfe and old Iron		1	0
A Carte and a harrowe, yowkes and Chaynes, 2 coulters		9	0
3 Kyne, 3 Calves	4	0	0
4 Steares, 2 hecfers	6	0	0
A Mare and a Colte		13	0
5 shuttes and a Sowe		13	4
Rye, Ottes, Haye In the Barne	1	3	4
The Rye and the Ottes In the feld	3	6	8
5 hennes, 2 capons, a cock		3	0
A fflyche of Bakon		2	0
[*£19.10.4*]	19	13	4

Note: The Will was dated 6th April and proved on 10th May 1576. The testatrix asked to be buried in Frensham churchyard and she made bequests of livestock to 8 children, of whom 4 sons and a daughter were from previous marriages. Her son John Manyer was the residuary legatee and executor. The overseers John Smyth and Thomas Bockham were each left 5s. Her own Aylling children were Jone, Richard, Robert and Thomas. Her husband's children were Oliver, Jone and Elizabeth Feld. An additional gift of a bed went to Thomas and the girls had household items and clothing. The silver rings were given to Jone Aylling and Elizabeth Feld. Robert Spore was given 4 bushels of oats after harvest. The 2 overseers witnessed the Will, as did Rychard Ansell, John Dennyng, Harry Huntingford and John Page. When Probate was granted, the executor was duly sworn before the curate of Frensham. In the record of the overseers' bond they were listed as husbandmen.

Ref: 1576 B 22/1 Will 1576 B 22/2 Inventory

Robert Holt **141**

of Witley, tailor; taken by John Barrat, Thomas Stynt, Thomas Tannar and William Payne, 9th May 1576.

	£	s	d
in Cattels	£	s	d
A Cow	1	6	0
One bulloc		13	4
One horse beast		10	0
4 yonge hoges		8	0
in brasse			
One Cauthorn and 2 cettels		8	0
2 potes		10	0
in pewtar, etc.			
4 plattars and one dysh		2	4
One chafing dishe and 3 candellstickes		2	0
One flock bedd, one bolstar, one covarlet and one bedstede		13	4
2 other flockbeddes, 2 covarletes, one paire of blanckes, 2 bolstars and beddstedes		13	4
in lenen			
one payre of Sheetes		6	8
3 payre of sheetes and one odd		11	8
2 table clothes and 2 napkyns		1	4
one old chest		5	0
4 cofares		5	0
2 cubbardes		16	4
2 tables, 2 formes		4	0
One Round table, 2 chayres		1	8
One fryeing pan, one spyt and one andiorn, pothangars, pothokes, one old pan and tryvet		2	4
One trow to knead, 2 tubes, one boule with other lomber		5	0
One Ceve, 2 verkynes, 2 peuter potes, one chaffere with other stone potes		5	4
His apparell		7	4
One ax, one byll, one augar, one shovell, one pannell, one old brydell		1	0
One payre of sheres and a presin iron and the shop bord		1	0
2 old sackes			10
One boulting huch, one poudering tubbe, 2 old tubes		1	4
One buckat, one old charne			3
One cock and 6 henes		1	2
Dyshes, spones and trenchares with all other lombery		1	0
	9	4	7
Debts to be deducted amounteth unto	7	8	0

	£	s	d
Remaineth	1	16	7

Note: The Will was dated 30th March and proved on 10th May 1576. The testator's wife Elizabeth was residuary legatee and executrix. She was given his house, barn and garden; the orchard, held of Hugh Turesley; a close of land called Fines, held of John Ede; and another garden plot, purchased on Jeffery Rolfe. These she could hold for 16 years, provided she brought up his children and paid the debts and legacies. After that she was to have an annual allowance of 6s 8d paid in half-yearly instalments for life. As long as the first son and heir was honest, hard working, did not try to sell his inheritance and was able to produce an heir, all should be well. However if problems arose, the order of succession was set down: Henry would be followed by William, Thomas, Margery and Sysley. The latter 5 children were each to receive £2 to be paid at the rate of 10s a year. Margery was left special gifts, including the christening sheet; and if any son chose a tailor's craft, he was to have the shears, pressing iron and board. The overseers who witnessed the Will, John Barrat and Thomas Tanner, were each given 20d. Laurence Stoughton and others were also witnesses.

Ref: 1576 B 35/1 Will 1576 B 35/2 Inventory

John Jewer, senior **142**

of Runfold in Farnham, husbandman; taken by Richard Hitchcock, John Adler and Henry Knight, 16th May 1576.

	£	s	d
In the hall			
2 tables, a forme, 2 bords and two tressells		1	10
A chayre, a stoole and potthangers			6
A posnett and a pann		4	0
A brass pott, a charger and a pottinger		6	0
A kettill of ye biggest, a little kettill, a caldron, a skimmer and 2 candelsticks		6	8
3 platters, 4 pottingers, 2 sacers, a peuter pott, 2 saltt sellers and 18 spoones		3	0
A ffryinge pann, trenchers, a ladell and wooden dishes			8
A fflitch of bacon and a gyrdiern		2	0
A wedge, a wimble, an agar, an ax, a hatched, a broch, a bill, a shovell with other lumber		1	8
2 spinninge wheles, a pare of cardes and a rele		1	0
In the chamber			
2 bedsteadles, a flockbeadd, a flock bolster, 2 hellinges, 2 blanketts and 2 pillowes		10	0
4 coffers, 4 shetes, 2 table clothes and 3 shertes		10	0
The apparell of the sayd John Jewer deasesed with other thinges		12	0
In the lofftt			
A beadsteadle, a flock bead, a bolster, a hellinge and a blanked		5	4
A quarter of maltt, 8 sackes, 2 baggs, a tubb, 3 sickels, one shelff with other lumber		15	0
In the outer chamber			
A powdring trow, 2 kyvers, 3 barrells, a kyve, tubbes, bowels, threase and canns with other lumber		5	0
In the barne			
The wheate and rye and 2 sythes	1	10	0
A ploughe sheare, coulter, 2 harrowes, 3 chaines, a pare of strops ffor the cartt, cartt sadle with the furniture therto belonginge		6	8
The wood within the gate		3	4
2 Kine	3	13	4
2 oxen, 2 mares, a little coltt, a waninge calf, a kow and 2 hackforthes	7	10	0

A yeltt with 4 shootes and poulterye		6	0
4 stalles of bees		8	0
In the fyeld			
Wheatt, rye and barley	3	0	0
Otes, peasen and beanes		16	0
Debts due	2	6	8
33 shepe and 6 lambes	6	0	0
The cartt, the lade and the rope		15	0
[*£30.19.8*]	30	15	8

Note: The Will was dated 23rd November 1575 and probate was granted to the executor John Jewer, his servant, on 5th June 1576. Three men bearing the name of John Jewer benefited by this will. John Jewer of Compton and his son Francis had bequests of stock and grain. John Jewer of Wayborne and his son Richard had a similar gift, with the addition of an iron-bound cart complete with ladder and ropes for carrying tall loads. John Jewer the young servant, not yet twenty, was left the residue of the estate after he had completed the administration. Three other servants were also beneficiaries. Jane Loyck, Elizabeth Jewer and Laurence Jewer, were given stock and useful household stuff. The two girls each had a spinning wheel and the boy a bedstead amongst the other goods. Small bequests also went to a godson William Stoner, to Agnes Aslett, to the daughter of Davis of Wrecclesham, to Walter Ide's son John and to John Aslett and William Stoner, the supervisors. No witnesses were recorded. The testator was buried at Farnham on 14th May 1576.

Ref: 1576 B 40/1 Will 1576 B 40/2 Inventory

John Mabancke **143**

of Egham, yeoman; taken by Richard Allen of Thorpe, husbandman, Willyam Bowllen, Thomas Steere, Henrye Cottrell, parishioners of Egham, 25th April 1576.

Stuff in the halle	£	s	d
One table, 2 formes, 4 stooles, one chayre and one coupboarde		4	10
One olde peynted cloathe			6
In the chambre benethe at thapper ende of the halle			
A playne besteade, one flocke Bedde with all thaparell thereunto belongeinge		10	0
3 playne Coffres		2	0
In the loafte overe the seide chambre			
One smale fether bedde, one blankett and one playne coveringe		6	8
A flocke beedde, a blanckett and one coveringe		3	4
One plancke, a paire of tresles and 4 borades		1	0
In the chambre at the lower ende of the halle			
Oene course bedde with all thapparrell		2	0
Lynen			
6 paire of sheettes		13	4
Tooe table cloathes, half a dosen of table napkynes and too hande towelles		6	8
In the kytchenne			
2 Brasse pottes		10	0
2 pannes of brasse and one posenett		13	4
6 pewter plattres, 6 dishees and 4 sauceres		10	0
One morter, one chaffinge dishe and tooe candlestyckes		2	0
Tooe spyttes, one paire of smale coabirones, one dryppinge panne, one fryeinge panne and one payre of potte hangers		2	0
Breweinge vesselles			
Tooe yelde fattes, too ale tobbes and one buckeinge tobbe		6	0
One poudreinge troughe, one knedinge trowhe, one cheese presse and one bowltinge tobbe		2	8

In Cattle			
Fowre Oxen	5	6	8
Tooe steeres	1	10	0
One heyefere		10	0
Three kyne	3	0	0
Tooe weanynge calves		8	0
4 lyttle boullockes	1	6	8
Tooe mares and one coulte	1	6	8
Tooe cartte nagges	1	6	8
70 olde sheepe	9	6	8
16 younge Lambes		16	0
One Sowe and 14 lyttle shoutts	1	17	4
Corne in the feildes			
Wheete groweinge uppon the grownde beinge fyve acres	2	0	0
One acre of barleye		5	0
4 acres of Rie	1	0	0
Five acres of smale oattes		12	6
In dry grayne			
In Rie 12 bushelles	1	0	0
In maulte one quarter		9	4
Necessaries for husbandrye			
One carte, one ploughe wyth other necessaries belongeinge unto husbandrye		16	0
One axe, one byll, one syth, one mattocke, one showell and one spade		1	6
One bushell and one fanne		1	4
Tooe Laddrs		1	0
One blacke byll and too sackes		1	4
One Saddle, one brydle and one pannell		2	6
Powtry abought the howse		1	0
Hys apryrell			
All hys wearinge Apparrell	1	6	8
The Lease of hys howse	3	0	0
	41	19	8
His debttes			
Oweinge to Wm. Hoale, weaver	7	5	0
To Thomas Goringe, smythe		1	8
	7	6	8

Note: The Will was written on 9th April and proved on 10th May 1576. The executrix and residuary legatee was his wife Jone who bound herself, together with William Snowmere of Thorpe, miller and Thomas Stere of Egham, husbandman, well and truly to administer the testator's estate. The overseers appointed were Robert Bateman and William Hoole. Three legacies of money were 10s to Edward Marloo Maybancke of Woking, 10s to Frances Wheatly of Chobham and £2 to the testator's brother-in-law William Hoole. His man servant William had 2 ewe sheep, his boy Roberte Shatoe had one ewe sheep and his maid Marye Davye had 2 ewes and 2 lambs. The poor men's box at Egham was given 3s 4d. The witnesses were Thomas Stere, Thomas Renalde, Willyam Snowmere and Willyam Hole.

Ref: 1576 B 51/1 Will 1576 B 51/2 Inventory

Willam Newman **144**

Vicar of Chertsey; taken by Thomas Holte, William Banister, John Heathe and Henrye at Wyke, 4th May 1576. [*The document is damaged and a few letters are missing.*]

	£	s	d
His apparell			
A coate, a dublet, 2 payre of hosen, An olde gowne and a worsted cassocke		13	4

A ioyned cupboorde	1	6	8
A lytle table, a payre of tressles and A rownde table		3	4
2 flock bedes with 2 payer of sheetes, 2 payer of blancketes, 2 coverlyttes, two bowlsters and A troockle bedsted	1	7	6
A standyng bedsted		8	0
A ffether bed, A bolster, 2 pyllowes, a coverlyd, a blanket and a payer of Sheetes	1	11	4
An other standinge bedsted, a flock bed with a bolster and a coverlyt		16	0
Two trookle bedsteds		5	0
A cawdron and two lytle ketles		18	8
A lytle ketle of 3 gallons and a lytle pan		3	4
A brasse potte and another lytle pan, a skellet and a potthookes		4	2
An other brasse potte and a possnet		4	0
A payer of potthangers, a payer of Andyornes and a tryvet		2	6
2 skylletes, a chafynge dishe and a skymer		2	0
3 potthangers, a tryvet and a payer of Andyornes		5	0
A ffryinge pan, a dryppinge pan, a payer of tonges and a cole rake		4	6
A styllytary of Leade		3	4
A latyn spice mortar with the pestle		1	8
Two pewter platters and a bason		3	0
7 pewter dyshes, 3 poryngers, one sawcer and a saltseller and a pewter cuppe		4	6
A treene bowlle, a treene platter and 12 treene dyshes, a bowll dishe and half dossyn of pewter spoones		2	2
A dragge, A ffagott hooke and a cuttyng knyfe			8
2 chamber pottes		1	0
A syde sadle, 2 brydles and a panell		10	6
A Buckyng tubbe, an old fate, a Kyver, 4 olde tubbes and 6 Kylderkyns		5	0
An axe and a Lantorne		1	0
Hempe and flaxe			6
3 turned chayres		3	4
A Hearne cubboorde		1	8
Two chestes		3	6
3 canvas sheetes		10	0
6 pyllowberes		6	0
Two dyaper olde table clothes		3	4
6 table napkyns and 2 cupboord clothes		5	0
2 shertes		5	0
A lynen tester of a bed		2	6
Fyve Joyned stooles		3	4
4 Kushens		2	0
An old Sylver spoon[*e and s*]ix pewter spoones		2	2
All the paynted clothes about the Howse	1	6	8
The glasse		16	0
Two shoottes		5	0
3 olde ketle bondes and a sawe with other olde Iron		2	0
A payre of bootes and a cap case		4	0
2 brasse candlestickes			8
A payr of skales of brasse		1	0
A lether bottle		1	4
A lynen wheele			6
2 basketes and a flasket and certayn olde boordes with other Lomber		5	0

[*£15.18.8*]	15	18	4

There is other goodes of the saide Deceassed which were gayged before his Deceasse for Debtes of money which is owing And as we understand, for not payment of the said money, full bought and solde of which goodes we can not well fynde the certayntee ther of.
And also what Duties of tythes and offringes are yet behinde, as Due to hym we knowe not

On 5th June 1576 this Inventory was exhibited by Henry Wikes, the Administrator of the goods and chattels. Ref: 1576 Ad 38

Thomas Northall **145**

of Guildford, saddler; taken by James Shaw and Henry Parkhurst, 25th June 1576.

	£	s	d
The hall			
A table with a frame		3	4
Two ioyned foormes		2	0
A cupbord		5	0
Two old chayers			8
3 paire of bell candelstickes		6	8
Two paire smale candelstickes		2	0
Two pewter pottes		2	0
One salte			6
An Alman ryvet with the furniture		10	0
Half hundred in weightes with a beame		4	0
Paynted clothes		1	8
The buttry			
One Cawdron		6	8
3 kettels		5	0
A chaffing dish			4
Three dryppeng pannes		2	0
A fryeng panne			6
Two spyttes		1	6
Treene vessels			6
A stone morter			4
An Aulmery			8
The Shop			
A counter		1	0
Rackes and shelves		1	0
The Strete chamber			
A standing bed with a paynted tester		5	0
A fether bed and a flock bed, a bolster, a coverlet, a blanket and a paire of sheetes	1	0	0
His apparell		13	4
The money in his pursse		3	4
A truckell bed with a flock bed and a paire of blanketes		5	0
Two chestes		2	0
Paynted clothes		3	4
8 paire of shetes		16	0
3 table clothes		7	6
The myddle chamber			
A bedstedell, a flock bed and a coverlet		6	8
Fyve Coosshens		5	0
Two keverletes		10	0

A carpet and two window clothes		3	0
A chest		1	0
Paynted clothes		1	0
The Inner chamber			
11 pewter disshes and 6 porringers		15	0
A bedsted with a tester of say		6	8
A fether bed, a bolster and two blanketes	1	0	0
Paynted clothes		1	8
A chest and a chayr		1	8
The back chamber			
A bedsted with a tester of canvas		5	0
A truckell bedstedell		1	0
Thre chestes		3	4
Paynted clothes		1	0
Thre pillowes		1	6
In the ketchin			
Two Cobyrons		2	0
Two pothangers		1	0
A fyre shovell, a fyre rake, a paire of tongues and a trevet		1	6
A paire of bellowes and a paire of pothookes			4
One brasse pot		5	0
Two kettels		3	0
Two platters, two pewter disshes and a sawcer		2	6
Tubbes and other vessels		1	0
A welbocket and a chaine		2	0
Shambels for butchers with a tylte		3	0
A lytle gryneng stone			6
	11	18	2

Note: The nuncupative Will was written on 13th June and proved on 17th July 1576. The testator's wife Margaret was to have a life interest in his house in Trinity parish, Guildford and land called Water Dene, near Guildford. At her death their son Bartholomew was to inherit the house and land and was to deliver to his brother Thomas Northall, vicar of Kerford, £20 "and the best fetherbed, bedstead and appurtenances". The appointed overseers James Shaw and Henry Parkhurst signed the Inventory. The widow and Bartholomew Northall of the same, shearman, bound themselves well and truly to administer the estate. The testator was buried at Holy Trinity, Guildford, on 12th June 1576, the day before James Shaw and Henry Parkhurst signed the official version of the nuncupative Will.

Ref: 1576 B 56/1 & 2 Will (n.c.) 1576 B 56/3 Inventory

Thomas Peytowe, the elder **146**

of Chiddingfold, yeoman; taken by John Osborne, Richard Aburrowe, Thomas Hall and William Eve, 18th May 1576.

		£	s	d
A lease of a Tenemente and certen Landes in Chidingefold called Ridgers		13	6	8
In the parlor				
A Joyned Table			1	8
Tenne Sylver spones		1	13	4
A Brasse pott			8	0
	[*£15.9.8*]	15	9	7

Administration of the goods and chattels was granted to Agnes Peytow on 5th June 1576. At the bottom of the Inventory in Latin is recorded the fact that the aforesaid Thomas Peytowe had died in 1550. Ref: 1576 Ad 42

Bartholemew Smethurst **147**

of Pirbright, yeoman; taken by Robert Russell, John Baker and Thomas Symons, 24th May 1576.

	£	s	d
in the haule			
Two tables, two foromes, to covers, foure Joyned stoles and a cubbert	1	0	0
in the kychinge			
Trene vessells		3	4
Brasen vessells	1	13	4
in the Buttry			
A Cubbert, 17 pewter platers and dishes, 9 saucers, 5 sautes, two pewter candellstickes and thre pewter quarte pottes and a pynt pott		13	4
Foure Brasen candellstickes, a drippinge pane, a dosen of spones, a chafern dishe		3	0
in the beed Chamber			
Two fether beedes, two flocbeedes, thre boulsters, thre pillowes, thre blankes, thre coverlites, Six payre of shetes, foure pillowe beres, foure table clothes, 8 table napkins and two table carpettes	3	0	0
Two Joyned bedstedells and two playne beedstedells and foure chestes		16	0
His apparell	1	0	0
In his purse		13	4
One carte with a payre of yorne bound wheles, two chaynes, two yokes, one payre of stroppes, an oxe harrowe and one smaule harowe and a plowe with the yornes therunto beloninge, a carte rope	2	0	0
In pultry		4	0
In hogges	1	6	8
Foure workynge Bullockes	8	0	0
Seven mylch Kene	9	0	0
Thre bullockese of two yeres of age	2	0	0
Six bullockes of a yere old	3	0	0
Five caulfes of this yeres weninge	1	0	0
A nagg and a mare	1	13	4
Corne in the Barne	1	10	0
Corne in the feldes, 12 acres of Rye	6	0	0
Seven acres of ottes and Barly	2	6	8
[*£47.2.8*]	47	8	0
The deptes of Bartholomewe Smethurst due to be payd unto the parties underneathe named as folowethe.			
In debte unto Mr Frannces Browne for Legaces unto fatherlese children of Chobham	16	0	0
Unto Mr Shawe of Gylford	1	12	0
Unto one Smythe		10	0
Unto Sharpe of Gylford		2	0
Unto Mr Frances Browne	4	0	0
	[*22*	*4*	*0*]

Note: The Will was written on 11th May and proved on 5th June 1576. The residuary legatee and executrix was the testator's wife Joan Smethurst. When goods were bequeathed the testator gave his brother's surname as Smethurst, but 4 of his own children, Thomas, Ales, Edward and Robert, were surnamed Bartholomew. Also among beneficiaries of gifts of livestock and crops, he named his son-in-law Anthony Dawe. Legacies included cattle in the heath, rye growing above the new ditch and the 21-year lease of a mansion house in Guildford called the Crowe. This lease was made over to John Whiting, one of 3 overseers; Harry Lee and Harry Brittwhisell were also to receive 5s for their pains. A bequest of a bed "with all his appurtenance" and valuable young livestock, was dependent on his daughter Ales marrying a person approved by her mother. Wearing apparel was given to the son Thomas; he, Edward and Robert, were to have livestock at Michaelmas next. In addition, Thomas and Edward were to receive an acre of rye when it was ripe, chosen by the overseers. The testator asked to be buried in Pirbright parish church or churchyard, giving 1s to the poor men's box. James Remnant and Jenkyn Walter, clerk, were witnesses to the Will. The burial was recorded on 14th May 1576.

Ref: 1576 B 77/1 Will   1576 B 77/2 Inventory

John Stynt **148**

of Milford in Witley; taken by Thomas Stynt, John Burckhust, Thomas Snelling, Stephen Matchwick, Nycholas Wodiar, with others, 4th January 1576.

	£	s	d
Brasse			
2 Cauthernes		8	0
1 brass pann		3	4
1 pap pann and one other pece of old brasse			6
1 pott of Brass		3	4
2 other old brass potes		2	8
1 Chaffing dysh of brass		1	4
4 Candellstyckes		1	4
3 payre of Sheres old			4
1 frying pann		1	0
1 broche, pothokes and pothangers		2	0
Pewter			
3 platters		3	4
4 peuter dyshes		2	8
6 Sausares		1	8
1 yene dyshe and 2 saltes			8
1 latten drypping pan and a tonell			4
1 Table, tressels and a forme		1	8
1 Chere			2
2 Tryvet		1	0
1 payre of bylles			3
4 old augers, 2 Chesels, 1 wymble and drawing knife			
1 hammer, 1 whip saw		1	8
2 axes, 2 byles, 2 shovels, 2 pronges		2	0
2 weges of yron, 1 pyncers			8
1 flock bede, 1 bolster, 1 Covering, 1 payre of blanckes		13	4
1 old bed, 1 bolster, 1 Covering, 1 payre of blancketes		8	0
2 bedstedes		16	0
2 Colfors		2	0
1 Cubard		2	8
1 bow with arrowes			6
1 knead trow			6
1 vate, 1 keve		1	4
4 tubes		1	0
3 stobynes		1	0
1 bushell			6

1 Kever, 1 boule, 1 Churme			6
3 steanes, 4 panches			8
1 klens seve, 1 trowell, 3 syves			6
2 turnes, 1 skaynar			6
1 Chese presse and 2 motes			6
1 host heare			8
2 sackes			8
old yron			8
Rey 10 heyls	1	0	0
Small otes 20 hyls		16	0
1 lode of hay		10	0
3 payre of shetes		4	0
4 oxen	6	13	4
2 table clothes		1	4
3 Keyne	3	0	0
1 twelvmothlyng bullock		10	0
3 horses beastes		13	4
A weayne, dong pot with chayns, ropes, etc.	1	0	0
1 plow with 2 old harrows, 3 sythes and gryneston		3	4
1 sow and 6 shoutes		14	0
his apparell		6	8
7 connyes of rey	2	6	8
20 wetheres, small	3	0	0
13 ewe shepe	1	12	6
14 teges shepe	1	3	4
1 cock and 3 hennes		1	8
1 bottell			6
2 stone cupes			2
1 pannell and 1 brydel		1	0
A bucket, old stoles, old tobs, Spones and Dyshes with all other Lumber		1	0
	28	15	7

To Thomas	5	0
To Robard	5	4
To Jone	1	0
Mr Jones	2	0

Note: The Will was dated 18th November 1575. A horse and a heifer for his eldest son Thomas and two tegs for John Stynt of Farnham, were to be chosen before the division of the goods was to be made. His wife Johanne was given one half and was named as executrix. The other half of the goods and cattle without and within doors was to be divided equally between the four children, Thomas, Robert, Jone and Jelyan. A shilling each was to go to the overseers Thomas Snelling and Stephen Matchwick. Probate was granted on 10th May 1576. The 5 named witnesses to the Will were Nycholas Edwardes, John Peto, Nycholas Woodiar and the 2 overseers. These last two responsible men, Stephen Matchwick of Witley and Thomas Snelling, smith, together with the widow, guaranteed the Administration Bond.

Ref: 1576 B 84/1 Will 1576 B 84/2 Inventory

William Todham **149**

of Horne; taken by John Wynchester of Tandridge and Robert Wyllat of Horne, 16th April 1576.

	£	s	d
2 Oxene	5	0	0
2 owld mares	1	6	8

2 Coltes	1	10	0
One steare of 2 yeares ould	1	0	0
3 Kenne	4	0	0
One Hecfare of one yeare owld		10	0
2 shottes of halfe yeare owld		3	4
One Acare and a halfe of wheat	1	0	0
2 Acars and a halfe of Ottes	1	5	0
One Colle Weayne, one Corne Weayne atyare for a payer of whells, 3 Tyttes, one Coltour, one Chane, one Towe		13	4
One axe, one byell			8
Howshold stoofe			
One fether bead, one bolstar, one Cowerlet, one blancat, one selynge		16	0
2 payer of shettes, 2 pelowbears, one Tabbell Clothes		13	4
2 Chesstes		2	0
One Cowbord		5	0
Carppytis		2	6
3 brace pottes, 3 bracce posnetts		18	0
One Cawthern, 2 pannes, one Chaffynge dyshe		7	0
6 Candell styckes		3	3
21 peaces of pewter		18	0
4 porryngers			
2 spettes		3	0
One pote huke, one potte hangar, one gyrdern, one brandyarne one Andyarn, one Drypping pane		2	6
4 tobbes, one vyrkyn		2	0
Saddell		1	0
One quarne		1	0
One ffryece Cotte, one Doblet and all his others Rapparell	1	0	0
[*£22.3.7*]	22	2	11

Note: The Will was written on 2nd April and probate was granted to the executor, his son John, on 9th May 1576. A daughter Margaret was given the major share of the family bequests including 'one Tabell Clothe that was hir mothers'. Two other daughters, Agnes and Joan, had benefit from the will to a lesser degree and there were arrangements made for the return of stock and money in other men's hands. The testator's wife Catharine was to repossess the goods she had brought to the marriage and also to have a third part of the lands and houses which were in his possession when they married. In order that his wishes should be fulfilled in every particular, the testator frequently gave the numbers, colours, ages and exact descriptions of certain livestock and household articles, as in the following examples: "my blake Kowe and one brase potte with out leages"; "my blake Kowe wyth the White bake and a payear of shettes wyth Hoke semes"; "one Cawthrene with 2 Eares"; "my Reade Kowe and my Read Huked Hacfar and the Calfe of the sam Kowe now awenyne". The son John was to benefit from the residue of the estate, first having paid the debts and legacies. Finally Jasper Lade and Thomas Chart were given 5s apiece for their pains taken as overseers of the Will, the latter witnessed by John Ingrame, Robert Wyllatt and Rychard Issted.

Ref: 1576 B 89/1 Will 1576 B 89/2 Inventory

Robert Wicker **150**

of West Molesey; taken by Robert Stackford, Henrye Fyssher and James Corneford, 4th May 1576.

	£	s	d
in the Halle			
One tayble, one forme, a payr of trestles		2	0
One cubborde, one Lytle Rownd tayble, one chayre and an other backe chayr		3	4

One paynted cloth		1	0
2 pott hanggars, a payr of tonges and a gyrdyron		1	0
in the parler			
One ffether bedd, a bolster, a keveryng and a bedstyd		13	4
A tester over the bedd		1	0
4 chestes and a forme		5	0
His apparell		6	8
Fyve payre of shetes		6	8
in the Lofte			
One fether bed, 2 bolsters, 2 pyllowes, 2 Keverledes, one bedstydd		10	0
A kevering		1	0
in the Kytchyn			
4 Kettles, 3 Cawtherns, 2 pannes, 6 bras pottes bygger and Lasser	3	0	0
3 spyttes		2	0
Drynck vessels and old chest		3	0
2 bottells, a frying panne, mylke booles wyth dysshes and spones		2	6
25 peces of puter, 3 puter pottes and 3 sawcers		15	0
2 chaffyng dysshes, 2 candellstyckes and a bras morter		3	0
A trevytt, a tubbe and sertyn old yron and a payr of cobyrons		2	4
Old Lumber		2	0
2 spynning Wheles		1	0
in the yarde			
A payr of old wheles, a payr of harrowes, a ploughe, a dong cart with sertyn Lumber		10	0
2 mares and 2 colttes	2	0	0
2 kyne and 2 bullockes	3	0	0
2 Sowes and 2 hogges		13	4
3 yooes and 3 Lambes		10	0
in the felde			
Of wheate and Rye 9 acars	3	6	8
Fyve acars of barlye	1	13	4
2 acars of tayres		10	0
An acarr of otes		3	0
6 gyes, 4 hens and a cock		4	0
	19	12	2
Debtes wiche I owe			
To William Wicker to be payd at Michellmas next	4	0	0
I do owe to Mystres Thorne, due at our Lady Day last past	1	14	2
I do owe to John Coper	2	0	0
I do owe to Mr Inwoode	1	0	0
I do owe to Frannces Lacke		10	4
I do owe to Robert Wattson	1	5	4
	[*10*	*9*	*10*]

Note: The list of debts was written by Lewis Price, the curate of West Molesey, at the end of the Will, which was dated 1st June 1575 and proved on 9th May 1576. The residuary legatee and executrix was the testator's wife Elizabeth. John Stackeford and Thomas Fyssher were to act as overseers. The testator asked to be buried in the churchyard of West Molesey and then proceeded to set down the equal portion of goods to be given to each of his 5 children when they should come of age. If John, Harry, Isabell, Jonne, or Alles should die, the survivors were to have an equal share of the legacy not so given. One share was half an acre of rye, half an acre of barley, a platter and a pewter dish. Robert Dowley and the curate Lewis Price were witnesses.

Ref: 1576 B 98/1 Will 1576 B 98/2 Inventory

Henrie Wilkyns **151**

of Great Bookham, husbandman; taken by Raphe Stevens, John Gardener, John by the Wood and Thomas Stambridge, 25th January 1576.

	£	s	d
The haule			
A table standing one a fforme being a stander of the house, also one old forme to the tabell belonginge		2	0
A Joyned cobberd		4	0
A potte hanger in the chymny			4
2 olde stolles			1
The paynted clothes			4
The kytchen			
A cawdran with a bayll like a kettell verie olde		2	6
A posnett with 3 litle skillettes		2	6
8 old platters		2	8
3 dishes			6
3 sawcers			6
An old grydyron			2
A spitte			4
2 candelstickes			4
Old Tubbes		1	8
The Chamb[*er*]			
2 old matrisses		1	4
2 paynted testers with the clothes about the chamber		2	6
2 blanickettes, 2 coverlettes		2	6
3 payre of sheittes, 2 old table clothes		4	0
2 old chestes		2	8
Waring geare			
A cote, a Jurkyne, a payre of hoosse, a ca[*n*]vis shurt		6	4
In his purse		1	0
The barne			
By estimacon 20 busshells of wheat and Rye	2	0	0
In barlie by estimacon	1	13	4
In hay and Tarres		10	0
An old phane and an old busshell with out eares			8
In fyve acres of winter corne, being wheat and Rye, being now soene one the ground	1	13	4
The cattle			
3 mayres	1	13	4
One cowe and a bullocke and a weanner of this yere	1	6	8
2 hoogg shutes		4	0
An old cart and thereunto belonging		10	0
Bacon in the Rooffe		2	0
	11	11	8

Note: The Will was dated 18th December 1575 and proved on 10th May 1576. The residuary legatee and executrix was the testator's wife Margaret, who was to have the tenancy of his tenement called Eastwick in Great Bookham, until their son John should reach the age of 21. He was to have his grandmother's cauldron and also the cupboard and table on a frame from the hall. The other 3 unnamed children had bequests of grain: 2 quarters of barley and 2 bushells of wheat. The overseer was the testator's cousin John Gardiner. Seven named witnesses were Rafe

Stevyens, John Marter, John Gardiner, Edmond Durdan, Thomas Marter, John Wylkines and James Rogers. The widow Margaret and the overseer John Gardiner, husbandman, bound themselves to see the administration of the Will carried out.

Ref: 1576 B 101/1 Will 1576 B 101/2 Inventory

John Sherwood **152**

of Shalford, carpenter; taken by Arnold Martyn of Guildford, shoemaker, John Segar of the same town, shoemaker and Richard Watlyngton of the same town, dyer, 21st February 1576/7.

In the hall	£	s	d
The table with the frame		3	4
The wenskot behind their back		3	4
1 Round table			6
2 paynted clothes		1	0
1 tryvet			6
1 andyron			8
1 pothanger with a payre of pothookes			6
A spynnyng whele			8
A brasse pot		8	0
A posnet		1	0
A brasse panne		4	0
A kettell		1	8
3 Candlestickes		1	0
3 platters		3	0
2 pewter dishes		1	4
5 sawcers		1	2
1 salt			8
4 pewter pottage dishes		1	4
2 old pewter dishes			8
1 pewter pot			6
2 buckets			6
2 tubes		1	4
2 kyvers		1	4
1 bowl dishe			2
A broken halfe busshell			4
An old fether bed and a bolster		10	0
An old flock bed		3	4
2 bedstedles		6	8
2 blankets		2	0
An Coverlet		1	8
[*line mutilated*] old cover		[*]	4
Fyve payre of shetes		18	0
2 pyllobees		1	0
3 Chestes		5	0
An old fetherbed		6	0
A pillowe			6
4 Kene	4	0	0
1 bullock		13	4
A wennyer		6	8
4 shootes		10	0
[*£10.3.0*]	9	18	0

On 1st March 1576/7 the Administration of the goods was granted to Johanna Sherwood, the widow. She and Arnold Martin of Guildford, shoemaker, bound themselves well and truly to administer the estate of the deceased. [*The year has been plainly written "1576" for the grant of administration and "77" altered firmly to "sixe" at the top of the document.*]Ref: 1576 Ad 48

1577

Note: Although no inventories are entered for that year, John Sherwood's Inventory (no. 152) which is registered in Winchester as 1576, may possibly belong to 1577.

1578

Thomas Barne **153**

of St Mary's, Guildford, smith; taken by George Myles, Anthony Webb and Walter Forde, 11th June 1578.

	£	s	d
in the Hall			
A table and the frame		2	6
An olde Cubborde		1	8
A Chayre and a stoole			6
A latten pott and three Candlestickes and a salt saller		2	0
Three olde Cushens			6
in the chamber			
A fether bedd and three olde bolsters and a Coverlet		10	0
A flockbedd, a bolster and a Coverlet		3	4
Three bedstedles, olde		3	4
5 payre of Sheetes and one table Clothe		5	0
One bed tester and a headclothe		1	0
4 Chestes		2	0
One troughe and a borde, olde			2
6 tubbes and twoe bowles		2	6
One broche, one pothanger, one dripping pann, one pothooke, one girdiron and a fleshe hooke		1	0
Foure litle Kyttles and an olde brasse pott		6	8
8 peces of olde pewter		5	0
One scomare, one bread grate, one dosen of Trenchers			6
One quart pewter pott, halfe a dosen of Tynne spones			10
An olde Cubbord		1	0
One olde horse myll		2	0
Foure grindstone handles, one spynder		2	0
Two olde winches or vices and a bokehorne		1	4
An Anvylde		5	0
[*£2.19.10*]	3	0	10

Note: The Will was written on 25th March and proved on 20th June 1578. The testator's wife Margaret was the residuary legatee, with the instruction that she should dispose and give those goods as she liked. Two of their sons John and Thomas Barne were appointed executors. No overseers were mentioned. The anvil and most of the working gear were to go to the son John. Anthony was to have a vice and 2 handles for the grindstone. Thomas was to have the horse mill in the street shop. The 5 children, John, Anthony, Thomas, Elizabeth and Agnes, were to be given specific household items after their mother's decease. These items included canvas sheets, a kneading trough, brewing and ale tubs, a keve, pewter platters and a dish, saucers, salts and a stone green sauce mortar. The testator asked to be buried in St. Mary's churchyard. Thomas Penntell, the curate there, wrote the Will which was witnessed by Thomas Welles and Walter Forde. The Parish Register records a burial on 6th April 1578 of Thomas Barne the elder, smith.

Ref: 1578 B 7/1 Will 1578 B 7/2 Inventory

William Bearde **154**

of Worplesdon; taken by Thomas Christemas, Davyd Cutler and Wylliam Chrochelow, 20th June 1578.

	£	s	d
4 smalle Ketteles		5	0
Too Lytell pottes of yerne		2	0
4 Kandellstyckes		1	0
A payre of potthookes			6
9 platters		6	0
Too dosen of spones		1	0
Too sawsers			6
A quarte and a pynte pott			8
4 Chestes		6	0
Stone pottes			8
His apparell		6	0
Too beddes, a Keverynge, one payre of shetes and a Tester		18	4
Owllde yerne towlles		3	4
A lytell table and a stowle		1	0
A lytell mare		6	8
A cowe	1	3	4
Tymbre		10	0
	4	12	0

Note: The Will was dated 13th May and proved on 20th June 1578. The testator's mead, called Sedgemeade, in the parish of Windlesham was bequeathed to his wife Mawde and her heirs for ever. She was to be executrix and residuary legatee. The overseers, Walter Creswell, gent. and Thomas Christemas, were given 5s apiece. The testator asked to be buried in the churchyard of Worplesdon. The parson there, John Cutler, was to have 2s. He witnessed the Will, together with Robert and William Doddiseworth and John Wheler. The burial of William Board was recorded on 18th May 1578.

Ref: 1578 B 8/1 Will 1578 B 8/2 Inventory

Thomas Bickenell **155**

of Frensham; taken by Edmond Lye, Thomas Connie and others, 27th November 1577.

	£	s	d
1 Kowe	1	6	8
4 yewes		13	4
1 heyfer		15	0
A gylding and a coulte	1	0	0
2 swyne		4	8
Cham[*ber*]			
2 bedstedes and one bede, with that that belongith to it		10	0
4 payer of Sheates	1	0	0
3 chestes		6	0
Ha[*ll*] and Ky[*tchen*]			
A table 3 chayers and a fourme		1	0
3 kettles, a brase pote and 2 little pape panes		16	0
2 platters, 2 porringers, a sawcer and 2 candelstickes		3	4
A broche, 2 frying panes, a gyrdian, a trevete, a payer of pote hokes and hanggers		3	4
In woodden vesseles		3	4
3 eadge toules		8	8

	£	s	d
5 hennes and a kocke		2	6
2 tournes, a lynen and a wollyn		1	8
In wearyng clothes		11	0
	8	6	6

Note: The Will was dated 22nd November 1577 and proved on 7th May 1578. The residuary legatees and executors were the testator's wife and son, Agnes and Thomas. The only other legacy was a 3-year-old heifer to his daughter Marie. He asked to be buried in the parish churchyard and appointed Thomas Lusher, gentleman, an overseer. The latter wrote and signed the will and was given 4d for his pains, together with the other overseer John Baulden, who made his mark. John was designated yeoman by the testator and tanner by Mr Lusher.

Ref: 1578 B 12/1 Will 1578 B 12/2 Inventory

Annys Channell **156**

of Chobham, widow; taken by John A Strete, Thomas Prytchat, John Gunnar, Thomas Wye, Nycolas Atfeld, John Sherrate and Wyllyam Sherrat, 21st April 1578.

	£	s	d
Of munnye in hir purse		10	0
For hir aparrell		13	4
5 kyne	5	0	0
2 telmonthynges and 2 Wenyears	1	10	0
26 shep and 9 lames	3	6	8
For 3 Jades	2	10	0
4 pyges		5	0
gese and hense		2	6
6 stales of bese		16	0
2 cartes, a plow, an oxe harrow and a lytle harrow, yookes and chaynes		16	0
For corne and heye in the barne	1	13	0
For 4 ackars of Rye and 4 of otes	3	0	0
For 2 bedes and ther furnitur	1	6	8
For brase and pewtter, boles, tubes, stoles and all othe houshold stufe	5	0	0
	26	9	2

Note: The Will was dated 13th April and proved on 7th May 1578. The residuary legatee and executor was the son of a previous marriage of the testatrix, Christopher Tayler of Guildford, shearman. Sums of 3s 4d each were given to Thomas Pritchett, Nicholas Feilde and Thomas Tayler, the overseers. The testatrix asked to be buried in the churchyard of Chobham, giving 12d towards repairs of the church. Her son Thomas Tayler was given £2, with £1 to each of his 4 unnamed children. Richard and Agnes Wattleton were each given a bed and bedclothes. John Smyth was given a coverlet. His wife and Prynce's wife each inherited a petticoat and "to owlde Elizabeth Woods" went " a smock and a Waste cote". A ewe each was given to Henry Tayler, Owyn Feilde and Roger Bekynsfeilde. The executor and John Hywood, vicar of Chobham, bound themselves well and truly to administer the estate. The 4 witnesses to the Will were the aforesaid John Hiwood, John Astrete, Harrye Pynson and Rychard Wattelton.

Ref: 1578 B 22/1 Will 1578 B 22/2 Inventory

William Foster **157**

of Wanborough; taken by John Ead, Thomas Paddecke and John Gunner, 5th April 1578.

In the Haule	£	s	d
One Cauldorn and one trifte		8	6
One table			6
Towe kettles, a brasse potte and a posenet		10	4

Three bowlles			8
A fryeinge panne, one candlesticke, one dripinge panne, towe peuter platters and a peuter potinger		2	2
One potte henger and one griderne			8
One axe and one ould byll		1	2
In the chamber			
One flocke beadde, one blanckett, a payre of shyttes and one coverlette		12	8
towe chestes		2	0
hys apparrell		2	6
in an other place			
One hogge of baccon		6	0
Towe toubbes with other lomberie		3	0
in the barne and abrodde			
Haye in the barne		4	0
For three kinne	4	10	0
One oulde mare and towe coltes	2	0	0
	9	4	2

Note: The Will was dated 14th February and proved on 7th May 1578. The residuary legatee and executrix was the testator's daughter Ellen, who was ordered to keep and use the livestock until Michaelmas to pay the rent and then to fulfil the bequests. The overseers William Chouter and Robert Seager were left 8d each. Ellen, John and Alice, three of the five children, had gifts of livestock: a brown cow, a bay mare, "a read garled cowe and a redde cowe" in that order. Thomas was given the great cauldron and the trivet in the hall. In the bequests of kettles and coffers, Ellen was to have the biggest and best and her younger sister Alice "the next to largest and the worser of the twayne". Alice did inherit the spinning wheel however. A certain Thomas

Lovell was given sheep and the third son Robert Foster was given 4s. The testator asked for christian burial in the parish churchyard. Henry Johnsonne, the curate, wrote and witnessed the signing of the Will.

Ref: 1578 B 37/1 Will 1578 B 37/2 Inventory

John Hays **158**

of Headley; taken by John Bristowe, Wylliam Langforth, John Newman and Richard Boxall, 20th August 1578.

	£	s	d
His apparell	2	0	0
In the haull			
A table, a forme, 2 ioyne stooles and a painted clothe		8	0
One fetherbed, a pair of blankets, a coverlett, a bolster, a tester and the bedsted	1	13	4
2 flockbeds, 2 pair of blankets, 2 coverlets, 2 bolsters and 2 bedesedes	1	0	0
One holland shete and 5 pair of canvas shetes		15	0
2 pillowes and 2 pillobers to the same		3	4
2 table Clothes of Canvas		3	0
One irebound chest and 4 Coffers		8	0
2 brasse potts, a caudron, 2 kettills, 2 posnetts, a skillet and 4 Candelstickes	1	10	0
One dosen of pewter, 2 saltes and a dosen of spones		13	4
2 broches, one andiron, a pair of pothookes, a pair of pothangers		4	0
A vate, a kiver, a bolting whiche and other od lumbrie		7	0
3 buckets, 2 boles, 3 dosen of trenchers		4	0

4 ale stannes		2	0
16 pound of woull		12	0
Chese	2	10	0
A sack, a bagge and 2 sives		1	4
Rye in the Barne	4	10	0
16 acres of oates	4	0	0
Hay	5	0	0
80 weathers	13	0	0
40 yeowes	5	6	8
40 lambes	3	13	4
4 oxen	7	0	0
7 kyne	8	3	4
4 bullocks	3	4	0
5 heiffer bullocks	3	0	0
5 wayninge Calves	1	6	8
2 mares and old horsse and 2 Coltes	3	13	4
20 hogges	5	0	0
8 small shuttes		8	0
14 gese, 6 duckes and other poultrie		6	8
A Cart, a pair of wheles, 3 yokes, 3 Chaines withe the appurtenances	1	10	0
A ploughe and a pair of harowes		5	0
A sithe, 2 hokes, 2 axes, 2 shovells, 2 bills and other old iron		4	4
An old lade and a dung pott		1	4
2 dosen of wattells		2	6
[*£82.9.6*]	79	15	10

Note: The Will was written on 12th July and proved on 23rd September 1578. The residuary legatee and executrix was the testator's wife Joan, who was to take charge of the £30 bequest to their son William, using it for him until he reached the age of 20. She was to distribute half a quarter of rye to those poor of the parish she thought had the greatest need. A sum of 6d was left to the Trinity church of Winchester, 2s to the poor men's box in Headley church, 4d to each of his godchildren and a ewe lamb to each of his nephews and nieces. The overseers were to be his friends, the brothers Mr Wylliam Beyll and George Beyll, who were each to have 13s 4d for their pains. The 2 witnesses were Wylliam Donnell, clerk and Mr Wylliam Beyll.

Ref: 1578 B 44/1 Will 1578 B 44/2 Inventory

Margaret Stansted **159**

of Woking, widow; taken by Thomas Purdam, Richard Colebroke, Thomas Child and Edmond Bonsey. [*undated*]

	£	s	d
In ready monye in her purse	10	0	0
A chayer			3
Fier wood		4	0
Hey		1	8
2 chestes and a fosser		5	0
7 stoles		1	6
A whelde chayer		2	0
2 fether bedes and a flocke bed, 2 fether boulsters and a flocke boulster and 3 Pillowes	2	13	4
4 coverlightes		7	0
4 blanckets		5	0
6 painted clothes, 3 curtens and a testerne		5	0
4 coshens		1	2

A nett with fethers, 2 basketes and a halfe pecke			8
A ffrise cassocke and a redd peticoate		6	8
2 bedsteades		2	6
A table and a paire of tressels			8
An Ieron beame, broken scales and 6 waightes		5	0
A pronge			1
2 brasse potes, 6 kettels, a panne, a scillat, a scimer, a friyngepan, a brotch, a payre of Andieres, a pothanger and pothokes	1	0	0
10 platters and disshes, 3 sacers, 2 potes, 2 saltes, 18 spones, a pece, a chameber pott, 4 candlestickes and a chaffinge dishe		10	0
5 tubbs and a butter churne	2	0	
A bredgrate, a pepper querne, 20 trenchers, 2 bowles, 4 disshes, 2 cruses, a drinckinge cuppe and a glasse		1	0
2 dowble rayles, 3 neckerchers, 4 kerchers and a payre of Ruffes		3	4
4 payre of shetes, a c[*u*]bberde cloth, a payre of pillowbers, a hatt and 2 capps and a towell		10	0
A payre of pillowberes, 2 aprons, a wallot and a fewe cloutes		1	0
A table, a forme and a c[*u*]bberd		6	0
A bedstead		2	0
A gunne, 2 swordes, 4 daggers, 3 hedpeces, a byll, a bowe and a sheffe of arrowes and an Alman revet		13	4
2 trowghs		1	4
	18	11	6

Note: The Will was written on 28th October 1572 and was not proved until 25th April 1578 by the widow's 3 daughters, Margaret Martyne, Margerie Champe and Elyzabeth Geffre. Margaret was singled out to take over the lease of 3 closes of land called Langstone, Langstone Piddell and the Buttone, held of John Mounger, citizen and mercer of London, to whom John Stansted, the late husband of the testatrix, had let a farm. The execution of the Will was the concern of the 3 daughters, but a son-in-law John Geffre, of Winkfield in Berkshire, was to be overseer and he was bound to administer the estate. The surname was written by another official "Jefferie". Five named witnesses were Thomas Thayer, John Snekell, John Davy, Richard Bedford and John Penne.

Ref: 1578 B 87/1 Will 1578 B 87/2 Inventory

Richard Tydey **160**

of Ockley; taken by Thomas Songhurst, Wylliam Worsfold, Walter Songhurst, John Margeson and others, 8th April 1578.

	£	s	d
Syx oxen	15	0	0
Foure workinge Steres	6	13	4
Foure thre yerelinge	5	0	0
Seaven keyne with calfes	10	0	0
Tow hecfors with calfes	2	6	8
Thre barreners	3	0	0
Syx tow yerelinge hecfers	5	0	0
Eight twelmonthing bullocks	4	0	0
Thre horse and a colt	5	0	0
Fourtene teggs	1	10	0
Syx shotts	1	0	0
One other Cowe and a bull	2	6	8

Eighte Acres of grene wheat	5	0	0
Eightene Acres of otts	6	0	0
The wheat, otts and hayne in the barne	4	0	0
Tow waynes and wheles, tow doncarts, one plowe, youckes, chaynes and harrowes	3	0	0
Tres standing and Tymber wrought	2	0	0
The bacon and beyfe in the Roughe	2	0	0
Wheat and malt in the howse	4	0	0
One Cawdren, tow brasse potts and seaven old brasse peces besides	2	0	0
Ten pewter platers, ten pewter dishes, one bason, foure porrengers, foure sawsers, thre salt sellers, one chamber pott and one pewter bottle	1	0	0
Syx laten Candelsticks, one chafingdishe, one Iron Morter and tow dosen of spones		10	0
Tow trefts, tow Iron spitts, tow girdirons, one Andiron, tow paire of pothokes, tow frying pans, one fire rake, one fire forke, tow oven peles, one latten ladle and one dripping pan		13	4
Tow fether bedds, one flocke bedd, thre Canvas bedds, syx coverlitts, five paire of blanketts, five bolsters, foure pillows, five quishens, one Joyne bedstedle and foure other bedstedels	5	0	0
Twelve payre of worne shetts	1	10	0
Foure table clothes, tow towells and syx table Napkins		10	0
One vate, one bruyng tubbe, one tun, foure kymnells, one Renninge tubb, one chorne, tow powdring tobbs, syx barrells, one bucking tubb	1	0	0
One dosen and halfe of mylke vessell, one chese presse and syx mylking buckets with all other wodden vessell		10	0
Foure chaires, one forme, one Table, tow stoles with all other ymplements and trumperye		5	0
One Mallard and five Ducks, one Cocke, tow henns and five chekens		3	0
His waring gere	2	0	0
Of Readye money in his porse		10	0
[*£102.8.0*]	102	18	0

Note: The Will was written on 10th February and proved on 20th June 1578, the executors being the testator's wife Joan Tydey and his son-in-law John Eversed. The overseers were named as Walter Songhurst and John Margesson. Their gifts of 3s 4d apiece for their trouble would have been well earned in carrying out all the minor bequests involving articles of clothing, money, grain, utensils and farming stock. William Nightingale, the sawyer, was given a medley jerkyn, while William Nightingale, the clerk, was to have the best "hosen and dublett". Edmond Lypscombe was given the testator's old frieze coat and Edward Ven benefited from the best medley one. To John Hytchurst went the best hat and the best fustian doublet went to John Tydey, one of the testator's four brothers. The buckskin doublet and the second best cloak were given to brother Matthew. Edmund was forgiven 6s 8d (a quarter of a debt of £1 6s 8d) and Thomas was repaid 5s and given a similar amount. George Tydey was a beneficiary too, but his relationship was not stated. Two servants Richard Carpenter and Agnes Maydman were given livestock. Margaret Shoo was given a bushel of wheat and three "old Mothers", namely Stone, Tyckner and Cooke, were each given 6d. Arrangements were made for the payment of money to his son William and daughter Elynor. The sum of 2d was left to the mother church of Winchester. Five named witnesses included the two overseers, with John Tydey, John Wright and William Chelson. The burial was recorded on 20th March 1577/8.

Ref: 1578 B 90/1 Will 1578 B 90/2 Inventory

William Wapshote **161**

of Chertsey; taken by Rychard Whetley, Rychard Bonsaye, John Wapshote the younger, Walter Wapshote and others, 5th May 1578.

	£	s	d
In redy mony in his purse		10	0
His apparell	1	0	0
A Bow and arrows with one blacke byll		3	4
4 Flocke Bedes and 2 Matryss	1	6	8
3 Coverynges, 6 blancketes	1	3	4
7 payer of Corse Shetes		14	0
One payer of fyne Shetes		5	0
3 pyllow beres, 2 Table clothes with all the other Lynnen in the Howse		4	1
2 Chestes		5	4
The paynted Clothes in the Chamber		5	1
The Hall			
The paynted clothes		3	3
The Cubbard		6	2
A Table, a forme and 3 Stolles		2	1
The Ketchyn			
One Cadron, 4 Ketles, 2 brasse pottes, one posnet	1	5	2
2 Candlestyckes, one Chafinge Dyshe, one Lyttle morter		1	9
All the pewter, viz. 6 platters, 12 dysshes, 5 Sassers, 4 porringers and 2 Saltes		16	10
One Treved, 2 Spetes, 2 potehockes and 2 pote hangers, a fyer pane, a payer of Tonges and one Cobyron		3	5
One Sythe, 4 syckles, 2 Axes, one byll, 2 fagot hockes		1	8
The Woden vesselles viz. 4 bowlles, 3 buckhetes, 8 Dysshes and 12 Trenchers		1	2
One salt troughe, one knedinge troughe and 4 alle vessells		5	0
An old shode carte with 3 payer of yokes, Chayns, Stropes, one small harow, one Oxe harow, 2 ploughes	2	6	8
6 Oxen	12	0	0
9 Kynne	11	5	0
15 Bullockes	10	0	0
5 weanynges	1	5	0
2 mares and one nage and 2 Coltes	3	10	0
30 Shepe	5	0	0
The swynne	1	0	0
The powltrye		2	1
The Corne in the feld viz. the rye	8	0	0
The Ottes	1	0	0
The gryndstone		1	4
2 Horse Collers and 2 payer of harnes		2	6
	64	15	4

Note: The Will was dated 26th April and proved on 7th May 1578. The residuary legatee and executrix was the testator's wife Joan. He left 4d each to the overseers, John Wapshote and Henry Crockeford and he asked for christian burial in the churchyard of Chertsey. Three of the poor folk were given specific bequests: 6d each to the Widows Brown and Doufell and a year-old teg to Edward Spong. A sum of £6 13s 4d was left to each of his children, John, William, Edward, Joan, Mary and Agnes Wapshote. If any should die, his or her inheritance was to be divided amongst the survivors. The sons were to inherit at the age of 20 and so were the 2 elder daughters. When the youngest Agnes reached the age of 11, she and her portion were to be governed by Henry Crockeford. She could claim her bequest at the age of 18 and each of the 3 girls could inherit on her wedding day, if that were earlier. The unexpired term of years of the lease of his house and land was to go to the son John, upon the decease of the executrix, but both were ordered to keep fences and buildings in good repair. A codicil in a shaky hand authorized the overseers to see that the children's legacies were reduced to £6 if the testator's wife should fall into poverty and be in need. Two named witnesses were Rychard Whetley and Water Wapshote.

Ref: 1578 B 96/1 Will 1578 B 96/2 Inventory

1579

George Collier **162**

of Worplesdon, yeoman; taken by Harrye Ockele, Thomas Christemas, Roberte Russell, Thomas Meryste and Steven Collier, 11th May 1579.

	£	s	d
In the Hall	£	s	d
A Tabell, a forem and a Stowlle		5	0
Too payntid Clothes and 5 cowsshenes		5	0
In the Chamber			
A bedstede, a bedd and all thynges belongynge to hit	1	0	0
6 Lytell Cofers and a litell Square Tabell		10	0
Aparell	1	0	0
In his poursse		13	4
In the Lofte over the halle			
Too bedstedes, to beddes, to Coverlyttes, too payre off blankes, to bowllsters	1	10	0
One bedd hangger with a haedd Clothe		2	0
A Chaere and a owlld payre of Stockcardes		1	0
A bedstede, a bedd, a Coverlyde and to bowllsters		10	0
A payre of Csckales with weyghts and certen hempe and a baskett of fethers		4	0
For Certen Cheses and a chese Racke and a lytell spynnynge wheele		3	4
9 payre of shetes, 3 table Clothes, 6 table napkynges and a towell	2	3	0
In the Kytchen			
5 broches, 4 awndyres, too Treftes and a gredyrne		10	0
7 kettelles, too bras potes and 4 pottengers	1	8	4
Certen pewter	1	3	0
Too pewter pott, 3 saeceers, 3 dosen of spoones and a Chafen dyshe		4	0
3 basons, 3 Kandellstycks		4	6
A morter with a pestell and 4 erthen pottes		2	0
Too lether bottelles and a Capcase		2	0
10 Toobes, 5 baryelles, 5 kevers, too Trowes		10	0
A Cooborde		10	0
12 bakone hooges	4	0	0
A quarter of corne and 6 sackes		13	4
4 dosen trenchers and a dosen of owden dysshes			6
A bowe and a sheve of Arowes		2	0
A bytell and 5 wedges, 2 axes, too bylles, too sithes		3	4
Hether unto there is nothynge preasyde but that goodes that are wythen the doores	17	19	8
22 Coopells of yewes and lambes	4	6	8
For 40 drye shepe	6	13	4

6 Oxen	12	0	0
Fyve horsebestes	4	0	0
Eyght Kyne	9	6	8
Nyne boolockes	6	0	0
Too other Steres	2	6	8
4 akers whete and Rye	2	13	4
3 akers of smalle otes		15	0
syxe shutes	1	0	0
A Karte and yernbownde wheeles wythe a payre of Strope, a payre of Rowndes, 3 yokes, 3 Chaynes	1	6	8
Too payre of owllde wheeles wythe a dogpott, an oxe harowe, a smalle haroowe and a plowe		16	8
4 hyves		10	0
For certen bourdes		3	4
Too yerne sledges, too Crowes, 4 hammers, a bushell, to peckes and too towlde daysheres		3	4
3 owlde geese, a gander, 9 younge gese, 10 doockes, 10 hennes and a Coke		4	0
A Lese taken of Robertt Smythe	1	0	0
A Lese taken of Harrye Crockforde	2	0	0
Summa there skore theryttene pownde fyve shelynges foure pence bye me John Cutler, Clerke and Thomas Merest [*signed*]	73	5	4

Note: The Will was written on 18th April and proved on 27th May 1579. The overseers were Harrye Ockele and Steven Collyer. The testator asked for a churchyard burial in Worplesdon; this parish and that of Pirbright were both left 3s 4d. A sum of £2 was given to the testator's nephew William Phellpe, with the remainder to his brother John Phellpe, if William should die unmarried. Two ewes and 2 lambs were also given. Joan Martyne, the testator's daughter, was left £1. Christian Hynd was to have 2 sheep. The godchildren were left 4d each and Edward Slarks was given a ewe and a lamb. The testator's wife Alice was given all the goods within the house and a half share of those out of doors; the other half share was given to the co-executor John Hynde. The 4 named witnesses were John Cutler, parson of Worplesdon, Robertt Smythe, Harrye Ockelee and John Cutler, the younger. The executors bound themselves to administer the estate. The burial was recorded at Worplesdon on 7th May 1579.

Ref: 1579 B 8/1 Will 1579 B 8/2 Inventory

Jonne Fulstone **163**

of Frensham, widow; taken by Rychard Harding, Symon Harding, William Valler, Richard Boxsall, William Somner and others. [*undated*]

In the halle	£	s	d
A Table, a Wainscote backe, formes, a painted cloth		10	0
Four chestes, four coffers and cowberd	1	6	8
On cawdren, four kettels, 2 brasse pannes, 2 brasse pottes	2	0	0
12 peces of pewter, 4 sawsers, 4 candelstickes, pewter pot		13	4
2 broches, Andierns, fryinge pan, grediern, pothookes		6	8
2 trowes, bolting wich, fates, barrels		13	4
A chese presse, butter churne, chese mottes		2	0
3 yoke of oxen and on ode ox at £3.6.8 the yoke	11	13	4
Otes thresshed		5	4
15 kynne prised at 20 shilling the kowe	15	0	0
13 yonge bullockes prised at 15 shilling a pece	10	15	0
7 weniers prised at 10 shilling the pece	3	10	0
30 shepe prised at 3 shillings a pece	4	10	0

				£	s	d
The Rye unthresshed in the barnne				3	0	0
Hey and Wotes				6	0	0
10 horsses prised at 5s. apeace				2	10	0
Pigges 26 prised at 18 pence apeace				1	13	0
Geace and hennes					5	0
Bacon at the Ruffe				2	6	0
Plough and carte with Implementes therto				1	0	0
7 horsebeast				8	0	0
Chese				1	10	0
The Chambe[*r*]						
Bedding apparrell				8	0	0
A todde of Woolle				1	0	0
Armory					5	0
Turnes, cheiers, disshes, trenchers					5	4
8 Acres of Rye and Wheat prised at 6 shillings and 7 pence the acre				2	6	7
				[*89*	*6*	*7*]

Note: The nuncupative Will was brought to Court on 24th April 1579. John Harding, senior, the father of the testatrix was the sole legatee to take all towards the upbringing of the children. Richard Harding and Thomas Beldam had elicited the wishes of the deceased the day before she died. Her father, being duly sworn, was granted administration of the goods.

Ref: 1579 B 17/1 Will 1579 B 17/2 Inventory

John Manfilde **164**

of Dunsfold, husbandman; taken by William Pulter and Robeart Rapley, 21st May 1579.

				£	s	d
The stofe in the Hall						
A tabell with trestelles and to formes					2	6
A rounde table, a cheare and to lytells stouls					2	4
A coberte					5	0
		9	10			
The brase and yron in the Hall						
A cawdren and a kettell					16	0
3 lyttell kettells and to small posnetts					7	8
A lyttell brasse pote and a lyttell yron pote					5	0
A spyte, a potehanger, a payre of potehookes and a gyrde yron					1	4
A dosen of wooden dysshes and wooden platters, a dosen of trenchers					1	0
8 flychesses of bacon				1	6	0
	2	17	0			
The backehouse						
A tro, a boultinge huche					3	0
4 keyvers and 5 tobes					6	8
A klen syve, a pecke, a meall syve						3
6 bolse, to earthen panes, a cherne					2	0
An old cheste						6
A fryinge pane, to sakes, a bage					2	0
A glase pote					1	0
A chese prese and 6 stens					1	0
		16	5			
The chambre						
The hanginges and a tester over the bede					4	0
A bedsted, a fetherbede, a boulster, a blancket, a payre of shytes, a coverlete				1	6	8
A bedsted, a flockbed, a payre of shytes, a sherde coverlet, a blanket					13	4

Three cofers and a cheste					6	0
His aparell and three shertes				1	10	0
Money in his purse					2	0
	4	2	0			
Another chambre						
A bedstede, a shrede coverlet, a blanket, a payr of shetes, a bolstere, a tester over a bede					16	0
Three pewter platters, 3 dysses, 2 sawsers, 2 saltes, half a dosen of pewter sponses					6	8
To latten candellstyckes					1	0
Three cofers and a tro, 2 baskettes					3	0
To bottelles, a bruse, a payr of sherres					1	0
4 cussens, a lyninge table cloth					2	8
To heginge bylls, an ax, a beck, a spytter					2	4
[*£1.12.8*]	1	13	0			
A chambre wherin is sartayn Lumbery						
6 busshelles of Acornes					2	0
Other trumpery					1	4
		3	4			
The whet an malte						
Halfe a quarter of whet					6	8
Halfe a quarter of otten malte					4	0
Hogs Larde					4	0
Foure hens					1	4
		16	0			
The cattell						
To yere heffers				1	10	0
2 yerelynges				1	0	0
Wayners					10	0
	3	0	0			
The hoges that be a lyve						
A sowe with 2 pyges					8	0
To shutes					8	0
		16	0			
The corne in the filde						
An akere of whet, an akere of Rye				1	6	8
To akers of otes					13	4
	2	0	0			
[*£16.13.3*]				16	13	7

Note: The Will was written on 6th May and proved on 27th May 1579. He asked to be buried in the churchyard of Dunsfold and he made a donation of 2s to the poor men's box. He arranged for his son Harry to receive 10s every half year, until his 24th year when he was to inherit the house and lands. Until that time the testator's wife Gylyan was to spend 6s 8d a year on repairs to the house, receiving the same allowance for herself when her son came of age. Gylyan was to be sole executrix and the overseers were Hary Manfilde and John Hurst. The widow and John Hurst of Alfold, husbandman, bound themselves well and truly to administer the estate. The witnesses of the Will were William Langborrowe, clerk, Robeart Rapley, Hary Manfilde, the elder and his son of the same name.

Ref: 1579 B 26/1 Will 1579 B 26/2 Inventory

John Rempnant, the younger **165**

of Pirbright, weaver; taken by John Russell, Stephin Rempnant, Henrie llee and John Martin the younger, 19th May 1579.

	£	s	d
His bodelie Apparell	1	0	0
In money in his purse		3	4
In the hall			
A table and a frame		3	4
A forme by the table			4
In Brasse, Pottes, panns and Kettells	1	10	0
A doosen of pewter platters and a doosen of Pewter podingers	1	0	0
2 Paire of potthangers and potthookes		1	4
A weavers Loome, with all thinges belonginge therto	1	0	0
In Bedding, Beddes, Blanckettes, sheetes, hellinges and coverlettes	1	6	8
A cheaste with a round lydd		3	4
An other cheast		1	8
4 other cheastes		4	0
A brasen cauldron		10	0
A Broche			6
A cheire with toobbes and treene vessells		3	4
A bowe and Arrowes		1	0
A bill, an Axe and a shoovell		1	6
A warr byll			6
2 old lytell cobbherdes		2	0
3 Acres of greene corne in the fild		15	0
4 Kyne and 2 heyfers	5	0	0
A coople of waynyng calfes		6	8
10 sheepe and 5 Lambes	2	0	0
2 Mares and 3 coltes	4	0	0
4 of the best hyves of bees	1	0	0
5 other hyves of bees		15	0
2 yong shewtes		3	4
4 lytell pigges		2	0
3 heenns and a cocke		1	4
Dettes owinge unto him upon specialties	6	10	0
Without specialties of John Rempnant thelder	1	10	0
Of Robert Russell, being suertie for one Exell of Woorplesdon	2	0	0
Of Edward White		9	10
Of Edward Westbroke	1	0	0
A Panell and brydell		1	0
	33	7	0

Note: The Will was dated 2nd May and proved on 27th May 1579. The executrix and residuary legatee was the testator's wife Alice. Sums of 2s each were left to the overseers, John Martin of Cowshote and Steven Collier, both of whom witnessed the signing of the Will, together with Steven Rempnant and Hugh Phillip, the curate. A sum of 6d was left to the poor men's box of Pirbright, in which churchyard the testator asked to be buried. John, one of his 2 sons, was to inherit his loom, the table and a form in the hall, the great chest and the best coffer in the loft. Each of his 4 children was given a stall of bees and household items. Edward had a lesser share than his 2 sisters Agnes and Jone, who had extra gifts of £10 and livestock. If any child were to die before the age of 21, the survivors were to divide any such share. His godchildren were left 4d apiece.

Ref: 1579 B 35/1 Will 1579 B 35/2 Inventory

1580

William Beston□ **166**

of St. Saviour's, Southwark, gentleman; taken by William Sym[*], Thomas [*] and Humfre [*], 1579. **Mutilated at top of document and there are several holes.*

	£	s	d
[* *]		5	0
[*An*] o[*l*]d flockbedd		5	0
[*An*] old feth[*erbed*]d and 2 bolsters		15	0
2 old bla[*nkettes*]		2	0
An old cover[*ing tap*]estrie lined		6	8
A testor [*of loc*]kr[*a*]m of red [*and*] yellow with a i[*o*]yned bedsted		5	0
A trundle bedd		2	0
A Dansk Chest		6	0
A buckes leather Jerkin		2	8
An old worsted Doublet		1	8
An old gowne faced with budg and lyned with white Cotton		10	0
Another old gowne faced with foxe and furred		3	4
An old paire of breches			6
A leather Jerkin		4	0
A furryd [*blank*] faced with foxe	1	15	0
2 nedlework Cushins		6	0
An old Cushin of flox			6
A Dagger		3	4
A Chest		3	4
A paire of turned sheetes		2	0
Another paire of old sheetes		1	8
A Table Clothe		2	6
A Dyaper Towell		2	6
A playne towell		2	6
Another Towell		2	0
2 pillowberes		3	0
An old pillowbere			4
4 table napkens		2	6
3 Course napkens		1	4
2 Shirtes		2	8
A Rapyer		1	0
3 flaskes, 2 tuche boxes and charges		2	0
A murrion and a coate of plate		6	8
An old harnes without splintes		1	4
2 old Chestes		7	0
A fetherbed, a flock bolster and twoe pillowes	1	3	4
2 blankettes		4	0
A covering lined with canvas		13	4
A shorte Carpett		2	6
3 bookes	[*no value given*]		
A Carpet of Dornix, a Cubord cloth and a Window cloth		9	0
3 old Cushens of tapestry		4	0
A paire of old shetes		2	0
6 platters, one bason, another bason and ewer, a plate, 5 Dishes 4 plate trenchers, 5 saucers, a porringer, a pynte pott, a salte waigheng 51 pounds and 3/4 at 6 pence a pound	1	5	10½
A pottle wyne pott, a quarte wyne pott, a pottle Ale pott, a quarte			

Ale pott, 2 chamber pottes - 23 pounds 3 quarters at 3½ per pound		8	10¾
A paire of large Candlestikes		3	8
An Iron pott		1	8
2 brasse pottes waigheng 9 pounds		2	7½
A kettle of Iron		3	4
An old fryeng pan			4
A Warming panne		2	0
A skymmer, a litle skellett		1	0
2 Spittes		1	2
A pestle and a spice morter			8
An old Byble		4	0
In Redye money	20	0	0
[£33.11.4¾]	33	16	0

Elizabeth Beston alias Bolton, sister of the Testator and Administratrix, was sworn to the truth of the above Inventory on 12th October 1580.

Note: The Will was dated 20th January 1572/3, when William Beston, citizen and girdler of London was a parishioner of Southwark St. Olave's; it was proved on 4th November 1579. The testator asked to be buried within the parish church and he intended his wife, Margaret Beeston, to be the executrix and residuary legatee. His cousin Cuthbert Beston, like himself a citizen and girdler of London, was appointed supervisor or overseer and was to have a black gown and the best gold signet ring. Bequests of money to the poor of the parish and to the local free school were to take effect immediately after the burial. Cuthbert was to distribute £1 annually, raised from the rent of his mansion, to buy faggotts or coals for those in the greatest need at Christmas time. The Fellowship and Company of Girdlers in the City of London was given £3 to make a recreation for the members. His wife's daughter Frances Bateman was to have £60 on her wedding day. A sum of £10 was bequeathed to Nicholas Blincowe, his wife's son. William Beston's own daughter Agnes Brooke was to be given money at the rate of £10 per quarter until £40 was complete. Thomas Wheler, Notary Public, had represented the widow Margaret as her Proctor when the Will was proved and the administration of William's estate was granted to her. She must have died before all the bequests were carried out. Bolton and Blincowe are names which occur in the parish register of St. Lawrence Jewry, the church connected with the Company of Girdlers.

P.R.O.Ref: PROB 11/61 ff 344,345 Will PROB 2/653 Inventory

William Chyttye **167**

of Godalming; taken by Richard Smyth, William Billinghurst, Henry Petow and Richard Carpenter, 13th March 1580/1.

	£	s	d
A lease of certaine land called Ocforde land within the parish of Witlye given and bequethed unto the above named William Chittey deceased by and in the last will and Testament of William Chytty his father late of Godallmyn aforesaid mercer deceased	30	0	0

The Inventory was produced on 14th March 1580/1 by the sister of the deceased, Cicelie Jackman alias Chittye, who was sworn to the truth of the document and was granted the administration of the goods.

Ref: 1580 Ad11

1581

John Cresey **168**

of West Horsley, husbandman; taken by John Hunte, Jasper Fulke, Edward Godard and Thomas Broker. [*undated*]

	£	s	d
Hys aparell			
A rycot Cote and a canvas dublat, a payre of rycot hose wyth the reste of hys aparell		13	4
In his purse		6	8
In the bed Chamber			
Won floke bed and the furnyter	1	0	0
Too Chestes, too payre of shetes		13	4
Too keteles and a braspot		13	4
Too peuter plateres, three saseres, won peuter dyshe, a peuter pot, won stonen pot, a dosen of spones		3	0
Too tobes wythe other eale vesseles, too woden platers, fower woden dyshes		1	8
Too kene, a hecfer, a boloke of a yere olde, a mare and a Coulte of a yere oulde	6	0	0
Too hoges		6	0
Won bill and a ax, a hand hoke, a hachat		2	0
Syxtene quar[*t*]ers of maulte and fife quarters of barley	10	0	0
Too pounde of buter, six Cheses		3	0
Three lodes of tember, fower plankes, three lodes of wod	1	6	0
Fower akers of wheate and a halfe, won aker of teres, won halfe aker of dredge	2	16	8
Too lesses	5	0	0
Won busshell, syx sakes		5	0
	29	10	0

Note: The Will was dated 20th March and proved on 10th May 1581. The residuary legatee and executrix was his wife Tamsin. The overseers Edward Godard and Jasper Fulke were each left 6s 8d. The testator asked to be buried in West Horsley churchyard. His mother, his son Edward and his maid Elisabeth Godard, were left £1, £10 and 6s 8d, respectively, with 12d to every godchild. The aforesaid Edward was also to benefit at the rate of 10s a year from 2 unnamed leases, the disposal of the remaining terms of years of which was set forth in case Edward should die. The testator's unnamed uncle and his wife were to share the benefit unless he were to die and she were to marry, in which case the remaining party would take all. Tamsin was to use the money for any child of the testator who might be born after his decease. This possible child would have prior claim to the £10 allotted to Edward, over the claim of the children of the testator's eldest sister. The 3 witnesses were the overseers and Thomas Broker. The executrix and Edward Godard of West Horsley, husbandman, bound themselves properly to administer the estate.

Ref: 1581 B 28/1 Will 1581 B 28/2 Inventory

Annys Dayer **169**

of Elstead, widow; taken by Thomas Ryeman, Wyllyam Bycnalle, Peter Bromehame and John Colyns, 30th March 1581.

	£	s	d
Her apparele	1	10	0
Alle the beddyng in the house	1	10	0
Alle the brase in the house	1	13	4
Alle the peuter in the house	1	0	0
Alle the Ier gere in the house		3	4

Too olde cobards		3	8
Foure olde cofrs		4	0
The wodden vessells in the house		10	8
The tabelle, forme and terusuls		2	6
The bakyne in the house		8	0
Too barryne kyne and too bolloks	2	13	4
Nyne shepe	1	6	8
The corryne and the haye in the barryne		18	4
One acker of smalle rye uppne the grounde		6	8
	12	10	6

Note: The Will was written on 12th January 1579/80 and proved on 10th May 1581. The residuary legatees and joint executors were her daughter Juliane and son-in-law Henry Mycenalle. Annys, the said Juliane's child, was given the major share of the household goods and clothing, each item specified as the best, some to be found in the chamber and some in the hall. The details of the goods and chattels were written in full only in the Will. The granddaughter's inheritance ensured that she was well provided for: a cow, 6 sheep and a heifer, a little vat, an ale barrel and a rick of rye, were of importance; in and around the hearth all necessities were available in the form of a cauldron, pot, brass laver and posnet, a broach, pothooks and a gridiron with hooks, as well as a table, trestles, a form and a cupboard; cooking equipment consisted of the 4 best platters, 2 pottingers, a chafing dish, salt cellar, "canstyke" and saucer; then came the best bed, coverlet and bedhangings, 2 bolsters, a pillow, 3 sheets, a long joined trough and even a bureau and 2 coffers; finally the best kercher, "rayle", waistcoat and petticoat; all were given to Annys Mycenalle. Annys Dayer's brother Whelar and his family, Annys and Elizabeth, had smaller bequests, as did her servant Richard Bookham and his unnamed children. John Page was given a sheep. Richard Bycnalle and other unnamed godchildren had small gifts of a few pence. The overseers were brothers Whelar and Bocame; witnesses were William Bycnalle and John Hedgarr. The executors, of Elstead and Richard Bookham of Thursley, husbandman, were bound well and truly to administer the estate of the deceased.

Ref: 1581 B 30/1 Will 1581 B 30/2 Inventory

William Fulston **170**

of Frensham. [*no appraisers given and undated*]

	£	s	d
10 ewes price 2s 4d	1	3	4
15 tegges - 2s 4d	1	15	0
A sowe hogg		4	0
A chest		1	0
His apparrell	1	0	0
A pig		1	0
In ready moneye	10	0	0
	[*14*	*4*	*4*]

Note: The Will was written on 12th January and proved on 10th May 1581. The residuary legatees and administrators were the brother and sister of the testator, Robert Fulston and Joane Fulston. A sum of 2d was given to the cathedral church of Winchester. The major bequest of £10 went to Jonne Foster, who was also given 6 ewes. John Foster of Frensham, weaver and John Harding, husbandman, bound themselves to see the administration of the goods and chattels carried out. Witnesses to the will were Richard and John Hardinge and William Summer.

Ref: 1581 B 46 Will and Inventory

Robert Rundell **171**

of Stockwell in Lambeth, yeoman; taken by Richard Mason, John Hamond, William Bonor, Raph Leveroke, Edward Heith and William Coe, 1st May 1581.

	£	s	d

7 kene and one bull		10	13	4
Two steres		2	13	4
7 yonge bullockes		5	0	0
2 oxen		4	0	0
8 horses		8	0	0
1 ould Mare with her colt		0	10	0
46 shep and 5 lambs		5	6	8
6 hodges		1	4	0
5 pigges		0	2	6
5 acres of whete		3	0	0
11 acres of Rey		6	0	0
1 acer and 1 haulf of tares		0	10	0
9 acers of barley		3	0	0
36 acers of otes		10	0	0
Otes in the barne		4	16	0
Rey in the barne		3	0	0
Mault		1	4	0
Haye		0	8	0
2 carners of a feild with hemp		0	5	0
1 long cartes		1	0	0
5 ould cartes		1	5	0
Plows and harrows, yokes and chaines		2	0	0
Horse harnes		0	6	8
Toles of husbandrey		0	10	0
Cartane timber			13	4
Cartane fire wood		1	10	0
	[*£76.17.10*]	42	8	10
In the house				
Two old tabells and formes		0	6	8
1 old cobbord		0	3	4
Chaires and stoules		0	2	0
3 Cushins		0	3	0
Certaine pewter		1	6	8
Brasse		3	6	8
Spites, Driping panes and trivetes		1	0	0
One Joyned bedsteed with a fether bed and the furniture		2	0	0
1 tabell, 4 Chestes, a presse		0	6	8
Furniter to scrue the presse		0	10	0
Linnin		3	0	0
His Apparell		2	0	0
A remnannt of wollen Cloth		0	10	0
Bedsteedes with 2 fether bedes and thire furniture		1	13	4
3 Chestes		0	3	0
A fetherbed tike		0	6	8
2 borded besteed and their furnitur		0	13	4
2 old Cobord		0	5	0
2 Chestes		0	2	0
Certaine bacon		0	2	6
Ould painted Clothes		0	10	0
A mault querne		0	13	4
Certaine powtrey		0	6	8
Ould Lombard		4	0	0
2 Leses of certaine ground		1	0	0

	24	10	10

Summa totalis one hundreth and one pound 8s 8d

Note: The Will was written on 10th April 1581 and proved almost a month later on 8th May. Money gifts were few: 2s apiece to his servants, 6s 8d to the poor of Lambeth and 6s 8d each to Richard Mason and Raphe Leverocke, the two overseers. Two kine were given to Robert Rundell of Feversham; one cow was given to his sister, Alice Beake of Sussex; 4 kine to John Jupe, his wife's son; and the residue was bequeathed to his wife Elizabeth, instructing her to educate and bring up his nephew Robert Kingestone and to be the executrix of the Will. The overseers witnessed the Will, together with the Minister, Richard Graynger and John Hamond. The burial was recorded in Lambeth on 16th April 1581.

Ref: 1581 B 96/1 Will 1581 B 96/2 Inventory

1582

William Becham **172**

of Thorpe; taken by John Goold, Richard Eyer and John Taylor, 8th January 1581/2.

	£	s	d
His aparell		5	0
In the Chamber			
A fether bed, a Coverlet, a bedsted, a payer of blanketes	1	0	0
A bedsted, a flocke bed, a blancket, a Coverlet, 2 bolsteres		13	4
Too payntyd Clothes			8
Too Chestes		3	0
Thre paier of shetes, 1 tabelclothe		10	11
In the Hawle			
A Couberd, a tabell, a forem, 3 stowles, a payntyd Clothe		7	8
In the Kychin			
4 pewter plateres, thre pewter dishes, 2 kandylstyckes, 2 sawseres, a pewter pote		7	4
A brasse pot, 2 Ketyles, a spyt, a paier of Cobelernes		5	0
3 Kyne	3	6	0
A mare and 2 Cowltes	2	0	0
A mawlt myle		13	4
A Cawdryn		5	0
6 Ierne weges, axe, a matocke		4	0
	10	1	3

Note: The Will was dated 20th November 1581 and proved on 30th May 1582. The residuary legatee and executrix was the testator's wife Elyzabeth. William asked to be buried in Thorpe churchyard and he appointed Richard Eyer of Thorpe, yeoman and John Goold as overseers. Tools and a cauldron were given to William's son John, household goods to his daughter Elizabeth and a 2-year-old bay colt to Thomas, the eldest son. The youngest son Thomas was to inherit the malt mill when both parents had died, meanwhile being paid 6d a year by his mother. The 2 named witnesses were the trusty overseers. Richard Eyre served also by being bound, together with the executrix well and truly to administer the estate.

Ref: 1582 B 7/1 Will 1582 B 7/2 Inventory

Bartholemew Bowdoxe **173**

of Albury, Parson; taken by William Attwell, Edward Rysbriger and Henry Rysbreger, 28th May 1582.

	£	s	d
For the money in his purse		3	4
For his Apparrell		6	8
Two fether bedes with the furnyture	5	6	8

One flockbede with the furnyture	1	6	8
Two truckle bedes with the furnyture	1	6	8
Two syngle flock bedes		10	0
Fyve payre of canvys sheetes	1	5	0
In the hawle			
One Joyne table and a forme		4	0
One coubbored		13	4
For chayares			8
One Joyne table		2	6
One square table, one forme, 4 stoles		6	8
Two Joyne chestes		13	4
One lytle square table, a lytle chest		2	6
3 chestes		3	6
One old coubbord		2	6
Foware smalle brass pottes	1	0	0
Two small Irne pottes		2	0
Two brass posnetes		5	4
One small cawdron		7	0
6 brass Kettles		13	4
One dossen peyter platters		15	0
6 peyter dysshes		4	0
3 pottengers		1	0
One payre cobornes, two pott hockes and 3 pott hangers		3	0
Sixe spyttes, 2 dripping panes, 2 tryftes, a payre of tonges		11	4
For paynted clothes		5	0
Fowre candellstyckes		2	6
One bruing fate, a tonning fate and 3 ferkens, one kyllderkyn, 3 stabbynes		9	0
Two small Kevers, 4 bowles		2	0
All his bookes	1	0	0
3 Kyne, 2 steres, 4 bullokes	8	10	0
One Mare and a nagg	2	0	0
Thre score shepe and lambes	10	0	0
Ten hogges and pygges		15	0
A cartt and whyles	1	6	8
A wollen whyle and a lynnon whyle		1	2
One gander and two geese		2	0
A Cok and 6 henes		2	4
One square table and a chest		6	0
	41	18	8

Administration was granted on 30th May 1582 to Jane, the widow. The obligation was registered upon the said widow, upon Edward Risbridger of Albury, yeoman and John Parkhurst of Guildford, clothier, who bound themselves well and truly to administer the goods and chattells of the deceased. A note is added giving the ages of the 4 children Bartholomew 20, Henry 19, Jane 28 and Ann 15. Then follow the words, "to stand to the order for the children".

Note: The burial was recorded on 20th April 1582. Ref: 1582 Ad3

Katherine Brand **174**

of Ockley; taken by Richard Winkworth and David Smith, 4th December 1581.

	£	s	d
18 shepes	3	12	0
One Cow at Gorg Pars	1	0	0

One bed, a boilster, with 2 worne coverletes		13	4
6 peaces of brase with a gridioure		18	0
13 peaces of pewter		12	0
One cofor, with 2 peare of shetes, with other Linen		10	0
2 wollen garmetes, more than half worne	1	0	0
One Brase pot		2	0
Certaine Iron		1	0
A old chopping knife			2
A Tod of wolle		17	0
A old table		1	8
2 Kevers			8
An old coverlet		2	4
In money of Late Delivered to him by Agnes Sone	2	10	0
A silver Ring		1	6
A pint bottle of Lether			6
[*£12.2.2*]	11	18	2

On 3rd February 1581/2 John Parkhurst and Catherine Bennett, administrators, were sworn to the truth of the Inventory. John Parkhurst provided the Administration Bond.

Ref: 1581 Ad 8

Peter Buckland **175**

of Kingston-upon-Thames, waterman; taken by William Dowsat, Davy Glinne, William Warde and Adrian Johnson, 29th May 1582.

				£	s	d
In the hall						
A table with a frame and a plaine forme and wainescote about the hall and 2 old chaires					6	8
A Joined coubberte and an old coubberte					13	4
The painted clothes, a nolde cradle, 2 Joine stoles and 7 bowe potes, 2 pewter candlestickes, a basen and a yewer and 3 salt sellers					8	0
2 andirons, a fire shovell, a paire of tonges, a pote hanger and a paire of bellowes					2	6
	1	10	6			
In the chamber above the hall						
A Joined bedsted with a seler, a flocke bed and a fetherbed, a paire of blancketes, a coverlet of darnixe, 2 bolsters and 2 pillowes				1	6	8
A Joined trucklebedestede, a woll bed, a coverlet, a blancket, a bolster and a pillowe					6	8
Another truckle bedstede, a flocke bed, a bolster and a pillowe and a coverlete					?	0
A Joined cheste, a cradle, 2 cofers and a litle plaine chest					4	0
	2	2	4			
In the chameber over the buttrie						
A Joined bedsted with a flocke bed, a fether bed, a bolster and a blancket				1	0	0
A litle Joined table with a frame, 6 Joined stoles					5	0
2 chestes, a plaine forme with certaine lumber					6	0
His aparrell				4	0	0
14 paire of shetes and 3s 4d a pece				2	6	8
3 table cloathes, a dosen of napkines, 3 towels and 6 pilloweberes					10	0
	8	7	8			
In the Buttrie						
10 platters, 8 pewter dishes, 6 saucers, 2 quart potes, a potle pot, 2 wine potes, 3 pewter cuppes, 4 porringers, a peweter botle and a smale pece				1	0	0

A knedinge troufe, a boultinge houtche and 2 ale toubes, 3 trayes, 2 dosen of trenchers, a dosen of dishes, a dosen of pewter spones with other old lumber					6	8
	1	6	8			
In the kitchine						
4 brasepotes				1	0	0
A breweinge panne and a litle pan, 3 litle ketles, a posnet, 3 latten candlestickes, a paire of pote hookes and a skimmer					13	4
3 spittes, a grediron, a paire of cobirons, a trivet and a frienge pan					3	4
A ladder in the Entrie					1	0
2 kine				2	0	0
A sowe and a shoute					6	8
	4	4	4			
In the yeard for the woode						
For baven, billet and other wood				1	0	0
A rowe bardge and 2 wheries with theire furniture belonging to them				6	13	4
	7	13	4			
				25	4	10

Note: The Will was dated 21st May 1582. William Iron and William Smeton were appointed overseers. The testator's wife and his son Edward were residuary legatees. Edward was given all the lands and tenements in Surrey and Middlesex; he was ordered to pay the debts of £30 and the legacies of £3 apiece to all the testator's children except Peter. No other names were given, but they could claim their inheritance at the age of 21 or on their wedding day. The testator asked to be buried in Kingston churchyard near his father. Robert Paltocke, William Dowsat and John Joyce, were witnesses to the writing of the will.

Ref: 1582 B 13/1 Will 1582 B 13/2 Inventory

George Burt alias Loveland **176**

of Worplesdon, husbandman; taken by John Elsted, William Underwood and John Miles, 23rd May 1582.

In the Hall	£	s	d
The tabell, the trestels, the frome, 3 benches, a cowbert, a kned trowe, a powlderinge trowe, 2 benches, two shelves, a bedstedell and a cheste, all these standerdes in the house	1	0	0
On brasse poot, 2 Kettels, on panne, two possnats and a skimer		12	0
Five platers		5	0
Sixe pewter dishes		4	0
Eyght sawsers		2	4
2 saultes, 2 pottingers and a pote		2	0
4 Dossen of spones		2	6
2 Kanstickes and a morter		2	6
On flock bed, a bedstedle, a boulster and a Hellinge		15	0
2 chestes, 2 fromes, 2 trestels		4	0
On Holland sheet		6	8
2 pillowes		2	4
2 payer of Kanvas sheetes		8	0
2 paynted clothes and a bed tester		3	4
3 stobines		2	0
2 kevers and a butter churne		2	0
On spit, 2 drippinge pannes		1	0
12 Dishes, 3 wodden platters, 2 bouls and 2 buckets		3	0
On pothangers, on pothockes		1	0
A chaier and a ioyne stole		1	0

His Apparell		10	0
Redie money in His pursse		3	4
4 Kine and a bulche of a yeare ould	6	0	0
3 suckinge Kaves		10	0
2 mares, 2 coultes	3	10	0
3 piges		3	0
A cart and a payer of wheels		3	4
A gander and a gose		1	0
A cocke and 2 Henes		1	0
4 Duckes		1	4
	16	2	8
His Debts that he owed			
Unto Harry Ockly	1	6	8
Unto Robert Pursse th elder	1	0	0
Unto Thomas Ockly	1	0	0
Unto Thomas Chrismas the younger	1	0	0
Unto William Butcher		15	0
Unto Thomas Stovole		?	0
Unto Annes Loveland		17	0
Unto John Davye	1	0	0
Unto William Russell	10	7	0
	17	11	8

Note: The Will was dated 2nd May and proved on 30th May 1582. The testator asked to be buried in the churchyard of Worplesdon and he left everything to his wife Joan, appointing her executrix and instructing her to bring up his children and to pay his debts. He gave 3s 4d each to his overseers, Robert Pursse the elder and Harry Ockley, yeoman. They witnessed the Will together with John Elsted. In the parish register the burial was recorded on 5th May 1581, but this must have been an error as the date on the Will was written in words.

Ref: 1582 B 15/1 Will 1582 B 15/2 Inventory

Richard and Margaret Clifton **177**

of Worplesdon; taken by William Clifton, John Miels, Thomas Stovoll, John Plonker and Thomas Farlie, 13th January 1581/2.

In the Hall				£	s	d
The table, the trestles, the forme, the Chaier and stolle					1	0
The Cowbert and the Cradell					5	6
On brasse poot, 4 Kettels, 1 possnat, a friynge panne					16	0
The Dishes and the trenchers						2
A gret and three pootes						6
A gridiron, A fier showelle and the poot hangers					1	8
	£1	4	10			
In the bed chamber						
The pewter					15	3
2 Kanstickes, on Morter					2	0
His Aparell					13	4
Her Aparell					16	0
The sheetes and the Aporne				1	16	8
Two Hattes					2	6
On flock bed, a matteris, a boulster, A pillow, 2 Blanketes, on Koverlet				1	4	4
[£5.10.1]	£5	9	1			
In the chees Lofte						
A bedstedle, a flock bed and a Koverlet					6	8
3 seckels and Kandelrusses						4

The cheese					7	6
On Harrow and on spitter					3	0
A mathock, a bettell and 2 weyges					2	0
		19	6			
In the malt lofte						
7 bushels of malt					8	9
12 bushels of Dredge					12	0
4 busheles of Otes					2	8
3 peckes of Bennes					1	4
4 Koffers					8	0
Two galones of gresse					2	0
Three hoges of Bakon and a halfe				1	0	0
The Powltery					4	6
An Axe and a Bill					1	0
Other Lomber About the House					10	0
The Bees					5	0
	3	15	3			
The Corne and the Cattell						
12 Bussheles of Wheat				1	8	0
4 Kinne				5	6	8
2 Hoges					7	6
Two Ackers of wheat upon the ground				1	8	0
3 geese					1	6
A mare and A coult				1	1	0
A cart and the wheeles					5	0
	9	17	8			
In Redie money				4	0	0
[*£25.7.4*]	26	6	4			

At court on 19th January 1581/2 administration of the goods and chattels was granted to John Clifton, brother of the deceased and Jane Chrismas, sister of the widow of the deceased. The estate was to be used for Jane Clifton, daughter of the aforesaid Richard and Margaret, deceased, on the direction of John Cutler, Rector of Worplesdon. Three men of Worplesdon, Christopher Clifton, husbandman, Thomas Chrismas, weaver and Robert Purse, tailor, bound themselves to see the administration well and truly carried out.

Note: Richard Clifton was buried on 26th December 1581 and Margaret on 11th January 1581/2.

Ref: 1581 Ad 11

Lawrence Elliott **178**

of West Clandon, husbandman; taken by Edward Symond, John Butt of West Clandon and William Butler of Send, yeoman, 23rd May 1582.

	£	s	d
In readye money in his purse		5	0
His Apparrell		10	0
A table and a fourme			6
2 flock beddes, 2 bolsters, one pillowe, 2 Coverletes, 4 paire of sheetes, one table Clothe	1	6	8
2 bedstedles		1	0
2 Chestes		1	0
2 small brass pottes and a brasse posnet		5	0
2 kettles, 2 panns		8	0
3 platters, 3 pewter dishes, 2 sawcers and one salt seller		3	4
2 latten Candlestickes			4

A paire of Pothangers, a paire of pothookes, a tryvet, a gred Iron, a litle spitt		2	0
The bakon in the Roofe		15	0
One ax, a bill, a spynnyng wheele, 3 boulls, 6 treen dishes, 6 spones, 6 trenchers, 3 tubs, 2 bucketes and a butter Cherne		3	8
8 bushells of barlye malte and 8 bushels of Dredge malt	1	0	0
2 acres of wheate	1	6	8
An acre of barlye		10	0
One acre of tares		5	0
5 Keene	6	5	0
One heiffer and one bullock of the age of one yere	1	6	8
One mare		16	0
5 Ewes, 5 lambs	1	0	0
4 shootes of the age of halfe an yere		?	0
4 Wayned pigges		4	0
One Cock and 6 henns		2	6
	17	5	4

Note: The Will was dated 20th April and proved on 30th May 1582. The residuary legatee and executrix was the testator's wife Joan. He asked to be buried in West Clandon churchyard and he gave 3s each to his overseers Thomas Butt and John Astreate of that parish, yeomen. He gave 20 nobles (£6 13s 4d) to his mother Julian, together with her flock bed and a red cow with a white back. A shilling was left to each of his godchildren and 10s to his sister Amye. His sister Mawde's son Richard Taplyn was given a cow and his brother Thomas Elliott, an old fallow cow. Witnesses to the Will were the overseers and Richard Fenne, William Marten and the writer Peter Churchar. The burial of Laurence Elliot was recorded on 22nd April 1582.

Ref: 1582 B 29/1 Will   1582 B 29/2 Inventory

Richard Exold **179**

of Frimley in Ash, husbandman; taken by Rychard Sawyer, Thomas Cortnys and Robert Gunner, 15th March 1582.

	£	s	d
In the hawle			
A Rownde Table, Two cobberdes		6	8
In the chamber			
One fflocke bedd, a bedsteed, a Coverlet, 2 bolsters and one paire of Canvas shettes		10	0
4 Chestes		4	0
Woll 8 pounds		5	0
Three smale brasse pottes, a possnett, 2 kettelles		16	0
5 platters, 4 pewter dysshes, 2 porridge dysshes, 3 Sawcers, 6 sponys and a salte seller		7	0
4 smale Candellstyckes, 2 ffryeng pennys, 2 broches, a Tryvett, a paire of pott hookes and a pott hangers		3	10
A bill, 2 Axes, 2 wedges, 3 Awgers with other workinge Toolys		4	0
Tobbis, bowles, with other Lomber		5	0
2 hennys			8
20 shepe	3	6	8
A mare	1	0	0
A hogge		2	0
A sythe		1	8
6 stawles of bees	1	0	0
3 Kyne and a heckfor	4	0	0
	12	12	6

Note: The Will was written on 18th November 1580. The overseers Edmond Benbryck and John Tornor were given 12d each for their duties. A sum of 4d was left to the poor men's box of Frimley and the testator asked to be buried in the churchyard of Ash. The residuary legatee and sole executrix was his wife Alyce. Their 4 children, John, Matthew, Henry and Agnes, were given livestock in the shape of bullocks and ewes and an equal share of the hives standing at Peperharow with those of John Jackman. The 3 eldest children were also to be given a brass pot when they reached the age of 21. The overseers and Anthony Stevyns made their marks when they witnessed the will. By the time probate was granted on 19th September 1582, the widow had moved to Farnborough. She and Edmund Benbrick of Frimley, gent., put up the Administration Bond.

Ref: 1582 B 30/1 Will 1582 B 20/2 Inventory

William Hampton, the elder **180**

of Seale; taken by William Harryson, John Budd, John Grove, constable of the hundred of Farnham and Edward Cranlye, 16th April 1582.

In the Hall	£	s	d
A table, a fourme, a payre of tressells		1	4
A bedd, a payre of blankettes, a bolster, a coverlett		10	0
Naperye		?	0
Thre old chestes		1	8
His apparrell		13	4
In his purse		10	0
His brasse		13	4
6 peices of peuter		5	0
A chaire with other implementes		2	0
2 flitches of bakonn		3	4
7 bushells of Rye		14	0
4 bushells of smalle woates		2	0
Old cartes, plowe and 2 harrowes, a bill, an axe with other ire geare belonginge to the plowe	1	0	0
6 hennes and a cocke		2	0
3 maeres and a colte	3	0	0
3 steares	3	0	0
6 kine	6	0	0
4 bullockes	2	0	0
6 hogges	1	0	0
6 acres of Rye and 7 acres of smale woates and acre of pease and tares	4	0	0
7 scoare of sheepe	25	0	0
[*£49.3.0*]	47	13	0

Note: The Will was written on 5th May 1567, while the testator was "walking and of good remembrance". He had already given lands and goods to his family during his lifetime, but he added instructions and minor bequests in this testament. The Will was proved on 25th April 1582 and the testator's wife Joan was made residuary legatee and executrix. A sum of 5s each was left to the overseers Robert Warner and Thomas Billinghurst. William asked to be buried in the church or churchyard of Seale and he gave 1s to the repair of the church, a sheep towards the needs of the poor and suitable refreshment for those of them who came to pray at his funeral. Beneficiaries included a daughter Agnes Waters, a son Richard Hampton, a daughter-in-law Agnes and William Hampton, her son. Also included were Alice and Ellen, Richard's daughters. A special bequest of £1 annual rent and any arrears due on some of his property, were to go to the aforesaid Agnes and William Hampton. There were 6 witnesses as well as the 2 overseers. John and George Austen, Robert Worsley, Hugh Tew and John Northall, signed their names. William Farley and the overseers made marks. The Administration Bond was provided by James and George Martyn. The burial was registered on 13th April 1582.

Ref: 1582 B 41/1 Will 1582 B 42/2 Inventory

Charles Holman **181**

of Walton-on-the-Hill, weaver. [*no appraisers given and undated*]

	£	s	d
One bed		5	0
Two coverleds		5	0
One blancat		3	0
One pillo and a boulster		3	0
Fife payre of shetes		10	0
Thre shertes		3	0
Sixe napkinges		2	0
Eyght cherchers		4	0
Foure hancherchers		16	0
Foure schests		5	4
Two platters		1	0
Foure pewter disshes		1	4
Two saltsillers			4
One candlestick			4
Thre payre of breches		5	0
Two doublets		3	0
Thre gerkinges		3	0
For lomes		13	4
One cubard		3	0
One bedsteddle			6
Sixe pounde 10 shillings which was left in Michills Hawards handes	6	10	0
	[*10*	*17*	*2*]

Note: The undated Will was proved on 29th May 1582. The residuary legatee and executrix was Anne Kempsoll, the testator's sister. Her three daughters, Anne, Mary and Briget, were to have £4, £1 and £1, respectively, to be recovered from the hands of Michael Hayward of Woldingham. Richard Kempsoll, also of Woldingham, was left the looms and tackle there. The testator had 3 other sisters, Mylesent, Alice and Dorothy, who were to have an equal share of his money left in his father's hands and the first 2 were also to have a pair of sheets. He asked to be buried in Walton churchyard and left a small bequest of 3s to William Matthew and another of 10s to his sister Anne, the executrix. The 4 witnesses were Thomas and Agnes Jutherye, Agnes Gardyner and William Mathewe. No overseers were mentioned. Charles Holman's burial is recorded as having taken place on 18th March 1582.

Ref: 1582 B 48/1 Will 1582 B 48/2 Inventory

William Luffe **182**

of Frensham, yeoman; taken by Martine Mannte, John Boxsoulle and William Prisone. [*undated*]

	£	s	d
His Aparell	2	0	0
3 beedes and all that belongeth ther unto	2	6	8
4 Tabell Clothes		4	0
The putter		13	4
3 brase potes, one Catherne, 3 kittells	2	0	0
3 Candelstikes, 3 Salters, a tin bottell, A doessene of spondes		3	0
4 stone Cupes			6
One doesune and a haufe of trine desses and A ladell and to doesene Trenshers			6
The Troues, toubes, chespres		10	0

One chiste 3 Covers		3	0
2 Cobordes		6	8
The Tabell, furmes and stoules		1	8
One pot hannger, pote hankes, Angers, a Trifte, a girdere, brogges		10	0
The axes, billes, shovelles		2	0
The nagers Wages and all the olde Iergere		?	0
One Wagon, one Weane, one ploughe and all that belongeth ther unto it	3	0	0
4 oxene, one stere	6	6	8
One gildinge, 3 mares, one coulte	3	13	8
6 Kine, A boule	7	3	4
6 boullokes	3	1	8
3 Waned Caves		10	0
8 skore and 8 shepe	28	0	0
26 lames	2	12	0
For swine	1	0	0
For bakene		?	0
The corne in the baren		18	0
The Corene in the feelde	2	6	8
For the Lente tilige	5	5	0
To quarters of dreages maulte	1	0	2
The sithis		4	0
For bees		2	6
One While and one paer of spinninge Cardes		1	0
One Rode sadell, one bridell, one old pannell		4	0
One Water carte, one dounge pote		1	0
One Coke, hinnes and doukes		2	0
[£75.3.0]	75	2	0

Note: When the Will was written on 25th April 1582, a wife and 7 children were named as beneficiaries. A sum of 1s was to be given to the poor men's box in Frensham church and 2s apiece was to be paid to the overseers Martin Mannt of Frensham and John Boxall of Elstead. Margaret, the wife and executrix, was to have the residue of the estate after every godchild had been given 1s. None of the children had yet reached the age of 21 years, when they were to receive a legacy of £8 each. At their father's decease they were to be given a ewe. The eldest son was to have 6 sheep and specific chattels, which were to remain in the house. The order in which the children were mentioned was as follows: John the eldest, Joan, William, Edward, Thomas, John the younger and Richard. Bartholemew Harding and William Greene acted as witnesses. The date of probate, 30th May 1582, was written on one of two copies of the Will bearing the memorandum "this will was soe defaced by reason of rayne being Carried from Guilford to Winchester from the visitation the xxxith of May 1582 in a Cloke bagge". The widow and Martin Mannte, also of Frensham, husbandman, bound themselves well and truly to administer the estate.

Ref: 1582 B 61/1 & 2 Will 1582 B 61/3 Inventory

Christopher Mellershe **183**

of Bramley in Shalford, yeoman; taken by Davye Warner, Robert Smyther and John Harper, 15th May 1582.

In the Hall	£	s	d
One Cubborde, one tabell standinge uppon a frame, one forme and a Chayer	1	6	8
Two pothangers, one andyron and a payre of Pothookes		3	4
In the parlour			
One fether Bedd, one flock Bedd, one Bedstedell, two Coverlettes, one			

blanckett, one fether bolster and two fether pillowes	4	0	0
One Table standinge uppon a frame, a Carpett and one forme		13	4
Two Chayers, two Joyne stooles and 6 Cusshens		6	8
In the parlour Lofte			
One fflock Bedd, one Joyne bedstedell, two Coverletes, three B[*l*]ankettes, two fether bolsters and two fether Pillowes	2	13	4
In the lofte without the parlour lofte			
One flockbedd, one bedstedell, one Coverlett, two blanckettes and one bolster		13	4
In the lofte over the buttrye			
One fether bedd, one bedstedell, one Coverlett, one blanckett and one bolster	1	10	0
A Table, one forme, two Chestes and the paynted Clothes		14	0
In the porche lofte			
One Joyned bedstedell, two Chestes and the paynted Clothes		14	0
In the Maydens Chamber			
One flock bedd, two bedstedelles, one Coverlete, two blanckettes, one bolster and three olde Chestes		16	0
8 payre of Canvas sheetes, three paire of Lokoram sheetes, one Hollande sheete, 3 table Clothes, 6 table Napkyns and two pillowebers	3	10	0
His apparell and money in his purse	3	0	0
In the ynner parlour			
One Joyned bedstedell, one foldinge table and two formes		16	8
In the kytchin			
All the brasse	3	6	8
4 spittes, one drippinge pan, one fryinge pan and one gridyron		13	4
All the pewter and lattyn	3	0	0
One powdringe trowe, one knede trowe, one boultinge hutche with Vates, bruynge vesselles, milke vesselles and all other woodden vesselles	2	0	0
Bylles, axes, sythes, Augers, spitters, bytle and wedges		16	0
Bakon, beef and Cheese	1	10	0
Rye and Maulte	3	0	0
Saddelles, Bridelles and bootes	1	0	0
Spynninge Wheeles and Cardes		5	0
A longe Bowe and a sheaf of Arrowes, a forrest Bill, a skull, a Cappe, a sworde and a Dagger		13	0
One plough, one Weane, two payre of wheeles with Yokes and Chaynes, Dongpottes, Ropes and harrowes with other ymplementes	3	0	0
4 sylver spoones	1	1	0
Shepe and lambes	18	0	0
Oxen and Steeres	28	0	0
9 Kene and a Bull	14	0	0
Bullockes	7	0	0
Wannyers	1	13	4
Horse beastes	6	13	4
Hogges	2	0	0
Poultry and geese		6	8
Rye and Wheate in the feildes	12	0	0
Otes and tares in the felde	10	0	0
The Soyle in the gate	1	0	0

[£141.15.8]	136	13	0

Note: The long Will was written on 16th November 1576 and proved on 30th May 1582. There was property in 7 parishes bequeathed by the testator to his wife Margaret, the executrix, as long as she remained a widow and to their 4 children, Thomas, John, Mary and Johane. His wish to be buried in the churchyard of Shalford carried with it a bequest of 3s 4d each to the poor men's boxes of Bramley and Shalford, together with a gift of 10 dozen of bread, 2 barrels of beer and sufficient cheese, to be given to the poor people at his burial. His dwellings in 1576 in the parishes of Bramley, Shalford and Dunsfold had barns, stables, gardens, orchards, lands, meadows, feedings and hereditaments. Named properties were Bedells in Bramley, Barates in Worplesdon, Blackhedge in Stoke, Skottesland in Shalford, as well as lands in Burpham. He had had in fee ferme 3 closes of John Durgate in Wonersh and also Edmunds, Rushetts and Babbs, in fee ferme of John Wintershall Esquire in Dunsfold. He left £30 each to his daughters. Household items were left to his sons, with the proviso that some were to be recognised as standards (i.e. fixtures) of the house, not to be removed. The 3 overseers were, a cousin George Austen, Robert Smyther and Thomas Chaundler, his son-in-law. They were to be arbiters should there arise any ambiguity, doubt, or question, within the next 4 years. The first 4 of the 6 witnesses made their marks, the other 2 signed their names. They were Robert Skydman, Robert and Thomas Smyther, John Gretest, Wyllem Hewett and Thomas Marlett. A bond of £4 was recorded as having been paid by Margaret, the widow and Thomas Chaundler of Shalford, yeoman, as security for the true administration of the estate. The burial was registered on 4th May 1582.

Ref: 1582 B 62/1 Will 1582 B 62/2 Inventory

John Russell, the eldest **184**

of Worplesdon, yeoman; taken by Richard Crosse, William Undrewoods, Thomas Coxe, Richard Standbridge, Thomas Stovall, Thomas Giles, Thomas Christmas, Thomas Boylett and William Clyfton, 7th May 1582.

	£	s	d
In the hall			
One table, a frame and 2 Joyned foremes		6	8
One olde coobboard and cooberd cloathe		1	4
A paynted cloathe		2	0
In the chambre			
A bedstedell, a testerne over it, A fether bedd, a bolster, the hanginges, A blanckett, A healinge and straw bedd undre the fetherbedd	1	4	0
2 chesteis, A presse, A chayere and a joyned forome		6	8
In the chambre behynd the hall			
The woorste fetherbedd, A beddstedell, a helinge, a blanckett, a bolster and a pillowe with the testerne over the bedd		13	4
A greate cheste, A roound table and one Joyned stoole		5	0
A Lytell bedd and all the furnyture belonging to it withe a paynted cloathe		2	0
A boultinge whitche			6
A Wynywinge sheete		2	0
His wearing Apparell, 2 coates, A cloke, 3 paire of bricheis, A letheren chircken, 2 dooblettes, 2 paire of lower stockinges, A hatt, A cappe, A gyrdell and powche, and 2 paire of shooes	1	10	0
A payere of Booates		2	6
In the garrett lofte			
2 old chestes, 4 earthen pottes and old yrone		3	4
5 bowles, 2 stobyns, 2 buckettes, A Steane and a table		4	0
2 Letheren bottells and 3 earthen pottes		1	4

In the Kittchin			
3 trowghes with lyddes		3	4
One old table, 3 tubbes and a busshell		2	0
An oste heire		2	0
A Sadell, Stirropps and gyrthes belonging to it, A pannell and bryedell		5	0
In the kittchin loft			
One chest and a yrone rake		1	0
3 Sawes, one Awger, a post axe, a pike axe, Drawinge knyffe and a wymbell		2	6
One hogge of Bakone hanging in the Kyttchin		5	0
One Troughe with a lydd standing abroade		1	0
4 paiere of sheetes, 2 table cloathes and 3 shirttes	1	1	0
A Bowe and Arrowes		2	0
A Woodd knyffe, A hanger, a buckeller, A howbard, A byll and a raven bill		4	0
2 olde Axles, a bill and a hattchett		1	6
2 Brassepottes, 2 Kettells, A panne, A skillett and a fryinge panne	1	0	0
7 pewter platters, A pewter disshe, A sawcer, 2 saltsellers, a chaffing disshe and 3 candlestickes		10	0
2 podingers, 2 brochies, 2 cobbyrones, A paiere of tongs and A dripping panne		5	0
2 Sackes		1	4
5 busshells of Rie and half a busshell of wheate in the howse		13	0
A Scoope and a Shoovell			8
A carte and wheeles, oxeharrow and ploughe, 3 hange yokes, 2 chaynes, a paiere of stropps, 2 pronges, a donge spytt, and a crow Leaver		17	8
4 payere of Harneyes, 2 Letheren collers, A flaggen coller, A trussing rope, 2 carte ropes, 2 letheren halters, 3 hempen halters, A paiere of Hames and a corde		12	0
A donge pott, a paiere of wheeles and the extree belonging to it, a donge Rake, A gryndstone, the spyndell and the trowghe belonging to it		6	8
One Oxe, 3 Kyne, A stiere of three yere old, A heickfer of three yere old, two heyfers of two yere old, A bull of two yere old, Two heifers of a yere old, A bull of a yere old and a waynyer of this yere	10	5	8
7 hogges and two pigges	1	6	0
20 loades of Donge		?	0
5 henns and a cocke		2	0
6 Loades of woodd in the meade, 3 loads of Billett in Crabb Wattmans A loade of great woodd in the gate and in crabb watmans, and a loade of woodd of Billett a hundred and a half without at the gate		19	10
3 Ladders		2	2
A hande barrow, a whele barrow and a busshe sythe		1	8
One graye Mare	1	0	0
One baye Nagge		10	0
In the Woorthe			
One Acre of Rye, an Acre and a halff of barlye and 3 quarter of a Acre of otes	1	10	0

3 Acres of pease in Suckcrofte and an Acre of pease in Shelvinge	1	8	0
In the Orchard			
One quarter of An Acre of Barly		3	0
4 Acres of Wheate	3	6	0
Of Beanes in the field		3	0
7 Lambes		15	0
	33	18	8

[*Written on the Will*:] Dettes that I do owe by specialties and without specialteys

To Thomas Yeade of Gwilford	15	0	0
To Mr Shawe of Gwilford	12	0	
I owe to Anthony Burroll, my cosen	5	0	0
To Thomas Russell of Burpham		6	4
I owe to John Russell my sonne in Lawe	1	6	8
To Valentine Cooke my man I do owe in the whole	5	2	4
	[*27*	*7*	*4*]

Note: The Will was dated 24th April and proved on 30th May 1582. The testator's wife Joan and his son John the younger, were residuary legatees, executors and beneficiaries of the gift of 12 acres of arable and meadow land for the ensuing 20 years. The testator calculated that the income from Sowthcrofte 4 acres, an adjoining meadow of 3 acres, Shelffeild 2 acres and Sowcrofte 3 acres, should pay his debts over the years. He asked to be buried in Worplesdon churchyard and he gave 6d to the poor and 4d towards the repair of the church. His daughter Jane Russell was given his cow called Jentill. His maid Elizabeth was given a white-faced heifer. His godchildren were each to have 1s and his son John the elder was to have his apparel, a cow and an old feather bed, when Joan should die. Sums of 3s 4d were left to his overseers, his brother William Russell and his cousin Robert Russell of Pirbright. Hugh Phillipp wrote the Will, which was witnessed by Wylliam Smythe, Richard Standbridge, Thomas Christmas the younger and Thomas Giles. Each executor was joined by 2 men when the Administration Bond was registered: John the younger was supported by Thomas Coxe and John Russell the elder, husbandmen; and the widow by Thomas Collens and William Underwood, husbandmen, all of Worplesdon. The burial was recorded on 25th April 1582.

Ref: 1582 B 76/1 Will 1582 B 76/2 Inventory

John Shaddatt als. Sherratt, senior **185**

of Woking; taken by Wylliam Shaddat, Anthony Garman and John Atwood the elder, 3rd May 1581.

	£	s	d
In Redie mone In his pursse			6
The aparell of his boddie		10	0
A Joyned table and a forme		5	0
A cubbord In the haull		5	0
Two flock bedes with theyr aparell		10	0
Fyve payer of sheyttes		13	4
Four playne bed stedylls		4	0
Thre chestes		6	8
A Round table, a cheyre and stolles		2	0
In brasse	1	0	0
In peuter		10	0
A chaffyng dyshe and fyve candylstyckes		3	0
A pothangar, pothoukes, cobyarns, trevettes and tonges		6	0
Tubbs, bouls, payll and butter chern		10	0
Chese presse and chese moattes		1	0
Shpynnyng wele and cardes		1	0

Spones and trenchers			4
Bakon In the house	1	5	0
In chesses		6	8
Half a quarter Rye		8	0
In oatmalt		7	0
Smale oates		1	0
Rye In the feylld	3	6	8
Oates In the feyld	1	0	0
Four workyng bullockes	5	6	8
Thre kene	3	0	0
Four bullockes	1	6	8
One ould toude		3	4
8 yeows and 8 lams	2	0	0
26 drye sheype	2	8	0
One sow and two shootes		6	8
A goose, a gander and gooles		2	0
Two henns and a cocke		1	0
An axe, byll, a shovell, a bettell and foure wedges		3	4
Two sackes and a bagg		2	0
Cart, dungcart, plow, harrows, yoakes, reapes, roapes, harnes and a ladder	2	10	0
In watter wood		10	0
	30	1	10

Note: The Will was dated 19th February and proved on 30th May 1582. The testator's son William was the residuary legatee and executor, who was to have the house and land after one year, meantime settling and calling in any debts. John asked to be buried in Woking churchyard. He made gifts of 6s 8d to his overseers, William Royden of Pyrford, gentleman and John Atwood the younger of Woking. The same sum was given to his son-in-law John Beckynfield, to his daughter's son John Russell and to his own son Gilbert Sherrett who owed him £6 13s 4d. This debt was to be reduced to £5 and discharged in full if that sum could be paid within a year. John and Robert Inwood, the sons of another daughter, were each given 3s 4d. The witnesses were John Watts, John Waterer and John Atwood the elder. The executor of Woking, husbandman and Christopher Taylor of Guildford, shearman, bound themselves well and truly to administer the estate. The spelling of the surname varies in the 2 documents, but in the Surrey musters it is consistent for Gilbert, John and William Sherrett; Shaddatt does not appear, nor does it in the lay subsidies of that time.

Ref: 1582 B 78/1 Will 1582 B 78/2 Inventory

William Stint **186**

of West Horsley; taken by Henry Whelere, John Hamshere and Nycholas Fenne. [*undated*]

	£	s	d
The hall			
A table, a forme, 3 Joynestolles, a chayre, a paynted cloth		3	0
Parler			
An oulde Fetherbed, a boulster, 4 pillowes, a coverlete	1	0	0
A bedstedle, 2 chests, a rounde table		3	4
Chamber			
An oulde Fetherbed, a boulster, 4 pillowes, 2 blanketes and a coverlett	1	0	0
In the lofte			
2 oulde Flockbedes, 2 boulsters, 2 pillowes, 2 blanketes, 3 coveringes, 4 chestes, 2 painted clothes, 8 payre of shetes, 3 littell table clothes	1	17	0
His apperrell	1	0	0

and in his purse		2	6
Chiching			
8 pewtere platters, 3 pewter dishes, 4 saseres, one dosen of spones, 3 saltsellers, 4 canddellstickes, 2 braspotes, 2 chaffingdyshes, 8 kettells, a panne, 2 spittes, a frying pan, a grediron, 2 trevates, 2 cobirons, 2 pothangers, a payre of pothookes, an over peelle	2	1	8
In the boulting house			
A bill, an axe, 2 wedges		1	4
A maltinge fatte, a knedinge trowe, a boulting huche, a boshell and certayne alle vessells with other lombere		6	8
An ost hare, 2 sakes		2	6
The frute		?	0
5 hennes and a cooke		2	0
The corne in the barne	6	13	4
3 Keene	3	0	0
3 bollockes, 2 small toudes and a coult	2	0	0
40 sheepe	5	10	0
6 hoges and 4 piges	1	0	0
For beese		5	0
A carte with bare whelles and a harowe		6	8
A sithe, 2 pronges, a dounge spude and a shovell		2	0
[*£27.2.0*]	26	17	0

Note: The Will was dated 18th October 1581 and proved on 30th May 1582. The residuary legatees and executors were the testator's wife Alice and his son Abell, both of whom were given 2 beds and bedding. Sums of 2s were given to the overseers John Hamshere and Edward Goddard. His godchildren were given 4d, the poor men's box 6d, Thomas Crouncher 6s 8d and a ewe, Rowland Stint £1 and William's daughter Ann £2. A ewe was also given to Elizabeth and Jasper Connyerste, Joan Lampone and Joan Saddler. Grain, mainly barley, was given to Rowland Stint, to his daughter Elizabeth Cleere and to his son Robert Stint. Lambs went to the Cleere children, to Chelsame's child and to Edward Goddard's children John and Tamsin. Robert's 2 sons were to share a stall of bees and Alice was to retain her 6 pieces of pewter and the salt she had brought to the marriage. Jasper Fulke, Alexander Stint and the overseers, witnessed the Will. The executor of West Horsley, carpenter and Edward Goddard of the same parish, husbandman, bound themselves well and truly to administer the estate.

Ref: 1582 B 81/1 Will 1582 B 81/2 Inventory

1583

Mathewe Byshopp **187**

of Leigh; taken by John Constable of Newdigate, John Bysshop of Charlwood, Edmunde Chesmunde and Richard Rowlie of Leigh, 14th May 1583.

	£	s	d
In the feildes			
6 Kine and heickfers	6	0	0
2 little Bullockes		13	4
One mare and one Colt	1	0	0
12 sheep and 3 Lambs	2	6	0
One Sowe and 2 shootes		8	0
One Acre and a halfe of wheat	1	0	0
3 Acres of otes	1	0	0
In the house			
In the Hall			
4 platters, 4 pewter dishes, 3 sawcers, 4 saltsellers			

and 2 Candlestickes		10	0
One Brass pott, 4 Kettles, one possnet and one skillet		10	0
One Cubbord, one table, one forme and 2 Chayres		8	0
Tubes and other Lumber		3	4
2 Axes, one Bill and one hatchet		2	6
In the Chamber			
One fetherbed and one flockbed with 2 Coverletes, 2 Blankettes, 2 Bowlsters and 2 Pillowes	1	0	0
3 Chestes		4	0
6 paire of Shetes and 2 table Clothes		13	4
His wearing aparrell		10	0
Purse, girdle and monie		6	0
	16	14	6

Note: Probate was granted on 15th May 1583. The nuncupative Will was signed with a mark by John Constable and John Bysshoppe. Mathew appointed his wife Elizabeth and his son Richard to be executors. He gave £4 each to his sons William and Mathew and £5 to his daughter Joan. One of the executors Richard Bysshop, husbandman and Oliver Cheseman, tanner, both of Leigh, bound themselves well and truly to administer the estate.

Ref: 1583 B 11/1 Will   1583 B 11/2 Inventory

Thomas Drewe **188**

of Chertsey; taken by John Tymmerton, Humfrey Drewe and Raphe Badger, 9th May 1583.

	£	s	d
A Bible		6	8
5 Kine, 1 bullocke of A yere old, A herfer, A mare and A colte	7	0	0
9 sheepe and 2 lambes	1	6	0
5 swyne		12	0
gesse and other pultrey		3	4
2 Acres of Rye		16	0
A fether bede and A mattresse		15	0
A coveringe, 2 blanckete, 2 Bolsters, 2 pillowes and 2 pillowe beares		13	0
6 paire of shettes and 2 table clothes	1	0	0
3 Borded bedstedes		3	0
3 chestes		4	0
A table boord, A forme and 2 chayers		3	0
A littell myll to grinde Mault		12	0
4 Brasse pottes, 4 Kettells, A grydyern, 2 fryenge panes, 1 spytte, A payre of cobyorns, a paire of tonges, A trifte, A chafinge dishe, 3 lattin candelstickes and a chaform	1	11	0
2 dossen of pewter dishes and platters, 4 sawsers, 4 pewter pottes, 2 pewter saltes	1	1	0
All the pay[n]ted clothes aboute the house		4	0
Wodden vessells and all other Stuffe and Implementes whatsoever not before spoken except his Apparell		10	0
His wearinge Apparrell		13	0
	17	13	0

The Inventory was presented by Katherine Drewe of Chertsey, the widow and relict of the deceased, on 15th May 1583. She, Thomas Hamly, clerk and Roger Watts, blacksmith, bound themselves well and truly to administer the estate. Ref: 1583 Ad 18

Richard Hiller **189**

of Albury, husbandman; taken by William Ticknor and John Astone, 15th May 1583.

	£	s	d
Money in his purse			3
His apparrell		6	8
One Simple Bed		6	8
His brasse and pewter and other smale ymplementes		10	0
One Cowe		18	0
3 shepe		6	8
Debttes to him owinge	1	10	0
	3	18	3

The inventory was presented by Agnes Hiller, the widow and relict of the deceased, who begged leave to administer the estate. She and Thomas Aborn of Albury, yeoman, bound themselves well and truly to administer the goods and chattells of her late husband. The same date was given as that at the top of the document. Ref: 1583 Ad 35

Thomas Ladd **190**

of Buckland; taken by William Stanton, John Lawrence and Thomas Whittlie, 26th April 1583.

Corne growing on the grounde	£	s	d
Three Acres of wheate growinge upon the grounde	1	16	0
One Acre of otes and a halfe growing upon the ground		8	0
4 Bushells of pease in the howse and teares		6	0
4 Bushells of wheate		9	4
4 bushells of Rie		7	4
A quarter of Barley Mault		12	0
4 Busshells of otes		2	8
3 Kine and one Calfe	3	6	4
4 small Bullockes	1	12	0
A mare and a Colte	1	6	8
16 Ewes and 16 Lambes	3	10	0
6 wheather Sheepe	1	0	0
5 small hogges		10	0
A goose and a gannder and 6 young goslinges		1	2
4 henns		1	4
One fetherbed and all the furniture therunto belonginge	1	10	0
One flockbedd and all the furniture therunto belonginge		10	0
A plaine Bedsteed		1	0
6 paire of sheetes	1	4	0
2 table Clothes and 4 napkinns		5	0
3 Chestes		5	0
A plaine Cubbord		5	0
All the wooden vessell		6	8
2 wheeles and 6 Traies		3	0
3 sikles and one pease hooke			8
One Brass pott, a Cawderane, 2 Kittles and one posnett		14	0
One Long spitt, a Trifft, a Cobborne, a paire of Potthangers and Pothoockes and a Dripping pann		5	0
A Dossen of peuter vessell		6	8
A Lattin Chafin Dish and Lattin Candlestickes		1	2
2 Salt sellers and a dozen of sponnes and one porrenger		1	0
A frying panne and a grediorne			10

3 Drincking pottes			3
A dozen of Trenchers and 6 Dishes			3
A Kneding Troffe and a Chees press		3	4
A Harrow		2	0
A Dounge Carte and a paier of ould wheeles		2	0
One paile			4
The painted Clothes in the house		2	0
2 sackes		1	8
All his working Tooles		2	6
A Certaine Lease of an acre of Lande	3	0	0
All his apparrell	1	0	0
A paire of Bellowse			3
In redie monie		5	0
His purse and girdle			4
A grindstone, a shale, a sive and a spitter		1	4
	[*26*	*10*	*1*]

Note: The Will was dated 14th April and proved on 14th May 1583. The residuary legatee and executrix was the testator's wife Elizabeth. A sum of 5s each was left to the overseers William Hall of Banstead and John Roffey. Thomas asked to be buried in the churchyard of Buckland, where he gave 3s 4d to the poor and to the repair of the church. Sums of £5 each were bequeathed to his daughters Catherine, Marie and Anne, each to be her sister's heir if any were to die before reaching her day of inheritance, her 21st birthday. The witnesses were the overseers together with Mr Edward Dalender, Mr Charles Dalender, Rafe Burges and others unnamed. The widow and William Hall of Banstead, yeoman, bound themselves well and truly to administer the estate. Thomas Ladd was buried at Buckland on 15th April 1583.

Ref: 1583 B 50/1 Will 1583 B 50/2 Inventory

Agnes Newdegate **191**

of Newdigate, widow; taken by Henrye Staunton, Wylliam Dibble and John Terrey, with others, 21st May 1583.

Cattall	£	s	d
Syxe Kyne	9	0	0
One Wainiyer		8	0
One geldynge	3	0	0
One saddle, a pyllyon, a sadleclothe with brydelles and gyrttes		10	0
2 hogges with powltrye		12	0
in the Chamber over the new parler			
3 fether bedes, one flock bed with coverletes, blancketes, bolsters and pyllowes and one bedstedle with sylke Curteyns and sylke tester	8	0	0
2 Chestes, one Chayre, 2 Cussyons and a Joyned stole and the lynnen in the lyttle Cheste	2	13	4
in an other Chamber within the same Chamber before			
One fetherbed, one flockebed with coverletes, blanckettes, bolsters and pyllowes, a bedstedle, one Cheste and one stole	2	13	4
in the Chamber over the olde parler			
One bedstedle, 2 fether beddes, one quylt with coverynge, blanketes, bolsters and pyllowes and Curteyns	2	13	4
4 Chestes, fourtie foure payre of shetes, 4 Table clothes, 2 dosen of table napkyns, 2 peces of new canvas, 3 peces of wollen Clothe, one Chayre, one table, one iron plate standynge in the Chymney, one pole Axe	14	10	0
in the lyttle Chamber			
Yerne, honnye and waxe and drynkynge glasses		6	8

in the olde parler			
A table, a fourme, a cupborde, a Cheste, a Cheyre, 2 stoles, 2 Carpettes and A payre of brandirons	2	0	0
in the Chamber within the new parler			
One Cubborde, 2 fourmes, a wycker Chayre with other implimentes		13	4
harnesse			
One Cosslet, one Almoner ryvet, a cote of plate, a case of pystoletes 2 gonnes, a bowe and shefe of Arrowes with other thynges therto belongeinge	5	0	0
in the hall			
3 tables with 3 fourmes		10	0
in the gate howse Chambers			
4 bedstedles, one fetherbed, 2 flock beds, bolsters, coverlettes, blanckettes and a table	2	13	4
in the kytchyn			
5 bras pottes, 3 posnettes, one great Cawdron, 4 bras pannes, 6 Kettles, a Chafynge dyshe, a skymmer, 6 Candlestyckes and one spyce morter	5	0	0
Pewter			
2 dosen of Pewter, one dosen of poringers and sawcers, a bason and Ewer and 2 other basons, 2 Candlestyckes, 3 saltes and one dosen of spones	2	10	0
in the Chamber over the buttrye			
A bedstedle and Trucklebed, one greate Cheste and A table		10	0
in the buttrye			
One Cupborde and A table		3	4
plate			
One goblet, one sylver salt with a cover, halfe a dosen of sylver spones	4	0	0
ymplimentes			
2 trevettes, one brandiron, one spyt, one gyrdyron one dryppynge pan with other implimentes, one fate, a tonne, 6 kylderkyns, 4 fyrkyns with all other woodden vessell	1	0	0
Corne			
Wheate and malte, whyte meate bacon and greane		13	4
Her Apparell and redye monye	13	6	8
	84	6	8

Note: The Will was written on 20th January 1581/2 while Agnes was thanking God for her good health and perfect memory and was proved on 4th July 1583. She asked to be buried near her husband Mr Newdigate in the church. She ordered £1 in money, a side of beef and beer to the value of £1, to be given to the poor at her burial. The residuary legatee and executor was her son Walter Newdigate. The overseer with a very neat signature was Thomas Eyer, gentleman, her son-in-law. Her daughter Eyer's 3 children, Thomas, Edmond and Elizabeth, were to share £20. If any should die, the survivors were to share his or her part. Eunice Wenham, another daughter, was to have a substantial proportion of the goods and chattells from various parts of the house. The witnesses were Thomas Eyer and William Lawe, the parson of Newdigate. The executor, of Newdigate, gent., bound himself well and truly to administer the estate. The burial was recorded on 13th June 1583. Ref: 1583 B 60/1 Will 1583 B 60/2 Inventory

1584

Richard Babbe **192**

of Wonersh, weaver; taken by Thomas Farley and Nicholas Monnger, 4th May 1584.

	£	s	d
In the hall			
One table, one forme, one paire of trestilles, 3 turnd cheires,			

2 boordes, one peynted cloth and one plonke used as a side benche		4	0
In the kichen			
4 kettles, 2 brasse pottes, one posnet, one chafing dishe, one gridyron, one fryeng panne, one broache, one brasen ladle, one pothanger and one paire of pothookes		10	0
2 troughes, one kned troughe and a silting troughe, one boulting hutche, one chese presee, one butter chirne, 5 boordes, 3 short plankes, 3 stobbins and 2 spynning wheles		6	0
In the lofte over the hall			
3 boordes, 2 formes, one trestill, 6 bolles, one kever, one old tubbe and 2 syffes		2	0
3 rounde thre legged stooles, certen erthen vessell and bad drinking cuppes, one bill and one axe		1	8
In the parlor			
12 peces of pewter, one saltseller, 4 latten candlestickes and 12 spoones		10	0
One ioyned bedsted, one cupborde, one table and 2 chestes		13	0
One flockbed, one bolster, 2 pillowes, 2 cuisshins, one paire of blankettes and one coverlett		15	0
In the lofte over the parlor			
One bedsted, one flockbed, one blankett, 2 bolsters, 1 pillowe, 3 litle old peynted clothes and one coverlett		10	0
5 cofers		5	0
Lynnen etc.			
4 paire of shetes, one table cloth, one bed tester of Lynnen and 2 pilloberes		8	0
3 kyne and one calf	4	0	0
One verey olde mare		3	4
His apparell		10	0
Money in his purse		3	4
One sowe and 2 litle shootes		8	0
One acre and one Rodmeale of otes		8	0
5 hennes and one cocke		2	0
Soyle in the gate		2	0
Beanes etc. in the garden		1	0
	10	2	4

Note: The Will was dated 23rd April and proved on 20th May 1584. The residuary legatee and executrix was the testator's wife Elizabeth. Sums of 2d were left to his overseers, his neighbours William Hewet and Thomas Charman. One son John was given 3 items of pewter and the other son William was given the greatest brass pot. A sum of 2 pence was left to the poor men's box of Wonersh. His kinsfolk the Sinke family were also beneficiaries: Richard was left a heifer; Thomas, Henry and Elizabeth, were left small items of brass or pewter. Witnesses were Richard Paige, Anne Palmer, widow, Thomas Sink senior and Joseph Kichin. The burial of Richard Bab was recorded at Wonersh on 1st May 1584.

Ref: 1584 B 4/1 Will 1584 B 4/2 Inventory

John Clifton, the elder **193**

of Puttenham; taken by Bartholmewe Hardinge, Thomas Avenell, John Coules and John Croucher, 4th May 1584.

	£	s	d
In the hall			
One table, a paire of tressles and a forme with a plancke		3	4
A pott hanger, a paire of potthookes and one old Trefet		1	0
In the Chamber			

A bedd, a boulster, a paire of blanketes, a paire of Sheetes, a Coverlett, a bedd Tester and a bedstead		18	0
One cheast or Cofer		2	0
All his wearing apparrell		13	4
Monie in his purse		2	6
Another bedstead and a chest		1	0
In the Loft over the hall			
2 busshells of Rie		3	0
3 bushells of barlie		3	0
One busshells of mault		1	2
One fate with other Lumberie		?	0
One Coulter, two ploughe chaines and other old yron		6	8
2 olde syths, 2 hookes and 2 sickles		2	0
One brasse pann, one brasse pott, fower old kettles, one olde frying pann and one gridyron	1	0	0
8 peeces of pewter, one olde salte and one olde Candestick		4	0
In the lofte over the shopp			
One old table with 2 old tubbs		2	0
One old bedde with all that belongeth thereto		10	0
An old andyron, a bill, an axe, a shovell and a hatchett		2	0
In the gardein			
14 stawles of bees	2	0	0
4 kyne and 2 bullockes	6	6	8
20 sheepe	3	6	8
One Mare and a Colte	1	0	0
One olde Carte, two harrows and the wattles		13	4
5 acres of wheet and rie upon the ground	2	10	0
6 acres of barlie, pease and tares	2	0	0
	22	16	8

Note: The Will was written on 13th April and proved by his two sons Thomas and John Clifton, the joint executors, on 20th May 1584. They were to share the residue of the estate, paying his widow Agnes 6s 8d yearly and making a single bequest of £1 each to a third son Robert and to the three daughters, Rose, Elizabeth and Margaret. The witnesses to the will were Bartholomew Hardinge, John Croucher and Henrye Johnsonne and the executors were recorded as husbandmen of Puttenham when they bound themselves well and truly to administer the estate. No overseers were named. The burial was recorded on 27th April 1584.

Ref: 1584 B 14/1 Will 1584 B 14/2 Inventory

Robert Fraye **194**

of Carshalton; taken by Thomas Whytocke and Richard Bothomlye, 8th May 1584.

	£	s	d
In Redy mony	9	0	0
His wering apparell		13	4
	9	13	4

Note: The testator was "verye sycke and lyinge at the mercye of god" when the nuncupative will was written on 6th May by the vicar of Carshalton, John Pearse. It was proved on 8th May 1584 by the testator's father Thomas Fraye and his brother-in-law John Warden of Carshalton, collier, they having bound themselves well and truly to administer the estate. The value of the apparell and the names of the appraisers, together with their marks, appeared as a note on the will. Thomas Fraye was left £6 and John Warden's children were left equal shares of £3. Thomas Fraye, Jone Warden, Margaret Blagge and Marrine Dilcocke acted as witnesses. No overseers were named. Robert Fray was buried on 8th May 1584, according to the parish register.

Ref: 1584 B 26/1 Will 1584 B 26/2 Inventory

Joane Hamptonne **195**

of Liddelinge in Godalming, widow; taken by John Byllinghurst and John Bauldinge, 27th April 1584.

	£	s	d
A flocke beadde, a boulster, a payre of sheetes, a payre of blankettes and a coverlette	1	6	8
A lockeram sheete and a blankette		4	0
Three oulde chestes		5	0
5 peuter potengers beynge oulde		4	0
A peuter potte, a salte seller and towe oulde candlestickes			10
Three kettelles of brasse		6	8
An oulde brasse panne		2	0
Towe broches or spittes		2	0
One oulde beaddesteaddle			8
Her apparrell		13	4
All her Linnen		9	0
A table		3	0
Towe oulde toubes, a fate, a kneadde troughe and other oulde Lumberie		5	0
10 sheep	1	10	0
One mare		13	4
In monye	23	0	0
	29	5	6

Note: The Will was written on 10th February and proved on 20th May 1584. Administration of the goods and chattels was granted to James and George Marline, the 2 sons and joint executors of the testatrix. She was most precise in her bequests to her six children and seven grandchildren, wishing quietness to ensue after her decease. The 4 married daughters were to receive, in common with James and George, £2 each through their husbands Thomas Byllinghurste of Littleton, Steven Machwicke, John Roker and Richard Bycker. James and George were to receive an additional 30s apiece. The younger generation comprising Anne, Mary and Henry Byllinghurste; George, Samuel and Thomas Marline, sons of James; and Joan Marline, daughter of George; were given household items, livestock, or in one case only, 10s. A bed and bedding, a cauldron and £1, were left to Joane Keene, who had been brought up with the testatrix. The sum of 5s was left to be distributed among the poor by the overseers Robert Warner and Richard Tanner. Henry Johnsonne wrote the Will which was also witnessed by Thomas Byllinghurste, while the testatrix was, as she said, "walkeinge and of good Remembrance". There is an entry of a burial on 19th April 1584 of "Alice" Hampton, widow and it is possible that this is yet another mistake of a name in that section of the parish register.

Ref: 1584 B 37/1 Will 1584 B 37/2 Inventory

William Netelfould **196**

of Abinger, husbandman; taken by Thomas Tydy, William Longhurst, Thomas May and John Lipscomb, 7th May 1584.

	£	s	d
Foure keine and one heyfore	6	13	4
10 teigs as ewes and wether teiges som of them havinge lames	1	13	4
One mare and a coult	1	13	4
One sowe and 3 shotes		6	8
One cock and one henn		1	0
Wheat upon the ground	1	13	4
Oates upon the ground	1	0	0
One harrow and one grindingstone with that which belongeth therunto		3	4

The bylles and axes, sythes and thowles, rynges and Iron weyges	3	0
2 flyches of bacon and a flyche of beife	2	0
2 chestes	1	0
One bede and one bedstedell with that which belongeth therunto	5	0
Mony In his Purse	1	0
His apperrell	5	0
One cobbord	2	6
One brasse pott, 2 kettles, one mortar, one girdiron, one spyte, one frieinge pan, with all other such Impelmentes	13	4
One tabell, with chayers, formes, towbs, keyvers, bowles, troues and other wodden vessell	3	0
	[15	*0 2]*

Note: The Will was dated 26th April and proved on 20th May 1584. The residuary legatee and executor was Edward, a son of the testator. Sums of 6s 8d were bequeathed to the overseers, Thomas Edwards of Ewhurst and Nicolas Marden of Reigate. Monetary bequests were spread over a period from the burial for a further 9 years. A shilling was left to the church at Abinger and a barrel of beer and a bushel of wheat to the poor. William Lipscomb the elder, Alice Nightingale and Catherine Wood, were to have 6d, 4d and 4d, respectively. Of 3 other sons, William was left £6 13s 4d in 2 stages and Thomas and Francis were left £1 each annually for 9 years. The 3 daughters Joan, Jane and Alice, were left £1, £3 and £2, in that order. Emery Dalton wrote the Will, which was also witnessed by Thomas Edwards, Thomas Tydy, William Longhurst, John Sponer, John Lipscomb and John Nightingale. The burial of William Netlefold was recorded at Abinger on 30th April 1584.

Ref: 1584 B 54/1 Will 1584 B 54/2 Inventory

Edward Scrafton **197**

of Godstone, weaver; taken by Thomas Plaw of Dormans, Wyllyam Grame and Rychard Wealler, 2nd May 1584.

	£	s	d
His pursse and gyrdle and mony		6	8
His Rayment	1	6	8
A table and forme		1	8
For Chayers and stooles		2	0
A brand yron, a pothanger, a payer of pothokes and a fyre rake, a fyre panne and a grediron		3	0
A coubbard	1	0	0
2 littell kyne and 2 littell haffers	3	13	4
18 shepe	3	6	4
A mare and 2 coltes	1	16	8
3 hogges and 5 suckynge pigges		9	0
2 geese and a gander, 4 hennes and a cocke		?	0
2 olde featherbeadds, 2 boolsters and 3 pillowes	1	13	4
2 coverleds and 3 blanckets		10	0
A flocke bead and 2 mattresses, 2 boolsters, one coverled and 2 pillowes		10	0
3 beadsteadles		10	0
6 Cheastes		10	0
For paynted clothes		4	0
12 payer of shetes	2	10	0
3 pillow cotes, 5 table napkynes		3	4
2 table clothes and 3 hand towells		2	6
4 payer of shetes		13	4

15 peces of brasse and an iron pot	1	10	0
30 peces of peawte of platters, dyshes, sacers and salts with porrengers and 3 candlestickes	1	0	0
18 tynne spones and 2 dosen of trenchers		1	0
A payer of towe combes and an old hytchell		2	0
A quarter of wheat, a quarter of Rye	1	8	0
4 bushellsof otten mawlt		4	0
3 loumbes with the tack lynges therto	3	6	8
3 spittes, 2 drepinge pannes, 2 fryinge pannes, a spice morter, a grate and 2 trevets		6	8
For baken and beife	1	0	0
A boultynge whiche, a fate, a bruynge toubbe, keelers, firkynes, trougges and all other lumberment	2	0	0
	30	14	2

Note: The Will was dated 20th April and proved on 18th May 1584. The residuary legatee and executor was the testator's eldest son Robert. The overseers were Edward's two brothers John and Robert Scrafton. There is a long list of bequests to his wife Julyan, to her two daughters Elizabeth and Alice, to his two younger sons William and Christopher and to his daughters Rose and Denise. His children would inherit their legacies at the age of 18, or at their day of marriage. Julyan was permitted to stay with the executor and the Scrafton children for 6 months and then she could take £2, a red cow, 4 sheep and the goods which she had brought with her when she married Edward. Witnesses were Richard Wealler, William Grame and the minister of Lingfield, Robert Spratt.

Ref: 1584 B 72/1 Will 1584 B 72/2 Inventory

1585

Thomas Astrete **198**

of Constables in Wonersh, husbandman; taken by William Tiknor of Woodhill, Richard Astrete of Smarcum, Phillip Gosden, Walter Strete and Herry Bikner, 11th February 1584/5.

In the hall	£	s	d
One table, one forme and 2 cheyres		2	0
One litle brasse pot and pot hookes and hangers, 4 kettles and One Skellet		11	0
One spit, one tryvet, one grydyron and cobyron		2	0
One bill, one spitter and one axe		1	4
All his pewter, 2 candlestickes, one saltseller and one cruse		3	4
One fether bed, two blanketes, one paire of shetes, one bolster, one coverlet		13	4
Foure cofers and a paire of shetes		4	0
His apparell		6	8
Money in his purse		2	6
2 Sythes and one beck		2	8
One cowe, one bullock, one wanyer and one sucking calf	2	10	0
28 ewes and tegges	3	0	0
6 old and bad wattles		1	8
Soile in the gate		3	4
One hog and one shoote		5	0
One acre of Rye		10	0
One fliche of bacon		3	4
2 hennes and a cock		1	0
2 hiles of Rye in the barnes		5	0
Hey in the barne		10	0

	9	18	2

Administration of the goods and chattels of the deceased was granted on 16th February 1584/5 to Agnes Astrete, widow, relict, who was sworn to the truth of the inventory.

Note: An entry in the Parish Register noted the burial on 25th January of Thomas Streat of Constables. Ref: 1584 Ad 2

Richard Bottomley **199**

of Carshalton, yeoman; taken by John Tegg, John Mathew and Robart Harman, 3rd May 1585.

	£	s	d
His apparell		6	8
One fether bed, a bolster, 1 coverlett, a blanket and a boorded bedsted		10	0
One other bed, a bolster, a coverlet and a boarded bedsted		13	4
A flock bed, a bolster, a covering, a boarded bedsted		6	8
A mattrisse, a bolster and coveringe		6	8
More a flocke bed, a strawshete, too coveringes and a blanket		6	0
Too pyllos		3	4
A ioyned coubberd		13	4
Thre chesstes		6	8
7 platters, 3 dysshes, 6 sawcers, thre poringers, 5 pottes, a sault, A dosin and a half of spoones and the chambre pottes of pewter	1	0	0
Foure payre of sheetes	1	6	8
8 payre of other sheetes	1	10	0
5 table clothes, a dosine and a half of table napkyns and too towels		18	0
5 pylloberes and a cobard cloth		6	8
A brasse pott, 4 kettles, 3 posnetes		13	4
An Iron drippyng panne, a frieng pane, too brand Irons, 2 spittes, a fyreshovell, a tonges, too pott hangers and a pott hookes		8	0
Too tables, 2 formes, one chaire, 3 stooles, 6 old cusshens		10	0
Three Lattin candlestickes, a spice morter and pestle, a chafyng dysshe and scomer		6	0
Paynted clothes		13	4
A boultyng Huche, a spininge wheele, a knedyng trough, a chese presse and other lumbre		10	0
6 stone pottes			8
A Laddre and other old tymbre		?	0
A racke, a manger, a Harrow, too paire of Harnes, a shovel, a donge spood, a dong rake		6	8
One kowe, threesmale Hogges	2	0	0
Corne sowen upon the ground	3	6	8
The lease of the house	1	0	0
	19	3	8

Note: The Will was dated 22nd April and proved on 28th May 1585. The residuary legatee and executrix was the testator's wife Johanne. She was to pay any charges incurred by the overseers Thomas Staunton and John Tegge. These 2 men and their heirs had a bequest, in the nature of trustees, of a tenement with appurtenances in Carshalton, recently purchased by the testator of John Gaynesford, gentleman, but they had to pay the previous owner 10s per annum, while the testator's daughter Johanne Stuarde and her heirs were to have the use of the property for ever. This same daughter was to be allowed to occupy her chamber in his own house and half the arable land, until Michaelmas 1587. After this date his wife was to pay his daughter 13s 4d out of the leasehold residence held of the aforesaid John Gaynesford. Witnesses were the overseers, together with Robert Harman and John Pearse, vicar of Carshalton. Two days after his Will was written the burial of Richard Bottomley was recorded on 24th April 1585.

Ref: 1585 B 12/1 Will 1585 B 12/2 Inventory

Henry Chytty **200**

of Eashing in Godalming, yeoman; taken by Wylliam Carpenter, James Stoner, Henry Sturte and Robert Peyto, 3rd May 1585.

	£	s	d
In the hawle			
In the parlor			
One table and one cobborde		16	0
In the chamber next the hawle			
One Jyned bedsted with 2 lytle cofers		16	0
In the lofte over the parlor			
One old Jyned bedste[*d*], one flokbed, 3 Covertletes, one fether bolster, 2 pyllowes and one chest, one lytle cofer	1	18	4
One lockerame shete, 5 payer of canvas shetes, one table clothe	1	3	4
Hys apparrell and mony hin hys purse	2	0	0
In the servants [*struck through*] loft over the chamber			
2 old bedstedes, one flokbed with a coverlet and one bolster and one old chear		8	0
In the chamber over the butrye			
One old bedsted, one flokbed, 1 bolster, one coverlet		6	0
In the mylke howse			
One butter cheren, 6 smale bowles, 1 fryinge pan with the old benchys and shelvys there, with erthen potes		3	4
In the buttrye			
2 kytles, 1 brasse pot, 1 posnet		17	4
2 candelstickes, 1 dosen half of pewter platters, 9 pewter dyshes, 2 sawsers, 3 saltselers, 1 yere dyshe with 6 sponys, 2 stone potes	1	8	0
2 awnd Irens, 1 broche with a dryping pan with 1 pothanger		4	0
One old chest, 1 stobyn, one sedecod, 1 cradle, 1 spyning whele, 1 basket		3	4
One prong, 1 axe, 1 bylle, 1 drawing knife, one hachet, 2 awgers, 1 rope, 1 Chesille, 1 botle		3	4
In the sellar			
2 fates, 4 fyrkyns, 2 Kefers, 1 stobyn, one chesepresse, 1 powdryng trough, 1 pecke and one buckin toobe		16	6
In the bakehowse			
1 Knede trowghe, 1 bowlting whiche, 1 lytle planke, 2 bukets 1 oste here		?	0
In Kytchin lofte			
2 bushell of malt, 6 pound of whyte wole with 2 sevys with 3 flychys of bakon		12	0
1 lanterne			6
Corne in the barne			
In the barlie barne of barley there		16	8
In the barne next the lane Whete there and Rie there	2	6	8
In the haye house serten gystes and bordes there		10	0
One dosen of watles		8	0
One wagen, 2 downgpotes, 1 ploughe, 1 harrowe with yowkes, chaynes and ropes	3	0	0
Serten tymber with some pales and Rayles with an old gryndestone		13	4
Rakes and sole in the gate		5	0
Catle			
3 oxen	5	0	0
4 Kyne	5	6	8

2 mares and a lytle geldinge	3	0	0
26 shepe, ewys and whethers at 3s 4d a pece	6	0	0
16 lambes at 18d the pece	1	4	0
6 smale hoges at 2s 6d the pece		15	0
The powletrye		5	0
Corne in the feld			
5 acres of whete at 13s 4d the acre	3	6	8
5 acres of Rie at 13s 4d the acre	3	6	8
8 acres of barlie at 10s the acre	4	0	0
4 acres of otys at 6s the acre	1	4	0
7 acres of pece and tares 6s the acre	2	2	0
8 lode of smale fagates standinge in the wode		10	0
Serten beanes and hastes in the garden		1	4
	56	4	0

Note: The Will was written on 23rd April and proved on 25th May 1585. The residuary legatee and executrix was the testator's wife Annys and the overseers were John Mellersh of Farncombe and Wylliam Chytty the elder of Godalming. The testator gave £1 to the repair of Godalming church where he asked to be buried and he gave 10s to the poor. His wife was to have a life interest in his house and lands, unless a son were to be born, in which case the son was to inherit at the age of 21. His daughter Annys was to have £60, which she would share with her sister should one be born. After his wife's decease and there being no male heir, the property was to go to John Chytty, the son of Wylliam Chytty his father's brother and his male heirs, paying £200 to the testator's daughter or daughters for the gift. The testator's sister Katheryne was given £1. Jone Peyto was to have all but £1 of the money owed by her father. It was recorded that John Cowdrey was the legal owner of the house, bought by him from Henry Chytty. Robert Peyto wrote the will which was also witnessed by John Chenill, Arnold Flodder,

Henry Sturte and John Edwards. The executrix and John Mellersh of Godalming, yeoman, bound themselves well and truly to administer the estate.

Ref: 1585 B 15/1 Will 1585 B 15/2 and 1585 B 15/3 Inventories

B 15/2: written by Robert Peyto; B15/3: neatly written copy with several small mistakes.

John Colton **201**

of Cobham, husbandman; taken by Robert Parishe, Robert Palmer, James Roger and John Peter, 30th April 1585.

	£	s	d
His weareinge apparrell	1	0	0
Monye in his Pursse		3	4
One old fether bed, 2 olde flockebeddes, 3 Bolsters, three Coverlettes, 3 blanckcttcs and 7 pairc of Shcctcs	2	10	10
4 olde Chestes		8	0
Pewter Platters, 6, the price		4	0
6 Pewter Dishes and 2 Sawcers		3	0
2 dozen of olde Spoones		1	0
4 brasse kettles, 2 Pannes and 2 brasse Pottes	1	12	0
3 Candlestickes and a Chaffingdishe		3	0
5 litle old Spittes and the pothangers and an olde paire of Cobbirons		5	0
2 smale olde Cubbordes		6	8
An olde Table, a forme and an olde Chayre		2	0
4 old Tubbes and a Cherne		3	0
2 Bowles and 2 Buckettes		1	0
2 olde Troughes		2	6
One quarter of Rye		12	0
A quarter of Barlye		12	0

3 Bushelles of Otes		3	0
4 Bushels of Maulte		6	0
2 axes and other his workinge Tooles		2	0
40 Sheepe and 16 Lambes	7	6	8
2 Litle Nagges and 2 Mares	5	0	0
3 kyne and a haifer	5	0	0
4 Bullockes	2	13	4
2 Calves		13	4
6 Shootes		18	0
1 Stale of Bees		1	0
A Carte, a Plowe and 3 olde Harrowes	1	6	8
4 old harnes and an old Pannell		5	0
8 Acres of Wynter Corne	4	0	0
5 Acres of Otes	1	5	0
2 Acres and a halfe of Pease, Tares and Beanes		10	0
	37	19	4

Note: The Will was written on 12th April and proved on 27th May 1585. The residuary legatee and executrix was the testator's wife Alice. The testator left 3s 4d apiece to the overseers, John and Antony Fenne of Byfleet and Robert Fenne of Pyrford. He left 2d to Cobham church and 6d to the poor. His 6 children were left sums of money: Mary was to have £5 three years after her father's death; William and Robert were to have £5 at the age of 25; Jane and Agnes were to have £3 6s 8d at the age of 21. Robert Parishe and John Thorp witnessed the beautifully written will.

Ref: 1585 B 18/1 Will 1585 B 18/2 Inventory

Elizabeth Cowicke **202**

of Ewhurst, widow; taken by Nicholas Dendye, John Butler and Ellis Dendye, 28th May 1585.

	£	s	d
Her wearinge gere or Apperre, wollen and Lynnen		10	0
In Redye money in her purse		10	0
In money owinge to her by Thomas At Ryde	6	0	0
In money owinge to her by John Longhurste	1	0	0
In money owinge to her by Henrye Cowicke		10	10
In money owinge to her by Nicholas Nitingale		10	0
	9	0	10

Exhibited on 5th June 1585 by the administrator, the executor being a minor.

Note: The Will was dated 29th April 1580 when Elizabeth was "somewhat sicklye but yet walking", but was not proved until 25th May 1585. Richard Atryde of Ewhurst was named as executor and residuary legatee. The overseers, John Butler senior and Raffe Dalton who wrote the Will, were each given 6s 8d. The 4 men chosen to carry the testatrix to the churchyard for burial were each to be given 6d. A sum of 5s was to go towards church repairs and £2 to the poor. Her godchildren were left 1s apiece and 7 gifts of 6s 8d were bequeathed to Annys Edsawe, Alice Young, Thomas Wheatland and Johanna, Mary, Ann and Edward at Ryde. The testatrix left 10s to Mary Staplehurst and 5s each to Johanne and Beatrice Stenynge. Thomas at Ryde junior was left £2. Elizabeth was indeed "yet of good and perfytte Remembrance" to dispose of all her money to a nicety. Ralph Dalton and Thomas Young signed the Will; Edward Dalton, John Butler senior and Richard Dendye, also acted as witnesses. When the Will was proved the executor was a minor, so he was represented by his brother Thomas Atryde of Ewhurst, yeoman. The bond lodged by Thomas was to be delivered to Harry Robinson.

Ref: 1585 B 22/1 Will 1585 B 22/2 Inventory

John Edwin **203**

of Wandsworth; taken by Phillip Horsam, Thomas White, Robert Woodd and Edward Busbe, 11th May 1585.

	£	s	d
In the parlor			
One table with a frame to the same, 4 Joyned stooles and a boorded stoole		5	0
3 Joyned settles		5	0
2 turned chaires		1	8
2 Wainscott Chaires		2	6
One Court Cubbard		1	4
Painted Clothes		10	0
2 greate Cushins and 5 smalle and a carpet		2	0
An other Carpet			6
in the chamber			
A bedsted, a mattresse, an ould coverlett, a blankett, a paire of sheetes and 2 boulsters		13	4
4 bottles			4
One Cubberd with a presse		10	0
A little table and an ould chaire		1	0
A Candle boxe, a flaskett, a baskett, an oulde Wheele			8
Painted Clothes		1	0
A doore, a boxe and an oulde table		1	0
in the west lofte			
A bedsted		2	0
One fether bed, three boulsters, a coverlet and a pillow		10	0
A little round table			6
Painted Clothes		1	0
A Wicker bed, a mattris and an ould Wood knife		1	0
2 Chesstes		4	0
in the chamber over the parlor			
The trundle bedsted and a mattris		1	0
The Wainscott		2	0
in the chimny chamber			
A Joyned bedsted with Curtaynes		10	0
A fether bed, 2 boulsters, 2 pillowes and a white rugge	1	0	0
A Court table and a Chest		1	4
Painted Clothes			4
in the great chamber			
A Cupbord with a presse		10	0
A deske and 2 grafting sawes			6
The bookes	2	0	0
An owlde wheele, a prong and boordes		1	0
in the hall			
An oulde Counter			6
3 stooles, 2 burd Cages, a Wheele, a brush and 2 Reele			8
An oulde table			8
in the buttery			
An a Cubberd and 2 kneading troughes and a boulting hutch		2	0
in the kitchin			
3 kettles		1	9
2 posnettes		1	4

A spice morter and a cullinder		1	0
2 brass pottes		5	0
1 Iron waight		1	0
One Chafing dishe			6
Ould lumber		1	0
3 Candlestickes		1	0
4 spittes		2	0
One paire of andirons		1	0
A paire of tonges and fire shovell			6
A paire of pott hangers and potthookes		1	0
A frying pann			10
Seven platters and a bason		5	6
3 pewter dishes		1	0
6 sawsers and a plate		1	0
3 dossen of spoones			4
2 flowre pottes			6
A pottle pott		1	0
A quart pott			6
4 porringers			6
2 little pewter Cuppes			6
2 salt sellers		1	0
A stone morter			3
2 firkins		1	0
A driping pan of yron			6
A paire of bellowes			4
8 paires of shetes	1	0	0
4 short table Clothes and a longe one		6	8
2 owld napkins			4
A sowe and nine pullen		6	0
[*£11.8.8*]	11	7	7

Exhibited by the administratrix on 3rd June 1585. No name given. Ref: 1585 Ad 22

John Farnham **204**

of Bisley; taken by John Cobbet the elder, Thomas Goring, John Vynsent and Robart Cobbet the elder. [*undated*]

	£	s	d
In his purse at his death		2	0
His wearing apparrell		5	0
A Cubburd with his Furnyture		?	0
A Table and a Forme in the hall		8	0
In Brasse		10	0
Wooden vessels and yron Stuffe		5	0
A cowe and a Bullock	2	10	0
A mare and a colt		13	4
In shepe	1	6	8
In swyne		?	0
A Flock bead with his Furniture		10	0
3 acres of Rye	2	0	0
A acre and halfe of oates		6	8
A old Cubbord and 3 chestes		10	0
A chere and a Stowle			6
Two axsis and a byll			8
Gese and hennes		2	0

	[*9*	*19*	*10*]

Note: The Will was dated 23rd April and proved on 25th May 1585. The testator's wife Joan was appointed executrix and the overseers were John Cobbet the elder and John Vyncent. A sum of 3d was given to the poor men's box at Bisley and to his son John went a ewe and a lamb. His son William was to have a ewe and a lamb; and a heifer which was to be rented out in his name for his profit, until he reached the age of 18 when he could claim it. The witnesses were Thomas Goring and John Symons of Bisley. The widow and John Cobbet of Bisley, weaver, bound themselves to see the Will administered correctly. John Farnham's burial was recorded in Bisley on 23rd April 1585, the same day his Will was written.

Ref: 1585 B 26/1 Will 1585 B 26/2 Inventory

Robarte Fenne **205**

of Pyrford, yeoman; taken by Wyllyam Rydon, John Frelande, Robarte Honor and Willyam Vynsent. [*undated*]

	£	s	d
In readye monye in his purse		10	0
His Apparrell		15	0
4 flocke beddes		15	0
4 Coverlettes		10	0
2 payre of Blankettes		6	8
7 payre of Sheetes	1	0	0
2 table clothes		3	0
6 Bolsters		13	4
2 Chestes		5	0
20 yardes of paynted clothes		3	4
4 Bedsteddells		8	0
One chayre and 4 ioyned stooles		2	0
6 pounde of Hempe			9
One cubborde		2	0
One table and 3 Formes and 2 payre of trestells		4	0
3 platters, 6 pewter dysshes, 2 salte sellers and one pewter candlestyke and 12 pewter spones		6	0
One brasse potte and 4 kettells		8	0
Potte hokes, Potte hangers, one grydeiron and a Fryinge Panne and a payre cobirons		3	4
One spytte			6
A Betell, 4 Wedges, an Ax, a Bill, a shovell and a Spade		2	4
One dosen trenchers			1
2 stone pottes and 2 Bottells			8
One trevet			4
9 tubbes		6	0
One Butter cherne, 2 Buckkettes, 4 wooden platters		1	6
One cheese presse and 3 Bowlls		1	8
One Brydell and a pannell		1	4
4 sacks		1	4
2 cheese mootes			4
One Hoste Hare		1	0
8 Bushells of Rye in the house		13	4
2 payre of sheeres and a pepper corne			6
One longe carte and a payre of shodde wheeles		15	0
2 dunge pottes and a payre of wheeles		5	0
One plow, one ox harrow and a small harrow		5	0
5 Kyne	5	0	0

40 sheape and 10 lammes	7	0	0
5 horse and mares and one colte	4	0	0
Harnes for 5 horses, a payre of ropes and 5 halters		6	8
A payre of stropes, an ox chayne and a strople yoke and a pronge		2	0
2 Awgers, a payre of pynsers, a hande Saw, a drawinge knyfe and dunge rake and a hammer		1	5
A Sythe and a cradell		1	8
The dunge in the gate		10	0
A ladder			8
A knedinge troffe			4
A Bow and 6 Arrows		1	0
9 shelves		1	6
12 acres of Rye	10	0	0
5 acres of otes	1	5	0
[*£38.1.7*]	38	1	3

[*Written on the Will:*] Dettes owynge by the sayd Robert Fenne

To John Fenne, my brother and	18	0
Elizabeth Fenne, my daughter and	10	0
To John, my sone	10	0
	[*1* *18*	*0*]

Note: The Will was dated 20th April and proved on 27th May 1585. The residuary legatee and executrix was the testator's wife Sara. The overseers were William Vynsent of Pyrford and John Vynsent of Bisley. Robert asked for a christian burial in Pyrford churchyard and gave 2d to the mother church of Winchester. His only individual bequests comprised one ewe to each of his 6 children, Elizabeth, John, Leonard, Richard, Edward and William. Witnesses were William Ryden, John Didlesson and David Davy.

Ref: 1585 B 27/1 Will   1585 B 27/2 Inventory

Robart Freelande **206**

of Ockham, husbandman and sawyer; taken by John Sawyer and Raphe Osborne of Ockham, yeomen, 4th May 1585.

	£	s	d
In the Hall			
A Cubberd		10	0
A paire of pot hookes		1	0
In the Chamber next the Hall			
His wearinge apparell	1	10	0
Two Chestes		5	0
Fower payre of Shetes		16	0
One course Table cloth		1	6
A flocke bed, one bolster, two pillowes, one pillowbere, one blanckett, one Coverlitt and a bedsted	1	0	0
In his pursse		15	0
In the Butterye			
A fryinge pann, a spitt and two dossen of Trenchers		1	6
Six pownde of yarne and a bottle		2	8
A brasse pann with a Civer		3	4
Seaven pewter disshes, Three platters and two salt sellers		7	0
In the Chamber over the Hall			
A forme and a Cheste with a paire of Tressells			10
A quarter of Mawlte		10	0
A Kettle, two brasse pottes and a paire of pothookes		12	0
A powderinge Tubb, a pronge, a halfe Tubb, two sackes and a forme		3	4

Two busshells of Rye		3	0
A Whipsawe with other workinge tooles		6	8
A sithe with a hedginge bill		2	0
Two Acres of Oates		10	0
In redie monye	5	11	6
A Lease taken of William Ryden gent., lying in Purforde	7	0	0
Owinge him upon Obligation to be payde on the feast daye of St. Thomas next comminge in the yere of our lorde 1585	11	0	0
Owinge him to be payde on the feast day of St. Bartilmewe next cominge	2	0	0
Owinge by Harrye David	1	0	0
	34	11	11

Note: The Will was dated 22nd April and proved on 25th May 1585. The residuary legatee and executrix was the testator's wife Katheryn, who was pregnant at the time. A £20 legacy was to be paid to the child, be it son or daughter, out of the messuage or tenement in Pyrford recently taken on a 31-year lease of William Ryden, gentleman. Sums of 2s 6d each were to be paid to the overseers: namely, his brother John Freland of Pyrford, who was also to have his working tools and William Rudford of Ockham. The testator asked to be buried in Ockham churchyard, giving 5s to the poor and 3s 4d towards the repair of the glass windows in the church. A number of monetary bequests went to his Freland brother and sisters John, Beatrice and Gillian; to his mother Elizabeth Bullen; and if his unborn child should not inherit the legacy, then £4 each to his Bullen brother and sister, Thomas and Marget. His mother-in-law Joan Budbroke, 2 godsons John Vincent and Richard Giles, a niece and nephew Mary and John Freland and a certain Thomas Hitches, also had bequests. Henry Studley, clerk, wrote the Will also witnessed by James Wylde, John Sawyer and Thomas Giles. The widow bound herself well and truly to administer the estate, together with George Taunton of Ripley, innholder and Ralph Osborn of Ockham, yeoman. The testator was buried a few hours after his Will was written.

Ref: 1585 B 28/1 Will 1585 B 28/2 Inventory

Thomas Freland **207**

of Windlesham, husbandman; taken by the overseers and others. [*undated*]

	£	s	d
The money in his purse			4
His apparrell		10	0
That which was bequeth to Edith being a table, a forme, a Coffer and a chest		2	8
more to Edith a brasse pott and a kettell and a spitt and 4 platters and a sausser		[*blank*]	
A dossen of pewter		5	0
8 peces of brasse		10	0
The beddes an bedstedles and the Coverlett		4	0
For the lininge		?	0
A table and a Chest and a Coffer with other Lomber		3	6
3 ackers of rie uppon the ground	1	0	0
3 ackers of otes upon the ground		7	0
2 kynne	1	6	8
A yearlyn bullocke		6	8
3 weaninge Calves		10	0
14 shepe	1	0	0
2 shuttes		2	8
A mare		10	0
Poultry and gesse		2	0
[*£7.3.6*]	7	5	6

Note: Filed with the Will and Inventory were instructions for folk remedies. In this case the kill or cure effect proved to be unfortunate.

Make A playstar with shyppes suet A punde
And with thys eache brucklyme, smallage and malowes
And with crumbes of weted breade sethe thes together
with parslye and make A playstar of yt
And bynde yt faste to the earde so hotte as yow maye Abyde yt.
make hym A drynke with Alle or beare
sett yt by the fyar and scrapke in yt
a good quantyty of kacke soppe and
drynke yt so hotte as yow maye.
also for barre Rye breade and harde chesse,
buttar mylke and be not much anggrye as lyttyll as yow maye.
make hym potagge with cleane paslye ofte.

Note: The Will was dated 31st May 1582 and was not proved until 28th May 1585. The residuary legatee and executrix was the testator's wife Margarett. The overseers were William Strett, John Wise and John Freman. Thomas asked to be buried in Windlesham churchyard. His son William was given a table, whereas his elder daughter Edith was given 12 household items, a pig, a half share of an acre of rye and an acre of oats. The other half share of the rye was given to Annes, his younger daughter, together with 8 household items. His godson Thomas Chutter had the bequest of a lamb. No witnesses were recorded.

Ref: 1585 B 29/1 Will 1585 B 29/2 Inventory 1585 B 29/3 Remedies

---

Elizabeth Fuller **208**

of Stoke next Guildford, a maid; taken by Richard Smither, of Stoke aforesaid, Lawrence Hardinge, Edward Browne and Edmund Chittie, 25th January 1584/5.

	£	s	d
In mony	4	8	0
4 sheetes		5	0
A flocke Bed with a Bollster, a simple blancket and seven paynted Clothes over and abowte the bed		6	8
A flocke Bed, souche a one as he is, with 3 simple blanckettes and a bad coverlette and a small bollster		4	0
All her woollen wearinge apparell	1	0	0
Her aporne and her hatte		6	8
The brasse and the pewter with a paire of potthockes		10	0
A spinninge whele with a paire of Cardes, a sallte and a stone cuppe		1	0
3 woodden platters and 4 dishes, an earthen platter and 3 earthen cruches and a litle pipkine and a baskette		10	0
A Candlesticke and a sickle			8
All her linnen wearinge apparell		13	4
3 ollde chestes and 3 or 4 ollde shellves		4	0
2 litle peeces of paynted clothes		1	8
A kever, an ollde Tubbe and a butter cherne			6
Other Linen fyttched awaye by her syster, the wyffe of Henrie Guyllame, which the praysers cannot come by to price			
A woullen wastecote and Clowth abowte her when she departed			10
	[*8*	*12*	*4*]

Note: The nuncupative Will was recorded on 20th January 1584/5 and Elizabeth bestowed small gifts of money, goods and apparel on 18 different relatives and friends, leaving 15s for the poor at her burial and 4s to the 4 men who should carry her to church. She had at one time been a aidservant in the house of John Browne of Burpham in Worplesdon and she forgave him the 5s at he owed her. She made a small bequest to Sara Browne, his daughter, of a little chest and 1s. enry, Alice, Joan and Susanne, the son and 3 daughters of Edward Browne of Stoke, were also membered, as was Jane Smallpeece of Trinity parish, Guildford and also the wife of poor man enry Hull. Her mother of Rogate, Sussex, were she still living, was left 15s, the largest bequest an individual. Two sisters, one called Annes, lived in Hampshire, a third was married to Henry wyllame alias Blowne and a fourth sister Alice lived with them. No parish was recorded for her other sisters Joan and Suzanne, but her brother Richard, who lived in Godalming with his wife nd worked as a shearman, was given a saffe garde. "All the residue of her goods and Cattles hatsoever she will and bequeathed unto the discretion of Mrs Smalepeece of Guildford to ispose of them as she should think best her owne paynes considered and having thus disposed er goods in the presence of Mistress Smalepeece of Holy Trinity Guildford, Edward Browne of toke and Edmunde Chittie of the same parish she departed this life". She died in the house of oodman Edmund Chittie of Stoke, a fuller and probate was granted on 16th February 1584/5 to e executrix, the said Mrs Smalepeece.

Ref: 1584 B 28/1 and 2 Will 1584 B 28/3 Inventory

---

lenry Lee **209**

f Sutton in Woking, husbandman; taken by Richard Burt, Henry Flanne, Richard Jeames, obert Wesbrooke and Richard Bedford of Sutton, yeoman, 6th May 1585.

	£	s	d
In his purse and his aparrell	1	0	0
The table in the hall and 4 stoles, 2 chares		6	0
A wollin wheele and a linen whele		1	0
Thre ould cubberds in the hall		16	0
Two fether beds with 2 fether boulsters and two coveringes and two blanckets and four pillowes	3	0	0
Two flocke beds, two ould coveringes, two ould boulsters	1	0	0
Four plaine bedstedles	8	0	
Thre painted clothes hanginge over the beds		3	4
Two ould chests		2	8
One ould table, trestles and forme in the chamber		1	8
One holland sheete		2	6
6 paire of canvas sheetes		16	0
2 paire of pillowbers		3	4
One ould table clothe with halfe a dosen naptkins and two ould towels		6	8
All the brasse	1	10	0
Thre ould candelstickes and a ould chafing dishe		1	8
All the pewter	1	0	0
2 spits, 2 andirons, one potehangers, two poothookes, a fire panne, a paire a tonges, a trefet, a girdiron		6	0
Ould tobs and lumber		5	4
Bucket, trenchers, a grate, dishes and bowles		1	8
Earthen pots			6
12 bushels a rye	1	0	0
A bushell a barly		1	4
A bill, an axe		1	0
6 hens and a cocke with a dosen a chicken		5	6
One goose and a gander with eight younge		3	2
Two sowes with six sucking pigges and sixe shootes	1	10	0
8 cople yeowes and lambes	1	14	8
7 tegges	1	1	0
Thre twelmonthe bullockes	2	0	0
Thre keene	4	10	0

Thre weaning caves		18	0
Thre ould cartinge towds and two cowls	3	6	8
Two strapt yookes, 2 chains and a paire a straps		5	0
A dunge carte and a carte with wheeles and round pinnes and two smale harrowes with ould plow irons with horse harnes with ropes and cart sadle		16	0
The dunge		2	0
The spitter and a shuwell		1	0
Ten hell a rye strawe		1	8
4 acres a smale woots an a acre a pese	1	11	8
4 acres a rye and a half and an acre a wheat and a halfe	4	0	0
For 2 flites a bacon		5	0
[*£35.6.0*]	35	1	0
Whereof To be inducted out for so muche mony owinge by the above named to Ruben Bicknould for 13 kilderkins beer at 3s 8d the kilderkin	2	7	8
To Steven Collier		10	0
Borrowed of William Forwes the beer bruer	2	0	0
To Henry Paine		10	0
To Richard Bucher		3	4
Borowed of Rooke	1	0	0
To John Cleocke		3	4
[*£6.14.4*]	7	12	4
And so remainethe there the debt debts payd [*£28.11.8*]	27	8	8

Administration was granted to Joan, the relict of the deceased, 25th May 1585.

Ref: 1585 Ad 40

Raff Mose **210**

of Mickleham, husbandman; taken by Raff Lucas, Thomas Roger, Thomas Mose and Thomas Lucas, 24th April 1585.

	£	s	d
Hys Weringe Aparell 3 shyrtes, 2 cootes, a gyrkin, hosen and showes	1	0	0
Money in hys purse			6
20 payr of sheetes	3	0	0
4 table clothes		5	0
A fether bedd, 2 floke beddes, 4 bed hyllers, 6 bowlsters, 2 pyllows, 4 blanketes	3	6	6
3 bedsteedels, 4 chestes		13	4
11 pewter platters, 6 pewter dysses, 2 sawsers		13	4
A quarte pootte, 2 sawltes and a lytle pewter potte		1	4
5 brasen candelstykes and a morter and pestle		3	4
3 brasse poottes, 10 keettles	2	10	0
2 posnetes, 2 chafinge dysses, 2 stonen pottes		3	4
A spytte, 2 brandyrnes, a cobyrne, a payr a pott hangers, a greedyrne, a treff, a byll and an axe		6	8
A cubbord		3	4
A table, a forme, stowles and cheers		3	4
Fates, covers and ale barels	1	0	0
11 fleiches of bacon	1	13	0
Mawlte in the howsse	2	10	0
The corne in the barne and horsse meate	4	0	0
8 Akers of wheat and Rye now groynge	5	0	0
13 akers of barly	6	10	0

6 akers of pease and teers	2	0	0
2 akers of wootes		13	4
6 carte horses and harnesse	8	0	0
A longe carte, a down cart, 2 plowes and 2 harows, cart ropes with other implementes	2	0	0
3 kyne, a hecfer and a bulloke	5	0	0
60 sheepe and 10 lambes	11	0	0
A sowe and 5 suettes	1	0	0
	62	16	4

Note: The Will was written by Rychard Ellis, rector of Mickleham, on 18th April 1585 and proved on 27th May. The bequests of money were to be paid at a time thought most expedient by the executrix, the testator's wife Joan. His son William was left £25, his son John £6 13s 4d, his daughter Joan £10, his daughter Jane £1 and each of his godchildren 4d. Richard and Joan Ellis were each left a ewe and a lamb. Another grandchild John Mose, the son of Thomas, was left the best brass pot after the death of his grandmother Joan, who was left a life interest in the lands called Mellams. Sums of 5s each were bequeathed to the overseers, Thomas Lucas of Headley, his wife's brother and William Lever, his own brother. Three witnesses to the Will were Raff Lucas, Wyllyam Lever and Thomas Gad. The widow and the rector bound themselves well and truly to administer the estate. The burial of Raffe Moze was recorded in Mickleham on 17th April 1585.

Ref: 1585 B 46/1 Will 1585 B 46/2 Inventory

John Procker 211

of Guildford, cardmaker; taken by George Miles, John Tomson and John Billie, 20th May 1585.

In the hall	£	s	d
A table and a forme		2	0
A Chaier and a Cupbord		3	4
A paintewd Cloth		1	0
2 Basens		1	0
6 platters		3	0
7 pewter dishes		2	6
10 Sawsers		1	8
A dosen and a half of flowre pottes		1	8
A pinte pott for wine and a pewter cuppe		1	0
3 Candellstickes, one of them pewter		3	0
An yron Raynge in the Hall			6
One Cubard Cloth			2
In the Parlor			
3 formes and a table		3	0
6 Cushines and a grene Carpet		1	0
2 bedstedelles, a fetherbed, a flockebed and curtynes	1	6	8
Painted Clothes in the Parlor		2	6
3 Chestes		3	4
In The Chamber next to the Street			
A table, a paire of Treselles, 2 formes		2	6
A fether bed, a flocke bed, a bedstedell, one Coverlit, 2 boulsters	1	6	8
His aparell		5	0
A Cheste		1	0
Painted Clothes		2	0
In The Chamber over the parlor			
2 formes, one Table, 3 treselles		1	4
3 flockebedes, 3 pillowes, 3 boulsters, 3 Coverlites, 3 bedstedelles	1	10	0

2 Quilltes		1	8
A standinge Cubard			6
2 bucketes with yron bayles			8
3 Quart pottes, 2 pint pottes		4	0
Woode		12	0
A bedstedell		2	0
3 pillowes of dowen		4	0
Lynone			
6 Table Clothes		6	0
2 paire of Lockrom Shetes		8	0
One Lockrom Shete		2	0
10 Canvas Shettes		10	0
4 pillowberes		2	8
4 Napkinges and one Cubard Cloth		3	0
The Kitchine			
Fowre platters		2	6
2 Chamber pottes		1	0
One bras pott		3	4
5 kettelles		5	0
2 pannes		2	0
2 skymmes and one posnett		1	0
One Chafyndishe		1	0
2 Morters, one of Stone		2	0
18 spones			10
2 dousen of Trenchers			2
A bord			6
2 Sh[*]		2	6
A paire of tounges, 2 ayngerens, a fryinge pan		2	0
A paire of pothokes, 2 potthangers, a Trefte and yron bare		4	0
A paier of Cardes and a spininge whell		1	4
2 drippinge panes		1	0
A fryinge pane			4
The Breuehouse			
10 Tubbes		5	0
A furnace, a keve, a bruinge fatte		10	0
8 kevers		2	8
A Troufe and other old Tubbes		3	0
A bagge of fethers		3	4
A well buckate and a stand and a seve		2	6
[*£11.17.4*]	12	0	3

Administration granted to "Johane, Relicte" on 25th May 1585.

Note: The burial at St. Mary's was registered as Richard Proctor, wool cardmaker, on 9th May 1585. Ref: 1585 Ad 56

Thomas Sayer **212**

of Cranleigh, yeoman; taken by Rychard Tyckner, Thomas Merser and John Mower, 14th May 1585.

	£	s	d
One tabell, one forme, one coberde, one chear wethe other stoles	1	0	0
One Joye bedsteadell, one flocke bed and all that be longethe to hem	2	0	0
In his chamber			
One flocke bed and a steadell		13	4

Wethe towe flocke bed and towe steadell	1	0	0
In the lofte			
One preasse, one cofer		13	4
One Joine tabell wethe tow other tabels, one Joyne forme wethe other chests, wethe fower covertobes wethe towe chestes In wolle one other cheste, three basskes (sic) weth towe bousshels of wheate	1	8	0
Towe peces of newe clothe 8 yardes		13	4
8 payer of shetes, one holen shett, one chrisnyg shett	1	10	0
In steane clothes			10
In the boutry			
One keaffe and fouere keavers and 5 stowbens, one bowlle wethe other smal vessell and other smal vessel		13	4
In course wolle and yeare		4	0
In and other chamber			
One poudryng trowe, two bolles, a cheane and towe formes weth a parre of skeales weth other smal thiynges		10	0
In the howse			
In whatte and Rye, in malte and wottes	1	18	0
8 sakes		6	0
One calrene and towe bras potes and one keitell weth other brase	3	6	8
One doesen and a halfe of peutr platres halfe a dosen peuter desshes, halfe a dosen of poringes and towe dosen of spones wethe saseres and salsellers, one cheafeng dyes, one laten mortre, wethe 5 laten canstiykes	1	6	8
In the kechen chamber			
One chespris, one knedeng trowe and breueng tobe, a bokeng tobe and towe bookes		5	0
In uden vessell and tranchers and drengken potes weth one grenynston		3	4
In yean tolles and iearnes and towe payer of pothengers and one pare of pott hooks, one broche, one deppyng panne, a freyng panne, a brandiarne, eiarne wages wethe uther towels		10	0
In baken in the Roufe	1	13	4
In greace		6	8
In corne in the felde		13	4
For uttes of the ground		10	0
In tember	1	0	0
In beanes		3	0
In geaes, olde and young		2	0
Three hecfores and caves	3	0	0
Three hogges, 5 peyeges		10	0
Towe tabell clotes, 6 tabell napkens		5	0
Hes parrell and mony in hes pors	1	0	0
	27	5	2

Note: William Fawden, parson of Alfold, wrote and witnessed the Will on 29th April 1585. Joan the widow was granted probate on 25th May 1585 and she had a life interest in her husband's considerable property, which she was to hold until the only son John reached the age of 25. The six daughters were each left £6 13s 4d to be paid at different times after the proving of the Will. The overseers, a cousin Richard Rickner of Northow and a brother John Greetyst, were charged with the care of the children if their mother were to die before they married or reached their majority: Anne, Jane, Elizabeth, Ellyn, Katherin and Margaret, were named in that order. A lease of Parkhooke field was given to the widow for her life and then to young John. The mansion house called Tilers in Cranleigh together with all barns, stables, buildings, orchards and gardens, were committed to her care, charging her to keep them in good repair. Also given was land called Sherelocks and Manningshill in Cranleigh and a house called Longhurst.

Ref: 1585 B 58/1 Will 1585 B 58/2 Inventory

Harry Skete **213**

of West Horsley; taken by Edward Stynte, James Redford and Thomas Broker, 20th May 1585.

	£	s	d
His aparell, a fryse Cote, a lethern Jarken, a whyghyte payre of hosse withe reste of his aparell		16	0
In his purse		3	0
In the hale			
A tabell, a forme, a cobord, a noulde paynted Clothe, 2 stoles, a Cheyer		7	0
2 floke bedes withe there furnyter	1	6	8
4 Chestes		5	0
3 bras potes, 7 keteles, a possnet, a panne, a skemer	1	13	4
8 platores, 5 peuter dysshes, 3 saseres, 2 saultes		13	4
3 Candellstykes, won chafynge dyshe, a dosen of spones		2	0
A broche, a fryinge pan, a Cobeyren, a trifte		3	0
A payre of pothokes and a pothangeres, a gerdyrne			10
2 axes, 2 billes, 3 weges withe the other impellmentes		4	0
3 payre of Canvas shetes, a payre of holon shetes, a payre of lokerom shetes, 3 tabell Clothes	1	13	0
2 stonen potes, 2 botteles, 3 woden platers, a dosen and a halfe of trencheres		1	0
8 tubes, a pouderinge troffe, 6 boules, a knedinge kever, a vate withe other lumber		16	0
A dunge carte, a longe Carte, a payre of wheles, a harow	1	0	0
A hekefor withe a Calfe, 11 shepe, a mare and a Coulte, 2 hoges	4	10	0
Fower henes and a koce, a gose and a gander		3	0
2 bussheles of wheate, a busshell and a halfe of maulte		6	0
3 akeres and a halfe of wheate, 2 akeres of barley, 5 akeres of wootes, 3 rodmeles of pease	5	14	0
Won leasse of manfeldes	4	0	0
[*£23.17.2*]	23	15	2
Detes to be payd of the same -	4	0	0
[*Listed on Will*] I doe owe Robert Stackford of Moulseye	3	0	0
paid+ I doe owe John Skeete of Estclandon		12	0
6 shillings paid I doe owe John Tayler of Ockinge		7	0
I doe owe John Goddard of Stroudstreate, the yonger, maried man		5	4
++ I doe owe Thomas Poore		3	0
I doe owe John Goddard, shoomaker		2	0
+ I doe owe Edward Stint		1	6
I doe owe my sister Lee		10	0

Note: The Will was dated 7th February and proved on 25th May 1585. The residiary legatee and executrix was the testator's wife Joan, who was to be guardian of his son Henry and to occupy Wrenneland in Little Bookham for that part of the 8 years for which it was held by licence of the Lord of the Manor, until the said Henry came of age at 21. Harry asked to be buried in West Horsley churchyard, giving 1s each to the church and to the poor men's box there. Sums of 5s each were to go to Thomas Tydy and John Elliote, the overseers. Apart from the gift of a sheep to his servant Robert Taylor, the only other bequests were of specific household goods and a cow to his 2 sons Henry and John. Each was to be his brother's heir in the event of an early demise without lawful issue. A large part of John's legacy was to count as standards of the house. The 2 overseers witnessed the will, as well as Edward and Alexander Stint, Richard West and James Ridford. The aforesaid James, yeoman of West Horsley and the widow were bound well and truly to administer the estate.

Ref: 1585 B 60/1 Will 1585 B 60/2 Inventory

Thomas Songhurst **214**

of Abinger; taken by John Astone, Walter Songhurst, Robert Smyth, John Eversed and others, 20th May 1585.

	£	s	d
Two keine	3	0	0
Two two yerelinge bullocks	1	6	8
Foure tege shepe and thre lambs		12	0
Foure shotts		13	4
The best fether bed and bedstedle with bolsters and pillows and all things belonginge ther unto	1	10	0
The second best bedd and bedstedle with bolsters and pillowes and all things belonginge ther unto	1	0	0
Foure paire of worne shetts		13	4
Two old chests		2	0
One old Cawdren		10	0
One other badd Cawdren		4	0
Thre smale brasse potts		15	0
Two old brasse panns		6	8
Two old posnetts		1	8
One chafer and one chafing dishe		1	8
One dripping pann and one frying pann and one girdiron		2	6
Five old pewter platers and five pewter dishes, thre porengers, tow sawsers and two saltsellers and one skummer		10	0
Two iron spittgs, one treft, one old andiron and a paire of potthocks and potthangers and a paire of tongs		6	0
Foure tubbs, thre barrels, one kymnell with other wodden vessells		13	4
Tow standing tables with formes and chaires		6	8
Axes, bills, wedges, with other Yplements and necessaries belonging to husbandrye		3	4
Two acres of grene wheate	1	6	8
Two acres of grene otts		13	4
His aparell		10	0
Of Redye Money in his purse		13	4
[*£16.1.6*]	15	11	6

Note: The Will was dated 30th April and proved on 25th May 1585. His wife Margaret was appointed executrix and residuary legatee. The overseers, Robert Smyth of Wotton, husbandman and Olyver Nye, were to have 3s 4d each above their charges for their pains. Great care was taken over the exact order of inheritance of the twelve acre Millfield alias Haynes. Instructions were given for the felling of the trees, "Leving allways standing all yong tres of ock and beche under the scantlen of 12 inches in compas about". Walter, John, Richard and Edmond, his four sons, had specific bequests, together with Thomas, son of Walter. The testator gave to the said Walter his best brass pot and his best iron spit, both to remain to the right heir male from heir to heir for ever, but Margaret to have them in her keeping for life. John Everseed and Alane Clarke witnessed the Will with others. The widow herself, Walter Songhurst of Ockley, yeoman and Robert Smyth of Wotton, husbandman, bound themselves to see it well and truly administered. As was his wish, Thomas Songhurste was buried in Abinger churchyard on 7th May 1585.

Ref: 1585 B 64/1 Will 1585 B 64/2 Inventory

Denise Towler **215**

of Tatsfield, widow; taken by Thomas Steven, John Woodden and Nicholas Burstowe, 10th May 1585.

	£	s	d
In the hall	£	s	d
A table, one forme and two trestles			8
One payre of pott hangers			2
Foure olde kettles and a little brasse pott		5	0
Foure olde platters of pewter and one bason of pewter		2	0
Two olde pailes			2
In the chamber			
One flocke bedd, one bolster, one pillowe, one coverlett, two blancketts and an olde painted tester		5	0
An olde cubbord and two chestes		5	0
Three shettes, one corsse table clothe, three olde kercheefes		4	0
Two gownes, two petticotes, one cloke and one olde pettycote		13	4
Two olde tubbes and an olde charne			4
The cattle			
Two kene	1	10	0
Foure sheepe		10	0
Two younge hogges		2	0
Two hennes			9
Debtes due to her			
In the hands of Thomas Lighe of Tatsfielde	1	0	0
	4	18	5

Note: The Will was written on 22nd February and proved on 27th May 1585 by the executor and residuary legatee, her son John Towler. The testatrix asked to be buried in the churchyard of Tatsfield and she gave 3s 4d towards the repairs of the church there. At the age of 21 her grandson John Banks was to be given 40s and a six-year-old cow. Her daughter Alice was immediately to be given 20s. At the same time a cow and 2 ewes were to be given to Alice Towler, the daughter of the executor. A ewe each was to go to 2 goddaughters: Elizabeth Isacke and Denise Wood, the daughter of her brother. A lamb was given to her godson John Multe. Two pounds of wool, not mentioned in the Inventory, together with her best gown, were given to the widow Johane Tymberton. The best and the second best petticoats were to go to Agnes Wastone and Agnes Hyrsillden, both of Westerham. Sums of 20d apiece were left to the overseers John Woodden and Thomas Steven, who witnessed the Will together with the writer Symon Tather, Nycolas Bristowe and Nycolas Wastone. John Towler, husbandman and John Heywood, yeoman, both of Tatsfield, bound themselves well and truly to administer the estate.

Ref: 1585 B 67/1 Will 1585 B 67/2 Inventory

Agnes Underwode **216**

of Worplesdon, widow; taken by Rycharde Crose, Johne Weale and Johne Russell, wheelmaker, 20th May 1585.

	£	s	d
The Halle	£	s	d
A table, 1 forme, the Benches		2	0
Twoe Andirons, 2 Broches, 1 Trevette with a drippinge pane		?	0
2 bras potes, 1 kettell, 1 cawderen, a postente		12	0
4 platters, 4 pewter dishes, 1 Sawser, 2 Candelstickes		4	0
The pothangers, the pothowkes, a Gridiron		1	8
The Lofte			
2 oulde bedes, 3 boulsters, 1 pillowe		10	0
Three Keverleedes		10	0

Twoe payre of Sheetes, a Table cloth		6	0
Twoe Chestes		2	0
The Chamber			
1 boulting houtch, 1 oulde cheste with other Lumber		3	4
Her Apparell	1	0	0
In her purse		2	0
Withoute			
One Coulte, one Sowe, twoe pigges		10	0
One Hive of Bees		4	0
	4	15	0

Note: The Will was dated 6th May and proved on 25th May 1585. The testatrix appointed as executor her only son Christopher . She presented the executor and the overseers, Richard Crose and John Weale, with a gift of 12d each. She asked to be buried in Worplesdon churchyard and she gave 12d to the poor. All her goods except the bees were carefully bestowed; a linen wheel and a woollen wheel not listed in the inventory went to Alice Watts. Christopher had the major share but her 3 married daughters also did well. Elizabeth Lashford, her husband Anthony and daughter Elizabeth, had money and goods, as did Agnes Elliate and her daughter Alice. Alice Watts and her daughter Frances also had a good share. The witnesses were John Cutler, parson of Worplesdon, Richard Crose and John Davys alias Tayler. The parish register records on 10th May 1585 the burial of the wife of Robert Underwode.

Ref: 1585 B 69/1 Will 1585 B 69/2 Inventory

Thomas Underwood **217**

of Bisley; taken by John Cobbet the elder, John Vincent and Robert Cobbet the elder, 1585, [*the name John Symons struck through*].

	£	s	d
In his Purse at his death		2	0
His wearing apparrell		5	0
A cubburde with all his ffurniture		13	4
In Brasse		3	4
In Kytchyn stuffe as wood and Iron		3	0
A Table in the hall and a cradle there and Stoles		1	8
A fflock bead with all his furniture		10	0
A matteris with his furniture		4	0
3 chestes		2	0
Tow kyne and tow bullockes	2	10	0
A mare and a colt		10	0
In shepe	1	10	0
In swyne		6	8
In Gese and hennes		1	8
3 acares of Rye and a halfe	2	0	0
Tow acares of oates		6	8
	9	9	4

Note: The Will was dated 6th May and proved on 25th May 1585. The testator appointed his wife Alice as his executrix, to pay his debts and legacies. His brother and his brother-in-law, Robert Underwood and John Rance, were made overseers. He gave 4d to the poor men's box. John Rance, who had stood as surety for debt, was to have the annual profits from the dwelling house held of Mr Lewsher until Alice was able to discharge that unnamed debt. Provision was made for his daughters Agnes and Jane, when they reached the age of 18, to have the use and profit of a red cow and a black cow, respectively. On similar conditions his son George was to have a black heifer, but in the case of his son William the profit on 10 sheep was to go towards his upbringing by whoever should undertake the care of the boy, recognising that the stock was finally to be given to him. John Cobbet the elder and John Symons witnessed the Will. The administrations bond was provided by the widow, by Robert Underwood of Stoke next Guildford, husbandman and by John Rawnse of Cranleigh, yeoman. The burial was registered on 7th May 1585.

Ref: 1585 B 70/1 Will 1585 B 70/2 Inventory

William Walter **218**

of Mitcham, yeoman; taken by William Jackson, William Longe, Robert Giles, John Everist, Edward Sone and George Frith, 20th May 1585.

	£	s	d
In the hale			
A Table, a Forme and a paire of Tresseles		3	4
A Cupbord and 2 lyttell Chayres, 2 stoles		5	0
A Cradell		2	0
2 Wheles		1	4
In the parlor			
2 bedstedes of bordes, 2 Flocke bedes, 3 kiveringes, 2 payre of blankettes, 2 bowlsters	1	13	4
6 Chestes whereof one waynestecote and 5 of bordes		16	0
A Cowpbord of Waynestecote and a chaire		8	0
5 Cowssions		3	4
14 payre of Sheites fyne and cowrse	2	0	0
8 table clothes, a dozen of napkins and 5 pillowbeares		13	4
A Testor of a bed of lynnen		2	0
A Cote, a payre of hose, 3 Clockes and a doblett	1	0	0
3 paynted clothes		1	0
In the chamber over the parlor			
A sadell and 10 pounds of hempe		4	0
In the lofte over the buttry			
A Bedstedle		2	6
3 peces of wollen clothe, 2 white, one Russett	1	10	0
One payre of Stocke cardes		1	0
One Bow and 6 Arrowes		1	8
In the entry betwene the hale and the parlor			
A bowltinge hutche		1	0
In the buttry nexte the parlor			
11 platters, 5 pewter dishes, a bason, 3 Sawsers, a pewter pynte pott, 3 Salte sellers, 5 pewter spones, 2 Candlestickes of latten, one morter of latten with a pestell	1	0	0
Tubes with other lomber		8	0
In the buttrye nexte the hale			
2 kylderkins, 2 Firkins, one cherne and 2 bottelles		3	4
In the sarvantes Chamber nexte the entry			
One olde bedsted, an olde kiveringe, a payre of Sheites and a boulster		5	0
A Cowlter and a shaire, 3 Sithes with other olde Iron		5	0
In the Kytchen			
2 brase pottes, one Caldron, 4 kyttes, a Chaffinge dishe, 2 Skyllettes, a payre of pothangers and a spite	1	0	0
2 Fattes to Brew withall and 3 towbes, 4 payles		13	4
In the Corne lofte			
3 quarters of Rye and 5 bussheles of Barley and 9 sackes	2	0	0
In the malte lofte			
Certayne malte	7	0	0
In the stable			
2 geldins, 2 mares and harnis belonging to them, a carte sadle and a ridinge pannell	5	0	0

3 Coltes	1	6	8
A Carte and a plowe, 2 payres of harrowes and a donnge carte	1	10	0
2 Oxen	5	0	0
4 kyne and 2 hayfayres	6	0	0
40 shepe and 20 lammes	10	0	0
14 hoges and piges	1	13	4
In the barne			
2 Fannes, 2 Pytche pronges and one bushell and a wynoinge sheite		5	0
Growinge in the Feildes			
13 acres of wheate and Rye	13	0	0
17 acres of barley at 18 shillings the acre	15	2	0
12 acres of beanes, peace, Tares and otes	8	0	0
Good Dettes			
John White of Mitcham, alekeeper, for malt	2	0	0
Wydow Etheridge of Mitcham for malt		15	0
Owinge more by John White for malte		13	4
Desperat Dettes owinge to the testator in his life tyme at Westram			
Owinge by Christopher Bawcome 29 bushells of malt at 22 pence the bushell [*£2.13.2*]	2	1	6
Owinge by Hew Johnson for malte	1	10	0
	96	0	4
Owinge by the said testator in his life tyme as ffolloweth			
Owinge to Mr Rutland his landelorde	5	0	0
Owinge to Richard Powell of Martyn	5	0	0
Owinge to a kynesman of the said testator dwellynge in Kent	3	0	0
	13	0	0
The chargis of the Funerall of the said testator			
Payed for the same	1	0	0
[Other debts listed in the Will:]			
Owing by the testator to Mr. Knowesberye of Wansworth 6 quarters of barleye	3	12	0
Owing to the testator by the Widdowe Deacon of West Throme		2	0

Note: The Will was dated 10th April and proved on 27th May 1585. The executrix and residuary legatee was the testator's wife Isabel. The overseers were William Jackson and William Long, both husbandmen of Mitcham. The family messuage, together with 18 or 19 acres of arable land called Nisils Hoult at Tonbridge in Kent, was the subject of detailed order of inheritance. Alice Walter, William's mother, was still to occupy the land with his brother John, as long as the old lady lived. Then it was to go to William's 2 sons, the next generation of William and John Walter. They were each to deposit on bond 100 marks [£66 13s 4d] to ensure an annual payment of £3 each to their mother Isabel. The boys were to have 12 wethers and the 3 daughters, Katherine, Ellen and Joan, were each given £6 13s 4d and 4 ewes. The Will was witnessed by the overseers, together with Robert Musgrave the curate, Edward Sooan, Richard Hargrave, Raphe Tissie and John Betts. The widow and the overseers bound themselves well and truly to administer the estate. The burial was registed on 14th April 1585.

Ref: 1585 B 72/1 Will 1585 B 72/2 Inventory

Geffrey Warde **219**

of St. Saviour's, Southwark, waterman; taken by John Wyngreve, Willyam Tychener and John Dorrell, 13th May 1585.

	£	s	d
In the Hall			
One table of wainskott with a frame and six ioyned stooles		13	4
A presse		16	0

An olde chaier and three small chaiers					1	8
An olde forme with a small matted chaier					1	0
Two olde quisshions						3
[*£1.12.3*]	£1	2	3			
In the Parlor						
Fyve lyttle kettles, 2 bigger kettles, two possenettes					12	0
Two olde frienge pannes, two drippinge pannes, an old iron pott, one gridiron, 2 spittes with a skymmer					4	0
A paier of small awndirons, two pott hangers, an olde paier of tongues with a fier shovell					2	0
		18	0			
Pewter						
A Pewter pottle pott, three quarte pottes with 3 pynte pottes of pewter					6	0
Nyne platters					10	0
Six disshes					4	0
Three sawcers with a small fruite dishe						8
A pynte pewter bottle for Aquavite					1	0
Three olde bowe pottes with three salte sellers					1	4
Syx small candlestickes and a chafing dishe					4	0
An olde cheste, a wasshinge bowle, two treene platters with a dozen and a halfe of trenchers					2	0
	£1	9	0			
In the chamber over the hall						
A standinge bedsted, an old fetherbed, a mattres, a strawe bedd, 7 pillowes with fethers, two bolsters, two coverlettes, a paier of sheetes with a broken trundle bedsted				1	6	8
6 paier of olde towen sheetes and one odd sheete with three flaxen sheetes				1	0	0
Two shorte towen table clothes with one flaxen table clothe					2	6
Fyve pillowbeers, two diaper napkins with 6 towen napkins					8	0
A blacke cloke havinge a cape of velvett with silke lace and halfe lyned with baies					13	4
An olde cloke withowte lyninge and a hatt					2	0
A clothe paier of breeches, an old frise Jerkin, a trusse with a frise gowne					13	4
3 shirtes and 3 bandes					5	0
A danske cheste and three other chestes					10	0
An olde wicker chaier						4
	£5	1	2			
In the chamber over the Parlor						
A bedsted with a halfe hedd, two flockes beddes, 2 bolsters and two old coverlettes					4	0
Three halfe tubbes, a stande, an olde cheste with a lynnen wheele					2	6
		6	6			
The Boates						
A Wherrie and a cocke, a rode, an ore, a broken ore, fyve skulles with barrettes and quisshions belonging to theim				2	0	0
A small ancker and an old rope					1	6
	£2	1	6			
In readye money					3	0
		3	0			
			[*£11.11.5*]	11	1	6

Note: The Will was written on 7th May 1585 and probate was granted to the widow of the deceased, the sole executrix Agnes Warde, three weeks later on 28th May. Geffrey Ward called himself a waterman of Paris Garden. The remaining term of years on his dwelling house there was bequeathed for life to his wife and the term of years remaining at her decease was to go to his son John Warde and daughter Katherine Spencer. Agnes was given half his goods and chattels. The other half was to be divided equally between the aforesaid two children by the overseers, his loving friends Robert Wayman and John Spencer. His servant Robert was given his "blewe goskines and white dublet of Canvas". Of the 5 witnesses to the Will, John Spencer, John Gardener, Robert Wayman, William Jackson and Arnold Saunders, only the last was able to write his name. The parish register of St. Saviour's Southwark records the burial of Jeffree Warde on 11th May 1585.

Ref: 1585 B 73/1 Will 1575 B 73/2 Inventory

William White **220**

of Collins Green, Leigh, yeoman; taken by Mr Richarde Lechford Esquire, Christopher Crouse and Richarde Bartelett, 29th April 1585.

	£	s	d
The Hawle			
One Table, one Forme, one Cupborde and one stoole	1	0	0
12 pewter platters, 12 pewter dishes, 11 porringers, 4 saucers, 3 fruite disshes, 2 smale pewter peeces, 2 saltes, 14 spoones, 5 Candlestickes, 2 flower pottes, 2 Chafinge disshes, one spice morter with a pestle there unto belonginge, 13 trenchers	2	10	0
The Chamber over the Hawle			
One Joyned bedstedd, One fether bedd, one bolster, 2 Coverlettes	3	0	0
One Joyned Table with a Carpett of Darnex		6	8
6 glasses and two litle viols			6
The Parler at the Easte ende of the Howse			
One Joyned beddstedd, One fether bedd, one Matte, one paier of sheetes, 2 blanckettes, one coverlett, twoe bolsters, 5 pillowes, a fringe of cruell hanginge about the bedde	3	0	0
One Joyned Table, 6 Joyned stooles, 6 cusshions		16	0
The Chamber at the weste ende of the howse			
One bedstedd of Carpenters worke, one olde fether bed, one bolster, 2 blankettes, one coverlett, a tester of buckeram over the bedd	1	0	0
One other bedstedd of Carpenters worke, one payer of sheetes, one old coverlet, one sheete nailed over the bedd		6	8
10 partelettes, 2 olde bondes, 12 course napkinges, 2 course aperns, 3 old chestes, one old Joyned Forme and one old Chaier	1	14	0
The lower Chamber in the weste ende of the howse			
One bedstedd of Carpenters worke, one old Fetherbedd, one bolster and one coverlett	1	13	4
6 chestes greate and smale		13	4
15 paier of sheetes	5	0	0
3 table clothes, two apernes, three handewypers		12	0
7 payer of sheetes and one odd sheete of the best sorte	4	0	0
3 dozen and three napkins of the beste sorte		15	0
2 table clothes of the beste sorte		10	0
Three towells		9	0
Divers peeces of fine lynnen	2	10	0
3 shertes, 6 smockes with other smale peeces of lynnen	1	0	0
4 upper boddies, 3 of taffaty and one of grograine, 3 stomachers	1	3	4
4 hattes		10	0
2 shertes, 2 dublettes, one paier of hose, 2 Coates and one Cloake	1	10	0
Two remnantes of wollen clothe		3	0

4 woemens gownes, 5 pettycoates, 2 kirtles, three savegardes	7	0	0
2 aperns, one paier of stockinges, one stammell waste coate and one peece of lyncie wolsye		10	0
15 pounde of lynnen yearne		15	0
One cupborde of Joyned worke	1	0	0
The mylke howse			
2 brasse pottes, 2 possnettes, 2 brass pannes, 4 kettles	1	16	4
2 kymnells, 6 traies, one charme with other woodden vessell		10	0
The Kytchin			
2 drippinge pannes, one handyron, one cobyron, 2 spyttes, one trevett, 2 pott hangers, 2 paier of potthookes, one gredyron, one choppinge kniffe, one fyer showell		7	8
One Ioytinge fatt, one cheespresse, one hempe brake, one old halfe pype, one powderinge troughe and 2 other old tubbes		19	8
In the Rowffe			
Of beeffe and baken	2	10	0
The bowtinge Howse			
One knedinge trowe, 2 lynnen wheeles, one woollen wheele, one Cheese presse, one old boultinge tubb, one wheele for a wheele barrowe with other smale peces		12	0
The lofte in the Easte ende of the Howse			
5 quarters and a halfe of maulte	3	6	0
One quarter of Oattes		6	8
2 quarters and a halfe of wheate	1	15	0
4 sackes, a seed cott, 3 olde tubbes and one showle		7	0
21 pounde of wooll		13	4
One other bedstedd		10	0
One sythe with a cradle thereto belonginge, one sawe, 4 awgers, pronges, wymbles, hammers with other suche like stuffe		10	0
2 saddles, one syde saddle and one rode saddle		6	8
2 buckinge tubbes, 2 paier of sheetes and certaine peeces of lynnen therin and one grynding stone	1	0	0
In the Feildes			
4 acres and a halfe of Wheate	4	0	0
7 acres and a halfe of oates	3	0	0
4 kyne with there calfes, 2 barrens and a bull	11	0	0
3 three yerlinges bullockes, 3 two yere linges and three yearlinge bullockes	7	0	0
9 hogges greate and smale	1	10	0
One Mare and 2 coltes	3	0	0
18 sheepe	3	12	0
One carte with the wheeles and 2 Harrowes	1	0	0
4 old geese and 12 gulles		7	0
6 hennes, 3 cockes		4	6
2 Turkies		2	0
In readye Monye			
In Redy monye		11	7
Debtes sperat owinge to the testator at the tyme of his Deathe			
Of John Smythe of Burstowe	1	9	10
Of Richard Charlewoode of Leigh		7	6
	96	3	7

Doubtefull debtes owinge unto the testator at the tyme of his decease
Of one Underwoode of Worpstone late father unto Cybill White late

deceased	5	0	0
Debts owing by the testator at the tyme of his Deathe.			
To John Croftes children of Charlewood	4	0	0
To Richard Lucasse of Betchworthe	1	0	0
To Thomas Towe of Worspestone		16	0
To Margarett White		14	0
To John Liffe of Ragatt	1	0	0
	7	10	0
Funealle expenses		5	8

Note: The Will was dated 16th April and proved on 4th May 1585. The testator asked to be buried in Leigh churchyard and he gave 3s 4d to the poor of the parish and 1s to the repair of the church. He appointed his wife Sibille executrix and residuary legatee. Sums of 3s 4d each were left to the overseers, William Bristowe of Leigh and George Francke of Cowlsdon. The considerable sums of 20 marks [£13 13s 4d], given to his 2 younger sons Francis and Henry and to his daughter Julian, were to be paid in that order at 2-yearly intervals, if necessary being raised by the overseers or responsible sureties by selling some of his goods or cattle. His eldest son William was left the 2nd best bed in the upper chamber at the east end of the house, together with the bedstead and bedding and the table from the hall. William's 3 children were each left 2s. Sums of 1s each were bequeathed to a godchild William Elzey, to Henry Wheeler and to William Turner. Richard Rowley the younger wrote the will, to which was added the mark of William Skotte and that of the testator. William White, the son of the testator, was granted letters of administration, his mother Sibille having since died.

Ref: 1585 B 77/1 Will 1585 B 77/2 Inventory

William Worsfold **221**

of Wotton, yeoman; taken by Lawrence attLee, John Hayne, Rychard Worsfold, John Eversed and others, 20th April 1585.

	£	s	d
6 oxen	15	0	0
five Steres	10	0	0
thre barrens	4	0	0
7 keine	13	6	8
8 towyerelings	5	13	4
7 twelvemonthing bullocks	4	0	0
Syx horse bease	10	0	0
12 smale hoges, 7 Wanyer pigges, 7 sucking pigs	3	0	0
7 score old shepe	28	0	0
40 lambs	3	0	0
syx acres of grene corne	4	0	0
11 acres of grene otts	4	0	0
wheat and mault in the howse	1	0	0
12 hoges of bacon	4	0	0
Tow paire of old shodd wheles, one wayne, tow dungpotts, one plow and ploweyrons, foure youks and chaines and thre old harrows	3	0	0
Tymber and woodd in Ockwood Land wrought and standinge	20	0	0
Tymber and wood in Hutchins and Sturks wrought and unwrought	40	0	0
One Joyne bedstedle, one fether bedd with bolsters and pillows and all things belonging to hym	2	0	0
One Joyne other bedstedle, one flocke bedd and all thinges belonging to hym	1	0	0
Tow other bedstedles with bedds and all things belonging to hym	1	0	0

Ten paire of shets	2	0	0
Tow Joyne cobberds	1	0	0
One Cawdron, one brasse pan, tow brasse potts, thre ketles, tow chafinge dishes, one laten ladle, one skummer, foure candlesticks and one laten morter	2	0	0
One dosen of pewter platers, foure porengers and to salt sellers		10	0
Foure iron spitts, a paire of potthangers, one trevett		6	8
One fate, one bruyng tubb and tun and all other bruyng vessells		10	0
All milke vessells and all other woodden vessells		6	8
Thre sadells		10	0
Tow tables, to formes, to Joyne stoles and to chaires		3	0
Gese, Ducks and henns		10	0
Debts owyng	30	0	0
One leace of sertayne yeares yet to come	10	0	0
Healing stone Causcers and pynnyng	3	0	0
Bills, axes, awgers, wedges and all other [*blot*] necessaries		10	0
Of Redye monye in his purse	2	0	0
His aparell	2	0	0
	[*231*	*6*	*4*]

Note: The Will was written on 7th April and proved on 25th May 1585. Alice, the testator's wife, was the residuary legatee and executrix, who was granted administration of the estate. Also bound well and truly to see this carried out was John Stere of Ockley, yeoman. The overseers were 2 other yeomen, Lawrence atLee of Abinger and Richard Worsfold of Ockley. William, his only son, was the major beneficiary of the livestock and implements. Elizabeth and Jane, the unmarried daughters of his present wife Alice, had gifts of £40 with 20 sheep and £20 with 10 sheep, respectively. Three daughters of his previous wife were each given £10: namely Johane, the wife of Thomas Dalton; Mary Worsfold; and Alice, the wife of Simon King. The 40s annual rent due on his property Huchyns in Wotton, from William Lamberte of Banstead, was to be paid to Alice Worsfold for life, then to William Worsfold, son of the testator, for life and then to his heirs. In addition Alice was to be granted free access to remove any "timber, woods, trees and stuffe felled and cut down, wrought and unwrought lying and being upon the lands called Huchyns". There were minor bequests to other young relatives: to Johanne Worsfold and William Dalton, to John Haine alias Cockes and to John Franckton, his own servant. The remaining years of his lease of Stirkes, a tenement and 20 acres of land, was given to his son William. The 6 witnesses were John Hayne, John Eversed, Rychard Worsfold, Lawrence Atlee, Robard Lilly and William Engler.

Ref: 1585 B 79/1 Will 1585 B 79/2 Inventory

1586

Richard Alyngham **222**

of Nutfield, yeoman; taken by John Turner, John Jones and John Laker, 9th May 1586.

In the Hall	£	s	d
2 chayers			6
A plannke table and a fourme		1	4
One brase pote, 2 kytelles, one cawdiron, 1 postnat and one Iron potte		10	0
Pott hangers and pothookes			8
3 fletches of bacon		3	0
3 platters, 3 pewter dysh[*es*], 2 sawsers, one salte and one porringer of pewter		4	6
6 tren platters, 4 dyshes, a dossen of trenchers, 4 spones and one skymer		1	4

A fyer rake, a payer of bellowes			3
2 candellstyckes			6
In the Kitchin			
One stande, one Keler, one fyrkyn, one charne, one fate, one shale, 2 syves		4	0
One olde chese prese and 4 old tubbes and other Lumber		1	4
6 mylke bowles		1	4
One olde malte quarne		2	6
In the litel chamber			
One chafe bedde, a boulster, 2 pyllowes, 2 blancketes and one coverlette		7	0
4 borded bedsteedes		3	4
In the bed chamber			
2 chafe beedes, 2 boulsters, 2 blancketes and one old coverlet		3	4
2 old chestes		2	8
2 Testers of lynen, 9 payer of sheetes, 3 table cloathes, 2 table napkynes and 2 pyllowebers	1	11	0
One stone of Towe		1	0
His apparrell		5	0
Money in his purse		1	6
A bushell of wheate		2	0
3 bushelles of Rye		5	0
One bushell of Otmell		1	0
17 bushells and a halfe of Ottes which her sone Peter is to delyver unto her after the next mowing of ottes		8	9
One loade and a halfe of haye		15	0
One sowe and 6 pygges		6	8
Necessary Toles as bylles		1	8
	6	5	2
Debtes that he dyd owe when he dyed		7	6

Note: The Will was dated 9th February and proved on 17th May 1586. The executrix and residuary legatee was the testator's wife Alice. His overseers were his son-in-law Andrew Marden of Reigate, husbandman and John Kyllick of Kings in Nutfield. He asked to be buried in Nutfield churchyard. His son Francis was to be given a 2-gallon brass pot after Alice's death. Amy, his daughter, was to be given a spinning wheel for linen and 5 useful items of hardware at her marriage or the age of 26. His son Peter as the lawful male heir was to have and to pass on to the next in direct male line, 4 items to be counted as standards of the house for ever: a malt quern, a kneading trough, a great trough and a great cauldron. There was a further bequest to Peter of the table in the hall, shelves and boards in the house and a comprehensive list of farming gear. William Mathewe wrote the will, on which Richard made a shaky mark. The widow and Andrew Marden bound themselves well and truly to administer the estate. The burial of Richard Allingham of Ropers is recorded on 22nd May 1586 in the parish register.

Ref: 1586 B 2/1 Will 1586 B 2/2 Inventory

Henry Bray **223**

of Reigate, tanner; taken by Christopher Cruste of Leigh and Robert Burstowe of Charlwood, 28th April 1586.

	£	s	d
His pursse and his gyrdell and the money in his pursse		2	0
All his apparell	1	13	4
1 ffeather bed, 1 strasheete, 1 payre of sheetes, 1 payre off blanketes, 1 covalet with the bedsted	1	13	4
1 fflocke bed and 1 payre off sheetes with that that belongeth thare unto		10	0

1 trettell bed with belong thairto		5	0
7 payre of sheetes, 2 table clothe, 6 napkynes	1	6	8
3 chestes		4	0
1 ffairbed, one bolster and 1 pyllow		13	4
1 table, a cowbord, 3 chayeres		10	0
1 dosen and a halfe off pewtar	1	0	0
1 chaffe bed and 1 coveryng		2	6
3 booshelles off wheate and Rye, 1 quarter off oten maulte		13	4
3 keatelles, 3 eyarne potes, 1 panne, 4 lytell possenates	1	6	8
10 trugges, 5 ffyrkenes, 2 Kymnelles, 1 tunne, 1 chese presse, 2 olde tubbes and 1 broche		14	0
2 lytell spittes		2	0
3 hogges of baken		10	0
6 keene, one bullock, 4 caulves	10	0	0
2 mares, one nag, 1 colte	4	0	0
5 pyges		10	0
3 akeres of wheat in grasse	1	10	0
3 akeres of ottes		10	0
3 lodes of tanne	1	0	0
30 ffattes and sistarnes, 4 peces of hoopes	8	0	0
1 tanne mylle		13	4
1 gryn stone			10
5 dyckeres off backes	40	0	0
6 dycker off over leather and a halfe	32	10	0
3 hynnes and 1 cock		2	8
[*£110.3.0*]	104	3	0

Note: The nuncupative Will was dated 19th April and proved on 17th May 1586. The residuary legatees and joint executors were his wife Clemence and his elder son Henry. The overseers were William Kelly of Horley and Edmund Chesman of Leigh. Two of those bearing witness to the promises made were Christopher Cruste of Leigh and John Shooe of Horley. The testator's younger son Richard was given £10 and the executors were instructed to keep the boy in school until he could write and read and cast accounts perfectly. His 3 daughters, Ann, Elizabeth and Margery, were each given £6 13s 4d and a year-old bullock. All these bequests were to fall due at 25 years of age or upon marriage.

Ref: 1586 B 8/1 Will 1586 B 8/2 Inventory

Thomas Filpe **225**

of Frensham, yeoman; taken by Thomas Lufe, Rychard Bristow and Thomas Upfould, 26th April 1586.

	£	s	d
His purse and his Aparell	2	0	0
Two feather bedes	2	13	4
5 floke bedes	2	0	0
The bolsters, pellowes and Cusiones	2	3	4
The Coverlettes and blankettes and Carpetes	3	6	8
6 peere of shetes	2	3	4
3 sellinges and two Cartaines	1	13	4
The Tabelle Clothes and Tabell napkenes	1	10	0
3 Joine bedstadeles	1	10	4
The plaine bedstadeles		14	4
All the Chustes	1	3	4
The painted Clothes		18	0
All the puter	2	14	0

Two basones, 3 Caffinge disses, one mortere and Candelstikes	1	0	0
All the brase	4	6	2
Broges, Angers, drippinge paines and one trifte		14	6
3 Colbordes	1	3	0
Tabeles, formes, Chaeres and stolles		6	6
All the wodden vessell	2	11	0
Axses, billes, shovelles and all olde Iere		16	0
One peere of sklles and Wattes		6	0
Cloth, Carene and Wooll	1	12	0
For malte and barlye	1	7	0
The baken		14	0
Sixe oxen	11	13	4
Sixe kine	11	0	0
5 bollockes	2	0	0
One gildinge, two mares and two Coltes	3	8	8
Wethers, tiges, Ewes and lames	20	12	0
The hogges	1	13	0
The Rie in the barene	2	10	0
The otes in the barene	1	13	4
The Rie and the otes upon the lande	8	0	0
One Carte, one plowe and all that belongeth therto	2	8	0
The bees		3	0
The Wattelles		8	0
Two Sithes		2	0
One lader and bordes		1	4
One Coke and hinnes		3	0
[*£105.1.10*]	106	0	10

Note: The Will was dated 20th March and proved on 16th May 1586. The testator's wife Tamsonne was made executrix and residuary legatee. Thomas Paine, yeoman and John Boxsoulle, husbandman, both of Frensham, were to have 5s between them as overseers. Thomas asked to be buried in Frensham churchyard, bequeathing 1s each to the church and to the poor man's box and 3 bushells of rye to the poor of the parish. A bed and bedding, useful hardware, his stuff at Headley, a great cupboard, 2 barrels and kevers for brewing, 2 bushells of rye, the best colt and 10 ewes, were given to his daughter Ann, with the addition of a great cauldron and a trough at her mother's death. His daughter Jane was given £3 already held by her husband, some hardware, 2 working steers, a colt, 10 ewes, 2 bushells of rye from Frensham and all the rye then at Headley. John and Joan, his brother and sister, were given his best coat and a bushell of rye, respectively. To John and Joan Alberry went 12d each, to his godson Thomas Heath a lamb and to each of his godchildren 4d. William Heath, William Grene and the 2 overseers were 4 named witnesses.

Ref: 1586 B 22/1 Will 1586 B 22/2 Inventory

William Kytchiner **226**

of Effingham, yeoman; taken by Raphe Edwardes of Effingham, gent., Myles Lustede of Dorking, George Edwoodes the elder of Great Bookham, and John Christemas of Binstead, 16th May 1586.

In the parlour	£	s	d
One Cloake London dye, one graye Russett cloakc and one mandellion	1	10	0
One Doubblett of Rashe, one leather Doubblett and one canvas Doubblett		8	0
One blacke ffryse Jerckinge, 2 paire of boote hose, one paire of bootes, one paire of stockins and 2 paire of breeches		9	0
2 hattes, 3 night capps and a scarffe		3	0
4 shertes, 2 bandes and one night capp		15	0
One old ffryse goune, mothe eaten			6

One Joyned beadsteed with the valence, 3 curtaines grene and Reade, 3 curtaine Roddes of yron, one ffether bedd with a bolster and 2 pillowes				1	10	0
2 Curtaines for the windowes with the Roddes					4	0
3 Coverlettes, 2 blanckettes and a litle Rugge				1	14	0
One Cuppbord clothe, one payre of sheetes, one pilleber					7	0
One Cuppborde, one table with a fframe, 3 Joyned stooles and one warminge panne				1	15	4
One close chayer, one setting stycke with a leade and one chiest					1	10
2 pewter candlestikes, 3 brasen candlestickes, 2 flowre pottes of pewter, one playte, 6 platters, 3 pewter dysshes, 2 porrengers, 7 sawcers, one salt seller, 2 brusshes and 4 table nappkins					16	10
[*£9.14.6*]	9	15	10			
In the haule						
One Table with a fframe, one Cuppbord, one Joyned stoole and 4 quisshins					10	0
One potthanger and one cobbyron					3	0
One curtayne with an yron Rodd, halfe a sheefe of Arrowes and a sculle					2	5
		15	5			
In the chamber over the haule						
2 flocke beddes, one bolster and 3 paire of sheetes					18	0
2 plaine beddstedes, one ffetherbedd, one bolster, one payre of sheetes, one Russett blanckett, one coverlett, one olde quylte and 3 chestes				1	2	6
	2	0	6			
In the owt howse						
3 awgares, one wrye byll, 2 axes, one squayer, 2 hammers, 2 yron wedges, one ffoote yron, 3 playnes, 2 chesells, one bowe wymble, one clevinge hatchett, one payre of styrropps, one lyne, one spytter, one mattocke, one payre of pynsowes, one Ripping axe, one crosse korfe sawe, one bearinge Bill, one wane Bill, 3 nettes, 2 gridyron, one payre of spunes, 3 Tubes and other lumberment					15	0
Half a loade of Tyles					5	0
	1	0	0			
In the kytchen						
One ffurnes of brasse				1	6	8
2 brasse potts, one kettle, one ffyer panne, one litle brasse panne and one cast posnett				1	0	0
One capon cowpe, one mowldinge boorde, one boultinge hutche, one knedinge trowghe, one pouldringe trowghe one kever, 2 tubbs, 2 fyrckinns, one byrde spytt, one litle barrell, one broche, 2 cobbyrons, one trevett and a paire of potthoockes					12	0
[*£2.18.8*]	1	18	8			
In the worckinge shopp						
3 loomes, 24 slayes and geeres, one warppinge barre and all that belongeth therunto, one wheele, scales and 28 pound weightes of lead, 7 shuttles with other ymplementes, one styllatorye and a lanterne				5	2	6
2 Rydinge sadelles, one pannell, 4 gyrttes, one horse combe 2 brydles and 2 chiestes					3	6
One pronge and a shovell						6
	5	6	6			
In the ffyeld and stable						
5 Acres of wheate and one Acre of pease				4	0	0
For hyrdles and woode					3	4

		£	s	d
One carte with the wheeles and 2 harrowes			11	4
All the haye			1	0
One Lease graunted by John Agmondesham esquire unto the said William Kytchener deceased		10	0	0
	14 15 8			
	[£36.9.3]	35	2	1

Note: The Will was dated 3rd December 1585 and proved on 16th May 1586. Thomas, the testator's son, was residuary legatee and executor. Sums of 13s 4d were given to the overseers, Thomas Rogers, his brother in law, and Thomas Kytchiner the elder of Binsted, his cousin. The latter's son, another Thomas Kytchiner, was named as heir to the freehold property in Effingham and Byfleet, if the testator's son should die without issue. Were both the young Thomas Kytchiners to die without issue, the land was to remain to George Ewdes [Edwoods]. The testator asked to be buried in Effingham churchyard. A list of more than 30 household items was left to Joane, his wife, amongst which was the best chest and the very worst latten candlestick. A sum of £2 was left to William Lee, his apprentice. Five pounds was to be paid to John Stanbridge alias Kytchiner, as soon as Leamgrove Coppice was felled or cut down. Rose, Thomas Monger's servant, was left £1, and her master was left a gown, a doublet, and a hat. Napkins were left to Margaret and Julian Atlee. John Burlace wrote the Will, witnessed by William Ovor and Anthony Wightman. On 14th May 1586 the burial of William Kitchyn was recorded in the parish register.

Ref: 1586 B 33/1 Will 1586 B 33/2 Inventory

Walter Songhurst **227**

of Ockley; taken by Raffe Astone, Robert Willett, Raffe Bax, John Eversed, and others, 27th April 1586.

	£	s	d
Tow oxen	6	0	0
Tow steres	4	0	0
Foure keine	7	0	0
Tow bulls	4	0	0
Thre horse	3	0	0
Tow wanyer calves		13	4
Foure lambs		8	0
Tow shotes		10	0
A wayne with shode wheles, youks, chaynes, plowes, harrows	2	0	0
Grene whete on the ground	3	0	0
Otts on the ground	2	0	0
Wheat and Rye in the barne	2	0	0
Ten busshels of barlye and barlye mault	1	0	0
Thre badd bedds with bedstedels and all things belonging thereunto	2	0	0
Dryed beyfe and bacon		13	4
Foure paire of worne shetts	1	0	0
Foure peces of brasse	1	0	0
Ten peces of pewter vessells		13	4
All manner of bruying vessells and all manner of wodden vessells	1	0	0
Potthocks, pothangers, trefts, girdirons, bill, axes with all ymplements and necessaries		10	0
One Ryke of haye	1	0	0
Layed out upon a leace hereafter to be made	15	0	0
His aparell	1	0	0
Of Readye money in his purse		3	4
	59	11	4
Debts owyng			
First Rychard Morer of Dorking	13	0	0

George Stere	4	0	0
William Chesman	6	0	0
John Astone	2	2	6
William Lyger	1	13	4
Robert Willett		12	0
William Chasmore		15	0
Robert Elis	1	0	0
	29	2	10

Note: The Will was dated 19th March and proved on 16th May 1586. The testator's wife Agnes was appointed executrix and residuary legatee. The overseers Robert Willett, husbandman, and John Eversed, both of Ockley, were to have 3s 4d apiece. These men were given authority to dispose of sufficient goods to pay outstanding debts and legacies if any future husband of Agnes should refuse to be bound by the testator's will. Walter asked to be buried in Ockley churchyard; he gave 20d to the poor man's box there and 2d to the mother church of Winchester. His godchildren received 6d apiece, and his son Thomas was given 6 silver spoons and 5 household items. Margaret, his eldest daughter, was left £10 to be paid at her marriage. Joan, another Margaret, Alice, and Elenor, his 4 younger daughters, were to have a like sum at their day of marriage or the age of 21, the survivors to have an equal share of the legacy of any sister who might not live to claim it. Three named witnesses were the overseers and John Songhurst. The widow and Robert Willett bound themselves well and truly to administer the estate. The burial of Walter Songhurste son of Thomas was recorded on 1st April 1586.

Ref: 1586 B 50/1 Will 1586 B 50/2 Inventory

John Walden, the younger **228**

of Horsell; taken by John Wapshott, Jon Goringe, Robert Simonndes, Wyllyam Collier, Wyllyam Scottier, and Walter Wapshott, 9th May 1586.

	£	s	d	£	s	d
In redye money		2	6			
His wearinge apparell	1	0	0	1	2	6
In the hall						
A Coubhorde, a table, a Settle of waynscote, a foroume belonginge to the table, 2 chayers and the painted clothes there				2	0	0
In the Parlour						
A standinge bedstedle, a floc bed and a short square table, 6 Joyned stooles, a chayer and a chest				2	3	4
In the chamer above the hall						
One oulde Bedstedle		1	0			
The Rie there		6	0			
The frenche wheate there		13	4			
The wooll there		3	4			
The scales and weyghtes			6			
A payre of Stocke cardes and a yoyned stoole		1	0			
The Scikles there			4	1	5	6
In the chamer above the Parlour						
A standinge Bedstedle, a Troucklebedstedle, twoo flocbeddes, and theyr furniture, a shorte square table, fowre chestes and the paynted clothes there and a pewter water pott				2	0	8
In the chamer benethe the entrie						
A Bedstedle		1	8			
Shetes there		1	8			
A cloke and blanket		5	0			
A spinninge wheele		1	0			
A presse there			4		9	4

In the chamer above the entrie						
A mattrasse, a payer of Sheetes, a Bollster, a Blankett, a helyer and a bedstedle					10	0
In the kitchinge						
4 kettles and a brasse pott	1	0	0			
5 new platters		6	8			
Three oulde peuter disshes		2	0			
Three saucers			6			
Twoo peeces of olde Peuter			6			
2 ere disshes			6			
Twoo Saltes		1	0			
One whyte candlesticke and twoo other laten candlestikes		1	8			
Twoo Trowes and other woodden vessell	1	0	0			
A frynge pann and a gredyron		1	0			
A fyer shovell, a paire of tonges, 2 cobyrons, a pothanger, a trifft, a spytt and a pothoke		7	4			
An awgur, a drawinge knife, a betle bound with yron, a wedge of yron, a byll and an axe		3	0			
A Sadle and 2 bridles		2	0	3	6	2
Abrode about the Baron						
His longe cart and his dounge carte		5	0			
The Plowe, yokes and chaines and stroppes		3	4			
Twoo horses		6	8			
Three hoogges		8	0			
Twoo Oxon	5	0	0			
fyve kine and 4 calvefes	9	0	0			
5 Twelmonnthlinge Bullockes	2	10	0			
His Pultrie		2	0			
His geese and duckes		4	0			
The Soyle		10	0	18	9	0
In the feelde						
His Sheepe	4	5	4			
His coppes wood	5	0	0			
All his other woodes	2	3	4			
All his wynter corne uppon the grounde	8	0	0			
His Summer tylleth as peese, Tares and Otts	1	0	0			
One lease unexpired	10	0	0			
An Oxe harrow		5	0	30	8	8
				61	15	6
Dettes owynge by John Walden as foloweth						
To Mr Sheeres				18	0	0
To Edward Remnand of Purbright				9	0	0
To Edward Simonndes of Chertesey				6	0	0
To the waldens of Wocking				1	0	0
To John Walden of Horsell					13	4
To Thomas Simonndes of Purbright					10	0
To John Thayer the elder of Horsell					3	4
				[*35*	*6*	*8*]

On 16th May 1586 Joyce Walden, widow and relict of the deceased, was sworn to the truth of the Inventory. She bound herself well and truly to administer the estate, together with Walter Harward of Merrow, gentleman, and John Astrete of Bramley, yeoman.

Ref: 1586 Ad 68

1587

John Atkynsone **229**

of St Olave's in Southwark, cooper; taken by William Chetone and Rychard Vascone. [*undated*]

	£	s	d
The ramente of John Atkynsone at his departure for his best hose and dobblete	1	0	0
For a oulde Cloke		4	0
For a oulde dobblete and a oulde payre of brechis and a oulde payre of netherstokes		3	0
More fore a oulde hate			6
More fore too oulde shyrtes		2	0
For too roste bandes and too plane bandes		2	0
For a oulde Chiste and a oulde dagere and too payre of oulde shoues		2	0
The monye that he hade in his pores wene he departede wase		2	0
	1	15	6

Note: The Will was dated 17th April and proved on 3rd May 1587. The executor and residuary legatee was the testator's brother-in-law John Blunden. Sums of £1 each were left to the overseers, his friends George Deacon, carpenter and Thomas Bywater, cooper. John had 2 sisters, Thomasyne Atkynsone and Dorothy Blunden, between whom he divided 3 properties in Essex. Heyler Lands in Great Burstow was leased to Thomas and William Daniell. A little tenement next to the Meal Market in Billericay was occupied by John Davison, shoemaker. These properties, less £1 a year from the rent of Heylerlands, were given to Thomasyne and her heirs. Dorothy and John Blunden were to have the annual sum of £1 already mentioned and a tenement in Burntwood occupied by Roger Holt on a special lease of £3 per annum. If either sister were to die without lawful children to inherit, then the surviving sister and her heirs would benefit. Roger Holt was to be allowed peacefully to complete his promised tenancy. John Hooper wrote the will, also witnessed by the overseers and the executor. The entry in the parish register for 19th April 1587 records the burial of John Atkinsonn, "servannte with Roberte Blunden, cowper".

Ref: 1587 B 2/1 Will 1587 B 2/2 Inventory

John Atwell **230**

of Fetcham, husbandman; taken by Thomas Blundell, John Kinge, George Gryffyn and Thomas Wodman, 2nd May 1587.

In the haule	£	s	d
2 greate kettles, one panne, 2 posenettes, a caldron, 2 pottes 4 litle kettles	3	13	4
2 spittes, one potthangers, 2 pott hoockes,a drippinge panne, 2 gobyrons, a trevett, a gyrdeyron and a hempe yron		5	0
2 tubbs, a foorme, 2 stooles, one chaire, 2 buckettes, 5 booles a kever, 12 woodden dishes, 2 woodden platters		4	0
24 peces of pewter, 4 candlestickes, a spycemorter, 2 Saltes	1	0	0
Olde tubbes and a cheirne		2	0
One Busshell and a half busshell and a pecke		1	0
3 trowghes, a cheese presse, a bracke, a paire of stocke cardes		12	0
Beddstedles and more trumperye tubbs		8	0
Woole		6	0
Hempe		1	8
3 chiestes		6	0
Linnen wheeles and woollen wheeles		2	0
2 cupbordes		8	0
One olde fether bedd, 2 bolsters, 3 pillowes and 2 blanckettes	1	0	0
One olde flocke bedd, a blanckett and a course healinge		10	0

10 paire of sheetes, 3 table clothes, 3 yardes of browne Russett	2	19	0
5 busshells of wheate, 3 busshells of Rye and Barleye and 12 busshells of Maulte	3	18	0
In the Barne, yarde and fieldes			
14 busshells of Barlye	2	2	0
All the haye	1	6	8
7 kyne and 3 calves	14	16	0
2 mares	2	0	0
3 litle hogges		9	0
5 Acres of winter corne	5	0	0
5 Acres of Barleye	3	6	8
6 Acres of codd ware and otes	2	0	0
42 sheepe and 9 lambes	6	4	8
4 staules of Bees		8	0
7 hennes and one Cocke		4	0
One olde carte, one olde dounge carte, one olde paire of wheeles, 2 ploughes, one harrowe, a fforme, a ladder		9	0
A bearinge Bill, one Axe, a pyckaxe with other trumperye geare		3	0
	54	5	0
Speratt dettes owing to the testator			
Thomas Wycke of Hedley	5	0	0
Raphe Longhurst of Letherd	5	0	0
	64	5	0

Note: The Will was dated 17th April and proved on 5th May 1587. The testator's wife Dorothy was appointed executrix and residuary legatee, being given the yearly rent of a house occupied by John Fox in Leatherhead towards the maintenance and upbringing of Elizabeth Atwell, his granddaughter, the child of his son Robert. He asked to be buried in Fetcham church, but he gave 3s 4d equally to the church repairs of both Fetcham and Leatherhead and to the poor of each of these parishes 13s 4d. Gifts of sheep were made to his brother Edward, to Edward's children and to Jane Hairbottle. Wheat was bequeathed to John Gryffin and Bartholemew Monccke. An annuity of 30s was left to his kinsman Arthur Atwell, from money due from Arthur's brother, Roger of Headley. John's son Robert was to have £4 when next he came into the country and Robert's daughter Elizabeth was to have the two debts of £5, listed at the end of the Inventory, when she married or reached the age of 21. This money was to be collected and held by Thomas Woodman, one overseer, supervised by John King, the other overseer. The Leatherhead house was willed to the said Elizabeth and her male heirs, or failing that, to his nephew Edward Atwell and his heirs. If Elizabeth were to die before the age of 21, the £10 was to be divided equally between Edward Atwell the younger and Arthur Atwell. The signatories to the document were the testator and the overseers, also George Hodgson, clerk and Bartholemew Moncke.

Ref: 1587 B 3/1 Will 1587 B 3/2 Inventory

John Barnard **231**

of Dorking, [*weaver*]; taken by Robard Nettelfould, Thomas Woode, John Stelwell and Richard Stelwell, 1587.

	£	s	d
There wollen apparrell	2	0	0
There lynen apparrell		13	4
For a fether bed, a boulster and pillowe		8	4
For a flocke bed and sted		2	6
For 3 pare of sheytes		10	0
For 5 pare of sheytes		18	2
For six pare of course sheytes		17	0
For tow pillowbeyres		1	0

For puter	1	0	0
For brase potes and panes, cetteles	1	6	0
For candelstickes and saltes		5	0
For tow tabel clotheyes		1	0
For tow tabel clotheyes		4	0
For tow hand tueles		2	0
For tow tabel napkinges		1	0
For fife chestes		10	0
For a bedsted			6
For hempe and toue		5	0
For tow pare of pothouckes and hangers		1	0
For a trevet		1	2
For a cobeyrne, a spite, a grideyrne		2	6
A dousen of spones			6
For a bed couvearinges		16	0
For a cobberd		3	4
For a bill and a axke		1	0
For disheise and trenchards		1	0
For a wolen while and a lynen while		1	4
For a tabel and a chare and stoules		2	0
For boules and towbes		3	4
For a hatte			6
For tow weveres loumes	1	0	0
For slessis		10	0
For wedges and a pickaxke	1	0	0
For ballanes and waytes		1	4
For oulde erne			8
A boshell and a peck		1	4
For poultrey		2	0
Mony in theyre pourse		2	0
	12	16	8

On 30th May 1587 Henry Elliott and Robert Rowe, uncles of Dorothy, Juliane and John Barnard, minors, were bound to administer the estate of the deceased. Also bound were George Robyns and Henry Rowe. John Barnard had been buried on 7th February of that year.

Ref: 1587 Ad 3

Richard Benet **232**

of Chiddingfold; taken by William Peto of Pickades and John Horner. [*undated*]

	£	s	d
His aparell		6	8
1 flockebed, 1 coverlid, 1 bowlster and a pare of sheetes		10	0
1 Lome with nessesarise to it		6	8
2 chests		3	4
7 platters, 5 sausers and 1 pewter dishe		6	0
4 ketteles and 1 brasse pott		7	0
2 candelstickes			6
1 cover, 1 tubbe and a chere		1	0
Disshes, tranchers, formes, a cradle		2	0
1 axe, 1 bill, 1 freinge pan, 1 pott hangger and a sheve		2	0
3 kine	4	0	0
A mare	1	0	0
2 shuttes		4	0

[*s and.d. corrected in same hand*]		9	2
[*faulty total*]	7	8	10

Note: The Will was dated 11th April 1587, leaving everything to his "wife, Mary, hopeing that she will bringe up my children vertusely". The widow was granted probate on 30th May 1587; witnesses to the will had been John Lloyd and Elyzabeth Osburn.

Ref: 1587 B 9/1 Will 1587 B 9/2 Inventory

Thomas Blake **233**

of Coulsdon; taken by Jefferey Payce, George Francke, Thomas Stonham, Thomas Hawkyns, with others, 5th May 1587.

	£	s	d
Corne			
16 acres of wheate	21	0	0
Of barley 6 acres	4	16	0
Of otes 16 acres	9	10	0
Of pesen and tares 7 acres	2	6	8
Wheate in the house 6 bussheles	1	10	0
Cattel			
Of shepe 3 score	13	0	0
Of lambes 26	3	0	0
Of oxen 2 steeres	4	0	0
Fyve kyne and fowre calves	10	0	0
To two yerlyng bullockes	2	10	0
3 twelmoneth bulockes	2	0	0
of horse			
Of horse fyve	8	0	0
2 coltes	1	10	0
of hogges			
12 hogges	2	0	0
Cartes, wheles, plowghes and harrowes and yokes, Reepes	3	0	0
beddes			
Two beddes furnished	6	0	0
Two flocke beddes furnished	2	0	0
of sheetes			
12 payre of shetes	4	0	0
10 table clothes	1	10	0
2 dyssen napkyns		8	0
chestes			
Fowre chestes		10	0
A presse		10	0
A cupbord		13	4
Tables, formes, chayres and stooles	1	0	0
Toobes, trowes, bowlles and all other wooden vessell	1	6	8
A payre of potthangers and two brandeyrons and a grydyron		5	0
Two spyttes		6	0
brasse and pewter			
A cawldron and 4 kytteles	1	2	0
A lyttle brasse pott and 2 chaffers		10	0
A morter and the pestell		2	6
Fowre latten candelstyckes		2	0
6 platters		9	0
8 pewter dysses		9	4

A dyssen pottengers		6	0
Two salte sellers		1	8
On dyssen spoones			9
A karrpett and halfe a dyssen quysshions		13	4
A syde saddle		10	0
A Rode saddle and a brydle		3	4
Fowre hennes		2	8
Gees, duckes		8	0
The horse harness		10	0
	112	2	3

Note: The Will was dated 4th May and proved on 31st May 1587. The executrix and residuary legatee was the testator's wife Johanna. The overseers were Jeffery Payce of Chipstead and George Francke. Thomas asked to be buried in the church or churchyard of Coulsdon and he gave 10s to the poor there. The 3 children of Thomas Fraye were to have their legacies invested by William Blake, the testator's brother and to have the principal sum and the interest. Thomas and John Fraye were to have upwards of £2 at the age of 21 and Johanna was to have upwards of £1 at the age of 16. They would benefit from a further half share of the goods from the farm if the testator's wife were to die before the expiry of the lease. William Clarke, the parson and Thomas Hawkins were witnesses to the will. The widow and Jeffery Payce bound themselves well and truly to administer the estate.

Ref: 1587 B 12/1 Will 1587 B 12/2 Inventory

Mawdlyn Boxold **234**

of Elstead, widow; taken by Henry Wheler, Thomas Reaves and Wylyam Wodache, 28th April 1587.

	£	s	d
In monye		10	0
Here aparell	1	10	0
The bedes in the house and all thyngs there to belonging	1	6	8
The wolle in the house		12	0
Three cheste		3	0
One cobard		6	8
The brase in the house	1	0	0
The peuter in the house	1	0	0
The woddyne vessell in the house		3	4
The Ire gere in the house		3	0
Fourtye wethere shepe	6	13	4
Thyrtye euse and tegs	4	10	0
Syxtene tegs	1	16	0
Syxtene lams	1	4	0
One smalle oxe	1	13	4
Foure kynne	5	6	8
Tooe heffers	2	0	0
Foure boulloks	2	13	4
Tooe boulloks of one yere old		6	8
Tooe caufese		6	8
One mare and thre coults	2	0	0
All the hogs aboute the hous	1	6	8
The Certe, the plowe and other Implements there to belonging	1	0	0
The koce and fyfe hense		1	0
One hyfe		3	4
The corne apone the grounde	3	0	0
The wots and pese apon the grounde	2	13	4

43 8 4

Note: The Will was written on 17th April and proved on 30th May 1587. Half of the residue of the estate was left to Henry Boxold of Elstead and a quarter each to John Boxold of Frensham and Johane Novell of Farnham, these being the three children of the testatrix. John Boxold, the elder son, had 4 children: Thomas, John, Elizabeth and Johane, each of whom had bequests of several items. Her second son Henry had 3 children: John, Henry and Richard. The gift to this John of the best yoke of oxen, the working gear, some grain and household items, could be used by his father until the day of his marriage. Richard Novell, his wife Johane and their children had bequests, as did Thomas Novell. Mawdlin Jewer, servant and a certain Hew Egar were 2 other beneficiaries. A reasonable load of hay from Elstead meadow was left to John Boxold, the elder son, annually for life. No executors were named when the Will was written by Gilbert Dutton and marked with their signs by the testatrix and the overseers. There followed a list of 4 debts owing to the testatrix: Robert Denier of Broke, Thomas Millet and John Boxold of Farnhurst, owed 20 shillings each and Thomas Ryckman owed 8 shillings. A memorandum then confirmed that Henry Boxold was to give his brother John the load of hay bequeathed by their mother, as long as they both should live. Henry then added his mark, witnessed by those people mentioned above. Administration was granted to Mawdlyn's 3 children, Henry, John and Johane. The 2 sons and Johane's husband, Richard Novell of Farnham, all husbandmen, bound themselves well and truly to carry out all the bequests under the supervision of the overseers, Thomas Luffe and Rychard Peyninge. These 5 men and Gilbert Dutton witnessed the final arrangements of the will.

Ref: 1587 B 13/1 Will 1587 B 13/2 Inventory

John Bristowe **235**

of Wotton, husbandman; taken by John Redford, Henry Palmer and Thomas Neale, 12th May 1587.

	£	s	d
One old Cowe and three Heckfers	5	13	4
Three litle Bullockes besides	1	10	0
One olde Mare		6	8
Fourtie sheepe	6	0	0
12 Lambes	1	0	0
Three smale Hogges		10	0
Two Acres of Rye verie sleight	1	0	0
Two Acres of verie smale Oates		13	4
One Flocke Bedd and a Mattaresse with the Furniture therunto belonginge		10	0
Foure payre of ould sheetes		10	0
All the Brasse and Pewter beinge verie old stuffe		12	0
One Litle old Cubbord with other old Woodden vessell		6	0
Two old Bedsteedes and two old chestes		3	4
One Bill, an Axe, a shovell, a Spitt, a pothangers		2	6
A Table, a Forme and two old stooles		1	4
His Apparell and two shillinges in his purse		6	8
	[*19*	*5*	*2*]

Note: The Will was dated 8th May and proved on 30th May 1587. The executrix and residuary legatee was the testator's wife Alice. His brother Henry Bristow and John Redford, both of Wotton, were appointed overseers. The testator asked to be buried in the local churchyard and he gave 5 sheep, £1 and a pewter platter, to his son Tobias and to each of his daughters Alice, Agnes and Elizabeth. His wife was to deliver these legacies 6 years hence and Elizabeth to have in addition "one waynier cowe calfe". If any of the 4 children should die, the survivors were to be equal heirs of the deceased. Robert Higham, the parson, together with John Redford and William Hall, all three of Wotton and Thomas Neale of Dorking, were witness to the signing of the Will. The administration bond was provided by the widow and John Sewell of Wotton, husbandman.

Ref: 1587 B 14/1 Will 1587 B 14/2 Inventory

Henrye Charlewood **236**

of [*Betchworth*] Surrey, tanner; taken by William Ponder, John Bell, Richard Hover, John Hewet and others, 3rd May 1587.

	£	s	d
20 over lether hydes	6	0	0
5 backes	2	0	0
3 loades of olde tanne		18	0
4 tanne vates and 1 little one		13	4
A tanne mill		13	4
The grounde vates and Cisterns		10	0
Certaine vate staves		6	0
3 bad kettles and A fryinge panne		10	0
2 little pewter dishes		1	0
A square table with a frame and forme		5	0
1 bad bed with thappurtenances		5	0
1 mare	3	0	0
2 paire of sheetes		6	0
His apparell		6	0
1 sowe		3	4
	[*15*	*17*	*0*]

Note: This is almost certainly the Inventory of a Betchworth man. Henry Charlwood's burial is recorded in the parish register on 25th April 1587. The first 3 appraisers all lived in Betchworth at that time. On 31st May 1587, Alice the widow of the deceased was sworn to the truth of the above Inventory and bound herself well and truly to administer the goods and chattels of her late husband. There followed a list of monetary bequests to the children, which she bound herself to honour. Marjorie's share was 20s, Thomas was to have 40s and Anne 46s 8d. Near the bottom of the document was written: "Bound, the widow. Leve a space for a surety and the vicar hath the bond to seale and return to Guilford 22nd June."

Ref: 1587 Ad 11

William Chittie **237**

of Godalming, clothier; taken by Nicholas Wylson, John Chenell and Arnolde Edwardes, 2nd August 1585.

In the Hall	£	s	d
One table with a frame and two formes thereunto belonginge		13	4
Two Carpettes for the same table		12	4
8 Cushinges		8	0
A benche clothe and a stayned cloth with a lettis		5	0
A Cupborde and a clofe for the same and a Cheyer	1	3	4
One Pothanger and one Andiron		2	0
In the parlor			
One table with a frame and one forme		6	8
One Carpett for the same table		3	4
One litle Cupborde		3	4
The stayned cloth in the same parlor		5	0
In the loft over the Shoppe			
One Joyned Bedstedle and one Bedstedle with a Stayned Cloth or coveringe	1	10	0
Two Fether beddes, one Flock bedd, two fether bolsters, fower fether pyllowes, 2 coverlettes and 2 blankettes	5	0	0
Two chestes, 2 tables, 4 stoles, one Cheyer, one Carpett and the			

stayned clothes for the same chamber	1	13	4
One Flite laide over the chamber		13	4
In the loft over the Hall			
Two bedstedles, two flock beddes, three blankettes, two bolsters and two coverlyttes	2	0	0
Three chestes and one table with trestelles		10	0
In the Chamber by the Shopp			
One bedstedell, one flock bedd, 2 blanckes, one Coverlitt and a bolster		10	0
8 paire of Canvas shetes, one paire of Locrome shetes and one Hollon shete	1	10	0
Three table Clothes		12	0
11 table napkyns		4	0
2 paire of Hollon pyllowberes, one paire of Locrome pyllowberes and fyve towelles	1	1	0
Brasse and pewter			
21 pewter platters, 13 pewter dishes, 6 sawcers, one bason, 3 wyndowe cupps and two pewter pottes	2	6	8
6 Candlestickes and one chafinge dishe		12	0
One morter		2	0
In the shopp			
4 paire of sheres, 8 Course of Handles and other shopp gere	1	16	0
One Winche presse and other thinges belonginge to it	1	0	0
Rackes			
Two paire of Rackes	1	0	0
In the Kytchin			
Two Caudrons, 2 pannes, 2 brasse pottes, fower kettles, one chafor and one posnett	3	1	0
One paire of andirons, 2 broches, one drippinge panne, one tryfte, one gerdiron and a paire of pothokes		13	0
In the bakehowse			
Two trowes and other tobbes		14	0
The Lease of the Howse	2	0	0
Kersies, Woll and yearne	45	0	0
One Geldinge, 2 Kyne and one calf	5	10	0
Corne in the fylde	5	13	4
Woode in the Gate		13	4
Three Hogges and 4 pigges		14	0
Heye in the Barne		16	0
For Cheese		6	8
For one Harrowe		1	8
His apparell and monye	5	6	0
[*£96.11.8*]	93	15	8

The Inventory was presented at Court for purposes of administration nearly two years after it was written. Alice Chittie, the widow, came on 3rd May 1587 and was sworn to the truth of the document. Also bound was John Chitty of the same place [*Godalming*], clothier.

Ref: 1587 Ad 14

Robert Crosse **238**

of Stoke Dabernon; taken by Mathew Fowches, John Yong and Thomas Charlewood.

[*undated*]

£ s d

Fyve ffether beddes and all that belonges to them	6	0	0
Twelve paire of sheetes	2	0	0
Foure Table cloates		16	0
Foure Cuboard cloathes		4	0
Foure Towells		2	0
Fyve Dozen of napkins		10	0
Eght platters and eght Dishes and eght Sawcers		10	0
Four paire of Candlestickes		4	0
Four Brasse pottes and a Cauldren and three ketles	1	10	0
His apparell of rayment	2	0	0
	13	16	0

Note: The Will was dated 23rd April and proved on 31st May 1587. The residuary legatee and executrix was the testator's wife Margaret. No overseers were appointed. The detailed bequests to his daughters Marie and Elizabeth gave them each a feather bed, bedding and a fair division of the goods. Their mother inherited about half the household stuff. The testator asked to be buried in Stoke Dawburne churchyard. The Will was witnessed by Thomas Lyffilde esquire, Thomas Vincent esquire and Thomas Ellis, clerk.

Ref: 1587 B 24/1 Will 1587 B 24/2 Inventory

Alice Furlonger **239**

of Chiddingfold, widow; taken by William Peto of Pickard and Thomas Peto of Gostrode.

[*undated*]

	£	s	d
3 gownse, 3 peticotes	1	0	0
4 kerchers, 3 Raeles, 3 corner kerchers, 3 neckercheres, 2 Wastcotes, 3 aprnes, a hatt and a girdill		6	8
A cabburd		6	8
4 platters, 5 pewter disshes, 1 basyn, 1 quart pott, 2 Sawsers and 2 salt sellers		6	8
2 brasse candelstickes, 1 morter, 1 chaffingdishe		2	6
18 tyn spones, 6 trene platteres, 12 treene disshes, 24 [*]?		1	8
1 Cawdron, 1 brasse panne, 5 ketteles, 1 pott and 1 posnett	1	0	0
1 spitt, 2 fryinge pans, 2 dridirns and 2 pare of shares		1	8
3 axes, 3 billes, 1 whipsaw, 1 hansaw, 1 pronge, 1 mattog and other workinge toolse		10	0
5 fleches of bacon and 5 fletches of beafe	1	0	0
1 chilling trow, 1 knedinge trow, 1 vate, 1 keve, 2 stobins, 3 kevers, 3 bowlse and 3 sheves	1	0	0
1 flockebead, 1 flocke pelow, a coverlid and a blanket		13	4
1 bedstid, 5 kofers and a paynted cloth		10	0
1 fyther beade, 3 pelowse, 1 bowlster, 1 coverlid and a blanket	1	6	8
3 flockebeades, 3 coverlides, 3 blanketes and 3 bowlsters	1	0	0
3 beadstids, a wheale, 3 shelves and 2 basketes		7	0
Woole		6	0
7 pare of sheetes, 2 beadtestors, 2 towels and a table cloth	1	0	0
A christeninge sheete		6	8
2 busshells of Wootten malt and 2 busshells of frenche Wheate		6	0
10 workinge oxen	25	0	0
4 kine, 2 heckfors and 4 yearlinge boollockes	14	0	0
2 horses	2	0	0
7 lambes		12	0
A sow and 6 pygges		16	0
6 acres of Wheat and Rye	4	0	0

	£	s	d
12 acres of Whootes	4	0	0
2 acres of fr[*e*]nche Wheat		13	4
2 plowes, 1 pare of yrons and a pare of plow Wheals		10	0
1 oxe harow and 1 horse harow		6	0
A waine, a doong pott and 2 pare of wheals	1	0	0
6 yokes, 6 cheans, 1 cottrell and a pare of stroppes	1	4	0
3 seithes and a grinding stone		4	0
4 hennes, a cocke and 2 Sackes		4	0
	65	0	10

Note: The Will was written on 9th April 1587 and probate was granted on 30th May of the same year. A sum of 4d was bequeathed for the repair of the church in Chiddingfold and 3s 4d for the poorest women of the parish. Anne, Mary and Catherine, the 3 daughters, were given items of household stuff; the two elder girls were to divide the apparel between them and they had gifts of money. Two of the 6 sons were named Edward. The elder was to have a 2-yearling bullock and the younger a year-old animal. A son Robert was given £5. The residue was to go equally to the other 3 sons: John, Thomas and Steven, who were appointed executors. The overseers, William Peto of Pickards and Thomas Peto of Gostrod, were given authority to judge and decide all manner of controversy that might happen to break out between the executors, to appoint the time of payment of the legacies and to withhold the bequests of any beneficiaries not amenable to their judgement. The 4 witnesses were Walter Marvyn, Richard Stockton, John Lloyd and Thomas Turner.

Ref: 1587 B 37/1 Will 1587 B 37/2 Inventory

William Giles **240**

of West Horsley; taken by Rychard Heglat, John Redford and Nycholas Fenn, 25th November 1583.

	£	s	d
On yoke of oxene	4	2	4
Mony oinge hem in dyvres places	5	18	4
For 9 cheepe	1	15	0
All his aparell		10	0
In hes purse		2	0
	12	7	8

Note: The Inventory was exhibited by Master West on 30th May 1587 and the fee paid, but there is no indication of any beneficiary.

Ref: 1587 Ad 27

Henry Graye **241**

of Bermondsey, loriner; taken by Richard Harrison, Roberte Cruchley, Samuell Watts, John Tailor and Edmond Rose, 5th May 1587.

	£	s	d
In the shoppe			
Sope, cheese, Baye salt, white salte, Onions and Butter	2	6	0
Vineger, Vergis, Candles, Cordes, glewe, packthreid, glasses, pottes, whiting, groceryе wares, haberdashe ware, with other Lumber	1	13	4
In the yarde			
Wood and Coles	1	3	0
In the hall			
A gowne, a cloke, one Jerkyn, one paire of Venetians, a capp and other things	3	0	0
A coverlet and 6 Cushions		17	11

	£	s	d
In the kitchen			
Bras, pewter and other ymplementes	1	4	0
A Cubbord, 1 settlbed, a Table, 4 ioyned stooles, 2 chaires, certaine painted clothes about the hall		16	6
In the Chamber			
One Bedstedd, one feather bedd and a Blanket, 2 sheetes, painted clothes, one looking glasse, 4 paire of sheetes, twoe dozen of napkyns, 2 table clothes, 6 hande towells, 4 shirtes, a Hatt and a forrest bill	3	0	0
The Remaynder of a lease of the howse		6	8
In Sperat debtes owing to the said testator at the tyme of his decease	3	0	0
	17	7	5
In doubtfull debtes owing to the said testator by divers and sondrye persons uppon scores and otherwise to the sum of	5	0	0

Note: The Will was dated 3rd March and proved on 27th April 1587 and the Inventory was exhibited on 13th May. The testator's wife Mary was the sole beneficiary and executrix. The 2 overseers named were his wellbeloved friends of London: Samuel Watts, ironmonger and John Gerratt, barber surgeon. He asked to be buried in the church or churchyard of St Saviour's, Southwark and gave no further instructions other than to beg the overseers to help his wife in settling his estate as he wished. Henry Graye wrote his own Will which was witnessed by Nicholas Draper, gent., John Spencer, Samuel Watts, Katherine Thomas, Izabell Simms, William Kirkham and others unnamed. It is unusual that the Will was written and proved, listing Henry as of St Saviour's, Southwark, where he asked to be buried and then when the Inventory was taken a week later, to be listed as of Bermondsey Street in the parish of St Mary Magdalen, Bermondsey. A certain Robert Ordimer represented the widow Mary and was duly sworn another week after that. The testator Henry Gray was buried in Bermondsey on 28th April 1587.

Ref: 1587 B 39/1 Will 1587 B 39/2 Inventory

Joane Hill **242**

of Ewhurst, servant; taken by Thomas Eeed and Thomas Kynge. [*undated*]

	£	s	d
One flocke bed, 3 sheetes, 2 Hylliars		6	10
2 brasse ketles		5	0
4 wooden platters			4
One cheste with lynene in it		2	6
One Coate		1	8
In money which was owinge unto her at that tyme of her death as followeth			
Of Thomas Edwards of Ewhurst	1	0	0
Of John Elliat of Hitchingefield in the Countie of Sussex, husbandman	1	2	0
	2	18	4

Note: The nuncupative Will was dated 1586 and proved on 30th May 1587. John Snellinge and Richard Launder vouched for the truth of the words spoken. Richard Launder made his mark at the end of the Will, which left everything to John Cockes, her master, as he had taken most pains with her. The said John Cockes was granted probate.

Ref: 1587 B 45/1 Will 1587 B 45/2 Inventory

Thomas Lipscomb **243**

of Cranleigh, husbandman; taken by Robart Flud, Richard Tycner, Antony Richbell, Edward Wakeley and Lawrence Serle, 27th April 1587.

	£	s	d
In the halle			
One table and a forme, one chare with other stoules		5	0
One payr of pothoukes, one annd Iron with other Iron Impelmentes a pertayninge to the fier, one brotche		3	4
One flockebead fornished		13	4
One other bed fornished		5	0
Olde painted clothes		1	4
4 chestes		4	0
3 payre of shetes with one locrome shete		13	4
One other bead furnis[*hed*]		10	0
The pewter vessele		13	4
One mortter, one chaffindishe, 2 candellstyckes		3	4
Toowe brase potes, 3 cettels, one bras pane withe other smalle vesseles of brase and Irone	1	6	8
Bruinge vesselles and bakeinge veseles and milke veseles and all woodden veseles		13	4
One byll, one ayx withe other workinge towles		5	0
Baken in the Roufe		6	8
2 kine, one haffor, one wainyer, one mar with a coult	7	6	0
One sowe and toow shoutes		6	8
Corne and otes one the ground	1	13	4
Toow table clothes with other lynen		3	4
His aparell and money in his porse	1	0	0
In the chamber			
One cobord		13	4
	[*17*	*6*	*0*]

Note: The Will was dated 18th February and proved on 30th May 1587. The testator's wife Elizabeth was appointed executrix and residuary legatee. Three witnesses were ordained according to the great trust and confidence Thomas reposed in them, so possibly he meant 'overseers'. They were Robert Flud, Antonye Rychbelle and Robart Stedman. He asked for a christian burial and gave his son Thomas a table with a form and a standing cupboard. Scrawled initials T L were written at the end of the Will.

Ref: 1587 B 55/1 Will 1587 B 55/2 Inventory

Margaret Parkehurst **244**

of Godalming, widow of Robert; taken by Lawerence Peitoe and Arnold Champion of Godalming, 16th May 1587.

	£	s	d
In the hall			
A table		1	6
A forme and 2 ioyned stoles		2	0
An olde planke for a bench			6
A Cubbord		6	8
A Carpet for a table		4	0
2 old Cubbord Clothes		2	0
An old painted clothe		1	0
In hir owne Chamber			
A bedstedle, a flock bed, an olde bolster, a paire of blankettes and a coverlet		10	0
3 old Coofers		3	4

4 boardes and 2 Joistes		2	0
An olde painted clothe over hir bedd		1	0
A Stockcarde plank and an other plank		1	0
An old bedsteadle, a flockbed, a coverlet and a paire of blankettes		6	8
Old Iron		2	0
A keade trowe, a vate, 6 old tubbes, 2 old stobins, 2 kevers and 2 old tubbes		4	0
4 plankes and 3 litle boardes		1	0
A litle Caldorne, 3 ketles, an old posnet, an old dripping pann, a litle Skymmer		10	0
4 Candlestickes, a morter and a pestel		5	0
5 old pewter disshes, 5 platters, 5 sawecers and 4 salt selers		7	6
2 litle pottes, 2 paire of potthookes, a pott hangar and a litle tryfte		2	0
20 wooden disshes, 12 trenchars and a wooden platter		1	0
2 old kettells			6
2 old spinninge wheeles and a skeaner		1	0
2 broches		1	8
3 old swordes		2	4
2 payer of sheares and 5 Corse of handles		16	8
2 presse plankes		2	6
2 dozen of presse bordes, 5 plankes and a borde		2	8
A pece of tymber for a spindle, 3 litle boardes and a skeave		1	8
An old paire of Rackes		10	0
An old Iron beame, a payre of skals and 7 leaden waightes		2	6
A paire of Canvas sheetes, one Locoram sheete and a table clothe		15	0
2 towelles, 2 pillowe beares, 4 holland kerchers, 3 Locoram kerchers, 3 Canvas apernes, a worsted aperne, a smocke and 3 wysottes		13	4
An old Cassocke and an old peticote		8	0
3 yardes of corse whyte clothe		4	0
A peece of a Carpet			6
12 staffe of teasels		18	0
tykes		2	0
An old brushe, an ax and an old hachet			6
2 old sackes and one old bagg		1	0
[*£8.18.0*]	9	3	6

Note: The Will was dated 18th April and proved on 30th May 1587. The executor and residuary legatee was Henry, the son of the testatrix. The overseer was John Periar. Jane, Margaret's daughter, was given the best canvas sheet and the best table cloth, all the linen in the coffer at the foot of her bed and the chest standing on the south side of her chamber. George Tewersleye was given a little bedside coffer and the bed and bedding from the middle room. The witnesses were John Periar, Lawrence Peito, William Grant, George Chittye and Francis Taylor. The executor and Richard Parkehurst, both of Godalming, shearmen, bound themselves well and truly to administer the estate. An entry in the burial register for 26th April 1587 lists Marget P'khurst, widow.

Ref: 1587 B 60/1 Will 1587 B 60/2 Inventory

John Parson **245**

of East Molesey, husbandman; taken by Thomas Wodroughe, John Beste, Edmond Dende and Robarte Parson, 5th May 1587.

	£	s	d
In the Hawlle			
A table, forme, cobbarde, stolles and a Settell		12	0

	£	s	d
In pewter wessell 15 peces		10	0
2 pewter potts, 4 candsticks		3	4
In brase potts and other old brasse		13	4
2 lattin bassens, 3 chaffingedishes, 2 skymmers		6	8
In the chamber			
In Bedinge with all that longs thereto	3	0	0
2 matteres with coveringes and bolsters		13	4
In shettes, 10 payre	1	10	0
2 tabbill clothes		3	4
2 shottes		6	0
	[*7*	*18*	*0*]

Note: The Will was dated 29th August 1584, leaving instructions to be carried out by Hollontide [All Saints' Day: 1st November] of the year of his decease, but probate was not granted to his wife Joan, the executrix and residuary legatee, until 31st May 1587. One son Robert was already in the position to arrange the delivery of loads of wood to Joan and to his brother Walter in 1584. At that time there were ewes, lambs and a cow in John's possession to be given as legacies between Walter's children Ellen and Alice Parson, Margaret Sherlock and the testator's wife, who was to have the right of cow pasture in Kingesford for the current season. The cow was to be hers for 4 years and was to go to Walter, if she did not live so long. The son Robert was to see that a financial agreement of 14 pence and 16 pence for the farming of the land, including fallowing, sowing and carrying dung, was carried out by William Durrant during the year. There were small gifts to Margaret Sherlock, John Person and John Dendy. Walter Parson was to be given half a bushell of barley by his mother. Witnesses were William Durrant, Edmund Dendy and Ralph Straddes. Thomas Woodroffe joined the widow in standing surety for the administration.

Ref: 1587 B 61/1 Will 1587 B 61/2 Inventory

John Peeter **246**

of Farncombe in Godalming; taken by William Carpenter, Henry Mellersh and John Warner, 15th May 1587.

In the hall	£	s	d
One table, a forme and 2 benches		3	4
One Cubbord with a Cubbord clothe		12	0
An old payneted clothe		1	0
An Andyron, a payre of potthangars and a grydyron		1	6
In the parlor			
A bedsteadle, a bolster, a pillowe, a Coverlet and a matt		14	0
One Chest and an old painted clothe		6	0
In the butterye			
A tubb, a firkin, 2 old pipkins, an old fryinge pan, a butter cherne, a chafeinge dish with other implementes		5	0
3 platers, 2 pewter disshes, 3 sawesers		5	6
About 5 pounde weight of old pewter		1	8
In the kychin			
2 ketelles, a litle brass pott and a skellet		8	0
2 old latin Candlestickes			10
One broache, 2 kevers, 2 spinning wheels with other lumbery		4	0
In the Chamber over the hall			
A plaine bedsteadle, a flockbed, a flockbolster and 2 paire of Canvas sheetes, a Coverlet, a blanket and a table clothe		19	0
In the Chamber over the parlor			
One Coofer, one powederinge tubb, one sacke and a shelf		2	6
In the Chamber over the kychin			
2 old sythes, a skeener and an old byll		2	0

With out the house			
An old mare and an old geldinge	1	3	4
A sowe, a shute and 2 pigges		8	0
An old payre of wheeles, a dungepott with harnes, a pronge and a hoggtrowe		4	0
3 acars of Rye	3	0	0
half an acar of wheate		10	0
3 Calves		12	0
his aparell		15	0
	10	19	8

30th May 1587 Administration was granted to Margaret, relict, who was sworn to the truth of the above inventory. Bound: the widow and William Perrye of Godalming, clothier.

Note: John Peeter's burial was recorded on 1st May 1587. Ref: 1587 Ad 58

Richard Pyggen or Piggen **247**

of Coulsdon; taken by Jeffrye Payce, George Franke, William Lamberte, William Hore and Thomas Hawkyns. [*undated*]

	£	s	d
Fower kyne and twoe Calves	8	0	0
Thirtye weather sheepe	7	10	0
Twentye ewes with their lambes	6	0	0
Tenn Tegges	2	0	0
One Crofte of barley	1	10	0
Halfe a acre of oates		5	0
One sowe hogge and two pigges		6	8
A Chamber			
A bedd furnished	2	10	0
Fower Chestes		14	0
Tenn payer of sheetes	3	0	0
Fyve table clothes		8	0
A dozen of table napkyns		10	0
Fower pillowberes		4	0
A nother Chamber			
A bedd and all that belongeth to itt	1	10	0
One cupborde		16	0
A table, a forme, chayers and stooles		6	8
Halfe a dozen of Cushions		3	0
The brasse	1	10	0
The pewter	1	0	0
Tubbes, troughes, bowles and all other lumber		10	0
In redye money	10	0	0
	48	13	4
Debtes dowbtfull			
Richarde Cuddington of Horley did borrowe of hym in money	5	0	0
Richarde Cuddington owethe for twentye weathers taken of hym	5	13	4
The saide Richard owethe for six Ewes	1	4	0
Frawnces Coxon of Croydon owethe	6	12	6
Goodman Wyndover of Croydon dothe owe for Coales taken in Frithe woode	2	0	0
Mr Poynes of Reygate did borrow of the testator	10	0	0
William Lamberd of Cowlsdon is indebted	10	0	0

	£	s	d
William Woode of Cowlsdon dothe owe	3	0	0
	43	9	10

Note: The Will was dated 9th April and proved on 22nd May 1587. The executor and residuary legatee was John Piggen, son of the testator. John was to give his mother £4 a year for life if he and the widow Maud did not live together. Her bequest was £10 in money, 20 pairs of sheets and a fully furnished bed. The testator's daughter Jonne and her unnamed son were given £10 and £1, respectively, as were Alse Slyter and her son. Aules, Catherine and Audery Marchant, were left 10s, 6s 8d and 6s 8d, in that order. Richard's brother William Piggen was forgiven his debts and bequeathed a quarter of barley. Two of William's unnamed sons were left 6s 8d, but Richard, his uncle's godson, was given 10s. No overseers were appointed. The witnesses were George Franke, Bartholemew Blake, Annyse Steven and Elysabethe Hethe.

Ref: 1587 B 61/1 Will 1587 B 61/2 Inventory

Thomas Richbeale **248**

of Ashstead, husbandman; taken by James Kyng, Hary Otwae, John Hamon, William Sims and John Mathye. [*undated*]

	£	s	d
Woon oxe	2	10	0
Three kyne and too kafse	6	13	4
Woon bowlloke of twelmont ooll		13	4
Too horse and thee harnnys	3	0	0
A mayre		4	0
A sowe and sixe pygs		12	6
Thee Karte and weelse and karte ladder, too rops	2	0	0
The don kart, a peary of plouewells and a rolar		3	0
The Ayouake and the Chane		2	6
Too ploues and that beelon too them		5	0
Fower horars and a safgarde		10	0
The grynstone and all that bee long to it			8
A yettynge trofe		3	0
All the brase	1	5	0
To cantyxe		1	1
All the peyter		15	0
Too paier of pothangers and a greddyon and too branyryeds		4	4
Three beads steddells and all that be lont to it	1	13	4
There tabel kosete, too napkyns, too pellabers		6	8
Fuwewer Chas		7	4
Too Cubbrds		8	0
A tabeell, three stoles		5	0
To Ceers		1	2
Ayle ffessyl		2	4
Too trofes		4	6
Too bolse, a Cimbel and a frying pan and the treys and a poddrynge tobe		2	0
The tobbs and a Chren		1	8
Too milse and a shale		1	4
A bussyl, a fan		1	4
A matholke 16 sousels		2	0
To byles, too bylhoucs, there oygers		2	6
Three weigsgis		1	2
Too bottelles		1	0
Spondes and dysshys and trynschers			6
Woon strefit		1	0

To paylse			6
Heyngyn klose		2	0
A hammar, a pare of pynsers			6
Hys wererynge klose		14	4
A kooke, too hens		1	4
The Corne and the graine Apon the grounde	13	8	0
	[*37*	*12*	*5*]

[*The following list of debts appeared at the end of the Will*:]

I doe owe to Thomas Mathew	£3	10	0	
to be payd at Michaelmas.				
To Roger Mathew	1	4	0	
To Michell Richbel		10	0	
to be payd upon Whitson Monday.				
To Thomas King		11	0	
To Thomas ffayerchild		14	0	
To Humfrey Westwood		10	0	
To Daborne of Letherhed		14	11	
To William King		6	5	
To Roger Richbeall	2	6	8	
To Susan Kirkham	2	0	0	
to be payd upon Trinitie Sunday.				
To Harry Ottie		8	0	
To Elizabeth Pinner		12	0	
To George Rumsey		1	8	
To George Dodson		1	2	
To Mr John Browne		8	4	
To Richard Robinson		3	6	
To John Glassington		16	0	[*£14.17.8*]

Note: The nuncupative Will was dated 30th April and proved on 31st May 1587. The testator's wife Joan was appointed executrix and residuary legatee. She was also made overseer and guardian of his youngest son Roger, until the boy reached the age of 21, when she was to pay the fines due to the lord of the manor. The testator made it plain that the bequests to his father's widow Helen Richbeale were to be honoured; if she decided to leave her daughter-in-law Joan, Helen was to have 6s 8d annually for 12 years, some corn, barley malt and a cow. A sum of £10 was to be given to the testator's son John Richbeale, 2s 6d to the parish clerk Richard Robinson and £18 was to be paid by Roger or his next heir to John Glassington in settlement of the sale of the house called Mammons and 4 parcels of land at Woodslie, Wimmers Bush and Straight Furlong. Joan was to settle the debts of the 17 people named above amounting to nearly £15. When Roger came of age, she was to have similar legacies to those given to Helen by his father. Five witnesses were Gowdfrye Codynton, Robart and William Girdyn, Rafe Glassington and Richard Robinson. The widow and John Glassington of Ashstead, husbandman, stood surety for the administration bond.

Ref: 1587 B 71/1 Will 1587 B 71/2 Inventory

John Russell **249**

of Pirbright; taken by Robert Russell, John Martyn, John Smithe, Thomas Smithe and Rychard fforde, 25th May 1587.

In the Halle	£	s	d
One table and two formes		5	0
Three Stooles		1	8
One Cubbard, one payre of andyrons and one fyre shovell		10	0
One Dozen of pewter, foure Candlestickes, two saltes and halfe a dozen of sacers	1	0	0
Halfe a dozen of Cooshins, three drinckinge Cuppes and a			

chaffinge dyshe		3	4
Ten bushelles of Rye, one dozen of sackes, one Bushell and a pecke	1	10	0
In the Kytchin			
Two brasse pottes, three Keetles, one trevyt, twoe potthangers with one greedyron with one skyllett	1	10	0
Two brotches, a bill, an axe and one shovell		3	4
In his bedd Chamber			
In his apparrell and in his purse	1	0	0
Foure beddes with the furnyture, fyve payre of Sheetes, two table Clothes with other Lynnen	3	6	4
Three Coffers, one lytle table and his swoorde		10	0
In the Hayse and abroade			
Eight Kyne	12	0	0
Three Styres and two hecfore bullockes	5	0	0
Three mares and three coultes	4	0	0
Two swyne, three henns and a cock		6	8
One Carte, two harrowes with the furniture	1	6	8
For thirtie Loade of woode	3	0	0
For certayne peeces of Roughe tymber	3	6	8
Two Closses of Rye contayninge by estymatyon eight acres	10	0	0
In Ready mony	6	0	0
Debtes owinge unto him			
Agnes Smith oweth him	1	10	0
Proctors wyddowe of Gyllford	1	0	0
William Bonnsie		6	8
Gyles of Brookewoode		6	8
Mawde Keene of Worplesdonne		16	0
[*£58.19.0*]	53	5	4

Note: The Will was dated 13th April and proved on 30th May 1587. The residuary legatee and executrix was to be his wife Cassandra and the overseers were his brother Robert Russell and Richard Foorde of Pirbright. His 5 children were all left £4 at the age of 21. Elizabeth, Joane and Alice could claim it if they married young, but John and Robert had to reach full age. His wife was left a life interest in the property, land, buildings and livestock, on condition that she brought up his children during their minority. Were she to marry, she was to put up beforehand sufficient security and bond to provide for all the legacies to be paid. The overseers were to have 2s apiece for their trouble and 2s was to be distributed to the most needy in the parish. Hugh Phillipp wrote the will, which was also witnessed by John Marten of Cowshott, John Smythe, Thomas Smyth and Robert Russell. The widow and Robert Russell of Pirbright, yeoman, stood surety for the administration bond. The burial of John Russell was recorded in the parish register on 21st April 1587.

Ref: 1587 B 74/1 Will 1587 B 74/2 Inventory

Robarte Seagare **250**

of Wanborough, husbandman; taken by Wylliam Costien the elder and Thomas Pursse, 26th May 1587.

	£	s	d
In the Hawle			
A table, a forme and a payre of tresselles		1	0
A lyttell cupborde		4	0
In the chamber			
One littell flocke beadde, a boulster, 2 payre of sheetes, one blanckette, a coverlette, a pyllowe and a pyllowe beare		10	0
A beadd steaddle		1	0

Hys wearinge apparrell		6	8
Monye in hys pursse		3	4
Towe chestes		2	0
In the Loafte over the chamber			
2 oulde flocke beaddes and 2 oulde boulsters		3	4
In the ketchine			
The brasse		5	0
3 pewter platters, one sauser, one pottenger, one salte seller and one chafeinge dishe		3	4
A broche, a lyttell fryeinge panne, a griddeirone, a trefte and a potte henger		2	0
The woodden vesselles with other lumberie in the howse		3	4
In cattell abroad			
One cowe and a lyttellbullocke	2	0	0
2 oxen	4	0	0
One horse beaste		6	8
3 tegge sheepe		7	6
One lyttell hogge		4	0
One carte, a payre of wheeles, yokes, chaynes and other thinges there unto belonginge		10	0
Corne in the feeld			
3 ackers of wheate	2	0	0
2 ackers of pease and tares		10	0
3 ackers of otes		15	0
	12	18	2

Note: The Will was dated 9th March and proved on 30th May 1587. The executors and residuary legatees were Andrew and Elizabeth, 2 of the testator's children. The appointed overseer was another son William, who was given 20d for his trouble. Robert asked to be buried in Wanborough churchyard and then made bequests of money to his immediate family. His wife Marianne was given 6s 8d for herself to use as she wished. Four of his sons, John, the aforementioned William, Henry and Thomas, were each left 20d. The witnesses were Henry Johnsonne who wrote the document and William Costien the elder.

Ref: 1587 B 77/1 Will 1587 B 77/2 Inventory

Robert Sheffeilde **251**

of Dorking, yeoman; taken by Mr Sheffelde, William Henne, Raffe Lucas and Thomas Hooker, 18th April 1587.

	£	s	d
4 Oxen	6	13	4
4 keyne and 2 bulokes	6	6	8
2 steere bullokes	2	0	0
4 horsse and mares	4	0	0
Waners of a yere olde		16	8
4 hogges		13	4
More 4 hogges small		10	0
A collte		5	0
Corne upon the grownde			
6 Akers of wheatt and Rye	3	6	8
A quarter of corne in the howse	1	0	0
A quarter of barlye and ottes		12	0
Howssholde stuffe			
2 bedes with bolsters, stedelles and 2 flocke bedes and a payer of blanckettes and 2 coveringes to the same	1	0	0

	£	s	d
7 payer of shettes	1	1	0
2 table clothes of towne		2	0
12 yeardes of narowe clothe	1	0	0
2 cheastes		1	8
4 pewter platters and 2 dyshes and 2 poryngers		4	0
A chaffynge dyshe			6
2 skillettes and an olde panne		4	0
4 ale vesselles, a tone and other bruynge vesselles		3	4
4 wooden platters and 6 dyshes and 4 lyttell bolles		1	8
A chayer and 2 stolles		1	0
A payer of potthookes			4
A bylle and a naxe		1	0
3 stone of wolle and yearne		5	0
A wenne, a olde doncarte and a payer of whelles and 2 yeokes and 2 chaynes with a plowe and all that longeth there unto	1	3	4
Fore hys a parrell thar ys a cott, a Dublett and a payer of hosse and a payer of shoues and a heatt and 2 shearttes		13	4
	32	5	10

Note: The Will was written on 26th March and proved on 17th May 1587. His daughter Margaret was left £20. The lands and tenements were left to his son Robert and his heirs, who was instructed to keep his grandmother in comfort. The widow Alice and the son Robert, as joint executors, were granted probate, they to have the residue of the goods and chattels. The overseers were John Sheffeilde of Westcott, Thomas Hooker and Raphe Lucas. Thomas Rusburgh wrote the will, also witnessed by Robert Sheffeilde, the son. The burial was recorded on 9th April 1587.

Ref: 1587 B 78/1 Will 1587 B 78/2 Inventory

Johane Shurloke **252**

of Send, widow; taken by Robert Small and John Inwood, 17th April 1587.

	£	s	d
Her apparell and monye in her pursse	1	0	0
All her beddinge in her howsse with all her Lynin	3	0	0
All her brass and peuter in her howss	2	0	0
All the wodden vesselles in her howsse		5	0
In her howsse 4 bushells of Rye		8	0
2 oxen	4	0	0
2 Kyne	3	3	4
One ster one hecver	2	0	0
All the corne one the ground	3	0	0
2 olde maers		13	4
5 shepe		15	0
2 shottes		5	0
All the carte and harrowe with the harnesses and yokes	1	0	0
	[*21*	*9*	*8*]

Note: The Will was written on 18th April, the day after the Inventory and it was proved on 30th May 1587. Richard Harward, clerk and vicar of Send, was paid 5s for writing both documents. The testator's 2 sons Robert and Abraham were appointed executors and a third residuary legatee was her daughter Allis. Robert was left the form and table in the hall and there was a comprehensive and complicated distribution of the livestock between her children and close relatives John Ride and his children John and Sara. Robert Small and John Inwood were appointed overseers. They were both local husbandmen who witnessed the Will and provided the administration bond.

Ref: 1587 B 79/1 Will 1587 B 79/2 Inventory

Agnes Songhurst **253**

of Ockley, widow; taken by John Steare, Raffe Astone, Raffe Baxe and others, 8th May 1587.

	£	s	d
Fyve keyne	11	0	0
Tow twelve monthinge bullocks	2	0	0
Thre wanyers	1	9	0
One Mare	1	5	0
Tow hogges		14	0
Too hogges of bacon, the best 13 shillings, the second 9 shillings	1	2	0
Thre flitches of dryed beyfe		8	0
Thre peces of brasse		16	0
Tow posnetts		1	8
Ten pewter dyshes, thre salt sellers, too dosen of spones, thre sawsers, thre porengers and one tynnen bottle		15	0
One lether bottle			11
Seaven boules and to trayes 3s 2d, syx wodden platters, nyne wodden dyshes, to old boketts and a dosen of tranchers 16d, thre ludging barrells 3s, one vat 5s, one kyver and one bokett 12d, thre tubbs 3s 4d, one churne 12d, to pecks and one sead codde 12d		18	0
One tycke, tow chaffe bedds, foure bolsters, foure coverlitts, five blankets 28s, six paire of worne shetts 18s	2	6	0
Tow table clothes 20d, five sacks and one bagge 4s, one ost hare 2s 8d		8	4
The best bedstedle 2s 6d, four old chests 3s 4d and to old chaires 8d		6	6
To baskets, one flaskett 12d, one grate 2d, a stonen pott 1d, to syves 2d, to Rudders 2d, to tornes 12d, one sheld 4d, the chese hopps 4d		3	3
One girdiron 10d, one paire of potthocks, one paire of potthangers 12d, one iron wedge 11d, to axes 12d, one hatchett 11d, to bills 7d, one syeth 11d		6	2
To harrows 7s 8d, thre youks, thre chaines, one plowe with irons, one chape, one paire of Rougs and horse stropps 6s 8d		14	4
One pott of grese 16d, syx pound of tallowe 20d		3	0
One busshell and a pecke of whete 5s, seaven busshells of oten mault at 18d, every busshell 10s 6d and seaven busshells of otts at 14d every busshell 8s 2d	1	3	8
The Wheate and Rye and otts upon the ground	4	13	4
One paire of old botts 8d, one old crosse karfe sawe 20d, one old ierkin 2s, an old shovell 6d, an old doblett 16d		6	2
For a chesse presse, a kneding trowe and hogge tubbe		1	0
Haye		1	6
One leace of certayne yeares yetto com	30	0	0
Of Readye money	10	10	0
	71	13	4
Debts owyng			
By Robert Willett	10	0	0
By Nycholus Willett ether	10	0	0
	20	0	0
Of Doughtfull Debts by William Chesman	5	0	0

Note: The Will was dated 29th February and proved on 30th May 1587, a year after that of her husband Walter, to which she refers indirectly. The 3 daughters-in-law were in fact her stepdaughters and "the portions of right" given to her 2 daughters were sums of £10 given by Walter. Agnes appointed Thomas Stere, husbandman, as her executor and trustee. John Stere and Raffe Bax, the overseers, were given 3s 4d each for their pains. She asked to be buried in the churchyard and gave 2d to the mother church of Winchester; to the poor of Ockley she gave 20d. Her godchildren were each to have 6d and Joan Dygons, her sister, was given £1 and all her best items of clothing including a hat and a smock. Her mother was to have the second best gown and the russet petticoat. Her servant Walter Hide was given £1 and her stepson Thomas Songhurst 10s as a token of goodwill. Her stepdaughters Margaret the eldest, Joan and Margaret the youngest, were given £3 6s 8d each. The promised legacy of £10 each left to Alice and Eleanor, her own daughters, was to be inherited on their wedding days or at the age of 21. These 2 girls were to inherit the residue of the estate equally, each to be the other's heir. If both should die, the legacy from their late father was to be divided: a half share for the three older girls, a quarter to Joan Dygons and a quarter to the poor of the parish. Four named witnesses were the overseers, Robert Willett and John Eversed. Thomas Stere and Raffe Bax, both husbandmen of Ockley, bound themselves well and truly to administer the Will. The entry of the burial was recorded in the parish register on 3rd May 1587 as Agnes Songhurst, wife of Walter.

Ref: 1587 B 81/1 Will 1587 B 81/2 Inventory

Richard Taylier **254**

of Cobham, husbandman; taken by William Wrenne of Cobham, yeoman and John Lysney of the same parish, fuller, 10th May 1587.

	£	s	d
In the Hall			
A fowlding Standard Table and a fforme, twoo Lyttle Stooles and a Chaire		2	0
Three Brasse pottes		16	0
Fowre Kettells and twoo ould Caldrons together	1	2	0
A possnett and two old Skellettes			8
A Chafinge Dishe			6
A Laver, three Latten Candlestickes and a Skummer		4	0
Old payntinges in the Hall hanging		1	0
An Awndyron, a Grydyron and potthangers, one spytt, a Toasting yron and twoo dripping panns		6	0
In the bed Chamber behinde the hall at the West end			
8 pewter platters, three pewter dishes, 4 pottingers, one Sawcer, one old Bason, a quart and pynt pott of pewter, one Salt Seller, six spoones		14	0
A Cupborde with a Lock and foure old chestes		8	0
Two boorded bedsteddes with Testerns paynted		2	6
For three paynted clothes there		2	6
In the Loffte at the West end			
Two boorded bedsteddes, twoo flockbeddes, two Koverlettes, two Blankettes, a Table with Trestles, twoo Chestes		13	4
In the Lofte over the Hall			
Fleece Wooll by estymation twoo stone		8	0
Hemp and Towe rough, by estimation 2 stone and Drest hemp by estimation fyve pownd weight		3	4
Lockes wooll half a Stone and the baskett together		1	0
4 payre of old Kardes			10
Two old Lynnen Wheeles		1	4
Rye by estymation half a quarter thresht and one bushell of Oattes		14	0
Three ould Barrelles			10
In the Entrie of the same house			
Twoo pease Hookes, twoo old axes, two Bylls and a pronge, one old			

shovell, one spade and 4 Syckells		3	4
In the Buttrie			
An old Bushell and a Bowlting hoouth and trowgh, two old Boles, a Trevett of yron, a Lyttle kettle, a frying panne, old payles, 5 Leather Bottells, three mylke boles, a Cherne, three cheese motes, 6 earthen pottes all praysed together		15	0
In the Kytchin			
Two busshells of Barley and a bushell of meale		8	0
A cheese presse, 4 old tubbes, two buckettes, a doong rake, a Tray and oother odd old Lumber, 14 new elme bordes, a Woollen Wheele, an old stoole		13	4
An Awndyron and an old Oast heare		1	4
In the Barne			
Twoo Hiles of Rye unthresht by estimation, a Ladder, a pronge, three Sackes, one ould Tubbe, a seed Codd and a Lytle cauch of Heye		8	0
In the yard or gate place			
A Carte and a Ploughe and plowgh yrons, twoo harrowes, ropes and harnes		16	0
Three old horses and mares and a Colte	2	13	4
24 Sheepe, 6 Lambes	4	13	4
A Hogge and a Young Sute		6	0
three geese and a gandard and 20 young goslinges, three Ducks and a Mallard		6	0
5 hennes and a Kocke		2	6
Six payre of Sheetes, 3 napkins, a Table cloth and two Towells	1	0	0
His Rayment altogether		13	4
In his pursse of money		1	0
Corne in the field standing			
Foure Acres of Rye and one Acre of Wheate	4	0	0
Two Acres of Tares standing, which were sowen to the Thirdes		10	0
Three Acres of Oattes standing	1	0	0
1 Acre of Barley standing		10	0
A Little plott of hemp standing		1	8
Two paire of Sheeares			6
	25	4	6

Note: The Will was dated 20th April and proved on 31st May 1587. The testator appointed his wife Elizabeth and his eldest son John joint executors and residuary legatees. Sums of 3s 4d were given to the 2 overseers: his wife's brother Anthony Metcalf of Walton-on-Thames and Mathew Fairchild of Stoke D'Abernon. Richard asked to be buried in Cobham churchyard and gave 12d to the poor. He asked that a debt of £5 to his son-in-law, James Nortridge of Cobham and £1 owing to Mathew Fairchild, should be paid as soon as possible. His copyhold dwelling house and lands in Cobham passed undivided to his son John, who before witnesses promised to pay his other sons, Anthony and James, £6 apiece within 6 years. These 2 were each given a bed, bedding and 2 pewter platters and dishes. His daughter Elizabeth was to be given rye at the next harvest and wool to make a coat. Except for the best cloak, James Nortridge was to have all the apparel. The grandchildren were each given a 2-year-old ewe. The witnesses were John Carpenter and John Melsham, both of Cobham and Richard Williamson, the vicar there. The executors provided the administration bond.

Ref: 1587 B 84/1 Will 1587 B 84/2 Inventory

William Whitfeilde **255**

of Kingston-upon-Thames, yeoman; taken by William Mathewe, butcher and Henry Bayard, paynter, 28th May 1587.

	£	s	d
A bedstedle praised at		8	0
A copbord at		2	6

A chayer			6
A table, a payer of tressels and a forme		1	4
Two old chestes at		2	6
An old chayre and a stoole			10
The paynted clothes		1	8
Two pewter dishes		1	4
Three woodden disshes and a sadell			1
An oulde boull and 2 stone pottes			3
An olde percer, an awger and a hammar			8
An olde sythe			6
2 butter firkines			3
A payer of Taylor's sheres			4
A payer of tonges and a reele			2
A whele			6
A paire of pothangers			6
A shovell and a pronge			6
A buckett			2
	1	2	7

There are desparate deabtes, but how mutche they are uncerteyn, for that one Thomas Fletcher, citizen and merchaunte taylor of London and others are bound unto the above sayd William Whitefeld to paie him, his executors and assignes 40 shillings for every acre of coppeholde land which the sayed William hath soulde unto the sayed Thomas Fletcher as shall come and happen unto him after the decease of Isabell Whitfeild, widowe, which as yeat is not knowne and therfore the debtes uncertine.

Note: The Will was dated 30th April and proved on 31st May 1587. The testator's wife Margaret was left a third part of the estate and his son-in-law James Lanckton was left the other two thirds and was appointed executor. Henry Bowrer, the overseer and Edward Fayerbanckes witnessed the Will. At the bottom of the document the date 4th July 1595 records the copying of the original by a notary public Edward Cole and its delivery to court by Roger Cole, notary public. A burial recorded on 23rd May 1587 names William Whitfeild a very old man.

Ref: 1587 B 90/1 Will 1587 B 90/2 Inventory

1588

Henry Atfeld alias Ripley, the elder **256**

of Worplesdon, husbandman; taken by Thomas Russell, John Browne, Henry Ripley alias Atfeld, John Milles and Richard Marlin, 17th May 1588.

	£	s	d
Redye money in his purse		5	0
His Waringe apparell	1	0	0
In the hall			
One Cubbord, one table, one Forme, Pewter vessell and brasse, Fyve fleches of Bacon and Tenne Cheses	2	10	0
in the Chamber within the hall			
Twoe bedstedles, 2 Coverlettes, one blankett, one Coverlett and 3 Chestes	1	10	0
in the Chamber above			
Twoe bedstedles, 2 flockbeddes, 2 Coverlettes, blankettes and a fetherbed	1	10	0
in the kitchin			
The ymplementes with axes and agers	1	0	0
Linen			
Fyve payre of Shetes, 2 tabell Clothes	[*1*	*10*	*0*]

Corne			
Barley and Marlt 3 quarters	1	4	0
Two quarters of Rye	1	0	0
7 akers of Wheat and Rye	5	0	0
4 akers of pease and wotes	1	6	8
Two akers and a half of tares		15	0
Thre akers of Barley	1	10	0
Cattell			
7 hogges	2	0	0
Fyve horse bestes, one Mare and 3 Coltes	13	6	8
Six kyne, two bullockes and 3 Waniers	13	0	0
10 Ewe Shepe and 8 lambes	2	0	0
Carttes, plowes, harrowes and harnes with all other ymplementes	3	0	0
Poulterye aboute the house		3	4
	53	10	8

Note: The nuncupative Will was dated 15th May and proved on 22nd May 1588. The testator gave all to his wife Millicent, trusting her to see all his children honestly brought up in the fear of God. She was sole executrix and the document was witnessed by John Browne, Alice Martyn, Elizabeth Ripley and Ann Marlyn. The administration bond was provided by the widow and Henry Atfeld alias Ripley of Worplesdon, husbandman. The entry of the burial is listed in the parish register on 16th May 1588 as "Ripley als. Atfielde Henry the elder".

Ref: 1588 B 1/1 Will 1588 B 1/2 Inventory

William Dibble **257**

of Newdigate, yeoman; taken by Henry Nedeler, John Constable, Henary Stantone and John Gardener, 15th March 1587.

In the halle house				£	s	d
The table, the furme, 2 chares, 2 Joynstoles					5	4
4 Cusshenes						6
One cubberde					10	0
The brase in the halle				2	2	0
The peuter in the halle				1	0	0
To ayxes, one byle, to pronges					1	4
One brase and one stone pote						4
	£3	19	6			
In the kichin						
The tables and the wooden dyshes					8	0
The Brase					12	0
The peuter					4	6
3 spytes, 2 drypingpans and other lumber					6	0
The Andiarnes in the chimnye, 2 pothangers, one pare of pothouckes, 2 gridiarnes					4	0
One pare of Bellose						4
	£1	14	10			
in the cheease house						
One chese prese, diveres tobes, bordes and wayghtes and one brase kettell					12	0
in the washing house						
One yoltinge fayte and other tobees					5	0
In the milck howse						
26 trougges and bowles					10	0
One kittell, 2 fryinge panes and other pottes					3	4

		£	s	d
5 cheastes and a bushell of peace, one pynt pott			3	6
	16 10			
In the Backhowse				
One ould cowberd with 2 kneadinge trowes and other tobes, dyches and pootes			7	0
Rye meall 2 busheles with an ould sacke			3	4
In the Garretes				
Ottees		3	6	8
Sickeles and other Impellmentes			1	0
	£3 7 8			
In the chambers in the west end of the house				
Maslen			12	0
One fetherbed, one bedsted, thre blanketes, one coverled, one bowlster, one pyllow and one pare of sheates		2	0	0
One cheste, 2 tobees, one chare, trenches and dyshes			3	0
Thre Sackes			1	6
	£2 16 6			
In the Middell chamber				
One fetherbed and bedsted furneshed		1	13	4
2 flocke bedees, 2 pare of Scheates, blanketes and coverletes		1	10	0
His warringe apparell and his monny		1	0	0
One cheaste with 15 pare of Scheates		3	10	0
Hempen Schates		1	0	0
One fflexen Scheat, one krystininge Scheat and one cheste			5	0
One coverled			6	0
3 flexen Scheates and a dossen of napkins			11	2
4 chestetes, one cowberde, 4 platteres			15	0
7 kandellstickes, one chaffing dysh, 4 calcers, 3 Scalcelleres and one lyttell bottell and to pottes			7	0
One chare, 2 byles, one baskett and other impellmentes			2	0
	£10 19 10			
In the moltinge Rome				
Rye and molte		2	3	0
8 flychees of baken, 3 beades of beaf		1	10	0
Tobes and other lomber			5	0
	£3 18 0			
The lease of the howse		20	0	0
4 pygges			12	0
Wheat and haye in the barne		1	6	8
One weane, chaynes, yokees, 2 plowes, 2 harrowes		1	10	0
6 kynne		11	0	0
7 oxsen		18	0	0
2 steares		3	0	0
4 horse and marees		4	0	0
3 Rykees and a half of haye		5	0	0
9 akerees and a halfe of ottees		4	10	0
7 bollockes		4	10	0
Wheat and Rye upon the ground 4 akerees		5	0	0
Dettes owinge unto him		14	0	0
	£92 8 8			
		121	8	2

Note: The Will was written on 15th March and proved on 21st May 1588. The residuary legatee and executrix was the testator's wife Annes, who was also left a life interest in his land bought of

William Wood of Newdigate. When Annes died the property was to go to his daughter Elizabeth and her heirs. His other daughter Annes was to have £30 at the age of 21 and the girls were given an equal share of bedding and pots and pans. The testator's sister Joan Burden was given £2, to be paid in 4 instalments and her children were each given a pewter plate. William asked to be buried in the church or churchyard of Newdigate and he left 6s 8d to the poor of the parish. Sums of 10s each were left to his friends Henry Nedeler and John Gardener, the overseers. The 3 named witnesses were Henry Nedler, Thomas Fuller and Thomas Bilkman. The burial was recorded on 18th March.

Ref: 1588 B 17/1 Will 1588 B 17/2 Inventory

Cornelius Eggen **258**

of St Olave's, Southwark, cooper; taken by Martyn Boman and [*] Stanforns, 1st May.

[*year not given*]

	£	s	d
In his purse		3	8
4 old bandes		2	0
A Dowblet and a paire of hoose of cloth, old		4	0
A ledder Dowblet old		1	0
A paire of black stockinges			4
A ledder Dowblet and briches	1	10	0
A other black Dowblet		6	0
A Clocke	1	0	0
A hatt		3	0
An old birdingpeice		3	4
	3	13	4
In Dowtfull Debte	3	0	0
In Desparait Debte	3	0	0
In Desperait Debte more		10	0
	[*10*	*3*	*4*]

Note: The nuncupative Will was written on 1st May and proved 23rd May 1588. The testator had been born in Falkenberg, either the port in SW Sweden or one of two small inland places in Central or NE Germany. He left everything he owned in England to William Proost of Southwark, joiner, making him his executor and asking him to see to the burial. The witnesses were Martin Boman and Danyel Heyendals. The entry in the parish register of a burial on 4th May 1588 records "Cornelys Eygen servannt with James Smithe, brewer".

Ref: 1588 B 21/1 Will 1588 B 21/2 Inventory

Richarde Fellowe **259**

of Esher; taken by Robertt Gouldwyar and Robertt Arrowsmithe, 20th May 1588.

	£	s	d
His monie in hys purse			4
His Apparryll		3	4
One bedstidell in the chamber		14	0
One owld fether bed		10	0
2 owld coverledes 2 ould blancates		4	0
To tables		7	0
One cubber		14	0
Peweter		6	3
Brasse		14	3
Owld tubs		1	0
One poore mare		16	0
One bulloke	1	1	0
Bees		7	0

Hougs			12	2
	[*£6.?9.4*]	6	8	4

Note: On 22nd May 1588 Alice, the widow, was sworn to the truth of the above inventory and was granted leave to administer the estate. She and Mathew Fellow of Esher, tailor, bound themselves to declare any further goods or chattels should they come to her hands, possession, or knowledge. Both deposited the required administration bond.

Ref: 1588 Ad 24

Thomas Howyke **260**

of Elstead; taken by Henry Wheler, John Adlae and John Stovole,15th May 1588.

	£	s	d
Fyrste in monye		3	4
More hys apparelle		10	0
More the beddyng		12	0
The brase in the huse	1	0	0
More the peuter in the house		1	0
More 1 cobard, 1 table, 1 forme		10	0
All the woddyne vessell		5	0
More the Iergere in the hous as toles and souch lyke		2	0
2 kyne	3	6	8
More 1 horse, a bad one		10	0
More 2 smale hogs		4	0
	7	4	0

Note: The Will was dated 27th December 1578 and was eventually proved on 22nd May 1588. The residuary legatee and executor was the testator's son Thomas. The overseer John Stovole was given 2s and the immediate family were the only other beneficiaries. He asked to be buried in Elstead churchyard and he carefully bestowed his goods on his wife Rose, his 2 other sons John and Richard and on his 2 daughters Joan the elder and Joan the younger. His wife was to have all that she had brought to the marriage. Part of her legacy, 2 sheep, were no longer included in the Inventory, neither was the spinning wheel bequeathed to the younger Joan, nor the sheets given to both daughters. Thomas, the son of John, was to inherit a brass pot after his father. Witnesses were the overseer and Edward Whals, curate. The burial was recorded on 10th May 1588.

Ref: 1588 B 34/1 Will 1588 B 34/2 Inventory

Joan Kidwelle **261**

of Rotherhithe, widow; taken by Christofer Shakelton, Griffen Barker, William Wisdale, Richard Miles and John Crane, 5th Dec 1587.

	£	s	d
In the Hawle			
An old waineskot Table with the frame and 6 Joynd stooles		8	0
Another short table		1	8
An old Cobard with a Deske uppon it		6	0
An old great Chiste		3	0
2 smale Joynd stooles			8
A fier shovell and a pare of Tonges		1	4
A pare of old Andiarns		2	0
A pare of pott hangers and 2 pare of pott hookes		1	0
A settell with a Back of old wainskott		10	0
A waineskott portall		8	0
The hangings of old stained Clothes		2	6
	2	4	2
In the parler			
A standing bedsted of wainskott		10	0

A Trundle bedsted		2	6
A Table of waineskott with 6 Joyned stolles		10	0
A fether Bed with the Bowlster	1	10	0
A flockbedd with a Bolster		1	8
A Covering of Dornex		5	0
An old Blankett		1	8
3 pillowes of Fethers		3	0
A littell Settell by the Bedside		2	0
A settell with the Backe of wainskott		16	0
The hangings of stained Clothes		2	0
	4	3	10
In the Chamber over the parler			
A standing bedsted of waineskott	1	10	0
A greate presse of waineskott	1	6	8
An old wainskott Table with 6 Joyned stoles		10	0
3 other old Joyned stooles		1	0
A Trunck for Apparrell		6	0
A Lyttell painted Chiste		1	0
A fether Bedd with the Bolster		13	4
1 old Danske Chist			8
A forrest Bill, a pike and a stonebowe		3	0
The hanginges of stained Clothes		2	0
	4	13	8
In the Chamber over the buttery			
3 old bedstedes of Carpenters woorke		3	0
An old fetherbed and 2 flockbedes with 3 flock Bolsters		10	0
2 Rotten Coverins and a Rotten quilt and an old Irish Rugg		2	6
An old Chist		1	0
The old hangings of stained Clothes		1	0
		18	6
In the Chamber over the hawle			
An old standing bedsted of wainskott		6	0
An old bedsted without a hed		1	8
2 old fether bedes with the Boulsters	1	0	0
2 Coverings of Dornex		5	0
A littell old Cubbard		1	4
The hangings of old stained Clothes		1	4
In the Buttery			
7 Brasse kettells and a brasse pan		13	4
2 Copper kettels		8	0
2 old Brasse pottes		3	4
2 Iron pottes		3	0
A Lyttell Latten Bason			8
5 Brazen Candlestikes		4	0
A Dripping pan			4
A frieng pann			4
2 Cheese knyves			4
2 spittes		1	4
An old warming pann		1	4
A spice morter and a pestle		1	0
A Brazen plate for a Candle			6
A Brazen Chafing dish		1	0
4 pewter platters		4	0

	£	s	d
3 pewter Dishes		2	0
2 Fruite Dishes		1	0
A pewter Bason		1	8
A pewter peece			4
5 pewter Drinking pottes		4	0
A pewter Chamber pott			8
2 pewter saltes			8
	2	12	10
The Lynnen			
11 pare of Sheetes	1	6	8
3 Table Clothes		5	0
24 Newe Napkins		8	0
6 Diaper Napkins		5	0
3 other plane napkins		1	0
1 shirtt		1	4
2 Bandes		1	8
2 Smockes		1	8
2 Drinking Towels		2	0
3 pillowberes		2	0
5 Dooble Kerchers		1	8
4 Crose Clothes			8
4 Neckegers		2	0
A Durance Apron and 2 white Aprons		2	0
A pare of Redd and grene say Coortaines		3	4
	3	4	0
There waring Apparrell			
2 pare of Breeches		10	0
An old Lether Dublett			6
A Cloake		12	0
A mans hatt Lynd with velvett		2	0
A womans hatt Lynd with velvett		2	0
2 Olde Cassox	1	0	0
1 stammet petticote		16	0
2 old Kirtells		10	0
A kersey waste cote		1	0
	3	13	6
Good Dettes which are to be recoverd Dewe to the Testator			
Oing by one Annes which lefte a petticote in pawne		18	6
Oing by one that left a Cloke in pawen		14	0
Oing by one that lefte a pare of Taffita breches		1	6
Oing in Redriff by one goodman Cok	1	5	0
Oing by Harie Clementes of Redriff		4	0
Oing by William Deane of Redriff		3	6
Oing by one Stevin Burde		18	0
Oing by ould goodwife Churchman		1	1
Oing by John Churchman of Redriff		1	9
Oing by goodman Browne the steward dwelling in Redriff		2	0
Oing by John Dawes of Redriff			7
Oing by Jeffery Vahan of Redriff		6	0
Oing by Thomas Risse of Redriff		8	0
Oing by Peter Wrighte of Redriff		4	6
Oing by one Morgan of Redriff		2	9
Oing by Mr Hendrik of Redriff		3	0

	5	14	2
Deptes Desperett			
Oing by one Georg		14	0
Oing by one John Danniell	1	7	0
Oing by one William Mylkens	2	6	0
Oing by one Edward Wood	1	0	0
Oing by one Thomas Rogers sailer of Redriff	2	0	0
Oing by one Androwe		8	9
Oing by one William Hill		8	3
	8	4	0
Some totalis of this invitory of all the goodes and good Dettes amountes to the some of	28	19	0
Deptes owing by the Testator			
Oing to Mr Tysse the Bruer of St. Katherins	19	2	6
Oing to Richard Doone the Baker in St. Toolis streete	3	5	0
Oing to the Landlord for a yers Rent	2	13	4
Oing to hir soone in Lawe Samewell Young which was for money Lent unto her	5	14	4
	30	15	2
Therefore Remains a lack of	1	16	2

Administration of the estate was granted on 23rd May to Susanna Young, daughter of Joan Kydwellye deceased, relict of Richard Kidwelly deceased.

Note: The parish register of Rotherhithe records the burial of Richard on 24th October 1587 and that of his widow Joane on 12th November 1587. Ref: 1588 Ad 35

Thomas Morer **262**

of Abinger, husbandman; taken by John Lee and Frances Morer, 20th December 1587.

	£	s	d
One Thabell, one Forme, one stole		1	0
2 benche, one shellff			4
One Lethell potte, one posnet, one morther with a pessell		5	0
One small Cathern, 6 Cetthelles, 2 skellette	1	0	0
One Branyerne, 2 pothehenger, one pothokes, a small Clever and one spette, 4 pare of sheres, one threvette, one gerderne		3	4
Pether plathers 6, 5 pether Desshers, 4 salltes sellers, 2 porengers, 2 sallssellers, one Dossone spones		13	4
8 pare of shettes and one shet, 4 thabellell clothes of hempen clotthe	1	6	8
One flocke bed, 2 pellos, one boster, one Cofferlette, 2 blanketts and the paynthed Clothes		16	0
3 Chestes		3	0
Mony in hes porsse		3	4
His Aparell		13	4
In the Lothe over the halle			
Bedstedell, one floke bed, one bollster, one shred heller, one blankette		4	0
One bedstedlle, one Flloke bed, one bollster, one pello, 2 blanketts		10	0
2 Chestes, one planke, one Forme		2	6
In Cheses - worth		5	0
One pothe of bother, one potth of gresse		5	0

In the halle			
Odene Fesselle		3	4
2 axes, 2 belles, 3 weges		2	6
In the Roffe			
5 hoges of Bakone	1	6	0
In the Kechene			
One netthrove, one panthryng throve with coffers, other lombrye		5	0
2 Thornes		1	0
2 olle styes		2	0
3 kene, one hekffer, one thell monithe boloke	6	0	0
One mare and a nage	1	6	8
11 shipe	1	10	0
6 shottes		8	0
In the Felle			
Whett 2 akers and hallffe, of Rey one aker and hallff	2	0	0
In the Barne			
Whett and Rey	1	0	0
Barly	1	0	0
Ottes		3	0
Pesses		5	0
Haye		1	0
10 Henes and A coke		4	0
4 hordells			8
	20	5	8

Note: The Will was dated 11th June 1587 and proved on 22nd May 1588. The residuary legatee and executrix was the testator's wife Agnes. Thomas asked to be buried in Abinger churchyard and he gave 5s to the poor folk there. Half his goods were bequeathed to his son Francis. John Astone, his son-in-law, was given rye and barley. Catherine and Joane Astone, daughters of John, were each given a ewe. Their father was made overseer and given 3s 4d for his trouble. He it was who witnessed the Will, together with Henry Latham, parson of Abinger, John Hunt and Francis More.

Ref: 1588 B 53/1 Will 1588 B 53/2 Inventory

Symon Tally **263**

of Guildford, vintner; taken by James Shawe, James Sharpe and Robert Marson, 10th April 1588.

	£	s	d
In the Hall			
One ffoldinge Table with a fframe and a fforme with an old Carpett		5	0
An old Cupbord with a Chaire and a Cupbord Cloth		5	0
Two Andirons, two pothangers, 2 pronges, a barr and a back to the Chimney, all of Iron	1	0	0
A Joyned Settle, a rodd wycker and the paynted Clothes		5	0
All the glasse in the Wyndowe		10	0
In his owne Beddchamber			
An old Bedstedle with a Tester of paynted Clothes with Curtens and 2 curten Roddes		6	8
A ffether bedd, a fflock bedd, 2 fether bolsters, a Coverlett of Tapestry and one wollen blankett	1	6	8
A Trundle bedstedle		2	6
A ffether Bedd, 2 ffether pillowes and a Coverlett of Dornex	1	13	4
A Joyned Table with a fframe and six Joyned stooles with a Chaire and an old Cupbord		10	0

6 Chestes with fowr lockes and keyes		13	4
A Joyned Presse		6	8
Two Andirons		3	4
12 payre of newe Canvas sheetes	3	0	0
55 payre of other Sheetes	20	0	0
14 ffether pillowes	1	8	0
Two newe quiltes		16	0
Two dozen and tenne Pillowberes	1	16	0
A large diaper table Cloth and 16 diaper Napkyns	1	10	0
3 bason ewre Towelles		3	0
16 Table Clothes and 6 Dozen of old table Napkyns	3	0	0
The paynted Clothes		2	6
A warmynge pan		1	4
All his Bokes		5	4
A newe bedd tyke and a bolster tyke		16	0
13 throme Cusshens	1	6	0
His apparell	6	13	4
In the Inner Chamber			
Two old Bedstedelles with painted testers		5	0
3 ffether Beddes, 4 ffether bolsters, a wollen blankett, an old Coverlett and an old quilt	3	0	0
Three Chestes		3	4
Two litle Andirons		1	0
The paynted Clothes		2	0
7 pound of course hemp yarne		1	8
In the Maydes Chamber			
Two old Bedstedelles		2	0
Two ffether beddes, two ffether bolsters, a fflock bolster, one wollen Blankett, two quiltes and an old Coverlett	2	10	0
Three Chestes		6	8
In the upper parlor			
A Bedstedell and a Trundlebedstedell and a paynted tester, 3 ffetherbedds, 2 Coorse canvas Tykes, 4 bolsters, 2 blankettes, 2 kyverynges, 2 Curteyns, a Mattres, one longe table with a Carpett, a longe fforme, 4 Cusshyns, one Chaire, one footestole and 2 Andirons	8	0	0
Glasse in the Wyndowe		6	0
In the greate Chamber			
A Bedstedell, one Bedd of Downe, one spare Tyke under the same Bedd, two bolsters of Downe, one ffether bolster, 2 blankettes, One Coverlett with ffyve Curteyns, one Trundlebedd, two ffether beddes, two bolsters, one course canvas Tyke under the same Beddes, two blankettes with a Coverynge, 9 Cusshyns, ffive fformes, 3 Joyned stooles, 2 Chaiers, one skryne, one lowe stole, 2 foote stoles, 2 drawynge Curteynes for the Wyndowes, one longe Table with a Carpett, one side Table with a Carpett and 2 Andirons	16	0	0
The paynted Clothes		2	6
In the two bedd chamber			
A Joyned Bedstedle, a trundlebedstedle, two fether beddes, two Canvas Tykes, 4 bolsters, two blanckettes, two Coverynges, two Curteyns, a side Table, a forme and a Close Chayer, 3 quyltes and the paynted Clothes	4	10	0
In Brokes Chamber			
A standinge bedstedle, a trundlebedstedle, three fetherbeddes, 2 course canvas tykes, 4 bolsters, 2 blanckettes, two Coverynges, a longe table with a Coverynge, one syde Table with two smale Coverynges, 7 Cusshyns, two fformes, one Chaire and two Andirons with 2 quiltes and the paynted clothes	7	0	0

In the stone Chamber			
A standinge Bedstedle, a trundlebedstedle, one Bedd of Downe, two fether beddes, two course canvas Tykes, 4 bolsters, 2 blankettes, 2 Coverynges, two Curteyns, a Mattres, a longe Table with a Carpett, 6 Cusshyns, three formes, fyve Joyned stooles one chaire, a side Table with a Coverynge, one Rounde Table and 2 Andirons, one Ironback in the Chimney, the paynted Clothes and 2 Quyltes	16	0	0
In the Taphouse Chamber			
A standinge bedstedle, a fether bedd, a course canvas tyke, one bolster, one blankett with a Coverynge, two Curteyns, a syde table, 2 formes and one Chayer, 2 Quiltes and the paynted Clothes	2	0	0
In the lower parlor			
A Joynedbedstedle and a trundle bedstedle, one fether bedd, two fether bolsters and a Coverlett of Dornyx		13	4
A Table with a frame, 2 formes and the painted clothes		6	8
In the further lodginge			
2 standinge Bedstedelles and a trundle bedstedle, 3 fether beddes, 2 flock beddes, a course canvas tyke, 6 bolsters, 3 Coverynges, 4 Curteyns, a Mattres, a Table with a Carpett, a forme, a chaire and two Andirons and two old quyltes	5	0	0
In the hether lodginge			
Two fether beddes, two Canvas Tykes, 4 bolsters and one old chayer	1	0	0
In the Crosse Chamber			
A standinge Bedstedle, a trundle bedstedle, 2 fether beddes, 3 fether bolsters, 2 Coverlettes,a Table, a forme and two Tresselles	3	0	0
In ffallettes Chamber			
A standinge bedstedle, a fether bedd, a flockbedd, a Coverlett, 2 fether bolsters and a Rugg, a Table with a fframe, a forme, a court Cupbord and paynted Clothes	4	0	0
A Muskett with all his furnyture, a bowe with a shef of Arrowes	3	0	0
In the Tapsters Chamber			
A lowe bedstedle, a fether bedd, a bolster, a Coverlett and a quilt	1	10	0
In the upper Kytchen			
All the brasse pottes, kyttelles and other vesselles of brasse, 3 Drippynge panns with spittes, Iron Rackes and other Lumbry	10	0	0
In the buttery			
Pewter platters, dishes, chargers, sawcers, Chamber pottes with other vesselles, all of pewter, two Candlestickes of pewter	4	0	0
3 old Cupbordes, 2 Chestes, a Round Table with other Lumbry		10	0
9 latten Candlestickes		10	0
In the two Sellars			
7 hogesheddes of wyne, a Butt and a half of Sack with other wyne	57	0	0
Wyne pottes		10	0
Sylver plate			
8 sylver bolles, 3 saltes, a Dozen and a half of spones, all of silver and 2 stone pottes covered with sylver	40	0	0
In the gate			
Aboute 30 loades of wood and certen Tymber in divers parcelles	7	0	0
Corne and hay in the Barnes	20	0	0
6 Acres of Rye in the ffeild	5	0	0
The Lease of a Mesuage in the tenure of John Tompson in Guldeford	10	0	0
Money in his purse	10	0	0
	291	15	2

Note: The Will was dated 4th December 1580 and proved on 21st May 1588. The testator asked to be buried in Holy Trinity church, Guildford at the discretion of his executor, his son James and his overseers, his friends George Parvys, James Shawe and George Austen. James was to inherit the residue of the estate and the overseers were given £1 each for their trouble. As befitted a man of consequence, Symon made a lengthy Will bequeathing a great deal of land in Guildford, Stoke next Guildford and Shalford to James, naming the properties and the previous owners in the latter two parishes. Presumably his messuages and tenements in Guildford were well known. Those in Stoke were :-
"Byndinges - messuages or tenements and lands purchased of John Purveys of Unsstead, Lands and tenements purchased of Mr Combes; 8 Acres of arable and pasture purchased of Sir William More, Knight and Thomas Jones, Gent.; Tenement and Messuage with garden etc purchased of John Browne; ½ Acre in the Common field, Stoke field purchased of John Wyntershall, Esq.; 1 Acre called the Quylles, parcel of Eyehorne, purchased of William Hoke; a Close of land purchased of Henry Monger; 1 Acre of land in Stoke field purchased of Thomas Coxe and Land called Bull Hill purchased of Henry Polsted, Esq".

From these lands James was to raise £3 per annum to pay the testator's wife Elizabeth an annuity for life. She was also given the sum of £53 6s 8d, to be paid in 4 equal instalments. Were Elizabeth to claim her third part of the estate, her dower as of right, the 2 previous bequests would become void. A bequest of £3 6s 8d was made towards the repair of the Guildhall, £1 was given to the poor, his unnamed servants were each given 3s 4d and his godchildren 1s. The mayor and approved men of Guildford were to take charge of £40 to be used for the benefit of William, son of Robert Tally, until he reached the age of 21, when the principal money would be his and the interest built up over the years would be shared equally between William and the mayor. The executor would receive a half share if William died young, but meantime he was required to bring up the boy without charge. George Parvis and George Austen witnessed the Will. A burial was recorded of Mr Symon Toyle on 8th April 1588.

Ref: 1588 B 63/1 Will 1588 B 63/2 Inventory

Richard Wicker **264**

of West Molesey, yeoman; taken by Thomas Fisscher, William Nyckollse and Thomas Byrchett, yeomen, 17th May 1588.

	£	s	d
In the parler			
His apparell		5	0
A Fether Bed and a flocke bed wyth all furneture	1	0	0
6 chestes, one wyth another		3	4
In the halle			
One Tayble, one forme, 2 chayres and one litle cubborde		3	4
3 Trevittes, a payre of pottehanggers and 4 spittes		3	4
All the Brasse and puter	1	2	0
All the Lomber		1	4
Thre dozen of Trenchers and disshes and a Laydle			4
5 Irone wedges			10
One Axe, 4 Awgers and wymbles			8
3 hammers			3
Fyve ould prounges			4
In the yarde and feeldes			
One Carte, one ploughe, one payre of harrowes and all the harnesse wyth ropes		10	0
2 Kyne and one Steare	2	10	0
3 Jaydes	1	10	0
3 hogges		6	0
10 shepe	1	0	0
All the wynter corne and sommer corne upon the ground when he dyed	3	0	0

	£	s	d
2 broode guysse and a gander, 4 hennes and a cocke		2	4
Sertyn ould hurdles and some litle fyre woodde		1	0
	12	0	1

Note: The Will was dated 19th April 1587 and proved on 22nd May 1588. The testator asked to be buried in West Molesey churchyard. His son Thomas was named as executor and residuary legatee and was given the 2 acres of lease land held of John Hamande, gent., provided he kept his mother Alice, "in all poyntes as becommeth an honiest man to use a woman of her Ayge, as shee hath bene used heretofore." The 5 named overseers were James Cornford, Robert Stackeford, Thomas ffyssher, Symonde Cooke and Thomas Butcher. The Will was proved by the executor. Richard Barton of Walton on Thames and John Pullin of West Molesey, both clerks, had witnessed it in the presence of the overseers. The administration bond was provided by the said Thomas Wicker, husbandman and James Burchett, blacksmith, both of West Molesey.

Ref: 1588 B 74/1 Will 1588 B 74/2 Inventory

1589

William Arnolde **265**

of Mickleham, yeoman; taken by Edward Roger, Rycharde Tuddam, Robert Sheffielde and John Mownte, 27th April 1589.

	£	s	d
In his purse		10	0
His wearinge Apparrell	2	0	0
In the Inner Chamber on hye			
A feather bedd, bolsters, pyllowes, Coverlettes, blankettes, a playne beddsteddle with a paynted Testerne	1	0	0
One bedd more in the same Chamber, a flockbedd with 3 blankettes, a Coveringe, Twooe bowlsters, 2 pyllowes and a playne bedsteddle with paynted Testerne	1	6	8
In the next Chamber to the same			
Table, frame with other Trumperye, an owlde Coveringe, 3 Cusshyns, 2 pyllowes, 12 payer of sheetes, ffower Table Clothes, a Towell, 4 Table Napkyns	4	9	0
In the Chamber belowe			
4 flocke beddes, 6 blankettes, 3 feather bowlsters, 2 playne bedsteddles, 2 paynted Testerns	2	0	0
In the Hall			
1 Table, 1 Joyned stoole, a paynted Clothe, 1 payer of brandyarns, pottehangers	1	3	4
8 pewter platters, 2 salt sellers, 1 pewter pott, 3 pewter dysshes, 1 bason, 6 poringers, 6 latten candelstycks, 1 Latten morter, 12 peuter panes, 1 Cubbarde clothe		16	0
In bras			
3 bras pottes, 4 bras kettelles, 2 pannes, 2 possenettes, 1 Cawdron in the furnace, 1 Chafinge dyshe, 2 owlde kettelles, 1 dryppinge panne, Tubbes and dyvers other Trumprey	3	0	11
Carte, Carte wheeles, a longe carte, 2 Dungcartes, 2 payer of wheeles, 2 plowes, 2 shares, 2 Cowlters, 3 harrowes and a seade coate	3	0	0
6 sackes, a wynowynge sheete and an oste heare		10	0
4 Kyne	6	0	0
3 heckfordes	3	0	0
4 Twooe yearelynge bullockes	3	0	0
6 Twelmonthlynges	4	4	0
Seaven score and seaven sheepe	26	0	0
33 Lambes	3	0	0

8 hogges and syxe pygges	2	1	0
The wheate in the barne 5 quarters	5	0	0
His heye in the barne and a quarter of Rye	2	10	0
His wheate nowe growinge on the grownde and Rye 17 Akers in the wheles	11	6	8
7 quarters of Mawlte	3	0	0
Axes, bylles, Ladders with other sundrye Trumprey, Rakes and forkes		6	8
[*89.4.3*]	90	0	0

Note: The Will was dated 27th February and proved on 14th May 1589. The executor and residuary legatee was the testator's son Raphe. His present wife Ellen was to have an annual income of £5 to be paid from his lands in Wotton and Mickleham, tenanted by one Gadd and Edmund Roger, respectively. Ellen already had a jointure (joint tenancy) of benefit to her for life. The testator asked to be buried in Mickleham church and he gave to the poor 6s 8d. His godchildren were left 6d each, his servants 12d, John Bosyer the younger of Dorking £1 and the overseers Richard Tuddam, butcher and Robert Sheffield of Tylehurst, yeoman, both of Dorking, received 3s 4d each. Seven of his wife's eight children, namely John, Christopher, Edward and Robert Wyllett, Joane Mownte, Elizabeth Howe and Margaret Shorye, were each left 10s. Agnes Wyllett was to have £5 if she would live with and serve his son Raphe Arnolde for 2½ years, being treated honestly by him. Any one of the beneficiaries in any kind of contention with the said Raphe would forfeit his or her legacy. The overseers witnessed the Will, together with the writer Thomas Rusburgh and others unnamed. The executor and William Moose of Mickleham, husbandmen, bound themselves to administer the estate.

Ref: 1589 B 1/1 Will 1589 B 1/2 Inventory

William Downing **266**

of Carshalton, shepherd; taken by Henery Warlinge and William Tanner, 1st May 1589.

In the Hawle	£	s	d
A spytt, one andyorne, A gredyorne, A fyre shovell, potthangers, potthoockes, one cheere, A tressell, one forme, 2 stooles, A fryinge panne and sertaine bordes		4	4
A meale and other lumbermentes		2	6
A fate and other old tubbes		4	4
A bushell, A pecke and halfe pecke, A showle and 2 old formes		2	0
The woodd aboute the house		4	0
A fetherbedd, A Strawe bed, 2 bowlsters, A coverlett, A coveringe, A bedstedle, A chaffbedd, A covering, one blanckett and one boulster	1	3	4
Nine payre of sheetes, one table cloth, one towell	1	1	0
A trevett, a hempe Irone and chees there		4	8
3 platters, 4 old pewter dishces, 2 sawcers, 2 saltes, a doszene of spones, 2 wollen wheles		6	8
4 kettels, one Irone pott, 2 chaffers		11	0
2 chestes and old coubburd		3	4
2 quarters of mault, A bushell of wheat, A bushell of Rie, 3 bushells of oottes	1	8	0
One half Acre of Rie, one half acre of barlye, one Acre of pece in the feeld	1	0	0
2 Stawles of bees		2	6
2 pygges, 2 hennes and a cocke		4	0
Candels in the house		3	0
The Lease of the house	1	0	0
Redye monye in the house		15	0
His apparell		10	0
Debtes owing unto the said Downinge at the tyme of his death			
One Brignall did owe		11	6
John Mathewe the yonger		9	10
John Kynsman		6	8
Hugh Harrishe		8	6

	11	6	2
Debtes owing by the said William Downing at the tyme of his death			
To Lowrannce Downinge	1	4	0
To William Downinge		12	0
To Thomas Downinge		12	0
To one Sanders		4	0
To Thomas Gosner		3	6
To the Tayler		3	4
To Lowrannce Downing		8	0
[*£3.7.10*]	3	7	8

The debtes of the said Downinge beinge discharged there remainethe cleer seaven powndes 18s 6d [*£7.18.4*]

The administration of the goods was granted to Elizabeth, the widow, on 14th May 1589. She raised the bond. Her husband had been buried on 19th April.

Ref: 1589 Ad 21

Richard Jennings 267

of Kingston-upon-Thames, fisherman; taken by William Dodson, John Phyllyppe, Thomas Philip and John Benson. [*undated*]

In the Hall	£	s	d
Two tables, sixe ioyned stooles, a Carpett and a forme		9	0
Foure olde chaires there		1	6
One olde Coberde with a bason and ewer and six flower pottes		3	0
All the painted cloathes there with two Curtens and foure olde Cushens		4	10
Twoe olde Andierns		1	6
		19	10
In the Chamber over the Hall			
One bedstedle with a father bedde, two blanketts and a pillowe	1	0	0
One olde Coberde with two basons and an ewer		1	8
One olde table, an olde chaier and a warminge pan		2	0
One platter, 5 pewter potts, a salt seller, 6 sawsers and one latin bason		7	0
13 paier of sheetts	2	6	8
fyve pillowbeares		5	0
8 table cloathes with 2 dozen of napkins	1	0	0
Two towells		2	0
6 olde chests		9	0
All the painted cloathes there		1	0
	5	14	4
In the Parlour			
One olde Coberde		2	6
One pewter bason, two pinte potts, two cups, a salte and two bowe potts		2	0
One olde gowne and one cloake		12	0
One olde presse		8	0
One Coverlett		12	0
Twoe olde bowes with their arrowes		2	0
One little table		1	0
The painted cloathes with an olde Curten there		3	4
	2	2	10

	£	s	d
In the Chamber over the Parlour			
One olde bedstedle with one olde fetherbed		6	8
Twoe olde chaiers and one olde cheste		1	8
The paynted cloathes there		1	8
		10	0
In the Buttrie			
Twoe Cawdrons		6	8
Three copper pan		3	4
Two little brasse pottes, 3 posnetts and a strainer		10	0
One olde Chafer		1	6
One olde table with the shelves			10
One olde cheste, a browne bill and a powderinge tubbe		1	4
Three olde wheeles and a bushell		1	0
	1	4	8
In the Lofte or chamber over the buttrie			
3 olde Chestes with all the lumber there		3	0
In the Kitchin			
Twoe little brasse potts		3	0
One Kittle and a pan		2	8
Thre brasen Candelstickes, one Chafendishe and one morter		2	8
10 olde peeces of pewter, one Chamber pott and one poringer		4	4
4 speets, twoe drippinge pans, an olde freyinge pan with a paier of Rackes and a pothanger		5	0
A grideron, one trevett, a paier of tonges, one fier sholve and a creeper		1	0
One olde dresser there and a shelfe			8
		19	4
In the Backhouse			
One olde Cheste with all the lumber there		2	4
One lease of an eight in Kingston	4	0	0
The Croppe of one acre of barley and one acre of tares	1	4	0
Owinge in desperate debts to the Testator		10	0
	5	14	0
	17	10	8

Note: The Will was dated 10th March and proved on 26th May 1589. A life interest in his messuage or tenement and 2 acres of arable lying in Westfield in Thames Furlong was given to his wife Maude unless she married, in which case it was to go immediately to his eldest son Robert. The said Robert was to have the best boat and the well boat, together with the equipment for fishing and laying wells. He was also given a bed and bedding, useful household goods and a piece of gold. At the age of 25 his second son George was to be paid £1 by each of the 2 executors, the testator's son Robert and his wife Maude. His daughter Elizabeth Benson and her husband John were given specific articles of clothing and household goods. Sums of £3 each and household stuff were given to the 3 other daughters, Johane, Alice and Anne, at their ages of 23, 25 and 23, respectively, or on their wedding days. The youngest Anne was to inherit the bed which had belonged to her maternal grandfather Robert Groves. The overseers Robert Norton and William Dodson, bricklayer, of West by Thames, were each given 5s. Robert Glover wrote the Will, which was also witnessed by Edward Fayrebanckes and William Averye. On 12th May 1589 the burial of Richard Genyngs was recorded in the parish register.

Ref: 1589 B 31/1 Will 1589 B 31/2 Inventory

Francis Lake **268**

of West Molesey; taken by James Corneforde and Simon Cooke, 24th Feb 1588.

	£	s	d
1 fetherbed, a Boulster, a coverlet	1	0	0
1 table Boorde, 1 Cubbourde	1	0	0
1 truncke, 2 chestes		4	0
2 olde pannes, 3 platters, 2 saucers		5	0
1 Andeirone, 1 spitte		1	0
1 spade, 1 hachet		1	0
1 Cloake, 1 Canvas Dublet	1	0	0
All his other Apparell	1	0	0
1 Browne mare		13	4
Sheepe and a Pigge	3	0	0
1 Cowe, 1 gander, 1 goose	2	0	0
Corne and maulte	2	0	0
Corne groweinge on the grownde	1	0	0
In money	5	18	4
Money oweinge to him		11	0
Woodde		6	8
	[*20*	*0*	*4*]
Debtes oweing me			
George Porter	1	5	0
Simon Cooke		19	4
William Gregory for a loade of Billettes		5	0
for a Bushell of Rye		4	4
	[*2*	*13*	*8*]

Note: The separate list of debts was written on the Will which was dated 13th February and proved on 14th May 1589. The residuary legatee and executor was the testator's brother Arthur, who was left the house at Appes after the death of their mother. Francis divided his stock, household goods, crops and apparel most carefully between the said Arthur and two other brothers, Charles and Robert. Sums of 5s each were given to James Corneford, his father-in-law and to Thomas Burchet, blacksmith, the overseers. He asked to be buried in West Molesey church, to which he gave 10s and the poor of the parish received £2. Gifts of clothing or money were given to Thomas Michaell, Nicholas Prior, Mother Blake, Agnes Stile, to the servants of his father-in-law, to Sible Hamones and to Dorothy Hawthornewhite. Witnesses to the Will were the overseers, also Robert Dowley, John Dally and Richard Child. The executor, husbandman and Thomas Burchett, blacksmith, both of West Molesey, bound themselves well and truly to administer the estate.

Ref: 1589 B 33/1 Will 1589 B 33/2 Inventory

William Mathewe **269**

of Albury, labourer; 10th May 1589. [*no appraisers given*]

In his chamber	£	s	d
A Symple bedd with the ffurniture and a cheste		10	0
7 sheape		14	0
His Apparrell		3	0
In monie in the handes of Thomas Lucocke		14	0
In the handes of Thomas Chenell of ffarlie		2	8
	2	3	8

Note: The Will was dated 6th May and proved on 13th May 1589. The testator asked to be buried in Albury churchyard. To his cousin Susan he gave a ewe and a lamb at Edward Risbridger's. His brother Henry of Cranleigh was left one half of his goods and his executor William Frances was to receive the other half. The Will was witnessed by Robert Cowper, clerk, the parson of Albury. The executor, a husbandman of the same parish, bound himself well and truly to administer the estate. A burial on 8th May 1589 recorded William Mathew occisus Henry Chesman. This may explain why no appraisers were named. Possibly the parson was urgently called to minister to his dying parishioner, the victim of manslaughter by Henry Chesman.

Ref: 1589 B 38/1 Will 1589 B 38/2 Inventory

John Molynge **270**

of Hambledon, Clerk and Parson; taken by Gyles Hull, gentleman, John A Streete, William Smalpece, John Monger, John Arnolde and Anthony Thorneden, 14th April 1589.

In the hall	£	s	d
A table and 6 Joyned stooles		5	0
One Cupborde		4	0
Two Cheyers with two litle stooles		1	4
Two Cousshinges		1	0
In the loft over the hall			
An olde bedstedle, two fflockbeddes and two bolsters, two paire of blanckettes, three Coverlittes,one olde paynted Cloth, two planckes and two pyllowes		18	0
In the Chamber over the buttery			
A Truckle bedstedle, a bolster, two coverlittes, three olde paynted Clothes, one plancke with two trestles and two Chestes		10	8
In the Butterye			
One Caudron, ffower kettles, two Iron pottes, one posnett, one Chafynge dishe and one Candlestick		19	0
6 platters, one bason, ffower pewter disshes, 6 Sawcers, two pottengers, 11spones, two salte sellers and a Tynnen bottle		11	0
Iron stuff			
One Tryft, a spytt, a Cobiron, a paire of pothookes, a paire of pothangers, a Gerdiron and a ffyer shovell		4	0
A Qualyver, a Murryan, fflaske and Tutcheboxe, a sworde and a Dagger		16	0
Lynnen			
Three paire of sheetes, two table clothes, two Hand towelles and 2 Half sheetes		13	4
Wodden Vessell and other stuf			
A kyve, a Wateringe vate, 6 kyvers, three pypkyns, one fyrkyn, one Stobbyn, two axes, two Hedginge bylles, a Watch byll and a spytter	1	0	0
Goodes Remayninge in the Handes of Frances Molynge, Wydowe late Wif of the saide John			
A standinge bedstedle, a flockbedd, a bolster, two pyllowes, a paire of blanckettes, two paire of Sheetes, one Coverlitt, one brasse pott, one Candlestick with other small thinges	1	5	0
His apparelll and monye in his purse	1	0	0
His Librarye in all		10	0
Cattle			
ffower Kyne, whereof one hath a calf, two Heckfors with two Calves, two twelmonthinge bullockes	12	6	8
9 Ewes, 9 Lambes, 6 tegges	3	3	0
A Mare	1	0	0
A Sowe and two shootes		18	0
Corne and hey			
Corne thresshed and unthresshed Rye, otes and heye	3	4	6

	£	s	d
A Carte and all necessarie thinges there unto belonginge, a Rode saddle, two Ladders, a pronge and a pannyll		8	0
Corne in the fylde			
Three acres of Rye	1	0	0
ffower acres of otes	1	6	8
Soyle and strawe in the Gate		3	4
One Quarter of Malt		5	0
	32	13	6

Note: The Will was dated 1st April and proved on 13th May 1589. Parishioners of Hambledon were to benefit from a bequest of 5s to buy a bible and 8 poor folk were to have 4s. A shilling was left to the poor of Godalming. His wife Frances was to have the best bed with its furnishings and all the goods she had brought to the marriage, together with £10. Her son John West was given the best bullock, whereas his son Richard Molynge was given 10s, as was Elizabeth Harmes. A son-in-law John Woolridge was to have £1 and the servant Elizabeth Mose was given a ewe and a lamb. The second best bed and its furnishings was left to Robert Jordan. The third best bed and its furnishings was left to Nicolas Dory, his son-in-law. Elizabeth Dorye, his daughter, was to have his best brass pan. This Nicolas Dory of Godalming, shoemaker and an unmarried daughter Mary Molynge were to be joint executors and to have equal shares in the residue of the estate. The overseers of the Will were to be William Smalpece of Hambledon and William Stinte of Bramley. These two men witnessed the signing of the Will together with Elisabeth Redfearne. The administration bond was provided by Nicolas Dory and Robert Jorden, both shoemakers of Godalming.

Ref: 1589 B 42/1Will 1589 B 42/2 Inventory

Richard Pagge **271**

of Horsell, husbandman; taken by Richard Stillman, James Dallye and Walter Warner, 12th May 1589.

	£	s	d
In his purse		1	0
For his apparrell		5	0
A fflocke bedd		3	4
Two paire of Shettes		5	0
For the bolsters, blankes and Coverlettes		4	0
Two bedstedles and ffyve chestes		6	8
For a Cobbard, a Table, a forme and Three stoles		8	0
One Brasse potte and a Cawdron, Two kettelles, a possnet		13	4
A friinge pane, a spitte		1	0
Tenn peices of pewter		5	0
Three Candellstickes and a Salt seller		2	0
For Three Toubes and a kned Troughe and a Cover		5	0
A Cowe	1	6	8
A Mare		13	4
A Sowe		5	0
An Acre of Rye		6	8
	5	11	0

The Inventory was exhibited at court on 13th May 1589 by Juliane, widow and relict of the deceased and administratrix of the estate.

Ref: 1589 Ad 44

Henry Parker **272**

of Farnham, yeoman; taken by John Terry, John Cox and Roberte Warner, 12th May 1589.

£ s d

Debtes owinge unto him and money in his purse	15	0	0
His waringe apparell		10	0
	15	10	0

Note: The Will was dated 18th April and proved on 13th May 1589. The testator asked to be buried at the discretion of his overseers, his friends John Cox and John Terry, to whom he left 2s each. He bestowed £1 10s amongst the 3 parishes of Farnham, Alton and Odiham: 3s 4d for church repairs in each and 6s 8d for its poorest people. He used the word "cossen" for his 4 nephews and nieces. Sums of 10s each were given to Thomas Parker and Joan Mason, the children of his brother Thomas. Eight great nephews and nieces, the three children of Joan Mason, the four children of Margery Harding and the one child of Margaret Parker were each left 3s 4d; the aforesaid Margery and Margaret were also children of brother Thomas. Rychard Mannen, son of the testator's sister Joan, was given £1. Two shillings was left to Agnes Ball, servant of Roger Serll of Warnborough. The residuary legatee and executor was his "cossen" John Harding. The Will was witnessed and signed by Wyllyam Petowe, John More and the two overseers. Henry Parker's burial was recorded on 3rd May 1589.

Ref: 1589 B 43/1 Will 1589 B 43/2 Inventory

Steven Penycod 273

of Elstead; taken by Thomas Lofe, Henry Boxhold and Robard Edsale, 29th April 1589.

	£	s	d
In monye		10	0
Hys apparell	1	0	0
The beddyng in the house		10	0
The brase and peuter in the house	1	0	0
One cobard, a bad one		1	8
One table, a forme with a stolle, certayne badgere		1	0
The woddenne vessell		6	8
The earthen vessel in the house			10
The carte harrose wyth the iergere in the house, bad gere		12	0
The horse bese aboute the howse	1	10	0
The hogs aboute the howse	1	0	0
The shepe and lamse	6	13	4
Thre kyne	4	0	0
Foure bullokes	2	0	0
The Rye in the felde	1	0	0
The Wotes in the fylde	1	0	0
The Rye in the baryn		2	0
The heyfes about the house		6	8
Thre hense one koce		1	0
	21	15	2

13th May 1589: Administration was granted to Anne, relict, who was sworn to the truth of the Inventory. Ref: 1589 Ad 45

Note: The parish register lists the burial of Steven Penycod on 9th April 1589.

John Rapley by West 274

of Chiddingfold, husbandman; taken by William Petowe, Richarde Aborowe, John Holloway and William Johnes, 22nd April 1589.

	£	s	d
All his wearinge apparell	2	0	0
2 Fetherbeddes, the steddles and all belonginge therunto	4	0	0
4 Flocbeddes, the steddles and all belonginge therto	3	0	0
8 payre of Sheetes	2	0	0
2 paire of Pillowbers, one towell, 6 Napkins		8	0

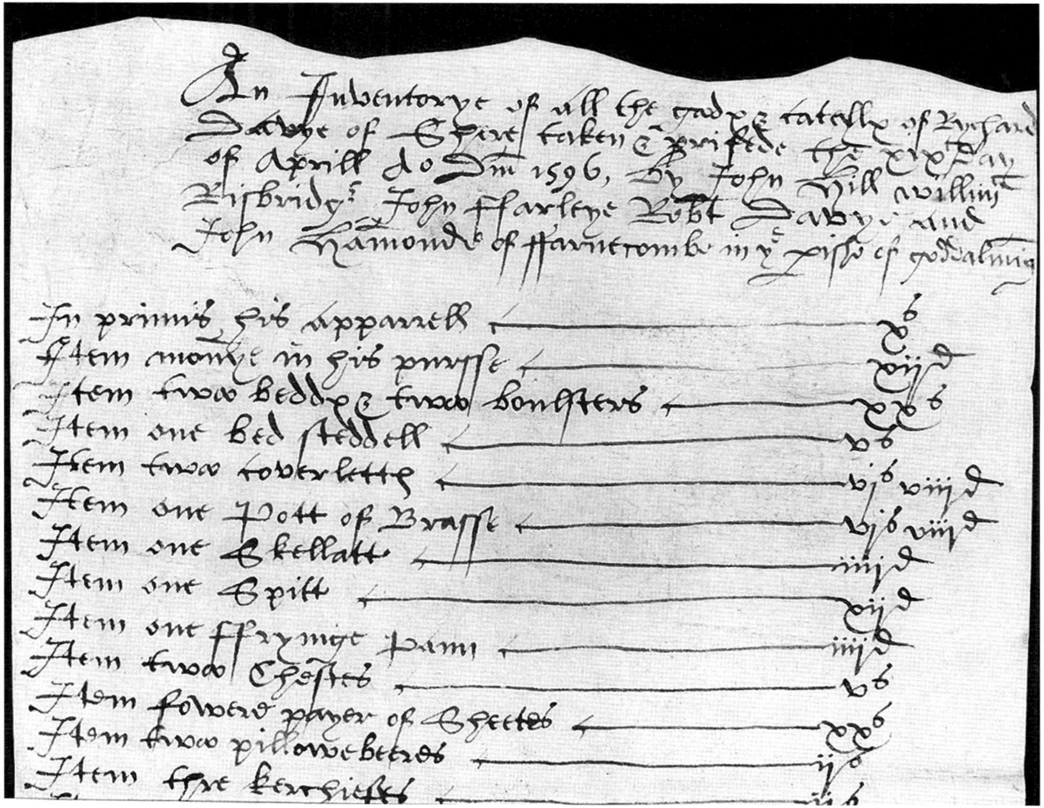

An Inventorye of all the goods & catells of Rychard Davye of Shere taken & praysede the xx day of Aprill Ao Dm 1596, by John Hill willm Risbridger John ffarlye Robt Davye and John Hamonde of ffarncombe in ye p[ar]ishe of Godalming

In primis his apparell — xs
Item monye in his purse — xijd
Item two bedds & two boulsters — xxs
Item one bed steddell — vs
Item two coverletts — vjs viijd
Item one pott of brasse — vjs viijd
Item one skellatt — iiijd
Item one spitt — xijd
Item one ffryinge pann — iiijd
Item two chestes — vs
Item fower payer of sheetes — xxs
Item two pillowbeeres — ijs
Item thre kerchieffs — ijs

Extract from original inventory 1596 Richard Davye of Shere: naming the appraisers
(350)

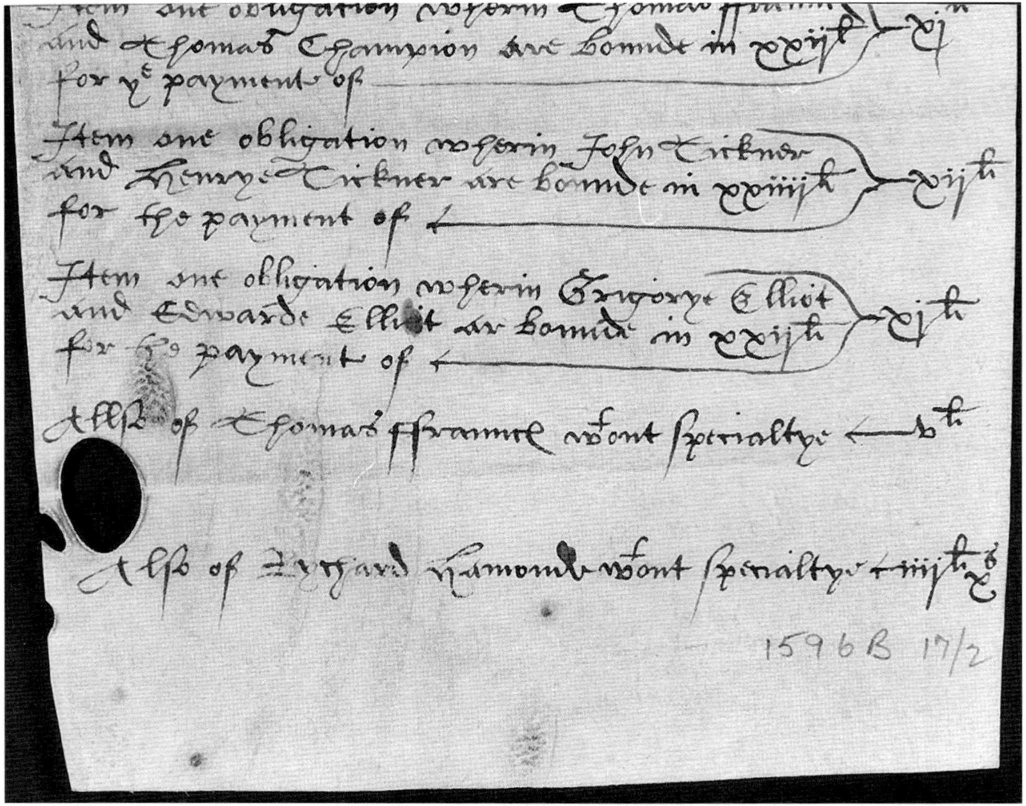

Item one obligation wherin Thomas ffraun[ce]
and Thomas Champion are bounde in xxijli
for ye payment of — xjli

Item one obligation wherin John Tickner
and Henrye Tickner are bounde in xxiiijli
for the payment of — xijli

Item one obligation wherin Gregorye Elliot
and Edwarde Elliot ar bounde in xxijli
for the payment of — xjli

Also of Thomas ffraunce wont speciallye — vli

Also of Rychard Hamonde wont speciallye — iiijli

1596B 17/2

Extract from original inventory 1596 Richard Davye of Shere: list of his debts of £43
(350)

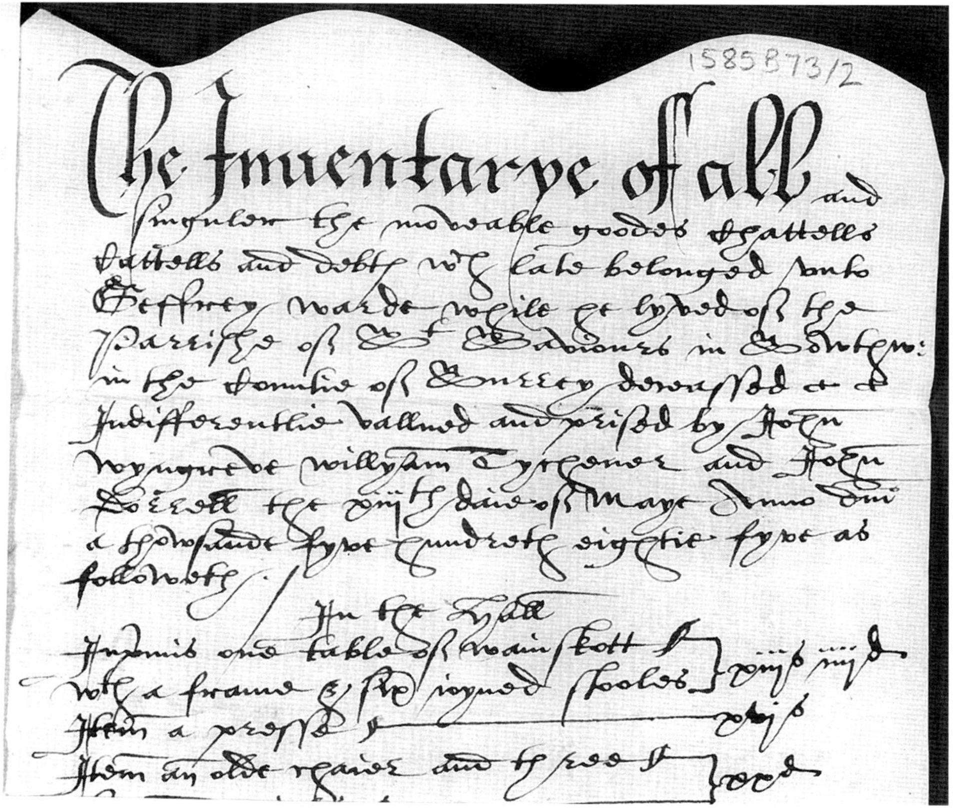

Extract from original inventory 1585 Geffrey Warde of Southwark: example of dating
(219)

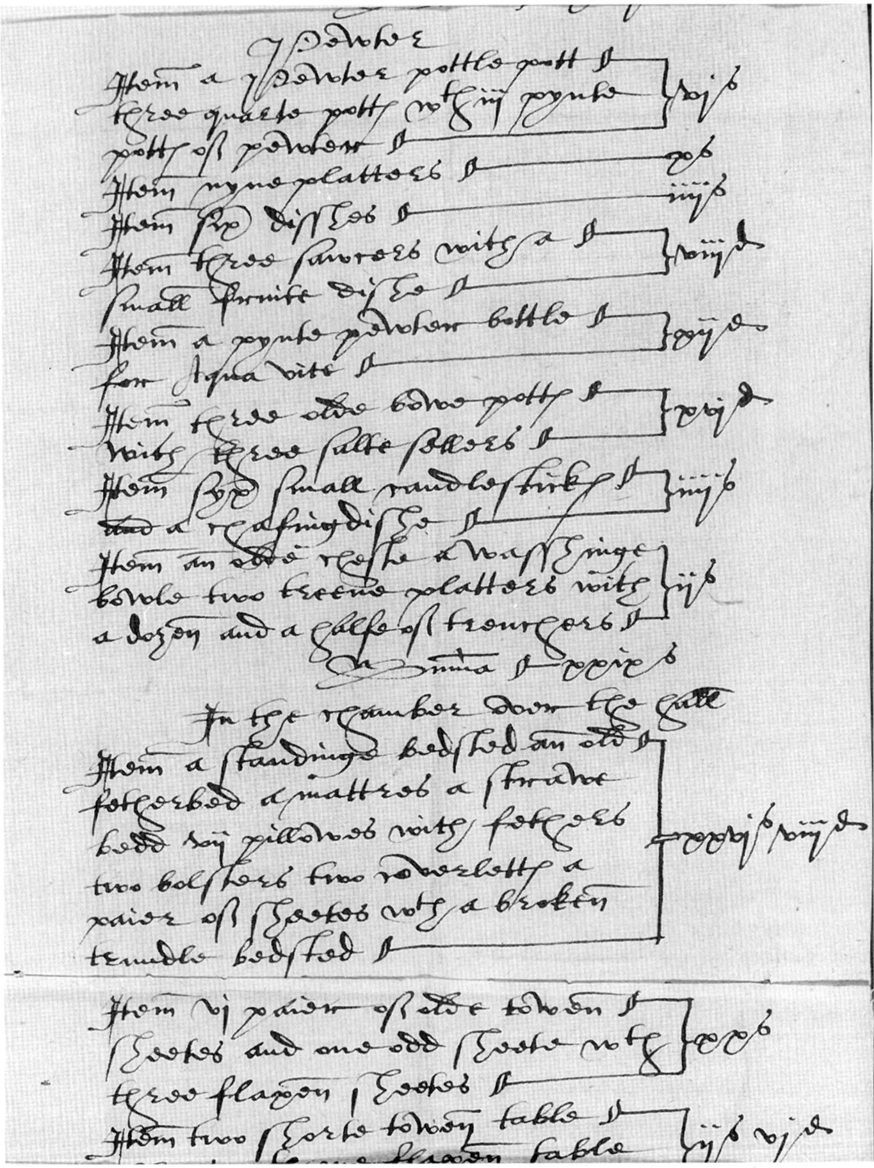

Pewter
Item a pewter pottle pott
three quarte potts with iij pynte
potts of pewter — xvj s
Item nyne platters — xs
Item sixe dishes — iiij s
Item three sawcers with a
small fruite dishe — xviij d
Item a pynte pewter bottle
for Aqua vite — xij d
Item three olde bowe potts
with three salte sellers — xvj d
Item sixe small candlesticks
and a chafingdishe — iiij s
Item an olde cheste a wasshinge
bowle two treene platters with
a dozen and a halfe of trenchers — ij s
Summa xxxix s

In the chamber over the halle
Item a standinge bedsted an old
fetherbed a mattres a strawe
bedd xij pillowes with fethers
two bolsters two coverletts a
paire of sheetes with a broken
trundle bedsted — xxxij s viij d
Item vj paire of olde towen
sheetes and one odd sheete with
three flaxen sheetes — xx s
Item two shorte [illegible] table — iij s vj d

Extract from original inventory 1585 Geffrey Warde of Southwark: list of his pewter including "a pynte pewter bottle for Aqua vite"

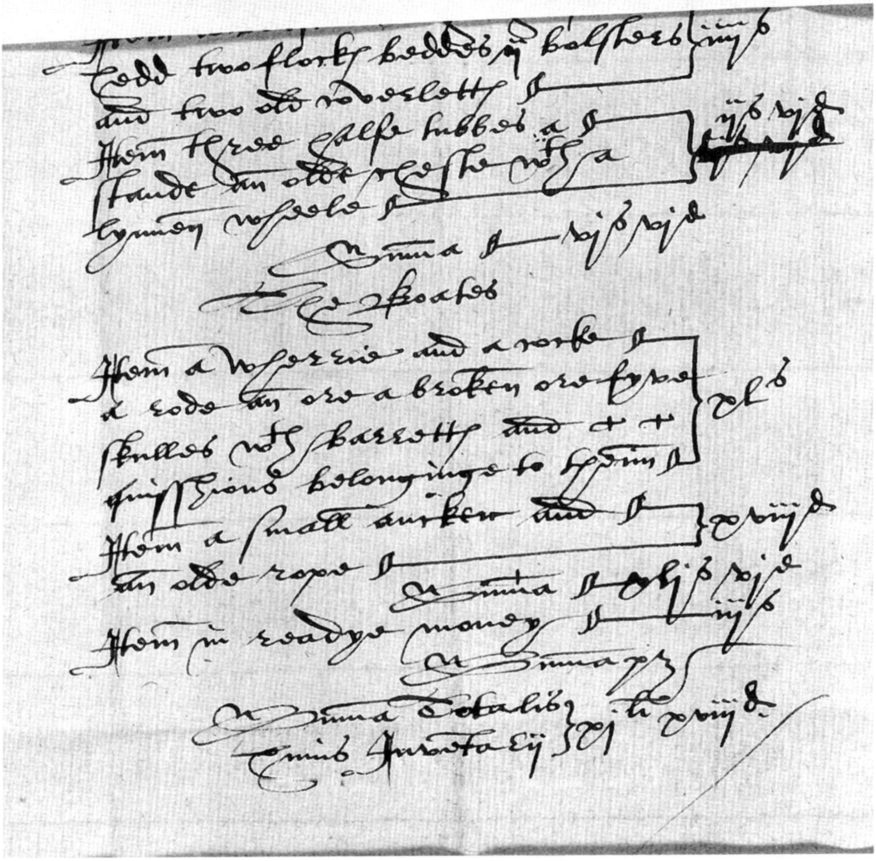

Extract from original inventory 1585 Geffrey Warde's wherry and a "small anker"

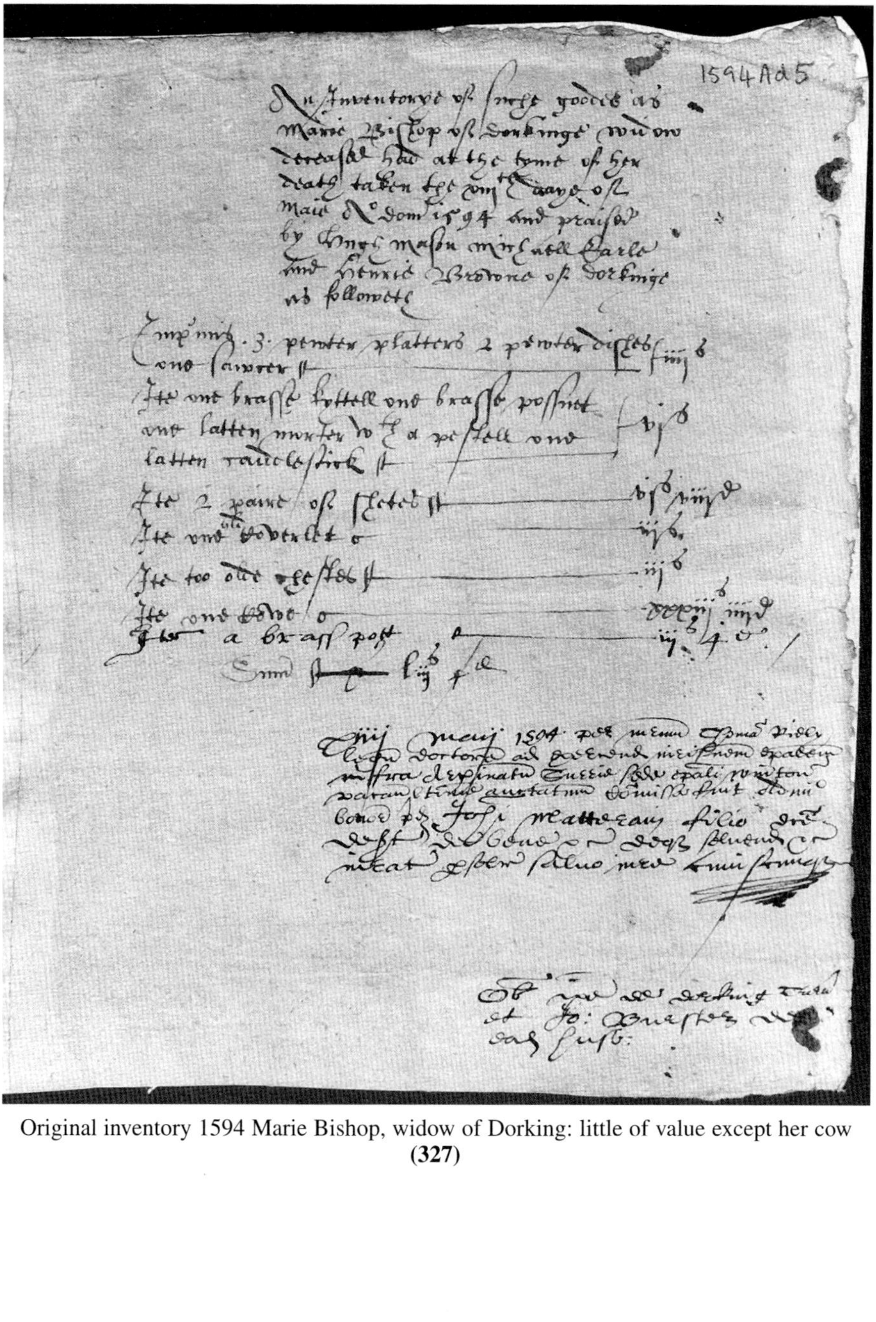
An Inventorye of suche goodes as Marie Bishop of Dorkinge widow deceased had at the tyme of her death taken the xiijth daye of Maie Ao domi 1594 and praised by Hugh Mason Michaell Earle and Henrie Browne of Dorkinge as followeth

Imprimis 3 pewter platters 2 pewter dishes one sawcer — iiijs
Item one brasse kettell one brasse posnet one latten morter wth a pestell one latten candlestick — vjs
Item 2 paire of sheetes — vjs viijd
Item one coverlet — iijs
Item too old chestes — iijs
Item one cowe — xxxs iiijd
Item a brass pott — iijs 4d
Summa liijs

[illegible]

Original inventory 1594 Marie Bishop, widow of Dorking: little of value except her cow

Nore farm, Shalford is mentioned in Robert Elliot's will of 1595

Robert Elliot and five other Shalford testators ask to be buried in Shalford church yard
(**335, 135, 183, 302, 351, 414**)

6 Coffers		12	0
A Presse		2	8
All the Brasse	2	0	0
All the Pewter	2	0	0
5 Candlstickes, an Ewer, a chaffinge dish, a Bason, a morter		10	0
Three Coopordes	1	10	0
8 Silver Spones	1	10	0
All the Woodden vessels	2	0	0
3 Tabls, Chaiers, formes and Stooles and trestles	1	0	0
All the Iron Ware that belongeth, house and all thinges els that belongethe therunto	1	0	0
Three Fliches of Beeffe and one Flich of Baken		14	0
Painted clothes		3	4
All his Furnyture	2	0	0
2 peeces of Woollen Clothe		10	0
2 dossen of pewter			10
Of redie money in his purse	1	0	0
All the haye and hard corne	6	0	0
4 Quarters of Wotten and Barlye mault	1	12	0
All maner graynes upon the ground namely rie, pece and woottes	10	0	0
6 oxen, yokes, weane, wheles, Chanes, harowes Dungcarts and all thinges beloninge therunto	20	0	0
Ten Kyne and nyne Calves and a Bull	20	0	0
Ten Bullockes	10	0	0
19 Hogges and Pickes	4	0	0
2 Mares and a Coulte	4	0	0
All the Sheepe	5	0	0
All the Powltrie		6	8
Bootes, Spurs, Boothose and Sadels		6	8
Wootmeale, Lard and Candles		6	8
A lease of Meade Lande	6	6	8
3 Steeres, 2 kyne with Houshould stufe that was in the keepinge of the executor	9	0	0
	[*124*	*19*	*6*]

Note: The Will, dated 17th March and proved on 13th May 1589, provided for the testator's wife Joan to stay in the best chamber of the house during her widowhood. It was carefully specified that she was to have a life interest in most of the best household stuff, which at her decease was to go to their son Thomas, the executor and residuary legatee. William Peto of Pickards and Robert Rapley, brother of the testator, were left 5s in consideration of their pains as overseers. Household goods, farm implements and stock, were to be distributed immediately by them to the two younger sons John and Robert. John was given the 6 oxen and most of the gear, as well as all the hard corn in the Rudgate Barn, a croft of oats of 3 acres in Netherland and 2 loads of hay. Robert was given a legacy of £30 to be paid in three instalments by the executor at two-yearly intervals. Were Thomas to default on the payment, or to refuse to prove the Will within a quarter of a year following the testator's decease, the overseers were empowered to distrain on the estate to fulfil Robert's legacy and the executorship would fall to John and Robert. There were small gifts of farm stock and money to John Randall the younger, Thomas Christmas and their families; to John Eides, to John Rapley's children and to the testator's godchildren. Chiddingfold church was given 2s and the poor of the parish half that amount. As well as his own chamber, a parlour was mentioned in the Will, which was witnessed by William Peto of Pickards, William Neman and John Rapley the younger. In the parish register there are no entries of burials from 1589 to 1593, but on the opposite page Thomas Stephen Cooper has written "John Rapley of West End, yeoman, was buried in the churchyard between 17th March 1588/9 the date of his Will and 13th May 1589 when Probate was granted T.S.C."

Ref: 1589 B 45a/1 Will 1589 B 45a/2 Inventory

Margaret Smallpece **275**

of Guildford, widow; taken by Morrice Abbott, Henry Nepp and Francis Hunt, 9th May 1589.

	£	s	d
In the Hall			
One Joyned Cubborde with a little frame theron and one Cubbord Cloth, three Chayers, five Joyned stoles, one Joyned forme, one carpett lyinge in the windowe, one paynted cloth to the chimney, three Cusshins and one other carpet for a table	1	8	0
In the Chamber over the Hall			
One Joyned Bedstedle, two fether beddes, two fether bolsters, two payre of blanckettes, 7 fether pillowes, two coverlettes with Curteynes of saye to the bedd and one Trundlebedstedle	5	0	0
All her apparell	4	0	0
Money in her purse		5	0
One Court Cubbord, fower chestes and one Joyned chayre	1	6	0
A bason and Ewer and two chargers of pewter, a dozen of pewter platters, a dozen of pewter dishes, a dozen of pewter Sawcers, half a dozen of pottingers, two little basons, three latten chafinge dishes with other smale peces of pewter	2	0	0
In the chamber over the Kitchen			
One Joyned Bedstedle, one flockbedd, a fether bolster, two coverlettes with curteynes of buckeram to the bedd and one great Joyned chest	1	10	0
One Joyned Chest, nyne payre of sheetes, one payre of fustian blanckettes, three payre of pillowbers, two table clothes, half a dozen of diaper table napkins, fowre diaper towelles, a dozen of lokeram table napkins, two lynnen curteynes for a bed, a cubbord cloth, two canvas Towelles	6	0	0
In the kytchen			
One plancke table, a payre of tresselles, two pewter quart pottes, three pewter pynte pottes, three pewter saltes, 7 pewter flower pottes, half a dozen of Candlestyickes and a little pewter pott and a pewter bottle		13	4
Three brasse pottes, two brasse chafers, three brasse skillettes, one Cawldron, five brasse pannes, a latten bason, five kettles, three fryinge pannes, a skimmer and a brasen ladell	3	10	0
Three spyttes and one drippinge pan, two payre of pothokes, one payre of pothangers, two payre of Andirons, a payre of tongges, a fyer pan, two gredirons, a stone morter, one axe with bowlles, dishes and erthen vesselles	1	0	0
In the boltinge house			
A moldinge borde, two tresselles, a boltinge hutch, one washing boll, a buckinge tubb, a powdring tubb with olde tubbes and other lumbary		4	0
In the gate			
One welbuckett, a rope and a chayne		2	6
The woode and cole		1	0
	27	10	10
Desperatt Dett owynge to the testator at the tyme of her death as foloweth			
Due by John Monck gent for Rent due to the testator at her death	4	0	0

Note: The Will, which was dated 11th January 1587/8, left a number of bequests to the poor, to her godchildren, to friends and to Dorothy, William, James and Thomas, the children of her late husband Thomas Smallpece, beside whom the widow asked to be buried in Holy Trinity church, Guildford. The residuary legatee and executrix was Dorothy Smallpece. The testatrix confirmed that her son-in-law Thomas Smallpece was to inherit the remaining years of the lease of the lands in Rusper, Sussex, called Chose alias Collys, Rowmede, Kettyllrede, the garden land and appurtenances. Most bequests were ordered to be paid out of the rent due from John Monck of

Rusper, gent., who occupied those lands. Sums of 4s were left to the overseers, her good friend George Austen and the aforesaid Thomas Smallpece. Witnesses were George Austen, Wyllyam Smallpece, Rychard Heath and George Hamond, who wrote their names and Thomas Jackman and Thomas Tuesley, who made their marks. The executrix Dorothy Smallpece, spinster, bound herself well and truly to administer the estate on 13th May 1589.

Ref: 1589 B 48/1 Will 1589 B 48/2 Inventory

Richard Smythe **276**

of Ham in Kingston-upon-Thames, weaver; taken by Henry Marlowe, William Fowler, Thomas Smythe, Richard Gyll, Richard Crosse and Rauffe Hoocke, 9th April 1589.

	£	s	d
Apparrell			
His apparrell	1	6	8
In the Chymney chamber			
A bedde with Furniture to the same	1	10	0
In the next Room			
The too Bedstedes with other implemendes and furniture	1	0	0
In the next chamber			
A bedde with the furniture and too olde chestes	2	0	0
In the Lower chamber			
An olde cubbarde, a bowlting whiche, a knedinge trough and an olde Tubbe		5	0
In the Folks chamber			
Two beddestedes with the furniture and an old cheste		10	0
In the seller			
In olde Lumber		5	0
	6	16	8
In the hall howse			
A ioyned table, fowrme and wainscott and other thinges	1	10	0
In Lynnen	1	10	0
In brasse, pewter, broches, cobbeirons and other Lyke implemendes	2	0	0
	5	0	0
In the Shoppe			
6 Lowmes furnished	2	0	0
In Corne in the feld	2	0	0
For tares and peas in the felde	1	0	0
For barlye in the barne	1	0	0
For hogges and powltrye	1	0	0
	7	0	0
	18	16	8

Note: The nuncupative Will was dated 8th April and proved on 14th May 1589. The testator gave his freehold land to his son Stephen, after the decease of his wife Christian. This land was to be considered full recompense for a legacy bequeathed to him by his uncle, Anthonie Tomkins. The testator's servant John Smythe was left 20s. Christian and another son Henry were made joint executors. The witnesses were William Fowler, Rauffe Hooke, Thomas Smythe, Richarde Gyll and Richard Crosse. The widow bound herself well and truly to administer the estate.

Ref: 1589 B 49/1 Will 1589 B 49/2 Inventory

Thomas Stroydwick **277**

of Alfold, husbandman; taken by John Shurlocke, John Ireland, William Barnard and John Puttocke, 25th April 1589.

	£	s	d
All his apparell	1	10	0
One Heickfer and a calf	1	10	0
2 shepe and one lambe		8	0
2 Chestes		4	0
His purse and the money therin		2	6
Owing to the testator at the tyme of his death by Edward Tanworth of Cranley	20	0	0
	23	14	6

Note: The Will, dated 9th April 1589, divided the livestock and money between four family groups: Stroydwick, Lenard, Erland and Tanworth. The bequests went to John Stroydwicke and his son, the brother and nephew of the testator; to Thomas, Anne and Richard, the children of the testator's unnamed sister and her husband John Lenard; to Elizabeth the daughter of John Erland; to Ann the daughter of Richard Erland; and to Edward, Jane and Ann, the three children of Edward Tanworth. There were some minor bequests of a few shillings to Alice Frances and Thomas Tikner's widow; and of a few pence to Jane Moyer, the daughter of Richard; to John Overington, servant to John Lenard; and to Annes Francis. John Puttock's three children, Nathaniel, Ann and Elizabeth, were given a ram then in the keeping of Richard Erland. The testator asked to be buried in Alfold churchyard. A sum of 50s was to be distributed among the poor of the parish by his executor John Lenard of Alfold, husbandman, in the presence of the two overseers John Erland and John Puttocke, tailor. Of the two witnesses to the Will, John Puttocke signed the document and marks were made by John Erland and the testator himself. On 13th May 1589 when probate was granted to the executor, he bound himself and so did John Weston of Guildford, butcher, well and truly to administer the estate.

Ref: 1589 B 55/1 Will 1589 B 55/2 Inventory

William Thatcher, senior **278**

of Chertsey; taken by Morris Denbighe, Thomas Day, John Rogers, John Holt, John Martyne and Bryan Latymer, 12th May 1589.

	£	s	d
All his wearinge apparell	1	13	4
In his purse		3	0
A sword and A dagger		3	4
In the Chamber over the Hall			
On Joined bedsted with a fetherbed, a mattrise and two bolsters, on pillowe, two blancketes and on coverledd	2	6	8
On Truckle bedsted with a fetherbed and a boulster, on pillowe, two blanckets and a coverled	1	0	0
Fower chestes and a table with a paire of Tressells and a strawe chaire		13	4
A paire of Andirons, a paire of Tonges, a paire of pothangers and two billes		4	0
Eight paire of Sheetes	2	0	0
Five table Clothes, a dosen of napkins and two towells	1	0	0
Two pillowe beers		2	0
In the Chamber over the Kitchen			
On borded bedsted with a flocke bed, An old coverled and a blancket		8	0
Two olde greate chestes and a wollen whele		10	0
In the Lofte over the Chamber			
A round table with a standerde, old tobbes, a Lynen whele and other old Lomber in the same chamber		2	6
Corne reddie threshte in the same Lofte		18	0

In the Haull			
On Joined table with a frame, on forme, two litle stoles and a litle chaire and a great chaire And A coubbarde		18	0
The painted clothes and fower cusshins		5	0
In the parlour			
A Joined bedsted with a fetherbed, two boulsters and a Pillowe, on Coverled and a blancket	2	0	0
On table with a frame, three stoles, two chaires And a Coubberde and a settle Coubarde And a chest		14	0
In the Kitchen			
On old Table with settles about the Kitchen		5	0
In the boultinge house			
On boultinge which, A kneddinge troughe and a chespresse		5	0
The brasse whatsoever	2	6	8
All Pewter whatsoever	1	3	4
In the buttrie			
A salt Troughe with Tobbes and other Lumber in the same Buttrie		8	0
The Cattell			
Fower oxen	7	0	0
Three kyne	5	0	0
Fower bullockes	3	0	0
Three Horses	2	10	0
Three score and three sheepe and tenn lambes	10	0	0
The Corne on the grounde			
Fower Acres of Rie	2	13	4
Sixe Acres of Otes and pease	2	0	0
In the Gate			
Five Hogges		18	0
3 pigges		2	0
A longe Carte and a donge Carte and two paire of shoade wheeles and A ploughe with two yokes and two chaines	2	0	0
A saddle and two briddles, a Carte sadle, thre harnnesse with other necessarie thinges therunto belonginge		6	8
For Gese, duckes and hennes		5	0
	55	4	2

Note: The six appraisers all wrote their own names except John Martyne, who used an unusual symbol ***..... Bryan Latymer's name was spelt in the same way at the beginning and end of the Inventory. Minor variations of spelling were to be seen with a final e at the end of Daye and Holte, no final s on Roger and Morres Denbe written in phonetic style. Administration was granted on 13th May 1589 to Margaret, the widow of William.

Ref: 1589 Ad 57/1

1590

John Boylett **279**

of Ash; taken by Henry Stevens, George Boylett, John Dayre, Thomas Gyles, John Jewer and William Carpenter 22nd May 1590.

	£	s	d
His apparell	1	0	0
Monye in his purse		6	8
In the Hall			
A table, a frame, two Cheyers, a Rounde table and a Stole		5	6
A Cupborde, a Joyned settle uppon a Benche and a paynted Cloth		10	0

In the Kytchyn			
Two brasse pottes, one posnet, two Cawdrons, two brasse pannes and an olde posnett	1	12	0
Seaven kettles, a skellett and a skemer		12	0
Two paire of Andirons, three broches, two paire of Pothookes, 2 paire of pothangers, a ffyer panne, a paire of fyer tonges, one Gerdiron, one fryinge panne and a tosting Iron		12	0
18 pewter platters, 9 pewter disshes, 5 sawsers, one salt seller, one dozen of spones and an old bason	1	10	0
7 latten Candlestickes and a latten bason		6	0
In the bedd Chamber			
One Joyned bedstedle and 3 playne bedstedles		5	0
Two ffether beddes of teeke, 2 flockbeddes, 3 teeke bolsters 4 fether pyllowes of teeke and 4 Canvas Pyllowes	2	6	8
5 Coverlittes		15	0
Two paire of blanckettes		5	6
Three paire of Locrome shetes, 7 paire of Canvas sheetes and 3 shorte table clothes	2	13	4
2 paire of Pillowberes		4	0
Two Chestes and 7 Coffers	1	0	0
In the upper Chamber			
A foldinge table, the paynted Clothes, a presse and a Chamber stole		10	0
In the butterye and Kytchin chamber			
4 Stabyns, a bulting hutche, a knedinge trough and a powdring trough		6	8
3 Vates, one Kyve, a barrell and a Virkyn		6	8
8 bowles, 2 kyvers, a butter chorne, a busshell, a half busshell and a bucking tubbe		8	0
4 sackes, 2 Tanckardes, 3 Crewses, 12 Woden Disshes and an old ffurnys		7	8
A spytter, a pyckaxe, a mattock, 3 old axes, 2 bylles, 4 wedges and other olde Iron		6	8
3 spynninge wheles, a paire of cardes, 3 buckettes, a chese presse with implementes thereto	[*no value given*]		
A table, 2 formes, a longe sawe and other toeles with dyvers other Lumbrye		8	0
One Carte, a donge pott and 2 paire of wheles	1	3	4
A plowe, an oxe Harrowe, 2 small Harrowes, a yooke, a chayne and a paire of Stropes		11	4
A saddle, a brydle, a pannell, a carte saddle with other Harnys and Ropes		7	0
9 stall of Bees	1	6	8
Fyve kyne	7	10	0
Two steres	3	6	8
7 Bullokes	4	10	0
7 Horsebeastes	6	10	0
Three Ewes and 2 Lambes		12	0
4 Wanyer Calfes	1	6	8
4 shootes		12	0
A Lease of certen landes called Monye Mores	2	13	4
Fyve acres of Wheate	3	15	0
Beanes and otes sixe acres	2	0	0
2 acres of Barlie		10	0
A Cock, Hennes and geese		6	0

Bacon in ye Roof			10	0
Wheate in ye Howse			3	4
	[£54.10.8]	54	15	0

Note: The Will was dated 20th February and proved on 1st June 1590. The executrix and residuary legatee was the testator's wife Bridget. Her brother William Carpenter and his brother-in-law Thomas Gyles were appointed overseers and given 5s each. The testator asked to be buried in the churchyard and gave 5s to the poor. He bequeathed a life interest in his dwelling house, orchard, garden, barn, stable and a close of land in Wick called Harris Croft, to his wife and after her, either to any child of his born after his decease, or to his elder brother George Boylet. His sister Alice Bignell of Worplesdon was given a cow, a 3-year-old heifer and a year-old calf. Agnes, Margaret and Judith, his wife's three daughters were each left a swarm of bees. His brother George was given the grey mare and George's two daughters were to have a lamb apiece. He ordered his writings and evidences to be taken from the house and delivered to two indifferent men. He signed the Will firmly and it was witnessed by William Smith, John Jewer, John Dayre, Hugh Goring and John Gronhill. The administration bond was provided by the testator's wife Bridget and her brother William Carpenter of Godalming, yeoman.

Ref: 1590 B 7/1 Will 1590 B 7/2 Inventory

Mawdlen Bromefeld **280**

of St Nicholas, Guildford. [*no appraisers given and undated*]

	£	s	d
In readie monie	40	0	0
Her Apparrell		[*blank*]	
	[*40*	*0*	*0*]

Note: The Will was dated 30th March and proved on 1st June 1590. The testatrix asked to be buried in the chancel of St Nicholas, Guildford, gave 5s to the poor and 6s 8d to the parson Thomas Key, whom she appointed overseer. The residuary legatee and executor was her son Richard. Her other sons, Harry of Hascombe, Simon of Shalford and Anthony of Bramley, were left £10, £10 and £20, respectively. Her brother-in-law Thomas Bromefeld was left £1, which would pass to his children should he predecease her. There were three other small monetary bequests: 4s to John Rofe of Tyting; 4s apiece to all her godchildren; and 2s 6d to one Grene, late servant of John Tomson of Guildford. Richard Ford and John Byrchitt were witnesses. The parish register of 14th May records the burial of Maud Bromfeild.

Ref: 1590 B 8/1 Will 1590 B8/2 Inventory

Robert Chaundler **281**

of Haslemere, husbandman; taken by John Humfrey, Robert Farnnden and William Meredith, clerk, 25th April 1589.

	£	s	d
All such debtes as were owinge to Robert Chaundler			
John Bridge	26	0	0
Walter Courte	11	0	0
John Marner	10	0	0
John Humfrey	4	8	0
Mr Lewis Thomas	1	6	0
Richard Boxold and Robert Farnnden	4	5	0
Richard Wakeford		1	8
	57	0	8

Note: The Will was dated 25th April and proved on 1st June 1590. The residuary legatee and executor was Richard Boxold, who was to pay the £10 legacies on 1st May 1591 to each of the testator's three sisters: Jane, the wife of John Gass; Anne, the wife of John Yalden; and Margaret, the wife of Thomas Wolridge. On that date three sums of £6 were to be paid by him to the overseers John Humfrey and William Meredith, clerk, to be invested for the Gase, Yalden and

Wolridge children until they married or reached the age of 21. The testator asked for a christian burial. He gave 6s to the poor of Haslemere and 5s for the repair of the church. An uncle, Harry Baker, his wife and four children: John, Richard, Harry and Alice, were beneficiaries. So also were Richard Aylling, Joan Smyth, his godson John Stede and the three children of Robert Farnnden: Richard, Peter and Toby. Three witnesses at the sealing of the Will made their marks: Thomas Hayward, Robert Billingshurst and Robert Chaundler. The two overseers signed their names. Richard Boxold of Haslemere, yeoman, the executor, bound himself well and truly to administer the estate. The burial was registered on 30th April 1590.

Ref: 1590 B 12/1 Will 1590 B 12/2 Inventory

Thomas Constable **282**

of Alfold, husbandman; taken by Olyver Mower, Thomas Tidy, John Leonard and John Balchyn, 22nd April 1590.

	£	s	d
Ready mony in his purse at the houre of his death		1	7
All his apparrell		10	0
In the hall			
All the brasse		11	0
All the pewter and spones		6	0
Three old latyn candlestickes			10
All the wodden vessell		3	6
Certen old axes, shovels, spitters, one little broache, one old saw and certen old Iron		3	10
One old wollen wheele and the Cardes		1	0
One old table, forme and stooles			6
All the Bacon and beef in the Roof	1	2	0
In the chamber			
Certen old chestes		1	0
The bedding and bedstedes	1	0	0
3 bushels of oaten malt and 3 peckes of wheate		5	0
Certen wollen yarne		5	0
The wheate and the oates on the ground	3	5	0
Hay and oates in the barne	1	0	0
6 Oxen	15	0	0
Three horses	2	0	0
6 hogges greate and small	1	0	0
The wayne, doong pott, wheeles, harrowes, yoks and chaines		16	0
One Cow, one heyfer and 2 twelvemonthinges	5	0	0
The Doong		6	8
Three little Lambes		4	0
The occupieng of the land untill Michaelmas next	1	0	0
	34	2	11
Debtes owing by the Testator			
To Thomas Tidy		3	0
To Thomas Jakman, his landlord		11	0
To Richard King		13	4
To Richard Jakman		9	0
To John Deane		8	0
To Henry Shoo		8	0
To the Parson of Dunsfold		3	0
To John Puttok, tailer		2	7
To William Laker		14	0

To William Symons			10
To John Ireland of Pigbush		4	10
To Maurice Buck		4	8
	4	2	3

Note: The Will was dated 17th March 1581 and proved on 1st June 1590. The executrixes and residuary legatees were named as Katherine, the wife of the testator and Christian, his daughter. Only Christian's name appeared in the record of probate. Sums of 3s 4d each were given to Thomas Tidy and William Crony, the overseers. John Shurlock and Richard Beldam witnessed the Will, which was written by the parson of Alfold, William Fawden. The testator asked to be buried in Alfold churchyard and that his debts should be truly paid. His godson Thomas Mower was left 12d and his own daughter Ellyn was to have a 2-year-old heifer, a ewe with a lamb, a ram teg and the worst save one hog of bacon in the roof. William Laker bound himself, as a husbandman of Alfold, well and truly to administer the estate.

Ref: 1590 B 14/1 Will 1590 B 14/2 Inventory

Walter Grene **283**

of Chobham, labourer; taken by John Hawoode, Rychard Mylton, Thomas Hooke and John Hedge, 5th September 1590.

	£	s	d
Of Munnye in his purse			10
For all his apparrell		5	0
In the hale			
A table, a forme, a cheyar, a paynted cloth, a brushe and a benche		3	4
For all the brase and pewtter		10	0
2 shelves and a coope, a gridioren, a payre of pothookes and a pothanger		2	0
For dishes, buckates and bowles		1	0
In the butry			
For all the erthen potes and panches, tubes and a whell		2	0
For a sellynge cloth, 4 shelves and a knedynge trough and a lytle table		1	0
For all the lynnan		5	0
In the chamber over the butrye			
2 bedes and all that longes to them		10	0
2 chestes and a tester of a bede		12	0
In the yeard			
3 piges		2	0
Henes		1	0
3 Kyne	3	10	0
For the haye in the barne	2	0	0
[*£8.5.2*]	7	14	0

Note: The Will was dated 30th August and proved on 17th October 1590; in this document Walter was classed as a yeoman. His executrix and residuary legatee was his wife Katherine. His good neighbour Thomas Hooke, his overseer, was given a bushel of apples for his pains. There were small bequests of goods: to Susan Taller went a mattress, bed and bedding; to Elizabeth Foster a brass pot; and to Susan Britten a pair of sheets. The witnesses were Thomas Hooke, Christopher Field and John Heywood, vicar of Chobham, who put up a bond for the administration of the goods and chattels.

Ref: 1590 B 19/1 Will 1590 B 19/2 Inventory

George Hannaway **284**

of East Clandon, husbandman; taken by Arnold Woddes, James Tydie, Thomas Atlee, Thomas Rogers and George Rogers, 17th May 1590.

	£	s	d
In his purse		2	0
All his apparell		6	8
One Cow	1	6	8
Fyve Staulls of bees		10	0
Two bedds with their furniture	1	0	0
Two Chestes		2	0
All the brasse		10	0
An old Cupbourd		2	0
All the peuter		3	4
One Latten Candlesticke			6
Old spads, bill, axe and showvell		1	4
One Acre of wheat		10	0
Two Acres of barley		13	4
A Fryinge panne, pothookes and spitte			8
A Sowe hogge and 3 pigges		10	0
A yonge mare		10	0
An old table and a forme		1	0
A dragginge forke			5
[*£6.9.11*]	6	9	7

Note: The Will was dated 7th June 1588 and proved on 1st June 1590. The residuary legatee and executrix was the testator's wife Anne, who was to inherit the house and land called Kyrrettes for a term of 60 years. When his wife died, the property was to pass to Jane, his daughter, she paying £1 at the end of the first year to another daughter Anne Shoare and £1 at the end of the second year to the third daughter Margaret Boulton. Jane was given eight items, including her bed and bedding, the dragging rake, some bees and a colt. John Shoare was left the best coat. The testator asked to be buried in East Clandon churchyard and he left 1d each to five poor neighbours: William Inwoode, John Atlee, John Fuharry, Agnes Inwood and George Rogers. Peter Churcher wrote the Will; George Rogers also signed, but George Hanway himself, Thomas Atlee and James Tydye senior, only made their marks. The overseers were Thomas Atlee and George Rogers. The latter of East Clandon, husbandman, together with the widow, put up the administration bond. The burial of George Hannaway was recorded on 16th July 1589.

Ref: 1590 B 23/1 Will 1590 B 23/2 Inventory

William Potter **285**

of Horsell, yeoman; taken by John Wapshot, Rychard Bonsey and John Walden the elder, 9th January 1584.

	£	s	d
His wearing apparell	1	0	0
In his Purse		11	8
In the Hall			
Painted clothes		1	0
Two Tables and a fforme		5	0
One Chayre			8
A ffyre shovell, a payre of Tonges, a gridierne and pothangers		2	0
Edged tooles		2	6
3 Pronges			8
In the Parlor			
One ffetherbed, 2 Boulsters, one Blanket and a Coveringe		13	4
The Bedstead		1	0

One ould Cheste and an ould Chayre			8
A Hearen Ambyre		1	4
The Bedseelynge and the hanginges		1	4
In the Chamber			
2 fflockebeds, 2 Bowlsters, one Blanket, 2 Coveringes		13	4
2 Bedsteades		1	8
Painted Clothes		3	4
6 Chestes		6	0
6 payre of Sheetes		13	4
One Table Cloth, 6 Table napkins and one Towell		2	6
A Round Table		1	0
One Lynnen Whelle and Two wollen wheles		1	0
25 [*pounds*] of Wolle		15	0
Three Bottles		1	0
In the Kytchen			
Tubbes, Bowles, Bucketes, Dishes and other Treane vessell		6	0
16 peeces of pewter		6	0
A dozen and a halfe of Pewter spones		1	0
2 Saltsellers			9
Two Brasse pottes, 4 kettles, one Cawedron, Two ffryeng pans and two skilletes	1	0	0
2 spittes and a payre of Cobbierns		3	4
3 Bell Candlestickes and a Latten morter		2	0
6 flytches of Bacon		13	4
2 Basketes			8
A Betle and 5 wedges		1	4
In the yarde			
One Cart with a payre of shodde Wheles, one Ploughe, one Harrowe, a dunge Carte and the horse harnes	2	0	0
7 Hoges and 4 Pigges	1	0	0
4 Oxen	5	6	8
5 Kyne	5	0	0
6 Bullockes	3	0	0
4 Horses	2	13	4
40 sheepe	4	3	4
4 Acres of Rye on the ground	2	13	4
The Corne in the Barne	2	0	0
4 loades of Haie	2	0	0
A Cock and 4 Henns		2	0
6 Sackes, a Bushell and 2 fflailes		8	0
Ould Iron		2	0
A Brydle		1	0
Wood in the yard		6	0
	39	9	5

Note: The Will was dated 10th December 1583 and the Inventory was taken a month later. Arrangements were made for legacies to be paid to four sons in turn at two-yearly intervals, starting in 1587 with that to William, then 1589 to Richard, in 1591 to Thomas and in 1593 to Henry. Probate was granted on 1st June 1590 to another son John, who was to have the residue of the estate and to act as executor. The only daughter mentioned was Joane; her legacy of £7 was to be paid at her marriage or when she reached the age of 27. The four boys were left £6 13s 4d each. William had the added favour of the right to a chamber in the house, coming and going at his pleasure until his marriage. Joane, the testator's wife, was left £5 if she survived him, but only £2 was to be at her disposal if she did not. Household stuff, including a round table which she had brought with her at her marriage, was given back to her. The testator's sister Thomasin

Bowyer was left 10s to be paid at the day of his burial. He gave 4d to the poor men's box and 3s to the repair of Horsell church, in which church or churchyard he asked to be buried. The overseers were Walter Wapshotte of Horsell and Richard Buttes of Weybridge. Four named witnesses were Richard Styleman, Christopher Bowyer, Henry Attewick and Robert Bust. The executor, registered as of Horsell, yeoman, put up the administration bond.

Ref: 1590 B 49/1 Will 1590 B 49/2 Inventory

John Pratt **286**

of Wrecclesham in Farnham; taken by John Grover, Rychard Brodbridge, John Holloway and John Shrubb the younger, 15th April 1590.

				£	s	d
In the Hall						
A table, a fforme and stooles					3	0
A Cubborde					3	0
Certen Pewter					5	0
Two Candlestickes and a salte					1	0
An Andyron, a pothanger, a payre of tonges and a payre of Bellowes					1	8
A table Cloth					3	0
		16	8			
In the Kytchin						
A brasse pott, 2 kettelles, 2 skellettes and a skymmer					6	8
A payre of potthookes, a spitt and an old drippinge pann					1	0
A Chese presse						6
A powdring trough					2	0
Two tobbes and other Lombrye there					2	6
On axe, a bill, a shovell, a mattok, a sythe and other small tooles					6	8
		19	4			
In the Chamber						
A flock bedd, a payre of sheetes, a Coverlett, two old bolsters and a bed tester					13	4
An old bedstedle of bordes					1	0
2 Coffers					2	8
Another bedstedle					2	6
An old flock bedd, a paire of sheetes and a simple Coverlett					5	0
Certen lumbrye in an other Chamber					3	6
His waringe apparell and money in his purse					15	0
	£2	3	0			
in the butterye						
Litle small thinges					2	6
A flytch of Bacon					2	6
A spinninge Whele and payre of Cardes					1	0
Soyle in the gate					1	8
A sowe and a litle shoot					10	0
A Cowe				1	7	0
3 small bullockes				1	10	0
3 acres of wheat and one acre of Rye				1	10	0
A payre of stropes and 2 Chaines					3	0
Certen yeres of a lease yett to Come				13	13	4
				23	0	0

On 1st June 1590 the widow Catherine and John Holloway of Farnham, husbandman, bound themselves well and truly to administer the estate, she having first been sworn to the truth of the Inventory. Ref: 21 M 65/D 3/158

Note: John Pratt had been buried on 7th April 1590.

John Tooth **287**

of Mickleham, husbandman; taken by Raff Arnold, Thomas Arnold and Rychard Woodstoke, 1st June 1590.

	£	s	d
Money in his pursse		5	0
Hys weringe aparell	1	0	0
In the hawle			
A table, formes, cheers, stooles and a cobbord		13	4
Fowre pewter platters, two pewter dysses, two sawcers, two saltsellers, a pewter pott, two stonen pottes		6	0
Three great kyttels, two Lytle kytells, a posnet, two Candelstykes	1	0	0
A spytte, a gobyrne and a trefthe		5	0
20 payr of sheetes, three table clothes, two napkyns, a bed hanger	5	5	0
Two fether beds, two flokbedes, fowr blankets and two Coverletts, fowre bowlsters, two pylows	5	0	0
Three playne bedstedels, three chestes	1	0	0
Two fates, fyve ale barels, a tonne wyth other Lumbermentes	2	0	0
8 fleges of bacon	2	5	0
In the howsse			
Thre quarters of wheat	4	0	0
Three bussels of Rye		7	6
16 Quarters of Mawlte	10	13	4
Fowr Akers of wheat now groinge	4	0	0
Two akers and a half of Rye	2	0	0
11 akers of barly	7	6	8
One aker of ottes		10	0
6 akers of pesen and teares	2	0	0
Fowr Carte horses	7	0	0
Three kyne and three bullokes	7	10	0
17 sheepe and 8 Lambes	5	0	0
6 hogges	1	0	0
A longe Cart, two Dunge Cartes, plowes, harowes, two payr of wheels, horse harnes	3	0	0
A byll and an axe, a share and a cowlter wyth other Lumbermentes		5	8
Fowr hennes and a coke		3	4
Horsse meat: hay, pease and tares		13	4
Fowre sakkes, three bagges		5	0
16 cheses		8	0
	[*75*	*2*	*2*]
[*These debts were noted at the end of the Will*:]			
Thomas Arnold owed	2	7	0
Wyllyam Arnold of Great Bowcham owed		7	4
John Arnold of Myckelham		8	9
	[*3*	*3*	*1*]

Note: The Will was dated 17th May and proved on 2nd June 1590. The residuary legatee and executor was the testator's son John. A shilling each was left to the overseers Thomas Arnold and Thomas Kumynge. Two daughters Joan and Mary were left £20, barley, malt and linen, in identical legacies. The third daughter Jane was left £30 to be invested and she was given linen and a young calf. Thomas Arnold and Thomas Drew witnessed the Will, the latter being given some barley. The son John, husbandman and Richard Ellis, Rector of Mickleham, bound themselves well and truly to administer the estate.

Ref: B 64/1 Will 1590 B 64/2 Inventory

James White **288**

of Long Ditton, labourer; taken by Richard Worman, Henry Martar and Robart Grenefeld, 31st May 1590.

		£	s	d
His aparell			6	8
in his Chambar				
A bedsted with a fether bed, a boulster with 2 blanketes and a koveryng			13	0
A flock bede with his fornetur			3	4
2 Chestes			1	4
6 payre of shetes			6	8
2 tabell Clothes and 6 napkens			1	0
In the hall				
A tabell with a frame and a forme			1	4
3 stoles				4
3 ketels and a posnet			1	8
A pot hangar and a trevat				4
A paynted Cloth and 2 Coshens				10
6 peutar deshes, 3 platars, 3 sawsers, 2 Candelstykes and a salt selar			2	6
2 tubes, 3 mylke bouls, 2 buketes			1	0
1 drynkeng pot, 4 deshes and a ladell				2
An axe, a bell and a spade and a byllhoke				6
3 hense and a Coke				8
1 shot and a pyge			1	4
2 heffer bulokes		1	0	0
A mare and a Coult			8	0
Corne on the ground		1	0	0
	[*£4.10.8*]	4	10	6
[*Listed on the Will:*] Debts which I do owe				
First to John Hook		1	13	0
To Waterman			13	6
To Thomas Cook			3	4
		[*2*	*9*	*10*]

Note: The Will was dated 11th May and proved on 2nd June 1590. The executrix and residuary legatee was the testator's wife Ellin. His overseer was Richard Wornam, husbandman, of Long Ditton. The testator asked to be buried in Long Ditton churchyard. His sisters Margery and Annis were left 6s 8d and 13s 4d, respectively. His daughter Alice was to have a cow and £2 on her wedding day or at the age of 21, to be paid by her mother Ellin or by his son Francis. The witnesses were Richard Wornam, Richard White, John Hooke and Thomas Woodward. The executrix and the overseer bound themselves well and truly to administer the estate. The burial was recorded on 8th May, but this may well have been an incorrect entry as the 11th May on the Will is plainly written "XI".

Ref: 1590 B 67/1 Will 1590 B 67/2 Inventory

John Woodclerk **289**

of Hersham in Walton-on-Thames, yeoman; taken by Anthonye Medcalffe, John Heywarde, John Hone and John Cleare, 20th May 1590.

	£	s	d
In the parler			
In money		1	0
His apparell, sword, dagger and gyrdle	1	1	0
Syxe shertes		8	0

	£	s	d
One symple bed, 4 pillowes, one bolster, 2 blanckettes, one kevering, one payre of bedstydles, 1 seeling and 2 paynted clothes		8	8
In the lofte			
One fether bed, one boulster, a shred kyverled, one blankett and a bedstidle		10	0
In another lofte			
2 blanckettes, one keverled, 1 boulster and 1 corded bedstidle		10	0
In the same lofte 1 fetherbed, 3 blancketes, 1 keverled, a bolster, 2 pyllowes and 1 payre of bedstidles		13	4
lynnen			
11 payre of shetes and one tayble cloth	1	2	0
4 pillowbeares, 1 speare cloth, 2 kerchers		4	0
5 chestes		10	0
10 olde Tubbes		5	0
3 cheares, a churn, a cubborde		5	0
A table, a forme and the bench		2	0
10 boules		4	0
6 buckettes		1	4
7 shelffes		2	4
Fyve boardes more and 2 duble quarters		2	4
2 Joyned stooles, 2 trestles, a lynnen whele and a rat trape		2	0
Sertyn hemp and Toawe		2	0
About 4 pound of woolle		1	4
brasse			
7 kettelles that are oulde		7	0
An olde panne, a chaffing dishe and a scommer		3	0
2 spyttes, a payre of Cob Irons, a payre of tongues, a treavytte, a payre of pottehanggeres		3	0
puter			
5 platters		3	4
4 puter disshes		1	4
4 sawsers			8
6 candlestyckes		1	8
2 saltes, 2 litle aquavite botles and a litle puter pot		1	0
One candlesticke, 6 spones and 6 trenchers		1	0
3 busshells of Rye		7	6
3 sackes and a bagge		1	8
3 wedges		1	8
A mattocke, a hatchett, an axe, a drawing knyf and a billhooke		2	8
3 billes and 1 hooke		1	6
2 spades and one shovell		1	6
2 roapes and 3 trestles		1	0
[*£8.13.10*]	8	15	6
In the yarde			
A sowe and 3 pygges		10	0
3 shootes		12	0
One Red cowe	2	3	4
4 kyne more	6	0	0
One heckfer at Burwood	1	6	8
A mare and a colte	2	0	0
A wanyer calfe		6	8
In the feelde			
An acre of Thynne grasse		6	0
An acre of Rye		12	0

A litle cloasse by the howse of Rye	1	5	0
A litle closse sowed wyth parte of peason		6	8
8 cople of shepe at 5 shillinges a cuple	2	0	0
22 other shepe at 3 shillinges and 4 pence a pece whice some doth come to	3	13	4
4 hense		1	4
7 guysse yong and olde		3	0
Certyn Rye standing at Burwode	3	0	0
An acre of otes		10	0
[*£33.9.10*]	33	0	6

Note: The Will was dated 19th May and proved on 2nd June 1590. The testator appointed as executors his wife Elizabeth and James Ellerie of West Molesey, husbandman. The residuary legatees in equal parts were the said Elizabeth and Henry Porter, his daughter's eldest son. Sums of 3s 4d apiece were to be paid to Richard Barton, clerk and John Feelder, a neighbour, the two overseers, before the Will was proved. The testator asked to be buried in Walton churchyard and he gave 3s 4d each to the church and to the poor of the parish. Elizabeth's son Thomas Wheeler had to hand over an unpaid debt of £12 and some farming implements to Henry Porter on Whit Sunday 1590. Robert, Isabel, Judith and Nycolas Porter were given valuable livestock. The best coat was given to Mosse and a sheep to each of his children. The servant Katheryn Smith and two neighbours, John Feelder and John Hone, had small bequests. Three named witnesses were Mr Anthony Standen, gentleman, Richard Barton, the vicar of Walton-on-Thames and James Ellerie of West Molesey. The aforesaid James and George Porter, yeoman, both of West Molesey, entered the necessary administration bond.

Ref: 1590 B 68/1 Will 1590 B 68/2 Inventory

1591

Richard Alden **290**

of Malden, yeoman; 18th April 1591. [*no appraisers given*]

	£	s	d
In his purse		1	0
His apparell		13	4
His bowe and arrowes		1	0
In the Hall			
A table, a bench and forme		5	0
A Cubberd		6	8
A Cubberd Clothe		1	0
Painted Clothes		5	0
2 Chayers, 3 Joyne stules		1	0
1 fire shovell, 1 paire of tonges, 1 paire of bellowes, 3 paire of pothangers, 2 spittes, 1 gridIron, 1 brandIron, 1 paire of Cob Irons		6	8
In the Kitchen			
1 greate Caudron ould; 1 kettell, 2 brasse pottes, 1 Lattine bason, 1 Candlesticke, 1 Drippinge pan, 1 Chaffinge dishe	1	2	0
1 Pan of brasse bequethed to his daughter Agnes		16	0
3 smale kettells, 1 brasse potte, 1 brasse Chaffer, 1 litle skilette, 1 ould pan, 2 ould Candlestickes		10	0
4 kilderkinges, 3 firkinges with other ould tubbs, 1 kneadinge troffe, 1 pouderinge troffe, 1 boultinge wich, 1 forme, 1 cherne with sixe bowels.	1	0	0
3 flyches of bacon		6	8
One quarter of Wheate	1	0	0
6 bushels of mault		15	0

	The Lower Chamber			
	1 besteede and a Fether bed furnished, painted Clothes and one round table and one Joyne stoole and three pillowes	2	0	0
	In the butterie			
	One Chese presse, one planke with one old Cubberd and an amerye and other shelfes		5	0
	The Milkhouse			
	Shelfes, Croutches		1	0
	The bed Chamber			
Doritie	One standinge bedsteede, 1 Fetherbed, 1 Coverlyd, 1 blanked, 1 Roughe, 1 boulster, 1 Chest, 2 Pewter Dishes, 3 payer of sheetes, 1 pare of pillowe beares which were bequeathed to his daughter Doritie	3	0	0
Agnes	2 Pewter dyshes, 3 payer of sheetes, 1 payer of pillowe beares, 1 Chest	1	0	0
[*ditto*]	8 payer of sheetes, 2 pilloweberes, 2 tableClothes, 6 table napkinges	1	13	4
Goodwife	3 Chestes, 1 stoole, 1 ronde table		5	0
	6 peeces of Pewter, 1 dozen of spoones, 2 porrengers		8	0
	5 payer of sheetes, 3 table Clothes, 3 napkinges		15	4
	1 troucle bed, 1 Coverlyd, 1 blanket, 1 flockbed, 2 boulster, 1 Pillowe		6	8
	1 Chest		3	0
	2 hampers			6
	1 browne bill			6
	1 forme			3
	The Chamber over the hall			
	Bedsteede, 1 flockebed, 1 Coverlyd, 1 blanked, 1 seelinge 1 painted cloth		6	8
	4 sackes, 1 bushell, 1peck, 2 fannes, 1 showell, with other trumperies		7	0
	Bourdes and other trumperyes		1	4
	21 peeces of pewter		10	0
	The mens Chamber			
	2 flockbed, 2 ould bedsteedes with other lumbermentes		6	8
	The garden			
	3 staules of bees		6	0
	Planckes and other boordes		1	0
	The Carthouse			
	1 Longe Cart with shoud wheeles, 2 Dung Cartes, 2 plowes, 3 harrowes	4	0	0
	1 seedecote, 2 shovells, 2 pronges, 2 Axes, 2 billes, 1 pare of Cartropes, 2 Iron wedges, 1 bilhooke, 4 augers 1 Ades, 1 mattogge, 1 pare of sheerges		8	0
	The stable			
	6 payer of harnes, 2 paynells, 1 bridell, 1 Sadell, 2 payer of fetters		13	4
	Remember 2 loades of 13s 4d			
	The hen house			
	6 hens and a Cokke		4	0
	Wheate 50 acres	60	0	0
	Otes, tares, beanes, barley	13	0	0
	Rackes, hoggtroffes		3	4

7 hogges	2	0	0
14 ewes and 14 lambes	5	12	0
5 sheepe	1	13	4
2 sheepe		18	0
2 Red kyne bequethed to his wyfe	3	6	8
3 kyne bequeathed to his sonne Nycholas	4	10	0
1 bull	2	0	0
6 horses	12	0	0
Hempe		2	0
Ten Acres of Fallowe	1	6	8
Dunge		13	4
One heffer beqeathed to Nan	1	10	0
Two kyne bequeathed to Nycholas	3	0	0
Two yerlinges bullockes	1	10	0
Heyffers	3	0	0
Stere	1	0	0
One Mare, 1 horse	1	13	4
Glasse in the Wyndowes		16	8
2 Crevetes		1	6
2 wheeles		1	0
2 kine that Thomas Aldeen of Ryckmonthworth at price and hyre	3	0	0
That Thomas Parker of Wallington oweth me	6	6	8
	[*147*	*19*	*1*]

Note: In the Will, written on 18th April and proved on 19th May 1591, the goods and chattels were most carefully listed, for instance "the broude shallowe brasse pan about eighteen gallones by estimation and one Chest lodged on the lyd" were part of the bequest to Agnes, the elder daughter. Her sister Dorothy was to have, amongst other things, the testator's own bed and bedding. "One longe Cart with shod wheles and two dung Cartes with bare wheles" were part of the bequest to his son Nycholas. "One Cowe which is nowe at Rickmansworth with Thomas Alden" was part of the gift to his trusty servant and kinsman Thomas Elborne. The other cow there was given to Jane Blake, the testator's daughter-in-law. The co-executors and equal residuary legatees were the trusty Thomas and the young Nycholas Alden, who was to claim his inheritance of the remaining years of the lease of the farm and a comprehensive list of implements and farm stock, at the age of 22. Agnes and Dorothy could claim £6 apiece, household stuff and a bullock, at the age of 18. The testator asked to be buried at Malden church, to which he gave 3s 4d. The overseers, his trusty friends Mr Roger Ewer of Malden and Nycholas Lane of Morden, were each given 5s; but his wife Jone was to have £6 6s 8d immediately and then £1 per annum and a chamber reserved for herself in the house if she wished to stay there. Meantime the farm was to be run by Thomas Elborne, using some of the profits towards the upbringing of the children. Jone's gifts were made with her comfort and convenience very much in mind, not forgetting to provide her with occupation in the shape of a linen wheel and a woollen wheel. The six witnesses were the vicar Rychard Dyer and Nicholas Lane, both of Morden, Richard Newman, John Browne, John White and Robert Huet.

Ref: 1591 B 2/1 Will 1591 B 2/2 Inventory

John Astone **291**

of Albury; taken by Edward Risbridger, Rafe Dalton, Henry Risbridger and William Callingham, 27th April 1591.

	£	s	d
In the hawle			
One table, one forme		6	8
One ioyned stoole, 2 cosheines and one shelfe		1	2
A qualiver with the Furnyture		15	0
In the parlor			
One bedd with Furniture, one Rownd table and one chest	1	13	4

2 paire of sheetes and one table clothe		13	4
In the chamber behinde the haule			
One bedstead and one chest		6	0
In the chamber behind the parlor			
2 bedds with their Furniture		10	0
One owld Cubborde		2	0
Six Fliches of bacone and foure peeces of beif	1	3	4
All the woodon vessells	1	13	4
3 brasse pottes and other brasse	3	0	0
4 peeces of pewter and one candlesticke and 8 spones		4	6
Spitts, drippinge panns, one Andiron, the pothookes and pothangers		3	4
One firepan, one lanthorne and 2 paire of sheares		1	8
Axes, bills and other tooles		4	0
His Apparrell	1	14	8
The monie in his pursse		6	8
Six oxen and steeres	16	0	0
2 bullockes and 2 horsses	2	0	0
5 kyne, 3 bullockes and 2 wonier calves	9	0	0
For four score sheape and lambes	21	4	0
Ploughes and chaynes, harrows and other thinges	4	3	4
Corne and malt		16	4
10 acres of Rye uppon the grownde	8	0	0
One acre of wheat	1	0	0
13 acres of otes	6	10	0
One acre of tares and pease		5	0
The tymber aboute one lode at		6	8
16 wattles at		8	0
7 hogges at	1	15	0
One wellbuckett and that belongeth therunto and one gryndstone		6	8
One Colte at		6	8
[*£5.0.10*]	5	4	10

Note: The Will was dated 10th April and proved on 17th May 1591. The executor and residuary legatee was his son Thomas, provided that all debts and legacies had first been discharged. The parson of Albury, Mr Robert Cowper, was given 6s 8d as one of three overseers, but Walter Butler of Cranleigh and George Stovold of Ewhurst had to share the same amount between them. The testator, of Stonehouse, gave 3s 4d to the poor, asking to be buried in a convenient place. His godchildren were each left 4d and his son John 20 sheep. His wife Jane was given all the furniture in the parlour. John made his mark on the Will, witnessed and signed by George Aldridge, Thomas Adeane and Raphe Stere. The executor, of Albury, yeoman, put up the administration bond. The entry in the parish register on 19th April 1591 listed John Stone of Stonehouse.

Ref: 1591 B 74/1 Will 1591 B 74/2 Inventory

Margarett Brigman **292**

of St Olave's, Southwark, widow; taken by Lawrence Emden, Peter Cleyman and David Frillichaven, 15th April 1591.

	£	s	d
3 olde fetherbeddes and twoo pillowes, fower quishons	2	10	0
One Spanishe bedsteede and a trussebedd		12	0
Eight paire of sheetes	1	10	0
3 Coverleetes and two blankeetes		17	0
Eight Smockes		11	0
Tenne Pillowberes		7	0

Fyve table clothes		6	0
Twelve napkins		5	0
Neckergeres, quoines and crose clothes		10	0
Certaine bookes		10	0
A smalle presse		10	0
A deale chiste		4	0
A cofer covered withe lether		10	0
3 pound of pewter		15	0
A table and 3 stoles		6	0
3 terned chaires, one whele and a smalle chist		3	0
One iron potte		2	0
Two Cassokes and one coate	1	10	0
Two Hattes		2	0
3 kettelles, one frienge panne, 2 spittes, one Grediron, one drippinge panne, one small Cupporde and one little table	1	0	0
3 golde ringes		13	4
In money	3	0	0
The Lease of the house	5	10	0
	22	17	4

Note: The Will was dated 16th April and proved on 4th May 1591. The Inventory and Will were exhibited by Mr Thomas Willett, notary public, on behalf of David Frelickhaven, the executor and residuary legatee. Two significant bequests were those of £2 to the Dutch Church and of the best pin pillow, a kirtle and an apron, to her goddaughter Sara, Peter Clement's daughter. Peter himself was given £10 and his father £2. Segrin and Jacob Frelickhaven also had bequests, as did Margaret the maid, Derricke Brooke and the widow Callais. The executor and Lawrence Endye witnessed the signing of the Will. On 19th April 1591 the parish register lists the burial of Margaret Biggeman.

Ref: 1591 B 8/1 Will 1591 B 8/2 Inventory

Margaret Charlewodd **293**

of Great Bookham, widow; taken by John Hylder, Robert Roger and Edmon Hudson, 9th May 1591.

	£	s	d
in the hall			
One table and a powdrynge trave		3	4
Brasse and pewter	1	0	0
All maner of yron		2	0
Stoles and dysshes, Trenchers, spoones and bottelles		1	6
in the Chamber			
A flocke bed and bedstedle withe all thynges therunto belongyng		16	0
2 Chestes and the small lynen in them and fyve payre of Shetes	2	6	0
In the mylkehouse			
Mylke bowles and mylke pannes with other thynges		2	6
3 busshelles of whete		10	0
In the loffte			
Wollen clothes and one payre of Shetes	1	0	0
All other thynges in the lofte		13	4
Redi money in her purse		2	0
One Aker of blade growyng in the felde		13	4
Anaker of pese		6	8
7 cheeses		2	0
2 shotelyng hogges		6	0
2 kene	3	0	0
Wodde in the gate		3	4

12 pounds of yarne at the wevers		4	0
	11	12	0

Note: The Will was dated 13th September 1587 and was proved by Agnes, the daughter and executrix, on 17th May 1591. This same Annys (Agnes) was to inherit the residue of the estate, with considerably more than the bequest to the son John Charlewodd of "a table clothe, a payre of hempen shetes, a brasse potte and a kettle, the lesscr of the twayne". The overseers appointed were Edmon Hudson and Wylliam Allyn, who both witnessed the signing of the Will, the latter by a double cross. Robart Shorter wrote the document and witnessed the same. No bond was taken.

Ref: 1591 B 15/1 Will 1591 B 15/2 Inventory

Thomas Crue **294**

of Windlesham, labourer; taken by John Atfeild and Thomas Chippes, 8th April 1591.

	£	s	d
His Apparrell			
A meddle Coate, a Dublet, a Jerkin, 2 paire of hose, 1 payre of shoes		6	8
In his purse			6
In the Chamber			
A [*] bedsted		6	0
A fetherbed, a boultster, a course coverlet		16	0
A flockbed, a bowlster, a coverlet		8	0
4 Chestes		4	0
The painted clothes		2	0
3 paire of sheetes		12	0
In another place			
The brasse		13	4
2 spitts, a paire of pothookes, pothangers, a gredron, a friyin pan		3	0
2 tubbes, 2 old bucketes, 4 Dishes		2	0
In the hall			
A old Cubbord		4	0
An old table and a forme		2	6
A bench bord			6
The pewter		10	0
An axe and a fagot hoke, a spade		2	0
A wheele and a paire of woole Cardes		1	6
A Cowe and a Calfe	1	13	4
A old Cowe	1	0	0
A old horse and a Coult	1	0	0
2 Ewes and 2 lambes and a teige		10	0
3 Eives of bees		7	6
2 hogges		2	0
	[*9*	*6*	*10*]

Note: The Will was dated 21st December 1590 and proved on 17th May 1591. The executrix, who was to have a life tenancy of the house and land so long as she remained a widow, was his wife Grace. The testator recorded that his sole heir was to be his son Thomas Crue, who was to have the kitchen immediately. He was also to inherit the bay mare, a hive of bees, 3 platters, a feather bed, a candlestick and a chest. Elizabeth and Margaret Crue, the two daughters, werc to have a platter apiece and a half share in a cow and a hive of bees. Thomas gave 1s to Symon Collier. He gave 2s to Windlesham church and asked to be buried in the churchyard. William Campian and Symon Collier, the two witnesses, both signed their names. The widow herself put up the administration bond.

Ref: 1591 B 17/1 Will 1591 B 17/2 Inventory

John Goringe **295**

of Worplesdon, yeoman; 1591. [*no appraisers given*]

	£	s	d
In his purse		10	0
His apparell	1	0	0
In the hall			
A dubell table, a table with a frame, 1 yoine form, 1 cobard, 1 paynted clothe, 1 chayr, 2 yoine stoolles, 2 coberne, 2 payre pote hangers, 1 payre of tonges	2	0	0
In the parler			
1 Joyne beedsted, a fether beed, a fether boulster, three pellowes, 1 table, 1 payre of tressells, a forme, 2 stayne clothes, 1 coverlate, 1 blanket 1 coberd	2	3	4
In the chamber			
1 bedested, 1 longe table with a forme, 1 payre treesells, 5 stayne clothes		10	0
In the chamber over the hall			
1 bedstedell with 2 flockbeds 2 cover= lates, 3 blankates, 4 boulsters, 1 pyllowe, 8 chesse, 1 table, a payre of treesells	1	6	8
In the old chamber			
1 bedstedell, 1 flokebed, 1 boulster		8	0
In the kychenne			
3 calldrens, 6 kettells, 2 pannes, 3 brasse pottes, 2 posnettes, 1 skyllet	4	0	0
1 skymmer, 4 broches, 2 dryping pannes, 1 potehannger, 2 potehookes, 3 buketes, 1 fier panne		5	0
In the bakehouse			
1 knedtrowghe with a cover, 1 boulting hutche, 1 chese presse, 1 forme		10	0
In the mylke house			
1 salt trowghe with a cover, 2 great boolles, 5 other booles with a buttercherne, 1 powdring tube, 1 salt tube, 2 frying pannes 6 earthen poottes, 1 sope boxe		13	4
In the mault lofte			
4 chesmotes with the followers, 1 hichell, 1 payre of tressells, 3 busshell oates, 2 bushells of maulte		12	0
In the butery			
1 bruing tube, 1 keeve, 6 alle tubes, 3 kyvers, 4 virkines, 1 wooden bottell, 2 letherne bottells, 5 stonen Jugges		13	4
In the spence loft			
With 2 bascats with a payre of scalles and smalle weittes with other trmperye		2	0
In the old chamber			
1 great cheste with a cover, 1 faate, 3 tubes, 1 half bushell, 3 syves, 2 whelles, 1 yre bound byttell and 6 yron weedges, 2 cobernes, 8 augers, 2 wimbells, 1 oaste heere, 1 wynnynge clothe, 4 sackes old	1	0	0
1 morter with a pestell, 5 candellstickes, 2 chafing dishes, 4 salts, 9 platter, 9 peuter dishes, 5 sacers, 1 dossen Sponnes	1	3	0
1 bowe, 1 sheave of Arowghes, 1 sword, 1 dagger, 1 gyrdell, 1 cape and a skulle		6	8
1 hoogge of baken		6	8
6 payr of sheites, 2 table clothes, 2 shertes	1	0	0

	£	s	d
4 Sythes, 3 axes, 4 bylles, 3 spytters, 1 shuffell, 2 stoppes, 1 pyke axe, 1 slege, 2 hammers, 3 pronges, 2 drage hookes		5	0
Wheate in the house	1	6	8
2 stalles of bees in the garden		6	8
1 grinstonne with a spyndell		1	4
	[*20*	*9*	*8*]

Note: The Will was dated 15th April 1588 and proved on 17th May 1591. The executrix and residuary legatee with a life interest in the freehold property was Alice, the wife of the testator. Sums of 2s 6d each were given to the overseers John Loveland and Robert Kyng. When Alice died, or were she to marry, the freehold lands were to go to John Hewett, the son of his daughter, together with four valuable household items to be counted as standards of the house. Alice Hewett, his daughter's daughter, was to have £2 at the age of 21. His maid Joan Coxe and Christopher Coxe were each to be given 6s 8d at the age of 20. Thomas Goring, his uncle's son, was to have an annuity of £2 for life, to be paid out of the freehold lands twice a year in equal portions. The testator desired his wife to be kind to his daughter Anne Maybonck and her poor children, paying her a legacy of £1. The poor of the parish were given 2s; his manservant William was to have £1; his godson Thomas, 12d; and his godchildren 4d each. The testator's daughters were to deliver the four standards to John Hewett when Alice died. They would have known the "Table Cubberd in the Hall and the great brase pott and the Calderne in the Kitchen". The great chest, also mentioned, was listed in the old chamber in the Inventory. Each of the three pages of the Will was signed by Thomas Shawe and John Harris added his mark. On the last page John Hall signed and William Underwood made his mark, as two additional witnesses. An entry in the parish register for 22nd April 1591 lists the burial of John Gorring.

Ref: 1591 B 25/1 Will 1591 B 25/2 Inventory

Richard Harrison **296**

of Bermondsey, St Mary Magdalen; taken by Lanncellott Johnson, Roger Hodgekines and Richard Mercer, 19th April 1591.

In the Kitchin	£	s	d
One Table with a frame and six ioyned stoles		12	0
One paier of Anndiornes, one paier of tonges and a fier shovell		1	0
Two Iron pottes and a copper kettle		8	0
Two spittes, one dripping pann, a frienge pann, a gridiron, potthookes and a slice		3	4
One old Cupbord		2	6
Nyne peces of old pewter		3	4
All the lomber		3	4
In the hall			
One presse Cupbord	1	0	0
One bedstedd	1	0	0
One Table with a frame and two settles		10	0
The payinted clothes in the same hall		5	0
In the Bedchamber			
One fetherbedd, two boulsters, two pillowes, two blanckettes, one paier of shetes, one Coveringe and one bedsted	3	10	0
Two Rugges		10	0
One old cheste		2	6
Two paier of shetes and other lynnen		13	4
One little bedsted, one flockbed, one keveringe, one boulster and one paier of shetes		10	0
Two old chestes		2	6
The leasse of the howse and grownd thre yeares yet unexpired	4	0	0
	13	17	10

Debtes owinge by the Testator at the tyme of his decease			
Owing by the testator at the tyme of his deathe as appearethe by his bookes the some of	16	0	0

The Inventory was exhibited for purposes of administration of the goods and chattels by his widow and administratrix Constance on 4th May 1591. She signed the document with a symbol. Ref: 1591 Ad 29
Note: Richard Harrison's burial had taken place on 20th April 1591.

John Hibbard **297**

of Great Bookham, yeoman; taken by Ralphe Crowcher and John Dudley, 14th May 1591.

	£	s	d
Brase			
One ould Caldren		6	8
2 Brase Potes		8	0
a Lyttle broken pane			4
Peauter			
3 ould peauter platters		1	0
3 newe pewter platters		2	8
2 peauter Dishes and 2 sasers		1	8
Apparrell			
One Ould Cheste with his apparell		13	4
Sheepe			
2 Eawe sheepe		6	8
2 Tegges		6	8
	[*2*	*7*	*0*]

Note: The Will, written on 26th April 1588, was not proved until 17th May 1591 by a son, Richard Hibbard, the executor and residuary legatee. He was left a range of pots and pans and the testator's dwelling house Bonetes, together with its land; also the profits from another property Estweke to hold in trust until his own son Robert reached the age of 21. The testator's son John was bequeathed three separate sums of money and useful pots and pans. John Francis was left 3 bushels of barley. The executor was to pay his brother John £1 3s 4d a year for three years. John Arnold, a tenant, was to repay 18s 6d and a further 7s was to be recovered from Rychard Hone of Cobham, butcher; all to go to John. Robarte Shorter wrote the Will, also witnessed by three men, William Arnolde, Ralphe Croucher and John Dudley, who made their marks. It is recorded that no administration bond was taken.

Ref: 1591 B 40/1 Will 1591 B 40/2 Inventory

Henry Kempe **298**

of Cranleigh, tailor; taken by Walter Howe, John Barker and George Martyn, 14th May 1591.

	£	s	d
One Table and a paynted Cloth		4	0
A brasse pott, 5 kettles, a Chafynge dishe and a paire of pothangers		17	0
4 Candlestickes and an other Chafyngdishe		3	4
A dozen of pewter vessell		10	0
A Drippynge panne and a fryinge pann			6
A Spytt, two wedges, a handbill, a handsawe and old yron		2	0
Woodden vessell and two tubbes		1	0
Three Flockbeddes, three Bedstedles, three Blanckettes, one Coverlett and two bolsters	1	6	8
Fower Chestes		6	8
Three payre of Sheetes and a table cloth		12	0
A Cubbord and a knead trough		4	0
His apparell		15	0

	£	s	d
Money in his purse		1	6
	5	3	8

Note: The Will was written on 14th April and proved on 17th May 1591. The executrix and residuary legatee was the testator's wife Elizabeth, who was asked to see him buried in Cranleigh churchyard. Rychard Kempe, his surviving son, was given the messuage or tenement in Cranleigh Street, bought of Thomas Redford by the testator and another son John at some previous time. Other bequests to Rychard mentioned a flock bed in the chamber where the testator lay, "a bedstedle in the Lower Chamber, a brasse pott being cracked in the bryme and one kettle without a bounde, a knedinge trowe with a mouldynge borde and one chafyng dish". Witnesses to the Will were Edward Tanworth, Walter at Howe, Walter Buttler, George Martyn, Wylliam Thornden and the writer Ralph Dalton. The administration bond was provided by Rychard Kempe of Cranleigh, tailor. Ref: 1591 B 45/1 Will
1591 B 45/2 [poorly spelt copy of Inventory] 1591 B 45/3 [well written copy]

John Lucas **299**

of Westhumble in Mickleham; taken by John Poulsdyn, John Saker, Vincent Doffyll and Richard Elis, clerk, rector of Mickleham, 28th April 1591.

	£	s	d
Hys weringe aparell	1	0	0
Money in hys purse		2	0
In the hawll			
A standinge table, a forme, a cubord, three chayers		10	0
Fyve pewter dysses, 7 pewter platters, two candelstykes, a morter and two salt cellers, three sawcers		13	4
Two aundyrnes, a pott huckes, pott hangers and a spytt		3	4
4 kyttels, two pottes, a posnett, a skelett pan and scommer	1	0	0
Tubbes, fates and other Lumbermentes	1	0	0
16 payr of sheetes, 6 table clothes, a dosyn of napkyns, two towells, a payr of pyllow beers	5	16	8
Two fether beddes and a flokbedd, two payr of blankets, two bowlsters, three pyllows, three coverlets	5	0	0
Three bedstedels		3	4
Fyve chestes		10	0
6 cowsyns and a dosyn of pewter spones		2	0
4 wedges, an axe and a byll: two stone weight of ledd		3	0
Corne in the howsse three bussels of wheat, two bussels of barly malte		15	0
Three akers and a halff of wheat now groynge, an Aker and a Rodd of Rye, fyve akers of pease and tares and one aker of wootes	5	0	0
Fyve akers of barly	2	0	0
Fowr kyne	6	13	4
An owld geldinge		13	4
14 wethers, 17 ews, three tegges and 7 lambes	7	0	0
A Cart wyth wheales, a harnes, a harow, a pronge and a grynstone		10	0
	[*38*	*15*	*4*]

Note: The Will was dated 16th October 1590 and proved on 18th May 1591. When the testator made his Will he was in perfect health and remembrance, walking about. He asked to be buried in Mickleham churchyard and he appointed his present wife Elizabeth executrix, giving her all he had. Thomas Rusburgh wrote the document and Vincent Duffielde and others unnamed witnessed it. Administration was granted to Elizabeth. John Saker of Betchworth bound himself to see this carried out.

Ref: 1591 B 49/1 Will 1591 B 49/2 Inventory

Elizabeth Michell **300**

of Epsom, widow; taken by Robert Palmer and John Crowcher, May 1591.

	£	s	d
In brasse		10	0
In poyter		5	0
All the woollen Cloths	1	0	0
All the waring lynnine		4	0
Seven sheetes and 2 tabellclothes		8	0
A flocke bed and a payer of blankets, a covering and a fethere boulster		6	8
Three Chestes, two bouls, one Cubbard, two tubbs, three stools		5	0
One hechill, one spite and one fryingpan			6
One Cow bullocke		10	0
	3	9	2

Note: The Will was dated 13th April and proved on 18th May 1591. The executor and residuary legatee was Elizabeth's son Robert. Another son William was given a bed, bedding and half her sheets, brass and pewter, except one special pan then in the possession of her son John, which was to be given to her daughter Elizabeth Maythey. She and the other daughter Joan Collins were to share most of the clothes, with Joan having first choice of cassock and petticoat. John Michell's wife was given two hats and the serving wench a petticoat. The witnesses were Robert Cole, minister, Beatrice Crowcher and Elizabeth Bird. The executor, a labourer, bound himself to carry out the administration.

Ref: 1591 B 55/1 Will 1591 B 55/2 Inventory

William Slatt **301**

of Chertsey, husbandman; taken by Henrie Atwickes, John Tymerton, William Thatcher and Henrie Crocford, 21st April 1591.

In the Hall	£	s	d
Certaine ymplementes		13	4
In the Chamber over the Hall			
One flockbedd with other ymplementes of Stuffe		13	4
In the next Chamber			
2 flockbedes with other furniture therunto		16	4
In the Butterey and in a littell Roome next it			
Certaine pewter and other houshold stuffe	1	0	8
In the Kichyn			
Potthanginges and old Stuffe		6	8
In the Barne			
Some Rye and other thinges	1	10	0
Certaine Corne growinge upon the grounde	2	4	0
Fower Oxen	5	16	0
2 Kyne	2	13	4
2 Steeres	1	13	0
A yerelynge Bullocke		5	0
2 Nagges	1	6	8
12 Sheepe and Lambes	1	13	4
A Carte, Plowe and Harrowes with the rest of the ymplementes belonginge to husbandrie	1	10	0
His Apparrell, Money and whatsoever goodes before not praised	1	2	0

	22	13	8

Note: The Will was witnessed by Thomas Hindley, minister, Allen Attfeild's wife and Marie Harme, on 14th April and probate was granted on 17th May 1591 to his widow Annis, the sole executrix. She was to inherit the residue of his goods after bequests to the testator's four children. Steven, the eldest, was to have £4 at the age of 23. The two girls Elizabeth and Amy and the younger boy William, were each to have a legacy of £2 at the age of 16 years or when they were married. A small bequest of 2s 6d was made to the poor of the parish of Chertsey. The overseers were named as Henry Atwicke and John Tymerton.

Ref: 1591 B 71/1 Will 1591 B 71/2 Inventory

John Stedman **302**

of Bramley in Shalford, husbandman; taken by Robert Smyther, Davy Warner and Thomas Chaundler, 11th May 1591.

	£	s	d
in the halle			
One table, one forme, one chayer, one spynninge whele and one stoole		2	0
Owlde vates		2	0
in the kytchen chamber			
Owlde trowes		4	0
Owlde chestes and coffers		5	0
Owlde fflocke beddes, keverlettes, blanckettes, bolsters and pillowes	1	0	6
Sheetes and one table clothe		14	0
Brasse and pewter	1	6	8
Milke vesselles, ale vesselles and earthen pottes		9	0
One littell spytt, one tryft, one awndiron, one payre of pothookes, one gerdiron and one fryinge panne		4	0
One owlde cauldron		3	4
His apparrell and money in his purse		15	0
Disshes, trenchers, spones and drinkinge pottes			10
2 candlestickes and one salte		1	0
Rye in the house	2	5	0
Maulte		13	4
Bacon in the Rooffe	1	10	0
4 oxen	10	0	0
3 kyne	6	0	0
5 bullockes	4	0	0
2 calves		13	4
Horses	4	10	0
Sheepe	8	0	0
Rye and otes	12	0	0
Hogges and pigges	1	13	4
Soyle in the gate		13	4
Weane, wheles, donge pott, yokes, chayne, harrowes, axes and billes	1	0	0
Lambes	1	0	0
Powltry		3	4
Beanes and hastyes		2	0
	59	11	0

Note: The Will was dated 28th February 1584/5 and proved on 17th May 1591. The residuary legatee and executrix was the testator's wife Jane. He asked to be buried in Shalford churchyard and he bequeathed 1s each to the poor men's boxes of Bramley and Shalford. His son-in-law Myles Mae was left £20 and 10 ewes. The six children of his son Robert Stedman were each given a ewe and his servant Susan Edwards was left 2 ewes. Two named witnesses were Richard Punter and John Mose. A cousin Robert Smyther of Tilsers and Thomas Mellershe were given 1s each, over and above their charges as supervisors. The widow and Richard Punter of Shalford, yeoman, put up the administration bond. The burial took place on 17th April 1591.

Ref: 1591 B 73/1 Will 1591 B 73/2 Inventory

Robert Stoner **303**

of Peperharow, husbandman; taken by John Jackman, Richard Jure, John Tanner and Edward Cowper, 19th May 1591.

	£	s	d
His purse and gerdle		2	0
All his apparrell		13	4
All his bedding		13	4
A little cofer with the thinges within it		2	0
All woodden vessle		5	0
A cupbord, table, forme and chaire		5	0
Brasse and pewter		3	4
A bill, axe, with all other old yron		1	6
2 harrowes		3	0
A cart, yokes, chaines, traces, ropes, wheles and dungpott with all thinges belonging thereto	1	0	0
A mare, a coult and a nage	2	0	0
2 stere bullockes	2	13	4
2 kyne and 2 heckfares	5	0	0
4 little young bullockes	2	0	0
20 shepe, Ewes and Wethers	3	6	8
10 Lambes		16	8
1 wayner calfe		5	0
Hogges and pigges		10	0
All the powltrie		5	0
A hyve of bees		2	0
3 akers and a halfe of Rye	1	10	0
8 akers of otes	1	6	8
Half an aker of pease		3	0
	23	6	10

Note: The Will was dated 8th May and proved on 19th May 1591. The executrix and residuary legatee was his wife Edith. Sums of 12d each were left to the overseers, his loving friends and neighbours John Tanner and Edward Cowper. These men were to put out to best advantage the legacies to his four children until they came of age: the boys John and Jefferie were to inherit the ox and horse teams with all the gear; the girls Grace and Alice were each to have a cow and 10 sheep. The testator gave 12d to the church and asked to be buried in the churchyard of Peperharow. No witnesses were named, nor was the Will signed on the surviving copy.

Ref: 1591 B 75/1 Will 1591 B 75/2 Inventory

Agnes Streete **304**

of Wonersh, widow; taken by John Bicknol, John Grethurst, Henry Harper and Tomas Ticknor, 9th April 1591.

	£	s	d
In the Hall			
On Cupborde standinge there		8	0
The Paynted Clothes hanginge ther		1	0
2 Chayres and one ioyned stoole		2	8
In the Chamber over the Hall			
On fetherbed, on Bolster, fower Pillowes, 2 Pillowbers, one payre of sheetes, on payre of Blanketes, on Helinge	2	10	0

2 bordes, 2 payre of Trestells, on forme, on Chayre		2	4
The Paynted Clothes there		10	0
Thirteene Busshells of Rye	2	2	0
Five Busshells of Otten malt		5	0
Fower Busshells of Otes		3	4
4 Pounde of Hoppes		1	0
In the shopp Loft			
3 Bedsteedells standinge there	1	0	0
2 olde flockbeddes, 2 payre of Blanketes, 2 Pillowes		10	0
2 olde chestes, on forme, on payre of scales and waytes		4	0
In the Kitchinge			
Seven Tubbes		6	8
Five Boules		3	0
On Table and on forme		2	4
3 brass Pottes and on Posnet	1	0	0
3 brass Panns		10	0
3 Kettells, on morter and Pestell and other old brass		10	0
On great Cadron		13	4
2 Spittes and on Cobiron		2	8
12 pewter platters		16	0
6 pewter disshes		4	0
4 old pewter platters and on saser		2	0
2 saltsellers and 2 sasers		1	0
4 brass Candellstickes and on Potled		3	4
2 dripping panns		2	0
On here Cloth		3	0
On Busshell			10
2 Sackes and on bagg		1	6
A broadstone ther		1	0
On Cheese press and a hen Coupe		1	4
Certayn old tooles and old Iron		3	4
In the Backhouse			
3 old Tubbes and on old barrell, 4 shelves and other wodden stuf		3	8
7 houshold loaves		4	6
The Bakon and beefe hanginge ther	1	9	0
3 benches, 2 shelves, on old Cage		1	0
Certayn earthen vessell with Larde		2	8
On borde, a payre of Trestells, on old fryinge pan and a bottell		1	2
A Butter Churne			10
In the Bedchamber			
Her wearinge apparell	1	0	0
2 payre of sheetes, 2 diaper Tableclothes with other linnen	1	0	0
On Coverlett and an old Carpet		6	8
On Tablecloth and on Cupbord cloth		1	0
Mony in her purse		5	0
In the Shopp			
On whele and on skeyner, on ioyned stoole, 2 Cusshions, a payre of billowes, on payre of Pothangers and pothookes		2	6
In the gate and in the feeld			
2 plankes, 2 bordes, on grindstone, a wheelbarrowe and on peece of Timber		2	2
5 Keyne and on bullock of a yeare old	11	0	0
The soyle and broome in the gate		12	0
The Haye there		15	0

The Hogges in the gate	1	3	4
Poultrye and geese		3	8
On Dungpot and wod in the gate, the Rackes and other old stuff		3	8
3 Acres and halfe of wheate and Rye in the feeld	2	18	4
2 Acres and half of Otes		17	4
The Beanes in the garden		1	8
	36	2	10

Note: The Will was dated 31st May 1590 and proved on 17th May 1591. The co-executors and residuary legatees were John and Christian Tickner and Mark and Agnes Frost, two of the widow's daughters and their husbands. The testatrix left 3s 4d each to her overseers, her loving neighbours Lawrence and John Street of Farnhill. She left a similar sum to the poor of the parish. John Astreete, her son's son, was left all the glass about the house, the hangings in the loft over the hall, 4 boards, a cow, some rye, a flockbed and bedding, a brass pot, a kettle and a platter. The executors were to pay 6s 8d apiece to Robert, Joan, Agnes and Christian Astreet; and to Edward, Jane, Alice and Agnes Frost. Phillis Astreet was given a cow and 30s. John Huett was to have a bullock or a 2-year-old heifer. The surviving children of the widow's daughter Joan were to have an equal share of a third of her estate at the age of 20, the money to be held in trust by the executors. Thomas Taunton, the vicar of Wonersh, signed the Will and John Bicknoll made his mark when they witnessed the document. The two sons-in-law John Tickner, husbandman and Mark Frost, tanner, both of Wonersh, bound themselves well and truly to administer the estate. The burial was recorded on 4th April 1591.

Ref: 1591 B 76/1 Will 1591 B 76/2 Inventory

William Ticknore **305**

of Albury, yeoman; taken by John Woode, John Tycknore of Haldershe, William Eased, William Callingham and Edmund Risbridger, 26th April 1591.

	£	s	d
In the hall			
Two tables, one Chayre, three rounde stooles and two cushynes		8	0
One Cupborde		12	0
Two brasse Cawldrens, two pottes and other brasse	2	0	0
14 peeces of pewter, one morter and two candlestickes		16	0
A qualiver furnished		15	0
In the parlor			
The bedd and furniture	2	0	0
In the chamber over the parlor			
Two beddes with their furniture, 3 ould chestes and table and a payre of tresselles	1	3	4
The wooden vesselles		13	4
In a backe chamber			
A bedd with furniture		6	8
6 payre of Sheetes and other lynen	1	10	0
Two spittes, the potthookes and the Andirons		6	8
His apparell	3	0	0
Money in his purse	1	0	0
Corne in the barne	3	0	0
11 skore sheepe at 4 pound the skore	44	0	0
30 lambes	2	6	8
8 oxen	20	0	0
8 kyne and 3 bullockes	14	13	4
4 horses	5	0	0
One Sowe and five shootes		15	0
Cartes, plouhes, harrowes, chaynes and such other furniture	1	10	0
Two Anuytyes for certen yeres yet to Come	20	0	0

For the fowldinge Wattelles		6	8
Billes, axes and workinge tooles		3	4
The soyle in the gate		3	4
Corne one grownd	10	10	0
	136	19	4

Note: Thc lengthy Will was first written and signed on 7th November 1579. A page was inserted and amendments made in another hand on 27th April 1584. Probate was granted on 17th May 1591. The executrix and residuary legatee was his wife Joan. The names of four overseers first written were deleted in favour of Mr Cooper, parson of Albury and John Gyles of Weston. Those men first chosen had been the testator's brother Rycharde Tycknore of Ropseyer, John Astone, Raffe Dalton and Thomas Chenell. William gave money to the church for repairs entailed in his burial therein. A sum of £2 was to be spent on bread, meat and drink, after the service. Money was given to 20 of the poorest people in both Wonersh and Ewhurst, with 6d for a knell and 2s for four men to ring a peal in both parishes. His godchildren and maidservants were remembered, though only Mary Person and William Gosden in the first group and Susan Baker and Agnes Durgate in the second group, were named. Most of his land holdings were given to his two daughters Joan Gosden and Jane Rydford, who were each left a cauldron. Each sister would become heir if there were no lawful issue of the other. In the first instance Jane would inherit Woodhill alias Woodland in Albury, Collyns in Dorking, Jaques Croft in Hascombe and Hillside in Albury. Her husband John Rydford was to have Marehouse land, Colemans and Wetherweeks in Cranleigh. Joan was to have a house and garden in West Street, Dorking. Her children were given Moonehall and Eldrishie in Ewhurst, her daughter Jane Gosden to hold them for 10 years and then her son William Gosden. Gifts of livestock went to five of the testator's manservants with an extra gift of money to a nephew, the last-named of the group: William Gosden, Bartholomew Tickner, John March, William Towe and Thomas Tickner. The two named maidservants were each to have a bequest of 10s and their unnamed colleagues were to receive 3s 4d apiece. The two fortunate godchildren were given 10s and the rest had to be content with the proverbial shilling. The testator made his sign of a five-pointed star on each of the three pages of the Will, which was witnessed by Thomas Street of Marehouse and John Stere. The widow bound herself to administer the estate. Her husband had been buried on 7th April 1591, his name being entered as William Tickner of Woodhill.

Ref: 1591 B 81/1 Will 1591 B 81/3 Inventory

1592

Thomas Aneve **306**

of Stoke next Guildford, yeoman; taken by Chrystopher Tayler, Rychard Fayrbrother, Robert Smyther, John Stoughton and John Brodbrydge, 6th May 1592.

	£	s	d
A table in the haule and a forme		3	0
His aparell		5	0
A trokelbed and a flokebed and all that longes to yt		5	0
In the lofte a standynge bedstedell and a flokebed and all that longes thereto		10	0
A table and a forme and a prese and 3 olde chestes		6	2
2 brase pottes and 2 ketteles and 6 olde plateres, 2 kandelstickes and 2 stoles and 2 olde chayeres and all other Lumber		7	0
	1	16	2

Note: The Will was dated 14th April and proved on 9th May 1592. Alice, the second wife of the testator, was to be executrix; she was to have all the goods and a life interest in two adjoining properties in Stoke towards the upbringing of the younger children. One of the overseers was his son Anthony, who was given the £1 due in fees for the use and maintenance of the common well behind the Stoke house; the other overseeer was Rychard Russell. Thomas, the eldest, was the testator's son by his first wife Margery Russell. He was left a house in Trinity parish, Guildford, situated with property of Gyles Abery to the West, with the testator's dwelling house to the East, Thomas Beersdall's land to the North and the king's highway to the South. Were Alys to interfere in any way with this gift, she would lose her dower. Thomas the younger was to inhabit a dwelling house in Stoke, recently occupied by Robert Smyther. John, another son, was to have the house next door, occupied by John Gunter. The only daughter Elizabeth was given £4 to be paid by Thomas the elder and Thomas the younger out of their rents. Witnesses to the Will were Thomas Oclye, William Maxman and Thomas Beersdall. The executrix was bound well and truly to administer the estate.

Ref: 1592 B 2/1 Will 1592 B 2/2 Inventory

William Atlee **307**

of West Horsley; taken by Harry Skete and James Rydford. [*undated*]

	£	s	d
Hys aparell			
Won Rycot Cote, too Rycot Jerkenes, the Canvas dublets, too payre of Rycot hosse, three shertes, won Hat, too payre of shooes	1	0	0
Halfe a quarter of wheate		8	0
Ten bussheles of maulte		13	0
Fyve yoes, fyve lames, three tedges	1	5	8
Fyve Rodmeles of wheate		17	0
Won aker three Rodmeles of barley		15	0
	4	18	8
[*A debt due to him written on the Will*:] Owynge me of Robard Waterer of Wokynge		6	0

Note: The Will was dated 1st May 1584 and proved on 9th May 1592. The testator's sisters Joan and Agnes were appointed executors. Sums of 12d each were left to John Elyot and Thomas Broker, the overseers. His brother Thomas was given the land of their late father in the common field and crops of wheat and barley in three half-acre plots in local fields. Joan and Agnes were given wheat and barley from other fields. The malt was given in bushel and half bushel, quantities to John Gate, Philip Fryland, Mother Jones, Richard Hunt, Robert Reder, Henry Tedder, Griffin's wife, William Fenson and Richard Gardener. Some of these beneficiaries had gifts of grain and livestock, too. William gave 12d to West Horsley church and asked to be buried in the churchyard. The overseers acted as witnesses, with Robert At Ryde, James Redford and Anthony Godard. The administration bond was provided by Thomas Broker of West Horsley, weaver. When the Will was made in 1584, wheat was given in Draylehurst and Hotche Holfes and barley was grown in Broadlande More, Ramsnet Hyll and Southgarden.

Ref: 1592 B 4/1 Will 1592 B 4/2 Inventory

John Cobbat **308**

of Bisley; taken by John Kobbat, Mathew Snellinge, John Hone the younger and William Bannister, 3rd January 1592.

	£	s	d
He hade in his purse		1	0
His a parrell		5	0
A tabell, a forme and a rounde tabell and a chare, to stoles		1	6
A cobbard with 6 oulde platters, to peuter pottes, thre canstickes		5	0
The brase		10	0
All the eyere weare		2	6
The beddinge of to beddes and that longethe to them		13	4
Thre oulde chestes		1	0
All the Lomber		4	4
A Cow and a mare	1	6	8
The corne upon the grounde and the fodder in the barne	1	10	0
Foure flytches of baken and 3 pigges		10	0
	[*5*	*10*	*4*]

Note: The undated, unsigned Will was proved on 9th May 1592. The testator appointed his wife Margaret and his son John co-executors and residuary legatees. Sums of 12d apiece were left to the two overseers, his cousin John Cobbat and John Hone the younger. He asked to be buried in Bisley churchyard. His son Richard was given the largest share of household goods: eleven items in all; his daughter Joan had seven items and his daughter Dorothy, five. The widow and John Hone the younger of Bisley, husbandman, bound themselves well and truly to administer the estate. The same John Hone and the cousin John Cobbat had previously witnessed the Will.

Ref: 1592 B 14/1 Will 1592 B 14/2 Inventory

John Feelder **309**

of Hersham in Walton-on-Thames, yeoman; taken by Thomas Dalley of Hersham, John Sleefeeld of Pyrford, John Sleefeelde of Byfleet, yeoman and Richard Barton, clerk, vicar of Walton, 21st April 1592.

	£	s	d
In the Parler			
One Russett cote wyth all the resedue of his Apparell		13	4
One Fether bed wyth all the furniture belonging to the same		13	4
4 Flockbeddes wyth all theyre furneture belonging to the same	1	0	0
10 payre of Course canvis shetes	1	13	4
Twoe payre of pyllowe beares		5	0
Fyve Chestes		8	4
Sirtyn paynted clothes		4	0
Sirtyn woolle and hempton toe		6	8
In the buttrie			
Twoe brasse pottes, 4 kettles, 2 pannes and 2 litle kettles	1	0	0
One dozen and a half of puter, one spitt, a gryd Iron and a fryinge panne		11	6
In the haulle			
One Tayble, 2 formes, one paynted cloth, 1 syde forme, 1 cheare, 2 AnndIrons, 1 payre of potthookes		6	8
In the Kytchen			
One kneding trough, 4 olde Tubbes and one hogg of baycon		8	0
An oulde heare cloth for a kylne or an oste		1	6
One saulting troughe, a boulting whyche and other loomber		6	8
In the yarde			
A carte and a dongcarte, 4 oulde horsses and mayres and the harness	3	0	0
3 oxsen wyth yokes, chaynes, stroppes and one plough	6	13	4
Twoe kyne, 2 heckfores and one calffe	4	10	8
Seaven shepe	1	8	0
One sow and 8 pygges		12	0
3 guysse, one cocke and 2 hennes		4	0
3 staulles of beese		6	8
In the feeldes			
Syxe Acres of Rye 12 shillings an acre	3	12	0
Two Acres of smalle otes		6	8
	28	11	8
Debttes owyng			
To Thomas Deacon of Walton, smyth	1	12	0
To his sister Listney		10	0
To Walter Man of Kyngston		2	6
	2	4	6

Note: The Will was dated 9th April and proved on 10th May 1592. The executrix and residuary legatee was the testator's wife Lucy. Sums of 3s 4d were given to the overseers, two of his cousins called John Sleefeld, one of Pyrford and the other of Byfleet. The testator asked to be buried in the churchyard of Walton. To each of his four children he gave a flockbed, bedding and useful hardware. Edward and John were also given a ewe and a lamb. Ann and Katheryn were also given a cow worth 30s and £5 in money. Lucy was to see these bequests made good when each child reached the age of 21, or was married. The overseers witnessed the Will, together with Richard Barton, vicar of Walton, John Cooke of Walton and John Woolfe of Hersham. The administration bond was provided by the widow and the vicar. John Feelder's death was recorded at the beginning of the Inventory as 13th April 1592.

Ref: 1592 B 20/1 Will 1592 B 20/2 Inventory

John Hellons **310**

of Walton-on-Thames, yeoman; taken by John Cooke, Thomas Deacon, Robart Venoe and Anthony Marchyn, 21st April 1592.

	£	s	d
In hys pursse		1	0
His apparell		16	0
In the Hale			
One table and a forme with a bantch, a cobard, three chayers, to Joyne stooles, to brandirons, fower potthangers, one fyer shovell and a pare of tonges, one pare of bellos		12	10
in the upper chamber			
A bedstedle with a ffetherbedd, one bolster and to pyllos	1	6	0
A truckell bedsted, a forme, a chayer of strawe and a voydynge cobard		4	0
in the chamber over the hale			
One bedsted, a fetherbed, too bolsters with a keverynge and a blanket	1	0	0
An other bedsted with a fflockebed, one keverynge and one blanket and too bolsters		10	0
One presse, one conter table		12	0
One cheste, in the cheste 11 pare of sheets, seven table clothes, seven dyoper napkynns, fower pare of pyllobeers, syxe towells	3	0	0
in the owter chamber			
One bedsted with a fflockbede, too bolsters, a keverynge and a blanket		12	6
Fower chests		13	4
In a chest: pewter 48 peesesse	1	10	6
8 candellstyckes, one brasen morter, three chaffyng dysshes		4	4
in an other chamber			
Too bedstedles, one Flockbedd, too keverynges, one blanket		8	0
in the Loffte called the Iron Lofte			
Fyve spytts wyth other olde Iron		6	8
In the Lofte over the cytchyn			
Too lynyn wheeles, one olde chesste with other lumber		2	0
in the chytchyn			
One table, one forme with bantches and bords		1	6
Fyve brasse potts, one chaffer, too possnets	1	10	0
Too cauderns, too pannes, fyve kettells, too scemers, one schylet, two frying panns	2	6	8
One gerdyron, too potthookes, one clever		2	0
In old pewter 14 peessess		5	6
Too buckets, fyve boles, too treys, one woolyn wheele wyth dysshes, trenchers and spoones		2	6
in the boultynge house			
Too troffs with too bords, a boultynge hutche, one busshell, 8 tubbs, syxe kevers, one yotynge fate		13	4

	£	s	d
The Mylk house			
Syxe shellfes, too Letheren bottells		2	0
In the bryckynge chaumber			
One bedstedle, an old fether bed, too bolsters, too cusshyns, one blanket		16	0
Sartayn paynted clothes		6	8
Fyve hynns and a cocke		2	0
Fower geese and a gander		3	0
On Sow shote		4	0
in the barne			
Three trusses off heye		1	0
Corne in the fyld			
Too Acres of wheat and three of Rye	2	0	0
Three Acres of barley	1	0	0
	[*21*	*15*	*4*]

[*Written on the Will*:] All these I doe Acknowledge my debttes as followeth

	£	s	d
To Barnard Edmondes of Kyngston	7	6	8
To William Symondes of London, shipwryght		15	0
To Thomas Wolmer of Walton		15	0
To John Cooke of the same		7	0
To John Guye		12	8
To Thomas Deacon of the same	11	0	0
To the same Thomas, more	7	0	0
To the same Thomas, agayne more	4	8	0
To Mr Robert Chelsome of Kyngston		8	0
[*32.12.4*]			

	£	s	d
Debttes owyng towardes mee as followeth			
Edward Querne of Reading	2	0	0
George Hammonde of Richmond for 2 lodes of billet for the Quene's use		6	8
[*2.6.8*]			

Note: The Will was dated 9th April and proved on 10th May 1592. The executrix and residuary legatee was Isabell, wife of the testator. Sums of 2s each were left to the overseers John Cooke and Anthony Machin of Walton-on-Thames, husbandman. The latter with Isabell provided the administration bond. John asked to be buried in the local churchyard. Isabell was left a life interest in all the freehold property, 3 cows and 5 acres of land in Walton called Buyrye Gasson owing suit and services to Sandon Court. This land was later to be inherited by his younger son Robert and his heirs. Robert, Elizabeth and Agnes, were later each to have a specific cow, which, incidentally, did not appear in the Inventory. These two daughters were also to have £5 apiece, paid by Isabell out of the freehold, or in the case of her death, by Clement Hellons, the elder son. Seven household items in the hall and a bed in the chamber over the hall, were to be counted as heirlooms or standers not to be moved. Joyce Willford and Mary Sleefelde, his two married daughters, were each given a feather bed. Clement's son and Joyce's daughters Joyce and Rose, were each given a platter. When John Hellons made his mark at the end of the Will it was witnessed by Richard Barton, the vicar of Walton, Thomas Deacon, Henry Dogwell and Robert Fenne, with others unnamed.

Ref: 1592 B 27/1 Will 1592 B 27/2 Inventory

Katheryn Lydgold **311**

of Walton-on-Thames, widow; taken by Wyllyam Buckwell and Edmund Hawcocke, 8th May 1592.

	£	s	d
One fetherbed and a bolster		13	4

One other fetherbed, one bolster and a strawe bed with a bedsted		16	0
An other fetherbed with a bolster, a strawe bed with a bedsted		16	0
To keveryngs, to blankets, a carpet and an old quylte, to bed hanger,to certyns	1	6	8
Tenne pare of sheets		16	8
Three chesstes		5	0
In pewter 17 platters and pewter dysshes		13	4
Fower pewter potts, syx candellstyckes, to chaffynge dysshes, a dosyn and a halfe of pewter trenchers		13	4
Fower table clothes and syx napkyns		10	0
Three towells and fower pillowe beares		10	0
A ioyne presse		10	0
Fower paynted clothes		3	4
Hyr apparell	1	0	0
8 peeses of brasse	1	10	0
To ioyne tables, one forme, a chayre		6	8
A dosyn of spoones		1	0
Syx kooshyns		2	0
[*10.3.4*]	10	13	4
[*A Memorandum on the Will*:-] My debttes howing			
To Oliver Warde	2	0	0
To Ellyn Lidgould that was	10	0	0
Whereof is in the handes of Thomas Rawnce senior of Kyngston, butcher of the same money,	9	2	0
but the same Thomas Rawnce is to pay and discharge the same £10 wholly			

Note: The Will was dated 13th August 1591 and proved on 10th May 1592. The executor and residuary legatee was William Woodman of Walton, yeoman. No overseers were appointed. Katheryn asked to be buried in Walton churchyard and she left detailed instructions about the disposal of her clothing and some of her bedding. The only other item mentioned was a great latten candlestick, which was given to Henry Young's wife Millicent, with a feather bed and a boulster. Young Thomas Rawnce was given six items. Katheryn's sister Agnes Rawnce was left the best black gown worn on holy days. The three other beneficiaries were Millicent Rawnce, Joyce Young and William Hudson's wife of Bookham. The four witnesses were Richard Barton, clerk, Thomas Deacon, Anthony Machyn and Edmond Hawcocke. The executor was bound to administer the estate.

Ref: 1592 B 34/1 Will 1592 B 34/2 Inventory

Robert Seith **312**

of Mitcham, yeoman; taken by Roger Tomson and William Jacson, 27th April 1592.

	£	s	d
In the Hall	£	s	d
One Table, one forme, three stooles and one Chaire		6	8
Six Cusshins and painted Clothes		4	0
Two pair of small andirons and a fire shovell, a pair of tonges and 2 pair of pothookes		3	4
In the Chamber over the hall			
One bedstead and a Truckle bedsteed with one fetherbed and a flock bed, two bolsters and three pillowes, one Coverlet and a pair of blanketes	2	0	0
2 Chests, a stoole and a small Deske and painted Clothes		14	8
In the maides Chamber			
One bedsteed of boardes, a mattresse, one old Coverlett a bolster and a pair of sheetes		6	8
In the Chamber over the Parlor			
Wheat thresshed	2	10	0

In the parlor			
A small Joind bedsteed, a fetherbed, a Coverlett and bolster a pillow and a pair of blanketes, a small stoole and a forme	2	0	0
Painted Clothes		2	0
In the Milk Howse			
A poudring tub, 10 booles, 2 shelves		10	0
In the Servantes Chamber			
A bedsteed of bordes, a mattresse, a Coverlet, a pair of blanketes, a pair of shetes and a bolster.		13	4
In the Buttrye			
Thre kilderkins, two firkins, a lether bottle		5	0
In the Kitchin			
One brasse pott, one litle brasse pott, a Chauldron and one Copper Chaldron, a skymmer, 3 brasse skillettes and a kettle	1	15	0
10 platters, 8 pewter disshes, 6 porengers, 3 pewter potts, 3 salts, 2 pewter basons, 4 pewter Candelstickes and two brasse Candelstickes	1	10	0
Two Coules, 2 hoghedes, two bruyng tubs and two half tubs		4	0
Two Iron tryvetes		3	4
Bacon in the rowfe	2	0	0
In the kitchin loft			
In Malt		13	4
One axe, 2 bils, one mattock, one spade and a shovell		2	0
A Cheesepresse		1	0
In the Stable and Yarde			
Six Cart-horse and 2 Twelmonthing Coltes	11	0	0
Harnesse for the horse		10	0
8 Drawing oxen	16	0	0
10 Steares of the bigger sort	14	0	0
8 two yearling bullockes	8	0	0
6 kyne	8	13	4
6 Twelvemonthing Calves	3	0	0
20 small shootes	2	10	0
10 piggs		10	0
Two long Cartes and two dongue Cartes	4	6	8
Two ploughes, two pair of small harrowes, one oxe harrow, 8 yokes and Cheines and a pair of Draftes	2	6	8
40 sheep and 12 lambes	10	0	0
In the barne			
Wheat unthresht	20	0	0
Barlie threst and unthresht	5	0	0
Wheat upon the ground	18	0	0
More in an other place	6	0	0
Rie upon the ground	16	0	0
Barlie upon the ground	8	0	0
Oetes upon the ground	4	0	0
4 geese and a gander, 40 hennes and 2 Cockes	1	0	0
In haye	2	0	0
Timber in the gate	1	10	0
In Linnen			
15 pair of sheetes, 6 table Clothes, 4 Towels, two dozen and a half of napkins, two pair of pillowbeirs	3	0	0
In the barne			
Two Fannes, one busshell and a skryne		13	4

[*182 4 4*]

Note: The Will was dated 30th March and proved on 9th May 1592. The executrix and residuary legatee was the testator's wife Helen. Of the three overseers, the most important, without whom no decision was to be made, was Mr Henry Sytern, parson of Ewhurst; Robert Gyles and William Swillinghurst of Mitcham were singly or together to assist in determining the just cause of any controversy between the executrix and Margaret, Joan, William and Elizabeth, four of his six children. He asked to be buried in Mitcham churchyard and gave 3s 4d for church repairs and 10s to the poor. To both Robert, his son and Frances, his daughter, a gift of £20 was made, each being the other's heir if one should die young. The four other children were likewise given £20, but at the age of 21 rather than 26. A gift of £1 went to his brother Henry Seith and to his sister Jane, the wife of Edward Russly of Kingston. The maid Joan, the manservant John Augustine and his brother-in-law Laurence Smith, were given 3s 4d, 5s and £1, respectively. The lease of Newbarn and the tithe of Mitcham, which the testator had of Mr Richard Burton, were given to the executrix provided that she brought up the four children in a manner befitting "their state and condition"; this last bequest would be revoked if any future husband of Helen's were to neglect them in any way. The overseers witnessed the Will, Henry Sytern and William Swillinghurst signing the document. Robert Gyles, Laurence Smith, Henry Seith and John Augustine made their marks. The parson of Ewhurst provided the administration bond.

Ref: 1592 B 51/1 Will 1592 B 51/2 Inventory

John Slarkes **313**

of Shere, yeoman; taken by John Mabank, Thomas Coxe, Henrie Martyne, Anthonie Slarkes, John King and Walter Lucock, 29th April 1592.

	£	s	d
4 Oxen	11	0	0
4 Kyne	9	0	0
2 steeres of two yeares olde	2	10	0
Five horse beastes	7	0	0
Fiftie Five sheepe, weathers, ewes and tegges and 13 Lambes	17	0	0
7 litle Hogges	1	15	0
Corne in the barne			
Of Wheate 4 quarters	3	4	0
6 busshells of Rie		9	0
3 quarters and a halfe of barlie	1	15	0
3 quarters of otes		18	0
12 busshells of French wheate		12	0
Upon the grounde			
10 Acres of wheat and Rie	10	0	0
9 Acres of barlie	6	0	0
6 Acres of pesen and tares	3	12	0
One Carte, one paire of wheeles and a paire of strapes	1	3	4
Two Dunge pottes, two Freethinges and one paire of wheeles		16	0
4 yokes and two chaynes		6	0
Two plowghes with their Furniture		10	0
The Horse harnes		10	0
3 Harrowes		8	0
Two paire of Fetters and a Lock		2	0
Two Acres more of Otes		10	0
In the Howse			
One presse in the halle	1	6	8
Two cheestes		4	4
10 platters, 6 pewter Dishes, 4 sawcers and 4 candlestickes	1	0	0
A scrine		10	0

In the Lofte over the Hall			
One bedd, one bedstedle and all furniture theirto belonginge	1	0	0
3 Cheestes		6	0
One other bedd and all theirto belonginge	1	0	0
In the litle chamber			
One bedd and all theirto belonginge		5	0
12 pound of Hoppes		5	0
In the Howse			
4 quarters of wheate	3	4	0
14 busshells of barlie		18	8
3 quarters of otes		18	0
20 busshells of French wheate	1	0	0
A Hatchell and Hempe		3	4
In the Chamber			
Pottes, ffirkins and other Lumber		8	0
In the Kitchin all the brasse	1	10	0
Fates, tubbes, bucketes and milke vessell		13	4
Axes, billes, spiters, broches, sythes and all other old yron in the howse		10	0
One Copboarde, one table and A Forme		17	0
10 Fliches of bacon	1	5	0
Hens, geese and duckes		3	4
Two stawles of bees		6	0
One Lease called John Landes	3	0	0
One other Lease called Holes in the tenure of Ambros Jonson	10	0	0
His Apparrell and money in his purse	2	0	0
	112	4	0
What Debtes are owinge unto him at his Decease			
His uncle Thomas Slarkes	1	5	0
Thomas Browne		2	6
What Debtes the said John Slarkes did owe at his Decease			
To Henrie Martine	14	10	0
To Ann Bracher	30	0	0
To Edwarde Slarkes	10	0	0
To Anthonie Slarkes	11	0	0
All other Debtes to Divers persons	11	2	0
	76	12	0

On 9th May 1592 administration of the estate was granted to Elena, widow of the deceased. She bound herself to administer the goods and chattels well and truly, as did Henry Marten of Pirbright, husbandman. Ref: 1592 Ad 95

Note: The burial of John Slarkes was recorded on 13th April 1592.

Walter Steven **314**

of Leatherhead, labourer, 27th April 1592. [*no appraisers given*]

	£	s	d
In the Hall			
A table, forme and cupbord with other shelves		1	0
7 peeces of brase		10	0
6 peeces of peuter with 7 spoones and a chaffin dish		4	0
A trivet and other cobbirons with spit, pothangers and gridiron		1	6
In the parlor			
2 chestes, a bedsted and bedtester with other ould tubbes		3	0
5 sheetes, 3 towne and 2 hemp, a floke bedd, a boulster, a pillow, 2 coverlydes and a blanket		15	0
His apparrell		10	0

In the yard				
A barren cow and a hekfare		2	13	4
The lease of his howse		2	10	0
	[*£7.7.10*]	7	7	11
Detes dew				
Robert Dee oweth			9	0
Nicolas Steevens oweth			9	10
Christopher Steven oweth		1	10	0
Money remaneinge yn his childrene handes		15	0	0
		17	8	10
		24	16	8

Note: The Will was dated 1st January and proved on 10th May 1592. The residuary legatees and executors were the testator's two sons Thomas and Walter. His three daughters, Ann, Elisabeth and Jane, were each to be given £5 on their days of marriage. No overseers were appointed, but Walter and Nicholas Steven of Leatherhead, husbandmen, bound themselves well and truly to administer the estate. Thomas Steven and Richard Lever had witnessed the Will.

Ref: 1592 B 54/1 Will 1592 B 54/2 Inventory

Thomas Tomson **315**

of Southwark, St Olave's, 24th April 1592. [*no appraisers given*]

	£	s	d
In the chamber			
1 gine bedsted		13	4
1 owld feather bed and 1 owld flockbed and 1 boulster, 1 coverlet of darnix and 1 blankett		15	0
1 Owld presse		5	0
1 little table with a frame		4	0
5 Owld gine stooles and 2 owld chestes		3	4
2 payer of Owld sheetes		5	0
the paynted clothe about the chamber		3	4
1 dozen of trenchers and 1 wooden platter and a peper querne			8
In the halle			
2 lyttle tables		3	0
1 fowrme and a little benche			8
2 wicker chayers and 1 turned chayer		1	4
2 little Iron pottes		2	6
2 little skillettes			8
5 pewter dishes, 2 sawcers and 1 porrenger		3	8
2 pewter cupps and 1 salte seller			10
1 spitt, 1 dreepinge pan, 2 Awndyerns and 1 fier shovell and 1 payer of pothookes		1	6
The paynted clothes about the halle		2	0
1 owld gowne, 1 cloake, 1 owld Dublett and 1 payer of breeches		16	0
2 shertes and 3 banndes		5	0
	4	6	10

Note: On 11th May 1592 the administration of the estate was granted to Elizabeth, relict of the deceased, who was sworn to the truth of the Inventory of the goods and chattels. The widow herself and William Crowlie of the same place, capmaker, provided the administration bond. An entry in the parish register for 15th April 1592 records the burial of Thomas Thomson, haberdasher.

Ref: 1592 Ad 101

1593

Christopher Curson **316**

of Dulwich in Camberwell; taken by John Heath, Nicholas Foster and John Bedle, 1593.

	£	s	d
In the Haule			
A table, a Cupbord, a forme, 2 stooles and a litle cheyr		6	8
Shelves and 2 wheeles		2	0
In the Kytchin			
4 kettles, 2 Caldrons, an Iron pott, one braspot, 3 spittes, 2 dripping pannes, a pare of pothangers	1	10	0
In the Malt house			
Milk bowles, Tubbes and shelves, a powldring trough with other lumber		10	0
In the Bowlting house			
Old Tubbes		2	0
In the Parlour			
A Presse, a bedstead	1	1	0
One Forme and 2 benches		2	0
A fetherbed, a bolster, a strawbed, a blanket, a coveringe with some old painted clothes	1	13	4
A cheir, 7 quishens, an other cheir		5	0
12 Brase Candlestickes		8	0
5 platters of puter, 6 puter dishes, 4 potingers, 2 saltes, 2 dozen spones, 4 drinkinge pottes, a puter Cuppe with other 2 puter pottes		18	0
A Cupbord cloth with a Deske			8
2 brushes and a Rubber			6
In the Chamber over the Parlour			
A bedstead, a wolbed, a coveringe, a bolster, a Blanket a pare of shetes		14	0
An other bedstead, a fetherbedd, a coveringe, a bolster, a blanket, a pare of shetes	1	6	8
15 puter platters, 9 puter dishes, 6 potingers, 6 sawcers, one salt and a pynt pott	1	10	0
6 old Chastes, an old bedstead		12	0
7 pare of shetes, a dozen of napkins and a Tablecloth	2	18	0
A Dublet, a Jerkin, a cloake, a hatt, a pare of hose, 2 pillobears and a shert		18	4
A quern with old Tubbes and other Lumber		10	0
A table, a bow, 2 pillows and old paynted clothes		5	0
A Table cloth, 6 napkins and a Towell		4	0
A pare of bellowes, fyrshovell, a pare of tonges, a stonepott, a litle brasmorter, wodden dishes and trenchers with handbills, an axe		3	4
5 pare of shetes and 3 tablecloths	1	5	0
A bedstead, a flockbed, a bolster, a blanket and a pare of shetes		6	0
6 hens and a cock		3	6
10 Duckes		2	6
In the barn			
Otes with straw, a bushell, a ffan and 2 quarters of wheate and Rye	3	6	8
3 old horses and their harnes	3	6	8
2 Cartes, 1 plough with yoks and chaines	2	6	8
5 oxen and 2 Steares	15	13	4

6 kyne, 2 bullockes and 4 calves	11	0	0
12 yonge beastes in the wood	7	12	0
3 mares and 4 Coltes	3	10	0
2 Loades of hay	1	0	0
2 pare of harrows, a seed codd and other lumber about the yard		6	0
2 hyves of Bees		2	0
Wheat upon the ground	2	16	8
Otes, pesen and Tares on the ground	2	10	0
One hogge and a litle bullocke		15	0
In grasse upon the ground	4	0	0
A lether bottell			4
	86	6	10

Note: The Will was dated 21st March and was proved on 31st May 1593. The executrix and residuary legatee was the testator's wife Anne. The two overseers were Edward Wilson and John Hall. A £16 legacy was left to his wife on condition that she remained a widow and would consequently be the more liberal a mother to her children and to his. Were she to remarry, the £16 was to go in equal shares to his sons, Henry, Edmund and Richard and to his surviving daughter Katherine. The churchwardens of Camberwell were to bestow most of 5s upon the poor of Dulwich. Sums of 2s 6d each were left to Agnes Badger and Richard Peare. The maidservant Agnes Bone and Anne, the daughter of his son-in-law John Goodinoughe, were each left a young cow-calf. The said John was forgiven a debt due a month after Lady Day last past. The testator's daughter Katherine was to inherit £6 13s 4d at the age of 22 or on her wedding day and his son Richard was to inherit £2 when he came of age. Cattle and horses were given to Christopher's three sons and to his two grandsons, children of Henry. Edward Wilson and Richard Peare witnessed the Will. The widow provided the administration bond.

Ref: 1593 B 18/1 Will 1593 B 18/2 Inventory

Richard Frayle **317**

of Woking, yeoman; taken by John Child the elder, William Clebroke and John Child the younger, 15th May 1593.

	£	s	d
Readye Monye in His purse		2	6
His warynge Aparill	1	0	0
In the Halle			
A Cobard, 2 Chayers, a Round table, 4 stooles, one paynted Cloth and a Cobard Cloth		18	0
In the Loware Chamber			
One standinge bedstead, 3 Feather bedds, 2 bolstars, one pare of sheettes, two Blancattes and one Coverlight	1	6	8
In the same Chamber allso 6 Chestes and 3 paynted Clothes		10	0
In an Upper Chamber			
One feather bed, one flockebed, 1 flock bolster, 2 owld feather bolstears, one pare of shetes and one helyer		13	4
In the Chamber over the hall			
One standynge bedstead, one playne bedstead, one trockell beadsted, one feather bead, 2 flockbeades, 1 feather bolstear, 3 flocke bolsters, thre pare of shetes, 3 pare of blancattes, 3 Coverlights, 3 other Blancattes, 2 other Coverlightes, five pellowes, 3 Chestes and one Cheare	1	4	0
In Lynnan 21 pare of shetes, one dossen and 10 Napkyns, 6 table Clothes, 4 Pilloweberes	2	16	8
In Lynnan yearne		10	0
In Platters and dishes of peuter 30 peses, 6 sacares, 1			

	£	s	d
porynger and 3 saltes		18	0
7 Latten Candellstix, one Morter and pestell, one skemer, one bastinge Ladle and a Chafange dishe		5	0
One pare of Andiorns, 2 pare of potthangars, 2 pare of pott Hoockes, 2 gridirons, 4 spettes and one trevett		6	0
In brasse 4 owld Cawdorns, fowre Lyttle brase pottes, 3 Litle panes, 9 small kytles, 3 Litell postenettes and one Colendar	£?	s	d
In all maner of Woodn vessell		5	0
His workynge Tooles		10	0
Rie in the howse	1	10	0
2 small Hoogges of bacon		9	0
4 Oxen, 3 horses, 5 kene and Heiffors, 7 bwllockes and 3 Calves	20	0	0
For 6 ½ Acars of Rie in the feld and for 4 Acars of Ottes	5	10	0
For Carte, plowe, yowkes, chaynes and harnes	1	0	0
For five Ewse and 9 Lames	1	8	0
For 3 Sowes and 9 small Hogges	1	0	0
	45	2	2

Administration was granted to Joan, the lawful relict and administratrix on 29th May 1593. She herself provided the administration bond. Ref: 1593 Ad 34

John Griffine **318**

of Fetcham; 14th May 1593. [*no appraisers given*]

	£	s	d
The Corne in the Close next the howse	2	10	0
The Tares in the next Close with the beanes		14	0
In the feeld 3 Ackers of barly and masekeline	2	0	0
The Corne in the howse of whete 5 bushels		10	0
On bushel of masekeline		1	4
On quarter of malte		11	0
On quarter of Barly		10	0
The quicke Cattell			
4 Kine, 2 Calfes and A twefe montinge Boolocke	7	16	0
A lettell horse and A mare	1	6	8
4 hogges, 4 shootes	2	2	0
Pwltery: All		5	0
Howsehowld Stoofe			
Tubes, sexteene, 1 fate, 7 bowles, A Cover, a Booshell, A kneding trow, A Chese Presse, A Cherme	1	0	0
1 Caudron, 1 brass potte, 5 Cettles and a skcllett	1	6	8
6 platteres, 3 pewter disshes, 4 sacers, A poringer, A pewter Cooppe, A latten Bason, A latten Chaffing Dishe, A pinte potte, 2 Saltes, 5 Candelsteckes, 6 spoones All these praysed at		18	0
2 fattes, 2 hande Billes, 2 other billes. A matthoocke, 2 Axes, A pronge		5	0
A potthanger, 2 Cobirnes, A trefte, A grideirn, A spite, A fring pan, potte hoockes, A peare of tonges		5	0
A table, a forme and stooles and 2 Boockes, 6 disshe, A joine stoole		3	4
2 Coburdes	1	0	0
4 peare of shetes	1	0	0
4 table Clothes		8	0
2 ould peelows		2	0

2 Beddes a fe[*ther*] and a flo[*cke*]	1	16	8
4 Chestes, A Cofer and A presse		8	0
1 Clocke, 2 Gerkins, 1 pear of hose, 1 peare of Stockinges, 3 shertes and a hatt	1	13	0
4 Sackes, an host hear, 2 painted Clothes		4	8
A Carte, a lettell Cart and A Dongcarte, A harow		10	0
3 Laders		2	6
Heay and tares in the baren		6	8
A fanne and A panell		1	8
	[*29*	*16*	*2*]

Note: The undated Will was proved on 29th May 1593. A life interest in all his goods was to go to his wife Joan. After her death, his cousin John Griffen, the executor, would be the residuary legatee. No overseers were appointed, but John King, George Griffen and Thomas Woodman made their marks as witnesses and Raphe Lambert signed the Will. The testator asked to be buried in Fetcham churchyard. He gave 3s 4d to the church and 4s to the poor. Bequests of money varied from 4d to some godchildren, to £1 for the favoured John Albroke and George Griffen. His brother's children Annes White, Francis, Alis and Annis Griffin and William Monke, were given small bequests. Harry Stint was the only person to be given livestock: a black cow. The executor of Fetcham, husbandman, was bound well and truly to administer the estate. It is possible that the entry of the burial of John Griffin on 21st December 1588 refers to the testator and that on 6th March 1596 to his cousin, the executor.

Ref: 1593 B 30/1 Will 1593 B 30/2 Inventory

George Hudshon **319**

of Little Bookham, clerk and parson; taken by Edmond Hudsone and John Albroke, 26th May 1593.

	£	s	d
In the Halle			
1 Joyne Table with a Frame, fyve Joyne Stooles, 2 Chayres, a paynted Cloath, a smale Table, a Lynnen Wheele		8	8
A payre of Potthangers and hookes, a payre of Tonges and a gridiron			8
In the Kitchine			
Brasse and Pewter with other Lumbermentes		10	4
In a Little Chamber			
A Bedstedle, a feather Bedde, a Flocke bedde with that belongeth thereto		17	0
In the Bake Howse			
A Bowltinge Hutche, two Keavers with other necessaries		2	6
3 ould Tubes		1	6
In Upper Chambers			
One Beddstedle		3	4
One Cheeste, 6 payr of Sheetes, 2 Table clothes with paynted clothes	1	8	0
A Gune, a head pece, a sword, a Flaske and a Dagger		6	0
In his Studye			
6 Bookes		1	0
In the gate			
2 Bigges		3	4
In the Barne			
Haye and strawe		1	8
In the Feild			
One Acre and a Rodmeale of Wheate		10	0
A Quarter and half of Mawlte		16	0
His apparell		13	4
Money in his Purse		1	1
	6	4	5

The Inventory was exhibited on 29th May 1593 and Letters of Administration were granted to Anne, the widow. The deceased was named as rector of Bokeham Parva. His widow and Edmond Hudson of Bokeham Magna put up the Administration Bond. Ref: 1593 Ad 43

Rowland Marden **320**

of Reigate, husbandman; 27th May 1593. [*no appraisers given*]

	£	s	d
1 acker and a halfe of wheate	1	4	0
1 acker and a halfe of Rye	1	4	0
1 acker 3 Roodes of ottes	1	6	8
A red hacked heyfor	1	10	0
A 2 yearlinge bolloke	1	0	0
4 hoges	1	6	8
6 payre of shettes	1	0	0
A brasse potte		8	0
A brasse panne		1	0
2 kettelles		3	0
6 platters		3	0
3 kanstikes			6
A quarte potte			8
All the beddinge		10	0
3 bedstedes		2	0
4 chestes		4	0
In the halle			
A table and a forme		1	6
A table and a forme		1	0
A cobberd of waynscote		6	8
2 chayres and a stolle		1	0
In the kitchen			
The stoffe		3	4
2 trestelles, a spitte, 2 payre of pottehangers, a gridiorne and a fringe pane		3	4
2 table clothes		2	0
His apparell		6	8
The goods	11	9	0
Debtes owinge by the said Rowlande Marden whileste he lived amountheth			[blank]

On 30th May 1593, Alice the widow and relict, legal administratrix of all the goods and chattels, was sworn to the truth of the above inventory. Robert Dalton of Reigate, husbandman and William Borer of Burstow, husbandman, bound themselves well and truly to administer the estate. Ref: 1593 Ad 58

Note: The burial was registered on 22nd May 1593.

Roger Marete **321**

of Fetcham; taken by Thomas Blondel, John Marter and Thomas Wodman, 24th May 1593.

	£	s	d
Twelve shepe	3	0	0
Foure lambs		10	8
His Aparrell with on Chest and his bou and arros	2	7	0
	5	17	8

Note: The Will was dated 16th April and proved on 29th May 1593. Roger's master John Kinge was appointed executor and given 8 of the sheep; the remaining 4 with their lambs were to be shared between Joan Swifte and Joan Arnold, who were also to have his chest. There was no mention of overseers. Three and a half yards of woollen cloth intended for his livery, two doublets and two pairs of venetians, were given to Roger Williter. The rest of his apparel, namely hat, jerkins, hose and shirts, were given specifically to William Williter, William Constable, Robert Tegge and Oulde Renolde. The named witnesses were Roger Wood, John Kinge, Thomas Wodman, William and Roger Williter, William Constable and Thomas Peter.

Ref: 1593 B 49/1 Will 1593 B 49/2 Inventory

Roger Mathew **322**

of Chadsworth, Thames Ditton, collier; taken by John Walter, James Kelette and Richard Perkis, 27th May 1593.

	£	s	d
A paire of Hoose and a dublet and a cloak with other waring Clothes		13	4
One Fetherbed and a bolster, a blanket and coverlet with a plaine bedsted and seeling	1	0	0
One Flockbed and a bolster, a blanket and coverlet with a plaine bedsted		10	0
16 paire of sheetes and 2 table clothes	2	0	0
4 old Chests, a Cubbard, 2 formes and a table, a paire of tressels and 2 old stooles		7	4
2 spinning wheeles		1	0
5 platters, 5 pewter dishes, 2 saucers and a salt cellar		5	8
4 Kettels, one brasse pot and a chafing dish		16	0
2 tubbes and 2 bucketts and 3 bouls, 3 trayes, 6 dishes, one doosen of trenchers, a Charne, a chesmot and a follower with a chesepresse		3	0
2 Cobirons, one trifte, a paire of pothookes, a paire of pothangers, a spit, a bill and an axe and a gridiron		2	6
4 Kine	4	0	0
16 sheepe and 2 Lambes	3	0	0
A mare		10	0
3 Hennes and a cock		1	4
A Hogge		3	4
One acre of Rye and 2 akares of Oates	1	10	0
	15	3	6

Note: The Will was dated 17th April and proved on 30th May 1593. The testator's wife Isabel and son John were appointed joint executors and residuary legatees. Sums of 2s 6d each were given to the two overseers William Parker of Thames Ditton and Bartholomew Roger of Sutton, both husbandmen, who with the widow put up the necessary bond of administration. The only bequests were of £2 apiece to his three daughters Elizabeth, Isabel and Joan, at the age of 16. Mathew Saunders, minister, signed the Will and the testator made his mark, as did Richard Perkis and William Parker.

Ref: 1593 B 51/1 Will 1593 B 51/2 Inventory

Agnes Peeters **323**

of Great Bookham; taken by Edmond Durdine and Raph Crowcher of Great Bookham, yeomen, 28th May 1593.

	£	s	d
Two Gownes, one Petycoate and a Saufgard	1	10	0
Three Working daies Pettycoates		3	0
Two Peeces of Wollen Cloth		13	4

One Peece of Lynnen		5	0
One Chest with lock and kye with fyve paire of sheetes and one ode sheete	1	0	0
One Chest with lock and kye and filled with small Lynnen		10	0
One other Lyttell Chest with small Lynnen		3	4
One Wollen Wheele, one Lynnen Wheele, one Paire of Wollen Cardes		2	0
One Nett with fyve pound of Lynnen Yearne		5	0
Two Hattes		2	0
Foure Platters, foure Pewter dishes, foure sawsers, 3 Pottes and three saltes		6	8
One Iron Posnett, one of brass, one brass pann, one Latten Candellsticke		3	4
One flock Bedd and one Coverlett		5	0
Foure Oulde Tubbs		1	0
Her Redy Money being Payable uppon a Bonde at Bartholomew Tyde Next	45	0	0
	50	9	3

Note: The two appraisers signed the document with their marks. Alice Stacie and Johanne Gray, the natural sisters of Agnes, brought the Inventory to court and their husbands were duly bound to see the goods and chattels well and truly administered. Matthew Stacie of Fletching in Sussex, sawyer and Edward Gray of Great Bookham, labourer, appeared on 29th May 1593 each to claim one third part for his wife. Richard Blundell, son of Henry Blundell of Dorking, laid claim to the remaining third share.

Ref: 1593 Ad 67

Thomas Peter **324**

of Fetcham, husbandman; taken by John Kynge, John Marter and Gorge Gryffyne, men of Fetcham, anno 1593.

	£	s	d
Three Kyne and on bolocke	6	3	4
On Mare		6	8
Four yonge hogges		18	0
To akers and a halfe of wheate	2	0	0
Four akers of barlye	2	8	0
To akers of peazen and otes and on aker of tares	1	4	0
On platte of beanes		3	0
For the poultorye		5	2
For geese and gozlynges		4	8
On longe Carte, on Dongcarte, on payer of Wyeles with all belongeinge therto	6	0	?
For the stufe in the barne		3	4
On beel, on axe and allother kind of tooles		7	0
To brase pots and a posnette		12	0
All the Resedue of brasse with an old panne		13	4
Four peuter platers and sixe peuter deshes, to sacers		11	0
On pynte potte, three goblets, to drynkinge potts, thre saltselers		3	0
Four Candelstyckes and on lytel spyce Morter		2	8
To bandirons, on speete, on frying pan, on gredyan		3	4
On bed, on bolster with all belonginge therto		13	0
To lyttall flocke bedds with all belongyng thereto		15	0
To Lyttell pillos		2	0
Three table Clothes		8	0
Eyghte payer of sheets	3	0	0
Seven napkyns		4	8

Five Chestes		10	0
On Coverlet		5	0
11 boosshels of Wheate	1	2	0
Hempe and flexe		7	4
Twentie pounds of Lynnen Yearn		9	8
Thre bedstedles		4	0
All hys apparrell	1	3	4
To quarters of barly and malte	1	2	0
On bakon Trofe with all woodden vessell and lumbermente	1	5	4
The Hoorss		8	0
Five staulls of beies		16	0
To Cobbards		10	0
Thre Tables, to Lynen whels, on old woollen whell, on old payer of Stockardes, to Chayers		12	0
Old Paynted Clothes and Woodden deshes		2	0
	30	13	10

Note: The Will was dated 24th February and proved on 29th May 1593. The executrix and residuary legatee was the testator's wife Joan, who was instructed to pay all the legacies before she married again. Sums of 2d each were given to the overseers Thomas Roger of Fetcham and John Kinge. The testator asked to be buried in Fetcham churchyard and gave 2s to the church and the same to the poor. Two of his six children were to be paid in the old-fashioned coinage of nobles: Thomas was to have 20 nobles (£6 13s 4d), 10 to be paid after 6 years and 10 after 12 years; Mary was to have 10 nobles (£3 6s 8d) on her wedding day or at the age of 20; some household items were also bequeathed to her. Of the three other sons, Robert was to have a cow, all the land and some items of furniture; Richard was given wheat and barley and some cobirons previously lent to him; and John was given malt and was excused repayment of a debt. Maude the other daughter was given malt. All the godchildren were to have 6d each. The witnesses were the overseers and Thomas Woodman. Nine days later on 7th April 1593 Thomas Peter was buried. The administration bond was provided by the widow and John King of Fetcham, husbandman.

Ref: 1593 B 59/1 Will 1593 B 59/2 Inventory

John Ridford **325**

of Wotton, yeoman; taken by Mr William Comber, Henry Bristo, Henry Astone, William Steevens and Robert Rogers. [*no date given*]

[*In his Chamber*]	£	s	d
One Rousset cloke of his, with the Reste of his aparell and the monne in his purse	1	0	0
The bedstedell, the bed all thinges belonging to it	1	0	0
15 pare of sheetes	3	6	8
In the other chamber			
A bedstedell, the bed and all thinges belonging to it and a prese and 4 chestes	1	13	4
4 tabelclothes, a Dossen and a halfe napkins	1	2	0
and 4 Kossens and a broshe		2	0
In the hale			
One tabell with a settell and formes and chayres with a Cuberd and a side tabell		13	4
In one other Chamber			
2 bedstedes and bedes with ther furnituer and one chest in that chamber and sertayn other thinges in the same chamber	1	10	0
In the Chichin			
The brasse and the peuter and an ould couberd and sertayn other impelments in that same Kichen	2	0	0

	£	s	d
One welbucket and a chayne		1	0
In the Buttery and the mylkehouse			
Sertayn Impelmentes		10	0
For Rye, moulte and wotes	2	0	0
One payre of andyerns and tonges and other peeses of ould Iorne		5	0
3 Oxsens with a ween, yokes and chaynes with one ploue and one harru and one Dung Carte	7	0	0
2 small Kyne, 4 bullokes and 3 wenner calfes	6	13	4
One horse, a mare and a coult	2	4	4
60 ould sheepe and 28 Lames	15	0	0
5 smale shootes		16	8
7 Acares of winter Corne standinge one the grounde	4	13	4
8 Acares of smale wottes	2	0	0
	53	10	0

Note: The Will was dated 22nd March and proved on 29th May 1593. The executrix and residuary legatee was the testator's wife Alice, who was to raise money from his property until his sons came of age. Sums of 20d each were given to the overseers Henry Bristowe and Robert Rogers, both of Wotton. He asked for christian burial and gave 3s 4d to the poor. His daughter Elizabeth was left £30 and the younger daughters, Mary and Sara, were left £20 each, to be paid when they married. The survivors would inherit the legacy, if a sister died young. When he reached the age of 21 his son Robert would inherit Kempslade and at the same age another son John would inherit Abrahams in Abinger, then in the occupation of John Sponer. Robert was to have one table, a settle with the benches and forme in the hall, also a watering vat and from the chamber at the west end of the house, a bed and bedding to count as "standerdes not to be removed". John was to have a bed and bedding from the loft over this chamber. The rector of Wotton, Robert Higham, signed the Will on which John Redford made his mark; Ralph Dalton had written the document, also witnessed by the overseers.

Ref: 1593 B 63/1 Will 1593 B 63/2 Inventory

John Todie alias Farrawle **326**

of Bagshot in Windlesham; taken by Thomas Baker, George Hawssard and Henry Stythurst, 9th April 1593.

In the hall	£	s	d
2 brasse Kettelles, one brasse pott		13	4
A basen and a ewer		2	6
3 platters, 4 pewter dishes, one olde Basen		5	6
3 porrengers, 1 fruite dishe, 3 pewter flower pottes, 1 sawcer		1	6
3 Joyned stooles		2	0
A payre of cobbirons and a pothanger		1	4
2 candlestickes, 1 salt, 1 quart pott		3	0
	1	9	2
In the Chamber			
2 old chestes		2	0
A fetherbed, a flocke bowlster and a coverlet and 1 painted cloth	1	0	0
2 payre of sheetes		6	8
A sworde and a dagger		6	8
3 cushins		1	6
	1	16	10
His apparell			
2 Dublettes and a Jerkin, 2 payre of hose and 2 cloakes	2	0	0
A mannge horsse		3	4
2 smale hogges		3	0

A weanier calfe		10	0
1 cowe prysed at	1	13	4
and she lies at pawne for £1.6.8			
And old Lanterne			2
	4	9	10
For the Lease of the house and the glasse aboute the house		13	4
For the haie that remaineth		3	4
For fuell and the Dunge in the yard		1	0
		17	8
[*£8.13.6*]	8	12	6
less pawn redemption			
	1	6	8

Administration of the goods and chattels of the deceased was granted to Thomasina, relict of the deceased, on 29th May 1593. The administration bond was provided by the widow and William Campion, clerk, of Windlesham. Ref: 1593 Ad 88

1594

Marie Bishop **327**

of Dorking, widow; taken by Hugh Mason, Michaell Earle and Henrie Browne, of Dorking, 13th May 1594.

	£	s	d
3 pewter platters, 2 pewter dishes, one sawcer		4	0
One brasse kyttell, one brasse possnet, one latten morter with a pestell, one latten candlestick		6	0
2 paire of shetes		6	8
One old Coverlet		3	0
Too olde chestes		3	0
One Cowe	1	13	4
A brasse pott		3	4
[*£2.19.4*]	2	13	4

On 14th May 1594 the Administration of the estate was entrusted to John Matthews, son of the deceased, of Dorking, turner. He and John Burster of the same place, husbandman, had raised the necessary bond. Ref: 1594 Ad 5

John Hone **328**

of Bisley; taken by John Kobbat the elder, John Avis, Thomas Goringe and William Hone, 1594.

	£	s	d
He had in his purse		1	0
His wearinge aparril		6	8
A table and a forme, to stoles		1	0
The brasse and pewter		3	0
A broche and a tryfte and potthockes			8
To flocke beddes with the bolsters and coverlyts and a blankat and apeare of shetes		7	10
A bedsted, to chestes and all other Lomber		3	0
Foure bushells of Rye in the house		6	0
Thre akars of winter corne one the grounde	1	10	0
Fyve akars of ottes on the grounde		15	0
On Cow, to heckefers and foure smale bollockes and a lyttell mare	5	0	0

On tegge		1	6
A Karte and a donge potte		3	4
Fyve hennes and a Coke		2	0
	[9	*1*	*0]*

Note: The Will was dated 23rd February and proved on 14th May 1594. The executrix and legatee for life of all his goods and unnamed lands in Bisley and Horsell was the testator's wife Alice. Sums of 12d each were left to the overseers Henry Atfeld and Thomas Goringe. John asked for a christian burial and he willed that after his wife's decease the lands should go to his son John and his heirs, or failing that, to his son Joseph and his heirs. John was given 2 steers and Joseph £5 at the age of 21. When his daughters Joan and Anne reached the age of 20, they were each to have a cow. Francis Taylor wrote the Will, which was witnessed by John Atfeld, John Kobbat the elder and Austin Woods. The widow and the said John Kobbat of Bisley, weaver, bound themselves well and truly to administer the estate. The dates on both documents were written firmly and clearly 1594, although at that time it was usual to record February as 1593.

Ref: 1594 B 30/1 Will 1594 B 30/2 Inventory

Christopher Mathew **329**

of Streatham, husbandman; taken by William Partyn, John Vilett and Richard Marson, 7th May 1594.

	£	s	d
In the Hale			
A table planke with a payre of tresseles, a forme, 4 Joyned Stoles, an old tourned Chaire and an olde Cupborde		8	0
An old Chiste and the paynted Clothes aboute the hale		2	6
In the Chamber over the hale next the streate			
A lyttle olde bedsteade, a fether bead, a coverlett of tapestrye, an old Darnex cuverlett, one boulster of ffethers, an other of fflox	1	0	0
2 Chistes and a lyttell spruse Cofer beinge olde		4	0
In the nexte chamber over the hale			
An olde ffeilde bedsteide, an olde ffether bedd, 2 old bolsteres of ffethers, one fflocke bolster, 2 white blankettes, an olde gray Rugg, an old coverlett and an olde Chiste		10	0
In Lynnen five payre of old towen sheetes, tow olde table clothes, foure olde napkins and an olde pillowbeare		12	0
In the chamber over the mylke howse			
An olde bedsteade and certeyn olde loumber		5	0
In the kytchin			
Fyve olde brasse kettles, tow olde brase panns		13	4
Three olde brase chafynge dishes, fyve olde brase candlestickes, a postnett and a morter of brasse		4	0
Tow olde skelletes, a warminge pann		2	0
3 lytell olde brasse pottes and 3 lytell olde brasse possnetes		8	0
12 platters, fyve dysshes, one lytell bason, tow pye plates, 3 sawseres of pewter		12	6
Tow quarte pottes, one candlesticke, one Chamberpotte, one littell goblett, all of pewter		2	6
Fowre lyttell spittes, tow potthangers, a payre of Rackes, a payre of pott hockes, a dryppinge pann, a gryrdiron and a payre of Cobirons all of Iron		5	0
An olde cupborde, 2 olde dresser bourdes and other lomber		1	0
Certayne olde bourdes and lomber in the mylke howse		1	0
3 Awgers, a nayle percer, a sawe, a bill and an ax		1	0
In cattell			
2 Kyne, 2 smale bullockes, 6 younge Sheepe	4	13	4

	£	s	d
4 olde horses with theire drawinge harnes	3	6	8
An olde longe Carte and an old Dounge Carte		10	0
The wheate of the grounde, the rent deducted		13	4
Three acres of otes in grasse, the rent deducted	1	0	0
The Lease of his howse and of the grounde thereto belonginge	2	0	0
Foure henes and a cocke		2	6
[*£17.17.8*]	17	7	8

On 15th May 1594 Cicelie, the relict of the deceased, was granted letters of administration of the goods and chattels. She bound herself well and truly to administer the estate, together with John Allen of Streatham, yeoman.

Ref: 1594 Ad 43

Richard Mychinall **330**

of Seale; taken by John Hampton, William Hampton and William Preston, 25th April 1594.

	£	s	d
His apperrell and 6 pence in monye in his pursse		3	4
A littell Sowe yelt		2	6
A Joyned bedstede, A fetherbed, a Coveringe and a paire of Blankattes	1	0	0
Three flockbedes, A standinge bedstede with Simple furniture	1	0	0
A Table and trusles, A chaire and a forme wythe Stowles		5	0
A Coupborde		8	0
A powderinge trowe, wythe other smale tubbes		6	8
One paire of lockerom sheettes, 3 paire of canvas sheettes and table napkines		10	0
3 coffers		3	4
2 lityll broches, a dripping pan and a trift		2	6
In Brasse and puter	1	6	8
A paire of potthookes, pott hangers and an andier		1	0
One buckinge hutche, a kever, a keeve, a lityll powderinge tubbe and a chaire		2	6
In pulterye		2	0
In Redye monye	14	0	0
[*£19.13.6*]	19	14	2

The appraisers used distinctive marks rather than signatures at the end of the inventory.

Note: The Will was dated 8th February and proved on 14th May 1594. The executrix and residuary legatee was the testator's wife Agatha. A sum of 5s each was left to the overseers, William Hampton of Hampton and Richard's son William, in whose hands £11 was already deposited for payment of the legacies within the ensuing 3 months after Richard's decease. His children and grandchildren had legacies of money: the 3 sons Thomas, William and John, were left 6s 8d, 6s 8d and 20s, respectively; the daughters Isabel, Katherine and Joan Jewer together with Joan's husband, were to have £5, £5 and £1 to add to the £1 already paid to the Jewers; Mary, Joan and Anne, Thomas's children and the Jewer's son William, were each given 2s. Richard asked to be buried in Seale churchyard, giving the minister 6s 8d and the church and the poormen's box 20d each. After Agatha's death the residue was to go to 4 of the children equally: John, Isabel, Katherine and Joan. Three named witnesses were William Hampton, Thomas Mychinall and Thomas Hogge. The burial was recorded on 8th April 1594.

Ref: 1594 B 45/1 Will 1594 B 45/2 Inventory

John Williamson **331**

of Elstead, wareburner; taken by John Stovall, Thomas Tribbe, John Hampton and Willyam Bromhall, 12th May 1593.

	£	s	d
Money in his purse	10	0	0
His apparrell	4	0	0
The stuffe in the parlar			
A standinge bedsted, on flockebed, a fetherbede, 2 bousteres, one coverlet, 7 quissinges, one old forme, hanging clothes	1	10	0
Stuff in the hall			
A cubbard, a tabell bord upon a frame, 2 formes, 2 chayers, 2 anIrones, a fyer panne, a payer of tonges, a payer of bellowes		13	4
The stuffe in the lofte over the hall			
One bedsted, a flockebed and one bouster, one coverlet, 3 tables and 2 trastells, 2 formes, 2 anIrons and on paintid cloth		14	0
The stuff in the loft over the parlar			
A bedsteed, 2 flockebedes, one bouster and 1 coverlet, 2 litell ioyned tables, one forme		16	0
In the loft over the buttry			
2 bedsteedes, 2 flockebedes, 2 bousteres, 2 coverletes, 4 pillowes, 4 chestes and coffers, in linnin 8 payer of shetes, five tabell clothes, 6 tabell napkins, 4 pillowberes	2	0	0
In the buttry pewter			
In pewter platters one doussin, in pewter disses sixe, 3 salt sellers, 10 sawceres, 3 pewter pottes, 2 doussin of pewter spones, Old wodde vessell	1	6	0
In the Chichin in brasse			
3 pottes of brasse, one great cathan, five kettelles, one chaffin dyshe, 2 great brasse posnettes, 2 litell posnettes, one ladell of brasse, five brasen candellstickes, on litell brasse panne, a fryinge panne, 2 payer of pothockes, 3 payer of Iron hangers, 3 spittes	1	13	4
In wodden vessells		5	0
3 flaggin bottells		1	6
In workin tolles		1	0
In bacon		6	8
All his Iron tolles for his trad and his ashes in the kill house	1	6	8
The wood in his gate	5	0	0
One sowe and 8 small shutes	1	13	4
His 2 guyldines	2	13	4
His saddell and bridell		4	0
His kinne and hayffers, 6 calfes	14	0	0
In corne			
In rye in the fild 9 aceres	3	10	0
In ottes 7 aceres	1	10	0
In barly 2 acers		10	0
His corne in the barne		12	0
One stalle of bees		3	4
In powtry		2	6
	54	12	0

Note: The Will was dated 2nd May 1593 and probate was granted to Juliane, the widow and executrix, on 17th April 1594, having first been sworn to the truth of the Inventory. She had previously bound herself to carry out the administration well and truly, together Robert Ansell, yeoman and Richard Gosden, yeoman, both of Elstead. The poor of Elstead were given 2s and the maintenance of the bridge was helped by 1s. His two sons Harry and John and his daughter Elizabeth, were left £16 each. A sum of £10 was left "to that child wherewith my wiffe is now great withall". Small amounts were to go to a sister Mabel, a godson John Ansell and the maid Margaret Farrell. His wife was to inherit the residue of the estate. Robert Ansell and Richard Gosden as overseers were given 3s 4d apiece and were to put the legacies of the children out to best advantage. The burial of John Wyllyamsonne was recorded on 4th May 1593, two days after the Will was written.

Ref: 1594 B 67/1 Will   1594 B 67/2 Inventory

1595

Tristram Blabye 332

of Southwark, gentleman; taken by Thomas Corslett, William Mairton, Henrye Wythers, Thomas Savadge and William Mairton, 9th May 1595.

	£	s	d
Certaine bookes all preysed together to the somme of	2	6	8
One course white rugg prise		5	0
One doublet, one cloake, one paire of breeches, one coat and one hatt		10	0
Two litle bedsteedes		5	0
4 shelfes to laye bookes on		3	0
One old table and one forme		3	4
Certen old lumber beinge some thinges of brasse and some yearthen and the rest wood		10	0
Two pewter candlestickes, one litle bason, eight dishes, sixe porringes, fyve sawcers, one salte, one half pint pott, one cupp and sixe old spoones		8	0
One litle featherbed and two flockbedes, two flockbolsters, one feather boulster, one flockepillowe, one old rugge and one olde cheker for a Coveringe	1	0	0
Sixe paire of course simple sheetes	1	0	0
Fyve old table cloathes, 14 old napkins and 14 old towells		6	8
One litle old Truncke, three litle old boxes, one old deske and two old stooles		6	8
Certaine old stooles and formes for children to sitt and write uppon		6	0
Certaine doubtfull debtes to the somme of		16	0
	8	6	4

On 23rd May 1595 Augustus Hulet, notary public, was duly sworn to the truth of the Inventory and granted Administration of the goods and chattels. Ref: 1595 Ad 6

Thomas Bushe 333

of Chertsey, husbandman; taken by William Bannister, William Thetcher, Edward Rogers, [*blank*] Redworth and William Locksmyth, 12th May 1595.

	£	s	d
In the Hall			
The table and forme with stooles and 2 Chaiers		2	6
An ould settle and an old Chest		1	6
Ould stayned Clothes			9
In the Chamber			
A table and 2 ould Chestes and a deske		5	0
An ould bedsteade of boardes with a Feather bedd and boulster and a coverlett with another ould bedstedd		16	0
The stayned clothes			10
In the kitchinne			
A kneadinge troffe and a Chese presse with other lumber		1	10

All the dishes, boules, trenchers and spoones		1	4
A spitt, a grediron, trifte and pothookes		1	1
3 ould tubbes and old lumber there		3	4
In the kitchinn Loft			
ould Lumber			10
In the butterye			
Trayes, boules and earthen dishes and pottes		5	0
In the loft over the buttery			
An ould tubb, 2 quarters with boardes and ends of boardes		1	0
In the old Chamber			
4 tubbs and a shelfe		2	0
All the brasse and Pewter	1	0	10
4 paire of sheetes		10	4
1 Axe, a bill and a spade			10
2 sackes, one bushell and a pecke		3	0
All the ould Iron		3	4
The fewell and the old timber for fire		4	0
The carte and ploughe with their wheeles and furniture		15	6
All the harnes and trayce Collers and attire		3	6
2 stalles of bees		2	8
The dunge in the gate		3	6
A horse harrowe		1	6
All the rye and wheate	10	10	0
All the barly	7	0	0
All the pease and tears	6	0	0
6 Kyne	10	0	0
5 bullockes	3	0	0
6 horse, nagges and Coltes	4	6	8
All the swyne		8	0
Hennes and duckes		2	6
[*£46.19.2*]	47	0	11

Exhibited on 21st May 1595 by Roger Cole, notary public. Ref: 1595 Ad 10

Roger Crose **334**

of Egham, yeoman; taken by William Attweicke alias Weekes, William Bourton and William Gybson, 3rd June 1595.

	£	s	d
In the Chambre within the Hall			
One bedsteede, one feather bedde, one feather boulster, one feather pyllowe and one Coverlett		16	0
In the Chambre over the Hall			
One bedsteede withe a feather bedde thereuppon and all furnyture thereunto belongeinge	1	0	0
Tooe flocke beedes and all the furnyture unto them belongeinge		13	4
10 payre of sheetes	1	6	8
Tooe table cloathes		3	0
Too pylloebeeres		1	0
5 cheastes		8	0
In the Hall			
One coupboorde		5	0
Tooe tables, one forme and the steyned cloathes		4	0
Too dooesen of pewter, bothe plattres and dyshes and fyve sauceres withe too pewter saltes	1	0	0
3 pannes, greate and smale, 3 kaytles of bras, greate and smale, three			

bras pottes, grate and smale and thre brasen Candlestyckes, lytle and greate, withe a posenet of bras	2	0	0
One fryeinge panne, one grydIron, one potthanger, one spytte and one Aund Irone		2	6
6 tubbes, one powderinge troughe, one wollen wheele and one lynnen, withe dyverse other Lombre		10	0
Cattle abroade in the feilde			
Fowre kyne	7	0	0
One boullocke of three yeare olde, tooe boullocks of one yeare old and one waynenyere	2	0	0
Tenne horses, mares and coaltes	5	0	0
Three skore sheepe	12	0	0
8 hogges, greate and smale	1	4	0
Corne in the feilde			
6 acres of rie	4	0	0
4 acres of oates	1	0	0
2 leases for yeres	6	13	4
His wearing apparell	1	6	8
[*£48.13.6*]	55	14	6

Note: The Will was dated 1595 and proved on 5th June that year. The residuary legatee and executrix was the testator's wife Agnes. Sums of 3s 4d each were left to the overseers William Bartholomew and William Atwycke. Roger asked to be buried in the churchyard of Egham and he gave 12d to the poor of the parish. Joane, Barbara, Elyzabeth, Sara and Margaret, his 5 daughters were each left 10s, with an additional gift of 10 ewes to the said Elyzabeth and her husband. When they were 21 years old his sons William, Richard and Thomas, were to receive £5, £5 and £3, respectively. At the writing of the Will, Thomas was given two indenture-hold leases of unnamed property in Egham. The deeds were handed over for safe keeping to be held by William Atwycke in trust until the said Thomas came of age. The overseers, William Gybsonne and others unnamed, witnessed the Will. The widow was bound well and truly to administer the estate.

Ref: 1595 B 10/1 Will 1595 B 10/2 Inventory

Robert Elliot **335**

of Shalford, yeoman; taken by Rychard Punter, John Jelley, William Punter and John Mellershe, 28th May 1595.

	£	s	d
For his appareill and mooney in his Pursse	1	6	8
For his Chestes and a Table and Tressels		7	8
For Bedes and bedstedles with the furnitures	2	0	0
For the Corne and Mault in the howsse	1	10	0
For the Woole		10	0
For all the Brasse		16	0
For the Pewter		5	0
For the Lynnen		6	0
For all the Wodden Vessels		8	0
For twoo broches and aundyrons and a fryeng pane		5	0
For Bills, Axes, sythes and suche lyke tooles		6	8
For Seaven Rudder Cattle	9	0	0
For fyve Shepe	1	0	0
For the Swyne	1	6	8
For three Acers of Rye and Wheate	2	0	0
For Wotes one the grownd	1	0	0
For Soyle in the Gate		6	8
	22	14	4

Debtes dew to the said Robert Elliott			
Of Nicholas Elliott	16	10	0
Of John Jellye	7	0	0
Of Thomas Bycknold	5	0	0
	28	10	0
	51	4	4

Note: The Will was dated 11th May and proved on 5th June 1595. The executrix and residuary legatee was the testator's wife Elizabeth. Sums of 2s each were left to the overseers Richard Punter, his cousin and Thomas Mellersh of Grafham. Six of his children, Joane, John, Henry, Robert, Thomas and William, were each to have £5, the sons at the age of 21 or 25 at the discretion of the overseers and his daughter on her wedding day or at the age of 25. Richard, the eldest son, was to have the iron-bound chest and 10s a year to be paid out of the profits from the half house, barn and land called Noreland, in which the executrix was to have a life interest. Robert asked to be buried in the churchyard of Shalford. The overseers and Henry Elliott witnessed the Will. On 23rd May 1595 the burial of Eliot, Robard of Bramley was recorded in the parish register of Shalford. The widow proved the will and was granted administration of the estate.

Ref: 1595 B 14/1 & 2 Will (2 copies) 1595 B 14/3 Inventory

Henry Feilde **336**

of Chobham, yeoman; taken by Henry Lee, Thomas Taylor, Thomas Whey, John Beedl, John Bruxed, Christopher Feeld and others. [*undated*]

	£	s	d
Money in his purss		10	0
His Apparrell	1	10	0
In the Haule			
Two Cupboardes, one Table and A forme	1	0	0
In the Chamber			
A bedsteadell and A bed and A Cupboard and A forme and paynted Clothes	2	10	0
In the lofte			
Three bedds	2	0	0
3 Chestes and paynted Clothes		6	8
In a Lower Chamber			
Chestes and divers Lombery	1	10	0
In a backer Lofft			
Lombering stouffe		10	0
In another Chamber			
wheris A great sort of Tubbes		13	4
In another Rome			
Loumbering stouffe		5	0
In the Chichen			
A Quearne with other stouffe	2	10	0
A brase Pott and brase panne	2	10	0
Puter and Candelstickes	1	0	0
Cobbarns, hanggers, Trevitts with spades and bills and other Loumbery	1	0	0
Linnen sheetes and tableclothes and other linnen	2	10	0
Bacon in the howse		10	0
Sixe Oxen	15	0	0
Eyght Kyne	16	0	0
Three Horses	5	0	0
Tenn bollockes	4	10	0
A shod payre of wheeles and A Carte and A Cartladder with			

A payre of Ropps	2	6	8
A horse harow and A Oxe Harroo and yookes with Chaynes	1	0	0
Two downg poottes with Too payre of wheeles	1	0	0
Uppon the Grownde			
Rye	4	10	0
Oattes	3	6	8
Fortye sheepp	8	0	0
Tenn Lambes		16	0
A Sow and eyght shoutes and sixe pegges	1	10	0
Gesse and hennes		3	4
A Leace	30	0	0
	113	17	8

Note: The Will was dated 15th April and proved on 5th June 1595. The executrix and residuary legatee was the testator's wife Alice, who was to have control of the property for 16 years before handing it over to the eldest son Henry. Sums of 6s 8d were left to the overseers Henry Lee and Thomas Taylor, both of Chobham. The testator asked to be buried in the local churchyard and he gave 6s 8d for church repairs and 13s 4d to the poor. The bequest to Henry, his son, went into great detail concerning furniture, household stuff and farming stock and equipment, as well as the quern to be a standard of the house, the scales, 28 pounds of weights and £10 in money. The other 4 children, William, John, Agnes and Amy, were each left £25, which they were to inherit at the age of 21. Two leases and two deeds concerning the unnamed freehold and indenture-hold lands were to be kept by the testator's brother Christopher during Alice's tenancy. Five ewes were to be given to each of the 5 children at the age of 16 and there were minor bequests to his mother Sherbon, to his sister Joan Cobbett, to Agnes Hunt and to Henry Gressell. The 4 named witnesses were Thomas Whey the elder, William Ryden, Henry Sponge and Nicholas Feild. The widow was bound well and truly to administer the estate.

Ref: 1595 B 16/1 Will 1595 B 16/2 Inventory

Roger Foster **337**

of Lambeth, victualler; taken by John Ward, Fraunces Hyde and John Ashbrooke, 25th May 1595.

	£	s	d
In the hall			
On littell old table		1	6
On old rotten cubbard		1	0
In the parlor			
On littell table with a frame		2	6
On old Joyned forme			6
On dishe, on salt seller, on porrenger, on pint pott, all of pewter			8
On old Iron pott		1	0
A paier of crepers of Iron, a paier of townges and a fier shovell		1	0
In the littell chamber			
On old half headed bedstead, on materas, on pillowe of fethers, on old darnix coverlett		3	4
On old chest without lock or key			6
In the chamber over the parlor			
On half headed bedstead, 2 old materasses, 2 boylsters of flockes, 2 old coverlettes, on old blankett		3	9
2 old Joyned stooles and on old backe chayre			9
2 payer of old towen sheetes		3	4
On old table cloth			6
2 table napkins and on towell			7
His wearing apparell worth not the praysing			
The Lumber aboute the house		1	3

	1	2	2

Administration was granted to Elizabeth, the widow of the deceased, on 3rd June 1595.
Ref: 1595 Ad 18

John Fuller 338

of Dorking, carpenter; taken by John Woodman of Colley, Myles Dudley, Edwarde Nettlefoulde and William Hyll, yeomen; 26th May 1595.

	£	s	d
In hys Purse gyrdle and Money therein		5	0
Hys wearinge Apparrell	1	10	0
A Cupborde		6	8
A Table and forme		2	0
One Chayre and 2 lyttle stooles			6
All the brasse	1	6	8
2 Trevettes, one gredyarne, 2 potthangers, one ffyre panne, one Andyarne, one payre of potthookes, 2 spyttes, 2 dryppinge pannes, one fryinge panne		10	0
2 shelves		2	0
2 Twooe Hyttchelles			6
4 Leathren bottelles		3	4
2 spytters, one shovell, 2 bylles and one Axe		1	0
6 syckles		1	0
All hys Carpenters Tooles	1	0	0
2 bushels of wheate, 8 bushels of malte	1	2	0
4 bedsteddelles and 4 beddes, bolsters, Coverlettes, blanckettes and all thinges thereunto belonginge	2	0	0
All the Lynnen	3	6	8
6 Chestes		10	0
One Cupborde		10	0
All the pewter		12	0
One brusshe and 2 payre of sheares			6
Paynted clothes		2	0
All woodden vessell, dysshes, trenchers, bowles, Tubbes, buckettes, busshelles and Trugges	1	6	8
Bacon and beefe		12	0
An oste hayre		1	0
Woole		15	0
Hempen yarne		6	8
2 pytche forkes			6
2 sythes		2	6
One Harrowe		2	0
Carte and wheeles		6	8
3 Ladders and fower Rackes		3	4
Hogge Troughes, planckes, bordes, wood Poles and other Trumperye	1	0	0
Tyles		5	0
Stalles and bees		5	0
Hogge	1	4	0
Horse beastes	1	0	0
A gryndstone		1	0
Beanes and hempe	1	0	0
3 Acres of Teares	1	4	0
7 acres of Oates	2	13	4
4 Acres of Rye	4	0	0
3 Acres of wheate	2	0	0

8 bullockes, greate and small and 3 Calves	8	0	0
9 sheepe and 5 Lambes	2	6	0
5 kyne	8	0	0
Tymber		3	4
Powltrey		1	4
	51	11	2

Note: The Will was dated 7th April 1593 and proved on 5 June 1595. The testator gave 6s 8d to the poor of Dorking and he asked to be buried in the churchyard near to his other wife. The residuary legatee and executrix was his present wife Alice, who was to take over all his lands until the Michaelmas following his decease. There were 8 sons and 2 daughters. Unnamed copyhold lands in Wotton occupied by Henry Palmer were to provide £10 legacies for Richard, George and Ursula, at 2-yearly intervals. The testator gave these lands to his son John the younger, so presumably after 6 years had passed the annual rent of £5 would be paid by the occupier to John himself. John the elder was to have the lands in Capel bought from William Palmer. Myles was to inherit the tenancy of the leasehold lands in Capel held of the elder and the younger George Hoover. Joan was to have her £10 legacy split into 2 bequests of £5, the first a month after her marriage and the second a year later. Unusually for sons, William and Edward were to have their £10 bequests at their days of marriage paid by the executrix. Robert was to inherit all the bedsteddles, cupboards, benches, tables and standers, in the house. John the elder was the only child not to be given a pair of sheets. Alice and Lawrence Peter were to share a year-old heifer; Richard Peter, godson of the testator, was to have a ewe and a lamb and a similar pair of animals was bequeathed to his grandson John, son of John Fuller. Representatives of 3 well-known local families were asked to act as overseers: George Evelyn Esquire, Edward Nettlefold and John Woodman of Colley. Thomas Rusburgh wrote the Will in the presence of John Fuller the elder and Myles Fuller, sons of the testator. George Evelyn signed his name and the testator made a complicated mark. The burial of John Fuller was recorded in the parish register on 20th May 1595.

Ref: 1595 B 18/1 Will 1595 B 18/2 Inventory

Elizabeth Goddard **339**

of Cobham, widow; taken by Robert Awncell of Cobham, innholder and Nicholas Rytchbell of the same, husbandman, 3rd June 1595.

	£	s	d
A Cassock of Russett and a Red pettiecote and other old woollen clothes	1	6	8
3 old smockes, 3 Lynnen Aperns, A worsted Aperne, An Aperne of Lyncie woolsye, 3 dowble kerchers, 4 course handkerchers, 4 Crosse clothes and 3 dozen of spoones		6	8
In her pursse in money	3	0	0
An old kettle, 2 old hattes and a womans Cappe, her hose and shooes		6	8
	5	0	0

Administration of the goods and chattels was granted to Robert Mersh, son of the deceased. Also bound to see this well and truly carried out was Richard Williamson, clerk, of Cobham. Dated 4th June 1595. Ref: 1595 Ad 21

Robert Hooke **340**

of Milford in Witley, yeoman; taken by John Payne, gent., John Barret, William Hooke, Nicolas Woodyer and William Burle, 9th May 1595.

	£	s	d
In the Hall			
One table with a forme, one cubborde, one chayre, 4 Cusshinges, one old paynted cloathe, one Carpet and one ioyned stole	1	0	0
In the Loft where he Laye			
One ioyned bedsted, one playne bedsted, 4 flockbeddes, 2 bolsters, one fether			

bolster, 4 fether pillowes, fyve Coverlettes, two payer of blankettes, the paynted cloathes there and the bedhanginge	4	5	0
Fyve playne Cofers		8	0
3 table clothes, 10 payer of sheetes, six table napkins, one bed hangeinge of Lynnen, one payre of pillowe beares	3	0	0
In the servantes chamber			
One old bedstede, one flockbed with a Coverlet and a payre of blankettes		10	0
In the kytchin			
One pann, 4 kettelles, 2 brasse pottes and two postnetes	4	3	4
4 broches, 2 payer of Andyrons, one drippinge pann, 2 potthookes, 2 pott hangars, one gridiron, one fryinge pann and one trevitt	1	6	8
In the buttrye			
One dozen of pewter platers, one dozen of pewter disshes, 3 sawecers, 2 salt cellers, 3 Candlestickes, 2 dozen of spones	2	0	0
In the bakehouse			
One knedinge trowe, 2 powderinge trowes, 2 keeves, 2 fates with certayne old tubbes, 2 barelles, 3 fyrkins with certayne bowels and buckettes		16	0
One cheese presse, one ax, a byll, a shovell with certayne Augers		3	0
His Aparell	1	10	0
Money in his purse		7	0
3 fflytches of bacon		13	4
Corne in the barne			
12 busshelles of wheate	2	8	0
20 busshels of Rye	3	6	8
8 busshels of barlye	1	0	0
16 busshelles of oates		16	0
10 busshels of oaten malt		12	6
Corne in the feilde			
Six acars of Rye	4	0	0
Two acars of wheate	1	6	8
One acar of barlye		6	8
10 acars of oates	2	10	0
3 acars of pease and tares		15	0
Cattell			
Three oxen	6	3	4
Fyve keene	8	13	4
One steere of 2 yeares old		18	0
2 bullockes of one yeare old	1	0	0
2 old horse beastes	2	6	8
2 smale coltes		16	0
Fyve smale hogges	1	0	0
44 wether sheepe	10	10	0
18 Ewe sheepe	3	12	0
17 Lambes	1	14	0
One wagan with dong pottes, plough, harowes, yokes and chaynes	1	10	0
4 hennes and a cocke		2	4
Debtes oweinge to hym			
John Hooke oweth	14	0	0
Thomas Bradfold oweth	12	0	0
[£101.9.6]	102	2	10

Note: The Will was dated 16th April and was proved on 5th June 1595. The residuary legatee and executor was the testator's son Henry Hooke. His daughter Alice was given half the money in the house on the day the Will was written, half the household goods, 10 ewes, 10 lambs, a cow, a heifer and the £14 to be repaid by John Hooke of Bramshott. Of this sum she was to have £4 and her children £10. Henry was to have the £12 repaid by Thomas Bradfold of Milford. The servant Jane Hooke was given £2, a flock bed, a pair of sheets and a pair of blankets. A sum of 10s apiece was left to the overseers: John Barratt the elder, of Witley and the testator's brother William Hooke, of Godalming. He asked to be buried in the parish church at Witley. Witnesses were William and Henry Hooke and Alice Barrat.

Ref: 1595 B 28/1 Will 1595 B 28/2 Inventory

William Marshall **341**

of West Horsley, labourer; taken by Jeffery Richbell, Nicholas Fenne and Anthony Neave, 4th June 1595.

	£	s	d
In his purse		1	0
His Apparell		6	8
His Bedd chamber			
One standinge bedsteade, one truckle bed with 2 flocke bedes, 2 coverings, 2 boulsteres, 2 payer shetes, one tester	1	0	0
3 payre sheetes, 3 Table cloathes, 6 Table Napkins, 2 lockeren pillowbeers, 5 chestes and one lytle Hamper, 1 bowe and arrowes, 1 pronge and one flicke of bacon		10	0
In the litle Roome nexte the Hall			
One Table, 2 litle formes and 2 stooles		2	6
In the Hall			
One Joyned coubarde, one chayer, one Joyned stoole, 2 cousheons, one cradle and painted cloathes, etc.		13	4
In one other chamber			
One standing bed with a teaster of wainescott, one playne bedstead, 2 flockbeds, 2 bowlsters, 2 coverletes, 2 Tables with Tressels, 4 formes	1	6	8
In the Kitchin			
One brasse pott, 2 lytle Kettles, 3 posnetts, 3 candlestickes		12	0
8 pewter platters,8 pewter disshes, 3 quarte pottes, five saucers, 1 chamber pott, 4 salt sellers, one pottinger, 1 chaufing dishe, 1 skimmer, one Tinninge Ladle, 1 dozen spoones	1	0	0
1 spitt, 1 Trevet, 1 payer cob Irons, one grediorne, 1 payer pothookes and pothangers, one payer bellowes, 2 axes, a byll and 3 wedges, one spitter, 1 Lanthorne, 2 latine drippinge panns and 1 payer sheres		6	0
1 boultinge Hutche, a Knedinge troughe, 1 salte troughe, a bruinge vessell, six stabins, 3 Kivers and 1 bowle, 1 friinge panne, 1 clensinge sive, one brasse pestle and morter with other lumber as dishshes, trenchers, etc.		13	4
One lytle crofte of wheate about one acre, one acre peason	1	4	0
One cowe	1	10	0
One mare		13	4
Six swine, small and greate	1	0	0
Geese and a gander, seven goslings, 4 henns and one cocke		5	0
In the gate soyle		2	0
	11	19	2

Note: The Will was dated 23rd May and Probate was granted to Joyce, the executrix, on 5th June 1595. The son Thomas was to have copyhold land in Little Bookham, previously bought from William's father Philip . Another son John and a daughter Joyce were each to have £3 at the age of 21. The residue was left to the executrix Joyce, his wife. The 3 witnesses were Nicholas Fenne, William Hiller and John West.

Ref: 1595 B 36/1 Will 1595 B 36/2 Inventory

William Mylton **342**

of Windlesham; taken by Thomas Chippes and John Freman, 16 December 1594.

	£	s	d
His apparell		3	4
In the Chamber			
A ffetherbed and a bedsted		6	8
Paintinge clothes		2	0
A chest and a linnen wheele		1	0
2 paire of canvas sheetes and a pillowbeere		7	0
In the hall			
A flockbed and a flock pillow and an old bedsted		5	0
A table and a forme		2	0
An old cubbard		2	0
In pewter		8	4
In brasse		8	4
An old trumpery in the hall		2	0
An old wheele and cardes		1	0
A paire of potthookes and potthangers and a trevet		1	0
His tooles		2	0
In Cattell			
An old mare and a Colt		13	4
2 litle bullockes and a Cow	1	6	8
6 smale sheepe		15	0
2 henns			8
In Rie		6	0
An acre of Rie in the grounde		6	0
A grinstone			8
Hives		4	0
	[*£6*	*4*	*0*]

Note: The Will was dated 21st July 1592 and was proved nearly 3 years later on 5th June 1595. His wife Ellen was appointed sole executrix; she was to have the use of his house and lands, both arable and meadow, for 4 years, after which his two sons William and John were to inherit all but one little meadow called Russet, which was to be shared between his two daughters Rose and Ellen. William was to have the tools; John a ewe; Ellen a feather bed, bedstead and the best brass pot; and to Rose was given the best pan. The testator asked to be buried in Windlesham churchyard. Thomas Chippes of Windlesham and Edward White of Egham were appointed overseers and were given 3s 4d apiece. The two witnesses were Thomas Chippes and William Campion. The administration bond was provided by the widow and the aforesaid Thomas Chippes of Windlesham, husbandman.

Ref: 1595 B 37/1 Will 1595 B 37/2 Inventory

William Phillip **343**

of Windlesham; taken by John Holte, Henry Phillipes and Thomas Martin, 19th May 1595.

	£	s	d
His apparel and the monie in his purse		6	8
An old ffether bed, an old coverlett and all the rest of the beddinge		15	0
2 old chestes and an old presse		5	0
An old bedstedle and an old fryinge pan		1	6
One payre of sheetes and a table cloth		3	4

In the Hall			
An old table			6
2 brasse pottes		15	0
An old pan and a litle kettle		4	0
In pewter		8	0
2 old Cubbordes		8	0
2 old tubbes and 3 bowelles and other lumber		2	0
An old byll and a pronge and potthookes		1	0
In the garden			
Ten hives and a halfe of bees	2	0	0
In the yarde			
2 kine, 2 heiffers and a bullocke	6	0	0
2 old Nagges	2	0	0
Weathers and ewes and lammes	7	0	0
A yonge sowe, 3 yonge shutes		12	0
The soyle in the yarde		5	0
The third of an acre of oates		2	0
£3 of monie that is owinge to him	3	0	0
	[*£24*	*9*	*0*]

Note: In the Will dated 27th April 1595, the testator asked to be buried in the churchyard of Chobham and he left his copyhold land called Pipersland jointly to his wife Elizabeth and his eldest daughter Agnes, whom he made residuary legatees and executors. The overseers John Holt and his kinsman Henry Phillip, of Chobham, were each left 1s. Agnes was left 10 sheep and the remainder were to be shared between his wife Elizabeth and his daughter Elizabeth, who was also given a brass pot. His daughter's child Ann Groave was left a ewe and 1½ hives of bees. The other 9 hives of bees were left between the two Elizabeths. A third daughter Joan was to inherit a red heifer. A codicil left the bed and bedding to his wife and a black heifer to the daughter Elizabeth. Probate was granted on 5th June and details of the debts owing to William were £2 due from Henry Atfeild and £1 from Old Thayre of Horsell. The Will was signed by John Ball. The testator made his mark, as did 6 more witnesses: John Hoult, Henry Phillip, Thomas Groave, Agnes Groave, Thomas Martyn and John Atffeild.

Ref: 1595 B 42/1 Will 1595 B 42/2 Inventory

Henry Rapley **344**

of Chiddingfold, servant; taken by Robert Kerne, Stephen Rapley and Henry Penicode, 9th June 1595.

		£	s	d
His wearinge apparrell			6	8
The mony in his purse			5	0
2 Cofers			6	8
A stall of bees			2	6
19 old sheepe and 8 Lambs		4	0	0
In Woole			13	4
Debts due unto me				
John Peito doeth owe		2	2	0
Henry Moore			17	8
John Bradfolde			11	0
Thomas Rapley my Brother		1	0	0
William Peito			10	0
Richard Bradfold			4	0
Thomas Millward	[*£11.5.4*]		6	6
Debts which I owe				
I owe to Thomas Millward		2	2	0

To John Penicot	[*£2.14.4*]	12	4
	[*£8.11.0*]		

Note: The Will was dated 17th May 1595 and probate was granted to the executrix, his aunt Elizabeth Rapley, on 5th June 1595. The poor of Chiddingfold were given 20s, as were each of Thomas Millward's four children: Elizabeth, Jane, William and Henry, whose legacies were to be paid on the day of marriage or at the age of 21. Elizabeth Peito and Laurance Holt were given 1s each and Thomas Christmas had 2s. Julian Jindens was to have the bigger coffer and his aunt Elizabeth Rapley was to have the lesser coffer and the residue of the estate. Witnesses to the Will were Robert Kerne, Henry Penycode, Laurance Holt, Thomas Christmas and the writer of the testament, James Shelley. The testator had asked to be buried in Chiddingfold churchyard and had appointed no overseers. He was buried, as he had wished, that same day 17th May.

Ref: 1595 B 45/1 Will 1595 B 45/2 Inventory

Elizabeth Stint **345**

of West Horsley, widow; taken by Robart Roger, Edward Taylor, John Eliote and Thomas Hunt, 1st May 1595.

	£	s	d
In here Pursse	1	0	0
All here Wearinge apparell	2	6	8
2 flocke bedes with ther furnitue to the same	1	13	4
4 payer and one sheet with one table Clothe		18	0
All the pewter		5	0
2 brasse pottes 2 kyteles and twoe Skyletes		15	0
2 Chistes and twoe powdering tubes		2	4
1 gred yoron and a scomer, 2 dosen of trencher, one Tube		1	2
Debte owinge unto here	13	6	8
3 bushelles and ½ of wheate and one of maulte		17	0
One Cuberde		2	6
	21	7	8

Note: The Will was dated 18th February 1594/5 and was proved on 5th June 1595. The executor and residuary legatee was her son-in-law John Hudson of Great Bookham, husbandman. The two overseers, Thomas Hunte of Birchateland of West Horsley and John Stint of Send, were given 3s 4d for their diligence. The sum of 12d each was to go to the poor men's boxes of West Horsley and Great Bookham. One daughter, the wife of William Storke, was left 10s and her two children 5s each. Four other daughters were left £1 and their children 10s each. The only named grandchild was Katherine Croucher. The daughters were Anne, wife of the executor; an unnamed wife of William Croucher; Constance, wife of Edward Taylor; and Elizabeth, wife of John Eliote. One year after the decease of the testatrix, the children's portions could go to their parents or to themselves, given suitable guarantees. The witnesses were Bryand Parre and John Stint. The executor bound himself well and truly to administer the estate.

Ref: 1595 B 57/1 Will 1595 B 57/2 Inventory

Robert Wardell **346**

of Lambeth Deane, blacksmith; taken by George Mortymer, gentleman and Robert Netlingham, 19th May 1595.

	£	s	d
In the Halle			
A table, a forme with two tressells		5	0
A Cupbord		1	6
3 Cheyrs, fyve stooles and paynted clothes		4	6
2 pare of Andirons, a fyreshovell and tonges		4	4
2 Spetes, a gridiron, a dripping pan, pothangers and a Chopping knyf		2	8

A brasspotte, an Iron potte, 4 kettles, a skillet, a chafing dish, a skymmer, a pestell and morter, 2 Candlestickes	1	8	0
3 quart pottes, half a pynte pott, 2 basons, 2 porringers, 6 platters, 4 sawcers, a salt and a puter bottell		13	4
A Chamberpotte, 2 bowles, 2 payles, a trey, a wooden platter, 4 dishes, a brush, a cupbord cloth, a quyshon and half a dozen of trenchers		3	4
In the parlour			
A fetherbed, a coverlet, 3 pillowes, a bolster, 2 blanketes and a bedstead	1	3	4
A forme, a Joyned stoole, 8 cofers or Chistes, a Cupbord, a bowe, a quyver of arrowes and paynted clothes	1	10	0
9 pare of shetes, 2 pillowbears, 3 table clothes and four napkins	2	15	0
His apparell	1	6	8
In the Chamber			
2 bedsteades, 2 flockbeddes, 2 coverlettes, 2 blanketes, a table, 2 tressells and paynted clothes	1	0	0
Tubbes and other Lumber		3	4
In the shoppe			
A pare off bellowes		13	4
An Anvell, a beacon, 9 sledges and hammers and three pare of tonges		13	4
A Vyce, a hammer, pincers and fyles		5	0
Old Iron		5	0
A trough, 3 blockes, a litle Cofer and weightes with Scales and a halter		2	6
In the yarde and Streete			
Seacole		5	0
Bavens, pooles and Talwood		6	8
Logges, a Gryndstone and a troughe		13	4
2 Ladders		1	0
A planke		2	0
A Cocke and fyve hennes		2	6
A Lease of an acre of ground called the barnyard		13	4
	15	4	0

Administration of the goods and chattells listed truthfully in the above inventory was granted to Winifred, the widow of the deceased, on 21st May 1595. Ref: 1595 Ad 60

Michaell Winge **347**

of Stoke d'Abernon; taken by William Cooke, Roger Davis, John Inwood and Edmond Hamford, 3rd June 1595.

	£	s	d
In the Hale			
One litle cubbard with table		6	0
One chaire with brandirons and other implementes		1	0
3 Kittles, one potte, one posnet		5	0
8 peces of pewter		2	0
In the litle chamber			
One bedde with thapurtenances		4	0
In the lofte			
2 beddes with boulsters, coverletes and one blanket		6	0
Twoe payre and one sheete		6	0
Three chestes		2	0
Paynted clothes		2	6
One cheese presse with other lumbermentes		1	0
Two kyne and one bullocke	3	10	0
Fower sheepe		12	0
Twoe pigges		1	8

	£	s	d
Corne in the blade		5	0
	6	4	2

Administration was granted to the widow, Anne, on 4th June 1595. Three people were bound that day. The widow, Roger Dewy of Stoke and George Bickerstaffe of the same, husbandman, provided the administration bond. Ref: 1595 Ad 64

1596

John Cooke **348**

of Walton upon Thames, parish clerk; taken by Thomas Deacon, Anthonye Machyn, Thomas Bouland, William Heathfeeld, with others, 13th May 1596.

In the haull	£	s	d
One Joyned Tayble, 1 litle round Tayble, 2 formes, 3 stooles, 1 chayre and A paynted cloth		2	6
One Cubberde, 1 platter, 5 disshes, 4 sawsers, one potte, all of puter with 2 candlestickes and 1 laver		13	4
2 Awndy Irons, 1 payre of potthanggers, 1 spytte and one payre of Tounges		2	0
In the lofte			
2 beddes wyth bedstydles, 1 blanckett wyth an oulde whyte Texterne and a kyvering	1	0	0
In the parler			
One bedstydle, 1 flock bed, 1 kyvering, a blancket and 2 paynted texternes		12	4
4 chestes, 3 paynted clothes		5	0
His apparell		10	0
In the backe lofte			
Ould lomber one wyth an other		5	0
In the buttrie			
One bras potte, 3 ketles, 1 chaffyng dysh and a Scommer		6	8
Tubbes, dysshes, yearthen vesselles one wyth an other and an ould hutch		5	0
in the yarde			
One chese presse and A lather		1	0
3 kyne	3	6	8
2 mares and A colte	1	1	0
One sowe, 2 sutes, 4 hennes and a cocke		7	0
2 Acres and a half of Rye and 1 yarde of wheate	1	5	0
1 acre and a half of Tayres		5	0
1 Acre and a yarde of barlie		6	8
32 shepe	4	10	0
	15	4	2

[*At the end of the Will appeared the following*:-]

Debttes howyng unto mee	£	s	d	
Robert Richbell 10 of ffagates		[*blank*]		
Goodman Fenne of Eavingham	1	0	0	
William Longhurste		6	0	
Waylter Longhurste		6	9	
John Kyng Junior	1	10	0	
Mr William Roger	1	15	0	
Anthonye Bryan senior one lode of byllett		[*blank*]		
Roger Bundell		19	0	that I gave to John my son moore
Humffray Smyth		7	0	

Thomas Woollmer	10	0
Thomas Noste	3	9
William Raunce	10	0
Rayff Payge upon A pawne		[* *]
William Buckwell, senior of byllet and tallwode and also in money	3	0
Wydow Ellice	3	8
Clement Hellonse	5	0
Mr Richardson, Sonburie	2	6
John Evens of Sondburie	2	4
Mr Seares	1	2
Thomas Graye	10	0
Goodman chypping one lode and a half of byllet		[* *]
Robert Rychbell for bynding of fagott	15	0
Thomas Wollmer one lode and a half of billett		[* *]
William Wooddman	3	8
Robert Mathewe	1	0
Nycholas Newman	1	2
Wydowe Wadbroke	2	0
Thomas Hathwell	1	0

Summa totall	10	1	0
Debttes owyng by mee for byllettes and other woodde the somme	3	12	2

Note: The introduction to the Inventory gave the date of death as 21st April 1596, two days after the Will was written. The testator gave 12d to the church of Walton and asked to be buried in the churchyard there. Probate was granted on 24th May 1596 to the co-executors and residuary legatees, his widow Agnes and their son Anthony. Agnes was to have the freehold for life, keeping it in good repair. If she should survive so long, she was to have the 14-year lease, held of William Wodeman, of an acre of ground by the Thames 'with the yerbydge About the same'. On her decease, another son John was to succeed his mother, paying annually '2 wheate cornes yf the same be lawffullie demanded', the rent having been all paid beforehand. Half an acre of meadow in the common Mead was to go likewise to Agnes and then to John, he paying 2d a year to the Queen 'holding of Sandon'. A cow at hire with Carpinter's wife was bequeathed to a son-in-law Thomas Taylor and a lamb each to two Taylor children. John's two children were also bequeathed a lamb. An extra item squeezed in at the bottom of the main Will recorded that John, the eldest son of the testator, was to have the copyhold for 3 years. The overseers Thomas Deacon and Anthony Machyn were to have 2s 6d apiece. The 5 witnesses were Richard Barton, the vicar of Walton, Edward Heard, Richard Reading and the overseers.

Ref: 1596 B 13/1 Will 1596 B 13/2 Inventory

William Cutt **349**

of Chertsey, husbandman; taken by Thomas Hamshire alias Wilkinson, John Cutt, John Walden and John Yonge, 3rd May 1596.

	£	s	d
In the Chamber over the Hall			
All his wearinge apparell and money in his purse	2	0	0
One Fetherbed and a ioynde Bedsted, a Coverled and a paire of sheetes, one flockbedd and a trundle Bedsted with a paire of Sheetes, a Blancket and Coverled, one ioynde Cubboorde and five Chestes with six paire of Sheetes in the same Chestes	3	0	0
In the Chamber over the Kitchin			
One fetherbed with a bedsted, blancket and Coverled and one Chest	1	0	0
In the Chamber over the Hall			
One mattris and ioynde Bedsted with that which belongeth thereunto		10	0

	£	s	d
In the Hall			
One Table with a frame, five ioynde stooles, one olde Cubboorde and a chaire with paynted Clothes		10	0
In the Kitchin			
Twenty peeces of pewter, two brasse potts, two pannes, a brasse Bason, 3 kitles, 3 spitts, a paire of Andirons, two paire of hangers, a paire of tonges, a Trivett with a Bucking Tubb and other Tubbs and Lomber	2	0	0
In the Buttry			
One old salte Tubb, one bowltinge Hutch and drinke Tubbs and bowles		5	0
In the Barne			
The Corne in the saide barne, Two Pronges and one fanne	2	2	0
In the Yard or gate			
One Longe Cart and a dunge Cart, a Plow, one litle harrow, two axes, a bill, a spade and a shovell	1	0	0
In the Stable			
A Geldinge and two mares with their harnais	3	0	0
Foure Kyne	5	0	0
Six bullocks, 3 of 2 yeres old and th other Twelve moneth olde	3	15	0
Forty Sheepe and 9 lambes	6	10	0
Five hoggs and 6 shootes	1	10	0
Foure henns and a Cock and two gese and a gannder		3	4
Sixe acres of Ry on the grounde	4	0	0
Two acres of barley on the ground	1	0	0
Foure acres of oates on the ground	1	0	0
All the Leases and interestes for yeares of all the landes and Tenementes that the said William Cutt was at his death possessed of	10	0	0
	48	5	4

Note: The Will was dated 15th April and was proved on 6th May 1596. The testator named his wife Ellyn as executrix. She was to have the first eight years of the lease of land held of the crown and the residue of the goods and chattels. Of the five children, the eldest son John was to have the remaining years of the aforementioned lease and some farming equipment. The eldest daughter Elsabeth would only come into a share if any of the three youngest children were to die before their £10 legacies fell due. The daughters Lettis and Ellyn were to benefit on their wedding days and the youngest son William was to have a double share: £10 from his brother John and £10 from his mother, who also had to provide the girls' shares. The overseers were John Cutt of Littleton, the testator's eldest brother and Thomas Hampshire alias Wilkinson. A sum of 3s 4d was to be given to the poor of the parish and the overseers were to take 1s each. The son John was to have a cart, a horse harrow and a plough. Three named witnesses were Thomas Handley, minister, Thomas Aunsell and Goodwife Walden. No bond was taken to ensure that the administration was well and truly performed.

Ref: 1596 B 14/1 Will 1596 B 14/2 Inventory

Rychard Davye **350**

of Shere, sawyer; taken by John Hill, William Risbridger, John Farleye, Robert Davye and John Hammonde of Farncombe in Godalming, 19th April 1596.

	£	s	d
His apparrell		10	0
Monye in his pursse		1	0
Twoo beddes and twoo boulsters	1	0	0
One bed steddell		5	0
Twoo coverlettes		6	8
One Pott of Brasse		6	8
One Skellatt			4

	£	s	d
One Spitt		1	0
One Fryinge Pann			4
Twoo Chestes		5	0
Fowere payer of Sheetes	1	0	0
Twoo pillowebeeres		2	0
Thre kerchiefes		2	0
Thre blanckettes		3	0
Fowere Kettelles	1	0	0
On chaffingdishe, one posnet, two candelstickes		4	0
One gridiorne, one shreddinge knyfe, one skimmer		1	0
One Trivett, one Anndiorne, one potthanger		2	0
Twoo wedges and one bittell		1	8
One olde Sawe, on sickell, one hayhoock, one Faggott hoock, one axe and a sheepe print		1	0
Fower platters		4	0
Nyne Pewter Dishes		5	0
Fower porringers, three sawcers		7	0
One olde Cubberde		3	0
One cheste		1	0
One Knedinge Troughe, one sault troughe, one table		5	0
One Beame, a payer of skales, twoo weightes		2	0
Twoo Augers, one wimbell			8
Thre olde Tubbes, one payer of tresselles		1	8
Six olde bordes		2	0
20 busshelles of Ottes		16	0
One Heyfor and a calfe	1	10	0
20 Sheepe Ewes and wethers	5	0	0
One Hogge		5	0
One obligation wherin Thomas Franncis and Thomas Champion are bounde in £22 for the payment of	11	0	0
One obligation wherin John Tickner and Henrye Tickner are bounde in £24 for the payment of	12	0	0
One obligation wherin Grigorye Elliot and Edwarde Elliot ar bounde in £22 for the payment of	11	0	0
Allso of Thomas Franncis without specialtye	5	0	0
Also of Rychard Hamonde with out specialtye	4	10	0
	[*£58*	*4*	*10*]

Note: No date is recorded for the writing of the Will, which was proved on 26th May 1596. The testator asked to be buried in the church or churchyard of Shere and he generously gave £4 to the poor there and a further £2 to the poor of Albury. John Hammond's widow was left £5 and the overseers, Goodman Farley and Henry Ventris, were left 6s 8d between them. William and John Davies were left £2 and £1 respectively. Most of the household goods were bequeathed to Robert Davies. Probate was granted to Alice, his widowed sister-in-law, lately the wife of his elder brother John and mother of the two girls, still minors, whom he had appointed joint executrixes and who were to inherit a bed and the chest containing his "wrightinges". The two nieces, Jone and Rachel Davies, would thus inherit the major part of the estate. No witnesses are recorded. A memorandum was added in which he mentioned the gifts to Mary and Richard Davies. The administration bond was provided by Alice, Raph Carpenter of Godalming, clothier and John Farely of Shere, shearman. The burial of Rychard Davy was recorded in the Parish Register on 17th April 1596.

Ref: 1596 B 17/1 Will 1596 B 17/2 Inventory

William Deringe **351**

of Bramley in Shalford, yeoman; taken by John Street, Richard Puntter and Steven Ticknor, of Bramley aforesaid, yeomen, 24th May 1596.

	£	s	d
In the Hall			
A Table with a frame, a forme and a Cupbord	1	0	0
In his bedde Chamber			
Two bedstedles and two fetherbeddes with their furniture and 3 Chests	4	0	0
6 paire of Sheetes, two table Clothes and 6 Napkins	1	11	8
In the servinntes Chamber			
A Course flockbed with his furniture and one old Chest		6	8
In the Butterie			
Brasse and Pewter and Tubbes and other Lumbry	2	0	0
Rye on the ground	4	0	0
Otes on the ground	3	6	8
34 sheepe and 3 lambes	5	0	0
Fvve Kyne, a bullocke and a waynyer	9	0	0
Two Steeres	4	0	0
One old Nagge or horse beast		13	4
Fyve hogges or Shooles		13	4
Certen workinge tooles and implementes of husbandrye		10	0
His apparell and money in his Purse	1	0	0
	37	1	8

Note: The Will was dated 1st May and was proved on 26th May 1596. The residuary legatee and executrix was his wife Agnes. The overseers appointed were Richard Conyngham and John Smyther. The testator's house and its contents at Crookham beyond Farnham was left to William Smyther the younger, at the age of 24. Meanwhile the goods there were "to be used as standerdes" by Agnes or his daughter Patience, if Agnes were to die or re-marry. The testator asked to be buried in the churchyard of Shalford and he gave 3s 4d to the poor of Bramley. His best doublet and best fryse coat were left to Richard Tickner and George Bignold. Jole Harrison was to deduct 4s from her rent when it next became due. His daughter Patience had gifts of a cow and an acre each of rye and oats. Patience, Mary and Anne, the three daughters of William Smyther the elder, were left household goods and livestock. Witnesses were John Mawdesley, clerk, George Steere and Steven Tickner. The burial of William Dyringe was recorded on 9th May 1596 in Shalford Parish Register.

Ref: 1596 B 21/1 & 2 Will 1596 B 21/3 Inventory

Robert Fowle **352**

of Oxted, husbandman; taken by John Ownsted, gent., A Wylliam Haywarde, John Brooker and John Eaton the elder, 16th April 1596.

	£	s	d
In his pursse		3	4
His Apparell	1	0	0
In the Hawle			
One Joyned Table with A frame and A foorme		5	0
One shelf, 1 olde Cubberde, 1 Little square Table, 2 Chayers and 3 Joyned stooles, 1 Ladder with other Impulmentes		10	0
More 2 payre of pothangers, 1 fyer shovell, 1 brondyron, 1 spitt, 1 payre of Cobyrons, 1 girdyron		5	0
In the Low Chamber within the Hawle			
1 Bedsteddull, 1 olde bedd, 4 olde Chestes, 1 Tester over the bed and 2 Chayer stooles with other stuffe		13	4

in the Chamber over the same			
1 fether bed, 1 bolster of fethers, 1 blancket and one Kyveringe	2	0	0
3 olde Bedsteddulls, 6 small Chestes, 1 Box, 2 flockbedds, 2 Bowlsters, 3 blancketes, 2 fether pillows with old payntted Clothes with other stuffe	16	0	0
In Another Lowe Chamber			
1 Bedsteddull, 1 fether bedd, 1 bolster, 1 Kyveringe, 1 Blancket, 1 pyllo of fethers with A tester	2	0	0
One Joyned Cubberd, 1 olde Cheste	1	0	0
2 Basons and A yoer, 10 platters, 6 pewter Dishes, 9 sawssers, 3 saltes, 6 porringers, 1 Drinckinge Cup, 1 quarte pot, 2 pynte potes and 1 half pynt pot, 2 Drypping pannes, 4 Candelstickes of Brasse, 1 Chamber pot	2	0	0
1 Forrest bill and A bowe		2	0
More 14 payre of sheetes	4	10	0
4 pillo Coates, 2 Fyne Tabull Clothes, 3 Course Tabull Clothes 1 Cubberd Cloth, 2 Hand tuells, 10 Tabull napkins	1	10	0
in the Kitchinge			
3 brasse pottes, 1 Chaffer, 1 Cawtherne of brasse and 10 other peeces of Brasse	2	0	0
1 Bunttinge Whootche, 1 bruynge vate with Dyvers Tubbs and other vessells of wood	2	0	0
in the Fieldes			
7 kyne	14	0	0
1 olde mare, 1 Colte of 2 years Adge	1	10	0
Fyve Hogges, Fyve Hennes and A Cock, 2 geese and a gander	1	13	4
3 Acres of whete and Rye	4	0	0
4 Acres of otes	2	13	4
2 bullox of Twelve monthes Adge	1	6	8
	44	18	0
Debtes owinge by the saide Robert Fowle to Wylliam Harlinge of Heaver	2	0	0
Debtes owing by hym for Rente Due at the feast Day of Thanuntiacion of our Lady 1596	4	10	0
More to Mr Houlton for Tythes		9	0
More to The overseer of my Husbandes wyll		5	0
	7	4	0
Desperat Debtes owynge to the sayd Robert Fowle from one [*blank*] Walker of Blechinglie, the queens Baylie	2	0	0
More of Thomas Wood the younger of Croydon, collier		7	0
	[£2	*7*	*0*]

Note: The Will was dated 8th April and was proved on 24th May 1596. The residuary legatee and executrix was the testator's wife Mary. Richard Hayward of Chelsham was named as overseer. He signed as a witness, but two Oxted men, Richard Hayward and Rowland Parker, only made their marks. The testator asked to be buried in Oxted churchyard. He gave his bed, bedding and 3 pairs of sheets, to his son Robert and made arrangements that his executrix should as soon as possible settle a debt of 24s owing to his brother Henry.

Ref: 1596 B 25/1 Will 1596 B 25/2 Inventory

Henry Ligeard **353**

of West Clandon; taken by John Symons and Thomas Cobat of West Clandon, 12th May 1596.

	£	s	d
Money in his pursse		2	0

His Apparell		10	0
2 flockbeddes with the coverlettes	1	0	0
3 bedsteeddes		3	4
4 paire of sheetes		8	0
On paire of fyne sheetes		10	0
4 litle chestes		5	0
2 old cubbertes		7	8
3 brasse kettells, on brasse pott, on posnet		10	0
14 pewter dishes and 3 saltes	1	0	0
On dosen of pewter spoones			10
On cheespresse and 3 cheesmottes		1	0
On Cherne			6
2 spyninge wheeles		1	6
A Spitt			6
On cobiron, on grediron			8
A pressing Iron and a payre of sheeres		1	6
A Spade			6
An Axe and a hedg bill			10
Tubbes, boles and other lumber		10	0
A table and a forme		1	0
2 Kyne	2	0	0
On yearling bullock		6	8
3 sheepe		10	0
An Acre and halfe of wheat in the field		15	0
2 Acres and halfe of barly in the field	1	0	0
An Acre of dredg		5	0
Halfe An Acre of taws		3	4
2 hogges		6	8
A mare		6	8
A henne and chikins			8
	[*£11*	*8*	*10*]

The Will was dated 19th April and proved on 26th May 1596. The residuary legatee and executrix was the testator's wife Margaret, who was to have a life tenancy of his house, lands and possessions, in West Clandon and to distribute any of his goods as she thought fit to his children. Henry asked to be buried in the local churchyard and he requested the parson John Ripton and another neighbour Edward Symmons, to be overseers. The inheritance of the property was settled on his eldest son Henry and his heirs, or failing that it was to go to his other son Thomas. The beneficiary was required to pay his remaining brother and sisters (unnamed) £1 apiece on taking possession. No witnesses were recorded. The testator was buried the same day.

Ref: 1596 B 46/1 Will 1596 B 46/2 Inventory

John Marner, the elder **354**

of Thursley; taken by John Patfold the elder, Richard Backham, William Heynes and William Gadde, with others, 5 May 1596.

	£	s	d
Five peeces of brasse		12	0
Brasse abroade		3	0
Pewter 12 peeces and 6 spoones		7	0
2 spites and a dripping pan and one Andiron		5	0
2 flockbedes		5	0
2 pillowes, 5 coverletes and 2 blanketes		13	0
A locrum sheete, A table clothe and other linnen clothe in all 6 peces		13	4

4 chestes		5	0
7 wooden vesselles		8	0
2 tables and two bedstedles		3	0
A cubberd		3	0
3 Leaden weightes and skales		2	0
2 Loomes with the appertunances		13	4
His apparell and other old lumpery		5	0
	4	17	8
Paid out of which sum for buriall expences and other such charges		16	0

On 26th May 1596 administration of the estate, well and truly declared in the Inventory, was granted to Agnes Ticknor alias Marner, daughter of the deceased. The two men who bound themselves to see this carried out were William Ticknor of Thursley, husbandman and Thomas Bradfold of Frensham, turner. Ref: 1596 Ad 45

John Marner, the younger **355**

of Thursley; taken by Thomas Heynes, Griffin Swaine and John Patfold, 10th May 1596.

	£	s	d
A flock bed and a beds[*ted*]le, a blanket etc		6	8
Two brasse ketles		4	0
A greate kever		1	6
A litle kever			6
Two litle platters			1
Trenchers			1
Dishes			2
Two earthen cans			4
Wooden vessels and tubbs		2	0
All other old lumperye			8
A payre of old sheeres			4
An old bill and an axe			4
An old broade axe			2
An old pickaxe			2
		17	0

On 26th May 1596 administration of the goods and chattels of the deceased was granted to Elizabeth, the relict, who was sworn to the truth of the above Inventory. She, the widow, together with Thomas Ticknor of Thursley, husbandman, bound themselves well and truly to carry out the administration of same. Ref: 1596 Ad 46

John Payne, the elder **356**

of Chobham, husbandman; taken by Richard Latham, John Woddes, John Millest, with others, 19th May 1596.

	£	s	d
Monye in his purss		1	0
His wearing apparell		10	0
In the Haule			
On Table and a forme		3	4
Tenn pewter disshes		5	0
8 platters, 6 sasers		6	0
2 Candelstickes, on salt		1	4
In the Kitching			
2 kettels with other brass		9	0
On Lytell cupbord		3	4

In an upper Chamber			
On fether bed, on boulster, 2 pillowes	1	0	0
4 payre of sheetes		13	4
2 Coverlettes, 2 blanketes		8	0
3 flockbedes, 3 bedsteedells		13	4
On Table cloth, 3 napkins with other Lynnen		5	0
4 Chestes, on standinge Table		13	4
In an out house			
4 Tubbes, a boulting hutch and other Lumbry stuff		13	4
Corne uppon the gronde	1	4	0
On Heyfer bullocke		13	4
2 Hogges		10	0
Geese and pultrye		2	6
2 staules of bees		6	8
The lease of the House	3	6	8
	[£*12*	*8*	*6*]

Note: The Will was dated 2rd April and was proved on 26th May 1596. The testator appointed his wife Agnes and his son John, joint executors and residuary legatees. A shilling apiece was left to the overseers John Woodes the younger and John Myllest. The testator asked to be buried in Chobham churchyard and he left his house and land to his wife solely for six years. After that she was to share equally with his son John, until such time as the survivor would inherit absolutely. The upper and lower parts of a close called Bandelands was given to his daughters Margaret and Elizabeth and their heirs. In every case the property was to remain to any surviving members of the family . The overseers signed as witnesses, together with Richard Latham of Horsell and Thomas Fysher. A codicil gave the kitchen and a little garden plot for herself for life to his daughter Elizabeth. The administration bond was provided by the widow and Richard Latham of Horsell, yeoman.

Ref: 1596 B 56/1 Will 1596 B 56/2 Inventory

John Pen 357

of Woking, husbandman; Niclas Chitty, John Civoke and Edward Davy, 4th May 1596.

	£	s	d
All his waringe Clothes bothe Wollan and Linnan		12	0
3 olde Canvas shettes and a tabel clothe		6	8
One ffloke bed, to bolsters, to pillowes, 4 olde Coveringes and to olde bedstedes	1	1	0
Olde payntted clothes in the chamber and in the Hall		5	0
4 olde Chestes		6	8
Woodden vesseles		6	0
To olde spininge Whelles		1	6
A nolde hand basket			2
To Troughes		3	0
One longe table, one pare of tresteles and a ffourme wythe other olde stoules		2	6
A betell and Iorne wedges with other towles		3	0
Other Iorne stufe		2	0
The brasse and the Peuter	1	0	0
3 olde Candelstickes and one olde Chaffingdish		2	0
5 peckes of Rie and one bushell of barly and halfe a bushell of malte		9	0
One smalle grinding stone, a nolde harow, 3 olde Sithes and a whele barro		4	0
The Rie and the Wottes on the ground in the Common felde		8	0

	£	s	d
The Rie and the benes on the grounde a boute the Howse	1	0	0
The ffire woode		2	0
The Dounge in the gate		1	4
One Hen			4
	6	16	2

Note: The Will was written 21st August 1590 and was proved 26th May 1596. The executors and equal residuary legatees were the testator's wife Betteris and John Clyfton. The testator asked to be buried in the churchyard of Woking. A bequest of 6d was made towards the repair of the parish church and to the common box for relief of the poor. A bushel of rye was given to Richard Bedford and the same plus his best leather coat, to John Sayer of Ripley. The overseers were Robert West and John Monger, to whom he gave 20d. Richard Davy, Robert Beldam, Wyllyam Collins and Richard Bedford, were the 4 witnesses.

Ref: 1596 B 57/1 Will 1596 B 57/2 Inventory

John Roger **358**

of Fetcham; taken by John Kinge and Thomas Woodman of Fetcham, 24th May 1596.

	£	s	d
11 Ewes and 11 Lambs	3	6	0
4 wether sheepe	1	0	0
2 wether teggs		8	0
2 Ewes		8	0
His wearinge aparrell with to yeardes of woollen clothe	1	7	6
	6	9	6

[*Written on the Will*:] The smale debtes

	£	s	d
Thomas Downinge oweth me		2	10
John Foster oweth me		3	6
John Seale oweth me 2 shillings, which I give to Thomas Stint		2	0
Thomas Roger, my Uncle, oweth me	1	10	0
Thomas Edsawe oweth me	1	5	0
	[*£3*	*3*	*4*]

Note: The Will was dated 13th May and was proved on 26th May 1596. The testator asked to be buried in Fetcham churchyard and he gave 10s to the poor of the parish. He appointed his uncle Thomas Roger his executor, giving him six wether sheep and the small debts for his trouble. His brother William was given the apparel and the two yards of cloth. The 11 ewes and 11 lambs went to his cousins Edward, Allis and Elsabeth Roger and two ewe sheep were given to Thomas Edsaw. £4 was left to his sister Katheren, 10s each to his sisters Mary and Agnes and he forgave his brother Thomas a debt of a similar amount. The witnesses were Thomas Stinte, Edward Rogers and Raphe Lambert. Only the last named was able to write. No overseers were appointed and a memorandum states that no-one was bound.

Ref: 1596 B 60/1 Will 1596 B 60/2 Inventory

John Steven **359**

of Cannon Court in Fetcham, yeoman; taken by Robert Sandes of Fetcham, gent., Thomas Roger of Bookham Court, yeoman and Rychard Blundell, yeoman, 13th May 1596.

	£	s	d
In the halle			
One table, one payre of tressels and a ffoorme		3	4
One lyttell table and a ffoorme		1	0
One Cubberd and 3 chayres and 4 lyttell stoolles		13	4
In the parler			
One Joyne bed, one ffetherbed belonginge to it, one bolster, 2 pylloes, 2 blankets, one coverlet and one strawe bed	3	13	4
One lyvery table and a carpett and 2 small ffoormes		6	0
2 chestes and 4 lyttell paynted clothes		10	0

6 Coosshens		4	0
In his bed chamber			
One greate chest and 3 other lyttell chests, one blankett and 3 keverings	1	13	4
A tester for a bed and 3 lyttell paynted clothes		10	0
All his aparrill and money in his poorse	1	0	0
In his maydes chamber			
One bedstedle, a flocbed, one keveringe, one blankett a nolde testor		11	0
In the mens chamber			
2 bedsteddels, 2 flocbedes, 2 keverletts and 2 blankets And in that chamber one matteris and one payre of blankets and bolsters to them belonginge	1	13	4
In the mylke howse or buttry			
One bruinge fate, one toone, 4 kevers, 3 small bolles and 4 troogges		16	0
2 kylderkyns and 7 open tubbes for ale, one saltinge troe, a powdring tub, a cherne, one doossen of woodden platters, 2 doosen of woodden dyshes, an ale syve, 4 doossen of trenchers, a dressing blocke		18	0
The pewter vessell			
2 doossen of platters and pewter dyshes, 8 sawsers, 4 salts, 2 quart pots and one pynte pott, 2 pewter cansticks, one basen, 2 dossen of spoones, 2 porringers	1	8	0
In the kytchyn			
2 kawderns, 2 brasse potts, one Iron pott, 8 kettels, 2 posnets	4	10	0
One chafynge dyshe, one lattyn basen, 4 lattyn kansticks one lattin morter and a skymmer		8	0
2 spyttes, a longer and a short, one payre of cobbearns, one Iron dryppinge pann, 2 whyte plate pannes for dryppinge		8	0
One ffriinge pann		1	0
Of Certaen pottes and crockes 2 doossen		3	4
One knedinge troff, a boolting hootcge and 7 buckets		8	6
In the garner			
One olde yeotinge ffatt and 10 olde dry tubbes		12	6
8 sackes, 2 bagges, one busshell, 2 ffannes, one pecke and a half pec		14	0
The syvves with other lumber there		10	0
Wheate in the garner 8 quarters	14	0	0
Rye 12 bushels	2	0	0
Barle 2 quarters	1	18	0
In the stable			
6 horse and ther harnes with some horse meate	18	0	0
2 Carttes, 2 payre of shodd wheles	4	0	0
2 doonge cartes, 5 harroes, 3 plowes with chyppes, coolters, shares, for every plow with other necesaries to them, with one shod cart, olde wheles	1	13	4
For the Cattell			
For 9 keene and 2 hecfors	24	15	0
One bulloc of 3 yere old	1	10	0
5 bullocs of 2 yere old	6	5	0
6 of one yere old	4	16	0
7 calves wayned this yere	2	16	0
One bull goinge with the kene	2	0	0

	£	s	d
Shepe			
Wether shepe 60	21	0	0
Yewes 36	9	0	0
Lammes 30	4	10	0
Tegges 20	4	0	0
Corne			
Of wheate 23 akers, of Rye 6 akers and a half	45	0	0
Of wotes 10 akers	5	0	0
Of pease and tares 24 akers	12	0	0
Of barle 31 akers and 3 roodes	32	0	0
Of dredge 5 akers	3	10	0
Of grasse 12 akers	6	0	0
Hogges 15 and one sowe and pyggs	5	12	0
The ssoyle	2	0	0
The lynnen			
Shetes 17 payre	6	16	0
Table clothes 7		13	4
Napkyns one doossen		10	0
Pyllobers 2 payre		4	0
Flex, hempe and Towe 30 pownde	1	0	0
In baconn 9 flytches	2	13	4
Befe in the Rooffe 4 peces		4	0
In malte 9 quarters	9	0	0
One Carpett for a longe table		3	4
3 bylles, 2 axes, one plowes hatchett, 2 wedges, 5 Awgers, 2 wymbels, a handsawe		6	4
Of home made cloth			
One yearde and a half of medle Russett		5	0
Of browne russett 6 yeardes		18	0
Of whyte Russett 4 yeardes and a half		9	0
Of hemppen cloth 4 ells		5	4
2 els of 3 quarterne cloth		1	8
5 bottells		3	0
4 Cart ropes		3	0
3 payre of ffetters and 3 horse lockes		4	0
2 wynnynge shetes, one of heare		10	0
One longe ladder and 2 short ones		5	0
Bees 3 stalles		10	0
3 pronges		2	0
10 hennes and a cocke		8	0
For 2 wallets and a hand towell		2	0
A chese pres and motes		6	0
2 trevets, a hitchell and a woollen whele		6	0
A barrill of varges		3	4
3 lynnen wheles		3	0
A flasket and a baskett		1	0
Pott hookes, a gredearne and pot hanggers		2	0
[*£285.0.0*]	285	0	8

Note: The Will was dated 21st September 1594 and proved on 26th May 1596. The testator asked to be buried in Fetcham church and he gave 3s 4d towards the repairs there. The residuary legatee and executrix was his wife Alice. Sums of 5s each were left to Thomas and Charles Woode and John Mylsame, the overseers. Bequests of money were spread over 4 years to his children. His sons Robert, John, Edmond and Thomas, were to have £4, £10, £6 13s 4d and £5, respectively.

His son William was given two yearling bullocks. His daughter Elizabeth was given £5, a year-old bullock and the great chest from his chamber. Alice and Francys were each given £1. A ewe was given to Francys Twyne and to his servants Lawrence Waker and Joane Gyles. John the shepherd was left 6d. William Cooke signed the Will and Thomas and Charles Woode made their marks as witnesses. The burial was entered in the parish register on 9th April 1596 as John Steven of Cannon.

Ref: 1596 B 65/1 Will 1596 B 65/2 Inventory

Agnes Tegg **360**

of Epsom, widow; taken by Thomas Woodman, John Burd and Raffe Pris, 12th May 1596.

	£	s	d
1 bedsted with a fetherbed and a boulster and a pillow and a coverled		13	4
A cooberd		7	0
1 ould cheste		1	6
3 payer of ould sheetes		10	0
3 ould smokes		1	0
3 nekercheyfes and 3 aporns and 2 kercheyfes		2	0
1 cassocke, 2 peticots and 1 save garde		6	8
2 olde hates and a cape			2
2 ould ketels		5	0
1 poyter platter and 1 dishe and 2 sausers		1	4
1 lattin chafing dishe			6
1 tabell and a furme		1	0
	2	9	6

Note: The Will was written on 11th April 1596 and was proved on 24th May. The overseers were to be her son Richard and her friend Robert Cole, vicar of Epsom. She left 12d towards the repair of the church. A sum of 20s was left to Maudlen Williamson to buy a heifer, but if she no longer lived, the bequest from the said Maudlen's grandfather was to be divided equally between Dorothy Burd, Thomas and Judith Hinde and Elizabeth Justins. The latter was left two chests, each with its lock and key. The great chest was beside the cupboard in the low chamber. Dorothy Burd had no additional bequest, but the other three did. Robert Hinde was to be the executor and he and his wife, the widow's son-in-law and daughter, were to inherit the residue of the estate. Three named witnesses were the vicar Robert Cole, John Turner and George Rofe.

Ref: 1596 B 67/1 Will 1596 B 67/2 Inventory

Richard Ticknor **361**

of Northowe in Wonersh, yeoman; taken by Thomas Mercer, Robert Smyther, Raffe Richbell, Raff English, Thomas Smyther and Raffe Mower, 25th May 1596.

	£	s	d
In the Hall			
One Table with a Frame and a forme		2	6
One Cupbord, an olde Chayer, 3 olde stoolles		13	4
In the Parlor			
One Table, three Joyned stoolles and two chestes		6	8
Two Bedstedles, two flockbeddes redy furnished	1	13	4
His apparell and money in his purse	2	0	0
One bedstedle and a bedd, one chest with other thinges		13	4
The Rye and Mault in the house	1	13	4
Two bedstedles, two beddes and fower chestes	1	10	0
Seven paire of sheetes with other lynnen	2	0	0
Ale vesselles, trowes and tubbes with other wodden vesselles in the house	2	0	0
The brasse in the house	2	0	0
The Pewter in the house	1	0	0

A Morter with a pestle and 2 Candlestickes		2	6
The Bacon in the Roof	1	0	0
Two spyttes, a Tryft, one andyron and two paire of pothangers		5	0
One yron bound Kettle, two yron wedges, augers, chizelles, billes and axes with other workinge toolles		5	0
Six Oxen and two steeres	22	0	0
Fyve kyne and a Barren	10	0	0
Yonge bullockes	6	0	0
Three horses	3	0	0
All the sheepe	2	10	0
Hogges and pigges	1	10	0
Fyve acres of Corne in the felde	4	0	0
Eight acres of Otes in the felde	4	0	0
The weane, yokes and chaynes, dongcartes and harrowes with other thinges therunto belonginge	2	0	0
The Henns with a Cock		3	0
Tymber and wood	1	0	0
The Donge in the gate		13	4
	74	1	4

Note: The Will, dated 23rd February and proved on 26th May 1596, was a lengthy document reciting the prescribed inheritance and rents due on three properties: Northowe in Wonersh and Eliottes and Leshemers in Cranleigh. The testator's wife Margaret was to have them for life only and she was the residuary legatee and executrix. Sums of 3s 4d were to be paid to the poor of Cranleigh, to the poor of Wonersh and to the overseers, his cousin Raffe Richbell and Raffe Mower. He asked to be buried in Cranleigh churchyard. After Margaret's death, Northowe was to go his eldest son Richard for life and then to the said Richard's son Richard. Eliottes was to go to William, a second son of the testator and to his heirs, or failing any issue then to Anthony, the youngest son. Leshemers was to go to another son Raffe and his heirs, or failing any issue to the testator's right heirs. The eldest Richard was charged with paying an annual rent of £1 6s 8d to Raffe At Stone and his heirs, as agreed by the testator in an indenture dated 1st January 1545, when he had bought the three properties from Raffe At Stone, deceased. Richard was to collect 6s 8d each from his brothers promptly each year. Bequests of £5 each were made to a fifth son John and to a son-in-law Anthony Richbell. The sum of £6 13s 4d was to be paid, on their days of marriage or at the age of 22, to his daughters Jane, Mary, Margaret and Katheryn and to Anthony at the age of 21. His son Raffe was to have a yoke of 2-year-old steers and Richard, the eldest, was given £2 6s 8d. The testator's grandchildren and his godchildren then living were each given 12d. Richard Ticknor made his mark at the end of the Will, as did the three witnesses Thomas Smyther, Nicholas Ticknor and Rowland Groave.

Ref: 1596 B 68/1 Will 1596 B 68/2 Inventory

Thomas Woodier **362**

of Dunsfold, labourer. [*no appraisers given and undated*]

	£	s	d
The Dettes that are owinge and belonginge to Thomas Woodier			
John Barker of Cranley and his wyfe	3	11	9
Daniell Ame		1	0
Mary Edwardes			4
	3	13	1
The Dettes that Thomas Woodier at his death dyd ow			
To George Martyn		4	0
To Antony Gyddes		1	0
To Antony Brother			6
		5	6

Note: The Will was written on 28th March and proved on 26th May 1596. The testator's cousin John Woodier was residuary legatee and executor. The witnesses were Richard Woodier and the clerk was William Langborrowe. The testator asked to be buried in Dunsfold churchyard and he gave 5s to the poor of Dunsfold and of Cranley. The same amount was bequeathed to Richard Woodier and to Harry Moar's wife of Wonersh. Thomas Ame, Thomas Cottrell and Annes Woodier, were to have 2s, 1s and 3s 4d, respectively.

Ref: 1596 B 76/1 Will 1596 B 76/2 Inventory

1597

Edward Crauly 363

of Ash, husbandman; taken by George Boylet, Alan Cournis and William Smithe, 12th April 1597.

	£	s	d
Moony in his purse		3	4
His apparell	1	0	0
In the haull			
A planke table, a round table, two formes		5	0
Too cheiers		1	0
An Upper chamber			
Too Joyne bedsteds, a fether bed, three bolsters, a payre of blankets, a coverlet, a bolster	3	0	0
A Lower chamber			
A playne bedsted, a flock bed, three bolsters, a payre of blanks, a coverlet, a whit Tester	1	6	0
To chests		6	0
The butterye			
A cubbard		5	0
Six standing barels, too beare barels, a boulting whche, a kever, a bruing fate, a powdring tubb, too woodden botels		13	4
The kichin chamber			
A bedsted, a flocke bedd, a payre of blankets and a bolster		13	4
The kichin			
Three brasse pots		16	0
A calderne		10	0
A pann, three ketels, too posnets		15	6
Certayne pewter		16	0
Fyve candlestikes, a chafing dishe		6	0
Too pothangers, too pothooks, a payre on andirons, a grediron, a trifoote, a payre of tonges, a broche, a fier pann		10	0
A payre of Scales		1	0
A payre of Shets		6	6
A Troghe		3	4
Fower olde tubbes, a kever, too bocats, a peck, a galon		10	0
A chese presse, a butter cherne		2	0
Three Augurs, too sawes, too drawinge knives, two weges		5	0
Certayne olde shelves withe other olde Stuffe		6	0
Too axes, too bills, too pronges		3	0
A here for an oste		5	0
To holow shovels and a spitter		1	4
A fliche of bacon and a brest of beefe		6	0
Too akers of green wheate	1	3	0
Three akers of rye	2	0	0
Too Stawles of bees		10	0

Too payre of olde wheles		10	0
Six oxon and fower horses	20	0	0
An ire bond cart	2	0	0
A Stacke of heye		10	0
A cow, a bull, a heyfer	3	13	4
Seven Swine	2	6	8
A plow, a harrow withe certayne yeoks and cheynes	2	0	0
	48	8	8

Note: The Will, dated 1st April 1595, was written on a folded sheet of paper. An amended version with the meaning made more obvious was written in another hand on an inside fold. Probate was granted on 19th July 1597 to George Wakeford of Ash, husbandman, Edward's trusted servant, the sole executor and residuary legatee. Henry Ede and Alan Courtneis were appointed overseers and were left 1s each. A like sum was given to William and Thomas Jewer, Agnes Michinall and Joan Purdum. Margaret Crauly was left 13s 4d. Edward Gelye was given a brass pot and Dorothy Billinghurst a brass pan. In the original document George Wakeford's legacy bound him to look after his master and mistress 'during terme of ther lyves', discharging the said Edward, his master, of all costs and charges whatsoever. The second version added 'during the tyme of his continuance under me in the house wherin I doo now dwell.' The witnesses were William Smith, Henry Gander and Henry Pullin. The burial of Edward Crauly was recorded on 11th April 1597.

Ref: 1597 B 18/1 Will 1597 B 18/2 Inventory

Richarde Edmeade **364**

of Chobham, husbandman; taken by Richard Bonsey, Richarde Elmer, Henrye Sponge, Walter Warner, John Payne, Christopher Feelde, with others, 18th July 1597.

	£	s	d
Monye in his purss		13	4
His Apparell	2	13	4
In the haule			
A Table, a forme and stooles		10	0
In an Inner chamber			
A flocke bedd, A bedsteedell and a Cupborde	1	6	8
In the Chamber over the haule			
On fether bed, A bedsteedell with that belongeth therunto, 2 Chestes	1	0	0
2 flockbeddes more with that belongeth therunto	1	0	0
Five payre of Sheetes, 2 Table clothes with other lynnen	1	1	8
In the kitchinge			
The brass and pewter ther with spoones and trenchers	1	13	4
On fatt, 2 troughes with other wodden vessell	1	1	8
On spitt, a tryfitt, pothangers, a bill, an Axe, 2 wedges of Iron, with other old Iron		3	4
In the feeld			
2 Oxen	5	0	0
3 kyne	4	10	0
4 bullockes and on weyned calfe	4	0	0
3 horses and one colt	3	0	0
6 sheepe	1	0	0
2 cartes, A plough, 2 Iron harrowes, yokes, cheynes, harnesses, with other Implementes	1	11	8
2 Acres of wheat, 2 acres of pease and tares, one acre of Barley	5	0	0
The hay reddy made		13	4
All the wodd which is cutt ther	3	0	0
The Lease of five acres of Lande geven by the Will	2	0	0

	£	s	d
On sow and 4 pigges		6	8
The geese and poultry		3	4
	[*£41*	*8*	*4*]

Note: The Will was dated 14th July and proved on 19th July 1597. The testator appointed his wife Agnes and his sons, John and Henry, executors and residuary legatees. A shilling each was given to the overseers, Christopher Feeld, Walter Warner and John Payne. Richard asked to be buried "in convenyent place" and gave 7s each to three good local causes: the poor, the church and the urgent repair of the causeway from Horsbridge to John Rogers' water gate. His son John was to pay 5s annually to Agnes, to his brother Henry, to his sister Agnes Elmer and to the maidservant Ellyn Buckland, from the profits of the years remaining on a lease of 4 acres of arable land and an acre of copse. The £1 was to be paid by John and divided equally among the survivors. Richard Elmer, the testator's son-in-law, was given the long cart, the plough and the ox harrow and Roger Elmer, the son of Richard and Agnes, was to have a black lamb. A lamb was given to the manservant Thomas Bonner. Henry Edmead, the other son of the testator, was given a house and land in Windlesham. In addition to her monetary gift, Ellen Buckland was given a heifer to be looked after by John until the first calf was born. The three overseers witnessed the Will.

Ref: 1597 B 27/1 Will 1597 B 27/2 Inventory

Henry Edwardes **365**

of Witley; taken by John Burll and Henry Smyth, 1st June 1597.

	£	s	d
A table and a forme and a payre of tressels		1	8
An old bedstead and bordes and one old colfer		1	4
An old Caldren		6	8
Certayne somes of mony owing hym at Dyvers mens handes	3	10	0
His Apparell and mony in his pursse	1	0	0
Recte £4.19.8	4	19	4

Note: The Will was dated 12th May and was proved on 19th July 1597. The executor and residuary legatee was John Edwardes, the brother of the testator. Henry Smyth was appointed overseer and the executor was asked to see the Will performed and the body honestly buried. There were three bequests of money to members of his family: £1 was given to his sister Joan Edwardes; 12s was to go to his other sister Alice; and his godson Henry, the son of William Edwardes, was left 10s. No witnesses were recorded. The executor, a husbandman, provided the administration bond. His parish was written as Ritlie, but the intial letter is more likely to have been W.

Ref: 1597 B 29/1 Will 1597 B 29/2 Inventory

Henry Eede **366**

of Ash, yeoman; taken by Thomas Inwood, Robert Vicary, Henry Dere and Georg Warner, 10th June 1597.

	£	s	d
Monny in his purse		10	0
His wearing apparell	2	0	0
In the hawll			
A table withe a Joyne frame, Two cubbard, fower cheiers, ann olde cubbard, a back of wenscott	1	10	0
In the lower chamber			
A cubberd and fyve chests		10	0
A Joyne bedsted, a fetherbed, a flock bolster, a pillow, too blankets, a coverlet, a trocle bed, a flock bed, a bolster, a coverlet, on payre of cutenes of Seye	2	13	4

An Upper chamber			
A Joyne bedsted, a fetherbed, a matryce, two blankets, a coverlet, a bolster, a troclebed, a fetherbedd, a matrice, a coverlet, a payre of blankets, a bolster, fower pillowes, a flocke bolster	3	6	8
Too small tabels, too litle formes, too chests, on Joyne Stoole		5	0
Too trocle beds, on flockbed, Thre coverlets, too blankets, a bolster, a pillow, a chest, a cheir	1	13	0
A chest and an olde cheyer		1	4
The kuchin			
A great troghe, thre shelves		5	0
A bruinge vate, fower kevers, eight bowles, a boulting whiche, three meale kevers, fyve chese moulds, a kneding kever, withe potts and erthen pannes	1	6	8
A wilby, a Rudder, too Sithes, a Seedcodd, Too Seeves		6	0
Eight brasse potts, fyve ketels, Two pannes, fyve posnetts, fower spitts, too Dripping pannes, a payre of Andirons, a grediron, a payre of potthangers	5	0	0
A dosen of dishes, too dosen of Trenchers, to dosen of spoones		1	6
A Vate, a chese presse, a gurner, a troghe, a henn coope		16	4
Twenty platters, twelve sawcers, Twelve poringers, 4 potingers, too basons, 3 salts, six candlestiks, a pestle and morter and a chafinge Dishe	2	3	4
Glasse Thirty foote		10	0
fyve cooshins		18	0
Three Steres	6	0	0
Too heyfers	3	0	0
Thre calves	1	13	4
Fyve bullocks	4	0	0
Six oxen	20	0	0
Three mares	4	6	8
Thirteene Lames	2	12	0
Eighteene yewes	3	12	0
Six Kyne	13	12	0
Ten akers of wootes	10	0	0
Too akers of barlye	1	0	0
Eleven akers of wheate	11	0	0
Beanes	1	0	0
Rye	1	0	0
Too Dung potts, on Long cart, 3 plowghes, on wagin, fower payre of wheles, two payre of irons	5	0	0
Six yeoks, Three cheynes, Thre payre of Straps, on oxe harro,	1	0	0
To ropes, Thre payre of cart harnys, thre payre of plow harnis, too prongs, To spitters, too billes, on axe, an iron barr, too iron weggis		16	0
To hives		10	0
Nyne hoggs, fower lytle piggs	3	6	0
A grin stone and a Lader		1	0
Fower sacks and a here clothe		5	0
Too bushels of wheate		12	0
Twelve bushels of oten malt	1	4	0
A cock and Six hennes		2	6
Nyne payre of canvas sheets	2	0	0
Six payre of Locorum sheets	2	0	0

	£	s	d
Six table clothes, six table napkins	1	5	0
	124	9	8

Note: The Will was dated 29th May and proved on 19th July 1597. The testator's wife Elizabeth was to be executrix and residuary legatee. Robert Vicary of Runfold and Alan Courtneys of Ash, the two overseers, were left 3s 4d apiece. Katheryne, Mary, Jane and Elizabeth, the four daughters, were to be paid £15 at the age of 23 years or on their wedding days. Different legacies went to each of the four sons. Stephen was to have £5 in 2 years' time and his son Stephen was to inherit a house and land at Wrecclesham after Elizabeth's decease. John was to have £5 at the age of 26. William was to have £20 at the age of 24. Henry was to have the freehold land in Chiddingfold and the implements of husbandry after Elizabeth's death. She was meanwhile to pay Henry £1 6s 8d annually and was to give him £5 if she wanted to dispose of the farming gear elsewhere. The overseers made their marks as witnesses to the Will, as did the testator himself. His burial was recorded in the Ash parish register on 31st May 1597.

Ref: 1597 B 23/1 Will 1597 B 23/2 Inventory

John Foster **367**

of Wrecclesham in Farnham, yeoman; taken by John Baldynge, John Shrube junior and Robarte Warner, 21st June 1597.

	£	s	d
All his wearynge apparrell and monye in his purse	1	10	0
In the bede chamber			
On flocke bede, on fether boulster, 2 fether pellowes, on flocke pellow, a paire of sheets, a paire of blanketts and a coverlytte	1	4	0
A bordyd bedsteddyll		1	8
A nother bede, a paire of canves sheetes and two old coverlytts		10	0
3 cheestes and a old chaire		3	4
In the halle and kichen			
A cubbard and a tabell, a paire of tresseles and 2 foormes		5	0
5 old platers, 3 porrengers, 3 sausers		5	0
3 brase potts		6	8
3 brase kettels		6	0
Two keyvers, with other lumbery		5	0
A lyttell barrell, withe other smale wodden vessylles		1	8
A veninge loome with other smale things		5	0
An axe, a byll, a pronge, a plowe chaine and a gridd yoron		2	0
A spite and a andyron		1	4
A lyttell cowe	1	13	4
A heiffer	1	10	0
Two lyttell shutts		6	8
Ther is Oweinge in redy monye in sartene mens hands the some of	19	10	0
A tabell clothe of canves and a wodden vessell		6	0
	28	12	8

Note: The Will was dated 6th May 1596 and proved on 19th July 1597. The executrix, with a life interest in all the goods, was John's wife, who was instructed to deposit the money in bonds with John Holloway to be increasing in value for the children. Sums of 18d apiece were left to the overseers, John Baldin and John Shrubb junior. The testator gave 4d to the church and 2s to the poor of Farnham to be given to them in bread at his burial in the churchyard. Elizabeth Holloway the younger was to have £6 and four household items. A brass pot was left to his daughter Jone Holloway and to his son Thomas Foster. After his wife's decease, the residue was to go equally to his three children Thomas Foster, Jone Holloway and Agnes Bristowe. In the event of Thomas's early death, his share was to go directly to his children Thomas, William, Jone and Jane. A debt of 15s due from Richard Mathew was to go to the testator's children at the age of 21 years. Robert Warner signed as a witness. John Holloway, John Baldynge and Steven Shrubb, made their marks. The administration bond was provided by John Holloway of Farnham, husbandman and John Ellridge of the same, miller. The testator's burial was recorded in the parish register on 18th June 1597.

Ref: 1597 B 31/1 Will 1597 B 31/2 Inventory

Thomas Hardinge **368**

of Tilford in Farnham, husbandman; taken by Thomas Preston, John Sowen, John Novell and Walter Craft, the writer, 15th April 1597.

	£	s	d
In the Hale			
A planck table, a forme, a Cubbard, 2 Stooles, a Chare, a painted cloth and a cubbard cloth		8	0
In the Chamber			
A bedsted and a flockbed and a paire of blangettes, a coverlett, a flock bowlster and painted bed tester		10	0
2 canvise sheetes and a locrum sheete		5	0
in the loaft over the hale			
An old bedsted and a flock bed, 2 blangettes, an old coverlett, a lynen bed tester and a flock bowlster		6	0
A Cheast with other lumbry		2	6
In the Little Loft			
A lyttle table with other lumbrie		1	0
In the kytchin			
3 little tubbes, a Tro with a planck, a vate, a little kyver, a bowlting which and a butter charme		5	0
A triff, a Cathron and 2 kittles, one little brase pott, a Chaffing dishe		8	0
One dusen of pewter, a driping panne with other lumbrie		8	0
In the Gate			
A Carte	1	0	0
A mare		16	0
A yoke and a chayne with other Lumbrie		1	8
3 tegges		6	8
In Corne	2	5	0
His wearing Apparell with money in his purse		3	4
	7	6	2

Note: The Will was dated 6th August 1591 and was proved on 17th July 1597. The executors and residuary legatees were the testator's wife Joan and his son John, provided that they could live together. Were this not agreeable, Joan was to pay John £22 and he was to go his way for her lifetime. The overseers, each to be paid 5s, were Richard Hitchcock and Henry Huntingford. Thomas asked to be buried in Farnham churchyard. He gave 4d to the church and 1s to the poor. His six other children were each given similar legacies of £10, to be paid in two sums of £5 at the end of the first and second years of their marriage, or if they chose not to marry, at the age of 24 and 25. If Annis, Gillian, Ann, Elizabeth, Thomas and Richard, were to die before inheriting the legacy, it was to be paid to the executors. The overseers made their marks as witnesses to the Will, which was signed by Daniel Craft, vicar of Farnham. The burial of Thomas Hardinge of Tilford was recorded in the parish register on 30th March 1597.

Ref: 1597 B 39/1 Will 1597 B 39/2 Inventory

Thomas Key **369**

of St Nicholas, Guildford, clerk and parson; taken by Thomas Crosse, Thomas Wells and John Hardinge, 1st September 1597.

	£	s	d
In the Hall			
A Joyned table and a frame and 6 Joyned stooles		9	0

6 Carpett Cushens		6	8
A Joyned Cubbard		10	0
A Joyned Chaire and a turned Chaire		2	6
3 old mapps		2	0
A dornix Carpett and a Cubbard cloth		5	0
A back of Wainscote		2	6
[£1.15.2]	1	17	8
In the kitchen			
A square Joyned Table and a forme, a ioyned Cubbard and a ioyned Chaire		13	4
2 paire of Andyrons, a c[*]paier of Tongs and a Trevett and 2 paier of potthangers		5	0
2 brass potts, a skillett, a Chaffing dish and 4 kittles of Brasse		13	4
8 peuter platters, 7 peuter dishes, 2 Chargers, a bason and Kiver, 3 fruite dishes, 3 pottingers, 2 plats, 3 salts, 3 Candlesticks, a quart pot and a pint pot, 2 beakers, 3 c[and]lesticks, 4 flower po[ts] of pewter	1	6	8
A Morter and p[estel]l of brasse		2	0
2 glasse Bot[t]les covered with lether		8	
A brush and a stone Pott			4
2 little Spitts		1	6
Wood in the gate	1	4	0
Old Tubbs		5	0
A Warminge pan of Brasse		1	8
	4	13	6
In the Chamber over the Hall			
A Joyned Bedstedle and a Trundle Bedstedle with Curtyn Rodds of Yron		13	4
A ffether bedd, a ffether bolster, 2 flockbedds, a flock bolster and a fether Pillowe	1	13	4
A Coverlett of Course Tapestry, an old Coverlett and a blankett		13	4
Curtyns for 2 bedds of green and Red sea	1	13	4
A paier of old Holland Sheets, 7 paire Canvas Sheets, 12 Pillowberes of Holland and Lockoram	1	10	0
5 Table Clothes, 18 Table napkins and 2 Cubbard Clothes	1	5	0
A little square Table and a wicker Chaire		3	0
2 Chests		1	4
[*£7.2.8*]	7	12	8
In the Chamber over the Kitchen			
A ioyned Bedstedle and a Trundle Bedstedle		9	0
2 old fflockbedds, 3 Coverletts, 2 flock bolsters	1	0	0
20 pound of wooll		13	4
A Muskett with sword and dagger and a soldiers Coat	1	0	0
2 Scottish daggers		2	6
His apparell and money in his purs	5	0	0
	8	4	10
Corne and Hay in the Barne	40	0	0
5 Kyne	10	0	0
A Nagg	2	10	0
2 Colts	1	6	8
2 Shelves		1	6
All his Books in his Study	6	0	0
A Lease of a Howse and certen Land at Ertington for certen yeres to come	10	0	0
In the handes of George Austen deliverd him in gold by the said Thomas Key in his life tyme	10	0	0

	101	16	10
Whereof geven to the widowe of the said Thomas Key for her maynetenance the said Lease, all the houshold stuffe and cattell and other thinges to the value of	40	0	0
Paid and allowed to Ryce Wight gent, deceased for so much by him layde out for detts owinge by the said Thomas Key in his life tyme and for carriinge and threshinge out of the Corne in the Barne and other necessary charge laid out after the death of the said Thomas Key, as appereth by a Bill of particulers in his owne hand and allowed amongest other things by doctor Ridley as ordinary in theis and other like Ecclesiasticall matters under his hand	37	6	0
Allowed to the said Rice Wight as so much by him paid and laid out for apparell, diett, Scholinge of the Children and other necessary Charges as appereth in a Bill of particulers under the hand of the above named George Austen	85	18	7

Note: The nuncupative Will was dated 18th August 1597 and proved on 19th April 1600. William Hopkins of Guildford, clothier and others, vouched for the meaning of the parson's last words: that he freely gave all he had to Sir George Moore, knight, George Austen and Rice Wighte, gent., desiring that they would be good to his wife and children. A series of documents recording the careful administration of the estate for the good of the children between 1598 and 1612 is held in the Surrey Local History Centre, Woking. The burial of Mr Thomas Key, minister of this parish, was recorded on 27th August 1597 in the register of Guildford, St Nicholas.

Ref: GMR LM 2011/43/1 Will GMR LM 1096 Inventory

Henry Martin **370**

of Farnham, glover; taken by John Searle, Thomas Marner, William Wheeller and William Pullen, 18th July 1597.

	£	s	d
In the Hale			
A Table and forme		1	4
An old cubbard and 2 old chaires		4	0
2 kittles, an old brasse pott, a broatche and a little pan		4	4
2 Candle[*stickes*], 3 pottengers, 3 Saucers and - [*s*]alts and a chafyng dish		3	0
A paire of Tongues, two paire of potthangers and an Angeron		1	0
Other Lumbrie		2	0
In the Shopp			
3 half hides, 9 sheepeskines and 2 Calves skins		6	0
Purses		1	0
2 dussen of gloves		5	0
2 paire of Sheires, a shavinge kyfe, A paire of hamppers and other Lumbrie		2	0
In the Loaft			
3 Chests		3	0
A bedsted		2	0
2 paier of sheets and 2 pillobers		6	8
An olde bedsted		1	0
A flock bed and a bolster		3	4
A flock bed and a flock bolster		3	4
Another flock bed and a bolster and 2 paire of blancketts and a paire of old sheetes		12	0
A paire of skayles		1	0
Waites		2	0
In the old howse			
A little haie		5	0
2 olde saddles		1	0
An old kiver		2	0

Skins not dressed		2	10
A shaving kyfe and a beame			4
A ax and a harrowe with other lumbrye		2	0
2 barrow pigges		8	0
His Apparell with money in his purse		10	0
	4	15	2

All the appraisers made their marks on 18th July 1597 when they had completed the appraisal. The document was written by Walter Craft and Letters of Administration were granted to Johanne Martin, the widow, the following day. Ref: 1597 Ad 60
Note: Henry Martin's burial was recorded in Farnham parish register on 14th July 1597.

Henry Martin **371**

of Worplesdon, weaver; taken by Henry Ockly, John Stening and Rychard Carpenter, 13th June 1597.

	£	s	d
All his aparille and 12 pence in his purs		10	0
A table, a form and a Coberd		5	0
4 flok bedes, two pair of blanketes, two boulsters, 4 Coverletes and 3 bedstedles	2	13	4
5 Chestes		6	0
in the buttrey			
4 tubes and all other wodstuf in the buttrey		6	0
3 brase potes	1	0	0
6 ketles and a Cawdern	1	0	0
6 pewter dishes and 6 spones and a sault		5	0
4 pair of Canves Shetes	1	0	0
3 kyne and two bullokes	6	0	0
A mar and two Coltes	2	10	0
An ould pair of wheles and a harow		6	8
An acre of whete	1	0	0
A Close of otes, Rye and pease	1	0	0
[*£18.2.0*]	18	2	4

Note: The Will, dated 18th May 1593, when Henry was "hole in bodie and mind" was not proved until 19th July 1597. The executrix and residuary legatee was his wife Anne. The sum of 4d was given to his overseer John Davies and 6d to the poor. He asked to be buried in Worplesdon churchyard. Some legacies were to be paid on demand: 12d each to the two daughters of his deceased son James and to his son Robert; 4s to his second son John; and to his sons William and Thomas, £1 each. His daughter Margaret was given 10s, the best cauldron and two pewter dishes. His daughter Alice was to have the other cauldron, "the worser bed save onc," and two pewter dishes. Catherine Martin, John's daughter, was left part of a stall of bees. The Witnesses were John Melishe and John Davies. The burial of Henry Marton was recorded on 4th June 1597 in the parish register.

Ref: 1597 B 52/1 Will 1597 B 52/2 Inventory

William Plogg **372**

of Peckham in Camberwell, yeoman, 5th April 1597. [*appraisers unnamed*]

	£	s	d
In the hall of the deceasedes Late dwelling howse			
One table, one forme, one cubbord, one square table, three chaires, two stooles, 2 andirons, one pothanger, one grediron, one fier shovell and one paire of tonges		6	8
One trevett, one pitchfork and one axe		1	0

In the parlor			
One Joyned bedsted, one fetherbed and the painted clothes	1	0	0
One Joyned table with a frame, one forme and one chaire		4	0
Three chestes, one cubard		8	0
Sixe quishions		2	0
8 paire of shetes and one paire of flaxen sheetes	1	10	0
Three Shirtes, 2 bandes and 3 towells		4	0
In pewter platters and dishes 11 and 5 porringers, 3 pewter pottes and 2 salt sellers		15	0
Fower brazen candlestickes, one morter and a pestell, one Latten pan, one scummer and 6 pewter spoones		4	0
3 tableclothes and 13 napkins		8	0
In the chamber belowe			
One fetherbed, one bedsted, one coverlett, one blanckett and one bolster	1	0	0
2 old chestes and the painted clothes		3	0
In the chamber over the parlor			
One bedsted, one mattris, one blanckett, one coverlett, one bolster and 3 pillowes		6	8
In the kitchen			
One kettle, one brasse pan and one chafer of brasse		4	0
Two spittes, one Iron pott and one dripping pan		3	4
6 traies for milke, 2 bowlls, 2 paire of milke tanckerdes, 1 bucking tub, 1 mylking pale, one cheese presse with the waite		5	0
One old bedsted with other Lumber		3	0
One frying pan and 2 dozen of trenchers		1	0
In old Iron		2	0
In Woll		6	8
Two lynnen Wheles and one Wollen Wheele		1	0
One gallon of beanes			10
One longe pitchfork			4
One long grayned staffe			2
The Testators wearing apparell			
Two clokes, 1 paire of breches, 2 dublettes, one paire of stockinges, one frieze coat, one hatt, one old gowne, one old peticoate and one paire of shoes	1	0	0
Corne on the ground and other stuffe in the barnes			
In pease and plowing	2	16	0
Hay in the barne		16	0
Two ploughe chaynes and one paire of Draftes		1	6
Cattell			
8 kyne	10	0	0
6 young bullockes	3	0	0
3 mares and 3 coltes	4	0	0
Two sowes and pigges		13	8
Two geese and 2 hennes		3	0
Two stockes of beese		3	4
Owing to the Testator by goodman Mitten for rent	3	6	8
	33	19	10

[*Written into Will*] Debts owing by the Testator

I do owe unto Mother Savidge £10 to be payd owte of my land that lyeth in Kent. The rent of it is £3.6.8 the yere and it is to be payd yerely during the terme of thre yeres yf she will be contentid so to receve it	10	0	0

I do owe unto John Bone dwelling at Dollitche twenty shillings	1	0	0
4 pence debt unto Mr Wilson, vycar of Camerwell			4
	[*£11*	*0*	*4*]

Note: The Will was dated 26th March and was proved on 21st July 1597. The executor, William Netlingham, was a son-in-law of the testator. The residuary legatees in equal part, with a life interest in the property in Kent, were the three daughters, Agnes Plogg, Elizabeth Glover and Philippa Netlingham. The overseers were Robert Netlingham and Henry Briggs the elder. Agnes Plogg was given four cows and £2. After the decease of his three daughters, the land and buildings were to remain to Benjamin Netlingham and his heirs for ever. Were his issue to fail then the legacy was to go to his grandson John Glover. After the debts were paid, three small bequests were to be distributed: a colt to Robert Kydwallett; £1 to Isabel Anscombe, his kinswoman; and £1 to Gardiner's children. William Plogg made his mark. The three witnesses signed their names: Henry Briggs the elder, Joan Wilsoone and John Glover, gardener. The testator's burial was recorded in the register of St Giles, Camberwell, on 31st March 1597.

Ref: 1597 B 57/1 Will 1597 B 57/2 Inventory

James Rysse **373**

of Hampton in Seale; taken by Roberte Tayler and William Reade, with others, 15th July 1597.

	£	s	d
His wearing aparell and a cheaste	1	0	0
Two heayves at 4 shillings the peace		8	0
8 sheepe at 4 shillings the peace	1	12	0
Money owinge by Rycharde Christmas	1	0	0
Money owinge by Williame Reede	1	0	0
Money oweinge by Henry Russell	1	15	0
Money oweinge by Elexandere Goodyer	2	0	0
Money in the handes of Elyzabeth Jwer wyddowe	8	0	0
	16	15	0

Note: The Will was dated 23rd March and was proved on 19th July 1597. The executrix and residuary legatee was his dame, Elizabeth Jewer, widow, so James was probably a servant in her employ. No overseers were named. He asked to be buried in the parish churchyard of Seale, all the usual duties having been discharged by the executrix. Wylliam Rysse, his brother, was left 5 nobles [£1 13s 4d] to be paid a year after his death. Sums of 3s 4d each were left to his two sisters Christiane Caterick and Amey Rysse. The three boys of William Reed were left 10s, so too were the children of Richard Christmas. A sheep each was given to Joan Jewer, Sander Rede and Elyzabeth Taylor. James made his mark on the document witnessed by Nicholas Waters, Richard Taylor and William Reed, the last two also making their marks. The testator's burial was recorded on 8th May 1597.

Ref: 1597 B 64/1 Will 1597 B 64/2 Inventory

Isabell Savage **374**

of Peckham in Camberwell, widow; taken by Henry Bettes, Thomas Newman and Henry Brigges, 25th April 1597.

	£	s	d
An old fflockbed, an old pare of Shetes, an old pillowbeare with a Coverlet		6	0
An old Chist		1	0
An old brasse kettell			10
All the Lumber with some wood		3	0
Dettes owing to the said Isabell			
William Netlingham	10	0	0
Peter Byrd	2	0	0

	£	s	d
Robert Cox		15	0
Henry Bettes	1	0	0
	14	5	10

[*From the Will*:]

William Netlingham, executor unto William Plogg doth owe unto me the some of £10 of la[*w*]full money to be Payed unto me or my assyners the 22 of May next being Trynyty Sooneday
Henry Bett doth owe unto me the some of 20 shillings to be payde to me or my assynes by Saynt Mykaell the arkeangell next comyng
Also Robart Cox doth owe unto me 20 shillings and yf it doth plese god to take me away owte of this worlde that then I gyve him 5 shillings of that mony and the rest, that is 15 shillings to be payde so sone as he can conveniently spare yt.
Peter Borde doth owe unto me the somme of 40 shillings

Note: The Will was written on 17th April and proved on 21st July 1597. Henry Bett and Henry Briggs the elder were appointed executors. This involved collecting the debts, which were to be delivered to Mr Wilson, vicar of Camberwell. The testatrix gave £1 to Thomas Numan, smith, in Kent Street Newington; he was also to have the money owed by Robert Cox and the bed and lumber in the house. The poor people of Peckham were given her wood and Mary Savidge was to have £1. The residue of the estate was to be given to the poor and fatherless of Camberwell at the discretion of the executors and the vicar. The witnesses were Henry Bett and Thomas Numan. The burial of the testatrix was recorded on 22nd April 1597 in the register of St Giles, Camberwell.

Ref: 1597 B 65/1 Will 1597 B 65/2 Inventory

Jefferie Smith **375**

of Sutton, yeoman; taken by George Franke, Thomas Rogers and Heugh Jewdery, 18th July 1597.

	£	s	d
In the Hall			
One Table, twoe formes, one chare, one Joyned cubberd, one other chare with a painted clothe	1	0	0
In the upper Inner chamber			
One Joyned Bedsted, one Truttle bed, one Table, 2 Tressells, one shelf, one forme, 4 stooles, 2 chestes, one boxe and one chare	1	10	0
2 featherbeddes, one flocke bed, 3 bolsters, 4 pilloes, 3 keverlettes, 4 blanckquettes	9	4	4
8 paire of sheetes, 2 table clothes, 8 napkyns and one Towell	3	6	8
In the Chamber over the Hall			
Of Wolle	25	0	0
2 quarters of breadecorne	4	10	0
3 quarters of Dredge Maulte	4	16	0
One Saddle, 22 pound of lynnen Yearne with other Lumber	1	0	0
In the Inner chamber nexte to the Hall			
One Joyned Bedsted, one truttle bed, one Joyned cubberd with a presse, 5 Chestes and one other bed	2	17	6
2 featherbedes, 3 bolsters, 5 pilloes, 4 keverlettes, 8 blanquettes	5	13	4
19 paire of sheetes, 8 table clothes and 12 napkyns	5	0	0
3 locorome shertes, 4 ruffe bandes, one kertchef		16	0
Of pewter 56 pound, 2 dozen of spones, 3 salte sellers, 2 pewter candelstickes	1	10	0
One other plater and a basen of pewter and alsoe a painted cloth		8	8
In the servanntes chamber			
2 bedsteddes, 2 matterices, 4 blanckquettes and also a Qualiver furnished	2	0	0
In the Boltinge howse			
2 kemnells and a Boltinge chest with other Lumber		10	0

In the kytchen			
9 kettells with a Caldron, 3 brasse pottes, 2 posnettes, 2 chafers, 2 chafinge dishes, 4 latten Candelstickes, 3 spittes, 2 skymmers, 3 paire of pothookes, one pothanger, 2 treftes, one grydyron, 2 spisemorters with 2 pestells, 2 drippinge pannes, a paire of Cobyrons with other thinges	5	0	0
In the kytchen Lofte			
Of Maulte	15	0	0
Of bakon	1	0	0
Of Otemell		6	8
2 Oste heres		16	0
In the Milke howse			
One Powderinge troffe, 2 powderinge Tubbes, one ffate, 2 Tunnes, one Chese presse with 8 kylderkynnes and other Lumber	3	0	0
Butter and Chese	3	10	0
3 Leatherne bottells, 3 fryinge pannes and 2 dozen of dishes		10	0
In the Stonehowse			
3 ffates and a Quarne with other Lumber and alsoe 40 Colesackes	5	3	4
In the Cartehowse			
4 Longe Cartes, 2 Dongcartes with 2 paire of shod wheeles with other Lumber	4	6	8
3 plowes with Coulters, 5 harroes and other Iron thereunto belonginge	1	8	0
In the other Cartehowse			
Wood Billetts and Boordes	2	0	0
5 Ladders		5	0
In the Barne			
Of Haye one loade ½		13	4
In the Gate			
One Welbuckett, rope, Wynche, rackes and grynstone		13	4
6 Hogges	2	13	4
Compost and Troffes		10	0
Poultrye		8	0
Hempe		10	0
In the Stable			
3 horsse with theire furniture	6	10	0
In the ffeild			
8 keyne	16	0	0
3 Bullockes	4	0	0
150 sheepe	37	10	0
20 Lambes	3	0	0
19 acres of Wheate	27	10	0
4 acres of Rye	5	0	0
32 acres of Barlye	32	0	0
14 acres of Otes	10	0	0
10 acres of Tares	5	0	0
4 acres of Peaze	2	13	4
3 half acres of Beanes	1	5	0
The Lease of his ffarme	10	0	0
His Wearinge Apparrell	2	0	0
Money in his pursse	1	0	0
[*£280.4.6*]	204	4	6

Note: The lengthy Will was dated 10th July and proved on 21st July 1597. The residuary legatee and executor was the testator's eldest son John. The overseers were left 3s 4d praying that Thomas Roger the younger, of Sutton and Simon Carpenter, of Cheam, would be good friends to John. His wife Elisabeth was given £30 and the large quantity of household goods which she had brought with her to the marriage and a gift of two cows and some grain. For the ensuing year she was given the lease of the house and land at West Cheam and the right to occupy the hall and the inner upper chamber in the Sutton house, provided she stayed unmarried. Elisabeth's two children, William and Elisabeth Harper, were given grain. His own daughters Elisabeth, Jonne and Ellen Smith, were given linen and £25, £30 and £30, respectively. John was to provide a living for the three girls and his two younger brothers, keeping Thomas at school for 1½ years and paying him £30 and giving Jeffery a cow, 6 wethers and £20, at times arranged by the testator. Jefferie senior's sister Charelton of Banstead and sister Roger of Wallington were given barley. The sum of 6s 8d was left to the church of Sutton and 13s 4d to the poor of the parish. The witnesses were Symon Carpenter, Thomas Franke, George Franke, Hew Judery and John Parker.

Ref: 1597 B 66/1 Will 1597 B 66/2 Inventory

Richard Stanbridge **376**

of Worplesdon, beer brewer; taken by Thomas Russell, Thomas Ockley and John Jenner, 12th May 1597.

	£	s	d
In his purse	1	0	0
His bedinge at	2	0	0
All the rest of his bedinge is at	3	0	0
All his waringe parrell is at	3	0	0
To tabeles and a forme		5	0
All his chestes and a chayre at		5	0
To brasepotes at		5	0
A caderrene at		5	0
A pane at		5	0
3 citteles at		5	0
5 plateres and to peter disshes at		4	0
3 canstickes		1	6
2 saltselleres at			6
A dussene of spones at			8
A dossene of trencheres at			2
2 cobordes at		5	0
3 payre of shetes		12	0
A payr of blanccketes		3	4
To boulstores at		3	0
2 payre of potehangers		1	6
A brandeiorne			6
A gergereirone			6
A broach at			6
and friinge pane			8
A tabelle clothe			8
A sacke			10
A bittele and 3 wedges		1	0
and to billes		1	0
On handsae			4
2 chiseles			4
A drainge knife			3
2 augeres			2
2 wimpeles			2
and a sorde and a gadere		3	0
A hate		3	4
His botes and his spores		1	6
A bridel and a scaddell		5	0

A greate kefe	1	0
All the bruinge fessell besides the kefe at	4	0
Halfe a busshell of rye	2	6
A hoste hayre	2	6
A mare at	16	0
A colte	10	0
A hodge at	3	4
A cart saddell and all that belonges to him	1	0
A siefe	1	0
A mackhoke		4
A war bill		6
A spitter		2
A loade of wode at	2	0
All his benes standing uppon the groune at the prise	1	0
[*£15*	*7*	*7*]

[*Written near the end of the Will*:] Robert Russell of Frenches must paye me at Mytsomer Day next commynge for a cowe and a calfe	2	12	0

Note: The undated Will was proved on 19th July 1597. The executrix and residuary legatee was the testator's wife. His overseers were John Russell, wheelwright and Thomas Busshelle, to whom sums of 5s apiece were to be paid within a month, if they could gather in the money. He bestowed money and goods where he knew they would be welcome. The value of 30s was to be bestowed on his poor neighbours in bread and beer at his burial. Poor widows and poor men of the parish were to have a share of £1. Nicholas Carter's wife was given 10s and the testator's sister's children £1, with an extra £1 for her eldest son. A gift of 16s was to go to John Rogers and his children and a like sum to Robert Christmas and his children. His two coats were given to Robert Christmas and John Crose; a pair of hose to Harry Bennet; and a doublet each to John Rogers, John Thatcher, William Underwood and Thomas Bennet. The three witnesses were Thomas Bayly, Thomas Ockley and John Jenner. The burial of the testator was recorded on 5th May 1597.

Ref: 1597 B 68/1 Will 1597 B 68/2 Inventory

Rychard Styllwell **377**

of Eashing in Godalming, husbandman; taken by John Flodder, Harry Sturte, Robert Peyto and Arnolde Smyther, 2nd May 1597.

	£	s	d
In the halle			
2 tables, 2 forme, one chear, 2 payer of tresseles		5	0
In the chamber where he laye			
One luned bedsted, 1 flockbed, 2 bolsters, 2 pyllowes, 2 coverlettes, 1 payer of blanckettes, 3 chestes and a forme		16	8
In the next chamber			
2 olde bedstedes, 2 flockbedes, 2 bolstares, 2 olde coverletes, 1 cofer, 1 forme	1	0	0
Lynen clothes, 3 table clothes, 5 shetys, 4 pyllowberes, 2 table napkynes	1	0	0
Hys apparrell	3	6	8
Mony in hys pursse		5	0
Pewtar vessell, 1 basen, 10 platteres, 11 pewter dyshes, 4 sawseres, 4 yerd dyshes, 2 dosen of sponys, 3 saltselleres	1	13	4
Brasse vessell, 2 pottys, 4 kytles, 2 pannes, 1 posnatt, 1 skellett, 6 old candelstykes	1	13	4
3 brochys, 2 awndIrones, 2 pothokes, 2 pothangeres, 1 drypynge pan, 1 fryinge pan, 1 gyrdIron and a fleshehoke		13	4
Wodden vesselles, 1 kedetrowgh, 1 kefe, 2 fates with serten barrelles, stobbynes, bowles, treas, bokettes, dyshes and a butter chearne	1	6	8
One shovell, 2 beckes, 1 axe, 1 bylle, 1 shythe, a longe hooke and a			

spynnynge whele		5	0
Halfe a tod of wolle		10	0
1 harrowe, 12 watles, 2 ladderes		10	0
A cocke and serten hennes		3	4
Catle			
3 kene and a heyford	8	0	0
1 bollock of a yere olde and 2 weyned calves	1	6	8
6 olde shepe and 5 lambes	2	0	0
4 smale hogges		12	0
Corne			
3 bushelles of french wheat		10	0
8 acres of wheat and Rye	10	0	0
4 acres of otys	2	13	4
2 acres of pease	1	6	8
Serten benys and Rotys in the garden		13	4
[*£40.10.4*]	42	10	4

Note: The Will was dated 27th April and was proved on 19th July 1597. The testator asked to be buried in Godalming churchyard and gave all he had to his wife Christine, making her executrix. The document was witnessed by 5 people: John Flodder, Harry Sturte and his wife Joan, Alyce Sturte, widow and Arnold Smither. It is recorded that no bond was taken by order of Mr Chancelor. The burial of Richard Stillwell took place on 29th March according to the parish register, but at least one of the three dates is probably an error.

Ref: 1597 B 69/1 Will 1597 B 69/2 Inventory

Thomas Thorp **378**

of Henley Park in Ash, yeoman 1597 [*no appraisers given*]

A note of his Cattell	£	s	d
4 oxen	10	0	0
A cowe that Wakford hath	2	2	0
A cowe that Hewghe Goaringe hath	1	19	0
A cowe that Pullen hath if he paye not £2 at Michelmas then he must deliver the cowe	2	0	0
5 steares and a bull and a hecfer	11	13	4
2 mares and a nagge and a suckinge colt	3	0	0
A yewe and a lambe		3	4
3 kine of Balgen, if he paye not £4 at St Thomas daie before Christmas, witnesse Ambros Duke	4	0	0
A yoke of oxen delivered by John Chuter the yonger, before Goodman Gyles, if he paye a £5 of Miclemasdaie	5	0	0
A colt of John Beddell, if he paie a £1 the 7th day of Agust	1	0	0
His grasse or groundes			
For Dearie that John Beddell hath taken to be paide the saide time the 7th daie of Agust	1	6	8
Dawes meade		[*blank*]	
Halfe of a meade at Aldershot where Huntingford hath the halfe		[*blank*]	
The money that is dewe to him			
Of A cawte as apperes by a bond is dewe at St Peter's tide	15	0	0
Of Huntingford at Miclemas as apperes bie a bond	5	0	0
Of Thomas Cawte and John Hinde miller to be paide on all saintes daie at Thomas Edwardes at Farnham	5	0	0
Of John Chuter the Father	2	0	0
Of Roger Borowe	3	0	0
Of John Tempet		19	0

	£	s	d
Of the bucher of Pirbright	1	3	0
Of Dare of Ashe		10	0
The whole of all 3 score and 14 pounds 16s 4d besides £2 which he gave for his buriall to the poore	74	16	4

Note: The nuncupative Will was dated 28th June and proved on 19th July 1597. The executor and a residuary legatee of one third part of the estate was his nephew Henry Thorpe, in the Will called "cosen", the eldest son of Thomas's brother William. No overseers were appointed. Thomas asked for christian burial, setting aside £2 as listed in the Inventory and also 10s for the poor men's box of Ash. The two younger sons of Thomas's brother Henry were to share the second of the three parts and his sister Avis Smith, of Brown Candover in the County of Southampton, widow, was to have the last of the three parts. The executor, a carpenter of Brown Candover, together with Richard Sutton of Abbots Itchen, husbandman, put up the administration bond. Francis Browne Esquire and Henry Jewre had been witnesses at the making of the Will. The testator was buried on 2nd July 1597 at Ash.

Ref: 1597 B 73/1 Will 1597 B 73/2 Inventory

Katherine Vine **379**

of Shackleford in Godalming, gentlewoman; taken by Thomas Marland, Davie Tanner, Richard Billinghurst and Nicholas Burle, 30th March 1597.

	£	s	d
In her purse	1	10	0
In the parlore			
A longe Table and five Joyne Stoles and three chayres and two syde Tables and two formes	1	10	0
Two Carpettes and sixe Cowshines with to Coubbart Clothes	1	0	0
One frame and one mappe		1	0
Two Anderongs			8
In the hall			
Two Tables, foure formes and Two payre of Tressells and a ronde Table		16	0
A Cubbarte	1	0	0
In the great Chamber			
One Bed of downe with a bolster and a payre of Pillowes with a bedsteadell	6	0	0
A payre of fusten blanckettes and a Coverlett and a white blanckett with a blew Quilte of damaske with five Courtines and the vallantes	4	0	0
In the same Chamber			
A pallet with a faire Coveringe and a bolster and a payre of fusten blanckettes and a payre of Pillowes	5	10	0
Sixe silke Cowshines with the hangynnes of blewe seay	2	10	0
A fether bed	1	6	8
Two greate Chestes with Two Joyne Chaires	2	10	0
In a nouter Chamber			
A fether bed with a bolster and a bedsteadell		16	0
Two Chayres and two Chestes with the hanginges		10	0
In the Studye Chamber			
A fether bed, two bolsteres with too blanckettes and bedsteadell with Curtines and vallantes	2	0	0
A Coubbart with the hanginges		5	0
In the Gallarie Chamber			
Two fether bedes, one bolster and Two blanckettes and a Coverlite with a bedsteadele Curtines and hanginges	1	10	0
Two Chestes and a Chayre		13	4
A bede with a blanckett		5	0
Two Chestes and a forme		2	6

A great Cofer in the Gallary		3	4
A syde saddell with the furniture		13	4
In the Garrett			
Two linen wheeles		1	0
In the Kittchen			
Foure brasse Pottes with a littell posenete	2	0	0
Three kettells and three pannes and a fiere panne with a Chafindishe with a brasen ladle and a skymmer	1	6	8
A Cawdrone of brasse		18	0
Three dripinge panes and six spites with two Griddians and foure payre of pothookes		13	4
Tonges and fiere panne and Chopping knyfes		3	4
A morter with the pessell		4	0
One Table and one payre of Tressells and a forme		2	6
One Coubbarte		2	0
A payre of Andirons		4	0
In the Bruhowse			
Three vaytes with the reste of bruinge thinges	1	10	0
A furnse of brasse		8	0
In the bake howse			
A great vayte and Two nead troufes and a boltinhuche and a nead Toubb	1	0	0
In the littell Butterie			
2 barrells, a butter Charme and a bole and a bread grate		6	8
In the great Butterye			
Sixe Puter Candelstickes and one salte		6	0
Three Puter Basons and three Eweres		6	0
Foure dosen of Puter, Two dosen of plates, foure poringers and eyght sawsers	2	2	0
Foure Puter Chamber pottes		3	4
Two barrells		2	6
Trenchers		1	0
In the Larder			
Two tables and three Tressells with a poudering troffe with boles and too Toubes with a shelfe		6	8
In the littell parlor			
A Table and a cheste with Toubes and other lumbber with a spytte		10	0
A trevitt with old iron and four iron wigges		6	8
A payre of scalles, beame and waytes		3	4
In a littell Store howse			
Glasses and a whele and some lumber		3	4
In a Clossett			
1 Chest with shelfes and Joynner toles		5	0
In the linen Chambber			
Foure payre of fine sheetes	2	0	0
1 dossen of Table napkines		4	0
6 Table Clothes		12	0
Her one aparell	6	0	0
1 fine gowne black	2	0	0
Two gownes	2	10	0
1 kirtell and a petycoate		[*blank*]	
In a linine Chest			
Three payre of pillowebeares, five holland napkines and a Damaske table clothe and a Damaske towell	1	6	8
In the feildes			
6 acares of wheate	6	0	0

Foure acares and a half of Rye	3	13	4
6 acars of ottes 8s. the acare	2	2	0
1 acare and halfe of teares and pease		8	0
Biles browne and a dogge and a saye		4	0
Foure fliches of bacon and too sydes of beffe	1	6	8
Tenne kinde and five bullockes and a calfe	27	10	0
Twentie and foure sheepe and seaven lambes	5	10	0
In the barne			
The Corne and heay	2	0	0
Foure hogges and foure smale piggs	1	10	0
Three horses	3	0	0
A Carte with olde wheles with harnese and furniture		5	0
Pottes and a leatherne bottell and glasse, a flogon bottell		2	0
Eyght Duckes and a mallard		4	0
To capones and sixe hennes and a cok		4	0
A Bushell and halfe a Bushell and a pecke and half a pecke		2	6
4 Bushells of malte and a peck of beans and a bushell and halfe of hoams	1	1	6
Dettes owinge			
John Bauldine the yonger	5	0	0
In wittensse whereof the Praysers have setto our handes and markes			
Giles Harrison, Richard Billinghurst, Thomas Marlyn, Davie Tanner, Nicholas Burle			
A bed in the littell Chamber which is lefte unpraised and forgotten which restethe untell they come again.			
Bowe and arrowes with the other harnesse at	2	0	0
	120	8	8

Note: The Will was dated 26th March and was proved on 27th March 1597. The executor and residuary legatee, if he survived his sickness, was Anthony, the youngest son of the testatrix. The overseer appointed to comfort and advise him was Christopher Reeves. Katherine asked for an escutcheon of the best to be set in the south side of the chancel to mark the site of her own burial and that of her father. She gave £1 to be distributed to the poor at her burial. The eleven beneficiaries were William, Richard, George and Anthony, her 4 sons; Mary, Elizabeth the younger, Elizabeth the older and Benett, her 4 daughters; Catherine Bell, her manservant John Juar and Christopher Reeves, the overseer. The list of individual items was wide-ranging and numerous, from William's 17 separate bequests to George's bequest of one cow. Of the four witnesses, Giles Harrison, Roger Dernelly, John Coolls and James Woodgier, the first two signed and the second two made their marks. Francis Taylor, the vicar of Godalming wrote at the bottom of the Will 'The executor beinge sick, is sworne to this wyll the second daye of Aprill 1597.' He was granted probate on the 27th of the month and the administration bond was provided by the same Anthony Vine of Farnham, gent. and Roger Darnely, also of Farnham, yeoman. The testatrix had been buried on 4th March according to the parish register, but this may be an error.

Ref: 1597 B 78/1 Will 1597 B 78/2 Inventory

1598

Richard Deane **380**

of Alfold, husbandman; taken by Oliver Mower, Richard Kynge, John Sherlock, with others, 24th May 1598. *Document mutilated - several ragged holes*

	£	s	d
Mony in his Pursse		2	0
All his Apparell	1	0	0
One Table with a forme and one bench		1	8
All the Brasse	1	0	0
One Iron pot		1	6

	£	s	d
All the Pewter		5	0
Chayres, stooles, benches and shelves		1	0
One Pothanger and two pot hookes			8
One Cupboord		5	0
Tubbes, boules, bucketes [*]shes, fyrkyns and all other Woodde[* *]		2	0
Two Bedes with [*] Coverletes and blanketes theru[*nto belonging*]	1	0	0
Two payre of Sheetes one [* *] and one Table Cloth		10	0
Three Chestes		1	6
Mault in the house		3	0
Two Turnes			10
Sackes, syves and basketes		1	4
One Powdering trow and a kneading trow		1	0
All the Earthen Crockes and Potes			1
Two sythes, one byll, one axe, one prong, one spytter and a shovell and all other tooles of husbandry		3	0
Old Iron and all other thinges of [*sm*]all value			2
One Cow, two bullockes and a Wayned calfe	4	13	4
Two horse beastes	1	15	0
All the Wheat and Rye growing on the ground	1	0	0
The Oates growing on the ground		15	0
Hay and straw about the house		3	4
A Donngpot, a Cart and a payre of Wheeles and a Harrow		4	0
The Doung and Rackes in the gate		3	4
Two Hoges		6	8
One Hen			4
The value of one lease of a Tenement and certeine landes wherin the said Richard Deane late Dwelt	2	0	0
The value of one lease of a Coppyhold called ffursyns lyeing in the said parishe of Alfould in the Countie of Surrey aforesaid	5	0	0
	21	0	10

Note: On 1st June 1598 Slicea, the widow, begged leave to administer her late husband's goods and chattels. John Hurst of Alfold, yeoman, bound himself well and truly to do the same.

Ref: 1598 Ad 17

Catherine Hills **381**

of Kingston upon Thames, widow; taken by John Dodson, cooper, Nicolas Foster and Robert Creswell, 24th May 1598. [*Part torn off right side*]

	£	s	d	£	s	d
In the Hall						
For 14 yardes of Waynscott					13	4
The Porttoll					3	4
One ioyne Table					6	8
Half a dozen of ioyned stooles					3	[*]
One owld Tabl in the Corner						6
The paynted Clothes					5	[*]
One owld Cubbord					5	0
One other Cubbord and a press					8	[*]
2 owld Chayres					1	6
One payre of Crepers						8
One payre of Andyorns					1	4
One ffyer shovell						2
One iorne to sett a fore the fyer						4
One payre of Tonges						4

A Slyce					3
2 tosteing iornes					2
A payre of Bellowes					6
2 Cusheinges					2
A payre of pothookes					2
	2	15	5		
In the Butterie					
For a Gerdiorne					6
For 2 Spittes					8
For a Warmeing pane				1	0
A Brasse pott				3	4
A Litell Scillet					6
A Chafeing dishe					6
More a drypeing pane					6
A Scumer					4
One Kittell				3	4
For 14 pound of owld pewtter at 4 pence per pound				4	8
For 2 Bowe pottes					4
For 2 quart pottes				2	0
For 3 pynt pottes				1	6
For 2 owld cupes and a salt					6
One pewtter Canndelstike					3
One pewtter Saltseller					4
2 Brasse Canndellstikes					8
Half a pint wyne pott					4
For wodden vessell					6
2 Stone Jugges					3
A posset pott					2
One Tannckard					2
2 owld Cubbord clothes					10
	1	3	2		
In the chamber over the hall					
One fether bed, one bowlster and one pillowe				16	0
A Bedsteadell				4	0
One owld Coverlett and blannket				3	0
One payre of owld sheetes				1	0
Her apparell				4	9
2 Towelles				1	4
Half a dozen of Napekins					6
3 pillow beers				1	6
2 hand towelles					8
A Wallet					4
One apporne					6
One payre of fflaxen sheetes				5	0
One payre of Tune sheetes				3	4
2 Tabl clothes				1	8
One chest of fure boord				3	4
One other owld chest				1	4
	2	8	3		
In the Chamber over the Butterye					
For one owld Tabl with the Tresselles				1	0
For the glasse					4
		1	4		

In the Parllor						
A Tabl, a fforme and a Benche					10	0
More a Carpet						8
Paynted Clothes					2	0
A waynscott chest					2	0
		14	8			
In the kitcheinge						
For the ffurnasse					6	8
One Trivatt						6
One owld Kitell						2
A Doore and Shelves					1	0
A measheing fatt					1	6
One owlde Tune					1	6
Twentie Civears and Tubbs at 6 pence a peece					10	0
A Tabl, tresselles and fframe					1	6
	1	2	10			
In the yarde						
The Bavein stake and Baveins					10	0
		10	0			
In the stable						
Too Ladders					8	0
The mannger and plannkes					1	6
A Hoges Tubb						2
		2	4			
				8	14	0

Administration of the goods and chattels was granted to Helen Syms of Kingston, widow, the natural daughter of the deceased, on 31st May 1598. She was bound to carry out the administration well and truly, together with Nicholas Foster, also of Kingston, cook.

Ref: 1598 Ad 34

Note: The burial of Catryn Hyll was recorded on 14th May 1598.

Henry Pencoste **382**

of Long Ditton, matchmaker; taken by John Walter, John Roger and Thomas Marter, 15th May 1598.

	£	s	d
Two fetherbeds, two boulsters and 4 pillowes	2	0	0
3 coverings, wherof two are simples and on blankett		10	0
Three course beddsteeds		5	0
Three chestes		6	8
Seven peare of sheets	1	0	0
Two pillowbeeres		2	0
His wearing apparrell		10	0
A flockbed, a boulster and a pillow		2	0
Two packeing sackes		3	4
Painted clothes		3	4
Five platters, 3 dishes, two sacers, 3 pottes, two saltes and on dosen of spoones - al of pewter		10	0
On dosen of trenchers			4
Two tables, two peare of trestles, two formes, two cheeres and two stooles		5	0
On caldron, fower kettles, on brasse pott and two skeletts	1	5	0
On spitt, on trevett, on peare of pott hookes, on peare of pott hangers and on frying panne		3	4

3 hundreth of matche	2	0	0
Five hundreth of towe	1	0	0
On washing boule, on washing tubbe, on churne, with other old lumber		12	0
On cheese presse		1	4
Two billes, two billhookes and on axe		2	6
Two spinninge whiles, peare of bellowes, a peare of scales and 3 leaden waights with a fann		5	0
On nagge, on mare and two coltes	5	0	0
Three sutes		10	0
Six lambes		15	0
Five kine	10	0	0
Fower bullockes of a yeare olde	3	0	0
Fower cowes	1	0	0
On peare of harrowes		10	0
Harnis for two horses and two pannels		6	8
Three ladders		2	6
On long carte with shodde whiles	2	10	0
On donge carte with whiles		13	4
Twelve acres of pese, tares and Otes	5	0	0
On acre of winter corne, Rye and wheate	1	0	0
	41	14	4

[*Written on the Will*:] Debtes which I owe

First to on Mr Eaton £10, as parcell of £24 whereof £14 is paid	[£*10*	*0*	*0*]
To one Mr Skilton	8	0	0
To Robert Ostler and Dally of Kingston for a cart and whiles bound	2	13	0
To Rose Marter	14	0	0
To John Brownent, parson of Long ditton	1	14	10
Dettes owing me			
John Rootes neere Cheley in Sussex	1	10	0
Robert Basemore	1	6	8
My sone Lawrance Pencoste hath in his keeping of myne 14 hundreth and halfe of towe and an hundreth of match			

Note: The Will was dated 7th May and proved on 31st May 1598. The residuary legatee and executrix was the testator's wife Elizabeth. Henry asked to be buried in Long Ditton churchyard and he appointed Mychael Pyburne, his brother, to be overseer. Henry made a mark instread of writing his name on the document, which was witnessed and signed by John Brownent, clerk and parson. The widow provided the administration bond. The burial had been recorded on 11th May 1597.

Ref: 1598 B 33/1 Will 1598 B 33/2 Inventory

Richard Pereson **383**

of Frensham, tailor, 10th October 1598. [*no appraisers given*]

	£	s	d
His Apperrell	1	0	0
A littell brasse kettell		3	0
A payre of sheres and his pressing Ire			8
Debtes whych are owing unto hime			
Wylliam Hayward	2	0	0
Ollyver Clere	2	0	0
Thomas Payne	7	10	0
He, the said Thomas, oweth for two ewe sheepe more		10	0
He oweth more for 6 yers rent of A close at 6s 8d yere: the sum	2	0	0
John Bettsworth, the sonn of John Bettsworth, the elder son of John			

Bettsworth of Combers in the parish of Studham, he oweth unto me	10	0	0
Richard Freborne he oweth unto me		19	0
Walter Courte he oweth unto me	1	0	0
Thomas Courte he oweth unto me	2	0	0
William Fachine he oweth unto me		10	0
Richard Lune he oweth unto me		19	0
Wylliam Tycner oweth unto me for twoe ewe sheepe, which he taketh to halfe the woole and halfe the Lamb		[*blank*]	
Henrye Curtnes oweth unto me		10	0
Robert Walkesoade oweth unto me		10	0
This debtes he, the said Richard, confesed to be owing unto hime in the presentes of Thomas Payne and Ollyver Cleare			
[*£31.11.8*]	32	1	8

Note: The Will was dated 7th October 1598 and proved on 27th February 1598/9. The executor and residuary legatee was the testator's brother William Pereson. From his inheritance William was to pay £7 each to their two sisters Jonn and Agnes Pereson, at or before the next Lady Day, 25th March. No overseers were appointed. The two witnesses Thomas Payne and Oliver Clare made their marks. The testator had asked to be buried in Frensham churchyard.

Ref: 1598 B 31/1 Will 1598 B 31/2 Inventory

Thomas Stilwell **384**

of Witley, yeoman; taken by Anthony Slarkes and Thomas Mathewe, 28th May 1598.

In the haule	£	s	d
A table and forme		3	4
A cubard, a chayre and 2 cushens		13	0
A litle table and 2 stoles		3	4
Pothangers, pothookes, 2 spytes and 2 cobirones		5	0
A cauthern and A great kettell		12	0
A brasse pott, 3 kettels, driping pann, tryvet, a litle pan, skyllet and one other litle kettell		12	0
An old table and a trough		2	6
4 truges, buttercherne, chesepresse and poudring trow		4	4
A vate with a stande		1	8
In wooll and maulte		2	0
in the Chamber			
A flock bedd, bolster and coverlett		8	0
A ioyned bedstede, one other bedstede, 2 bolsters, 2 pillowes, 2 blankes and A coverlet	1	4	0
One other bedstede, linen tester, an old flockbed and 4 colfers		10	4
A table, 2 stoles, A flasket, 2 payre of shetes, a table cloth and one other sheete		14	8
His apparell and mony in his pursse	1	0	0
in the kytchen			
6 peuter platters, 2 dishes, 2 sausers, 2 saltes, 3 candelstickes and A driping pann		9	0
A gryndstone		1	4
Weges, shovell, spytter, 2 pronges, a beck, an axe, a byll, 2 Augers and drawing knyfe		3	4
without Dores			
One barryn cowe	1	13	4
A mare with a colte and one other colte	1	10	0
Fyve hoges, one shepe and 3 staules of bees	1	7	0
2 acres of wheate, one acre ½ of otes and twelve wattels	2	18	0

A litle carte and doung pot with other tacklinges		4	0
2 ladders, harrowes, sythes and donge		12	0
A bucket, sack, dishes and spons with all other lombery		2	0
Owing unto hym	7	0	0
[£22.16.2]	23	0	2

Note: The Will was dated 25th May and was proved on 1st June 1598. The residuary legatee and executor was the testator's son Robert. A shilling was left to the overseers, his neighbours Henry Flutter and Thomas Burle. One daughter Jelyan was left £3; the other Elizabeth was left £5 and the greatest kettle. Four members of the Chamber family had smaller legacies: £1 went to Margaret and 6s 8d each to Ellyn, Thomas and Sara. George Matchwick of Witley, husbandman, was left 1s. Both overseers and Lawrence Stoughton witnessed the Will. The executor provided the administration bond.

Ref: 1598 B 44/1 Will 1598 B 44/2 Inventory

1599

Edward Aburne **385**

of Weston in Albury, husbandman; taken by Robert Cowper, parson of Albury, William Risbridger of Shere, Thomas Mabanck, George Aldridge and John Maynarde, 19th April 1599.

	£	s	d
In the Hall			
One Joyned table, one Joyned forme, two Joyned stooles, one Cubberd and a Lytle Chayre, two Andyrons and a Creeper of Irone and two Iron potthangers	1	13	4
In the Buttery			
One old Cubberd, ffower old Tubbes, a kneding Keever, one boulting Hutch, Sixe trugges, Sixe woodden dishes		6	8
In pewter Vessell: Three Basons and one Ewer, ffower platters, Eleaven pewter dishes, ffyve pewter sawcers, a Dossen of spones, ffower pewter pottes, one dowble pewter salte, two pewter Cuppes	1	0	0
In Brasse: Two brasse poottes, three small kettelles, three old porsnettes, two Candelstickes, one Cullender, one old Chafing dish	1	1	0
In the outer Chamber			
One Joyned Bedsted with a ffetherbed and the furniture, one old Cubbard, two Chestes and one boxe, one Chayre Covered with leather	2	10	0
In the Chamber over the Hall			
One ffayre Bedsted, Joyned, with a ffetherbeed in it and the ffurniture, ffower Chestes, One Cubbard, Sixe old Cushions, one warmeing pann, a payre of Andirons of Iron and Brasse	6	13	4
In Lynen; Seaven payre of Sheetes, ffower Table Cloathes, Twelve Table napkins, Three pillowbeeres	3	0	0
One Bill, one axe, one Spitter with other workinge tooles for husbandry		3	4
His wareing apparell and money in his purse	3	6	8
In Cattell of all sortes			
Two kyne	5	0	0
One mare and one mare Colte of two yeres old	5	0	0
Sixetene old Sheep and Eight Lambes	5	13	4
ffower litle Hogges and two pigges		13	4
One harrowe		3	4
	[*£36*	*4*	*4*]

Note: The Will was dated 8th April and proved on 24th May 1599. The residuary legatee and executrix was the testator's wife Agnes. His friends, the overseers John Maynard and Thomas Mabanke, were trusted to share the goods and chattels fairly for the relatives, were Agnes to re-marry. Edward asked to be buried in Albury churchyard and he gave his dwelling house with its lands to Agnes to hold until his son John reached the age of 26. Were John to die without lawful issue, the house and land was bequeathed to his daughter Rebecca and her heirs, or failing her, to his nephew John Chittie and his heirs. Edward made his mark, but the two witnesses Thomas Mabanke and George Aldridge signed their names. The widow provided the administration bond. The burial of Edward Aborne was recorded on 9th April 1599 in the parish register of Albury.

Ref: 1599 B 1/1 Will 1599 B 1/2 Inventory

William Arnoulde **386**

of Reigate, yeoman; taken by Robert Tomson and John Sparke, 8th April 1599.

	£	s	d
Five payer of Sheetes and a table Cloathe	1	2	0
Thre yarde kerchers, a corner kercher, two hand towells, fowre handkerchers and fowre shertes		10	0
A rounde Cappe			6
A bushell bagge			4
Two pursses and a girdell		1	0
A blacke Cloake, a fustian Dublett, a payer of venetians, a payer stockinges and all his owlde apparell	2	6	8
A felte hatt and a nightcappe			10
A Latten Candelsticke			8
A flocke bead, two fether boulsters, two pillowes, two pillowbeers, a Coverlett and two blanckettes	1	10	0
Three sherte bandes, two payer of oulde gloves, a payer of fustian sokes, a payer of garters and a litle box			8
Three Chestes and a Chayere		6	0
In readye monye	17	8	6
	23	7	2

Note: The Will was written on 1st March and proved on 23rd May 1599. His three executors and residuary legatees were John Woodman of Colley, the elder, Benjamin Cooper and Robert Ware. A son-in-law William Myles and two daughters-in-law, Joane Sharpe and Mary Pledge, had bequests of money. There were other minor bequests, including the share of his woollen clothing between five men: Thomas Wonham, the father, Vincent Pullen, William Hubbard, Edward Ware and James Edwardes. Two kinswomen, Canber's wife of Chipstead and Arnold's widow of Merstham, were each left 6s 8d. The testator asked to be buried in the churchyard of Reigate near to his wife and he gave 20 dozen of bread to be shared by the poor there after his death. His longest chest was bequeathed to John Killick, the servant of John Woodman of Colley. No overseers were listed. The two witnesses Robart Tomson and Richard Banester signed their names. The burial of William Arnold of Combe was recorded on 7th April 1599 in the parish register of Reigate, St Mary's.

Ref: 1599 B 2/1 Will 1599 B 2/2 Inventory

Margerett Bennet **387**

of Farnham, widow; taken by John Dearing, John Searle, Christopher Stanes and Hugh Powlter, 10th April 1599.

	£	s	d
In the Chamber			
An olde bedsted, a flocke bed, a bolster, a pillowe, an olde Coverlet, a blancket and an olde tester		8	0
3 sheetes and 2 pilloweberes		8	0
A warminge pan		1	8
An olde cheste			6
Her wearinge apparill	1	6	8
In the Halle			
A table, 2 tressles, a forme, a Joyned stoole, an olde Chaire and a little			

Cubard				5	0
2 Iron Andirons, a fire shovell, a pere of tonges, a girdiron and pothangers				3	4
In the kitchine					
A brasse Cadron, a brasse pan, 2 brasse potes, a brasse skillet, a little kettle and an old chaffinge Dishe				18	0
An olde trowe and other olde tubes				2	0
In the gate					
A Cowe			2	0	0
			5	13	2

Note: The Will was dated 17th March and was proved on 24th May 1599. The residuary legatee and executor was the son-in-law of the testatrix, William Wheeler, husband of her daughter Joan. She asked to be buried in the churchyard of Farnham, where she was at that time a parishioner. No overseers were appointed. Most of her household goods were specifically given to her immediate family. Of her own generation her friend Joan Bicknell, widow, was given her best furred gown and her sister Alice Cocknaw, a worsted gown. The other bequests went to her son Samuell Bennett and his wife; to her daughter, Margerett Cooke; to Alice Bennett; and to her grandchildren Alexander and Margerett Wheeler, the children of William and Joan. Robert Bristowe wrote the Will, also witnessed by John Dearing and John Searle. The burial of old mother Bennett was recorded on 20th March in the parish register of Farnham.

Ref: 1599 B 4/1 Will 1599 B 4/2 Inventory

John Brownewend **388**

of Long Ditton, clerk and parson; taken by Thomas Jenckins, George Taylor and John Smalpece, 14th May 1599.

				£	s	d
In the hall						
A table and a frame and 7 Joyned stooles					10	0
A lytell table , a Joyned Cubbard with a Descke, a Joyned forme servinge as a benche and three turned chaires and a payre of bellows					10	8
A fire sholve, a paire of tonges, a paire of Awndyrons, a paire of Cottrels of Iron with hokes to hange pott or kettell over the fyre					6	8
A Lyttell Cubbard of boxes and a shelf					1	4
	£1	8	4			
In the Chamber next the hall beloe						
A Lytell Joyned bedstead, a liverie table, towe Joyned stooles, a deske of burd made to go into the bedd, a hamper and a strawe chaire					8	6
A fether bedd, towe pillowes, three blanckettes a rougge, a Canopie and a bedd matte made of hey				1	6	8
	£1	15	2			
The Chamber over it to the west end						
One Joyned bedstead with a testor and another bedsteade without a tester, one Joyned stoole and a shelf					8	6
One fether bedd, one bolster, towe blanckettes, a Dornackes coverlett, a bedd matte made of hey					16	0
	£1	4	6			
The next Chamber over the hall						
A Joyned bedstead, a trouckell bedstead, a Joyned Cubbard, a Lyverye Cubbard, 4 small Joyned stoles, fower chestes and one boxe				1	0	0
His Lyberarie of bokes there worthe				5	0	0
To wyndowe Cusshins of neadellworke and fowre of tufte						

mockadoe olde					6	6
2 olde grene Cubbard clothes of grene carsey					1	6
A fetherbedd, a mattrisse, one bolster and a bolster tyke, three pillowes, five blanckettes, towe coverlettes mad of wollen yarne, courteyns and vallence of grene seye				2	6	4
Towe gownes, three clockes, towe dublettes, towe cottes, three payre of breatches, sixe payre of stockinges, towe hattes, towe gyrdels, seven shertes, eight bandes, sixe handkerchers and sixe nyght Cappes				7	6	8
Sixe pewter platters, fower pewter disshes, towe Custard disshes, sixe frute dysshes, one pie plate, sixe sawcers, nyne poryngers, towe basons, fower salt sellers, towe chamber pottes, towe pewter pottes, 12 sponnes, towe candelstickes of Latten				1	3	4
A paire of Awndyrons, a fire sholve, a paire of tongges, a Lokinge glasse and a wicker Chaire					3	4
	£17	7	8			
The next rome within that Chamber						
A Corslett furnyshed				1	10	0
One Joyned stole, three shelves, five dossen of trenchers and a Capcase					3	4
A hand baskett, divers glasses for waters and to drincke with and towe brusshes					3	0
21 paire of sheetes, sixe payre of pyllowberes, fower dossen of table napkins, nyne table clothes, twelf towels, three Lynen Cubbard clothes				5	5	0
	£7	1	4			
In the Buttrye						
A bread bynne, a beare stond, towe shelves, a tobbe for vergis, three coverd baskettes and one hand baskett					2	8
A paire of bottes, sporres, slyppers and showes					5	0
20 pound of Lynen yarne					10	0
		17	8			
The maydes Chamber						
A bedsted, a wollen wheale and a Lynen wheale, a paire of wolle cardes, towe sicles and one shelf					2	6
One flockbedd, a bolster and a blanckett					5	0
		7	6			
The lofte over the Maides Chamber						
9 burdes, a Joyned benche, a chese racke, a paynted clothe, a hekchill and towe paire of wyndinge blades					6	8
11 pound of course yarne and a parsell of Roughe hempe					3	4
		10	0			
The Mylkhouse						
A table of a frame, a forme, five shelves, a haire Cubbard, a powdringe tobbe, a Charme, six Ches mottes, a littell tobb to salt chese, towe boxes of ot meales and salte, one gratte, fower butter pottes, 14 mylke boules, a paire of wodden scalles and a butter fyrkine					10	0
The boultinghouse						
A boultinghouche, towe knedynge vessels, a floure bynne, a vessell to washe in, sope, one bucking tobbe, a moulding burde, a chopping burde, three Lether bottels, towe drynking Jugges, 6 trene disshes, towe cupp disshes, a choppinge						

knyf and a mynsynge knyf		4	10
The Kechine			
Three brasse pottes, towe Kettels, three skellettes, one chafing dishe, one skymer, one bedd panne, one brasen Ladell, one slice, one bastinge Ladell, a morter and pestell, a brassen oven, a stillytorie with feate, three drippinge pannes, fowre spittes, one girdyron, towe fryinge pannes, a tryvett, towe cobyrons, a fende, a pothanger, towe paire of pothokes and one Iron peale	1	18	6
A cowpe, a dresser burde, three buckettes, a salt toubbe and a kyver		2	0
The Lofte over the ketchine			
A bedsteade with a paynted testor		2	6
A flocke bedd, a bolster, 2 blankettes of wollen yarne, coverlett		5	0
21 burdes and a shelf		7	6
An old saddell, brydell, old yron, a matthockes, old awgers, a garden Racke, a paire of carte ropes		2	8
In the nexte Lofte			
A hepe of wheat by estymacion 16 busshels, a heape of ottes of 20 busshels, a heape of barley of 3 bousshell	2	18	4
Three old sackes and towe bages and an old chese presse		3	10
Flaxe in grasse groing in the garden		2	0
Billett, faggott, baven and wod in the yarde		10	0
[*£7.7.2*] £7 17 2			
In the barne			
Unthresshed wheat and rye by estymacion	3	0	0
A heape of Rie in the barne not clene by estymacion worthe		10	0
Strawe and the hey in the barne worthe		6	8
The donge in the yard by estymacion worthe		6	8
Ottes in the barne worthe		8	0
A fanne, a busshell, a pecke, a half pecke, 2 pronges, a flaile, 2 corne sholves, a shodd shulve, a spade, an axe, a hedginge bill		3	4
A Longe carte, a donge carte with wheales to them, a ploughe, a paire of harrowes, a pece to make a carte boddie	1	10	0
The harnysse for 6 horse with halters, a stable pronge with 2 pannels		6	8
2 Ladders and a wheale barrowe		2	6
2 drie tubbes to put corne in		1	4
3 mares and towe geldinges	15	0	0
5 kyne and 3 bullockes of a yere olde	10	0	0
One sowe hogge		6	0
One Cocke, 6 hennes, on Mallard and 2 duckes		3	4
In grasse of the ground one acre and a half wheat and rye, towe acres barley, towe acres pease and three acres and a half of tares	2	16	8
Tithe wood in the woodes not yet brought out of the woodes worthe	2	0	0
In reddy money in the house	2	0	0
Deptes owinge him at his decease			
William Bose owethe for tithe heye 1598		4	4
Richard Hubbard owethe for tithe hey 1598		1	0
Richard Berry oweth for ottes		3	6
Barnard Edmondes owethe for 13 lod of tythe wood in Copte grove	3	0	8
Joseph Hoke owethe for ottes		3	6

Dover and Bose owethe for strawe						4	0
Humfrey Stynte owethe for strawe and for a busshell and a half of ottes						1	9
Thomas Wodward owethe for plowinge						3	0
Penticostes weddowe owethe for plowinge parsell of 14s						9	0
		£43	11	11			
[£81.11.3] £81 11 7							
He owethe to Tyffine of Kingston for 14 kylderkins beere		1	15	0			
So comethe the rest to	*[£79 16.3]*	£79	16	7			
Moreover there was owinge to hym at the daie of his deceasse in good deptes		£95	0	0			
So the whole comethe to	£174 16 7	*[£174*	*16*	*3]*			

Note: The Will was dated 3rd May and proved on 23rd May 1599. The testator asked to be buried in the chancel of Long Ditton church. The residuary legatee and executrix was his wife Jane. His brother and his cousin, both clerks, were appointed overseers, Richard of Banstead signing the Will Brownwend and Thomas of Cheam signing Brownent. His seven children were to be paid their legacies when they left their mother's care. Sums of £20 each were bequeathed to his sons John, Robert, Thomas and George. The sum of £30 each was left to the daughters, Jane, Frances and Margery. Two beneficiaries who were left £1 each and made their marks on the Will, were the widow Margaret Fletcher and a servant John Starr. Sara Baker the maid was left £2. These last three bequests were to be paid as soon after the funeral as they should be demanded. The widow and Thomas Roberts of Long Ditton, yeoman, provided the administration bond. In the parish register it was recorded that John Brownent, rector of this church, was buried on 5th May 1599.

Ref: 1599 B 6/1 Will 1599 B 6/2 Inventory

Andrew Fellmore **389**

of Farnham, servant with John Harding; 31st August 1599. *[no appraisers given]*

	£	s	d
His Apparrell	1	0	0
One obligacion wherein Richard Trigg of Privett standeth bound for the paiment of £14.6.0 by obligacion forfeited	14	6	0
	15	6	0

Note: The Will, written by Walter Crafte on 15th July 1599, appointed the testator's sister Elizabeth Fellmore executrix and legatee of £10. His brother Henry was to have £4 at the age of 21. His uncle Humfry Tanner was asked to invest Elizabeth's money for a year and Henry's money till he came of age. The residue was to be used to pay the funeral charges and the overseers were named as Humfry Tanner and George Walker, both of whom witnessed the Will, together with Robert Courtnes and Walter Crafte. The back of the document recorded 1st September 1599 as the date that the executrix was granted Probate. The said Elizabeth Fellmore, spinster and Humfry Tanner of Frensham, sawyer, provided the administration bond. The burial had taken place on 16th July.

Ref: 1599 B 16/1 Will 1599 B 16/2 Inventory

1600

John Boughton **390**

of Wotton, husbandman; taken by John Hayne of Wotton, yeoman; John Boughton of Warnham, Sussex; John Tayler and Roberte Butler, husbandmen, 6th May 1600.

the hall	£	s	d
One table, one fframe and a fforme		3	4
3 Kettles, a bell posenat and an old brasse potte		12	0
2 pewter platters, fyve pewter dishes, 2 latten Candlestrickes, one			

Chaffeinge dishe and a pewter saltseller		6	8
One Brandiron, a payer of potthookes and one potthanger, one old Chayer and an old Cradle		2	6
2 Awgers, a hand sawe and a Wymble, an old axe, an old Shoovell and a spitter, 2 pronges, one bill and a shavinge knife, a payer of Sheeres		3	0
the Lowe Chamber			
One old Cubberd, an old Kneedinge troughe and a siltinge or powdringe troughe		2	0
One Kilderkine, one Firkine, 2 Keevers, three old tubbes, 6 Wooden mylke vessells, one Chorne, sixe Woodden platters and 6 Wooden dishes		7	0
One spitte and an Iron drippinge pane, one pewter pynte pott		1	8
the Upper Chamber			
2 bedsteddles, one flocke bedd, one boulster, 2 old Keeveringes and 2 old blanckattes and a Iron shooinge horne		13	8
2 payer of sheetes, 6 old Chestes and an old table, one wollen whele and a fliche of bakon		13	4
2 acres of Whete and Rie	2	0	0
2 acres and a halfe of Ottes	1	0	0
3 Kyne with there Calves	5	0	0
2 too yerelinge hecfers and one two yerelinge bull	3	0	0
3 twelvemonthinges	1	10	0
3 hogges beinge halfe yere old		12	0
3 hens and a Cocke		2	0
His apparell and monye in his purse		13	4
Debtes certeyne and uncerteyne	10	0	0
Debtes owinge by John Boughton deceassed			
to John Hayne		18	0
to Robert Butler	6	13	4
to John Boughton of Warnham		14	3
to Edward Goodden	1	15	0
Oweinge at Horsham for certen wares sett by the said John Boughton deceassed of diverse men	3	5	2
to John Margeson		7	0
to Richard Lillye		2	0
to George Ditcher		2	6
to Ralfe Backes		1	4
Oweinge to fyve of the Children of the said John Boughton deceassed, beinge there grandfathers giftes to the value of which was to either of the fyve children 30 shillings a peece	7	10	0
Value of Inventory	[£*27*	*2*	*6*]
Debts owing to others	[£*21*	*8*	*7*]
Residue	[£*5*	*13*	*11*]

Note: The nuncupative Will, dated 25th April, was proved on 8th May 1600. The executrix and residuary legatee was his wife Katherine, so that she could maintain herself and bring up the rest of his children. The overseer was his brother-in-law Robert Butler, who was to ensure that a £4 legacy to the testator's son John was invested within 6 months and so to accrue until John was 21; of this money 30s was due as a gift from the boy's grandfather and the rest was to be paid out of the estate. Four other unnamed children of the testator inherited a similar 30s bequest. The Will is most interesting for the wish "to be buryed within the Christian buriall of the Chappell yeard of Okewood", at the southern end of the parish of Wotton. John Boughton and Robert Butler, both of Warnham, Sussex, husbandmen, were recorded as witnesses. The widow and Thomas Borer of Wotton, husbandman, put up the Administration Bond.

Ref: 1600 B 4/1 Will 1600 B 4/2 Inventory

Richard Edmed **391**

of Horsell; taken by Thomas Theiare, Richard Simondes, John Woodes and John Taylor, 7th April 1600.

	£	s	d
Monie in his Purse	1	0	0
His Apparrell	1	0	0
In the Parlor			
A bedsteed and a fetherbeed all thinges belonging to it	1	10	0
A Coobert		8	0
The Pewter upon the cobbart		12	0
3 chestes, a press, 2 painted clothes		7	0
A peece of new cloth	1	10	0
In the hale			
A Table, a forme, chaires and stooles		8	0
In Pewter a chafindish, a morter		6	0
A paire of Cobb Irons, a spit, a paire of poothangers		3	0
In the upper chamber			
2 flockbeedes, sheetes, blanketes, pillowes and beadsteades	1	10	0
1 chest, a Litell board, a sowrd		4	0
12 bushels of Rie	1	6	8
2 Bushels of Wheat		5	0
A quarter of Barlie		12	0
4 Bushels of otes		3	0
7 bushell of mault		10	6
5 paire off sheetes, 3 Table clothes, a Towell	1	2	0
In the Butterie			
5 boles, a butter churne and other implementes		5	0
In the Chitchinge			
In Brasse and other implementes	1	0	0
A yocke of oxen	5	0	0
A yocke of steers	4	0	0
6 Bullockes	4	0	0
6 Kine	8	0	0
3 horse, 2 cooltes	4	0	0
Shepe	2	0	0
For all the Corne one the growne	8	0	0
A plow, harrow, yockes and chaines, A carte	2	10	0
In hogges	2	0	0
A bill, an axe, a spade		2	6
Duckes and Geese and other pulterie		6	0
	[*£54*	*0*	*8*]

Note: The Will was dated 3rd April and was proved on 8th May 1600. The executors and equal residuary legatees were his wife Millicent and two of his sons John and George. Sums of 3s 4d were given to the overseers John Woodes and John Taylor. Millicent, having promised to be a good mother to his children, was given a life interest in his land, which after her decease was to go to his son Harry, together with a yoke of oxen, a horse, a good cart and farming implements. The testator gave 12d to Horsell church and asked to be buried in the churchyard there. A ewe and a lamb were given to Agnes Estwell and to John, Millicent and Elizabeth, three of Henry Edmead's children. Edward Parker, clerk and the overseers witnessed the Will. The Administration Bond was provided by the widow of Horsell and Thomas Thaier of Pirbright, husbandman.

Ref: 1600 B 16/1 Will 1600 B 16/2 Inventory

Thomas Grace **392**

of Kingston upon Thames, blacksmith; taken by Robert Sturmy, baker, John Dent, maltman and James Hubberstye, tailor, 5th May 1600.

	£	s	d	£	s	d
In the Hall						
A plancke table with two tressels, a forme and benches at					2	6
A cubbord with a deske to it and a cubbord clothe and a settle of waynscott at					1	6
Fyve turned smalle chaires with thre quissions at					1	0
The painted clothes						8
Two Andirons, a fyershovell, a paire of tonges and two paire of potthangers at					1	0
		6	8			
In the parlour						
An olde table with a frame, a forme and the benches at					2	0
Two olde ioyned stooles with the painted clothes					1	4
A paire of olde Andirons and a paire of hangers at						6
		3	10			
In the kytchen and Buttrey						
An old fornace with dyvers brewinge vessels and tubbes at					10	0
Thre olde kettles, two chafinge disshes, sixe candelstickes, a spice morter, seaven quarte pottes and fower pinte pottes of pewter at					7	4
Two pewter platters, sixtene pewter disshes, one Bason, one salt seller, sixe sawcers and a dozen of spoones					8	10
A kettle at					1	8
Two smalle brasse pottes at					5	0
Two Iron pottes at					2	0
An olde Chafer at						4
An olde warmynge pann at						6
	£1	15	8			
In the Chamber over the Hall						
Two olde bedstedles with painted testerns, two flock bedes, two fether boulsters, two flocke boulsters, two pillowes and two Coverletes at					10	0
A litle plancke table with two tressels, two formes with the painted clothe at					1	0
		11	0			
In the Chamber over the parlour						
Two headles bedstedes of olde bordes with a truckle bed, thre olde fether bedes, two blancketes, thre fether boulsters, fower pillowes and thre olde coverletes at				1	10	0
Fower olde chestes at					4	0
Olde painted clothes						4
	£1	14	4			
Lynnen						
24 payre of flexen and towen sheetes at				1	16	0
14 table clothes and towels at					7	0
Fyve pillowe beares					1	8
Two dozen of napkyns at					4	0
	£2	8	8			
In the lofte over the Kytchen						
Twelve busshels of malte				1	1	0
	£1	1	0			
In the yarde						
Fower smalle hogges and a hen at					13	4
Fower peeces of Tymber at					1	4

An olde Busshell						6
Fyer wood and hovell at				1	0	0
	£1	15	2			
The Lease of the testator's dwellinge house at					10	0
His apparell and money in his purse at					6	8
		16	8			
In the Shoppe						
Two Anviles, one paire of bellowes, sledges, hammers and other tooles belonginge to a smyth at				5	0	0
	£5	0	0			
All the Lomber aboute the house at					2	0
		2	0			
				15	15	0

Note: The Will was dated 28th March and proved on 7th May 1600. The residuary legatee and executrix was the testator's wife Katheryne. Sums of 1s each were left to the two overseers, his friends Robert Sturmye, baker and John Dent, maltman. His tenement and shop near Cooke Row in Kingston Market Place was left to his son Robert and his heirs for ever. For default of such lawful heirs, the property was to remain to the testator's daughter Elyzabeth Swyllier, wife of William Swyllyer of Mitcham and her heirs. For want of such issue, then the lawful next heirs of Thomas himself were to inherit. This bequest was dependent on the payment of 5s at each quarter day for life to Katheryne. His daughter Elyzabeth was to have £1 a year for four years only. Robert was left the tools of the trade and any moveable items in the tenement or shop. The testator made his mark, but the three witnesses signed: James Dent, James Hubbarste and Edward Fairebanck. It was recorded on the Will that no bond was taken.

Ref: 1600 B 21/1 Will 1600 B21/3 Inventory

Richard Harding **393**

of Dockenfield in Frensham, yeoman; taken by Phenix Browne, gent., John Harding of Sprakley, John Chaundler and William Newman, 20th June 1600.

	£	s	d
His Wearing Apparrell	4	0	0
In the High loft over the Hall two fether bedes furnishd	10	0	0
There 3 ioyned chests	1	0	0
Therin 12 paire of sheets	2	5	0
More six tableclothes and 2 dozen of Napkins	1	0	0
More 4 pillowe beeres		10	0
There a table and 3 ioyned stooles		7	0
A chaire and forme		2	0
Andirons		2	0
Windscoate	2	0	0
In an other chamber by a flockbed furnishd	2	0	0
More there a table and forme, stole and chaire		3	0
In the shop chamber a flockbed furnishd, a table,a chest and a chaire	2	0	0
In the maidens chamber 2 flockbeds furnishd	1	0	0
In the shop a flockbed furnishd		5	0
There a loome, a table and tresle with other Lumbry		10	0
In the Hall A table and forme, 2 chaires, 3 stooles and a cubberd, 3 greene carpets and 6 cushions together with windescoate and painted clothes	3	0	0
In the kitchin 8 flitches of Bacon	2	0	0
A farnace		10	0
2 brasse pots, 3 ketles, a brasse pan and a cawdron, 2 brasse skillets, 2 other litle skillets and 3 brasse candlesticks	2	0	0

4 dozen of pewter, 3 candlestickes, 4 saltes, 6 pewter dishes, 2 basons and 3 chamber pots	2	0	0
2 dozen of Trenchers and a dozen of Spoones		1	0
In the cheese Loft 17 cheeses		10	0
In the Bakehouse a bolting whitch, a kneading trowe, a powdring trowe with other implements		10	0
In the Buttry 10 barrells and other drinke vessels		10	0
In the milkehouse trugs and other milke vessels		10	0
In the kitchin loft of wheat and Rye a quarter	1	0	0
There a quarter of Mault		12	0
There tubbs and other wooden stuffe		5	0
A powdring tubbe and a cheese presse		3	0
In the gate Powltrye 12 hennes and a cocke		5	0
8 Stales of bees	1	0	0
A plowe and a cart unbound, 2 paire of wollen wheeles, a paire of smal harrowes and an oxe harrowe	2	0	0
Abroad in the feilds 2 yoake of oxen	11	0	0
10 kine	17	0	0
19 young bullocks	12	0	0
A mare and an old gelding for the cart	3	0	0
2 mares, 2 colts and a nag	5	0	0
15 weaning pigs	1	6	0
27 hogs	8	0	0
6 Acres of wheate	6	0	0
4 Acres of Rie	4	0	0
2 Acres of barly	1	0	0
9 Acres of Oates	4	10	0
3 Acres of french wheate	1	0	0
8 Acres of grasse	4	0	0
More 4 Acres of Oates	1	10	0
20 Tunne of Timber	3	0	0
Owing for wyne and Carriage	6	0	0
	132	16	0

Note: The Will was dated 6th June and was proved on 24th September 1600. The residuary legatee and executor was the testator's son Robert, but this legacy did not include the wainscot and standards in the dwelling house. Sums of 10s each were left to the overseers, his cousin John Harding and his brother John Chaundler. Richard asked to be buried in Frensham church, giving £2 to the poor of the parish. A bullock was given to each of his 19 grandchildren, the oldest animal to the oldest child "in order as they grow one after another." The children of his son Robert were Elizabeth, Constance, Katherine, Jane and Bridget. Daughter Marryan's nine children were Walter, Robert, Abraham, Elizabeth, Constance, Jane, Joan, John and Marryan. Daughter Jane's family were John, Richard, Robert, Constance and Jane. Apart from bequests to his three eldest children, the testator gave generously to his son Abraham and especially to his son John, who was to inherit all the unnamed freehold and copyhold land and tenements. Robert Bristowe wrote the Will, which was witnessed by the overseers. The executor of Dockenfield, yeoman and Richard Holney of Frensham, clerk, provided the Administration Bond.

Ref: 1600 B 24/1 Will 1600 B 24/2 Inventory

John Kent alias Newbery **394**

of Farnham, glover; taken by Willyam Welch, John Terrey and Phillip Warner, 27th May 1600.

	£	s	d
In the Hall			
A Table with a frame, 2 chayers, 2 Joyned stooles and 4 other stooles		8	0

A Joyned cubbard with a cubbard cloth of dornix and a settell		12	0
Paynted clothes and 3 shelves		3	4
2 Andyrons, 2 pott hangers, a payer of Tonges, a fyer pronge and a barre of Iron		6	0
A Byble with other bookes		13	4
2 Quisshens of dornix		3	4
In The Parler			
A Joyned bedsted		4	0
A paynted Tester with a vallence		3	4
A Tyke fether bed, a fether bolster, a flock bolster, a coverlett of List and two blanckettes	2	6	8
A cubbard, a presse, a Round Table and 2 coffers		10	0
4 payer of sheetes	1	0	0
3 Table clothes of canvas, 4 pillow beeres, 4 Table napkins		13	4
In The loft over the Parler			
A Joyned bedsted with a vallenc		10	0
A Tyke fether bed with a bolster and 2 blanckettes of List	3	6	8
A court bedsted		2	6
15 yeards of wollen cloth	1	10	0
A sqware Table with a frame		3	4
A great chest and 2 coffers		10	0
2 swords, a Rapyer and 2 daggers, a bowe, a sheafe of Arrowes, a red capp with a skull		13	4
In The Loft over the Butterey			
A bedsted, a flock bed, a coverlett, 2 blanckettes and a bolster		13	4
In The Loft over the Hall			
A bushell of Wheat, 8 bushells of barley, 7 bushells of Messelin, 4 bushells of Rye, 12 bushells of Maultt	3	11	4
7 pownd of hoppes		3	4
4 Tubbes with other lomber		3	4
In The Loft over the Shopp			
5 Toddes of wooll	5	0	0
A beame, a payer of skales and a Tod waight		3	4
2 Lynen wheeles, a Wollen wheele with other Lomber		5	0
In The Bakehowse			
A bowlting Hutch, a Trow, a kneding Keever and 6 Tubbes		6	8
4 shelves, 2 bottells, a bushell with other Lomber		3	4
In The Butterey			
A brasse pan, 5 brasse kettells, 2 brasse pottes, 6 brasse candelstickes	2	3	4
12 pewter platters, 10 pottingers, 8 sawcers, 2 pewter pottes, 2 salt sellers, 2 chamber pottes, 2 pewter cuppes, 2 fruitt dishes,a frying pan and a dripping pan	1	13	4
2 broches		1	0
7 Tubbes, a powdring Trow, a forme, 8 shelves with other lomber		10	0
10 cheeses		5	8
A brasse morter, a bred grate		2	0
8 smale bowles		2	6
3 fletches of bacon	1	0	0
5 sackes		2	6
In The Shopp			
7 dossin and a halfe of sheepes lether		11	4
Horsse lether Tawed		7	0
A dossen and a halfe of buckes skins	3	3	4
20 does skins	1	6	8

12 sheepe skins Tawed		3	0
6 lether pursses		1	6
2 sachells and a dossin of gloves		3	6
27 lambe skins		5	6
12 smale wooll fells		7	0
The Implements in the shopp		10	0
3 dossen of wooll ffells	2	10	0
3 dossen of doe skins in the pittes	1	16	0
2 hundred of sheepes pelttes	2	0	0
8 dossen of calves skins	2	0	0
5 horsse hydes in the pittes		15	0
2 drench Tubbes, a bucking Tubb, a Trow, a bealme and a Knyfe, an aporn, a blocke		6	0
A hooke, a Lather with other lomber		1	6
In The gate			
2 Lode of wood and a lode of ffaggottes		10	0
A cheese presse, 3 cheese fates with Sawed Tymber		13	4
In The Stable			
A Rack, a manger, a Whelebarrow, 3 shovels, a prong, a mattock, an axe, 4 bylles, a harrow, a harrowinge harnesse, a coller		8	0
A leasse of an acre and a halfe of grownd	2	0	0
An acre and a halfe of barley growing	1	0	0
2 acres and a halfe of otes and ffetches growing	1	0	0
Halfe an acre of wode growing		13	4
For hastyes, beanes and onyons growing		5	0
A gelding, brydell and saddell	2	0	0
5 kyne and 2 Heyffer bullockes	10	0	0
Hogges and 4 pigges		16	0
A ewe and a lambe		6	8
His apparrell and money in his pursse	3	0	0
In detts owing to the testator	16	10	0
In Ready money	18	0	0
	103	18	10

Note: The Will was dated 3rd May and was proved on 8th May 1600. The residuary legatees and joint executors were the testator's wife Margaret and son John. Sums of 2s 6d were left to the overseers, his friend William Welch and his brother-in-law Thomas Marner. The testator asked to be buried in Farnham churchyard near the door, where some of his children already lay. He gave 1s towards church repairs and £1 to the poor of the parish. Margaret was to have Hatch Close in Wrecclesham for life, with the right to bestow it where she chose; she was also given four cows and her own bed and bedding. His daughters, Jane and Margaret, were given two heifers between them and £10 when they married. His daughter Elizabeth and her son John were left £5 and £2, respectively. His brother Thomas Marner was given three doeskins and his sister Alice Stevens was left 3s 4d. Robert Bristowe wrote the will, which was witnessed by Phillip Warner and William Welch. On 5th May 1600 the burial of John Newberry als. Kent was recorded in the parish register.

Ref: 1600 B 37/1 Will 1600 B 37/2 Inventory

Elizabeth Lambert **395**

of St Thomas the apostle, Southwark, widow; taken by John Launce and George [?]Brunname. [*undated*]

	£	s	d
One oulde feterbeed and one boulster and foure pilles	1	0	0
Foure oulde coverledes and three blankites		16	0

	£	s	d
Three courtens and a pece of ane oulde vallient		2	0
One oulde beedstead		5	0
Sixe ould chistes		10	0
One oulde cubberd and one tabble and one oulde beence		5	0
Foure stoules, three cheares, a lettel table		5	0
One wicker flasket, tow basketes, one candellcas		1	0
One ould buffing goune	1	0	0
One certell, tow petticottes, tow wascottes		13	4
Foure pare of flacksonne shettes	1	6	8
Towe pare of towne shettes, a halfe shet		6	0
One dusen of oulde napkkinges		2	0
Three smockes, eight apernes		5	0
Sixe olde pilleberes		1	6
Five ould neckengers, tow neckclothes		5	0
Five ould cerchers		2	0
Five ould tabblclothes		4	0
Four oulde dipper tabllclothes		6	0
Sertting ould putter lumberment		12	0
Five ould cettles		8	0
Tow ould brasse potes		4	0
Tow sceeletes, a warming panne, a chafer and a spice morter		3	0
Sertten ould Irne and brase lumberment		6	8
Tow bickernhedes, a pare of bellowes		10	0
	[*£9*	*19*	*2*]

Note: The Will was dated 29th March and proved on 6th May 1600. The executors and residuary legatees were Thomas Corsley and Nicholas Eliott. No overseers were named and no bond was taken. A scarlet petticoat was given to Alice, wife of Thomas Corsley. The wife of Richard Salter, the apothecary, was given the best black gown and a costermonger's wife living at the Three Cranes was to have the widow's felt hat. Her great dripping pan and her washing bowl had been promised to "the daughter of that man who dwelleth at the sign of the Three Buckes in Cornewall Street in London." Elizabeth willed her "body to be buried where it should please God to provide for it." Richard Hall, scrivener, neatly wrote the will, signed by him and Joan Wyllssone as witnesses.

Ref: 1600 B 29/1 Will 1600 B 29/2 Inventory

William Parkes **396**

of Richmond alias West Sheen, carpenter; taken by Thomas Gisbie, Thomas South and John Marshall, 25th April 1600.

	£	s	d
In the Hall			
On cupborde, on table and forme		17	4
The Wainescott and bentch there		5	0
A holberde and Bill		2	0
In the Parlor			
On bedsted, on fether bed, on boulster, on pillowe, 3 curtens, on rugg of greene color and 2 blancketts	2	0	0
On truckle bedsted, on court cupborde, on table, six stooles, a litle cupborde, an old chaire, 3 cushens, a carpett, a setle and the painted clothes there, also a litle paire of andirons	1	0	0
In the chamber over the Parlor			
A standing bedsted, a truckle bedsted, on fether bed, on boulster, on pillowe, on blancket, on coverled, 3 curtens	1	0	0
A rounde table, a carpett, a cort cupborde, an olde chaire, 2 formes, 2 creepers and the painted clothes there		16	0

In the chamber at the staires hedd			
A half heded bedsted, a flockbedd, 2 coverleds, on boulster, a litle table and an emptie chest		9	0
In the chamber over the Kytchen			
Two bedstedds, the on seeled, the other half heded, on blanckett, on boulster, on olde pillowe		10	0
2 chestes, a box and a flaskett		4	0
In the chamber over the Butterie			
On bedsted, a painted cloth over it, a fether bed, 2 boulsters, on blanckett, on covering	1	0	0
On table, on chest, a litle stoole, 2 andirons, a paire of tonges, a paire of bellowes and the painted clothes there		5	0
In the litle roome next the yarde			
An oulde bedsted, 2 bordes, 3 tresselles and a litle forme		2	0
In the kytchen			
Fower brasse pottes, 2 brasse chafers, a morter and pestle of brasse		16	0
Fower ketles, on with another, on brasse pann, on bason, 2 chafing dishes, on skillet, 3 skimmers, 2 ladles, 6 candlestickes, a cullender, a payre of skales of brasse and an ould morter		5	0
2 driping pannes, on frieing pan, 6 spittes, a paire of rackes, 2 trevetts, a paire of tonges, 2 old iron slices, 3 paire of pott hangers, a fleshe hooke, a creeper, an olde gridiron, a clever and a shredinge knife, an iron peele, 2 iron pottes and a paire of bellowes		5	0
Pewter			
Twelve dishes, 4 porringers, 2 quart pottes, a bason, 2 saltes, an dosen of spones, on beaker, 5 chamber pottes		14	0
Linnen			
Seven paire of sheetes, on dosen of napkins, three table clothes	1	6	8
A parcell of timber	1	0	0
A litle table, 2 olde formes, the dressers, a wheele, a bowle, 2 ould Jugges		2	0
His weareing apparell	1	0	0
His leases	10	0	0
[£23.19.0]	23	18	0
The debts which he oweth			
To Mr Goodwin of Dorkin	7	14	0
To on Roger Reinoldes	5	0	0
To Ellen Parkes	6	13	4
To Mr Stanton of Kingston		18	0
To Water Mann		10	0
	20	15	4

Note: The Will was written on 21st February and was proved on 7th May 1600. It was witnessed by Thomas Browne, clerk and Rafe Fletcher. This same Mr Rafe Fletcher, a good neighbour, was appointed overseer. The testator's wife Joane was to be the sole executrix and she was to inherit all his goods and chattels, on condition that she divided the estate among five of his six children in equal portions. His daughter Sara, the only one named, was to be omitted from any share, but her daughter Sarah was to be given a silver spoon. Wiliam's children were only to have their legacies if they were to continue in dutiful obedience and to behave themselves in loving and good sort towards their mother. These same legacies would fall due at their marriage or when their mother died.

Ref: 1600 B 42/1 Will 1600 B 42/2 Inventory

John Stanton **397**

of Ripley in the parish of Send, fuller; taken by Rychard Maybanke, Wylliam Stanton and John Inwode, 24th April 1600.

	£	s	d
His apparell and monye in his pursse	2	0	0
In the halle			
2 tables, 2 setteles, 2 formes, 2 olde chayars		10	0
One pare of Cobards, 2 pare of pothangars, 1 griderne, 2 pare of tonges, paynted clothes, 2 wyndowe certines and one ffyer panne		5	0
One Severall Rome in the halle		12	0
In the butterye			
13 pewter platters, Towe dosen pewter disshes, 1 dossen of Sawsers, 9 porrengers, 6 saltes, 4 pewter pottes, one pynte potte, Towe bassens, 2 chaving dishes	2	18	0
In the Kychin			
5 bras pottes, 7 kettelles, 6 skyllettes, 3 dripping pans, one brassen ladell, 2 brassen Skymmers, one morter with a pestell, one warming pan, 8 lattin candellstykes	3	14	3
More 6 bras pannes, 2 Cawddernes, one bruinge ffurnis, 6 spyttes, 4 pare of potthangars	7	0	0
More one bruinge ffatte, 2 tonnes, one Cowbard, 10 kylderkynes, boles, treas and all other wooden vesselles	5	0	0
One myll to grynde malte		16	0
One welbokytte with a wynche and a chayne		2	0
4 chamberpottes		4	0
One charne, 1 ffryinge pan, 1 pare of shuges		4	0
1 dossen of Sackes and wyningshette		1	8
In the parlor			
One standinge bedstede, 2 cortens, 2 cortene Rodes, 3 floke bedes, 3 fether bolstares, one fether pyllowe, 2 Rugges, 4 pare of blanktes, 11 Cosyanes, one bede Tyke	6	4	0
2 olde bedstedes, 2 flokbedes, 2 pare of blankettes, 2 bolstares	1	0	0
4 Cowbars, one presse, one table, one Settell, 1 Forme, one wyndowe curtin, 3 Cawbord clotes and the paynted clotes	3	8	0
All the wull in the howsse	5	0	0
In all the howsse tenne chestes	2	0	0
30 pare of shettes, 12 tabell clothes and Towelles and napkines 3 dosen, 1 dossen and a halffe of pillebers	20	10	0
A pare of Fustion blankes		13	4
3 olde bedstedes, 3 flokebedes, 2 bankes, 4 Coverleyttes, 3 floke bolsters	1	0	0
1 floke bede, one flokebolster and 2 coverlettes of darnyxe	1	5	0
4 standing steddes and a trendell bede, 2 Fetherbedes 3 fetherbolstars, 3 flokbedes, 3 floke bolstoors, 2 pare of blankettes, 4 Coverlettes, 2 qyltes, 1 tabell, 1 fforme, a settell	9	0	0
3 Joyned stolles waynscotte and paynted clottes and a pare of Andyans	1	10	8
One Joyned tabell, one benche, 3 fformes		3	4
2 standinge steddes, 2 fetherbedes, one flokebede, 3 ffether bolstars, 2 fether pyllowes, 1 pare of blankytes, Twoe coveringes of darnyxe and 2 qyltes	6	12	4
One pare of Andyarnes, 1 fyre pane		2	0

	£	s	d
1 Standinge stedell, 1 tyndlle bede, 1 fether bolster, 2 ffether beddes, 1 floke bolster, 1 fether pyllowe, 1 pare of blankyttes 2 Coverlettes, 2 curtins and one pare of Andyarnes	5	2	0
2 tables, one fframe, 2 fformes, 3 Joynede stolles, 1 Chayare, 4 bedposes and one benche	1	0	0
In the chamber over the halle			
2 tables, 2 frames, a fforme, 2 Chayars, 5 Joynede stolles and the paynted clothes	1	0	0
2 standinge steddeles, 3 curtins, 2 fetherbedes, 2 fether bolsters, 2 fether pyllowes, 2 pare of blanktes, 2 Coveringes of orris, 2 wullin Carpites	12	3	4
The waynscotte bytwne the Towe chambers and the paynted clothes	1	0	0
In the barne			
Heye	8	0	0
Ottes	3	0	0
8 kyne, one bull	15	0	0
2 maeres with 2 coltes, one nage	7	0	0
56 sheppe	11	8	0
9 hoges	5	0	0
Sixe peces of tymber	1	10	0
All the wood abowte the howsse	2	0	0
6 hundred of borde	1	0	0
Certeyne tres standinge in a grove at Ryde Farme	3	10	0
10 tres in Horsse Crose	2	10	0
2 pare of shode welles, one longe carte, 2 Dungcartes, Towe harrowes wythe the Furniture		16	0
2 pare of ffullars Rakes and 2 pare of ffullars sheres		10	0
A betell and wegges, 1 axe, 1 byll, 2 spytters, 2 showelles		12	0
The leasse of the Ine callede the Gorge	30	0	0
All the glasse abowte the howsse	2	0	0
	195	17	3
Debtes owinge by the said John Stanton to the value of	-80	0	0

Administration of the goods and chattells of the deceased was granted to Ann, relict on 8th May 1600. Ref: 1600 Ad 56

William Valler **398**

of Frensham, yeoman; taken by Wylliam Norris, John Morer and Nicholas Robinsone, with others; 16th June 1600.

	£	s	d
One Cowple of working Steeres	5	6	8
Too Steers of too yeres of Age	3	6	8
Fower Keene	8	0	0
One Bull	1	13	4
Three Bullockes of A yere old	2	8	0
Fower wayned Calves	2	0	0
Too mares	4	0	0
One Gildinge	3	10	0
Three Cowltes	4	10	0
Twelve Ewes	2	8	0
Eight Lambs	1	6	8
Too Sowes and 15 piggs	2	6	0

Theirteene Shuttes	2	12	0
His Apparrell and monye in his purse	3	6	8
One featherbedd with all that belongeth to it	3	0	0
Too flockbedds with all that belongeth to them	1	6	8
Three Cheasts and one Coffer		17	0
Three Trowghes		6	0
All the wodden vessell	2	0	0
Three brass potts		18	0
Fower Kettles		13	4
One Cawdron and one pann		10	0
Fower small skilletts		1	8
One Bason, a Chaffingdish and three Candlestickes		5	0
Thirtie peeces of pewter	1	6	0
A dosen of spoones and an halfe		1	0
One Joyned Table and too formes		5	0
One Cowbbord, too old Chayres and too Joyned Stooles		6	0
One payre of Locrum sheats		6	0
Too payre of Canvas sheates		10	0
Three Table Clothes and Six table napkins		8	0
20 pound of woll		15	0
7 flitches of Bacon and one gallon of grease	1	8	0
All the Cheese in the howse	1	0	0
Wheate and Rie in the howse three bushells		8	0
Fower bushells of mault		8	0
3 broaches, too Aundirons and one dripping pann		8	0
Too Triffettes, too potthangers, A girdiron and too old frying panns		4	0
Carte, A plowgh with yokes, Chaynes and Harrowes	2	0	0
Too Axes, too bills, one shovell, one spitter		2	0
Three Sithes and fower Sickles		4	0
A Calyver furnisht		13	0
Too Short Carte Roapes		2	0
A Becc, three Iron Wedges, too Augers, one Handsawe, one wymble and A little Hammer		3	0
A payre of Scales, an Iron beame and some waightes		2	6
A wynn sheate, A heare Cloth, A sack and two bagges		6	8
A Saddle, too bridles and one pannell		5	0
Three Stoane potts			8
One Stayned Cloth		1	6
One Sive and a Ridder			4
A payre of sheeres and A Brush			8
One Ladder and three hogg trowghes		1	6
Fyve Acres of wheat on the grownd	5	10	0
12 Acres of ottes	6	0	0
Tenn geese and 4 Ducks		6	0
A lynnen wheele, A wollen whele and A payre of Cards		2	6
Six Henns and A Cock		3	0
	80	9	0

Note: The Will was dated 1st June and proved on 20th October 1600. The co-executrixes and residuary legatees were his wife Margaret and the youngest of his five daughters, Constance. Sums of 3s 4d apiece were given to the overseers Richard Boxhold and John Valler, his brother. The testator asked to be buried in the parish churchyard, giving 12d to the poor there, 12d to the poor of Hedley and 12d towards the repair of the bells of Frensham. His gifts of livestock were to be delivered within a month if lawfully demanded. A ewe was given to three married daughters and a granddaughter: Joan, wife of Stephen Golding, vicar of Amport; Ann Weston; Alice Bawlden and Elizabeth, her daughter. The other children of Alice and John Baulden were each to have a lamb. Isabel Soane, the fourth married daughter, was given a ewe and a lamb. Her husband William, servant to the testator, was given a cow, two ewes and a year-old colt. John Valler, his son, was to have a year-old calf. Witnesses were John Read, Nicholas Robinson and Edmund Fullick. The Bond of Administration was put up by the executrixes of Dockenfield, Stephen Golding of Amport and Ralph Weston of Hedley.

Ref: 1600 B 64/1 Will 1600 B 64/2 Inventory

Henry Wheeler **399**

of Elstead, husbandman; taken by Richard Gosden, Henry Stovoll, Richard Millat and Edward Wheeler, 8th May 1600.

	£	s	d
In money		4	0
His apparrell	1	10	0
One bedstedle and the bedding in the house	2	10	0
3 Chestes		5	0
Woodden vessels		6	8
The brasse in his house	1	3	4
His pewter		6	0
All his Iron thinges		3	4
One table, two stoles, one linen Wheele, one Woollen Wheele, two boards		5	0
Two Hoges of bacon		16	0
His other Cattayle	8	0	0
One litle cart and two horses	1	0	0
His sheepe	3	6	8
Two hoges		8	0
Two hens and one Cock		1	6
His Corne on the ground, rye and oates	3	10	0
His beanes		2	0
	23	17	6
A true noate of thos debtes which I Henry Wheeler owe at the tyme of my death			
To Richard Gosden	9	2	0
To John West	2	3	0
To Thomas Snelling		3	0
To John Wheeler		14	8
To Thomas Waker		3	4
To Henry Stovol		8	4
To Joane Wheeler		8	0
To William Wheeler on loade of hay			
To Henry Wheeler alias Webb		1	0
	[£*13*	*3*	*4*]

Note: The Will was dated 1st May and was proved on 8th May 1600. The executrix and residuary legatee was his wife Jane. Sums of 12d apiece were given to the overseers Robert Aunsell and Edward Wheller. The testator asked to be buried in Elstead churchyard and he gave 3s 4d to the poor there. He gave to his brother Edmond a cow bought of John Stovoll. His brother Thomas was given a ewe and his brother John Walker was given all his best apparel. A ewe was to be shared by the two children of his sister Agnes. The testator made his mark on the document, which was signed by Edward Welch, curate, Philip Wheeler and Henry Stovoll.

Ref: 1600 B 70/1 Will 1600 B 70/2 Inventory

1601

Henry Cartwright **400**

of East Molesey. [*no appraisers given and undated*]

	£	s	d
Goodes in the letel chember			
1 standenge bed forneshed	2	0	0
1 tabel and painted cloth		3	4
Goodes in the chember or lofte			
bedstedes and bed		10	0
10 payer and one shete and cheste	2	0	0
Goodes in the chamber over the khengn			
1 bed and bed sted		13	4
1 flocke bed, blanked and cerlet		5	0
1 old tabel and tobes		3	0
Part of a coslet and bo and aroes		5	0
Goodes in the chember over the halle			
1 bed forneshed	1	10	0
2 cotes, 2 dobletes, 1 per of breches, 1 cloke	2	0	0
6 pelous		15	0
1 gret chest		5	0
2 old ches, a old tabel and a hamper		3	0
1 sword, 1 per of pontes, 1 per of beles an abotl		5	0
Godes in the letel chamber next the chen			
1 fether bed forneshed	1	10	0
5 per of shetes and 1 tabel cloth	1	10	0
3 old ches, 1 tabel, 1 cher		6	8
Godes in the chem			
2 potes, 3 ceteles, 1 chafer, 1 warmenge pane		15	0
necere lomber in the khechen		5	0
Godes in the hall			
puter	1	0	0
pres, tabel, stoules and payntenge	1	0	0
3 younge bolokes	3	0	0
Corne on the ground	3	0	0
in money	15	0	0
	38	4	4

Note: The Will was dated 11th March and was proved on 28th May 1601. The executrix and residuary legatee was the testator's wife Ann, who was also given £5 to be paid at Michaelmas from a bond due at that date from Gowers Taylor. Sums of £5 each were given to his goddaughter Em Peamore and to Constance Fullwell; Constance was also to have a heifer and a bed and bedding when she came of age, her share remaining to Em if she were to die young. Em's father John was to invest the money and her mother, nee Cartwright, was to have Henry's "usual Seale ring of gold." Henry's sister Margaret was given £1 and John Best, at court, William Jenings and John Brookes of the court were each given apparel. Henry signed his Will, as did Thomas Foster and George Hamond. Thomas Hurleston made his mark. These last two men witnessed the surrender of an acre of copyhold land lying in Swan, butting upon Pepper Acre. The testator had asked to be buried in the churchyard at East Molesey. The Administration Bond was provided by the widow, Richard Barton of Walton upon Thames, clerk and Mr Browne of Wick in Middlesex, fisherman.

Ref: 1601 B 14/1 Will 1601 B 14/2 Inventory

William Dynes **401**

of Godalming, husbandman; taken by John Westbrooke, Henrie Peitoe, John Anthonie and Roberte Champione, 27th May 1601.

	£	s	d
In the Hall			
Two tables and on litle foorme		9	0
One cubbord and on cubbord clothe	1	0	0
Two stooles and on old chayre and 3 boords		2	0
In the parlor			
One standing Bedsteed with curtaines, on fether bedd, one bolster, three pillowes, 2 blankets and on coverlett	5	10	0
In the chamber over the parlor			
One Bedsteed with a painted tester, on litle fether bed, on bolster, two blankets and on coverlett	1	6	0
Two boords		1	0
In the chamber over the Hall			
One standing bedsteed, on fether bed, on flokbed, one bolster, two pilloes, on blankett and on coverlett	3	6	8
On truckle Bedsteed, on flockbedd, on bolster, on blankett		13	4
One cubbord with a cubbord cloth and on court cubbord		13	4
Fowre chestes	1	0	0
In the kytchinne			
On furnace, on Caldron, five kettles, three brasse pottes, two skillettes and a skimmer	3	10	0
One brewing trough with a cover, on forme, 3 shelves, 8 trugges, 2 kevers, 6 boledishes, 4 buckets and on lynnen wheele		14	6
Three Andirons, 2 paire of potthookes, 2 paire of pott hangers, 2 spittes, on payre of tonges, on fyer shovel, on grydiron, One tryvett	1	0	0
In the milke howse			
Fowre shelves, 7 bottles, ten earthen pottes, on stone morter, on butter cherne		7	4
In the Brew house			
One stande, on foorme, on shelf, on Coope, on brewing fatte, on keve, 3 kevers and 2 Tubbs		7	0
In the Butterie			
Three kilderkins, foure firkins, three shelves		7	0
Six pounds of woolle		4	6
Six pounds of hopps, 4 pounds of towe, on paire of scales, with a beame and on hetchell		5	0
One gallon of Larde		2	0
Pewter			
Seven platters, fyve dishes, 3 basins, 3 fruite dishes, five sawcers, two pottingers, on dozen of spoones, 2 saltes, on quart pott, on pynt pott, 2 drinking cupps, on Aquavita bottle, 2 bow pottes, on Tunnell and ffower candlestickes	1	15	0
One frying panne, on chafing dishe and on plate candlestike		3	4
One old bedd with certaine Lumberie		6	8
Lynnen			
Twelve paire of sheetes	3	0	0
Foure pilloes and seven pillobeers	1	1	0
Fyve table clothes and 23 table napkins		15	0
His apparell and money in his purse	6	13	4
Corne in the howse			
Wheate twentie and on bushels	3	6	8

Rye twentie and eight bushels with three bushels of pease	4	0	0
Barlie six bushels		13	4
Barlie mawlte and dregge mawlte 26 bushels	2	12	0
Oates 3 quarters	1	4	0
Corne sackes 13		13	0
Implementes of husbandrie in the Gate			
One wagon, 2 Cartes and 2 dung pottes	5	0	0
Plowes, harroes, yoakes, chayne and horse harnes	1	6	8
Tymber and fyer woode	4	0	0
Fowre Rackes		5	0
Fowre spitters, 2 Axes, on hatchett, on pikaxe and on Bill		5	0
In the Barne			
Two long ladders, on shorte ladder, 3 pronges, 2 dungrakes, on saddle and a brydle and certaine boordes	1	0	0
Seven pounds of lynnen yarne		7	0
Seven flitches of Bacon	1	3	4
Corne in the fielde			
Fyve acres of Wheate, 11 acres of Rye, five acres of barlie, nyne acres of oates and on acre of beanes, pease and carrotes	30	0	0
Cattle			
Six oxen	17	0	0
Eight steares	18	0	0
Twentie two kyne and on Bull	51	15	0
Twelve bullockes of 2 yeares olde	15	8	4
Twelve bullockes of on yeare olde	12	0	0
Eyght horses and mares	26	0	0
Fowre score and foureteene sheepe and 35 lambs	31	6	8
Foureteene hogges	3	0	0
Money owinge to the testator	7	0	0
	272	0	0

Note: The Will was dated 21st May and proved on 29th May 1601. The executrix and residuary legatee was the testator's wife Blanche. The loving friends chosen to be overseers were Valentine Castillion, gentleman and Robert Champion, yeoman. The testator asked to be buried in Godalming churchyard and he gave £1 to the poor. The sum of £40 was left in trust to each of his sons John and Peter, until they were 21 years old. The money was to be raised on his goods as soon as possible. His daughter Frances was to have £30 at the age of 18 years, or on her wedding day. If John or Peter died young, his £40 was to be divided between his brother and sister. Blanche's son Thomas Newman and a nephew Richard Dynes, were each to have £2. The overseers acted as witnesses. Blanche was sworn to the truth of the Will on 28th May before Francis Taylor, the vicar. It was she who provided the Administration Bond. The burial of William Dynes was registered on 23rd May 1601.

Ref: 1601 B 21/1 Will 1601 B 21/2 Inventory

Henry Harper **402**

of Dunsfold, husbandman; taken by John Tickner, John Punter and Thomas Chaundler, 27th May 1601.

	£	s	d
His Aparill		10	0
In his purs		1	0
A bead with all things belonnging ther to		12	0
Five peses of pewter		5	0
Bras		2	0
3 Candellstickes		1	0

3 Chestes		5	0
A playn bedstedle		1	0
Two Andirns		2	0
3 stools			8
2 kushens		1	0
A bunting huch		2	0
Wooden vessell		1	0
A tabell and A foorme		2	0
Serten Debtes as by perticulers Apereth	14	0	0
	16	5	8

Note: In the Will, dated 27th March and proved on 29th May 1601, the overseers were requested to arrange for the testator's burial in Wonersh churchyard and to distribute the 3s 4d bequeathed to the poor men's box of that church amongst his poorest neighbours. Jane Lenegar was to have 4s; and three other women, Johan Strett, the wife of Richard Strett, Annis Hays and Annis Jones, the wife of Henry Jones, were to have 3s 4d each. His lands and tenement called Waterhatch in Dunsfold were bequeathed to Millicent, his daughter. Failing any lawful heirs of hers, the bequest was to pass to his nephew William Hayes, the eldest son of his sister Annis and her husband William Hayes. Millicent was appointed sole executrix and residuary legatee. Sums of 6d apiece were left to the overseers Henry Chaundler and William Hayes. John and Thomas Tickner made their marks and John Kichen and Thomas Chaundler signed the Will as witnesses. Probate was granted to William Hayes, next of kin to Millicent, the testator's daughter, an idiot, the executrix named in the will. The Administration Bond was provided by the said William Hayes and by Thomas Tickner, both of Wonersh, husbandmen.

Ref: 1601 B 35/1 Will 1601 B 35/2 Inventory

John Inwood, the elder **403**

of Send, yeoman; taken by Richard Mabanke, Daniell Mabanke and William Stannton, 25th May 1601.

	£	s	d
The money in his purse	2	0	0
The apparrell of the deceased	3	0	0
In the hall			
One table with a Couple of tresselles, a setle, two formes, 6 Cushions, one Chaire, one Cubbord with a Cubbord Cloth and the painted clothes	1	3	4
One paire of Andirons, a fire pane, a fire pronge, a gridiron, two paire of potthangers		5	0
A ioynde table, a ioyned settle, two ioyned formes, one Carpett and sixe Cushions		13	4
A Cubbord and a Cubbord cloth		10	0
In the parlor			
A ioyned bedstedd, a matt, a strawbedd, a fetherbedd, three blanckettes, a Coverlett and one great olde chest	3	0	0
In the chamber over the parlor			
A lyvery bedstedd, a flock bedd, one paire of blanckettes, two Coverlettes and one chest		12	0
In the lofte over the parlor			
One standinge bedstedd, one trendle bedstedd, one strawbedd, one flockbedd, a fetherbedd, three blanckettes and a Coverlett	2	0	0
A presse and two chestes		6	8
In the buttry			
25 pewter platters, 13 pewter dishes, fyve pottingers, 8 sawcers, a tynne plate, a bason and Ewer, 1 quarte pewter pott, fyve dozen of pewter spoones, a brasen morter with a pestle, one pewter ladle and one chamber pott	3	0	0

In the howse next the Buttry			
One brewinge fate, two tunns, two Coolers, a tunninge bowle, a powdringe tubb, 9 Kilderkins, 1 powdringe troughe, 6 leather bottles, 1 wodden bottle, a little tunninge dishe and 6 stone potts	1	15	0
A paire of scales with an Iron beame and weightes		5	0
In the Kitchin			
A litle ffornace		13	4
A knedinge troughe, a boultinge whiche and diverse other dry vesselles		6	8
Three small spittes and two drippinge panns		6	8
Two brasse pottes, two kaldrons, two kittles, three posnettes and a brasse pan	3	0	0
A hanginge Cubbord, two cheese presses, a fryeinge pann, a dozen of trugges, three bowles, a butter chearne and tenn cheese motes	1	0	0
One borde or stand, three stooles, a litle powdringe tubbe, two kyvers, a racke for cheese and 6 buckettes		5	4
Two bedsteddles, three Coverlettes and a paire of blanckettes	1	0	0
In the lofte over the Mylkehowse			
Fyve quarters of Malte	5	0	0
8 shelves, a cheese racke, two paire of tresselles, two Joinde stooles, two kyvers, two little tubbes and a trapp for rattes		5	0
Twenty cheeses		13	4
Fyfteene hogges of bacon with some beefe	8	0	0
Lynen or nappery in the howse			
15 paire of sheetes, sixe table clothes, 2 dozen of napkins, fyve hande towelles, fower pillowes and foure pyllowe beeres	6	0	0
Implementes of husbandry			
All the workinge tooles in the howse, two axes, foure billes, two betles, sixe wedges, sixe olde Scythes, two spitters, two shovelles, a mathoke and a Crowe leaver		10	0
Corne in the Garner and on the ground			
8 quarters of wheate	10	14	4
Tenn quarters of Rye	10	13	4
Fyve quarters of Otes	2	10	0
Corne on the ground beinge 14 acres of wheate	14	0	0
Rye on the ground 20 acres	13	0	6
In barley three acres	2	0	0
Peaze and tares 9 acres	4	0	0
Of great Otes 19 acres	9	10	0
Of small Otes 15 acres	7	0	0
Of ffrench wheate tenn acres	3	6	8
Cattell			
Thirteene oxen	40	0	0
18 kyne and one bull	31	13	4
Foure steers	10	0	0
Tenn bullockes of two yeres of age	12	0	0
Tenn bullockes of one yeres olde	8	0	0
Tenn wayned Calves	4	0	0
Horses, nagges and mares with their Coltes	10	0	0
Swyne small and greate	5	0	0
35 couples of Ewes and lambes	10	0	0
One hundreth and ten of dry sheepe	27	10	0
All the powltry, geese and duckes		16	0
Cartes, ploughes and other Implementes of husbandry			
Two large Cartes with their wheeles	4	0	0
Three dunge Cartes with their furniture	1	10	0

Two ploughes, with yokes chaines and other thinges belonginge unto the same, with one oxe harrow and small harrowes	2	6	8
A lease of a certeyne tenemente with the appurtenances for certeyne yeres to com called Prues	40	0	0
The interest, lease and terme of yeres of the decesed yet to com of a ferme called Send Barnes	2	0	0
[*£331.1.6*]	310	1	6

Note: In the Will, dated 14th May and proved on 29th May 1601, the gift of the freehold house and land purchased from John Farrante a year since was to go to the testator's son Thomas, with £40. Were Thomas to die without lawful issue, then this property near the highway from Woking to Guildford was to go to Richard, his youngest son and his heirs. The same Richard was given 20 marks [£6 13s 4d] and another son George was given £10. The testator's daughters Katherin, Margaret and Anne, were each given £40, two cows and two pairs of canvas sheets and in addition Anne was given the christening sheet. These legacies were to be paid to the sons within a year, but the daughters were to receive theirs either at the customary age of 21, or on the day of their marriage. There was the usual proviso that on the death of any sister her portion would be divided between the survivors. Sums of £1 apiece were given to John Wheatlye and James Coxe, the testator's sons-in-law. Two godchildren John Wheatlye and Joan Coxe were to have two ewes and two lambs apiece, whereas their unnamed brothers and sisters were each given one lamb. The testator asked to be buried in the churchyard of Send. He bequeathed 6s 8d to the church there and £1 to the poor of both Send and Ripley. His son John was appointed the only executor and residuary legatee. The aforesaid sons-in-law were to be the overseers. The Will was written by the vicar Richard Harward. Daniel and Richard Maybanck, the other two witnesses, made their marks. The Administration Bond was provided by the executor and William Stanton of Ripley, yeoman.

Ref: 1601 39/1 Will 1601 B 39/2 Inventory

John Skete **404**

of Chobham, husbandman; taken by John Houlte, Henry Phillipp and Edmond Brockys, with others, 10th April 1601.

	£	s	d
His apparrell and money in his purse		10	0
A Table, a Cupborde, one forme and two smale stooles		5	0
Two olde fflockbedes with the thinges belonginge unto them		8	0
One bedd and bedsteddelles with the thinges perteyninge thereunto		9	0
Fyve Sheetes		5	0
Five pewter dishes, fower platters, 2 sawcers, 2 saltes, a pinte pott, 2 brasse candlestickes, A brasse potte and a brasse posnett, 3 kettelles		12	0
Other brasse and pewter there		7	0
A paire of pothookes, pothangers, 2 spittes and other olde iron		2	0
Fyve kyne	6	0	0
Sixe bullockes	3	0	0
A Mare and a Colte	1	6	8
A horse Colte	1	0	0
2 Henns		1	0
3 acres of Rie in the feilde	2	0	0
The Tyme of the lease of His House	1	0	0
More beddinge, Viz 2 flockbeddes, 2 Coverlettes, thre blankettes thre boulsters, one bedsteddell, thre Chestes	1	0	0
A boultinge hutche, a knedinge troughe, 2 olde tubbes		2	0
	18	17	8

[*Written at the end of the Will:*]

I owe my brother Robert Skeet	2	10	0
Richard Collyer of Aldbury	1	4	0

Thomas Lee of Cranley owes me	2	18	0
John Tucker oweth me	1	0	0

Note: The Will was written on 2nd April and was proved on 29th May 1601. The testator named his son Arthur Skete as executor and residuary legatee. Elizabeth, his wife, was left the lease of the house and land in Chobham and specific stock, crops and household stuff. A son John was to have two heifers and four household items. A daughter Jane was left £5 at the age of 18 and five items. Another son George was left £4 at the age of 23 and two items. The sum of £2 was to be divided between Elizabeth's six children: Elizabeth, Henry, Frances, Ann, Rose and Richard. The testator appointed his brother George Skeete of Chobham, husbandman and his cousin Henry Feeld, also of Chobham, to be overseers. The Will was witnessed by the vicar Thomas Taunton, with Robert Skeet and both the overseers. The aforesaid George Skeete was granted administration of the estate during the minority of his nephew Arthur. The Administration Bond was provided by George and by Arthur Davy of East Clandon, husbandman.

Ref: 1601 B 50/1 Will 1601 B 50/2 and 1601 B 50/3 Inventory

Nicholas Smalpeece **405**

of Guildford, haberdasher; taken by Thomas Smalpece, Thomas Crosse, Thomas Haynes, John Sackvile and John Millett, 6th May 1601.

				£	s	d
Reddy money in his purse				30	0	0
His apparell				13	6	8
	£43	6	8			
In the Shopp						
Eight dozen and a half of untrymmed hattes				5	0	0
Fyftene hattes called Shelles				3	15	0
Fyve other shelles				1	2	6
Eleaven other shelles				1	16	8
12 mens hattes lyned with taffata				3	0	0
Fower feltes lyned with velvet				2	0	0
6 feltes lyned with taffata				1	2	0
Nyntene other feltes lyned				2	5	0
Twenty unlyned hattes				2	0	0
4 Dozen of hattes unlyned				2	10	0
Nyne feltes unlyned					12	0
4 Cullored shelles lyned in parte and 2 bandes					18	0
Eight Dozen and 7 hattes course cullored with bandes for Children				7	4	0
4 Dozen and a half of Course cullored feltes with bandes				1	16	0
3 Dozen of Cipers black				3	12	0
Nyne dozen roll bandes				2	13	?
Bandes for Childrens hattes					3	0
Sixe night Cappes worsted					4	0
One dozen and a half of Cipers					15	0
64 Cipers bandes				3	13	0
Chestes, cupbordes of weynscott, hampers and tyltes in the shopp				4	0	0
3 feltes					6	0
Two dozen of feltes for women				2	8	0
A stele glasse					1	0
	£52	16	6			
In the hall						
A drawinge table, 6 Joyned stoles, a litle table, two cushen stoles, a Cushen Chayer and two litle stoles				2	0	0
12 Cushens, a Carpett and 2 Cupbord Clothes				1	13	0
2 andirons, a payer of tonges and a fier shovell					13	4

Stayned Clothes and 2 picktures 6 8

£4 13 0

In the parlor

A table with a frame, a forme, a Cushen Chayer, one other Chayer, 3 Joyned stoles, 2 litle stoles, a paier of brandirons, 6 Cushens and a Carpett 1 10 0

£1 10 0

In the great Chamber

A Joyned bedstede with Curtens, valens and Roddes 4 0 0

A fetherbedd, a fether bolster, 4 fether pillowes, a grene Rugge, 2 blankettes, a matteris and a truckle bedstede 6 0 0

A table with a frame, a forme, 3 Joyned stoles and two Chayers 10 0

3 windowe Cushens, a Carpett, a windowe Clothe, hanginges of Orrys worke old, 2 table picktures, a payer of Andirons, 2 windowe Curtens and roddes 4 0 0

£14 10 0

In the litle streat Chamber

A bedstedle with Curtens, valens and roddes, a fetherbedd, 2 fether pillowes, 3 Coverlettes, hangings of Orris worke, old, 2 small cobirons, a table frame, 2 Joyned stoles, a Court cupbord and a Curten 10 0 0

£10 0 0

In the Chambers called James Parsons Chambers

A Joyned bedstedle, a flockbedd, a flockbolster, a fether bolster, a table with a frame, painted Clothes, a windowe Curten and rodd 1 10 0

A table with a frame, a settell with painted Clothes and a boxe 5 0

£1 15 0

In the Gallery

A table, old, a Chayer, painted Clothes, Mappes and benches, a Curten and a Curten Rodde 1 10 0

£1 10 0

In the Maydens Chamber

A bedstedle, a truckle bedstede, two flockbeddes, 2 flock bolsters, a white Rugge, a Coverlett, 2 blankettes, a great Chest and 1 10 0

£1 10 0

In the Chamber over the Kitchen and entrye

A bedstede, two fetherbeddes, two fether bolsters, a truckle bedstede, a flock bedd, a flockbolster, 2 fether pillowes, a Coverlett, a Rugge, a blankett, Courtens, testers, Curten Roddes, a Joyned presse, paynted Clothes, 2 Chestes, 2 boxes and 2 andirons 10 0 0

A Close stole 5 0

Two truckle bedsteddes, one fether bedd, a flockbedd, 3 flock bolsters, 2 Coverlettes, 2 blankettes, 2 Chestes and one old table 2 0 0

£12 5 0

Napery

24 payer of shetes, one table Cloth of Damaske, 6 other table Clothes, 6 Dozen of table Napkins, 12 pillowbers and 12 towelles 14 13 4

£14 13 4

Sylver plate

One sylver gylt salt, 5 goblettes, 2 dozen and one spones 25 0 0

£25 0 0

In the litle Inner parlor

A Joyned Bedstedle, a truckle bedstede, a presse, a table and one old Chest 1 10 0

A still					5	0
	£1	15	0			
In the buttery and seller						
A table with a frame, a bynne with the shelves and two skrenes					13	0
6 pewter candlestickes, 5 latten candlestickes, 4 pewter pottes, 2 tynnen beakers, ffower pewter saltes, 4 flower pottes, 32 platters, 30 pewter dishes, 12 Chargers and basons, 12 porrengers, one Ewer, 3 dozen and 4 sawcers, 3 chamber pottes and one dozen of spones				6	4	4
A hand basket and trenchers					2	0
A Muskett, bandeleers, flaske and titch box, sword and dagger, thre Murrions, a rest and a souldier's Coate				1	0	0
Standes, tubbes and lumbry in the seller					10	0
Two Tune of Iron				18	0	0
	£26	9	4			
In the kitchen						
6 brasse pottes				3	10	0
6 kettelles					12	0
A Cawdron and a brasse panne				2	0	0
5 skelletes and one Chaffinge dish, a warminge panne with an Iron handell					10	0
A qualyver					5	0
8 spittes					8	0
A payer of Rackes, 4 payer of pothangers, 3 payer of potthookes, two andirons, 4 drippinge panns, two payer of tonges, a Cole racke, one fyer shovell, an Iron Jack, the old Iron about the hearth, a table and a forme and other lumbrey				1	12	0
	£8	17	0			
Corne in the house						
20 quarters of Malt and barley				20	0	0
6 quarters of wheat				8	0	0
	£28	0	0			
In the servantes Chamber						
A flockbedd, a flockbolster, a blanckett and one borded stedle					10	0
		10	0			
Cattell						
6 oxen				18	0	0
Thre old horsbestes				3	0	0
Thre keene, one calf and 7 bullockes				12	0	0
4 Cart with shodd wheles, yokes, Chaynes, donge pottes, ploughes and other ymplementes of husbandry				3	0	0
	£36	0	0			
Corne in the feild						
11 acres of Wheat and Rye				22	0	0
22 acres of barley and 2 acres of otes				22	0	0
5 acres of peaze and tares				5	0	0
	£49	0	0			
In the bakehouse and brewhouse						
A furnes				3	0	0
Two old tables, a knedinge troughe, a bultinge hutche, an oven peele, a bushell, a half bushell, a peck and 2 Gallons, a Cooler, a vate and other lumbrey, a sesterne of leade , a welbuckett, a Rope and a Chayne				4	0	0
4 welcurbes, a grindestone, wood in the gate and other lumbrey ther				3	0	0

4 hogges, 4 pigges and the poultrey				1	8	0
	£11	8	0			
Debtes owynge by specialtie to the testator						
Debtes by specialties				133	0	0
Debtes by booke and otherwise				62	0	0
	£195	0	0			
Woodes felled						
21 trees, the wood and tymber				4	0	0
A lease of certen landes at Chagden for 4 yeares to come				1	0	0
	£5	0	0			
				522	8	10

Note: The Will was dated 10th March and proved on 29th May 1601. The executrix and residuary legatee was the testator's wife Annis. Sums of 10s apiece were left to the overseers, his cousin Thomas Smalpeece and his son-in-law James Parson. Four of his five children were left property; his daughter Annis was the exception. A gift of £10 in money was made to her and to her son, the testator's godson. James, his only son, was given all houses and lands in Holy Trinity, Guildford; St Mary's, Guildford; Shalford; two acres in Stokefield; five acres near the hospital there; and a further holding of the shop and dwelling house ready furnished with wares and household stuff then owned by the testator. This major bequest was to go to James upon his mother's decease. The bequest, under the same condition, of two tenements and lands in Farnham, then occupied by John Austen and Roger Hawarde, was made to James Parson, the husband of a second daughter Alice, who was given £10 in her own right. The third daughter Dorothy was to be paid £40 at the age of 17 and the Dye House, leased to Henry Kemp with the stock worth £40, was to be handed over to her at the end of Kemp's lease. The fourth daughter Elizabeth was to be given £40 at the age of 17 and the promise of lands at Slovelgrene after the decease of the tenants Richard Lee and his wife. All the godchildren were left 12d apiece. The poor of three Guildford parishes were left sums of money: Holy Trinity, St Mary's and St Nicholas, were left 4 nobles (£1 6s 8d), £1 and 13s 4d, respectively. Two maidservants Julien Parson and Elizabeth Stent were each left 6s 8d. His manservant Edward Forde was given a cow. His goddaughter Joane Snelling was to be paid the £10 which he had held in trust for her. Witnesses to the Will were Henry Beedel, Philip Champion, Thomas Parkhurst and James Parson. The entry in the parish register of Holy Trinity on 29th April 1601 lists the burial of Mr Nicholas Smalpece, some time mayor.

Ref: 1601 B51/2 Will 1601 B 51/3 Inventory

Mathewe Snelling **406**

of Windlesham; taken by John Attfeild, Henry Lee and Jasper Strangwith, 26th May 1601.

				£	s	d
His apparell and money in his purse					10	0
In the Hall						
A table, two Cubeardes and a forme					16	0
In the Chamber						
A flock bed, bedsteed and a coffer					10	0
In the loft above						
A bed, a bedsteed and a chest					10	0
Six bushells of Rye				1	0	0
Half a quarter of oates					4	0
Brasse and Pewter				1	6	8
Sheetes and other lynnen				1	0	0
Summa	£5	16	8			
A yoake of oxen and a yoke of steares				8	0	0
Foure kyne				6	0	0
Foure yonge bullockes and two weaninge Calves				3	13	4
Two Mares and a geldinge				4	0	0

Twenty sheepe	4	0	0
Foure swyne	1	0	0
Two stalls of bees		13	4
A Cart and other implementes of Husbandry	1	10	0
Two Spitts, a trefeet and potthangers, axe, bill, shovell and pronge		2	0
Eight acres of Rye	6	0	0
Nyne acres of Oates	3	0	0
Three acres of French Wheate	1	0	0
Summa [*£38.18.8*] £38 16 8			
Summa totalis [*£44.15.4*]	£44	13	4

Administration of the goods and chattels of the deceased was granted to Jane, the widow, on 29th May 1601. She was bound well and truly to administer the estate, together with John Attfeild of Windlesham, yeoman. Ref: 1601 Ad 37

Annys Stonner **407**

of Ash; taken by Thomas Inwoode, Hewgh Hamman, George Warner and William Moone, 25th Jan 1600/01.

	£	s	d
In the hale			
One table, one forme and one Cubbarde and one Chaire		3	[*]
For woodden v[*es*]sells		6	[*]
For Brasse, Pewter and a gergar		13	[*]
For two beddes, two bowlsters, two Coverlettes and 3 blanckettes and two bedstedes	1	6	8
3 Chestes		1	4
For 3 paire of sheetes and two table clothes		10	0
For 3 kyne	4	0	0
For one Waynninge bullock and one Waynning colt		10	0
For one Mare		14	0
For 4 hogges		12	0
For all kinde of graine	1	2	0
For haye		10	0
For wearinge Apparell		6	8
[*8d missing*]	10	15	4

On 29th May 1601 the administration was granted to Agnes Eade, widow, niece of the deceased. William Moone of Farnham and George Warner of Ash, husbandmen, were bound well and truly to administer the goods and chattels. Ref: 1601 Ad 39
Note: Notice of the burial was entered in the parish register of Ash on 26th December 1600.

Thomas Wye, the elder **408**

of Chobham; taken by Henry Lee, Henry Ra[*n*]son, Henry Sponge, Michaell Matthew, Thomas Tayler, with others, 19th May 1601.

	£	s	d
Mony in his purse	1	0	0
His apparell	2	0	0
In the Haule:			
A longe Table, six Stooles with a foorme		10	0
A payre of Cobirons		6	8
In the lytell parlor			
A bedsteedell, a fether bed with his furnyture, fower Chestes, 2 Cupbordes	2	0	0
In an other chamber			
One bedsteedell more		9	0

On bedsteedell, a flockbedd and bolster, one chest		10	0
In the new Chamber			
A bedsteedell, a bed and boulster and coverlett, a lytell Table and chayre	1	0	0
In the servanntes chamber			
Certayne beddinge		5	0
In the milke house			
A powdringe troughe, a boultinge hutche, a great boule with other wodden vessell ther	1	0	0
A querne, a cheese presse		10	0
In the kitchinge			
One Table and a foorme, 2 brass pottes, 2 spittes with other furnyture ther	2	0	0
3 brass Candellstickes with the pewter ther		13	4
The Lynnen in the house	1	0	0
The Rye and Ottes in the house		10	0
In the feeld			
9 Acres of Rye and on Acre of wheat	10	0	0
11 Acres of Sommer grayne	5	10	0
7 sheepe and five lambes	2	0	0
10 kyene and a bull	16	0	0
11 yonge bullockes	9	0	0
4 wayninge calves	1	6	8
The hors beastes	4	0	0
The Cartes and wheelles with ther furnyture	4	0	0
The hogges and swyne	2	13	4
The Leas of Brooke house	3	0	0
The Cockes and hens and other poultry		10	0
	[*£71*	*14*	*0*]

Note: A letter from Thomas Crompton to his friend Dr Ridley, concerning the administration of the estate advises the lawyer that "it is not material whether the Administration be granted unto [Thomas Wye, the son] him onlie or to both Thomas and his Mother in Law" [the widow] as "they will well agree." The document was signed Tho: Crompton and then a personal message was initialled "Health and harty comendacions to you and yors." It is then recorded in another hand that in the administration of the goods of Thomas Wye of Chobham, Thomas Wy the son appeared and Anna Wye, widow, renounced her rights to the same. The Administration Bond was provided by Thomas Wye and Henry Spong, both of Chobham, husbandmen and Henry Purdham of the same parish, shoemaker, on 28th May 1601.

Ref: 1601 Ad 49/1 Inventory 1601 Ad 49/2 Letter of Administration

---

1602

Harrye Charlewood **409**

of Sutton, labourer; taken by Thomas Rogers, George Tye and Heugh Jewdery, 29th April 1602.

	£	s	d
In the Hall			
One Table, one cubberd, one chayre and certen formes and shelfes, one fyershovell and 2 cobyrons		6	8
In the kytchen			
One ffornace, 2 mouldinge boords and other lomber		13	4
In the butterye			
One Cauldron, one kettle, 2 other kettells, 3 brasse pottes, one Iron potte, 2 chafers, one lyttle brasse potte, 6 platters, 3 pewter Dishes, 4 sawcers, 2 porringers, 2 salte sellers, 2 pewter candelstickes, one latten candelsticke, one pestle and morter, 2 spittes, 2 pothookes			

and a gryddyron, 2 pewter chamber pottes, 3 shelves, one troffe and other necessaries	2	10	0
In the Parlor			
One Table, 2 tressells, one forme, one ioyned bedsted, one keverlett, one blanckett, one flockebedd and one flocke bolster	1	0	0
In the Chamber over the Buttery			
One ffetherbed, one boulster, one blanckett, one keveringe, 2 pillowes	2	0	0
4 chestes and 2 cofers		10	0
14 payre of sheetes, 4 table clothes, 10 napkyns	2	13	4
2 payre of pillowbeers, one christeninge sheete	1	0	0
In the Chamber over the parlor			
One table, a payre of Tressells, one flockebedd, 2 bedstedes, one coverlett, one blanckett, one bolster	1	0	0
In the Gate			
3 keyne, 2 hogges	4	0	0
One Mare and a colte	2	0	0
One quarne, rackes, ladder and other thinges		6	8
In the feilde			
Of Wheate, barlye, peaze, beanes and tares	5	0	0
His wearinge apparrell		6	8
	23	6	8

Administration was granted on 20th May 1602 to Emma, relict of the deceased. She was bound, together with Hugh Jewdree of Sutton, yeoman, well and truly to administer the estate. Ref: 1602 Ad 8

Adrian Chutter **410**

of Weybridge; taken by William Porter and William Leger, inhabitants of Weybridge. [*undated*]

	£	s	d
He had in his pursse		1	6
The apparell that he did weare		5	0
In the haule			
One cubberd		6	8
A table with a frame and one bench		3	4
2 stooles, a chaire, a paire of handirons and a payre of potthangers		1	6
In the Buttry			
One brasse pott, 2 litle kettles, a halfe a dozen of small peeces of peuter with tubbs and other trash		5	0
The Chamber overe the haule			
One standinge beadstead, a truckel bead, one flocke bead, a boulster, a pillowe, a coverlid, 2 ould chests, three ould paynted clothes		15	0
The chamber over the buttrye			
One standinge beadstead and an ould beadstead, one flockbead and coverlid, a boulster and a blanked		5	0
Three paire of course sheetes, 2 tablclothes and cubberd cloth and a pillowbeere		7	6
One mare and a coult	1	0	0
One cowe	1	0	0
Sixtene sheepe and yearlings at a half a crown a peece	2	0	0
2 piggs		2	6
Four henns and a cock		1	8
[*£6 14 8*]	6	0	4

Note: The Will was signed but not dated and was proved on 21st May 1602. The testator's wife Elizabeth was the sole executrix, who inherited the residue of the estate. His eldest son Edward was forgiven a debt of 10s. His daughter Joane and his younger son Edward were given a ewe lamb; two sons bearing the same name were not unusual in those days. The witnesses were William Leger, Edward Coffin and William Hookes. No overseers were named, nor was an Administration Bond recorded, but the testator asked to be buried in Weybridge churchyard.

Ref: 1602 B 10/1 Will 1602 B 10/2 Inventory

Margerye Clarke **411**

of St George the Martyr, Southwark, widow; taken by John Mortimer, Henry Burch and John Tayler, 15th May 1602.

		£	s	d
In the hall				
One table and foure ioyned stooles			12	0
A forme and a settell			3	4
A standing bed and a trucklebed			6	8
An ould featherbed, an old boulster and an ould pillow			10	0
An old Rugg and an ould blancket			8	0
Three ould Curtaynes and the frindge			2	6
Two ould Chestes			3	0
One wicker Chayre and a stoole			1	6
One warmeing pann			1	0
A payre of Andirons and two slices			1	6
A halbert			1	6
The paynted cloth in the hall			8	0
Seaven crosclothes				6
Foure ould pillowbeers			1	0
Two towells				8
Foure Diaper napkines			2	0
One dozen of napkines			3	6
Tenn napkines			1	6
Two smockes			2	0
One neckercher			1	0
One ould hatt			2	0
One Deske				8
Foure payre of sheetes			16	0
One old flockbed, one old blanket, a shredden coverlett and two old boulsters			3	0
	[*£4 12.10*]	4	13	4
In the chamber within the hall				
One half headed Bedstead			1	0
One ould featherbed, an old coverlett, an ould payre of sheetes and an ould boulster			13	4
An old presse			5	0
One peece of new cloth			10	0
Two stuffe gownes			10	0
Two stuff kirtles			12	0
An old peticoate			2	0
An old Chest				4
	[*£2 13.8*]	2	2	5
In the Garrett				
Two halfeheaded bedsteades			3	4
One featherbed and a boulster		1	0	0
Two payre of pillowbeares			4	0

A blanket, a coverlett and a mattris			6	0
Seaven payre of sheetes		1	4	0
Shopp clothes and towells and one Chest			4	0
Two ould wheeles			1	0
		3	2	4
In the kitchin				
For seaventye one pound of pewter at 5 pence per pounde		1	9	7
A Copper Kettle			5	0
Thirty eight pound of brasse at foure pence per pound			12	8
Three Candlestickes			2	0
An iron potte			2	0
A gridiron, a dripeing pann and a fryeing pann			1	0
A fyershovell, tonges and pothookes and one iron barr			1	6
Three spittes and three payre of pothangers			1	4
Three stooles with some other lumber			1	4
An ould table				10
A payre of bellowes, a Candlemase and a chopeing knife				8
An ould cupbord with half a dozen trenchers			1	0
Two treyes and an ould boule				9
An ould wicker Chayre				6
	[£3.0.2]	2	19	9
In the Shopp				
Three chayres with Cushians			1	6
Three looking glasses			2	6
Two brasse pottes and a kettle			3	4
Twelve porringers and an old bason			1	6
Fyve Candlestickes and three branches			3	0
Six brushes			2	0
Fyve paire of sissers, foure komes and two cases			3	0
A warmeing pann, a payre of tonges and a slise			2	0
A Chest			1	6
Two dozen and fyve clothes			3	4
A fornace with a cover and a ladle			3	0
One box and a tubb				8
Paynted clothes			2	0
	[£1.9.4]	1	9	0
In the Seller				
Seaven old tubbes			2	0
	[£15.0.4]	14	8	11

Note: The Will was dated 12th May and was proved on 19th May 1602. The executor and sole beneficiary was the widow's servant James Holland, to whose loyal, cheerful and single minded service towards herself and her business interests she paid tribute. The witnesses were William Harris, John Mortymer, Margerie Neale, widow and John Griffith, the first of whom wrote the document. The proctor James Ireland, notary public, came in person to present the Inventory which he had signed and to swear to its veracity and that of the aforesaid will. Probate was duly grated to the worthy James Holland and "No bond was taken upon this will".

Ref: 1602 B 11/1 Will 1602 B 11/2 Inventory

Thomas Lawsson **412**

of Walton-on-Thames, husbandman; taken by Master Thomas Inwood, John Lawsson, Anthonye Machyn and Thomas Deacon, yeomen, 8th May 1602.

	£	s	d
In the haull			
A Tayble upon a frame, A Cubborde, a forme, 7 Stoolles, a syde Tayble, a plancke, a butter churne, 3 buckettes, 2 kyllderkyns, 12 wooden disshes, a payre of Awnd Irons, a payre of potthanggars, A payr of bellows, A payre of tongues, 3 lattyn candlestickes, 2 ston Jugges, 1 saulte seller, a paynted cloth, A Choping knyfe, a payre of sheyres, A spitt, a drypping pan and a laydle		13	4
In the parler or chawmber			
A Joyned bedstidle, A flock bed, 1 blanckett, a payre of shetes, 1 boulster, a pillow, a square litle tayble, 3 bras pottes, one Cawthern, 3 ketles, 6 peses of puter, 1 sawlte seller, 1 chafyng dish, A dozen of puter spones, a frying pan, a spitte, a payre of potthookes, 10 boulles and disshes, A payre of skaylles, 3 leade weyghtes, 2 paynted clothes, A dozen of trenchers, 2 firkyn tubbes, a butter tubb	1	5	0
In the lower chaumber			
1 boarded bedstidle, a fetherbed, 2 boulsters, 2 pillowes, a payre of shetes, 2 blanckettes, one other bedstidle, a mattris, A litle syde tayble, 2 chestes, 2 paynted clothes, a payre of shetes, a tayble cloth and all his weyring apparell praysed with 8 pence in his pursse	1	13	4
In the lofte over the Chamber			
6 chestes, fyve payr of shetes, 4 Tayble clothes, 1 Towell, 3 payre of pillow beares, 1 large shete, a bed seiling cloth, 18 table napkyns, 8 puter platters, 3 puter disshes, 3 sawcers, 1 puter quarte potte, A wyne pyntte, 2 Sawlttes, 2 lattyn candlestyckes, fyve poundes of hempteere, 3 poundes of hempen toe, 3 poundes of woolle and a shelff boarde	1	15	0
A woollen whele and a lynnen whele and 3 leyther bottelles		2	0
In the kytchyn			
A kneyding trough, 3 Sives, 2 prongues, a spade, An hoste heyr cloth, a yoltynge fatt, a yeelde fatt, a buckyng tubbe, a bill hooke, a bill		12	0
In the stayble			
3 stoned horsse and a mare	4	0	0
In the yarde			
3 kyne, 2 Calves	4	0	0
A ploughe, 2 ould harrowes, a long carte, a payre of shodde wheles, a litle olde doung potte cart	1	0	0
Debbtes owing to hym			
Of John Poole for ploowyng and harrowing		8	8
Of Humffray Smyth for plowing		9	2
In Wallton feeldes corn on the grounde			
Fyve Acres of wheate and Rye	2	12	0
4 Acres of barlye	1	12	0
6 Acres of Tayres and oattes	1	16	0
An Acre of barlye on the backsyde		10	0
2 Acres of payse and tayres next to the wharffe		13	4
[£23 1 10]	23	3	4

Note: The Will which was dated 1st May was proved on 20th May 1602. The executrix and residuary legatee of half the estate was Margery, wife of the testator. The other half was to go to their unborn son or daughter, if the child should survive. Were his wife to remarry, her father Edward Arthour of Esher and John Connye junior of Walton, the two overseers, were to take charge of the child's half of the estate until he or she came of age. They were to be paid 12d for their trouble. Thomas asked to be buried in the churchyard of Walton. He gave a steer to his mother and a white ewe and a lamb each to his servant John Tynsley and his servant maid Katherine. The five witnesses were John Lawsson, John Beckynsfelde, the two overseers and the vicar Richard Barton. The Administration Bond was provided by the widow and Edmond Parkines of Esher, husbandman.

Ref: 1602 B 26/1 Will 1602 B 26/2 Inventory

Thomas Manorie **413**

of Puttenham, tailor; taken by Bartlemew Hardinge, John Cooles, Nicholas Hardinge and John Billinghurst, 19th May 1602.

	£	s	d
In the haule			
One table and a forme and an olde Chaier		5	0
One Cubbarde		13	4
In the Parlor			
One plank or table apon a frame with a forme, two ioyned stoles		5	0
In the parlor Chamber			
One fether bed and a bolster with a litle flocke bed liynge under and a bolster filled with flokes, a paire of blankettes and a Coverlett of Carpett Worke and a bedstedle and a paire of Pillowes	2	10	0
Two Lytle Chestes		3	0
In an other Chamber			
One flock bed with two bolsters thone filled with ffethers, a paire of blankettes, a Coverlet and a bedstedle	1	6	8
An old litle ffether bed with a paire of blankettes, one bolster filled with flokes and an old Coverlett		16	0
Six paire of Sheetes	1	10	0
Two table Clothes		5	0
Two brasse pottes, fowr Kettles whereof two be smale and one skyllett and one other kettle	1	6	8
14 peeces of pewter beinge divers sortes, three pottengers, 3 sawcers and one Chamber pott	1	0	0
Two Litle Candelstickes, a salte and a litle pewter pott		2	6
A fflock bed and bolster, a paire of blanckettes and an old Coverlett, A Litle bedstedle made with bordes		10	0
One Powdringe troughe and the Cover		3	4
Three troes, three bowles and a butter Cherne and a Litle Chese presse		4	0
A knedinge kever, three firkyns with 4 Tubbes and other Lumber		7	0
A paire of Cobirones, a paire of tonges, a old fire shovell, a paire of Pothangers		3	4
A broche, a friynge pan, a girdiron and a dripinge pan		2	6
a Shop borde, a paire of tailors sheres and a pressinge iron		3	4
An old sack, a busshell bagg and a peck		1	0
Six pewter spones			3
His wearinge Aparell	1	13	4
Money in his purs		3	4
4 Acres of Wheate Lyinge in the Comon feldes and one Acre of Rye	4	0	0
3 acres and a halfe of barley	2	0	0
2 acres of oates		13	4
One acre of peese and fowr acres of tares	1	13	4
One Cowe, a bullock of a yere old and a Weyninge calffe	2	13	4
A Litle Nage and one Colte	2	0	0
Three wether sheepe and six ewes and fowr Lambes	2	6	8
A Litle saw Hog and two yonge barrow hoges with two weyninge piges	1	0	0
	[*£30*	*11*	*3*]

Note: The Will was dated 21st April and proved on 21st May 1602. Before two witnesses, Bartholemew Harding and Robert Manorie, Thomas appointed his wife Margaret and his daughter Marcy as executrixes and joint beneficiaries. The Administration Bond was provided by the widow and George Stanlock of St Nicholas, Guildford, yeoman. The burial of Thomas Manerie was recorded in the parish register on 26th April 1602.

Ref: 1602 B 28/1 Will 1602 B 28/2 Inventory

John Mawdesley **414**

of Bramley in Shalford, clerk; taken by Robart Babb of Bramley, yeoman, John Brabant, tanner and William Stint, tailor, 7th May 1602.

	£	s	d
In the Hall			
One table standinge uppon trestles, one forme and twoo planckes used for seats		2	6
In the Parlor			
One Table on a frame with a Carpit, one forme and one other litle table		5	0
Twoo Chaires, 8 ioyned stooles, foure great, three small, one litle chaire, seaven Cushions and one Cupbord		18	0
Twoo paire of pothangers, one paire of Andirons, one paire of Pothookes, one fire shovle, one paire of Tonges, one Iron used before the fire and a girdiron		5	4
One Lantiron, one paire of Bellowes and one paire of Snuffers		1	0
In the Chamber over the Parlor			
One standinge Bedstedle with a bed tester, one Trucklebed, twoo flocke beddes, twoo bowlsters, twoo Coverlittes, twoo blanckittes and one old Canopie	1	4	0
In the same Chamber three litle Chestes, one Truncke and a boxe with lockes and keyes		11	0
In the Chamber over the Butterie			
One litle bedstedle, one flockbed, one boulster, one pillowe		10	0
In the Hall Chamber			
Twoo bedstedles, twoo fetherbedes, one flocke bedd, one boulster, foure Pillowes, three Coverlittes, three blanckittes and one Coveringe	4	0	0
In the same Chamber Thirteene paire of Sheetes, five Pillowe beares, twoo dozen and eight of Napkyns, foure table Clothes and sixe hand towelles	3	4	0
In an other Chamber adioyninge to the Hall Chamber			
Twoo spinninge wheeles, one plancke and a paire of trestles		2	0
In the Butterye			
Eleaven pewter platters, five pewter dishes, twoo fruyte dishes, foure porringers, one pewter bason, 9 sawcers, three saltes, five pewter Candlestickes, one pynt pott and a half pynt pott, 15 spoones, one pewter bottle and five Chamber pottes	1	10	6
In the same butterye ffoure kettles, one Iron pott, one posnett, 3 skellettes, one fryinge panne, three dripinge pannes, foure spittes, one skymmer, one Iron Morter with a pestell, one Chaffinge dishe, one Choppinge knyffe, one shreadinge knyffe and a bastinge spoone		18	8
In the same butterye 16 wodden dishes, twoo woodden platters, twoo dozen of Trenchers, twoo buckinge Tubbes and twoo buckittes		2	0
In the Bakehowse			
One boultinge hutch, twoo knedinge tubbes, one powdringe tubbe, foure kevers, three firkins, one Churne, one secke, twoo bagges and other old woodden vessell		9	6
In the Bookehowse			
Bookes	1	0	0
Beanes and hasties and suchlike growinge in the Backside		3	4
One acre and a half of Rye nowe growinge	1	0	0
One Cowe	2	0	0
One Nagge	1	15	0
One sadle, bridle and other furniture belonginge		5	0
One Sowe and a yonge shoote		10	0

	£	s	d
Foure hennes and twoo Chickyns		2	0
His wearinge apparell	4	6	8
Money in his purse		3	4
	[*£25*	*8*	*10*]

Note: The Will was dated 13th April and was proved on 21st May 1602. Samuel, the testator's son, was named as the executor, who at his coming of age would inherit land and appurtenances called Cuckewes or Cuckoo Frost in Thorncombe Street, Shalford, then occupied by Richard Caringham. He might inherit money from its sale and he was given all the books. All other possessions were to be divided equally into four parts by the overseers: Thomas Edwards of Clifford's Inn, London, gent; William Risbridger of Shere, yeoman; Richard Caringham the elder of Bramley, yeoman; and John Smither of Bramley, beer brewer. These four friends were to have 3s 4d for their trouble, Thomas Edwards being responsible for either selling the Cuckewes property, or keeping it in trust for Samuel. The four major beneficiaries were the wife Alice, two daughters Martha and Mary and the son Samuel. A second son William was to be paid £1 6s 8d within six weeks, made up of equal amounts of 6s 8d to come from Alice, Martha, Mary and Samuel. The children were to be informed of the value of their inheritance, which was then to be kept by Alice, as long as she remained a widow and with the agreement of the overseers. William Stinte and John Cockes witnessed the Will. Probate was granted to Alice, the widow, during Samuel's minority. She and William Bromham of Dunsfold, yeoman, put up the Administration Bond. On 13th April 1602 in the parish register of Shalford the burial of "Master John Moselie the curat of Bramlie" was recorded. When he signed his will on both pages he had written John Mawdesley and the two witnesses had each time signed themselves John Cockes and Wylliam Stinte. On the inventory this spelling was repeated by Wylliam Stinte. John Brabant made his mark and Robart Babbe signed thus.

Ref: 1602 B 29/1 Will 1602 B 29/2 Inventory

Alice Mychel **415**

of Frensham, Shottermill, widow; taken by William Osburne, William Cacroft, William Gilford and Thomas Farandell, 7th May 1602.

In the Loft whear she Laye	£	s	d
Hire purs and Redye mony		10	0
Hir woollen a parell and one hate	3	6	0
Hir Lynane clos		10	0
11 Shetes, 3 peloue caces and 2 tabell clothes	1	10	0
On fethere bede, on boulstere, 3 pelous, a paire of blankates, on coverlet of blue and red	2	4	0
On flocke bede, on boulster, on peloue, 2 Blankates, on coverelete of rede and blue		15	0
On Joynd bede stedell, on other bedestedell with cords and mates to them		17	0
2 cofers with Lockes		5	0
In the Lofte over the hall and the other Loft			
2 chestes with Lockes		5	4
On borden bedestedele and 4 Small cofers 2 bedmates		10	0
On Rodesadell with sterupes and girtes, on syde sadell with 2 girsts		6	8
On cote of male with 6 earthen cruches		2	6
3 shilfes		2	0
In the hall			
On tabell, on forme, on cheire, 2 stoles		6	0
A payre of pot hangers, a payre of fire tonges, a payre of Brand Irnes, a fyre shovell		6	0
10 peces of peuter and 2 candelstyckes		10	4
On Irne pot, 3 kyttels of bras, on bras pan, on bras Scyllat, on cafer			

of bras, 3 Cyllates of bras, on ladell of bras, on fryingpane, on cymere, on payre of belas and on peuter pote, on chafinge dyshe, 2 broches, on Irne oven peayle, on cleaver	1	7	0
3 qushshens		1	8
In the butterye			
2 fyrkens, 3 tubes, 4 trugges, one butter chearne and for odene vessell and bordes		13	0
In the Shope			
8 Eles of canves		10	8
On turne, on bushell and a cever		4	0
3 Irne weges, on slege, on chayne, 2 spiters, on shovell, on axe and a bill		8	4
A Sacke and 2 bages		1	0
4 Lodes of wode		10	0
For bens and pasone		4	0
Detes			
Mr Edward Tanere	3	0	0
of [* *] Yee of Thursley	1	6	8
[£20.12.2]	20	10	1

Note: The Will was dated 10th February and proved on 21st May 1602. The executor and residuary legatee was the eldest son of the testatrix, William Sherin. The sum of 3s apiece was left to the overseers William Osborne of Pitfold in Frensham and William Cacrofte of Frensham. She left 12d to the poor of each of three parishes: Frensham, Haslemere and Linchmere. Her two elder married daughters, the wife of Richard Lylye of Abinger and Joan the wife of Thomas Packing of Horsham, were left 3s 4d each. The youngest daughter Joan, the wife of Robert Nye of Ewhurst, was left £1, as were the two younger sons Myles Sherin of Wotton and John Sherin of Warnham. Robert Parsones signed the Will as a witness and John Lassame made his mark. The information in the two copies of the Will is substantially the same, but there are variations of wording and spelling.

Ref: 1602 B 31/1 & 2 Will 1602 B 31/3 & 4 Inventory

Richard Myllest **416**

of Chertsey, husbandman; taken by John Bonsey, William Scotcher, John Drew, Henry Byndinge, Richard Penn and Henry Myllet, 13th May 1602.

	£	s	d
The apparrell of the deceased and the money in his Custodie at the tyme of his decease	1	10	0
In the Hall			
One Table, one olde forme and an old Cubbord		4	4
Two chaires and three olde stooles		1	4
Foure shelves, 2 benches and 2 foote and a halfe of glasse		2	2
In the lofte over the hall			
One plancke, 2 shelves, 2 formes, 2 lynen wheles, a pair of stockcardes with other lomber in the same		3	0
Corne in the same lofte		15	0
In the lofte over the low Chambers			
An olde bedsted, a fockbedd, a flockboulster, an olde fetherbedd, a blanckett and a Coverlett		6	8
Three Chestes, a paire of scales and other lomber		4	0
The Malte and otes in the same lofte		18	6
In the low chamber next the hall			
An olde bedsted with painted clothes over it, an olde flockbedd and strawbedd, one fether boulster and a flock boulster, a paire of blanckettes and one Coverlett and an olde fether pillowe		8	2

A new peece of white cloth and an other Coverlett and an olde yellow blanckett and a white blanckett, two chestes and the shelves and other olde lomber		12	0
In the other low chamber by the Mylkhouse			
An olde bedstedd, an olde flock bedd and Mattrice, an olde fether bolster, an olde redd Coverlett lyned with Canvas, one olde chest, certeyne tubbes, a square plancke legged and other lomber		8	0
In the Mylkhouse			
A salt troffe, a forme, certeyne boules, panches, dishes and pottes, a cheese presse and fattes and shelves and lomber		8	0
In the buttery			
Certeyne drinke tubbes, shelves, pottes, trenchers, boules, spones and other ymplementes		2	6
In the kitchin			
An olde Chest, a boultinge which, old tubbes, certeyne axes, billes and other ymplementes of husbandry, three sives and other olde lomber		4	0
Brasse and Pewter and other ymplementes for huswivery			
One Caldron and a banded Kittle	1	0	0
Three brasse pottes, three skillettes, fyve small Kettles, 1 brasse panne and two brassen Candlestickes	1	8	10
1 gridiron, 2 spittes, 1 paire of Cobirones, one paire of Pothangers and two triftes		4	6
Seven pewter dishes, fyve platters, two saltes, two pottingers, two sawcers, 1 Chaffingdish, a litle pewter pott, one dozen spones		10	0
Fyve stone Jugges			6
In the barne			
The Corne threshed and the strawe and hay and a seed Codd, a scyth, a sive and a ffann and a halfe bushell and a pecke and ladders and poles and other ymplementes of husbandry		13	4
One pronge and two paire of Shires		1	2
In the stable and stawle			
The horse Collers and traces and a panell, with the moveable rackes and mangers and other ymplementes moveable pertinent to the stable		2	6
In the gate or backside			
The dunge or Compost in the same gate and the fewell	1	0	0
A litle longe Carte and dunge Carte and one paire of wheles, one harrowe and other ymplementes for husbandry, a gryndestone and a swynes troffe		6	8
Lynen			
Fyve paire of Course sheetes, two table Clothes, halfe a dozen of Napkins and other course lynen for the usuall busines for the housholde	1	0	0
Corne on the ground growinge			
Halfe an acre of wheate and foure acres and a halfe of Rye	5	0	0
Two acres of barley and one acre and halfe of peaze and thre acres and halfe of Otes	5	0	0
Cattell			
Foure mares, Coltes and fyllies	1	10	0
Three kyne, one heifer and three bullockes	8	10	0
Sixe and thirtie sheepe, one with an other	5	5	0
Two Swyne		10	0
The Pullyne, as geese, henns, Cocke and Chickins		3	4
Debtes sperat and disperat	10	0	0

All the leases, interestes and termes of and for yeres whereof the deceased was at the tyme of his decease possessed	10	0	0
	58	13	6

Note: The Will was dated 13th April 1602 and probate was granted on 21st May to Joan, the widow and executrix. In 1602 neither had the son John reached the age of 22, nor the daughter Joan, the age of 20, when they were to receive £10 apiece and 12 sheep. If they died before that legacy fell due the money was to be divided amongst the testator's nieces and nephews. A share of all the goods and chattels, together with the stock and the leases of two coppices with responsibilities for felling, fencing and rent, was to go in three equal parts to his wife and two children. John Drew and Henry Bynding were appointed overseers. Henry Lloyd alias Myllett wrote the Will, which was also witnessed by the overseers and John Bonsey.

Ref: 1602 B 32/1 Will 1602 B 32/2 Inventory

Robert Ropley **417**

of Chiddingfold; taken by Wallter Tydye, John Peyto and Robert Quennille, 1602.

	£	s	d
Mony in his purse			6
His apparylle	1	0	0
One coberd		6	8
The table and the forme and the cheyere		1	8
The peyter veselle all at		8	0
The Brase pote and ale the reste of the Bras att		5	0
4 Kyne and cous	6	13	4
More 2 Hecvers	2	13	4
Mor 2 Twelmonth Bulloks		16	0
More the corne on the g[*r*]ounde		13	4
More 2 akers of otes	1	0	0
Mor otes in the houes and in the barne		10	0
More 3 bedds and all that longs to them	2	0	0
Mor 3 covers		6	0
Mor in tobs and troggs		3	4
The broche and drippinge pane		1	0
More 4 shots		6	0
[*£17.4.2*]	19	4	2

Administration of the goods and chattells was granted to Johanna, the widow. Bound also on 21st May 1602 to see this well and truly carried out were William Bromham of Dunsfold, yeoman and John Ede of the same, yeoman. Ref: 1602 Ad 34

Note: The burial of Robert Ropley was recorded in the parish register on 14th March 1602.

Jone Stynt **418**

of East Clandon, widow; taken by Richard Butler, Arthur Davye and John Jourdan, 19th May 1602.

	£	s	d
A flock bed and all that belongeth unto the same	1	0	0
Pewter and brasse	1	0	0
A cupboard and a litle presse		13	4
Thre chestes		6	0
In Wylliam Attlee his hand - debt	7	0	0
In Wylliam Saunder hand - debt		6	8
In Lypscombe hand of Shere	2	0	0
	[£*12*	*6*	*0*]

Note: The Will was dated 13th April and was proved on 21st May 1602. The executor and residuary legatee was William Stynt, son of the testatrix. Her brother Thomas Attlee and John Jourden of East Clandon were appointed overseers. The widow asked to be buried in the churchyard of East Clandon and she gave 12d to the poor there. Alexander Addams wrote and signed the will as a witness, adding "and John Sexton of Elstead," in a firm hand. There followed "John Sexton his mark 1X". The burial of Jone Stint, widow, was recorded in the parish register on 16th April 1602.

Ref: 1602 B 47/1 Will 1602 B47/2 Inventory

Robert Warner **419**

of Woodham in Chertsey, yeoman; taken by William Roidon, gent, William Claverley, Henry Crockford the elder, Henry Crockford the younger, John Wheatley, Salomon Myllest and John Warner, 10th April 1602.

	£	s	d
The ready money in the purse of the deceased		3	4
All the apparrell of the deceased	1	0	0
In the hall			
One Cubbord, a table and tresselles, one Chaire and certeyne stooles		6	8
In the Chamber			
The best bedd, boulster and other the furniture to it		16	0
The bedstedds and two other olde bedds		6	8
In the upper Chamber			
Three small chestes		5	0
A table borde, a paire of tresselles and 2 olde tubbes		1	8
Three baskettes and three Syves		1	0
An axe, 1 bill and other workinge toles for husbandry		1	8
Pewter and brasse			
8 platters, a Chafinge dish, a morter, two Candlestickes, a drippinge pan and halfe a dosen of Spones and other olde pewter		10	0
Three kitles, one brasse pott and 2 posnettes		10	0
Implementes for huswyvery as buckettes, bowles, trenchers and other lumber not afore declared		5	0
Old lynen as sheetes and a table cloth		5	0
Corne			
In the fielde fyve acres of rye and one acre of wheate	6	0	0
Three acres of otes	1	0	0
Cattell			
Foure kyne	5	6	8
Three mares	4	0	0
25 Ewes and lambs	3	0	0
Foure hogges		13	4
Foure henns and a Cocke		1	4
One longe Cart, a plough, a dunge pott and two olde harrowes and the harnes for the draughtes	2	3	4
The Compost or dunge in the gate		2	6
	26	19	2

Note: The Will was dated 15th January 1597 and was proved on 21st May 1602. The executrix and residuary legatee was the testator's wife Elizabeth. Sums of 20d each were given to the overseers Thomas Beriman and Richard Myllest, both of Chertsey. The testator asked to be buried in the churchyard of Chertsey and he left 2s 6d to the poor there. His younger son Richard and his daughter Joan were each to be given £5 when they came of age: he at 21, she at 16. Henry, the elder son and his brother and sister were to have two platters and a pewter dish, but Henry was to have the biggest platter. Robert Warner the manservant and Alice the maid, were each left 12d. Two thirds of the value of his land and buildings at Woodham were to be given in trust to his wife, towards the payment of his debts and the upbringing of his children for 17 years. The table and benches in the hall and the salt trough were to remain as standards in the house until Henry should succeed. Robert Rydon wrote and signed the Will, on which William Claverly and Henry Crockford made their marks.

Ref: 1602 B 53/1 Will 1602 B 53/2 Inventory

Bartholomewe Williamson **420**

of East Clandon, yeoman; taken by Richard Butler, John Jurden and Arthure Davye, 19th May 1602.

	£	s	d
Money in hys Purse	6	0	0
His apparrell	5	0	0
Eleaven sylver spones	1	5	0
Thre golde Rynges	1	5	0
Two great sylver pynnes, one smale sylver pynne and one payer of sylver hokes		4	0
In the parlor			
One Joyned bedsteddle, one ffether bedd, Two ffether bolsters, one ffether pillowe, one payer of blankettes, One Coverlett, one payer of Curtynes, One forme and one warmynge pane	3	10	0
In the Hall			
One Joyned Table, one Joyned forme, one Joyned Cubbard, one Joyned Chayer, 3 Joyned stoles, 3 Copper bazons, one Pewter bason and ure, 3 whit candlestickes, 2 lattyne Candlestickes, syxe Pewter platters, syxe Pewter disshes, syxe frute dysshes, one Pewter platt, one bazon, ffyve sawcers, syxe porrengers, 3 salte sellers, fower Pewter pottes, 3 Lattyne Chafinge disshes, 2 Andirons, one fier shuffell, Two payer of pott hangers and one payer of billos	3	0	0
In the Kytchen			
Fower brase pottes, ffyve Kyttelles, 3 spittes, Two pannes, Two posnettes of brase, a Collender, Two payer of Andirons, one fier pane, One fryinge panne, One Iron Dryppinge pane with other Lumber there	2	10	0
In his bedchamber			
One Joyned bedsteddle, one Truckell bedd, 3 ffether beddes, 3 ffether bolsters, One fflocke bedd, one fflocke bolster, Two payer of blankettes, ffower Coverlettes, one payer of grene Curtines with Valyans and 3 fether pillowes	5	0	0
One greate Joyned Chest, one little chest, one turned Chayer, Two Trunckes, one little Joyned table, the paynted Clothes and one Deske	1	0	0
Seaven payer of Canvas shettes, Thre ffyne shettes, Two Pillobers tosseld, Thre payer of fflexen shettes, Two payer of Canvas shettes more, halfe a dozen of Dyaper napkyns, one Diaper Table Clothe, Syxe table Clothes of canvas, 2 dozen of Table napkyns, 2 ode napkyns, one Diaper towell, 2 fflexen towelles with other wearinge Lynnan	5	0	0
In the Outter Chamber			
One Joyned Presse, one playne bedsted with a paynted tester, One ffether bedd, one fflocke Bedd, one fflocke bolster, one blankett, Two Coverlettes, Two greate Chestes with other Lumber there	3	0	0
His Firste Wyfes apparell viz: Two Clothe gownes, 3 Redd Pettycotes, 3 Kyrtelles, One Mantell of Stammell, One hatt faced with Velvatt	3	0	0
Money owinge by sondrye persons	150	0	0
Two Wayned pigges with bordes and other stufe		15	0
One Bybell and other bookes		10	0

[£*190 19 0*]

Note: The Will was dated 25th March and proved on 21st May 1602. The co-executors were the testator's second wife Joan and his brother-in-law John Derricke of Guildford. Bartholomew left 10s to his overseers Alexander Adams, parson of East Clandon and William AtLee, with the request that they should call the executors to account every three months, to ensure that the interests of his four children, the residuary legatees, were being well served. The repair of East Clandon church, the poor of the parish and a certain John Sexton, each had a bequest of 10s. His wife Joan was given £30 and plenty of bedding. His son Francis was given the bed and bedding in the parlour and a white basin and ewer. His three daughters Elizabeth, Agnes and Mary, were to have £10 at the age of 21, or on their wedding day. They were each to have a gold ring and two silver spoons. Elizabeth was to have the ring which had belonged to Bartholomew's first wife and Mary was to have in addition a pair of silver hooks and two silver pins. Richard Butler and John Sexton made their marks as witnesses to the signing of the document by the testator. The mark, 1X, is similar to that on Jone Stynt's will. The burial was recorded in the parish register on 17th March 1602.

Ref: 1602 B 57/1 Will 1602 B 57/2 Inventory

1603

Thomas Chittye **421**

of Haslemere, husbandman; taken by Robert Quennell of Chiddingfold, John Penicod and William Howard of Haslemere and John Burle of Farnham, 4th May 1603.

	£	s	d
His apparell	2	0	0
In the loft over the hall			
Two bedsteadeles		12	0
Three flock bedes	1	10	0
Three blanketes, three hillinges, two bolsteres, three paire of Canvis sheetes, one locorom sheet, two pillowberes	3	10	0
Two Chestes, one table and painted Clothes		10	0
In the hall			
One Cubberd, one Chaire		8	0
Three platteres, three pewter dishes, two sawseres, one Candlestick, two saltes, a dozen of spones		8	0
In the Chamber next the hall			
One flock bed, one bedsteadle, one Coverlid, one sheet, one bolster, two table Clothes	4	0	
In the Kichine			
One brasse pote, two iron pottes, three kettles, one posnet	1	10	0
Two tubes, two boules, foure truges, one kewer, one butter churme		12	0
One spitt, two girdirones, one paire of pot hangeres, one woollen wheele, one bill, one axe		6	0
Two standeres, one keefe, one barrell, one powdering tube, a wooden vessell and other lumbry		6	8
Foure busheles of wheate, 10 busheles of barlye maulte, foure busheles of oatten maulte, foure busheles of barlye, three busheles of oates	1	13	0
Foure fliches of bacon and two fliches of beefe	1	0	0
Six oxen	15	0	0
Two horses	3	0	0
Thertene eues and lambes	8	18	0
Six dry sheepe	1	4	0
Six kine and Caules and one bull, five bullockes, foure steeres, one mare	24	0	0
Seaven acres of hard corne	9	0	0
Three acres of barlye	2	0	0
Tenne acres of oates, on acre of pezen and tarres	5	10	0

Two paire of great iron bound wheeles, one paire of small iron bound wheeles, three harrowes, 2 paire of unshod wheeles, one wagin, one plow with yoakes and Chaines, two dunge pottes		4	10	0
Six hogges, foure hennes and a cock		1	10	0
Mony due		1	15	10
	[*£90 17.6*]	93	0	6
His debtes				
To John Smither and Thomas Burle		3	6	0

Note: The Will was dated 17th April and was proved on 10th June 1603. The residuary legatee and executrix was the testator's wife Katherene. His sons or their assignees were to inherit certain legacies on the death of the said Katherene. The eldest Henry was given a yoke of oxen, three sheep and £2. The second son John was given £6 13s 4d. The third son William was to have the best cow and the best mare or horse. The sum of 3s 4d apiece was left to the overseers John Penicod and William Howard of Haslemere, who were witness to the Will. The Administration Bond was provided by the widow and Nicholas Heyward, also of Haslemere, bellowsmaker.

Ref: 1603 B10/1 Will 1603 B10/2 Inventory

Richard Constable **422**

of Abinger, yeoman; taken by John Stere, John Evershede, Richard Lyllye, John Margesson, William Morgan, William Tydye and John Lylly, 10th May 1603. [* *Large illegible patch*]

	£	s	d
Redy Mony in his Purse		3	4
His Apparrell		16	0
In the Hall			
One Table with the forme and Banche and a Cubburde		10	0
Two Brase Pannes and two Kittelles and a Posenette	1	6	0
Thre Platters, 6 Pewter dishes and thre Sasers		10	0
One Candellstick, 2 Saultes and 6 Pewter Spownes		1	6
One Spit, One Brandiron and one Paire of Pothangers		4	0
In the Parllor			
One flocke Beede and a Beedstedell with a Coverleight, a blanckett and Boulster		18	0
In the Kittchenn			
One old Vatte, one Bucking tubbe, a old Brewing tubbe, a small Barrell and two old Tubbes		6	0
In the Kittchenn Chamber			
A kneadinge Troughe, a Chesspresse with other Instrumentes Belonginge		5	0
In the Milck house			
Thre Trudges and Thre Bowles, A Churne and Thre Buckettes		2	6
In A other small Chamber			
A Wollen Whell, A lynnen Whell and Two Barrelles		2	0
In the Loft over the Hall			
One Beed Steddell and Thre Cheastes		9	6
In A other Loft			
One Chafe Beed with all thinges Belonginge		6	8
In the Loft over the Kittchenn			
One Chafe Beed with Certaine old Beedes		3	0
Thre Paire of Shetes		[* *]	
Two Table Clothes		[* *]	
Two S[* *]		[* *]	
One Bushell of Wheate in the house [* *] of peasen and tares upon the ground abought the value of [* *] per Acre		[* *]	
[* *] of Otes upon the Grounde abought			

the value of 6 Acres and a halfe			[* *]
Of Hea and Strawe	1	0	0
Of Otes in the Barne and in the Gatte		10	0
Of Rye in the Barne		4	0
One Cow and a Bullocke of the Age of one Yeare Olde	2	15	0
One Coult of the Age of two Yeares	1	10	0
One Sowe and fower Pidges	1	10	0
One Corne Weane and a dung Cart with Rounges and Linces to the sayd Wean	1	0	0
Thre Yokes and two harrowes		13	4
One Plough with the Irones		6	8
One Grindstone with the Winche		3	0
Thre Chaynes, A axe, a Bill, one smal ludg Chayne, one chape, a paire of dubble Hokes with other old Iron		10	0
William Chessman Indepted	1	5	6
Twoe kyne and one horse	6	0	0
	32	11	10

[*accounted for: £22.11.0 - amount missing: £10.0.10*]

Administration was granted to Elizabeth, relict of the deceased, in October 1603. The obligation was committed in trust to Mr Griffeth, curate of Abinger, to see the same sealed by the widow and her sureties and returned safely into the office. The order was completed by the widow and John Lellie of the same, husbandman. Ref: 1603 Ad 12
Note: The burial was recorded in the parish register on 25th April 1603.

William Deacon **423**

of Ockham; 4th May 1603. [*no appraisers given*]

		£	s	d
In the Hall				
A table standing upon Tressells with a fourme			3	4
A Cubboord			16	0
2 old chayres			1	0
2 smale Andirons			1	0
2 owld Tryvetts			1	4
About 6 yardes of owld paynted cloathes			1	8
A potthanger with potthookes			2	6
A fyer pan, 2 spitts and 2 old gredirons			2	6
	£1 9 4			
In the chamber next the Hall				
A Bedsted			3	0
An old testern of paynted cloth to it				8
4 playn chestes			5	4
3 old shelves framed together to lay apperell on			1	0
An owld rownd table				4
About fyve yardes of ould paynted cloathes			1	4
An old fetherbed with two blanquetts, 1 coverlett, 1 bolster and 2 pillowes unto it			1	10
	£2 1 8			
In the upper Chamber				
2 ould playn bedstedds			4	0
An old paynted tester and on paynted cloth			1	4
One playn old chest			1	4
2 old flockbedds			6	8
Therto belonging 1 blanquett, 2 bolsters and 2 old coverletts			5	0

	£0	18	4			
In the litell Roome at the stayr hed						
A linen whele					1	2
A woollen whele						10
	£0	2	0			
In the Bakehowse						
A kneading Trough					1	0
A bulting Hutche						6
A kneading Cover						8
6 bolls					2	6
fyve bolldisshes						6
A salt Tubb					1	0
An old chearn						8
An old cheese presse						6
8 earthen crocks						8
2 old bucketts						8
2 fryeng pannes					1	8
2 brasse potts and a possnitt					7	0
4 litell Kettuls					3	0
3 lether bottells					1	4
4 syves						4
4 basketts						8
An old sawce tubb						4
A coople of smale Rundletts						10
2 fyrkin tubbs					1	4
A peck measure						2
1 smale caldern and 2 kettells					7	0
6 platters and fyve disshes of pewter					8	8
6 sawcers, 3 porengers and 3 tyn salt sellers					2	6
3 old brazen cansticks					1	0
8 spoones of pewter						6
16 woodden disshes, 3 dossen of trenchers and 4 stone potts					1	5
2 litell glasse bottells						3
A saw and A shaving knife						8
	£2	7	4			
In the lofte over the bakehowse						
A bedsted, A flockbed, A blanquett, A coverlett, A bollster and A seede codd					12	0
A trowell						2
	£0	12	2			
In the Kytchyn						
A mawlding block with buckyng tub and brewing tubb					2	0
A skayner, 2 garden rakes, a mollspade with other lumber					1	10
3 iron wedges, a bond betell, 2 bills					1	6
An ax, A prong, 2 awgers, 1 Chizell, 1 wimbell, spitter and shovell					2	0
	£0	7	4			
The Lynyn in the howse						
6 payre of owld coorse hempen sheetes				1	0	0
1 old lockram shete					2	6
2 flaxen table cloathes					3	0
4 old napkins					1	4
	£1	6	10			
Corne on the ground						
3 akers and halfe of wheat				2	13	4

2 akers and halfe of Rye				3	0	0
1 aker and halfe of tares					15	0
4 akers and halfe of great oates				2	13	4
Halfe an aker of smale oates					2	0
	£9	3	8			
Cattell						
4 kyne				6	0	0
2 oxen				6	0	0
4 yerelinges				4	0	0
4 horses				4	6	8
2 wayned calves					13	4
6 hogges				1	0	0
	£22	0	0			
In the Barne and stable						
An old cart with shodd wheeles				2	0	0
A yoake with A chayn and payr of strapps					2	6
An old dung cart					3	0
An ox harrow and 2 smale harrowes					8	0
The Cart harneys with the plow, cart saddell, bridells and a paynyell					15	0
	£3	8	6			
His apparell with mony and the lease of his howse						
2 cloakes and the rest				2	0	0
Mony in his purse					6	8
The lease of his howse for 6 yeres worth fyve markes yerely above the rent				10	0	0
	£12	6	8			
Alicie Relicte				56	3	10

Note: The Will dated 4th May was proved on 10th June 1603. In the document, 12½ lines were written in the usual form, but the testator's last wishes were contained separately in "A note of the rehersals of William Decon of Occham of his last Will and Testament by hym gyven as followeth." Everything was recorded on one sheet. His wife Alice and William Deacon were nominated as executors in the presence of Thomas Freland of Uptons, Mathew Ham and George Freland. Thomas Deacon was given two bullocks and William Fuller one. The only other specific bequests were that he should be buried in Ockham churchyard and that named goods should go to William, Annis and Joan Deacon, his children. The brass and pewter were to be equally shared by them and the linen by the two girls, who were each to have a joined bedstead and bedding. William was to have a table and form and Alice the best cupboard. Annis was given a brown cow and Joan a red one. Annis was to have an acre of rye growing in the Worefield and Joan an acre of wheat growing on the lower side of the close to the westward. The burial was recorded in the parish register on 5th May 1603.

Ref: 1603 B14/1 Will 1603 B 14/2 Inventory

Anthony Fen **424**

of Byfleet, yeoman; taken by Hendrye Wild and Robert Harme the younger, 2nd May 1603.

	£	s	d
In the Hall			
A plank Table, a fforme and a Bench		3	4
A Cobiron, a Spit, an iron showing horn, a payr of Pothookes and Pothangers		2	0
In the Chamber			
2 bord bedsteds, a fflockbed, a ffetherbed, 3 sheets, a blancket, a coverlet and a table cloth, an olde Chest and a broken Cubberd.	1	6	8
His wearing Apparell		13	4
In his purse		5	0

In the Buttry			
The Brasse and Pewter		13	4
An olde Cheese presse and certain bowles and other lumber		10	0
A busshell of Ote malt		1	0
A fflitch of Bacon		3	0
In the Barne			
Rye		6	0
On the ground			
Growing Corne	7	10	0
Pease and Beanes growing		3	4
In the Stall			
A yoak of Oxen	4	10	0
2 Horses	2	10	0
2 Milch Kyne	3	0	0
4 Bullocks	3	0	0
20 Sheepe	5	0	0
4 Showts	1	0	0
A Cart furnished and a Plow and an Harrow with furniture	1	0	0
An Axe and a Bill and other Husbandry tooles and other trifles		3	4
	32	0	4

Note: The Will dated 5th April was proved on 10th June 1603. The co-executors and residuary legatees were the testator's wife and his son Allen. The sum of 2s each was given to the overseers, his good friends Anthony Smith and Richard Porter. He asked to be buried in Byfleet churchyard and he gave 6d each to five of the poorest people in the parish. If any further benefit was to accrue to him after the writing of the Will, it was to be divided equally between his wife and six children. A year after his death £6 apiece was to be paid to two sons William and Anthony and to three daughters Agnes, Joan and Elizabeth. Anthony was to have two ewes, two lambs, the great brass pot and the long chest. Agnes was to have one ewe and one lamb and so was her sister Elizabeth, who in addition was given the great chest. George Pen and the overseers signed the document. The testator and Robert Harme the younger made their marks.

Ref: 1603 B 15/1 Will 1603 B 15/2 Inventory

John Flodder **425**

of Eashing in Godalming, yeoman; taken by John Edwardes, Arnolde Flodder, Henry Sturte, Robert Peyto, Wylliam Lane and Edward Peyto, 16th May 1603.

	£	s	d
Hys apparel preysed at	1	13	4
Mony in hys pursse at the tyme of hys death		6	8
In the halle			
One table with a forme, 3 chears, a coslet with a pyke furnesshed and a paynted cloth	1	15	0
In the parlor			
One table with a forme and a carpytt, one cobberd with a clothe to cover the same, 6 cussynes and a olde paynted clothe there		16	0
In the chamber within the parlor			
One Joyned bedsted, one table with 3 stooles, one fetharbed with a bolster, 2 fethar pyllowes, one coverlett, one payer of blanketes, one chest and a Rugge to cover the bed withall presed at	3	0	0
In the lofte over the parlor			
One Joyned bedsted with a flockbed, one bolster, one coverlett, one blankett, 7 cofers and a pece of new wollen clothe	2	13	4
More one pece of new cloth of 5 yerdes		15	0

Lynnen clothes			
4 payer of canvas shetes, 3 table clothes, 3 olde hollen shetes, 3 payer of hollen pyllowbers, 4 table napkyns presed at	3	0	0
In the servantes chamber			
2 olde bedstedes, 2 flokbedes, 2 coverlettes, 2 blanketes, 2 shetes, 2 bolsters	1	6	8
In the lofte within the same chamber			
Serten tymber [*] plowes and youkes with some bordes there preysed at		11	6
More there 6 bushelles of wheat presed at	1	0	0
More there of mawlte and barlye 16 bushelles	1	1	4
More there serten sythes with snedes and cradles and a lynnen whele presed at		10	0
In the kytchyne			
Of brasse: one Cawdron, 6 brasse pottes, 3 pannes, 5 kytles, 3 skelletes, 2 basones, 6 Candlestykes, a scuymer, a brasen ewer, one chaffynge dyshe, a frying pan presed at	5	16	6
Pewtar vessell: 12 platters, 12 pewtar dyshes, 4 potyngers, 3 sawsers, 3 salt sellers with some sponys	1	8	6
Serten wodden vesselles: 2 old trowes, 3 fates, 5 kefers, 2 kefes, 6 stobbynes, 2 barreles, 2 vyrknes, 1 powdrynge tubbe, 1 bukynge tubbe with serten buketes, dyshes, trenchers, a butter chearne and a chese presse	3	12	0
In the kytchin lofte			
Cheses and otemeale		8	0
2 letheren botles and an hoste hear		12	0
3 broches, 1 awnd Iron, pothokes, pothangers, a fyer pan, a gyrdIron, a fyer shofell		16	0
9 flytches of bacon and 2 flytches of befe	2	10	0
Shoveles, axes, bylles, awgers with other tolys		12	0
Rye in the barne 44 bushelles presed at	4	8	0
Hey in the barne preysed at		10	0
A fanne to wynow with all		1	0
A wagon with wheles, dong pottes, plowes, harrowes, youkes, chaynes and all thynges thereto belongynge	5	13	4
A well Rope with a bukett and a chayne thereto		6	8
A grynde stone and hogge trowghes		4	4
A ladder with Rackes and one gate		12	0
Serten tymber and wod in the gate	2	0	0
In Watles for the folde and one Ironbound whele		10	0
The soyle in the gate	4	0	0
Catle			
4 workynge oxen	9	0	0
5 kene with 3 Calves	9	0	0
4 heyfordes and 2 bullockes	7	0	0
20 whethar shepe	5	0	0
11 ewes and lambes with them	3	6	8
More 4 whethar shepe	1	6	8
3 mares presed at	4	0	0
12 hogges preysed at	4	6	8
10 weyned pygges presed at		15	0
Corne in the feld			
Of wheat and Rye 23 acres	23	0	0
Of barlye 13 acres	12	0	0
Of pees and tares and otys 25 acres	12	10	0
Serten corne at sowthwode presed at	4	0	0
Serten beanes in the garden presed at	1	0	0

[*£148.4.2*]	148	13	8

Note: The Will was dated 28th December 1601 and was proved on 10th June 1603. The co-executors and residuary legatees were the testator's wife Agnes and Richard and Henry, two of his sons. There were four overseers: John Edwardes, Henry Sturte, Robert Peyto and William Lane, who were each given 5s. The testator asked to be buried in the church or churchyard of Godalming and he gave £1 for church repair and £2 to the poor of the parish. The two closes or crofts of land called Grove Closes of 6 acres, bought from Henry Cartwright and Jone, his wife, were left to Henry and his heirs for ever. Another son John and the four daughters Julyan, Jone, Agnes and Elizabeth, were each left £1. An extra £1 was to be added to the money held as stock for Thomas Flodder. Awdry Flodder, like Thomas a relative and servant, was to have £3 to complete the £30 money held on her behalf by her master. John's godchildren were to have 1s each. A servant Jane Porter was left £3 and Sisselye Porter £2 in money. The three executors put up the Administration Bond. The appraisers, with the exception of Arnold Flodder, witnessed the Will. On 28th April 1603 the burial of John ffludder the elder of Eashinge was registered.

Ref: 1603 B 16/1 Will 1603 B 16/2 Inventory

Henry Flutter **426**

of Bartley in Witley, husbandman; taken by John Jure, Richard Eede, Robert Stilwell and Thomas Burel, 7th May 1603.

	£	s	d
In the Haule			
A table planck, forme, chayre and one stole		3	4
One Cubard		10	0
4 peuter platters, 4 peuter dishes and one salt		5	6
In the kychen			
One old brasse pott, 2 old ketles, 2 old brase posnetes, one Iron pott and Iron posnet		9	0
Two Vates		5	0
One spytt, pothangers, pothokes and grediron		1	6
A boulting huch and a keade trough		2	0
2 stobyns, a litle tub, 3 boules and A bucket		3	4
In the Cambers			
A flockbed, a bolster, a blanket, coverlet, 2 shetes, matt and bedstead	1	10	4
2 other olde flockbedes with the furniture and beddsteades	1	9	0
One payre of canvas shetes and A table cloth		3	4
One colfer		1	6
His Apparell with mony in his purse	1	10	0
Abrode in the feldes			
Six oxen	14	10	0
Fyve keyne and thre calves	10	13	4
Tenn Steres, bullockes and Hefers	11	0	0
Two Mares and three coltes	8	13	4
19 Sheepe and eight lambes	4	16	4
Fyve hoges and fyve piges	1	18	0
Fyve acres of Wheate and Rye	5	0	0
11 acres of otes	5	10	0
The Dounge in the gate		5	0
A Wagon with wheles, plowes, dongpot and harrowes with all tacklinge to them	3	18	2
A bill, axe, spitter, 2 pronges, a sawe, 2 Augers, drawing knife and 2 weges		2	6
A bushell and a sacke with all other lumbery in the house		1	8
In mony by bondes certayne and desparat	119	0	0
	192	2	2

Note: The Will was dated 30th April and proved on 10th June 1603. The executrix and residuary legatee was his wife Margery. Sums of 5s each were to be paid to the overseers, Anthony Slarkes of Shere, tailor and David Tanner of Shackleford, husbandman. They were given the power to withhold money from the widow and give it to the children, if she failed to govern them well. The testator asked to be buried in Witley churchyard. Three ewes and three lambs were given to Thomas, William, John, Henry and Elizabeth, his children. All but John had in addition articles of clothing, linen, or household goods. His servant Thomas Gretest was given two ewes and two lambs. The children were eventually to inherit the money lent out during the testator's lifetime, to be paid to them at the behest of the overseers. They were also to have a fair share in half the estate when they came of age, the boys at 21 and Elizabeth at 20. Witnesses to the signing of the document were Lawrence Stoughton, Robert Stilwell and Thomas Flutter. The widow and the overseers put up the Administration Bond.

Ref: 1603 B 17/1 Will 1603 B 17/2 Inventory

Richard Francklyn **427**

of Farnham, shoemaker; taken by John Tylley, John Marten, John Hole, John Frensham and Thomas Newbery. [*undated*]

	£	s	d
In the halle			
A Cobbard		12	0
A lyttell square tabell with a frame		1	8
A Chare		1	0
2 Joyned stoles and one lyttell s[*t*]ole		1	4
A lynen whele			6
One blancke			6
7 yardes of paynted Clothes		1	8
A bybell		9	0
6 fote of glase		1	8
A paire of bellouse			3
In the kytchen			
2 brase kettels		4	0
A brase pan		1	6
A brase pott		2	4
2 postnetes		2	6
A brasen morter and a pestell		2	0
5 brasen Candellstyckes		3	0
A brasen skymer			4
2 pewter platters and 3 pottengers, 3 saucers, a pewter dyshe, 3 spones and 3 sault sellers, one bason		7	0
A payre of andeyrnes, a payre of tonges, a fyre shovill		4	0
A brotche, a gyrdeyrne, a dryppynge pan, a fryinge pan		2	6
2 payre of pothokes, 2 potthangers		1	6
A boultynge whyche, 2 kevers and 2 barrels		3	0
A bockking tobe			6
3 plankes		2	0
A bottell			10
3 meale bagges			8
A huche with other lomber		2	0
A bockett and A seve			6
In the lofte			
2 fether bedes, a fether bolster, 5 fether pellowes, 3 olde koverlytes	2	12	0
A bedstedell		12	0
A Joyned Cheste		8	0
4 Coffers		3	0
A Corte Cobberde and A Chayre		1	8

2 Cobburde Clothes, 2 quysshines		2	6
2 payres of Canvas shetes, one lockorom shete, A lockorom bed tester		13	4
A payre of pyllobeares		2	6
A bed, A Coverlyte, A bolster		4	0
A bedstedell and A cheste		3	0
A wollen whele, A watchbyll		1	0
A flocke bede, A plancke and 2 tresteles		3	4
In the shope			
2 dossen and 6 payres of new shoes	1	6	6
For bordes and leases, A Cottyng knyf and A hamer and other thinges		3	4
For lether		9	0
For peces		2	0
In the backe syde			
Wode and tymber and faggottes and poles and A shovele and an axe and 2 wedgges and other lomber	4	3	0
His apparrell with mony in his pourse	1	13	4
[*£16.13.3*]	16	13	4

Note: The nuncupative Will was dated 29th January and was proved on 10th June 1603. The co-executors and residuary legatees were his wife Agnes and his only child William. There was a single bequest of 40s to James Twyne. The five witnesses to the Will were William Wealch, George Wrothe and Robert Warner, who signed the document and William Frinsham and Christopher Garye, who made their marks. The burial was recorded the day after the Will was written.

Ref: 1603 B 21/1 Will 1603 B 21/2 Inventory

Symon Harding **428**

of Frensham, yeoman; taken by John Figge and John Hardinge of Frensham, 18th March 1603.

	£	s	d
In the bedchamber			
Money in his purse		10	0
His apparrell	1	0	0
A bedsted and bed furnished	2	13	4
A presse cubbard		13	4
A chest and three cofers		8	0
A paire of blankets, 4 paire of sheetes, a coverlet, a canvas bolster and a bedsted, a fether bolster and 2 paire of pillowes	2	4	0
Seven cushions		2	4
A payre of Holland sheetes, 2 table clothes and 2 hand towels		10	0
In an other chamber			
A flock bed furnished		10	0
A quarter of wheate	1	4	0
9 bushells of barlie		12	0
A quarter of oaten maulte		5	0
8 Cheeses		5	0
In an other chamber			
An old flock bed and bedstedle		5	0
In an other chamber			
A quarter of french wheate		8	0
Two quarters of oates		10	8
In the parlowe			
A table and forme and 2 ioynd stooles		10	0
A round table, a chaire and a chest		3	4

	£	s	d
In the Butry howse			
18 peeces of pewter and sixe sawcers		14	0
3 salts, 5 pewter dishes, a dozen and a halfe of spoones		3	4
3 candlestickes		2	0
A pestell and morter		1	0
In the milk house			
An old cubbard		6	0
In the Hall			
A table and forme, 2 chaires and 2 ioynd stooles		4	0
In the Kitchin			
A cawdron and an old brasse potte together with the rest of the brasse	2	0	0
3 litle spits and a paire of Andirons, a trift, a gridiron and other fire stuffe, as pothangers, potte hookes, fire shovell and Tonges		8	4
Two paire of sheeres			8
Beame and skales and weight		4	0
Spinninge wheele and cards and stockcards		1	8
11 bushels of small oates		3	8
An old flockbed and blankets		1	8
A loome with the Appertenances		10	0
An old hayre with sieves		2	6
A kneading trowe and bolting whitch		2	0
2 vautes together with all the rest of the wooden vesseles	1	0	0
A bryne trowe and a cheese presse with the cheese moates		5	4
Milk vessels and butter chorne		4	0
A gallon of Lard		2	0
12 pound of butter		3	4
Three little cuppes and old bottells		1	0
7 hogs of Bacon	3	10	0
Tooles of husbandrie, 2 bills, an axe, a spade, wedges, agres, Sythes and suchlike		10	0
A bushell, a peck and halfe peck, a seedcod and sackes		4	0
A plow and a carte with a Ruther harrow and 2 small harrowes, yokes and chaines and other things belonging to the cart	3	0	0
4 bushels of wheate and 12 bushels of Rye in the barne unthreshd	2	2	0
Oates and Hay	3	6	8
For drie sheepe	5	0	0
For 14 couples of ewes and lambes	2	16	0
2 yoke of oxen and a yoke of steeres	12	0	0
6 keene, wherof 4 have calves	11	0	0
13 bullockes	10	0	0
For swyne	2	8	0
For dounge		10	0
3 horses and 2 coltes	6	13	4
A stall of bees		5	0
A grinding stone		1	0
10 hennes and a cocke		5	0
Wheate and rye, 8 acres	5	6	8
Oates, 9 acres	3	13	4
	92	5	6

Note: The Will was dated 27th February and proved on 10th June 1603. The executrix and residuary legatee was his wife Joane. Sums of 3s 4d apiece were given to the two overseers, his cousin John Harding and his son-in-law John Baker. The testator asked to be buried in Frensham churchyard and he gave 12d to the church and 6s 8d to the poor of the parish. His seven children had a variety of bequests. Robert was given 3s 4d; William had five valuable pieces of furniture; John inherited one of the best bedsteads, a loom and the shop tools. In three years Alice was to be given £20, but her three sisters were to have livestock at once: Elizabeth Baker, a 2 year old heifer; Constance Coome, a one year old steer; and Katherine, a 2 year old heifer. Two relatives Elizabeth Baker and Elizabeth Heather were each given a ewe lamb and to his godchildren went 6d each. The Will was written and signed by William Wilkins. The other witnesses were the John Harding of Spreakley, John Baker and John Figge. The widow and John Harding of Frensham, husbandman, provided the Administration Bond.

Ref: 1603 B 26/1 Will 1603 B 26/2 Inventory

Thomas Hart, the elder **429**

of Windlesham, yeoman and carpenter; taken by John Osborne, John Attfeild, Henry Lee and William Aneave, 25th March 1603.

	£	s	d
His apparell and money in his purse	2	0	0
In the Hall			
The Table and the Cupboard and the other furniture		10	0
In the loft over the hall			
A flocke bed and the furniture, a Table and a Cupboard and other furniture	1	10	0
In the litle Parlor			
A ffeather bed and the furniture, a table and two Chests	2	0	0
In the backe loft			
A bed and a chest		6	8
The brasse and Pewter	1	10	0
The Lynnen	1	0	0
The Iron and the Edge tooles		6	8
Other tooles and Implementes of a Carpenter	1	0	0
Two fflytches of Bacon		10	0
The Rye in the Barne	2	0	0
The hay in the Barne	1	0	0
The ffrench Wheate		6	8
The Rye on the ground	4	0	0
The Oates on the ground	1	0	8
Foure Oxen and foure steares	13	0	0
A Cowe and a Calf and three heiffers	5	0	0
Foure Horses	4	0	0
Eghteene Sheepe	3	0	0
Two shootes and other poultrey		6	8
The Cartes and plowes, yoakes and Chaynes	1	6	8
[*£45.14.0*]	46	12	0

Note: The Will was dated 14th March and was proved on 10th June 1603. The executor and major beneficiary was the testator's eldest son Thomas, who was to take over the house, land and stock, paying Gylian the widow £3 6s 8d quarterly for life and providing her with a room, a bed, bedding and linen and to allow her free access for her comings and goings. The overseers John Attfeild and Henry Lee were given 12d apiece. The testator asked to be buried in Windlesham churchyard and he contributed 3s 4d to be invested for the poor. The six younger children had bequests of money to be paid a year after Gylian's decease: John was to have £2, William £5, Roger £10, Maude £3, Joane £4 and Margaret £10. A certain Gylian Bignoll had to wait three years for her £3 bequest. Two ewes and two lambs were to be shared by John and Thomas, the sons of the executor and John Child's two sons were each to have a lamb. A godchild Thomas Attfeild was given 12d. Robert Maynwaringe, rector and Henry Lee signed the Will and John Attfeild made his mark. The executor of Windlesham, yeoman, bound himself well and truly to administer the estate of the deceased.

Ref: 1603 B 28/1 Will 1603 B 28/2 Inventory

George Ireland **430**

of Guildford; taken by John Moore and Edward Smalepeece, 10th June 1603.

	£	s	d
One gelding with bridle and sadle	2	0	0
Pewter and Lynnen		10	0
His apparrell and money in his purse	2	0	0
Detts owing unto him	1	0	0
	5	10	0

Administration was granted on 10th June 1603 to Mary, relict of the deceased.

Ref: 1603 Ad 34

Richard Mannam **431**

of Waverley in Farnham; taken by Mr Frances Jaye, Nicholas Harrison, Richard Haman and William Hampton, 21st March. [*no year given*]

	£	s	d
Monie in his Pursse		10	0
His Apperrell		10	0
2 flock bedes, 3 Blankattes, 3 bolsters, 3 pillowes and 2 Coverlettes	2	0	0
A Cheste of Linninge	1	3	0
5 chestes		18	0
2 bedstedles		5	4
One Copborde		13	4
2 Joyned tables and one ioyned forme		6	8
A brewinge tubbe, a buckinge tubbe with other woodden vessell		12	0
Brasse and puter	1	10	0
A brotche, a paire of andiers, a paire of pottehookes, a paire of potte hangers and a girdiron		5	0
A powderinge troughe with other certaine woodden vessell		2	6
3 sithes, one shovell, one bill, an axe and such thinges		4	8
3 quarters of Dredge malt	1	10	0
3 busshells of french whett		2	6
4 busshels of rie		9	8
21 busshels of ottes		10	6
11 busshels of teares		15	0
22 pound of woole and yarne		15	0
Butter and Cheese		8	0
4 sackes		3	4
2 harrowes and a paire of harnesse		5	8
A bottell and a handsaw		1	8
2 quarters of otes in the barne		10	0
6 busshells of Dredge		6	0
3 busshels of pesse		6	0
One Lode of haie and a quarter	1	0	0
2 hogges of bacon	1	1	0
9 kinne and 7 calves	21	0	0
24 sheepe and 10 lames	6	0	0
One stere and a hecfer	3	0	0
2 Wanier calves and the thirde partte of an other	1	10	0
3 live hoagges		18	0
2 acres of corne on the ground and the third parte of an other		10	0
	50	1	10

Administration was granted to Johanna, relict of the deceased, on 5th April 1603.

Ref: 1603 Ad 45

John Mors 432

of Guildford, musician; taken by John Derrick senior, John Derrick junior, Thomas Derrick and John Abbott, 6th June 1603.

	£	s	d
In the owtewarde chamber called the Hall			
One ioined tabell with a frame, twoo ioined formes, two ioined stoles, one old torned chaire, one olde Cobberde, one other cobberde, wodden Disshes, platters and trenchers		13	4
Fyve platters, fyve Disshes, eight frute Disshes, nyne Sawcers, Fower saltesellers, two candelstickes, one olde Bason, twoo cupps and one porrenger of Pewter and twoo latten Chafinge disshes		12	0
One old Pott, thre kitteles, greate and small and one Skyllett of brasse, one Latten Panne, one olde paire of Tonges, twoo olde andirons, one olde ffyre panne, one littell spitt, one littell gerdiron, one paire of Pott hokes, one paire of Pott hangers and one paire of olde bellowes with other lomber		5	0
His Wearinge apparell	1	0	0
In his bedchamber			
One ioined bedsteddell, one fetherbedd, one fether bolster, twoo olde coverlettes and one trukell bedstedd	1	6	8
One base Viall		10	0
Thre paire of fflexen shetes olde, fyve paire of olde canvas shetes, twoo olde chestes, one boxe, one standinge bedsted with halfe a hedde, one olde flockbedde, one olde flock bolster and one olde coverlett	1	5	0
Money in his purse		2	6
	5	14	6

Administration was granted on 10th June 1603 to Jowse, relict of the deceased. The widow herself provided the Administration Bond. Ref: 1603 Ad 49

Note: The burial of John Morse had been recorded in the parish register of Holy Trinity Church on 3rd May 1603.

Katherine Mower 433

of Cranleigh, widow; taken by Robert Smither and Thomas Smither of Cranleigh and Thomas Knight, 6th June 1603.

	£	s	d
In the bedchamber			
3 fetherbedes, a flockbedd, 4 boullsters, 4 pillowes, 2 Coverledes, 4 blancketes, 16 payer of Sheetes, napkins and other linen Conteyned in a littell Chest in the same Chamber	8	0	0
One beddsteddell, 1 presse, 3 Chests with other small lumber	1	13	4
In the hall			
6 brasse potts, 4 dozen of pewter, 6 brasse Candellsticks, 2 oulde kallderns, 2 kettells with other small trifels	4	0	0
In the kitchine, buttrye and milckhouse			
Barrells, tubbes and such other stuffe		13	4
2 silver Spoones		6	8
2 silver pinnes and hookes		2	0
Her wearinge apparrell and mony in her purse	4	10	0
In the handes of Thomas Mellershe	10	0	0
In the handes of Richard Mower	17	0	0
In the handes of Raphe Richebell	2	0	0
In the handes of Thomas Chalke	1	0	0

In the handes of Thomas Smither	1	0	0
In the handes of William Darcknole	1	0	0
One goulde Ringe		13	4
[*£51.18.8*]	52	3	8

Note: The Will was dated 3rd May and proved on 10th June 1603. The executor and residuary legatee was Anthony Godwyne, son-in-law of the testatrix. The sum of 2s each was given to her friends Thomas Knight and Thomas Cowper, the overseers. She asked to be buried in Cranleigh churchyard and she gave 10s to the poor of the parish of "the older sorte of peple". Elizabeth Knight was to have £1 and Thomas Knight a brass cauldron. Mary Allen, the daughter of Henry Allen, was left £20 to be invested for her until her day of marriage or the age of 21; Mary was also to have a feather bed and other bedding, the best brass pot, her mother's wedding ring and a piece of gold worth 15s. Were Mary to die before claiming her inheritance, the £20 was to be evenly divided among her brothers and sisters. Henry Thackham and Richard Mower signed their names, Rowland Grobbie and the testatrix made their marks. The Administration Bond was provided by two men of Cranleigh: Anthonye Godwyne, blacksmith and Thomas Smither, husbandman.

Ref: 1603 B 38/1 Will 1603 B 38/2 Inventory

George Osborne **434**

of Farnham, yeoman; taken by John Figge, Robert Costreat and William Terrey, 27th September 1602.

	£	s	d
In the Hall			
2 Joyned Tables, 2 Joyned stooles		6	8
A cobbard		6	0
2 waynscot backes and 2 chayers and olde paynted clothes		8	0
In the backer Chamber			
2 ffether beds, 1 bolster, 1 pyllow and 1 fflocke bed	2	13	4
A payer of olde blancketts, 3 coverletts and an olde qwilltt	2	0	0
2 bedsteds and an olde bed tester		10	0
1 carpett and 10 olde cusshens		10	0
1 silver saltseller, 3 littell silver bowles, one of them gillt and 12 sylver spones	8	0	0
2 mazer disshes edged with silver	1	0	0
18 pewter platters great and smale, 9 sawcers, 6 porringers, 4 salt sellers, 2 pewter candelsticks and a basen and yewer, 2 pewter potts and a chamber pott	1	10	0
An olde chest and an olde forme		2	0
In the loft over the butterey			
An olde bedsted		2	0
In the loft over the shopp			
1 bedsted, 3 cheasts, an olde Table, an olde forme		13	4
13 payer of sheetes	2	6	8
2 payer of pillowbeeres, a Lynen bed tester, 2 Table clothes, 11 napkins, a cobbard cloth and a hand Towell		13	4
An olde payer of sheetes		2	0
In the kitchin			
An olde ffurnase, 2 broches, a fyer pronge		8	0
A moldinge table and an olde plancke		1	0
4 brasse pottes, 2 brasse pannes, 4 kettells, 7 brasse candelstickes, a baster and an Iron drippinge pane	2	0	0
2 payer of Iron andyrons, a fyer pan and a fyer pronge		3	4
A brasse chaffing dishe, a brasse morter and pestell, 2 bressen flowerpottes		4	0

In an other chamber			
An olde fether bed, a flock bed, 3 olde bolsters, 2 pillowes and 1 coverlett and a payer of blancketts	1	10	0
An olde chest		4	0
In the barne and the gate			
1 cow	2	0	0
Wheat in the barne	2	0	0
Barley in the barne	2	13	4
Otes in the barne	1	0	0
ffetches in the barne		5	0
A lode of hay		14	0
His Apparrell and money in his pursse	3	0	0
	37	6	0

Note: The Will was dated 28th July 1589 and was proved on 10th June 1603. The executor and residuary legatee was John More, nephew of the testator. The sum of 6s 8d apiece was given to his friends Robert Wyne and Robert Philips, the overseers and £1 was bequeathed to the poor of Farnham. The More family, two daughters Agnes and Joan and the aforesaid John More, inherited George's considerable property in three counties. Agnes was given George's house in West Street, Farnham, with a parcel of land of four acres called Wheatearth, precisely delineated: it abutted to the south, east, north and west, on land of William Greene, John Brewer, to the Waverley Field and land of John Figg, in that order. Agnes was also given a furnace, two tables, frames and wainscott in the house. Her sister Joan was given a house in Castle Street occupied by Widow Jackson. She was to have the testator's own feather bed and bedding and the cupboard in the hall of his own house. John, the nephew, was given six separate lots of property; some in the occupation of William Wickman was in East Borne, Hampshire; there was a house and 40 acres in Sussex at Fernhurst and 20 acres with a tenement in Heyshot in the same county, both in the occupation of William Shorter; a house and garden in Downing Street, Farnham, occupied by Thomas Knight; two houses with orchard and garden occupied by John Hewitt and William Serell; and a two-acre close lying north of the Farnham to Alton highway and bordered on its east, north and west sides by land of Edward Quinby, gentleman, Cobygate Lane and land of Robert Mannery, completed the inheritance of John More. Simon Beading was given the best gown. His wife and daughter, both named Joan, were given £3 each. Another daughter Dorothy and the son John Beading were given £2 each. The testator's sister Porytt, the wife of John Polling, was given £1 a year for life, to be paid by John More out of the land. George More, son of John More, was given a silver bowl partly gilded. Each godchild was to have 4d. The witnesses were Simon Beading, Joan Rowland and Thomas Knight, who was the writer of the five large pages of the Will, each inscribed G O by the testator. The executor, John More of Farnham, yeoman, provided the Administration Bond. The burial was recorded on 4th August 1602 in the parish register.

Ref: 1603 B 42/1 Will 1603 B 42/2 Inventory

James Raunger **435**

of Frensham, weaver; taken by John Hardinge, Robert Richardson, Oliver Fanner and William Trigge, 15th January 1603.

	£	s	d
In the Hall			
A table and forme		1	0
A cubbard and a cloth on it		3	8
A cloath and 4 bords		2	0
A chaire and a cradle, a ioyne stoole and other stooles		2	0
A paire of pothangers and hookes, a spit and gridiron		2	0
8 peeces of pewter and 2 salt sellers and 2 sawcers and 6 spoones		6	0
2 ketles, a pan, a pott, a skillet and 2 brasse candlestickes		9	4
A bible and 6 other bookes		8	0

In his bedchamber			
His apparrell		13	4
A bed furnishd		18	0
5 chests		6	8
2 shelves and 3 plankes			6
In a litle chamber			
A flockbed and an old coverlet		4	0
A cradle and a spinning whele and an old tubbe		1	6
In an other litle chamber			
A paire of stockcards, a quilling toorne and a seed codd		2	8
A loome and all things apperteyninge		5	0
Foure paire of geeres		5	0
In the kitchin			
2 kevers, a bushell and a peck		4	0
2 tubbes and buttercharne		1	0
A boltingwhich and a toorne		1	8
A cheesepresse			4
A spitter, an axe and other tooles of husbandrye		1	8
A sawe		2	0
In the barne			
Haye and stubble	1	10	0
Oates and oate strawe		16	8
Rye on the ground	1	13	4
2 sheepe		6	0
A colte		10	0
A pigge		1	0
6 hennes		2	6
2 flitches of bacon		8	0
Summa	20	7	10

Administration of the goods was granted to Grace, widow of the deceased, on 10th June 1603. She provided the Administration Bond. Ref: 1603 Ad 55

William Richardson, the elder **436**

of Byfleet, yeoman; taken by John Harme and Anthony Smyth, 17th May 1603.

	£	s	d
In the Hall			
His wearing Apparell		6	8
In his purse Money		3	4
A Plancke table, a bench, a backboord, a foorme, a painted cloth, 2 chayres and a cubberd		11	0
In the Parler			
A plain bedsted, a painted cloth over the bed, a fetherbed, a bolster, 2 pillowes, a coverlet, 2 blankets, a Bynne and painted clothes about the Parler	1	0	0
In the Chamber over the Parler			
2 boord bedsteds, 4 Chests, a painted cloth over a bed, 2 fetherbeds, 2 blanckets, 2 coverlets	1	12	0
A byll, a bow and a pikestaff		1	4
8 payr of sheets, 4 pillowbers, 2 tablecloths and 9 napkins	1	10	0
In the loft over the hall			
10 pound weight of yearn, half a flitch of bacon, 4 busshels of dredge malt, a cheese rack and 2 shelf boords		8	0
In the loft over the buttrie			
A boord bedsted, a flockbed, a coverlet, a blanket, a payr of stockardes, a wheele and other lumber		10	0

In the buttrye			
A little foorme and 5 boords and other trifles		2	0
In the kitchin			
3 little kettles, 2 little brasse pots and 2 posnets brasse		10	0
9 pewter platters, 4 disshes, 4 sawcers, 2 porringers, a candle stik, a chamber pot, a salt seller and 6 spoones		10	0
One pere of Andirons, pothooks, 2 pothangers, a dripping pan, a frying pan and 2 spits		5	0
A kneading trough, a salt trough, a boulting hutch, a cheese presse and a butter cherne		3	4
Buckets, tubs, bowles, woodden disshes and such lumber and some erthen pots		5	4
2 prongs, a beetle and 2 wedges, a bill and other iron tooles and scales and waights		2	8
In the barne			
2 ladders, straw, a flayl, a plank and other olde boords		1	8
In the yeard			
ffyer wood		1	4
In the Garden beanes etc growing		2	2
Rye growing	1	7	0
2 bullocks, a calf, 2 hogs and 2 hennes	1	6	8
	10	19	6

Note: The Will was dated 7th March and proved on 10th June 1603. The executor and residuary legatee was his son William. The sum of 8s between them was given to his good friends, Henry Harme the younger and Richard Porter, the overseers. The testator asked to be buried in Byfleet churchyard and he gave 12d to the parson there. He was moved to order his heir to give £1 to the poor after his death, or if he should be restored to health, it would be given by his own hands. His wife was to have 10s and all the household stuff and apparel which she had brought to their marriage. Her daughter, married to John Harme, was given a pair of sheets. His daughter, married to Robert Goddard, was given a bed and bedding, 13s 4d for a petticoat cloth and £1 annually for life, half of which would be paid at Michaelmas and half on Lady Day. Sums of 10s for the five Harme children and £1 for the five Goddard children, were to be invested at the choice of their parents in lambs or bees. The testator gave 8s apiece to his sister Frances Nickson and her daughter Frances. Gifts to the Wylde family were 2s 6d to George the elder and to Joan, a goddaughter; and 12d to Harry. Another goddaughter Elizabeth Wheeler, daughter of John, was to have 2s 6d. Gifts of 10s were made to Mistress Adams and her daughter Sara Waterer. Alice Porter, sister of Richard, was given 2s. Combes the ferryman at Shepperton was given 6d and the same "to one Ride that Combes knoweth that brought the flownder to me on the pole to St Mary Overies". Combes was to distribute 12d among John Marloe's children and the same was to go to any of Cooke's children still living. Robert Smith of Hoods was given his best hat and Smith's wife and Agnes, their daughter, were to have 12d apiece. The same sum was given to John Porter's wife, to Agnes Banister and to Robert Porter, Thomas Wheeler's servant. A note at the side made a further bequest of 12d to Elizabeth Gregory. George Pen the parson, Richard Porter and John Harme, signed the Will. The testator and Robert Harme the younger made their marks.

Ref: 1603 B 48/1 Will 1603 B 48/2 Inventory

Richard Southe **437**

of Ash, taken by Mathewe Gullsoune, Henry Hazell, Gilbart Lambole and John Dare [*no day or month*] 1603.

	£	s	d
in the hall			
One table, one Cubbard, one Chest, towe dry fattes with other shelfes	1	0	0
Towe pott hanggeres, one paire of pothookes, towe girdirones, one paire of Andirones with one dogge of iron and one spit, one paire of tounges, one fier shovell		5	0

in the parlor			
One table with a frame and halfe a dozen of stooles and one benche and one Lyttell syde table, one Lyttell Cheare and a Lyttell stoole		12	0
Six quoshinges, towe window quoshinges, one Lyttell Carpett cloothe, a few small bookes with tow small glasses		6	8
in the backe howse			
One querne, foure Ceveres, four tobbes, one boltinge huche, three firkines, a yotinge fatte, one bushill, one peck with other Lumber		13	4
Some brass Ketteles, tow brass pottes, tow posnettes, one brass morter and one paire of hookes	1	13	4
in the buttery			
Halfe a dozen of puter platteres, with a dozen of small puter platteres and foure sauseres, half a dozen of porrengeres and one bason, six Candelstickes of puter, tow dozen and halfe of spounges, three saltes, towe Lyttell puter Cuppes with a Chamber pott	1	0	0
One fryinge pan, one bastinge Ladeell, one scummer, one butter Churme, three shelfes and a stand with other Lumber		3	4
in the shopp			
Foure paire of sheeres, one sheere bord, ten Corse of handeles, three tournes, one Scraye with other Lumber	1	10	0
One hulbard, one other bill, Ax, three weedges, three daggeres, one swoord		3	4
in the Loft over the hall			
One beame and Scakeles with wayghtes		6	8
Towe wooll baskettes, one paire of Stokkardes, one frame, one heare Cloothe		3	4
Three flychees of bacon, sixteen Lyttell Cheeses		12	0
in the Loft over the Parlor			
One standinge beedsteed with a truckell beedsteed, six Coferes	1	0	0
Towe fether beedes, towe fether boulsteres, six fether pillowes	3	0	0
Towe flockes beedes, towe flokes boulsteres, towe mattes for beedes, foure Coveringes, one paire of blankites	1	10	0
Eight paire of sheetes, foure bourd Cloothes, a dozen of napkines, three paire of pillow beares with a Christninge sheete	4	0	0
A Lyttell Chamber over the buttery			
One bedsteed, towe Coferes, one flocke beed, a flocke boulster, a paire of blankettes and one Coverled		13	0
His wearinge apparill	1	6	0
Money in his Purse		3	4
Three quarters of Otes, halfe a quarter of rye, towe bushilles of barleye	1	10	0
A Carte with harness	1	0	0
Wood		6	8
Towe akeres of Rye, foure Akeres of barley, one halfe aker of Otes	4	0	0
Grasse in the Orchard, beanes and pease		5	0
Foure Kine and Calfe, one bull	8	0	0
Seven steares, one Heiffer, three weaninge Calfes	8	0	0
Three horses	5	0	0
One Sowe with eighte pigges and five shewtes	2	0	0
Fyteene Geeze, eight henes and one Coke with six Chickines		3	4
For Dyeres weedes	1	0	0
	51	7	4

Note: The Will, written in 1603, was proved on 10th June. The executrix and residuary legatee was the testator's wife Amy. Sums of 6d apiece were left to John Dare and John Monger, the overseers and 3s 4d to the minister. The testator asked to be buried in Ash churchyard. He left £5 to each of his five children: Thomas, Margery, Cysleye, Frances and Jayne. Mathew Gullsoune wrote both documents. The testator and the overseers made their marks on the Will. The burial was recorded on 5th May 1603. The widow of Ash and William Hasell of [?], tanner, provided the Administration Bond.

Ref: 1603 B52/1 Will 1603 B 52/2 Inventory

Henry Sponner **438**

of Abinger, yeoman; taken by John A Stone, John Lypscombe, Davye Tydye and John Sponner, 9th May 1603.

	£	s	d
Mony in his Purse	2	0	0
His Warring Apparrell	2	0	0
In the Hall			
One Table, one forme and the frame Belonginge		5	0
One Cubberd		16	0
One Pothangeres with a Iron Bare and a Brandiron		2	6
One Chare, Two Stolles and eight Quishinnes		5	6
In the Parller			
One Beed with all thinges theirunto belonginge	2	0	0
One Table		2	0
One Coliver and all furnitur Belonginge	1	5	0
In the Loft over the hall			
Two Beeds with all thinges theirunto Belonginge	2	13	4
Thre Cheastes, thre Stowles		7	0
In the Loft over the Parller			
One Beed Steddell with all belonging, one Cheast		15	0
In the Loft over the Buttery			
One Beed furnished		10	0
A Shelfe and a Cheaste		3	2
Of Lynnen Yearon 13 poundes and 4 poundes not Spune		7	0
In the Kittchen			
Five kittelles, two Pottes, thre Postnettes, 12 peeces of Pewter fower Saultes, two dussen of spones, thre porringers, fower Saseres, two spittes, one Treft, a dripping pan, a pair of pothangers and a pair of pothockes	2	5	0
One vatt, one Bucking tubb, fower Bowles, one Chespresse		10	0
6 Hodges of Bacon	4	0	0
Otes and mault two Quarters		16	0
In the Mylk house			
6 Troudges, two Bowles, one kneading trough, one Churne, one Bunting huch and the Banches		10	0
In the Butterry			
One Powderring trough and the Beffe in the said trough		11	0
Thre kiveres, two Barrells, thre tubbs, one frying pann, thre prongs, two axces and one Bill		9	4
Thre Candellsticks, one Chaffingdishe, one morter and two waytes of leade		6	4
Tenn Paire of Shettes	2	0	0
Fiv Table Clothes		10	0
Thre Sacks		2	0
Wheat one the ground 12 Acres	15	0	0
17 Acres of Otes	8	10	0
8 Oxcen	20	0	0

10 Kinne	16	13	4
Fowre Bullockes of the Age of one yeare	3	0	0
Thre other Bullocks of the Age of Two Yeares	3	0	0
Eight Wanyer Calves	3	0	0
Sexe Horsses	8	0	0
Threskore and Tenne Ewes and weathers	20	0	0
Seven and twenty Lambs	4	0	0
Seven hodges and Two Pidges	3	0	0
Weannes, Dungcartes, ploughes, harrawes, Chaynes, yoks and all other Instrumintes whatsoever belonging to Husbandrey	2	10	0
In the Barne and house			
Wheat	1	16	0
Twenty Bushelles of Wheat and Rye Myngelled	2	10	0
In the Barne			
8 Bushelles of Otes		6	0
of Trannsformed stufe of tymber and of Cordwood in Wickes	10	10	0
Fourty Stack of Wood in Redford	5	0	0
Of Wood in Pistley	2	10	0
Of Wood in the Fishfould	6	0	0
The Lease of the Weckes Woode	20	0	0
	180	15	6

Note: The Will was dated 25th April and was proved on 16th June 1603. The co-executors and residuary legatees were his two sons Henry and William. Sums of 10s each were to be paid to the overseers, his brother Robert Sponner and John Lyllie. The testator asked to be buried in Abinger churchyard. The overseers were to distribute 10s to the most needy poor in Abinger and 5s in Ockley. His wife Joan was to inherit the best bed and bedding, her own choice of chest, six of the best pieces of pewter and two kine of her own choosing. William, the younger son, was to inherit the lands, woodlands and copses, in Abinger called Stubbings or Vulvinnes. Annis Daulton, the younger daughter, the wife of Raphe Daulton, was to have a life interest in the house and three acres of land called Bennatts in Ockley. After her decease the property was to go to her children, or if there were none, then to the aforesaid William Sponner. The testator's father Raph Sponner was to have the annual gift of 12 pounds of wool to be made by the executors on St John the Baptist's Day, 29th August. Another gift to son William was that of two black five-year-old oxen. Amy Hunt, the elder daughter and wife of John Hunt, was left £9. Their four children Anne, Elizabeth, John and Jane, were each to be given £4 at the age of 16 by the executors. A son-in-law Raph Daulton, who occupied part of the land called Weecks, was given 20 of the best oak and beech trees growing there chosen for him by the overseers. Raph Sponner, the testator's brother, was given 10 of the best beeches growing on that part of Weacks occupied by Henry Sponner, the elder son of the testator. Both men were to have free access for felling and carrying the timber so given. Four of the servants, John Shoe, Henry Shoe, Robert Beldame and Thomas Gates, were each to have a ewe at Michaelmas, 29th September. One witness Richard Margesson signed the will; John Mower, Richard Butler and the testator, made their marks. The executors and John Lyllie, all husbandmen, put up the Bond of Administration.

Ref: 1603 B 54/1 Will 1603 B 54/2 Inventory

Robert Steele **439**

of Frensham, husbandman; taken by Richard Geale of Sandhurst, yeoman and John Hardinge and Oliver Fanner of Frensham, 23rd March 1603.

	£	s	d
In his bedchamber			
Money in his purse		2	10
His wearing apparrell	1	0	0
A flockbed furnish with a paire of sheets, a paire of Blankets, a coverlet, 2 pillowes and a bolster, with a stedle and appurtenances	1	3	4
Sixe chests and an old Tubbe		10	0

	£	s	d
A cubberd and a chaire		2	6
In another chamber			
A certaine of Tubbs and other wooden vessells		10	0
In a chamber over that			
A flockbed, a coverlet, a sheete, a fether bolster and pillowe, a bedstedle with a clothe over it and an other old bed standing by and 2 paire of sheetes	1	6	8
French wheate foure bushells		4	0
Five pound of lambs woll		3	4
A bushell and halfe of oaten mault		1	8
In the chamber over the hall			
3 quarters of oates	1	0	0
Wheate and rye 2 bushells		5	0
2 pound of woll		2	0
In the Kitchin			
A cheespresse and a moate and a wheele and cards		1	8
3 Sythes		3	0
In the Hall			
A table		1	0
10 bords and a forme		2	6
A cubbard		8	0
10 peices of pewter, 2 sawcers and 2 candlestickes, 2 Saltsellars and a dozen of spoones		13	4
3 ketles, a brasse pot, 2 brasse skillets		10	0
A paire of pothangers and other fier stuffe		1	0
A basket, 2 boles, 3 stooles		1	0
3 hogges of bacon	1	6	8
Tooles of Husbandrie, 2 bills, 2 axes, a sawe, a wimble, an agre and a paire of sheeres		3	0
In the gate, barne and feild			
6 stalls of bees	2	0	0
3 kine	6	0	0
2 heyfers	3	6	8
Heyfers of a yeere and vantage	2	0	0
A yoke of oxen	4	13	4
A yeerling steere		10	0
8 shootes and 2 yearling hogs	2	6	8
A horse and mare	3	0	0
A cock and 2 hennes		1	6
A paire of cart wheeles		5	0
Dounge and wood and skilling and skaffold poles	1	0	0
In the barne			
Wheate and oates	3	6	8
Haye	2	0	0
In the feild			
3 acres of Wheate and rye	4	0	0
Sheepe, 23 couples of ewes and lambes, one rambe and 4 ewe teggs	9	0	0
A paire of harrowes and harnes		3	4
[*£53.15.8*]	52	15	7

Administration of the goods and chattels was granted to Elizabeth, the widow, on 10th June 1603. She was bound to administer the estate, together with Thomas Treg of Frimley and John Treg of Frensham, husbandman. Ref: 1603 Ad 62

Henry Sturte **440**

of Eashing in Godalming, husbandman; taken by John Kene, Thomas Matchwyke, Robert Peyto, Henry Joyse and Rychard Clyfton, 4th June 1603.

	£	s	d
Hys apparrell preysed at	2	0	0
Mony in hys pursse at the tyme of hys death		5	0
in the halle			
1 table with a frame, 2 formes, 2 cobberdes, 2 chears, 2 Joyned stoolys	1	13	4
in the lofte over the halle			
One Joyned bedsted with a flockbed, 2 bolsters, one Coverlett, one payer of blankettes, one lytle table	1	10	0
in the lofte where he laye			
One Joyned bedsted, one flockbed, 2 bolsters, 2 pyllowes, one coverlett, one blankett, 2 chestes and 4 cussenes	2	2	0
in the servauntes chamber			
One olde bedsted with a flockbed and a coverlett		6	8
the lynnen clothes			
2 table clothes, one payer of lokeram shetes, 3 payer of canvas shetes, one payer of pylowbers, 6 table napkynes	1	14	0
in the kytchyn			
4 brasse pottes, 4 ketles, 2 skelletes, 2 payer of pothokes, 2 payer of pothangers, one broche and a lytle awndIron	2	0	0
pewtar vessell			
7 platters, 5 pewter dyshes, 4 sawsers, 2 salt sellars, 2 Candlestyckes, a morter with a pystle and a dosen of sponnys		16	0
serten wodden vesselles			
as 3 vyrkynes, one kefe, one fate, one knede trowghe, one powdryng trowghe, one chese presse, with other tubbes, trees, bowles, bukettes and other lomberye	2	0	0
Rye in the howse - 6 bushelles		12	0
8 bushelles of mawlt and 4 bushelles of barlye		16	0
8 flytches of bakone	2	0	0
serten chesys preysed at		5	0
3 tod of wolle	3	0	0
Catle			
6 oxen and a stere preysed at	14	0	0
5 kene	8	0	0
3 bolockes	3	0	0
2 weyned calves		13	4
3 mares	5	0	0
4 skore and 17 shepe	19	12	0
35 lambes	3	10	0
10 hogges and 12 weyned pygges	3	18	0
Corne in the felde			
Of wheat 26 acres preysed at	30	0	0
Of Rye 8 acres	8	0	0
Of barly 8 acres	5	6	8
Of otys 6 acres	3	0	0
Of pece and tares 6 acres	3	0	0
Of french wheat 3 acres	1	10	0
Of grasse 4 acres	2	0	0
In the garden benes and other frute	1	0	0
One wagon with wheles and doung pottes, youkes, chaynes, plowes,			

harrowes, harnes, traces and other nessesaryes thereto belongynge	3	0	0
Soyle in the gate preysed at	2	0	0
Serten fold watles		4	0
One axe, 1 byll, shovelles, awgers and other nessesary tooles of husbandrye		2	0
A well Rope and a bukkett		5	0
A Hoste hear and sackes, one halfe bushell with sythes and sycles		10	4
Serten hennys and cooke		2	0
	138	13	4

Note: The Will was dated 27th May and was proved on 10th June 1603. The co-executors and residuary legatees were Joan, the wife of the testator and Henry, the son. Sums of 2s 6d apiece were given to the overseers Henry Joyse and Richard Clifton of Godalming. Jane, daughter of the testator, was to inherit, when she came of age or when she married, a comprehensive collection of household goods: two heifers, 20 sheep, wheat, rye and £5 in money. He gave £1 to his sister-in-law Alice Sturte and 10s to his own sister Susanna, whose son was to have two ewes. His godchhildren were to have 6d apiece. Thomas Matchwyke and Robert Peyto signed the Will, written by the latter, a clothier of Godalming and together with the widow, he put up the Administration Bond. As Henry was still a minor when his father died, his mother herself was granted letters of Administration. On 29th May 1603 the burial of Henry Sturt of Eashing was registered.

Ref: 1603 B 56/1 Will 1603 B 56/2 Inventory

Arthur Talbot **441**

of Kingston upon Thames, bricklayer; taken by Richard Chelsham, John Chelsham and William Monday, 6th June 1603.

In the hall				£	s	d
One prese wyth a Coberd Clothe				1	0	0
One tabell wyth a frame and 8 stooles					12	0
One Corte Cobard, to Chares an to small stooles an to boxes					13	4
The wenscote wyth the panted Clothes and on portele of wenscote				1	10	0
Halfe a dosen of grene Cushens and to other					8	0
One payer of andyerns, on fyer shovell and on payer of tonges					3	0
	£4	6	4			
The Chamber over the hall						
One Joyned bedsted, on fether bead, to fether bowlstars, on Coverlyd, one blanket, one payer of read Cortens wythe the rods, on strawe bead				4	0	0
One trondell beadstead, one flocke bead, one Coverlyd and on blanket, to bowlsters				1	0	0
One halfe headed bedsted, one flock bead, to bolsters, to Coverlyds, to mates				1	10	0
One presc				1	10	0
3 Ches and one Close stoole an one screwe pres					17	0
The panted Clothes, on wyndowe Curtene wyth a rod, on still, one flarsket, on slyce				1	2	0
	£9	19	0			
The Chamber over the Cychen						
On standinge beadsted, on feather bead, to feather bolsters, on flocke bead, one payer of grene Curtens and rodes, to blankets, to Coverlyds				12	17	0
One trondell beadstead, on flocke bead, 4 blankets, on quylte, one bolster				1	12	0
On frenge for a bead, on square tabell, 3 carpetes and on Courte Cubard				4	0	0
To chers, one troncke, to boxes wyth one frame				1	14	0
One wycker Chayer, the panted Clothes, one grene wyndowe Curten					13	4
11 pylows, to silver spoones, to brushes				2	5	0
	£23	1	4			

The Lynen						
18 payer of shetes, 15 tabell Clothes, 9 payer of pylowbers				22	4	0
4 Cubard Clothes, 6 longe towells, 7 drynkeinge Clothes				2	0	0
7 dosene of napkyns, 15 hansqweles an a pece of newe Clothe				4	12	0
The Chyld bead lynene				3	0	0
One pece of newe Clothe				1	0	0
	£32	16	0			
The Cychene						
18 pewter platers, 5 pewter dyshes, 12 frut dyshes, 19 sasers and to plates 8 pewter poryngers, 4 pewter basons, 6 pewter Candellstycks, on pewter quarte pot, one pynte pote, on pewter botell, to pewter potes, to Cupes, 4 pewter salte sellers, to dosene of sponnes				3	10	0
The bras						
5 bras potes, 5 kyteles, 5 posnets, on warminge pane, on Chafen dysh and 3 brasen ladels				3	2	4
On payer of rackes, an yeren, 3 drypinge panes, 3 spytes, on grydyerne, to payer of pot hangers an to payer of pothooks, on payer of belowes, on fyer showele, on payer of tonges, on fryen pane, on payer of andyerns					17	6
On tabell with a forome					10	0
To bybels and other small bookes					16	0
	£8	15	10			
In the backsyde						
5 lode of lathe				6	5	0
14 newe bordes					13	0
Pavinge tyll and lyme					16	0
The fyerwood				5	4	8
4 Chatherne of se Cole				2	8	0
	£15	6	8			
The lese of the hows wherin the testator duelled				10	0	0
His warynge aparell				7	0	0
Money in his purse				5	0	0
Debtes due to the testator				5	0	0
The Lomber aboute the hows				3	0	0
	£30	0	0			
				124	5	2

Note: The Will was dated 16th May and proved on 10th June 1603. The executrix and residuary legatee was the testator's wife Margaret, not doubting that she would be a kind, loving and natural mother to her children and his. He appointed his very good friends, William Nicholls and John Wonham, to be his faithful overseers. He asked for christian burial and gave 10s to the poor of Kingston. He made it plain that his eldest son John was eventually to inherit the first property in Kingston, in which his wife was to have a life interest: there were four tenements under one roof in Heathen Street, adjoining the ground of George Snellinge, gent. His second son Arthur would inherit the second property on similar terms; this was a tenement, also in Heathen Street, lately purchased of Thomas Paltocke, mercer, deceased. His oldest daughter Ruth was to have £13 6s 8d at the age of 21 or when she married. Were Margaret to marry again, she was to pay £10 each to Meryam and Elizabeth, his two other daughters, at the age of 21 or when they married. Arthur Talbot made his mark on each of four pages of the Will. John Wonham and Edward Fairebanck signed as witnesses. On 27th May 1603 the burial of Arthur Talbott, bricklayer, was registered.

Ref: 1603 B 57/1 Will 1603 B 57/3 Inventory

Thomas Westbrook **442**

of Pirbright, husbandman; taken by Robert Russell, Edward Remnant, Thomas Smyth and Georg[*e*] Marten, 26th April 1602 or 1603 [*no year given*].

	£	s	d
For thre flook beedes withe thre kovrings	1	0	0
For to paier of shets and two boulstors		10	0
For thre kettles and two bras poots		6	8
For halfadosson of peutor and fowr kanstekes and a chafing desh and a salt		6	0
For a koobord and a tabl and a pair of andiorns with a pair of poothangrs		5	0
For koorn in the hous	1	0	0
For korn in the barn thre hill		3	0
For korn upon the ground	3	0	0
For two akrs of otes and halfanakur of pes and half anakar of barley		6	8
For 6 oxen	10	0	0
For 5 ken and 4 kaves	5	0	0
For 13 boolokes	6	0	0
For one hors		10	0
For two hooges and 5 piges		5	0
For 20 shep and 4 lames	3	0	0
For on kart with yokes and chaines and a plow with a harow	1	0	0
For thre chestes and two tobs and two bokkets		3	0
For ax and bell and a shovell and two wadges		2	0
For two sithes		1	0
	[*£32*	*18*	*4*]

Note: The Will was dated 2nd April 1602 and was proved on 10th June 1603. The co-executors and residuary legatees were his wife Joan and his son William. Sums of 12d apiece were given to Edward Remnant and Thomas Smithe, the overseers. The testator asked for christian burial. He gave £5, two ewes and two lambs to each of his sons George, John and Thomas. John was also to have a three-year-old heifer and Thomas, one of two years old. Austin Woodde signed the document as a witness. The testator and Robert White made their marks. The executors provided the Administration Bond.

Ref: 1603 B 59/1 Will 1603 B 59/2 Inventory

George Whittingham **443**

of Farnham, innkeeper; taken by Robert Aston, Robert Hardy, Edward Fildar and William Mauncell, 25th May 1603.

443A

	£	s	d
In the great Chamber			
Wynscot and glasse	3	0	0
2 bedes, 2 bolsters, 2 Coverlettes, 2 blanckettes, a standing bed and a truckell bed with Curtteyns	5	0	0
2 tables, 2 formes, a Joyned stoole and five Cushens, 1 an Iron, 1 fier shovell, a Wickett Chaire	1	0	0
In the red chamber			
1 standinge bedsted, 1 bed, 1 coverlett, 1 blanckett, 1 quilt, 1 table, 1 forme, 1 chaire, 1 bolster and the glasse	3	4	0
In the Chamber called the broad stares			
1 standinge bedsted and a truckell bedsted, 2 fetherbedes, 2 bolsters, 2 Coverlettes, 2 blanckettes, 1 quilt and Curtteyns	5	0	0
2 tables, 3 formes, 1 side cubbard, 2 Chaires, 2 smale Carpettes,			

2 Cushens, 1 aniron, Wynscott and glasse	2	0	0
In the servanntes Chamber			
1 flocke bed and a strawe bed		10	0
In the yowlow chamber			
2 fether bedes, 2 bolsters, 2 coverlettes, 1 blanckettes, 1 standinge bedsted and a truckle bedsted and curtteyns	4	0	0
1 table, 1 forme, 1 side cubbard, 2 carpettes, 2 anirons with paynted Clothes and glasse	1	0	0
In the greene chamber			
1 fether bed, 1 bancket, 1 coverlett, 1 bolster, 1 standing bedsted and a truckle bedsted	1	10	0
2 tables, 2 formes, 3 carpettes, 1 sidcubbard, 1 quilt, 1 chaire, 1 Cushen		16	0
In the Chappell chamber			
2 fether bedes, 2 bolsters, 2 Coverlettes, 3 blanckettes, 1 standing bedsted and a truckell bedsted	3	10	0
1 table, 2 sidcubbardes, 1 forme, 2 carpettes, 2 chairs, 4 Cushens, 1 aniron and hangings and glasse	1	0	0
In the new chamber			
2 fether beds, 2 bolsters, 2 Coverlettes, 1 blanckett, 1 standinge bedsted and a truckle bedsted, Curtteynes and vallens	3	0	0
1 Long table, 1 sidecubbard, 2 carpettes, 4 formes, 1 chaire, 1 Cushen 2 anirons and glasse	1	0	0
In the ston chamber			
1 standing bedsted, 1 coverlett, 1 Long forme, 1 side Cubbarde, 1 aniron, 1 chaire		13	4
In the Parlor			
1 fether bed, 2 bolsters, 1 Coverlett, 1 blanckett, 1 standing bedsted and Curteyns	2	4	0
2 tables and frames, 2 formes, 1 stole, 1 carpett, windscott and paynted clothes and an Iron back	1	10	0
In the Taphouse			
4 hogsheds, 8 kilderkins of beare	3	10	0
In their bedchamber			
1 fether bed, 2 bolsters, 1 coverlett, 1 blanckett, 1 standing bedsted, 1 other bedsted, 1 flockbed, 1 flock bed and 1 old Coverlett, 4 Chestes and 1 trunck	2	0	0
In the maides chamber			
2 flock bedes, 2 flock bolsters, 2 Coverlettes, 2 blanckes, 2 old bedstedes		16	0
In the Hale			
1 table and fram, 1 other table and frame, 3 formes, 1 sittle, windscot and paynted clothes, 1 aniron and glasse and a Cubbard, 1 Cubbard cloth	2	6	8
In the Sellor			
2 hogsheds of wyne white and claret	12	0	0
5 gallens of sacke by estymacion in a runlett	1	0	0
3 emptie castes		7	0
Standes		1	6
2 pottle pottes, 6 quart pottes, 5 pinte pottes, 1 half pinte pot, 1 quarter of a pint pot		18	0
1 Joyned stoole			10
2 tunnells and a perche		1	0
3 emptie runlettes		2	0
In the old hale			
1 table and frame, 1 Safe, a stell, 1 forme and Lumbry		13	4
An old quare table and a paire of playing tables		3	4

In the Brewhoose			
1 smale furnas, 1 vate, 2 keeves, 1 keeller, 12 smale kivers, 6 hogshedes, 10 kilderkins, 2 bucking tubbs, 1 hop sive, 2 meshinge shovells, 1 skoope, 1 tap hose, 1 tunnell, 3 standes, 1 little troo, 2 battenders	4	6	4
In the kitchen			
22 platters	1	2	0
20 pottengers		10	0
34 sawsers and plattes		7	6
1 bason and ewer		2	0
15 pewter candlestickes, 2 quart pottes, 1 pinte pott, 2 beckes		8	0
4 saltes		3	0
10 Chamber pottes		7	0
2 brasse pannes, 1 brassen hanginge candlestick		3	6
4 kittles and 1 old kittle	1	0	0
4 brasse pottes, 3 skillettes	1	1	6
1 Iron pott		1	10
2 motters, 1 gratter		3	6
1 little Cubbard, 1 choping boarde		1	6
1 bowle 3 trease		1	0
3 bassens, 6 porrengers		3	0
1 warminge pann, 2 chaffing dishes, 4 spittes, 1 girdiron		8	0
2 driping panns, 1 bastinge Ladle, 2 anirons, 1 iron barr		8	8
2 smale anirons, 1 fier shovels		1	6
2 brassen Ladles, 2 skemmers		1	6
1 iron Oven peele, 3 potthangers, 2 pair of potthooks		4	6
2 tables, 2 formes, 3 little Joyned stooles, 3 shelves		5	0
3 fletches of pig bacon		10	0
In the Bakehouse			
1 bowlting which, 1 kneding trow, 2 tables, 1 powdring tubb with other Lumbry		6	6
1 fryeng pann, 2 earthen pottes, 1 bottle		1	8
In the Napry			
16 paire of canvas sheetes	5	6	8
6 pair of Lockrum sheetes	2	0	0
1 old pair of holen sheetes		6	8
5 canvas table clothes		10	4
1 diaper table cloth		4	0
11 pillows and 11 pillowbers	1	8	0
3 Duzen of napkins		9	10
3 towells		6	8
3 old Chestes		3	0
In the gate			
Woode and faggates	6	0	0
Rackes and Manngers		12	0
A presse and Lader		3	0
A Watring trow		2	0
A brasen Laver		1	0
2 selver bowles	3	12	0

Att the Antolop: **443B**

In the hale			
4 boxes with Lockes and keys		4	0
1 half back of windscot, 1 bench, 1 portall of windscot, the stayned clothes, 1 glasse window		8	6

In the greene chamber			
The stayned clothes, the windscott and a table		11	0
The glasse		3	0
Glasse		3	0
In the great chamber			
A back of windscot, stayned clothes and glasse in the east window and a portall	1	4	0
In the new chamber			
The stayned clothes and glasse		10	0
In the Orian chamber			
The stayned clothes and glasse		7	0
In the Little parlor			
Stayned clothes and glasse, a bench, 1 peece of windscott		13	4
In the great parlor			
The stayned clothes, wyndscot, a bench, the glasse, 1 portall	1	6	8
His apparell, 1 cloke, 2 dublettes, 1 pair of hose, 2 paire of stockins, 2 hates, 3 shertes, 4 bandes, 1 frise Jerken	1	17	0
	104	17	8

Administration of the goods and chattels of her late husband were granted to the widow Juliane on 10th June 1603. Also bound to see this well and truly carried out was Richard Hammond of Godalming, shearman. Ref: 1603 Ad 76

Note: The burial was recorded on 9th May 1603.

Henry Woddes **444**

of Chobham, husbandman; taken by John Hoult, John Tayler, Thomas Shrubb, with others, 1st June 1603.

	£	s	d
Mony in his purss		10	0
His apparell		13	4
In the hawle			
A Table with a frame, a ffoorme, 2 Joyned stooles, a chayre		8	0
A Cupborde ther		10	0
In the Chamber next the haule			
A bedd and bedsteedell with his furnyture	1	0	0
3 Chestes and a lytell Cupborde		8	0
In an over chamber			
A bedd and bedsteedell with his furnyture		10	0
In the loft over the haule			
A bedd and bedsteedell with his furnyture		16	0
In the kitchin			
The brass and Pewter	1	6	8
The Tubbes and other Lumbry ther		10	0
A payre of potthangers, a spitt, a payre of Cobirons with other such Iron stuff ther		3	4
The Linnen			
Seaven payre of sheetes and a Table Cloth	1	8	0
2 Oxen, 2 Steeres	7	6	8
2 Kyne	2	13	4
8 Bullockes	7	0	0
A wayninge Calfe		5	0
4 hors beastes and a colt	4	0	0
The Corne in the Barne		8	0
7 acres of Rye in the feelde	5	0	0

4 Acres of Otes in the feeld	1	6	8
3 Acres of Pease, Tares and french wheat	1	0	0
Half an Acre of barley		3	4
12 Ewes and 6 Lambes	3	0	0
6 hogges		18	0
A Cart, yokes and chaynes and other such furnyture	2	0	0
The hens, geese and Duckes		3	4
An Ax, A bill and a pronge		2	0
	[*£43*	*9*	*8*]

Note: The Will was dated 19th May and proved on 10th June 1603. The executrix and residuary legatee was the testator's wife Agnes, who was given his house and lands at Windlesham for 12 years. The sum of 12d apiece was given to the overseers, John Hoult and John Taylor. His children Henry, William, Christopher and Ellyn, were each given a heifer, £2 in money, a pair of sheets, a platter and a dish; his son Christopher was also left a bed and bedding. His servant Elizabeth Huntingford was given 12d. If Agnes were to die before the 12 years had expired, the rents and profits of the Windlesham property were to go equally to any surviving children. The vicar Thomas Taunton and Thomas Geyles signed the document.

Ref: 1603B60/1 Will 1603 B 60/2 Inventory

Thomas Wodier **445**

of Witley, husbandman; taken by Richard Eede, Robert Payne and William Byde, 20th April 1603.

	£	s	d
In the haule			
One Cubard		6	8
One brase pot and 2 ketles		5	0
2 peuter dishes and 2 sausers		1	0
2 buckets, 2 boules and 3 stobyns		1	2
A table planck and forme			6
A whele and cardes			6
Pothangers and pothookes			6
An ax and spytter			8
In the chamber			
3 colfers		2	0
2 payre of canvas shetes		2	6
One old flockbed, bolster, blanketes, coverlet and a bedsteade		6	8
His Apparell and mony		3	4
8 bushels of otes		5	0
A basket			4
In poted butter 12 pound		3	0
A fryinge pan and knead trow			8
A pannell and sursingele			8
Abrode in the feld etc			
One Jorny of Rye		13	4
Thre iornyes of otes	1	0	0
Rye, otes and straw in the barn		5	0
One cowe and calfe	2	9	4
One sowe hoge		4	6
Thre flyches of bakon		16	0
2 stoles with all lombery		1	0
Dounge in the gate		2	0
A stone pott			1½
	7	11	5½
Debtes to be deducted	-5	0	0

2 11 5½

Note: The Will was dated 1st April and was proved on 8th June 1603. The executrix and residuary legatee was Joan, wife of the testator. She was to have a life interest in his house and lands in Witley, which at her decease were to be inherited by William Wodier, his elder brother's son. The overseers Lawrence Stoughton, vicar of Witley and John Myles of Thursley, his brother-in-law, were to have 3s 4d each. The testator asked to be buried in the churchyard of Witley. He instructed William Wodier to pay, within two years of receiving his inheritance, £5 each to William and Nicholas, the eldest sons of his cousin Nicholas Wodier. The overseers witnessed the Will. A memorandum stated that no bond was taken. Joan, the executrix, was duly sworne before Francis Taylor on 1st June 1603.

Ref: 1603 B 61/1 Will 1603 B 61/2 Inventory

GLOSSARY

Almain Rivets, **alman rivett,** light, flexible armour of German origin.
Arras, **arys,** see Orris.
Auger, **ager,** carpenter's tool for boring holes in wood.
Aumbry, aulmery, large cupboard with doors used for food and later for books, clothes & linen.
Bands loose, turnover collar or strips of white material worn at the neck which succeeded the ruff.
Banker, **benker,** bench cloth or carpet.
Beak, **beck,** pointed end of anvil.
Bettle, heavy wooden mallet usually strengthened with iron rings.
Bickernheads, beakiron, an anvil with two pointed ends.
Bickhorn see Bickernhead.
Bill, bele, implement with metal blade fixed to a long handle, used for hedging.
Bondes see Bands.
Brake, toothed implement for dressing flax and hemp.
Brandiron, iron grid with short legs and long handle used to support cooking vessels over an open fire.
Broach, broche, a long rod of metal or wood used to thrust through meat to be roasted in front of the fire. The revolving device was supported on cobirons.
Buckler, small, round shield.
Budg, lambskin with wood dressed outside.
Buffin, buffing, coarse cloth used for gowns.
Burling iron, tool used for removing scruffy locks from sheeps wool.
Cap case, small travelling case or band box.
Ceiling, **sellynge cloth**, covering over top of four poster bed.
Chafing dish, held burning fuel and used to head vessels placed upon it.
Chamlet, camlet, a rich fabric of Eastern origin but later adapted to include wool, hair, silk, cotton or linen.
Chequer coverlet, probably patchwork.
Chips, chyppes, strips of wood to hold fast the plough share.
Cleftes, wedges.
Clense sieve, klens seve, strainer.
Clout, piece of iron fixed to the axletree to prevent wear.
Coddware, possible peascods or stems of beans.
Coffer, coofore, a wooden box or chest for storing clothes or valuables.
Coliver, caliver, *see Qualiver.*
Combe, connye, 4 bushells, measure of grain.
Coppes, wooden part of ox-harness, movable frame attached to front of wagon or cart.
Corslet, **coslet**, body armour.
Cotterels, cranes or bars to hang pots over the fire.
Couch of Hay, cock of hay.
Coule, cooler, large cask for carrying water.
Coverlid, coverlet, covering for bed.
Crocks, cruches, small earthenware pans.
Cross clothes, knitted kerchief, a headcloth.
Cruel, **crewel**, woollen embroidery on linen.
Cruse, crewse, drinking cup of earthenware or wood.
Cypress, cipers, rich fabric.
Dansk, imported from Dantzig.
Denshires, daysheres, turning irons.
Dicker, a bundle of ten hides or skins.
Dornick, **dornax**, heavy fabric of Flemish origin used for hangings, carpets, vestments, etc.
Dredge, a mixture of oats and barley sown together.

Dungpot, tub attached like a pannier to the flank of a packhorse, in which manure was carried to the fields.
Ells, eles, measurements of 42 inches.
Extree, axletree, beam or bar connecting two wheels.
Fente, remnant of cloth.
Firkin, small cask holding nine gallons.
Flasket, long shallow basket with handle at each end.
Flite thin pieces of wood.
Fold pitcher, **pecher**, heavy iron to make holds to take base of hurdles for the sheep fold.
Followers, wooden blocks used as weights in cheese moulds and cloth presses.
Forest bill, used for topping branches. **Brown** and **Black**, black painted and used as weapons by soldiers.
Foscer, fossett, a small iron-bound chest used to contain documents, jewellery or valuables.
French wheat, imported from the Continent, cheapter to buy and worth less as a crop.
Frethings, type of hurdle to extend height at side of cart, cart ladder.
Frieze, fryse, coarse woollen cloth.
Galles, goolles, gulles, goslings, small species of goose.
Garlyd, speckled.
Gell, Yell vat, vat used to hold new fermenting beer.
Genytes, carpenter's adzes.
Gergere, **gergar**, piece of iron.
Gilt, Yelt, young sow.
Gorget, gorcete, armour covering the throat.
Gyrtes, girths.
Gystes, joists.
Hair, **hearne cupboard**, one covered with hair cloth.
Hair Cloth used to cover frame on which barley was spread during malting process.
Halberd, howberdes, combined spear and battle axe on long handle of 5 to 7 feet.
Hanger, for suspending a pot over fire, or a device made of leather with straps and pad to which the scabbard of a rapier could be buckled for safe carrying, or cloth hanging over bed.
Hasties, hastings, an early ripening pea.
Haulms, hoams, odd straw.
Healing, helyer, hillinge, bed covering.
Heifer, hexford, a young cow before it has had a calf.
Hill, heyl, hyl, shock or stook containing 10 sheaves.
Hitchel, hatchell, tackle for dressing hemp or flax.
Holland, hollon, fine linen.
Hopps, hoops or moulds for cheese.
Host Heare *see* Hair Cloth.
Hovel, stack of corn.
Hutch, chest used for storing clothes
Bolting Hutch, bin used for sifting flour to separate it from the bran.
Jack, coat of mail, plated iron over quilted leather upper garment *see also* TOOLS & HEARTH.
Jade, an old horse.
Jerkin, girkyn, close-fitted short coat often of leather.
Journey, a measure of land for crops.
Keeler, coolers used in brewing.
Keeler ?*see* Cooler
Keeve, kefe, wooden, cooling bowl or vat used in brewing.
Kerchief, kercher, cloth used to cover a woman's head.
Kerf cut made by a saw, a notch, also a long horizontal cut made partway through a board for the purpose of bending.
Kersey, coarse narrow cloth, usually ribbed with origins in Kersey, Suffolk.
Kimnel, kemnell, wooden tub.
Knead Trough, dough bowl.
Lade, ladder, framework fixed to side of the cart or wain for high loads.

Latten, latyn, alloy of copper, zinc, lead and tin, similar to fine brass.
Laver, washing basin, finger bowl.
Leases, threads for sewing shoes.
List, lyste, strips of cloth or patchwork.
Lockram, lokeram, linen fabric.
Loriner, lorimer, maker of metal work for harness, bits, bridles, stirrups.
Mandilion, mandellion, a look overcoat with a standing collar buttoned at the chest only.
Martelmas, corruption of Martinmas: 11th November.
Maslin, mastlen, a mixture of wheat and rye sown, grown and harvested together.
Mazer, maser, bowl or drinking cup with a foot.
Medley, cloth woven in different coloured wool.
Mockado, mockeadoo, woollen cloth imitating velvet.
Morion, murrion, a helmet without face covering.
Motes, moates, moulds for cheese.
Netherstokes, stockings.
Nihil, nechell, none, an early form of the word.
Oast hair *see* Hair Cloth.
Orris, orris work, lace of various patterns in gold and silver.
Ostery, ostrye, possibly entry or gatehouse.
Pancheon, panche, large shallow earthenware bowl.
Pannel, paynyell, pad used as a rough saddle.
Partlet, partelettes, ruffs, collars, neckerchiefs.
Peck, measure for 2 gallons of dry goods.
Pillowbeer, bere, bear, pillow cases.
Pipkin, small earthenware cooking pot.
Points, pontes, dagger.
Portall, portele, fixed wooden screen between the door and the fire to keep out the draught, often of wainscott.
Posnet, possenette, a small metal 3-legged cooking pot with a handle.
Pottinger, small basin.
Powdering, pickling or salting.
Puke, superior woollen cloth
Pullen, poultry.
Qualiver, a light portable gun.
Quarters of wood, wood for panelling.
Quilling, winding of thread or yarn onto a spool.
Rail, rayle, woman's neckerchief.
Rash, fine serge cloth, sometimes of silk.
Reaps, reppes, reap hooks, scythes with serrated edges.
Reaps for ploughs
Renning, use of rennet to curdle milk in cheesemaking.
Ridder, probably riddle, a coarse sieve.
Rodden, wicker.
Rodesaddle, riding saddle.
Rodmeale, rodmeles, a quarter of an acre.
Rongs *see* Rungs.
Roste, ? rose coloured.
Rounds, rowdes, radds or rades - rails of a wain or cart.
Rubber, brush or material for polishing.
Rudder cattle, horned cattle usually oxen.
Rudder *see* Ridder.
Rung, rail (in a cart).
Runlet, rundlett, a cask for liquor of varying capacity.
Russett, a coarse homespun cloth, reddish-brown or grey in colour.
Ruther, rother - horned beast.

Rycot, patchwork or variegated design and pattern.
Safeguard, **saufgard**, outer skirt or petticoat worn by women to protect their skirts when riding.
Say, **seye**, a very fine cloth resembling serge, in early days often silk with wool.
Scrub, **skrubde**, a breed of cattle distinguished by their small size.
Seedcod, **seadecodde**, basket carried at waist level for hand sowing of seed.
Setting Stick, implement for making or setting the pleats in ruffs.
Shred shrydd, usually a coverlet.
Shutes, young pigs.
Skeiner, **squirm**, implement on which plyed yarn was placed.
Skillet, 3-footed metal cooking pot with handle.
Skilling, **shilling**, a lean-to or outhouse.
Skimmer, **scummer**, a cooking utensil.
Slayes, **slessis**, an instrument for beating down the weft of cloth during weaving.
Slice, fire shovel for removing ash from break oven.
Snead, snede, handle for a scythe.
Spear the screen between door and fireplace to keep out draught.
Spence loft, a store place.
Spitter, spade.
Spokeshave, spookshawe, a drawing knife for dressing spokes or other curved work.
Stammel, fine worsted cloth usually red.
Stean, **stene**, glazed earthenware pot.
Stilitory, **styllytary of lead,** a still, apparatus for distillation of liquids.
Stobbin, stabyn, stubbin, stuppin, wooden vessells connected with brewing; perhaps a wooden pan made by turning the inverted stump or junction between trunk and roots of easily-orked wood such as field maple.
Stonebow, form of crossbow or cataput using stones for killing birds and small animals.
Strapt, strople yoke, yoke make of cord rope or twine.
Sursingle, a girth going over the pannel or rough saddle.
Talwood, wood for fuel cut ot a particular size.
Tawed, made soft, white and pliant by steeping in a solution of alum and salt.
Tester, texterne, ceiling of bed made of wood or material.
Thrum, throme, coarse wood embroidery.
Tick, **teek**, closely-woven linen or cotton for mattresses, pillows etc.
Tilts, **tights**, **tyttes**, covering often for waggon or wain.
Tod, 28 pounds or 2 stone.
Toft, messuage with right of common.
Touch, tuche box, box used for carrying priming powder for a musket.
Toud, todd mare, perhaps hard worked mare.
Towen, **towne**, coarse quality sheets made of the shorter fibres of flax or hemp.
Treen, wooden (of trees).
Truss: a close-fitting body garment worn by men and women, or
a travelling bed which could be dismanted and trussed-up.
Tunnell, tonell, funnel.
Turn, tourne, wheel.
Vanntage, advantage i.e. profits arising.
Vargis, vergis, verjuice, crab apple vinegar.
Vats, vautes, fats, wooden vessels.
Venetians, hose or breeches of a particular fashion originally imported from Venice.
Waine, ven, weane, a wagon with four wheels.
Wallet, bag with two pouches for carrying goods or a pedlar's pack.
Warming pan, long-handled, lidded metal pan filled with hot coals for warming beds etc.
Watchet, **wageot**, pale blue.
Which, whych, *see* Hutch.
Wool Cards, wooden frames with rows of iron teeth for combing fibres of wool prior to spinning.
Wort, worthe infusion of malt to ferment it and make beer.

Wysotte, waistcost.
Yardland, about 30 acres or so.
Yoer, ewer.
Yoll *see* Yell.
Yolting vat, vat for soaking or steeping.

For further reading :

Milward, Rosemary, *A glossary of household farming and trade terms from probate inventories* (Derbyshire Record Society 1982)

Raymond, Stuart, *Words from wills and other probate records 1500-1800, a glossary* (Federation of Family History Societies 2004)

ABBREVIATIONS USED IN ENTRIES

a	appraiser
Abr	Abraham
ad	administrator
Adr	Adrian
Agn	Agnes
Alex	Alexander
And	Andrew
Ant	Anthony, Antony
Art	Arthur
b	beneficiary or residuary legatee
Barb	Barbara
Bart	Bartholomew
Ben	Benjamin
Berm	Bermondsey
c	creditor of the testator
Cass	Cassandra
Cat	Catharine, Catherine
Chas	Charles
Chri	Christian
Chris	Christopher
Con	Constance
Corn	Cornelius
d	debtor of the testator
D'Ab	D'Abernon
Dan	Daniel
Dor	Dorothy
e	executor and residuary legatee
E.	East
Edm	Edmund
Edw	Edward
elder	the elder
Eliz	Elizabeth
ex	executor only
Fra	Francis
Geff	Geffry, Geoffrey
gent.	gentleman
Geo	George
Greg	Gregory
H.T.	parish of Holy Trinity
Hum	Humfry, Humphrey
husb.	husbandman
Hy	Henry
Isa	Isabel
Jas	James
Jeff	Jeffrey
Jn	John
jnr.	junior
Joh	Johane, Johanna
Jud	Judith
Jul	Juliana, Juliane
Kat	Katherine
lab.	labourer
Lau	Laurence
Law	Lawrence
Mart	Martin
Mat	Matthew
Mgt	Margaret
Mgy	Margery, Marjorie
Mich	Michael
Mill	Millicent
My	Mary
Nat	Nathaniel
Nic	Nicholas
o	overseer
Oli	Oliver
Pet	Peter
Phil	Philip
Ra	Raff, Ralph
Reb	Rebecca
Reg	Reginald
relict	widow of the testator
Ric	Richard
Rob	Robert
Rog	Roger
Row	Rowland
s	bound as surety
Sam	Samuel
Sar	Sarah
Sim	Simon, Symon
snr.	senior
St Geo	parish of St George
St M	parish of St Mary
St O	parish of St Olave
St Sav	parish of St Saviour
Ste	Stephen Steven
Sus	Susan, Susannah
Swk	Southwark
Thas	Thames, or on Thames
Tho	Thomas
Tim	Timothy
Tris	Tristram
w	witness to the will
W.	West
Wat	Walter
Wm	William
yeo.	yeoman
yngr.	the younger

APPENDIX I

Entry No	Testator	Parish	Date of Will	Date of Inventory
1	**Botley**, Chri	Lingfield	24 Nov 1556	17 Apl 1558
2	**Burgies**, Jone	Kingston	7 Apr 1558	26 Apl 1558
3	**Cole**, Jn	Limpsfield	26 Jan 1557/8	25 Apl 1558
4	**Copsell**, Hy	Lingfield	1 Jun 1558	n.d.
5	**Lewer**, Jn	Newdigate	30 Aug 1557	3 Oct 1557
6	**Tolley**, -	Charlwood	-	7 A[pr] 1558
7	**Bekeham**, Jn	Farnham	3 Nov 1558	16 Jan 1558
8	**Braye**, Edw	Cranleigh	16 Aug & 10 Sep 1558	1558
9	**Chesman**, Tho	Wotton	10 Apr 1559	n.d.
10	**Chittey**, Wm	Godalming Ea	21 May 1559	13 Jun 1559
11	**Codde**, Miles	Weybridge	31 Oct 1558	22 Nov 1558
12	**Frysbee**, Jn	Morden	23 Dec 1558	23 Dec 1558
13	**Goryng**, Nic	Morden	2 Feb 1558/9	2 Feb 1558/9
14	**Peerson**, Ric	Frensham P	26 May 1559	26 May 1559
16	**Tornor**, Joan	Kingston Ham	-	26 Jan 1558/9
17	**Clemente**, Jn	Nutfield	16 Apr 1559	1 Oct 1560
18	**Lylley**, Rob	Wotton	4 Oct 1560	n.d.
19	**Banester**, Jn	Chertsey	3 Jly 1561	n.d.
20	**Byckenall**, Jn	Puttenham	31 Mar 1561	5 May 1561
21	**Cacot**, Jn	Bletchingley	10 May 1559	n.d.
22	**Chenell**, Wm	Wonersh	15 Jly 1560	1561
23	**Collen**, Wm	Thursley	16 Apr 1561	n.d.
24	**Davy**, Pet	Send	3 Apr 1561	14 Apr 1561
25	**Fanner**, Oli	Frensham	14 Feb 1561	8 Mar 1561
26	**Forde**, Ric	Guildford	28 Jan 1560/1	24 Feb 1560/1
27	**Glover**, Geo	Guildford St M	22 Apr 1561	15 Jly 1561
28	**Haywarde**, Tho	Farnham Rf	1 Dec 1560	25 Jan 1560/1
29	**Hedger**, Hy	Thursley	14 Jan 1560/1	10 Feb 1560/1
30	**Lamboll**, Chris	Ockham	8 Mar 1560/1	8 Apr 1561
31	**Lucas**, Ric	Horley	21 Mar 1560/1	13 Apr 1561
32	**Mabanke**, Wat	Hambledon	4 Feb 1560/1	14 May 1561
33	**Mowse**, Rob	Tandridge	15 Mar 1560/1	27 Mar 1561
34	**Moyr**, Tho	Alfold	2 Jun 1561	13 Jun 1561
35	**Mychell**, Joan	Chertsey	26 Feb 1559/60	25 Feb 1560/1
36	**Roger**, Wm	Fetcham	1 Jan 1561	n.d.
37	**Saker**, Jn	Betchworth E	12 Apr 1561	26 Apr 1561
38	**Selwode**, Rob	Guildford H T	7 Nov 1560	22 May 1561
39	**Shudde**, Jn	Shere	15 Dec 1560	3 Jan 1560/1
40	**Steyll**, Bart	Frensham	22 Dec 1560	6 Jan 1560/1
41	**Thorne**, Chris	Ewell	23 Feb 1560/1	22 Apr 1561
42	**Whyte**, Wm	Dorking	23 Feb 1559/60	24 Feb 1559/60
43	**Wyght**, Tho	Shere	31 Mar 1561	n.d.
44	**Peter**, Jn	Capel	27 Jan 1561/2	31 Mar 1562
45	**Stere**, Tho	Capel	22 Jan 1561/2	19 Feb 1561/2
46	**Hawle**, Joan	Farnham	9 Oct 1563	2 Nov 1563
47	**Hull**, Jn	Hambledon	1 Oct 1562	20 Jan 1563 & 30 Jun 1564

Entry No	Testator	Parish	Date of Will	Date of Inventory
48	**Juer**, Allys	Farnham Rf	18 Oct 1563	2 Nov 1563
48	**Juer**, Hy	Farnham Rf	18 Oct 1563	2 Nov 1563
49	**Mannte**, Pet	Farnham Rf	19 Oct 1563	19 Oct 1563
50	**Alyngham**, Nic	Horley	17 Jan 1564/5	19 Jan 1564/5
51	**Amy**, Mgt	Cranleigh	10 Apr 1565	2 May 1565
52	**Bonyon**, Jn	Chobham	15 May 1565	28 May 1565
53	**Marlyn**, Mgt & Ric	Chobham	27 May 1565	30 Apr 1565
54	**Morrell**, Tho	Merton	30 Jan 1564/5	30 Jan 1564/5
55	**Oliver**, Ric	Godalming	1565	29 May 1565
56	**Taylor**, Rob	Horsell	21 May 1565	n.d.
57	**Worthyngton**, Ant	Horsell	26 Feb 1564/5	13 Apr 1565
58	**Amias**, Wm	Reigate	11 May 1566	22 May 1566
59	**Elvyn**, Wm	Horne	10 Mar 1565/6	15 Apr 1566
60	**Walker**, Nic	Kingston upon Thas	26 Sep 1565	10 May 1566
61	**Bet**, Jn	Fetcham	10 Dec 1562	13 Apr 1567
62	**Birle**, Wm	Hascombe	20 Apr 1567	4 May 1567
63	**Hardynge**, Bart	Frensham Westend	8 Apr 1567	28 Apr 1567
64	**Harfell also Harper**, Jn	Wonersh	7 Apr 1567	2 May 1567
65	**Hill**, Nic	Ewhurst	15 Apr 1567	25 Apr 1567
66	**Rawstricke**, Jn	Kingston	24 Mar 1566/7	16 Apr 1567
67	**Sherube**, Ste	Farnham Wr	14 Apr 1567	28 Jun 1567
68	**Webb**, Tho	Farnham	-	20 May 1566
69	**Andrew**, Rob	Kingston	1568	n.d.
70	**Beste**, Jone	Gatton	27 Jun 1558	n.d.
71	**Meede**, Tho	Worplesdon	11 Apr 1568	n.d.
72	**Otwey**, Tho	Ashtead	27 Apr 1568	9 May 1568
73	**Basyngton**, Ric	Camberwell	16 Apr 1569	16 May 1569
74	**Byrche**, Geo	Witley	12 Oct 1568	23 May 1569
75	**Altham**, Rob	Tooting Gr Bec	-	24 Apr 1570
76	**Baker**, Wm	Dunsfold	-	15 Jun 1569
77	**Chyty**, Tho	Ockley	20 Mar 1569/70	11 May 1570
78	**Constable**, Jn	Ockley	6 Apr 1570	23 Apr 1570
79	**Hoke**, Jn	Chiddingfold	-	n.d.
80	**Marshar**, Rob	Farnham Wr	30 Jan 1569/70	28 Mar 1570
81	**Northall**, Jn	Guildford	-	20 Mar 1570
82	**Westbroke**, Jas	Compton next Guildford	22 Apr 1570	25 Apr 1570
83	**Winne**, Jn	Farnham Wr	8 Feb 1569/70	28 Mar 1570
84	**Bundell**, Rob	Ditton Thas	1 May 1571	12 May 1571
85	**Elyot**, Jul	Godalming Cat	18 Apr 1571	19 May 1571
86	**Gylman**, Ric	Bletchingley	10 Apr 1571	17 May 1571
87	**Hedger**, Ric	Thursley	28 Apr 1571	16 May 1571
88	**Monnyarde**, Jn	Horne	11 Sep 1570	16 Apr 1571
89	**Osborne**, Ric	Haslemere	-	19 May 1571
90	**Parker**, Nic	Betchworth Brockham	12 Apr 1571	11 May 1571
91	**Tew, Too**, Hugh	Farnham	-	28 Jan 1570/1
92	**Warner**, Tho	Farnham	4 Apr 1571	20 May 1571
93	**West**, Fra	Haslemere	-	7 May 1571
94	**Wysdome**, Rob	Capel	5 May 1571	5 May 1571
95	**Channell**, Wm	Farnham Wr	6 Nov 1571	5 Dec 1571

Entry No	Testator	Parish	Date of Will	Date of Inventory
96	**Holt**, Jn	Alfold	-	7 Apr 1572
97	**Lypscombe**, Jn	Abinger	16 May 1567	25 Feb 1572
98	**Machyke**, Rob	Thursley	7 Jun 1566	21 Apr 1572
99	**Starr**, Sence	Ditton Long Tol	4 Feb 1571/2	1572
100	**White**, Alice	Betchworth Brockham	14 Aug 1571	26 Mar 1572
101	**Bonwick**, Pet	Horley	22 Jun 1572	n.d.
102	**Boxold**, Hy	Elstead	1571	2 Dec 1572
103	**Clebroke**, Rob	Ockham	-	1573
104	**Ede**, Wm	Farnham Wr	4 Apr 1573	29 Apr 1573
105	**Fagatere**, Ric	Pirbright	7 May 1573	18 May 1573
106	**Foxe**, Tho	Kingston Surb	10 May 1573	12 May 1573
107	**Fulston**, Tho	Frensham	12 Feb 1572/3	22 May 1573
108	**Fylden**, Rob	Swk St S	6 Apr 1573	18 Apr 1573
109	**Fynnes**, Giles	Tandridge	14 Apr 1573	16 Apr 1573
110	**Hardewyn**, Rob	Byfleet	18 Mar 1572/3	4 Apr 1573
111	**Isam**, Jn	Horsell	30 Oct 1572	28 May 1573
112	**Lyllye**, Chris	Abinger	24 Apr 1573	19 May 1573
113	**Marlyn**, Geo	Puttenham	-	6 Jan 1573
114	**Martyn**, Tho	Compton	-	24 Mar 1572/3
115	**Mathewe**, Edw	Woking	22 Apr 1573	28 Apr 1573
116	**Payne**, Geo	Horley	25 Oct 1568	18 Apr 1573
117	**Punter**, Hy	Send	31 Mar 1573	1 Apr 1573
118	**Reves**, Agn	Frensham	29 Dec 1572	25 Feb 1572/3
119	**Reynolde**, Tho	Egham	23 Feb 1572/3	10 Mar 1572/3
120	**Snellinge**, Dor	Guildford St M	5 May 1572	12 May 1572
121	**Warner**, Tho	Wonersh	6 Apr 1573	21 Apr 1572
122	**Waters**, Jn	Rhithe	20 Jly 1570	2 May 1573
123	**West**, Edw	Godalming	4 Feb 1573	16 ... 1573
124	**Woodward**, Rob	Swk	-	n.d.
125	**Dakin**, Tho	Seale	28 Jun 1574	8 Jly 1574
126	**Hayward**, Tho	Farnham Wr	28 May 1570	26 Apr 1574
127	**Penvey**, Tho	Chiddingfold	26 May 1564	21 Jun 1574
128	**Allen**, Tho	Frensham P	-	5 May 1575
129	**Browne**, Jn	Cranleigh	-	n.d.
130	**Chaundler**, Agn	Haslemere	13 May 1575	30 May 1575
131	**Geale**, Rob	Byfleet	-	24 Apr 1575
132	**Gosden**, Jn	Wonersh	16 Apr 1575	25 Apr 1575
133	**Lake**, Rob	Molesey W	15 May 1563	n.d.
134	**Mantill**, Jn	Swk St G.	-	6 Apr 1575
135	**Petoe**, Ste	Bramley in Shalford	24 Apr 1575	17 May 1575
136	**Turner**, Tho	Compton next Guildford	8 Jan 1574/5	27 Apr 1575
137	**Waterer**, Jn	Shalford	19 Apr 1575	17 May 1575
138	**Aslet**, Jn	Farnham Rf	28 May 1574	21 May 1576
139	**Brodebridge**, Wm	Farnham T	26 Apr 1575	4 May 1576
140	**Feld**, Eden	Frensham	6 Apr 1576	11 Apr 1576
141	**Holt**, Rob	Witley	30 Mar 1576	9 May 1576
142	**Jewer**, Jn	Farnham Rf	23 Nov 1575	16 May 1576
143	**Mabancke**, Jn	Egham	9 Apr 1576	25 Apr 1576
144	**Newman**, Wm	Chertsey	-	4 May 1576

Entry No	Testator	Parish	Date of Will	Date of Inventory
145	**Northall**, Tho	Guildford	13 Jun 1576	25 Jun 1576
146	**Peytowe**, Tho	Chiddingfold	-	18 May 1576
147	**Smethurst**, Bart	Pirbright	11 May 1576	24 May 1576
148	**Stynt**, Jn	Witley Milford	18 Nov 1575	4 Jan 1575/6
149	**Todham**, Wm	Horne	2 Apr 1576	16 Apr 1576
150	**Wicker**, Rob	Molesey W	1 Jun 1575	4 May 1576
151	**Wilkyns**, Hy	Bookham Gt	18 Dec 1575	25 Jan 1576
152	**Sherwood**, Jn	Shalford	-	21 Feb 1576/7
153	**Barne**, Tho	Guildford St M	25 Mar 1578	11 Jun 1578
154	**Bearde**, Wm	Worplesdon	13 May 1578	20 Jun 1578
155	**Bickenell**, Tho	Frensham	22 Nov 1577	27 Nov 1577
156	**Channell**, Agn	Chobham	13 Apr 1578	21 Apr 1578
157	**Foster**, Wm	Wanborough	14 Feb 1577/8	5 Apr 1578
158	**Hays**, Jn	Headley	12 Jly 1578	20 Aug 1578
159	**Stansted**, Mgt	Woking	28 Oct 1572	n.d.
160	**Tydes**, Ric	Ockley	10 Feb 1577/8	8 Apr 1578
161	**Wapshote**, Wm	Chertsey	26 Apr 1578	5 May 1578
162	**Collier**, Geo	Worplesdon	18 Apr 1579	11 May 1579
163	**Fulstone**, Jonne	Frensham	n.d.	n.d.
164	**Manfielde**, Jn	Dunsfold	6 May 1579	21 May 1579
165	**Rempnant**, Jn	Pirbright	2 May 1579	19 May 1579
166	**Beston**, Wm	Swk St O & St S	20 Jan 1572/3	79
167	**Chyttye**, Wm	Godalming	-	13 Mar 1580/1
168	**Cresey**, Jn	Horsley W	20 Mar 1580/1	n.d.
169	**Dayer**, Agn	Elstead	12 Jan 1579/80	30 Mar 1581
170	**Fulston**, Wm	Frensham	12 Jan 1581	n.d.
171	**Rundell**, Rob	Lambeth St	10 Apr 1581	1 May 1581
172	**Becham**, Wm	Thorpe	20 Nov 1581	8 Jan 1582
173	**Bowdoxe**, Bart	Albury	-	28 May 1582
174	**Brand**, Kat	Ockley	-	4 Dec 1581
175	**Buckland**, Pet	Kingston	21 May 1582	29 May 1582
176	**Burt als. Loveland**, Geo	Worplesdon	2 May 1582	23 May 1582
177	**Clifton**, Ric & Mgt	Worplesdon	-	13 Jan 1581/2
178	**Elliott**, Lau	Clandon W	20 Apr 1582	23 May 1582
179	**Exold**, Ric	Frimley Ash	18 Nov 1580	15 Mar 1581/2
180	**Hampton**, Wm	Seale	5 May 1567	16 Apr 1582
181	**Holman**, Chas	Walton on Hill	n.d.	18 Mar 1582
182	**Luffe**, Wm	Frensham Ch	25 Apr 1582	n.d.
183	**Mellershe**, Chris	Bramley in Shalford	16 Nov 1576	15 May 1582
184	**Russell**, Jn	Worplesdon	24 Apr 1582	7 May 1582
185	**Shaddatt als Sherratt**, Jn	Woking	19 Feb 1581/2	3 May 1581
186	**Stint**, Wm	Horsley W	18 Oct 1581	n.d.
187	**Byshopp**, Mat	Leigh	-	14 May 1583
188	**Drewe**, Tho	Chertsey	-	9 May 1583
189	**Hiller**, Ric	Albury	-	15 May 1583
190	**Ladd**, Tho	Buckland	14 Apr 1583	26 Apr 1583
191	**Newdegate**, Agn	Newdigate	20 Jan 1581/2	21 May 1583
192	**Babbe**, Ric	Wonersh	23 Apr 1584	4 May 1584
193	**Clifton**, Jn	Puttenham	13 Apr 1584	4 May 1584

Entry No	Testator	Parish	Date of Will	Date of Inventory
194	**Fraye**, Rob	Carshalton	6 May 1584	8 May 1584
195	**Hamptonne**, Joan	Godalming	10 Feb 1584	27 Apr 1584
196	**Netelfould**, Wm	Abinger	26 Apr 1584	7 May 1584
197	**Scrafton**, Edw	Godstone	20 Apr 1584	2 May 1584
198	**Astrete**, Tho	Wonersh	-	11 Feb 1584/5
199	**Bottomley**, Ric	Carshalton	22 Apr 1585	3 May 1585
200	**Chytty**, Hy	Godalming Ea	23 Apr 1585	3 May 1585
201	**Colton**, Jn	Cobham	12 Apr 1585	30 Apr 1585
202	**Cowicke**, Eliz	Ewhurst	29 Apr 1580	28 May 1585
203	**Edwin**, Jn	Wandsworth	-	11 May 1585
204	**Farnham**, Jn	Bisley	23 Apr 1585	n.d.
205	**Fenne**, Rob	Pyrford	20 Apr 1585	n.d.
206	**Freelande**, Rob	Ockham	22 Apr 1585	4 May 1585
207	**Freland**, Tho	Windlesham	31 May 1582	n.d.
208	**Fuller**, Eliz	Stoke next Guildford	20 Jan 1584/5	25 Jan 1584/5
209	**Lee**, Hy	Woking	-	6 May 1585
210	**Mose**, Ra	Mickleham	18 Apr 1585	24 Apr 1585
211	**Procker (Proctor)**, Ric	Guildford	-	20 May 1585
212	**Sayer**, Tho	Cranleigh	29 Apr 1585	14 May 1585
213	**Skete**, Hy	Horsley W	7 Feb 1584/5	20 May 1585
214	**Songhurst**, Tho	Abinger	30 Apr 1585	20 May 1585
215	**Towler**, Denise	Tatsfield	22 Feb 1584/5	10 May 1585
216	**Underwode**, Agn	Worplesdon	6 May 1585	20 May 1585
217	**Underwood**, Tho	Bisley	6 May 1585	1585
218	**Walter**, Wm	Mitcham	10 Apr 1585	20 May 1585
219	**Warde**, Geoff	Swk St S	7 May 1585	13 May 1585
220	**White**, Wm	Leigh	16 Apr 1585	29 Apr 1585
221	**Worsfold**, Wm	Wotton	7 Apr 1585	20 Apr 1585
222	**Alyngham**, Ric	Nutfield	9 Feb 1586	9 May 1586
223	**Bray**, Hy	Reigate	19 Apr 1586	28 Apr 1586
225	**Filpe**, Tho	Frensham Ch	20 Mar 1586	26 Apr 1586
226	**Kitchiner**, Wm	Effingham	3 Dec 1585	16 May 1586
227	**Songhurst**, Wat	Ockley	19 Mar 1586	27 Apr 1586
228	**Walden**, Jn	Horsell	-	9 May 1586
229	**Atkynsone**, Jn	Swk St O	17 Apr 1587	n.d.
230	**Atwell**, Jn	Fetcham	17 Apr 1587	2 May 1587
231	**Barnard**, Jn	Dorking	-	87
232	**Benet**, Ric	Chiddingfold	11 Apr 1587	n.d.
233	**Blake**, Tho	Coulsdon	4 May 1587	5 May 1587
234	**Boxold**, Maudlin	Elstead	17 Apr 1587	28 Apr 1587
235	**Bristowe**, Jn	Wotton	8 May 1587	12 May 1587
236	**Charlwood**, Hy	Betchworth	-	3 May 1587
237	**Chittie**, Wm	Godalming	-	2 Aug 1585
238	**Crosse**, Rob	Stoke D'Ab	23 Apr 1587	n.d.
239	**Furlonger**, Alice	Chiddingfold	9 Apr 1587	n.d.
240	**Giles**, Wm	Horsley W	-	25 Nov 1583
241	**Graye**, Hy Berm	St M	3 Mar 1587	5 May 1587
242	**Hill**, Joan	Ewhurst	1586	n.d.
243	**Lipscomb**, **Lypscombe**, Tho	Cranleigh	18 Feb 1587	27 Apr 1587

Entry No	Testator	Parish	Date of Will	Date of Inventory
244	**Parkehurst**, Mgt	Godalming	18 Apr 1587	16 May 1587
245	**Parson**, Jn	Molesey E	29 Aug 1584	5 May 1587
246	**Peeter**, Jn Godalming	Farncombe	-	15 May 1587
247	**Piggen, Pyggen**, Ric	Coulsdon	9 Apr 1587	n.d.
248	**Richbeale**, Tho	Ashtead	30 Apr 1587	n.d.
249	**Russell**, Jn	Pirbright	13 Apr 1587	25 May 1587
250	**Seagare**, Rob	Wanborough	9 Mar 1587	26 May 1587
251	**Sheffeilde**, Rob	Dorking	26 Mar 1587	18 Apr 1587
252	**Shurloke**, Joh	Send	18 Apr 1587	17 Apr 1587
253	**Songhurst**, Agn	Ockley	29 Feb 1587	8 May 1587
254	**Taylier**, Ric	Cobham	20 Apr 1587	10 May 1587
255	**Whitfeilde**, Wm	Kingston upon Thas	30 Apr 1587	28 May 1587
256	**Atfeld als. Ripley**, Hy	Worplesdon	15 May 1588	17 May 1588
257	**Dibble**, Wm	Newdigate	15 Mar 1588	15 Mar 1588
258	**Eggen**, Corn	Swk St O	1 May 1588	1 May 1588
259	**Fellowe**, Ric	Esher	-	20 May 1588
260	**Howycke**, Tho	Elstead	22 Dec 1578	15 May 1588
261	**Kidwelle**, Joan	Rhithe	-	5 Dec 1587
262	**Morer**, Tho	Abinger	11 Jun 1587	20 Dec 1587
263	**Tally**, Sim	Guildford	4 Dec 1580	10 Apr 1588
264	**Wicker**, Ric	Molesey W	19 Apr 1587	17 May 1588
265	**Arnolde**, Wm	Mickleham	27 Feb 1589	27 Apr 1589
266	**Downinge**, Wm	Carshalton	-	1 May 1589
267	**Jennings**, Ric	Kingston	10 Mar 1589	n.d.
268	**Lake**, Fra	Molesey W	13 Feb 1589	24 Feb 1589
269	**Mathewe**, Wm	Albury	6 May 1589	10 May 1589
270	**Molynge**, Jn	Hambledon	1 Apr 1589	14 Apr 1589
271	**Pagge**, Ric	Horsell	-	12 May 1589
272	**Parker**, Hy	Farnham	12 Apr 1589	12 May 1589
273	**Penycod**, Ste	Elstead	-	29 Apr 1589
274	**Rapley By West**, Jn	Chiddingfold	17 Mar 1589	22 Apr 1589
275	**Smallpece**, Mgt	Guildford	11 Jan 1588	9 May 1589
276	**Smythe**, Ric	Kingston Ham	8 Apr 1589	9 Apr 1589
277	**Stoydwick**, Tho	Alfold	9 Apr 1589	25 Apr 1589
278	**Thatcher**, Wm	Chertsey	-	12 May 1589
279	**Boylett**, Jn	Ash	20 Feb 1590	22 May 1590
280	**Bromefeld**, Maudlin	Guildford St N	30 Mar 1590	n.d.
281	**Chaunder**, Rob	Haslemere	25 Apr 1589	25 Apr 1589
282	**Constable**, Tho	Alfold	17 Mar 1581	22 Apr 1589
283	**Grene**, Wat	Chobham	30 Aug 1550	5 Sep 1590
284	**Hannaway**, Geo	Clandon E	7 Jun 1588	17 May 1590
285	**Potter**, Wm	Horsell	10 Dec 1583	9 Jan 1584
286	**Pratt**, Jn	Farnham Wr	-	15 Apr 1590
287	**Tooth**, Jn	Mickleham	17 May 1590	1 Jun 1590
288	**White**, Jas	Ditton Long	11 May 1590	31 May 1590
289	**Woodclerk**, Jn	Walton Thas Her	19 May 1590	20 May 1590
290	**Alden**, Ric	Malden	18 Apr 1591	18 Apr 1591
291	**Astone**, Jn	Albury	10 Apr 1591	27 Apr 1591
292	**Brigman**, Marg	Swk St O	16 Apr 1591	15 Apr 1591
293	**Charlewood**, Marg	Bookham Gt	13 Sep 1587	9 May 1591
294	**Crue**, Tho	Windlesham	21 Dec 1590	8 Apr 1591

Entry No	Testator	Parish	Date of Will	Date of Inventory
295	**Goringe**, Jn	Worplesdon	15 Apr 1588	1591
296	**Harrison**, Ric	Berm St M	-	19 Apr 1591
297	**Hibberd**, Jn	Bookham Gt	26 Apr 1588	14 May 1591
298	**Kempe**, Hy	Cranleigh	14 Apr 1591	14 May 1591
299	**Lucas**, Jn	Mickleham Westhumble	16 Oct 1590	28 Apr 1591
300	**Michell**, Eliz	Epsom	13 Apr 1591	May 1591
301	**Slatt**, Wm	Chertsey	14 Apr 1591	21 Apr 1591
302	**Stedman**, Jn	Bramley in Shalford	28 Feb 1585	11 May 1591
303	**Stoner**, Rob	Peperharow	8 May 1591	19 May 1591
304	**Streete**, Agn	Wonersh	31 May 1590	9 Apr 1591
305	**Ticknore**, Wm	Albury	7 Nov 1579 & 27 Apr 1584	26 Apr 1591
306	**Aneve**, Tho	Stoke next Guildford	14 Apr 1592	6 May 1592
307	**Atlee**, Wm	Horsley W	1 May 1584	n.d.
308	**Cobbat**, Jn	Bisley	-	3 Jan 1592
309	**Feelder**, Jn	Walton Thas Her	9 Apr 1592	21 Apr 1592
310	**Hellons**, Jn	Walton Thas	9 Apr 1592	21 Apr 1592
311	**Lydgold**, Kat	Walton Thas	13 Aug 1591	8 May 1592
312	**Seith**, Rob	Mitcham	30 Mar 1592	29 Apr 1592
313	**Slarkes**, Jn	Shere	-	29 Apr 1592
314	**Steven**, Wat	Leatherhead	1 Jan 1592	27 Apr 1592
315	**Tomson**, Tho	Swk St O	-	24 Apr 1592
316	**Curson**, Chris	Camberwell Dul	21 Mar 1593	1593
317	**Frayle**, Ric	Woking	-	15 May 1593
318	**Griffine**, Jn	Fetcham	n.d.	14 May 1593
319	**Hudshon**, Geo	Bookham Lt	-	26 May 1593
320	**Marden**, Row	Reigate	-	28 May 1593
321	**Marete**, Rog	Fetcham	16 Apr 1593	24 May 1593
322	**Mathew**, Rob	Ditton Thas	17 Apr 1593	27 May 1593
323	**Peeters**, Agn	Bookham Gt	-	28 May 1593
324	**Peter**, Tho	Fetcham	24 Feb 1593	1593
325	**Ridford**, Jn	Wotton	22 Mar 1592/3	n.d.
326	**Todie als. Farrawle**, Jn	Windlesham Bag	-	9 Apr 1593
327	**Bishop**, Mary	Dorking	-	13 May 1594
328	**Hone**, Jn	Bisley	23 Feb 1593/4	1594
329	**Mathew**, Chris	Streatham	-	7 May 1594
330	**Mychinall**, Ric	Seale	8 Feb 1594	25 Apr 1594
331	**Williamson**, Jn	Elstead	2 May 1593	12 May 1593
332	**Blabye**, Tris	Swk	-	9 May 1595
333	**Bushe**, Tho	Chertsey	-	12 May 1595
334	**Crose**, Rog	Egham	1595	3 Jun 1595
335	**Elliot**, Rob	Shalford	11 May 1595	28 May 1595
336	**Feilde**, Hy	Chobham	15 Apr 1595	n.d.
337	**Foster**, Rog	Lambeth	-	25 May 1595
338	**Fuller**, Jn	Dorking	7 Apr 1593	26 May 1595
339	**Goddard**, Eliz	Cobham	-	3 Jun 1595
340	**Hoke, Hooke**, Rob	Witley Milford	16 Apr 1595	9 May 1595
341	**Marshall**, Wm	Horsley W	23 May 1595	4 Jun 1595
342	**Mylton**, Wm	Windlesham	21 Jly 1592	16 Dec 1594
343	**Phillip**, Wm	Windlesham	27 Apr 1595	19 May 1595

Entry No	Testator	Parish	Date of Will	Date of Inventory
344	**Rapley**, Hy	Chiddingfold	17 May 1595	9 Jun 1595
345	**Stint**, Eliz	Horsley W	18 Feb 1593/4	1 May 1595
346	**Wardell**, Rob	Lambeth	-	19 May 1595
347	**Wingle**, Mich	Stoke D'Ab	-	3 Jun 1595
348	**Cooke**, Jn	Walton Thas	19 Apr 1596	13 May 1596
349	**Cutt**, Wm	Chertsey	15 Apr 1596	3 May 1596
350	**Davye**, Ric	Shere	n.d.	19 Apr 1596
351	**Deringe**, Wm	Bramley in Shalford	1 May 1596	24 May 1596
352	**Fowle**, Rob	Oxted	8 Apr 1596	16 Apr 1596
353	**Ligeard**, Hy	Clandon W	19 Apr 1596	12 May 1596
354	**Marner**, Jn	Thursley	-	5 May 1596
355	**Marner**, Jn	Thursley	-	10 May 1596
356	**Payne**, Jn	Chobham	23 Apr 1596	19 May 1596
357	**Pen**, Jn	Woking	21 Aug 1590	4 May 1596
358	**Roger**, Jn	Fetcham	13 May 1596	24 May 1596
359	**Steven**, Jn	Fetcham	21 Sep 1594	13 May 1596
360	**Tegg**, Agn	Epsom	11 Apr 1596	16 May 1596
361	**Ticknor**, Ric	Wonersh	23 Feb 1596	25 May 1596
362	**Woodier**, Tho	Dunsfold	28 Mar 1596	n.d.
363	**Crauley**, Edw	Ash	1 Apr 1595	12 Apr 1597
364	**Edmeade**, Ric	Chobham	14 Jly 1597	18 Jly 1597
365	**Edwards**, Hy	Witley	12 May 1597	1 Jun 1597
366	**Eede**, Hy	Ash	29 May 1597	10 Jun 1597
367	**Foster**, Jn	Farnham Wr	6 May 1596	21 Jun 1597
368	**Hardinge**, Tho	Farnham T	6 Aug 1591	15 Apr 1597
369	**Key**, Tho	Guildford St N	18 Aug 1597	1 Sep 1597
370	**Martin**, Hy	Farnham	-	18 Jly 1597
371	**Martin**, Hy	Worplesdon	18 May 1593	13 Jun 1597
372	**Plogg**, Wm	Camberwell Peck	26 Mar 1597	5 Apr 1597
373	**Rysse**, Jas	Seale	23 Mar 1596/7	15 Jly 1597
374	**Savage**, Isa	Camberwell Peck	17 Apr 1597	25 Apr 1597
375	**Smith**, Jeff	Sutton	10 Jly 1597	18 Jly 1597
376	**Stanbridge**, Ric	Worplesdon	n.d.	12 May 1597
377	**Styllwell**, Ric	Godalming Ea	27 Apr 1597	2 May 1597
378	**Thorpe**, Tho	Ash	28 Jun 1597	1597
379	**Vine**, Kat	Godalming Sh	26 Mar 1597	30 Mar 1597
380	**Deane**, Ric	Alfold	-	24 May 1598
381	**Hills**, Cat	Kingston	-	24 May 1598
382	**Pencoste**, Hy	Ditton Long	7 May 1598	1 May 1598
383	**Pereson**, Ric	Frensham	7 Oct 1598	10 Oct 1598
384	**Stilwell**, Tho	Witley	25 May 1598	28 May 1598
385	**Aburne**, Edw	Albury	8 Apr 1599	19 Apr 1599
386	**Arnoulde**, Wm	Reigate	1 Mar 1598/9	8 Apr 1599
387	**Bennett**, Marg	Farnham	17 Mar 1598/9	24 May 1599
388	**Brownewende**, Jn	Ditton Long	3 May 1599	14 May 1599
389	**Fellmore**, And	Farnham	15 Jly 1599	31 Aug 1599
390	**Boughton**, Jn	Wotton	25 Apr 1600	6 May 1600
391	**Edmed**, Ric	Horsell	3 Apr 1600	7 Apr 1600
392	**Grace**, Tho	Kingston	28 Mar 1600	5 May 1600
393	**Harding**, Ric	Frensham D	6 Jun 1600	20 Jun 1600
394	**Kent als. Newbery**, Jn	Farnham	3 May 1600	27 May 1600

Entry No	Testator	Parish	Date of Will	Date of Inventory
395	**Lambert**, Eliz	Swk St T	29 Mar 1600	n.d.
396	**Parkes**, Wm	Richmond Sheen W	21 Feb 1599/1600	25 Apr 1600
397	**Stanton**, Jn	Send Rip	-	24 Apr 1600
398	**Valler**, Wm	Frensham	1 Jun 1600	16 Jun 1600
399	**Wheeler**, Hy	Elstead	1 May 1600	8 May 1600
400	**Cartwright**, Hy	Molesey E	11 Mar 1600/1	n.d.
401	**Dynes**, Wm	Godalming	21 May 1601	27 May 1601
402	**Harper**, Hy	Dunsfold	27 Mar 1601	27 May 1601
403	**Inwood**, Jn	Send	14 May 1601	25 May 1601
404	**Skete**, Jn	Chobham	2 Apr 1601	10 Apr 1601
405	**Smalpeece**, Nic	Guildford	10 Mar 1600/1	6 May 1601
406	**Snelling**, Mgt	Windlesham	-	26 May 1601
407	**Stonner**, Ann	Ash	-	25 Jan 1601
408	**Wye**, Tho	Chobham	-	19 May 1601
409	**Charlewood**, Hy	Sutton	-	29 Apr 1602
410	**Chutter**, Adr	Weybridge	-	n.d.
411	**Clarke**, Mgy	Swk St G.	12 May 1602	15 May 1602
412	**Lawsson**, Tho	Walton Thas	1 May 1602	8 May 1602
413	**Manorie**, Tho	Puttenham	21 Apr 1602	19 May 1602
414	**Mawdesley**, Jn	Bramley in Shalford	13 Apr 1602	7 May 1602
415	**Mychel**, Alice	Frensham Sh	10 Feb 1601/2	7 May 1602
416	**Myllest**, Ric	Chertsey	13 Apr 1602	13 May 1602
417	**Ropley**, Rob	Chiddingfold	-	1602
418	**Stynt**, Joe	Clandon E	13 Apr 1602	19 May 1602
419	**Warner**, Rob	Chertsey	15 Jan 97	10 Apr 1602
420	**Williamson**, Bart	Clandon E	25 Mar 1602	19 May 1602
421	**Chyttye**, Tho	Haslemere	17 Apr 1603	4 May 1603
422	**Constable**, Ric	Abinger	-	10 May 1603
423	**Deacon**, Wm	Ockham	4 May 1603	4 May 1603
424	**Fen**, Ant	Byfleet	5 Apr 1603	2 May 1603
425	**Flodder**, Jn	Godalming Ea	28 Dec 1601	16 May 1603
426	**Flutter**, Hy	Witley	30 Apr 1603	7 May 1603
427	**Francklyn**, Ric	Farnham	29 Jan 1602/3	n.d.
428	**Harding**, Sim	Frensham	27 Feb 1602/3	18 Mar 1603
429	**Hart**, Tho	Windlesham	14 Mar 1602/3	25 Mar 1603
430	**Ireland**, Geo	Guildford	-	10 Jun 1603
431	**Mannam**, Ric	Waverley	-	21 Mar ....
432	**Mors**, Jn	Guildford	-	6 Jun 1603
433	**Mower**, Kat	Cranleigh	3 May 1603	6 Jun 1603
434	**Osborne**, Geo	Farnham	28 Jly 1589	27 Sep 1602
435	**Raunger**, Jas	Frensham	-	15 Jan 1603
436	**Richardson**, Wm	Byfleet	7 Mar 1602/3	17 May 1603
437	**Southe**, Ric	Ash	1603	1603
438	**Sponner**, Hy	Abinger	25 Apr 1603	9 May 1603
439	**Steele**, Rob	Frensham	-	23 Mar 1603
440	**Sturte**, Hy	Godalming Ea	27 May 1603	4 Jun 1603
441	**Talbot**, Art	Kingston upon Thas	16 May 1603	6 Jun 1603
442	**Westbrook**, Tho	Pirbright	2 Apr 1602	26 Apr ....
443	**Whittingham**, Geo	Farnham	-	25 May 1603
444	**Woddes**, Hy	Chobham	19 May 1603	1 Jun 1603
445	**Wodier**, Tho	Witley	1 Apr 1603	20 Apr 1603

APPENDIX II: PARISHES

Entry	Testator	Will	Burial	Inventory	Probate
	Abinger				
97	Jn Lypscombe	16 May 1567		25 Feb 1572	7 May 1572
112	Chris Lyllye	24 Apr 1573	12 Apr 1573	19 May 1573	20 May 1573
196	Wm Netelfould	26 Apr 1584	30 Apr 1584	7 May 1584	20 May 1584
214	Tho Songhurst	30 Apr 1585	7 May 1585	20 May 1585	25 May 1585
262	Tho Morer	11 Jun 1587		20 Dec 1587	22 May 1588
422	Ric Constable		25 Apr 1603	10 May 1603	Oct 1603
438	Hy Sponner	25 Apr 1603		9 May 1603	10 Jun 1603
	Albury				
173	Bart Bowdoxe		20 Apr 1582	28 May 1582	30 May 1582
189	Ric Hiller			15 May 1583	15 May 1583
269	Wm Mathewe	6 May 1589	8 May 1589	10 May 1589	13 May 1589
291	Jn Astone	10 Apr 1591	19 Apr 1591	27 Apr 1591	17 May 1591
305	Wm Ticknore	7 Nov 1579/27 Apr 1584	7 Apr 1591	26 Apr 1591	17 May 1591
385	Edw Aburne	8 Apr 1599	9 Apr 1599	19 Apr 1599	24 May 1599
	Alfold				
34	Tho Moyr	2 Jun 1561		13 Jun 1561	2 Jly 1561
96	Jn Holt			7 Apr 1572	7 May 1572
277	Tho Stoydwick	9 Apr 1589		25 Apr 1589	13 May 1589
282	Tho Constable	17 Mar 1580/1		22 Apr 1589	1 Jun 1590
380	Ric Deane			24 May 1598	1 Jun 1598
	Ash				
279	Jn Boylett	20 Feb 1590		22 May 1590	1 Jun 1590
363	Edw Crauley	1 Apr 1595	11 Apr 1597	12 Apr 1597	19 Jly 1597
366	Hy Eede	29 May 1597	31 May 1597	10 Jun 1597	19 Jly 1597
378	Tho Thorpe	28 Jun 1597	2 Jly 1597	1597	19 Jly 1597
407	Ann Stonner		26 Dec 1600	25 Jan 1601	29 May 1601
437	Ric Southe	1603	5 May 1603	1603	10 Jun 1603
	Ashtead				
72	Tho Otwey	27 Apr 1568		9 May 1568	11 May 1568
248	Tho Richbeale	30 Apr 1587		no date	31 May 1587
	Bermondsey St Mary				
241	Hy Graye	3 Mar 1587	28 Apr 1587	5 May 1587	27 Apr 1587
296	Ric Harrison		20 Apr 1591	19 Apr 1591	4 May 1591
	Betchworth				
236	Hy Charlwood		25 Apr 1587	3 May 1587	31 May 1587
	Betchworth: Brockham				
90	Nic Parker	12 Apr 1571	19 Apr 1571	11 May 1571	22 May 1571
100	Alice White	14 Aug 1571	25 Mar 1572	26 Mar 1572	8 May 1572
	Betchworth, East				
37	Jn Saker	12 Apr 1561	12 Apr 1561	26 Apr 1561	8 May 1561
	Bisley				
204	Jn Farnham	23 Apr 1585	23 Apr 1585	no date	25 May 1585
217	Tho Underwood	6 May 1585	7 May 1585	1585	25 May 1585
308	Jn Cobbat			3 Jan 1592	9 May 1592
328	Jn Hone	23 Feb 1593/4		1594	14 May 1594
	Bletchingley				
21	Jn Cacot	10 May 1559		no date	17 Jly 1561
86	Ric Gylman	10 Apr 1571		17 May 1571	22 May 1571
	Bookham Great				
151	Hy Wilkyns	18 Dec 1575		25 Jan 1576	10 May 1576
293	Marg Charlewood	13 Sep 1587		9 May 1591	17 May 1591
297	Jn Hibberd	26 Apr 1588		14 May 1591	17 May 1591
323	Agn Peeters			28 May 1593	29 May 1593

Entry	Testator	Will	Burial	Inventory	Probate
	Bookham Little				
319	Geo Hudshon			26 May 1593	29 May 1593
	Bramley in Shalford				
135	Ste Petoe	24 Apr 1575		17 May 1575	18 May 1575
183	Chris Mellershe	16 Nov 1576	4 May 1582	15 May 1582	30 May 1582
302	Jn Stedman	28 Feb 1585	17 Apr 1591	11 May 1591	17 May 1591
351	Wm Deringe	1 May 1596	9 May 1596	24 May 1596	26 May 1596
414	Jn Mawdesley	13 Apr 1602	13 Apr 1602	7 May 1602	21 May 1602
	Buckland				
190	Tho Ladd	14 Apr 1583	15 Apr 1583	26 Apr 1583	14 May 1583
	Byfleet				
110	Rob Hardewyn	18 Mar 1572/3		4 Apr 1573	29 Apr & 20 May 1573G
131	Rob Geale			24 Apr 1575	18 May 1575
424	Ant Fen	5 Apr 1603		2 May 1603	10 Jun 1603
436	Wm Richardson	7 Mar 1602/3		17 May 1603	10 Jun 1603
	Camberwell				
73	Ric Basyngton	16 Apr 1569	3 May 1569	16 May 1569	23 May 1569
	Camberwell Dulwich				
316	Chris Curson	21 Mar 1593		1593	31 May 1593
	Camberwell Peckham				
372	Wm Plogg	26 Mar 1597	31 Mar 1597	5 Apr 1597	21 Jly 1597
374	Isa Savage	17 Apr 1597	22 Apr 1597	25 Apr 1597	21 Jly 1597
	Capel				
44	Jn Peter	27 Jan 1561/2		31 Mar 1562	4 May 1562
45	Tho Stere	22 Jan 1561/2		19 Feb 1561/2	4 May 1562
94	Rob Wysdome	5 May 1571		5 May 1571	21 May 1571
	Carshalton				
194	Rob Fraye	6 May 1584	8 May 1584	8 May 1584	8 May 1584
199	Ric Bottomley	22 Apr 1585	24 Apr 1585	3 May 1585	28 May 1585
266	Wm Downinge		19 Apr 1589	1 May 1589	14 May 1589
	Charlwood				
6	- Tolley			7 A[pr] 1558	1558
	Chertsey				
19	Jn Banester	3 Jly 1561		no date	25 Aug 1561
35	Joan Mychell	26 Feb 1559/60		25 Feb 1560/1	24 Apr 1561
144	Wm Newman			4 May 1576	5 Jun 1576
162	Geo Collier	26 Apr 1578		5 May 1578	7 May 1578
188	Tho Drewe			9 May 1583	15 May 1583
278	Wm Thatcher			12 May 1589	13 May 1589
301	Wm Slatt	14 Apr 1591		21 Apr 1591	17 May 1591
333	Tho Bushe			12 May 1595	21 May 1595
349	Wm Cutt	15 Apr 1596		3 May 1596	6 May 1596
416	Ric Myllest	13 Apr 1602		13 May 1602	21 May 1602
419	Rob Warner	15-Jan-97		10 Apr 1602	21 May 1602
	Chiddingfold				
79	Jn Hoke			no date	9 Oct 1570
127	Tho Penvey	26 May 1564		21 Jun 1574	2 Oct 1574
146	Tho Peytowe		1550	18 May 1576	5 Jun 1576
232	Ric Benet	11 Apr 1587		no date	30 May 1587
239	Alice Furlonger	9 Apr 1587		no date	30 May 1587
274	Jn Rapley By West	17 Mar 1589		22 Apr 1589	13 May 1589
344	Hy Rapley	17 May 1595	17 May 1595	9 Jun 1595	5 Jun 1595
417	Rob Ropley		14 Mar 1602	1602	21 May 1602

Entry	Testator	Will	Burial	Inventory	Probate
	Chobham				
52	Jn Bonyon	15 May 1565		28 May 1565	2 Jun 1565
53	Mgt & Ric Marlyn	27 May 1565		30 Apr 1565	2 Jun 1565
157	Wm Foster	13 Apr 1578		21 Apr 1578	7 May 1578
283	Wat Grene	30 Aug 1550		5 Sep 1590	17 Oct 1590
336	Hy Feilde	15 Apr 1595		no date	5 Jun 1595
356	Jn Payne	23 Apr 1596		19 May 1596	26 May 1596
364	Ric Edmeade	14 Jly 1597		18 Jly 1597	19 Jly 1597
404	Jn Skete	2 Apr 1601		10 Apr 1601	29 May 1601
408	Tho Wye			19 May 1601	28 May 1601
444	Hy Woddes	19 May 1603		1 Jun 1603	10 Jun 1603
	Clandon, East				
284	Geo Hannaway	7 Jun 1588	16 Jly 1590	17 May 1590	1 Jun 1590
418	Joe Stynt	13 Apr 1602	16 Apr 1602	19 May 1602	21 May 1602
420	Bart Williamson	25 Mar 1602	17 Mar 1602	19 May 1602	21 May 1602
	Clandon, West				
178	Lau Elliott	20 Apr 1582	22 Apr 1582	23 May 1582	30 May 1582
353	Hy Ligeard	19 Apr 1596	19 Apr 1596	12 May 1596	26 May 1596
	Cobham				
201	Jn Colton	12 Apr 1585		30 Apr 1585	27 May 1585
254	Ric Taylier	20 Apr 1587		10 May 1587	31 May 1587
339	Eliz Goddard			3 Jun 1595	4 Jun 1595
	Compton				
82	Jas Westbroke	22 Apr 1570		25 Apr 1570	22 Jun 1570
114	Tho Martyn			24 Mar 1572/3	18 Jly 1573
136	Tho Turner	8 Jan 1574/5		27 Apr 1575	19 Sep 1575
	Coulsdon				
233	Tho Blake	4 May 1587		5 May 1587	31 May 1587
247	Ric Piggen	9 Apr 1587		no date	22 May 1587
	Cranleigh				
8	Edw Braye	16 Aug & 10 Sep 1558	1 Dec 1558	1558	3 Mar 1559
51	Mgt Amy	10 Apr 1565		2 May 1565	2 Jun 1565
129	Jn Browne		May 1574	no date	28 Apr 1575
212	Tho Sayer	29 Apr 1585		14 May 1585	25 May 1585
243	Tho Lipscomb	18 Feb 1587		27 Apr 1587	30 May 1587
298	Hy Kempe	14 Apr 1591		14 May 1591	17 May 1591
433	Kat Mower	3 May 1603		6 Jun 1603	10 Jun 1603
	Ditton. Long				
288	Jas White	11 May 1590	8 May 1590	31 May 1590	2 Jun 1590
382	Hy Pencoste	7 May 1598	11 May 1597	1 May 1598	31 May 1598
388	Jn Brownewende	3 May 1599	5 May 1599	14 May 1599	23 May 1599
	Ditton, Long Tolworth				
99	Sence Starr	4 Feb 1571/2	17 Mar 1571/2	1572	8 May 1572
	Ditton, Thames				
84	Rob Bundell	1 May 1571		12 May 1571	22 May 1571
322	Rob Mathew	17 Apr 1593		27 May 1593	30 May 1593
	Dorking				
42	Wm Whyte	23 Feb 1559/60	24 Feb 1559/60	24 Feb 1559/60	20 May 1561
231	Jn Barnard		7 Feb 1587	87	30 May 1587
251	Rob Sheffeilde	26 Mar 1587	9 Apr 1587	18 Apr 1587	17 May 1587
327	Mary Bishop			13 May 1594	14 May 1594
338	Jn Fuller	7 Apr 1593	20 May 1595	26 May 1595	5 Jun 1595

Entry	Testator	Will	Burial	Inventory	Probate
	Dunsfold				
76	Wm Baker			15 Jun 1569	12 Jun 1570
165	Jn Rempnant	6 May 1579		21 May 1579	27 May 1579
362	Tho Woodier	28 Mar 1596		no date	26 May 1596
402	Hy Harper	27 Mar 1601		27 May 1601	29 May 1601
	Effingham				
226	Wm Kitchiner	3 Dec 1585	14 May 1586	16 May 1586	16 May 1586
	Egham				
119	Tho Reynolde	23 Feb 1572/3		10 Mar 1572/3	29 Apr 1573
143	Jn Mabancke	9 Apr 1576		25 Apr 1576	10 May 1576
334	Rog Crose	1595		3 Jun 1595	5 Jun 1595
	Elstead				
102	Hy Boxold	1571		2 Dec 1572	29 Apr 1573
169	Agn Dayer	12 Jan 1579/80		30 Mar 1581	10 May 1581
234	Maudlin Boxold	17 Apr 1587	24 Apr 1587	28 Apr 1587	30 May 1587
260	Tho Howycke	22 Dec 1578	10 May 1588	15 May 1588	22 May 1588
273	Ste Penycod		9 Apr 1589	29 Apr 1589	13 May 1589
331	Jn Williamson	2 May 1593	4 May 1593	12 May 1593	17 May 1594
399	Hy Wheeler	1 May 1600		8 May 1600	8 May 1600
	Epsom				
300	Eliz Michell	13 Apr 1591		May 1591	18 May 1591
360	Agn Tegg	11 Apr 1596		16 May 1596	24 May 1596
	Esher				
259	Ric Fellowe			20 May 1588	22 May 1588
	Ewell				
41	Chris Thorne	23 Feb 1560/1		22 Apr 1561	23 Apr 1561
	Ewhurst				
65	Nic Hill	15 Apr 1567		25 Apr 1567	missing
202	Eliz Cowicke	29 Apr 1580		28 May 1585	25 May 1585
242	Joan Hill	1586		no date	30 May 1587
	Farnham				
7	Jn Bekeham	3 Nov 1558	before 20 Dec 1558	16 Jan 1558	18 Jan 1558/9
46	Joan Hawle	9 Oct 1563	17 Oct 1563	2 Nov 1563	23 Nov 1563
68	Tho Webb			20 May 1566	16 Jly 1567
91	"Hugh ""Tew, Too"""		25 Oct 1570	28 Jan 1570/1	6 Oct 1571
92	Tho Warner	4 Apr 1571	13 Apr 1571	20 May 1571	22 May 1571
272	Hy Parker	12 Apr 1589	3 May 1589	12 May 1589	13 May 1589
370	Hy Martin		14 Jly 1597	18 Jly 1597	19 Jly 1597
387	Marg Bennett	17 Mar 1598/9	20 Mar 1599	24 May 1599	24 May 1599
389	And Fellmore	15 Jly 1599	16 Jly 1599	31 Aug 1599	1 Sep 1599
394	Jn Kent als. Newbery	3 May 1600	5 May 1600	27 May 1600	8 May 1600
427	Ric Francklyn	29 Jan 1602/3	30 Jan 1603	no date	10 Jun 1603
434	Geo Osborne	28 Jly 1589	4 Aug 1602	27 Sep 1602	10 Jun 1603
443	Geo Whittingham		9 May 1603	25 May 1603	10 Jun 1603
	Farnham Runfold				
28	Tho Haywarde	1 Dec 1560		25 Jan 1560/1	2 Jly 1561
48	Allys Juer	18 Oct 1563	21 Oct 1563	2 Nov 1563	13 Nov 1563
48	Hy Juer	18 Oct 1563	19 Oct 1563	2 Nov 1563	13 Nov 1563
49	Pet Mannte	19 Oct 1563	25 Oct 1563	19 Oct 1563	13 Nov 1563
138	Jn Aslet	28 May 1574	6 May 1576	21 May 1576	5 Jun 1576
142	Jn Jewer	23 Nov 1575	14 May 1576	16 May 1576	5 Jun 1576
	Farnham Tilford				
139	Wm Brodebridge	26 Apr 1575	3 May 1575	4 May 1576	10 May 1576
368	Tho Hardinge	6 Aug 1591	30 Mar 1597	15 Apr 1597	17 Jly 1597

Entry	Testator	Will	Burial	Inventory	Probate
	Farnham Wrecclesham				
67	Ste Sherube	14 Apr 1567	6 May 1567	28 Jun 1567	14 Jly 1567
80	Rob Marshar	30 Jan 1569/70	14 Feb 1569/70	28 Mar 1570	12 May 1570
83	Jn Winne	8 Feb 1569/70	28 Mar 1570	28 Mar 1570	12 May 1570
95	Wm Channell	6 Nov 1571	9 Nov 1571	5 Dec 1571	7 May 1572
104	Wm Ede	4 Apr 1573	10 Apr 1573	29 Apr 1573	29 Apr 1573
126	Tho Hayward	28 May 1570	23 Jan 1574	26 Apr 1574	2 Oct 1574
286	Jn Pratt		7 Apr 1590	15 Apr 1590	1 Jun 1590
367	Jn Foster	6 May 1596	18 Jun 1597	21 Jun 1597	19 Jly 1597
	Fetcham				
36	Wm Roger	1 Jan 1561		no date	21 May 1561
61	Jn Bet	10 Dec 1562		13 Apr 1567	missing
230	Jn Atwell	17 Apr 1587		2 May 1587	5 May 1587
318	Jn Griffine	no date		14 May 1593	29 May 1593
321	Rog Marete	16 Apr 1593		24 May 1593	29 May 1593
324	Tho Peter	24 Feb 1593	7 Apr 1593	1593	29 May 1593
358	Jn Roger	13 May 1596		24 May 1596	26 May 1596
359	Jn Steven	21 Sep 1594	9 Apr 1596	13 May 1596	26 May 1596
	Frensham				
25	Oli Fanner	14 Feb 1561		8 Mar 1561	21 May 1561
40	Bart Steyll	22 Dec 1560		6 Jan 1560/1	21 May 1561
107	Tho Fulston	12 Feb 1572/3		22 May 1573	29 Apr 1573
118	Agn Reves	29 Dec 1572	24 Feb 1572/3	25 Feb 1572/3	29 Apr 1573
140	Eden Feld	6 Apr 1576		11 Apr 1576	10 May 1576
155	Tho Bickenell	22 Nov 1577		27 Nov 1577	7 May 1578
156	Agn Channell	22 Nov 1577		27 Nov 1577	7 May 1578
164	Jn Manfielde	n.d		no date	24 Apr 1579
170	Wm Fulston	12 Jan 1581		no date	10 May 1581
383	Ric Pereson	7 Oct 1598		10 Oct 1598	27 Feb 1598/9
398	Wm Valler	1 Jun 1600		16 Jun 1600	20 Oct 1600
428	Sim Harding	27 Feb 1602/3		18 Mar 1603	10 Jun 1603
435	Jas Raunger			15 Jan 1603	10 Jun 1603
439	Rob Steele			23 Mar 1603	10 Jun 1603
	Frensham Churt				
182	Wm Luffe	25 Apr 1582		no date	30 May 1582
225	Tho Filpe	20 Mar 1586		26 Apr 1586	16 May 1586
	Frensham Dockenfield				
393	Ric Harding	6 Jun 1600		20 Jun 1600	24 Sep 1600
	Frensham Pitfold				
14	Ric Peerson	26 May 1559		26 May 1559	12 Oct 1559
128	Tho Allen			5 May 1575	22 Jun 1575
	Frensham Shottermill				
415	Alice Mychel	10 Feb 1601/2		7 May 1602	21 May 1602
	Frensham Westend				
63	Bart Hardynge	8 Apr 1567		28 Apr 1567	missing
	Frimley Ash				
179	Ric Exold	18 Nov 1580		15 Mar 1581/2	19 Sep 1582
	Gatton				
70	Jone Beste	27 Jun 1558		no date	11 May 1568
	Godalming				
55	Ric Oliver	1565		29 May 1565	missing
123	Edw West	4 Feb 1573		16 ... 1573	20 May 1573
167	Wm Chyttye			13 Mar 1580/1	14 Mar 1580/1
195	Joan Hamptonne	10 Feb 1584		27 Apr 1584	20 May 1584
237	Wm Chittie			2 Aug 1585	3 May 1587
244	Mgt Parkehurst	18 Apr 1587	26 Apr 1587	16 May 1587	30 May 1587

Entry	Testator	Will	Burial	Inventory	Probate
	Godalming Cateshall				
85	Jul Elyot	18 Apr 1571		19 May 1571	21 May 1571
	Godalming Eashing				
10	Wm Chittey	21 May 1559		13 Jun 1559	16 Jun 1559
200	Hy Chytty	23 Apr 1585		3 May 1585	25 May 1585
377	Ric Styllwell	27 Apr 1597	.. Mar 1597	2 May 1597	19 Jly 1597
425	Jn Flodder	28 Dec 1601	28 Apr 1603	16 May 1603	10 Jun 1603
440	Hy Sturte	27 May 1603	29 May 1603	4 Jun 1603	10 Jun 1603
	Godalming Farncombe				
246	Jn Peeter		1 May 1587	15 May 1587	30 May 1587
401	Wm Dynes	21 May 1601	23 May 1601	27 May 1601	29 May 1601
	Godalming Shackleford				
379	Kat Vine	26 Mar 1597	.. Mar 1597	30 Mar 1597	27 Apr 1597
	Godstone				
197	Edw Scrafton	20 Apr 1584		2 May 1584	18 May 1584
	Guildford				
26	Ric Forde	28 Jan 1560/1	5 Feb 1560/1	24 Feb 1560/1	21 May 1561
81	Jn Northall		10 Mar 1569/70	20 Mar 1570	12 May 1570
145	Tho Northall	13 Jun 1576	12 Jun 1576	25 Jun 1576	17 Jly 1576
211	Ric Procker (Proctor)		9 May 1585	20 May 1585	25 May 1585
263	Sim Tally	4 Dec 1580	8 Apr 1588	10 Apr 1588	21 May 1588
275	Mgt Smallpece	11 Jan 1588		9 May 1589	13 May 1589
405	Nic Smalpeece	10 Mar 1600/1	29 Apr 1601	6 May 1601	29 May 1601
430	Geo Ireland			10 Jun 1603	10 Jun 1603
432	Jn Mors		3 May 1603	6 Jun 1603	10 Jun 1603
	Guildford Holy Trinity				
38	Rob Selwode	7 Nov 1560	8 Nov 1560	22 May 1561	6 Dec 1561
	Guildford St Mary				
27	Geo Glover	22 Apr 1561	25 Apr 1561	15 Jly 1561	4 Jun 1561
120	Dor Snellinge	5 May 1572	9 May 1572	12 May 1572	29 Apr 1573
153	Tho Barne	25 Mar 1578	6 Apr 1578	11 Jun 1578	20 Jun 1578
	Guildford St Nicholas				
280	Maudlin Bromefeld	30 Mar 1590	14 May 1590	no date	1 Jun 1590
369	Tho Key	18 Aug 1597	27 Aug 1597	1 Sep 1597	19 Apr 1600
	Hambledon				
32	Wat Mabanke	4 Feb 1560/1		14 May 1561	21 May 1561
47	Jn Hull	1 Oct 1562		20 Jan 1563 & 30 Jun 1564	15 Apr 1563
270	Jn Molynge	1 Apr 1589		14 Apr 1589	13 May 1589
	Hascombe				
62	Wm Birle	20 Apr 1567		4 May 1567	missing
	Haslemere				
89	Ric Osborne			19 May 1571	21 May 1571
93	Fra West			7 May 1571	21 May 1571
130	Agn Chaundler	13 May 1575		30 May 1575	22 Jun 1575
281	Rob Chaunder	25 Apr 1589	30 Apr 1590	25 Apr 1589	1 Jun 1590
421	Tho Chyttye	17 Apr 1603		4 May 1603	10 Jun 1603
	Headley				
159	Mgt Stansted	12 Jly 1578		20 Aug 1578	23 Sep 1578
	Horley				
31	Ric Lucas	21 Mar 1560/1		13 Apr 1561	28 Apr 1561
50	Nic Alyngham	17 Jan 1564/5		19 Jan 1564/5	1 Jun 1565
101	Pet Bonwick	22 Jun 1572		no date	27 Apr 1573
116	Geo Payne	25 Oct 1568		18 Apr 1573	27 Apr 1573

Entry	Testator	Will	Burial	Inventory	Probate
	Horne				
59	Wm Elvyn	10 Mar 1565/6		15 Apr 1566	23 May 1566
88	Jn Monnyarde	11 Sep 1570		16 Apr 1571	22 May 1571
149	Wm Todham	2 Apr 1576		16 Apr 1576	9 May 1576
	Horsell				
56	Rob Taylor	21 May 1565		no date	2 Jun 1565
57	Ant Worthyngton	26 Feb 1564/5		13 Apr 1565	2 Jun 1565
111	Jn Isam	30 Oct 1572		28 May 1573	20 May 1573
228	Jn Walden			9 May 1586	16 May 1586
271	ric Pagge			12 May 1589	13 May 1589
285	Wm Potter	10 Dec 1583		9 Jan 1584	1 Jun 1590
391	Ric Edmed	3 Apr 1600		7 Apr 1600	8 May 1600
	Horsley, West				
168	Jn Cresey	20 Mar 1580/1		no date	10 May 1581
186	Wm Stint	18 Oct 1581		no date	30 May 1582
213	Hy Skete	7 Feb 1584/5		20 May 1585	25 May 1585
240	Wm Giles			25 Nov 1583	30 May 1587
307	Wm Atlee	1 May 1584		no date	9 May 1592
341	Wm Marshall	23 May 1595		4 Jun 1595	5 Jun 1595
345	Eliz Stint	18 Feb 1593/4		1 May 1595	5 Jun 1595
	Kingston				
2	Jone Burgies	7 Apr 1558		26 Apl 1558	27 Apr 1558
66	Jn Rawstricke	24 Mar 1566/7		16 Apr 1567	missing
69	Rob Andrew	1568		no date	11 May 1568
175	Pet Buckland	21 May 1582		29 May 1582	missing
267	Ric Jennings	10 Mar 1589	12 May 1589	no date	26 May 1589
381	Cat Hills		14 May 1598	24 May 1598	31 May 1598
392	Tho Grace	28 Mar 1600		5 May 1600	7 May 1600
	Kingston Ham				
16	Joan Tornor			26 Jan 1558/9	missing
276	Ric Smythe	8 Apr 1589		9 Apr 1589	14 May 1589
	Kingston Surbiton				
106	Tho Foxe	10 May 1573	10 May 1573	12 May 1573	20 May 1573
	Kingston on Thames				
60	Nic Walker	26 Sep 1565	13 Feb 1565/6	10 May 1566	26 Jun 1566
255	Wm Whitfeilde	30 Apr 1587	23 May 1587	28 May 1587	31 May 1587
441	Art Talbot	16 May 1603	27 May 1603	6 Jun 1603	10 Jun 1603
	Lambeth				
337	Rog Foster			25 May 1595	3 Jun 1595
346	Rob Wardell			19 May 1595	21 May 1595
	Lambeth Stockwell				
171	Rob Rundell	10 Apr 1581	16 Apr 1581	1 May 1581	8 May 1581
	Leatherhead				
314	Wat Steven	1 Jan 1592		27 Apr 1592	10 May 1592
	Leigh				
187	Mat Byshopp			14 May 1583	15 May 1583
220	Wm White	16 Apr 1585		29 Apr 1585	4 May 1585
	Limpsfield				
3	Jn Cole	26 Jan 1557/8	1 Feb 1557/8	25 Apl 1558	27 Apr 1558
	Lingfield				
1	Chri Botley	24 Nov 1556		17 Apl 1558	27 Apl 1558
4	Hy Copsell	1 Jun 1558		no date	9 Nov 1558
	Malden				
290	Ric Alden	18 Apr 1591		18 Apr 1591	19 May 1591
54	Tho Morrell	30 Jan 1564/5	2 Feb 1564/5	30 Jan 1564/5	1 Jun 1565

Entry	Testator	Will	Burial	Inventory	Probate
	Mickleham				
210	Ra Mose	18 Apr 1585	17 Apr 1585	24 Apr 1585	27 May 1585
287	Jn Tooth	17 May 1590		1 Jun 1590	2 Jun 1590
265	Wm Arnolde	27 Feb 1589		27 Apr 1589	14 May 1589
	Mickleham Westhumble				
299	Jn Lucas	16 Oct 1590		28 Apr 1591	18 May 1591
	Mitcham				
218	Wm Walter	10 Apr 1585	14 Apr 1585	20 May 1585	27 May 1585
312	Rob Seith	30 Mar 1592		29 Apr 1592	9 May 1592
	Molesey, East				
245	Jn Parson	29 Aug 1584		5 May 1587	31 May 1587
400	Hy Cartwright	11 Mar 1600/1		no date	28 May 1601
	Molesey, West				
133	Rob Lake	15 May 1563		no date	22 Jun 1575
150	Rob Wicker	1 Jun 1575		4 May 1576	9 May 1576
264	Ric Wicker	19 Apr 1587		17 May 1588	22 May 1588
268	Fra Lake	13 Feb 1589		24 Feb 1589	14 May 1589
	Morden				
12	Jn Frysbee	23 Dec 1558	23 Dec 1558	23 Dec 1558	30 Jun 1559
13	Nic Goryng	2 Feb 1558/9		2 Feb 1558/9	missing
	Newdigate				
5	Jn Lewer	30 Aug 1557		3 Oct 1557	28 Apr 1558
191	Agn Newdegate	20 Jan 1581/2	13 Jun 1583	21 May 1583	4 Jly 1583
257	Wm Dibble	15 Mar 1588	18 Mar 1588	15 Mar 1588	21 May 1588
	Nutfield				
17	Jn Clemente	16 Apr 1559	1 Oct 1560	1 Oct 1560	5 Oct & 31 Oct 1560
222	Ric Alyngham	9 Feb 1586	22 May 1586	9 May 1586	17 May 1586
	Ockham				
30	Chris Lamboll	8 Mar 1560/1		8 Apr 1561	21 May 1561
103	Rob Clebroke		11 Jun 1573	1573	27 Jun 1573
206	Rob Freelande	22 Apr 1585	22 Apr 1585	4 May 1585	25 May 1585
423	Wm Deacon	4 May 1603	5 May 1603	4 May 1603	10 Jun 1603
	Ockley				
77	Tho Chyty	20 Mar 1569/70		11 May 1570	12 May 1570
78	Jn Constable	6 Apr 1570		23 Apr 1570	12 May 1570
161	Wm Wapshote	10 Feb 1577/8	20 Mar 1577/8	8 Apr 1578	20 Jun 1578
174	Kat Brand			4 Dec 1581	3 Feb 1581/2
227	Wat Songhurst	19 Mar 1586	1 Apr 1586	27 Apr 1586	16 May 1586
253	Agn Songhurst	29 Feb 1587	3 May 1587	8 May 1587	30 May 1587
	Oxted				
352	Rob Fowle	8 Apr 1596		16 Apr 1596	24 May 1596
	Peperharow				
303	Rob Stoner	8 May 1591		19 May 1591	19 May 1591
	Pirbright				
105	Ric Fagatere	7 May 1573		18 May 1573	30 May 1573
147	Bart Smethurst	11 May 1576	14 May 1576	24 May 1576	5 Jun 1576
249	Jn Russell	13 Apr 1587	21 Apr 1587	25 May 1587	30 May 1587
442	Tho Westbrook	2 Apr 1602		26 Apr	10 Jun 1603
	Puttenham				
20	Jn Byckenall	31 Mar 1561		5 May 1561	21 May 1561
113	Geo Marlyn		29 Oct 1572	6 Jan 1573	29 Apr 1573
193	Jn Clifton	13 Apr 1584	27 Apr 1584	4 May 1584	20 May 1584
413	Tho Manorie	21 Apr 1602	26 Apr 1602	19 May 1602	21 May 1602
	Pyrford				
205	Rob Fenne	20 Apr 1585		no date	27 May 1585

Entry	Testator	Will	Burial	Inventory	Probate
	Reigate				
58	Wm Amias	11 May 1566	17 May 1566	22 May 1566	24 May 1566
223	Hy Bray	19 Apr 1586		28 Apr 1586	17 May 1586
320	Row Marden		22 May 1593	28 May 1593	30 May 1593
386	Wm Arnoulde	1 Mar 1598/9	7 Apr 1599	8 Apr 1599	23 May 1599
	Rotherhithe				
122	Jn Waters	20 Jly 1570		2 May 1573	6 May 1573
261	Joan Kidwelle		12 Nov 1587	5 Dec 1587	23 May 1588
	Richmond West Sheen				
396	Wm Parkes	21 Feb 1599/1600	26 Feb 1599/1600	25 Apr 1600	7 May 1600
	Seale				
125	Tho Dakin	28 Jun 1574	1 Jly 1574	8 Jly 1574	20 Jly 1574
180	Wm Hampton	5 May 1567	13 Apr 1582	16 Apr 1582	25 Apr 1582
330	Ric Mychinall	8 Feb 1593/4	8 Apr 1594	25 Apr 1594	14 May 1594
373	Jas Rysse	23 Mar 1596/7	8 May 1597	15 Jly 1597	19 Jly 1597
	Send				
24	Pet Davy	3 Apr 1561		14 Apr 1561	21 May 1561
117	Hy Punter	31 Mar 1573		1 Apr 1573	20 May 1573
252	Joh Shurloke	18 Apr 1587		17 Apr 1587	30 May 1587
397	Jn Stanton			24 Apr 1600	8 May 1600
403	Jn Inwood	14 May 1601		25 May 1601	29 May 1601
	Shalford				
137	Jn Waterer	19 Apr 1575		17 May 1575	18 May 1575
152	Jn Sherwood			21 Feb 1576/7	1 Mar 1576/7
335	Rob Elliot	11 May 1595	23 May 1595	28 May 1595	5 Jun 1595
	Shere				
39	Jn Shudde	15 Dec 1560	30 Dec 1560	3 Jan 1560/1	21 May 1561
43	Tho Wyght	31 Mar 1561	1 Apr 1561	no date	21 May 1561
313	Jn Slarkes		13 Apr 1592	29 Apr 1592	9 May 1592
350	Ric Davye	no date	17 Apr 1596	19 Apr 1596	26 May 1596
	Stoke D'Abernon				
238	Rob Crosse	23 Apr 1587		no date	31 May 1587
347	Mich Wingle			3 Jun 1595	4 Jun 1595
	Stoke next to Guildford				
208	Eliz Fuller	20 Jan 1584/5	ob. 20 Jan 1584/5	25 Jan 1584/5	16 Feb 1584/5
306	Tho Aneve	14 Apr 1592		6 May 1592	6 May 1592
	Streatham				
329	Chris Mathew			7 May 1594	15 May 1594
	Sutton				
375	Jeff Smith	10 Jly 1597		18 Jly 1597	21 Jly 1597
409	Hy Charlewood			29 Apr 1602	20 May 1602
	Southwark				
124	Rob Woodward		27 Apr 1573	no date	28 May 1573
332	Tris Blabye			9 May 1595	23 May 1595
	Southwark St Geo				
134	Jn Mantill			6 Apr 1575	26 Apr 1575
411	Mgy Clarke	12 May 1602		15 May 1602	19 May 1601
	Southwark St Olave				
229	Jn Atkynsone	17 Apr 1587	19 Apr 1587	no date	3 May 1587
258	Corn Eggen	1 May 1588	4 May 1588	1 May 1588	23 May 1588
292	Marg Brigman	16 Apr 1591	19 Apr 1591	15 Apr 1591	4 May 1591
315	Tho Tomson		15 Apr 1592	24 Apr 1592	11 May 1592
	Southwark St Olave & St Saviour				
166	Wm Beston	20 Jan 1572/3		79	12 Oct 1580

Entry	Testator	Will	Burial	Inventory	Probate
	Southwark St Saviour				
108	Rob Fylden	6 Apr 1573	14 Apr 1573	18 Apr 1573	27 Apr 1573
219	Geoff Warde	7 May 1585	11 May 1585	13 May 1585	28 May 1585
	Southwark St Thomas				
395	Eliz Lambert	29 Mar 1600		no date	6 May 1600
	Tandridge				
33	Rob Mowse	15 Mar 1560/1		27 Mar 1561	16 Apr 1561
109	Giles Fynnes	14 Apr 1573		16 Apr 1573	22 May 1573
	Tatsfield				
215	Denise Towler	22 Feb 1584/5		10 May 1585	27 May 1585
	Thorpe				
172	Wm Becham	20 Nov 1581		8 Jan 1582	30 May 1582
	Thursley				
23	Wm Collen	16 Apr 1561		no date	21 May 1561
29	Hy Hedger	14 Jan 1560/1		10 Feb 1560/1	2 Jly 1561
87	Ric Hedger	28 Apr 1571		16 May 1571	21 May 1571
98	Rob Machyke	7 Jun 1566		21 Apr 1572	7 May 1572
354	Jn Marner			5 May 1596	26 May 1596
355	Jn Marner			10 May 1596	26 May 1596
	Tooting Bec, Great				
75	Rob Altham			24 Apr 1570	11 May 1570
	Walton Hersham				
289	Jn Woodclerk	19 May 1590		20 May 1590	2 Jun 1590
309	Jn Feelder	9 Apr 1592		21 Apr 1592	10 May 1592
	Walton on Hill				
181	Chas Holman	no date		18 Mar 1582	29 May 1582
	Walton on Thames				
310	Jn Hellons	9 Apr 1592		21 Apr 1592	10 May 1592
311	Kat Lydgold	13 Aug 1591		8 May 1592	10 May 1592
348	Jn Cooke	19 Apr 1596	ob. 21 Apr 1596	13 May 1596	24 May 1596
412	Tho Lawsson	1 May 1602		8 May 1602	20 May 1602
	Wanborough				
158	Jn Hays	14 Feb 1577/8		5 Apr 1578	7 May 1578
250	Rob Seagare	9 Mar 1587		26 May 1587	30 May 1587
	Wandsworth				
203	Jn Edwin			11 May 1585	3 Jun 1585
	Waverley				
431	Ric Mannam			21 Mar	5 Apr 1603
	Weybridge				
11	Miles Codde	31 Oct 1558		22 Nov 1558	2 Apr 1559
410	Adr Cutter	no date		no date	21 May 1602
	Windlesham				
207	Tho Freland	31 May 1582		no date	28 May 1585
294	Tho Crue	21 Dec 1590		8 Apr 1591	17 May 1591
342	Wm Mylton	21 Jly 1592		16 Dec 1594	5 Jun 1595
343	Wm Phillip	27 Apr 1595		19 May 1595	5 Jun 1595
406	Mgt Snelling			26 May 1601	29 May 1601
429	Tho Hart	14 Mar 1602/3		25 Mar 1603	10 Jun 1603
	Windlesham Bagshot				
326	Jn Todie als. Farrawle			9 Apr 1593	29 May 1593

Entry	Testator	Will	Burial	Inventory	Probate
	Witley				
74	Geo Byrche	12 Oct 1568		23 May 1569	24 May 1569
141	Rob Holt	30 Mar 1576		9 May 1576	10 May 1576
365	Hy Edwards	12 May 1597		1 Jun 1597	19 Jly 1597
384	Tho Stilwell	25 May 1598		28 May 1598	1 Jun 1598
426	Hy Flutter	30 Apr 1603		7 May 1603	10 Jun 1603
445	Tho Wodier	1 Apr 1603		20 Apr 1603	8 Jun 1603
	Witley Milford				
148	Jn Stynt	18 Nov 1575		4 Jan 1575/6	10 May 1576
340	Rob Hoke	16 Apr 1595		9 May 1595	5 Jun 1595
	Woking				
115	Edw Mathewe	22 Apr 1573		28 Apr 1573	20 May 1573
160	Ric Tydes	28 Oct 1572		no date	25 Apr 1578
185	Jn Shaddatt als Sherratt	19 Feb 1581/2		3 May 1581	30 May 1582
209	Hy Lee			6 May 1585	25 May 1585
317	Ric Frayle			15 May 1593	29 May 1593
357	Jn Pen	21 Aug 1590		4 May 1596	26 May 1596
	Wonersh				
22	Wm Chenell	15 Jly 1560		1561	21 May 1561
64	Jn Harfell/Harper	7 Apr 1567	28 Apr 1567	2 May 1567	missing
121	Tho Warner	6 Apr 1573	18 Apr 1573	21 Apr 1572	20 May 1573
132	Jn Gosden	16 Apr 1575	17 Apr 1575	25 Apr 1575	18 May 1575
192	Ric Babbe	23 Apr 1584	1 May 1584	4 May 1584	20 May 1584
198	Tho Astrete		25 Jan 1584/5	11 Feb 1584/5	16 Feb 1584/5
304	Agn Streete	31 May 1590	4 Apr 1591	9 Apr 1591	17 May 1591
361	Ric Ticknor	23 Feb 1596		25 May 1596	26 May 1596
	Worplesdon				
71	Tho Meede	11 Apr 1568		no date	missing
154	Wm Bearde	13 May 1578	18 May 1578	20 Jun 1578	20 Jun 1578
163	Jonne Fulstone	18 Apr 1579	7 May 1579	11 May 1579	27 May 1579
176	Geo Burt als. Loveland	2 May 1582	5 May 1581	23 May 1582	30 May 1582
177	Ric & Mgt Clifton		26 Dec 1581/11 Jan 1581/213 Jan 1581/2		19 Jan 1581/2
184	Jn Russell	24 Apr 1582	25 Apr 1582	7 May 1582	30 May 1582
216	Agn Underwode	6 May 1585	10 May 1585	20 May 1585	25 May 1585
256	Hy Atfeld als. Ripley	15 May 1588	16 May 1588	17 May 1588	22 May 1588
295	Jn Goringe	15 Apr 1588	22 Apr 1591	1591	17 May 1591
371	Hy Martin	18 May 1593	4 Jun 1597	13 Jun 1597	19 Jly 1597
376	Ric Stanbridge	no date	5 May 1597	12 May 1597	19 Jly 1597
	Wotton				
9	Tho Chesman	10 Apr 1559		no date	20 Apr 1559
18	Rob Lylley	4 Oct 1560		no date	8 Dec 1560
221	Wm Worsfold	7 Apr 1585		20 Apr 1585	25 May 1585
235	Jn Bristowe	8 May 1587		12 May 1587	30 May 1587
325	Jn Ridford	22 Mar 1592/3		no date	29 May 1593
390	Jn Boughton	25 Apr 1600		6 May 1600	8 May 1600

INDEXES

EXPLANATORY NOTES

1. All reference numbers refer to the key number ascribed to each Inventory/Will and not to page numbers. For complete list see Appendix 1.
2. Square brackets and italics have been used for additional information and for author's comment
3. Asterisks indicate that the original document is damaged or illegible.
4. Compilation of the Indexes:
   a) Index of Items The index has been classified into sections (see list of classified headings below). To produce a more useful index, modern spellings have been used for the individual items in preference to those actually used in individual Inventories. The date of the first appearance is given. The underlined reference numbers refer to items in Wills which have been included in the additional Notes to the Inventories.
   b) Index of People The index includes all the various spellings of each name. Please note the following :
      i. Entries in capitals refer to the testators.
         e.g. **ARNOLDE**: Wm 265[of Mickleham, yeo.]
      ii. **Bold type** indicates the most commonly occurring version of the surname.
      iii. Additional information is placed in square brackets following the key reference number of the Inventory/Will, using the following sequence: - the elder, the younger, junior or senior; place of abode; quality or trade; function or role.
         e.g. **Bax(e)**, Backes: Ra 227[*a*], 253[of Ockley, husb., *a,b,o,s,w*], 390[*c*

   c) Index of Properties The full parish references appear in Appendix II which stands as a place index. The Index of Properties adds sub-names and Out-County names.

INDEX OF ITEMS: CLASSIFIED HEADINGS

BUILDINGS & ROOMS

FURNITURE & FURNISHINGS

BEDS & BEDDING

LINEN & NAPERY

APPAREL

WEAPONS & ARMOUR

BOOKS, JEWELLERY, MONEY & MUSICAL INSTRUMENTS

HEARTH FURNITURE

COOKING, EATING & DRINKING

BAKING

BREWING & MALTING

DAIRY

SALTING

WASHING

HOUSEHOLD MISCELLANEOUS incl. STORAGE CONTAINERS & VESSELS

WEIGHTS & MEASURES

STORED GOODS & PRODUCE

STOCK-IN-TRADE: GOODS, TOOLS & EQUIPMENT

CLOTH TRADE incl. HOUSEHOLD SPINNING, WEAVING & ROPEMAKING

TOOLS & AGRICULTURAL IMPLEMENTS

CARTS, PLOUGHS etc., HARNESS & TACK

LIVESTOCK

GROWING CROPS

INDEX OF PEOPLE

INDEX OF OCCUPATIONS AND STATUS OF TESTATORS

INDEX OF PROPERTIES

<u>OTHER COUNTIES</u>